FOURTH EDITION

Interviewing in Action in a Multicultural World

Bianca Cody Murphy
Wheaton College

Carolyn Dillon
Boston University

BROOKS/COLE
CENGAGE Learning™

Australia • Brazil • Japan • Korea • Mexico • Singapore • Spain • United Kingdom • United States

BROOKS/COLE
CENGAGE Learning

Interviewing in Action in a Multicultural World, Fourth Edition
Bianca Cody Murphy, Carolyn Dillon

Aquisitions Editor, Counseling, Social Work and Human Services: Seth Dobrin

Assistant Editor: Arwen Petty

Editorial Assistant: Rachel McDonald

Media Editor: Dennis Fitzgerald

Senior Marketing Manager: Trent Whatcott

Marketing Coordinator: Darlene Macanan

Senior Marketing Communications Manager: Tami Strang

Content Project Management: Pre-PressPMG

Creative Director: Rob Hugel

Art Director: Caryl Gorska

Print Buyer: Judy Inouye

Rights Acquisitions Account Manager, Text: Roberta Broyer

Rights Acquisitions Account Manager, Image: Leitha Etheridge-Sims

Production Service: Pre-PressPMG

Photo Research: Pre-PressPMG

Copy Editor: Daniel Nighting

Compositor: Pre-PressPMG

For product information and technology assistance, contact us at **Cengage Learning Customer & Sales Support, 1-800-354-9706**

For permission to use material from this text or product, submit all requests online at **www.cengage.com/permissions**
Further permissions questions can be e-mailed to **permissionrequest@cengage.com**

Library of Congress Control Number: 2010921449

Student Edition:
ISBN-13: 978-0-8400-3209-6
ISBN-10: 0-8400-3209-9

Brooks/Cole, Cengage Learning
20 Davis Drive
Belmont, CA 94002-3098
USA

Cengage Learning is a leading provider of customized learning solutions with office locations around the globe, including Singapore, the United Kingdom, Australia, Mexico, Brazil, and Japan. Locate your local office at **www.cengage.com/global**

Cengage Learning products are represented in Canada by Nelson Education, Ltd.

To learn more about Brooks/Cole, Cengage Learning, visit **www.cengage.com/brookscole**

Purchase any of our products at your local college store or at our preferred online store **www.CengageBrain.com**

Printed in the United States of America
2 3 4 5 6 7 14 13 12 11

To our students

Who taught us how to teach

To our clients

Who taught us how to practice

To our teachers

Who taught us to learn from our students and our clients

Bianca Cody Murphy, Ed.D., is Professor and Chair of the Psychology Department at Wheaton College in Norton, Massachusetts. She is a licensed psychologist and has a clinical practice with Newton Psychotherapy Associates. She has conducted numerous workshops and training programs for mental health professionals around the country and has published professional articles and book chapters on clinical work with lesbian and gay clients, on peace psychology, and on families exposed to environmental toxins. Dr. Murphy has served as the Chair of the Committee on Women and Chair of the Board for the Advancement of Psychology in the Public Interest of the American Psychological Association. She has been President of Psychologists for Social Responsibility. She is the recipient of the Distinguished Professional Contribution Award from the Society for the Psychological Study of Lesbian, Gay, and Bisexual Issues (Division 44) of the American Psychological Association.

Carolyn Dillon is Clinical Professor Emerita, Boston University School of Social Work, where she has won teaching excellence awards from both the Alumni Association and the student body. She received the Metcalf Award for teaching excellence and was the recipient of the "Greatest Contribution to Social Work Education" award from the Massachusetts Chapter of the National Association of Social Workers. She has practiced for 40 years as a Licensed Independent Clinical Social Worker and has also tutored in English through her local library. She is a member of the National Association of Social Workers and was a longtime affiliate of the Council on Social Work Education and the Massachusetts Society for Clinical Social Work. She has published and spoken widely about the need for professional self-care and stress management and has consulted with social workers in health and mental health settings. She is also the author of *Learning from Mistakes in Clinical Practice.*

Contents

CHAPTER 4
Attending and Listening　　　　　　　　　　97

CHAPTER 5
Support and Empathy: A Sustaining Presence　　127

CHAPTER 6
Exploration and Elaboration   157

CHAPTER 7
Assessment, Formulation, and Goal Setting   185

CHAPTER 8
Planning for and Evaluating Change   **221**

CHAPTER 11
The Clinical Relationship: Issues and Dynamics   307

CHAPTER 12
The Clinical Relationship: Addressing
Self-Disclosure and Other Boundary Issues   337

CHAPTER 13
Working with People in Crisis   367

CHAPTER 14
Endings and Transitions   409

CHAPTER 15
Professional Issues: Ongoing Education and Self-Care 439

Preface

Interviewing in Action in a Multicultural World emphasizes and illustrates the relational, interactional, and multicultural nature of practice in the twenty-first century. It is based on our RE-VIEW PRACTICE Method of clinical knowledge and skills development. We believe that students can best learn when they read about skills, view seasoned clinicians using the skills with clients, and practice the skills through role-plays and skill application exercises, receiving feedback from instructors and peers. Thus, we have developed an integrated learning package whose elements build upon each other. The comprehensive yet easy-to-read text is accompanied by a 2-hour DVD containing video clips in which real-life clinicians demonstrate and reflect on key skills discussed in each chapter. The Companion Website includes student self-exploration activities, essay questions, Web links, and other resources.

Special Features of the Package

1. *Realistic for today's practice environments.* The text and DVD video clips address the complexity of issues that clinicians confront and the limited time and resources available to them. They also address important issues affecting clinical work, such as managed care, evidence-based practice, and the use of the Internet and other technologies.
2. *Experiential learning.* The book, the Instructor's Manual, and the Companion Website contain nearly 400 individual and group exercises for use at home, in class, and in distance learning. They include suggestions for role-plays, personal reflections, essay questions, video activities, classroom discussions, and journaling—all to forward growth in knowledge and in use of self and skills.
3. *Cross-cultural and multicultural.* Multicultural considerations for effective clinical practice are integrated throughout the book, video clips, Companion Website, and Instructor's Manual. Cultural issues are addressed in all aspects of clinical work from preparation and engagement of clients to ending.
4. *Difference and diversity.* Discussion of the influences and issues of class, gender, ethnicity, sexual orientation, age, spiritual affiliation, and disability are infused throughout the text content and are well represented in the DVD video clips, the Companion Website reflection and essay questions, and the Instructor's Manual.
5. *Relationships as well as skills.* Learning how to establish and maintain a productive and caring working alliance is every bit as important to effective work with people as is education about the phases, skills, and mechanics of professional interviewing. The text and video clips highlight the unfolding nature of clinical relationships and the ways in which they can help both clients and clinicians grow and change through mutual feedback and shared responsibility for outcomes.

6. *Beliefs, values, and social norms.* The text and Instructor's Manual exercises and students' own Web-based self-exploration and journaling exercises encourage and assist in the development of greater awareness of students' own values, beliefs, and social norms and how these affect all aspects of their professional relating and work.

7. *Clinician first-person accounts.* The book contains relevant, often touching stories from the field in which seasoned clinicians share personal accounts of their real-life experiences with clients. Students see that the implementation of skills is not always on target as clinicians reflect on what they learned from baffling challenges and memorable missteps. As students are exposed to many different clinicians, in different settings, from different disciplines, with different theoretical orientations, they learn that a practice principle or skill can be actualized in many creative ways, depending on the setting; on the particular needs, background, and culture of the client; and on the conditions in the moment or the surround.

8. *Concrete examples.* The text is replete with clinician–client dialogues demonstrating how skills may be implemented. The accompanying video clips show actual clinicians using these skills in clinical situations in which the relationship and the work unfold with varied effects. The clinicians periodically comment on their selective choice and use of skills, comparing the effects of skills used at different points in the interview or the work.

9. *Applicability to many disciplines.* Although we use the generic term *clinician* in the text, we provide practice examples from a variety of settings (group home, outpatient clinic, office, home, job, hospital, street corner) and professional roles (employee assistance worker, rehabilitation counselor, social worker, school psychologist, human service worker, criminal justice professional, drug counselor, milieu therapist, and psychiatric nurse clinician). We believe that more and more practice will occur in interdisciplinary teams and groups and that we need to move toward a shared practice language that can facilitate dialogue and collaboration.

Earlier editions of the book/video learning package have been used by beginning and advanced students of social work, psychology, counseling, human services, criminal justice, and nursing. They have also been used by other professionals wishing to refine or update their knowledge and skills. These disparate learners tell us they have used our materials with a common goal of relating and working more effectively with clients, and we have been very gratified by the positive feedback from them as well as from instructors using our learning package. They tell us that they like the book's lucid explanation of concepts, its down-to-earth language, its realistic practitioner examples and narratives, the chapter exercises and opportunities for students to video record themselves in action, and the illustrative companion video clips keyed to specific text content. Instructors have commended the Instructor's Manual and its numerous chapter-by-chapter exercises and suggestions for learning activities within instructional groups. Accordingly, all of these mutually enhancing elements have been preserved and expanded in the updating of this fourth edition.

Students and instructors tell us that this package speaks directly to their own experiences, illustrating how to form and tend effective relationships with clients, carry out thoughtful and productive assessments and develop realistic goals, and begin to evaluate progress and outcomes. They say that they have benefited from content and class discussion about self-disclosure, maintaining one's professional self while remaining human and authentic, and spotting and dealing with inevitable missteps. Instructors and students also like the way the book and video uniquely represent diversity in both clients and clinicians—something they may not see often in educational programs, in agency life, or in learning materials and videos. Instructors and students have also appreciated the absence of clinical jargon, formality, and distance in the text and video clips. The fourth edition preserves these traditions.

What's New in Our Fourth Edition

Since we wrote the first edition of our book in 1998, the field of clinical practice and the world in which it occurs have continued to change dramatically. Evolving areas in clinical practice include increased attention to global and multicultural issues in practice; evidence-based practice; the heightened influence of technological advances in research, treatment, and practice management; and the strengths perspective's new companion, the emerging field of Positive Psychology. There is heightened attention to spirituality and its integration into clinical practice. We have added content on each of these developments, and their treatment applications are given added attention throughout this new edition.

- The phrase "We live in a global society" is repeated almost daily in the media due to the cross-national effects of economic, ecological, political, and population shifts. People move from one country to another, either by choice or in forced migrations to avoid war, persecution, or starvation. There are more multinational companies, further shrinking the globe as people travel around the world for business. Clinicians, too, move around the globe to provide services in countries facing natural disasters or war, to collaborate on research or teaching, or to increase their knowledge by attending international conferences. As a result of all of these phenomena, there is significantly more research on cross-cultural and multicultural counseling every year. In every chapter, we have expanded and updated the content, readings, exercises, and examples of working in a multicultural context with clients from different cultural groups.
- Technological advances in the information management and communications fields in the last decade have led to the development of rapid global communication on a scale unparalleled in human history. People now routinely use email, cell phones, search engines, Web pages, electronic databases, online chat rooms, text messaging, "tweets," and videoconferencing. We have included new information about the use of technology in assessment, record keeping, and clinical practice management in many chapters, including material about online counseling as a new clinical environment in Chapter 3; on the use of virtual reality technology (VRET) in behavior treatments in Chapter 10; and on the ethical issues of online practice in Chapter 2.
- Since it was first introduced in the late 1990s, the field of Positive Psychology, with its emphasis on growth and well-being, has had a major impact on clinical work. We include a discussion of "positive ethics" in Chapter 2, positive psychological approaches to assessment in Chapter 7, and positive interventions designed to help clients feel differently and create more empowered well-being for themselves in Chapter 9. We discuss posttraumatic growth in Chapter 13.
- We have enhanced our content on evidence-based practice, distinguishing it from empirically supported treatment in Chapter 1, and we have included new information about empirically supported treatment in a number of chapters. We discuss the empirical evidence demonstrating the importance of the relationship in effective treatment outcomes, and in Chapter 8 we explore some of the challenges of applying empirical studies in clinical settings.
- In response to the global epidemic of suicide and to requests from colleagues, we have added a significant new section on suicide to Chapter 13 (Working with People in Crisis). We moved this crisis chapter (formerly Chapter 8) to situate it after our discussion of relationship and boundary issues.
- We have continued to increase the content regarding the importance of spiritual and religious beliefs, practices, and faith-based initiatives in the everyday lives of people around the world. We emphasize the importance of eliciting, assessing, and working with clients' spiritual beliefs, networks, and other resources whenever such actions are appropriate and client-centered. For example, in Chapter 7 we discuss ways to integrate spirituality into

assessment. Clinician–client examples illustrate a variety of ways clinicians can show respect and creativity in working with spirituality from a strengths perspective.

- We have included more examples of working with a variety of clients including rural clients and traumatized veterans.
- We have added new exercises, self-exploration questions, essay questions, and suggested readings in many chapters.

About the Book

Chapter-by-Chapter Overview

Chapters highlight the history, nature, values, structures, and traditions of clinical practice, and discuss the relational, ethical, and multicultural nature of practice today, emphasizing that self-awareness and knowledge of others different from ourselves have crucial to sensitive and informed practice.

Chapter 1 focuses on the student's clinical learning pathway and anticipated challenges. We describe our RE-VIEW PRACTICE Method and its integration of read/see/do/get feedback activities that forward learning.

Chapter 2 addresses the bedrocks on which clinical practice depends: multiculturalism and ethics. We highlight the importance of multicultural practice and have students think about identity development, difference, and diversity, as well as multiple dimensions of identity. We discuss the skills and knowledge that clinicians need in order to work in our multicultural world. The second half of the chapter focuses on professional codes of ethics and common ethical dilemmas that clinicians face. We emphasize the importance of ethics in protecting and affirming clients and in guiding clinicians, and we offer frameworks for decision making when dilemmas arise. Sections of actual ethics codes from various professional organizations are included in the text.

Chapters 3–5 approach the clinical process as a unique kind of talking, with rules, roles, mutual expectations, boundaries, layers, and the requirement of intentional, client-centered behavior on the part of the clinician. Chapter 3 explores planning and preparation for work with clients of varying backgrounds, experiences, communication skills, strengths, and service needs. We discuss special issues related to the great variety of interviewing environments (home, shelter, medical setting, street, agency office, online, workplace and faith-based sites, scenes of disaster) and review strategies for maintaining clinician safety in high-risk situations. We incorporate a fresh appraisal of confidentiality concerns and steps that can be taken to protect clients and their personal material. In Chapter 4, students learn and practice basic attending and listening skills and learn about the nuances of nonverbal communication. We also address issues for those communicating in a nonnative language, including the use of translators and interpreters. In Chapter 5, we discuss support and empathy as well as empathic failures, noting that empathy is a mutual process. Students learn to develop a sustaining presence that will serve as a holding environment for all ensuing clinical work and to watch for processes that can interfere with empathic responsiveness.

Because clients need to be able to explore and articulate their stories to develop reasonably attainable, meaningful, and practical goals, Chapter 6 addresses skills of exploration and elaboration, discussing the use of well-timed questions, prompts, probes, reflection, and other techniques for helping clients elaborate their stories. Care is taken not to press for disclosure when working with people whose family or cultural norms and styles discourage the sharing of personal or intimate information.

Chapters 7 and 8 examine the issues and skills of assessment, goal setting, contracting, and evaluation. In Chapter 7, assessment and formulation frameworks guide students in completing an assessment, conceptualizing their findings, and writing assessment summaries or reports. Students learn how to help clients set goals for their work together based on the formulation. In Chapter 8, we discuss the stages of change. Strengths are actively identified and utilized to animate change work. Motivational Interviewing skills are demonstrated as a means of helping to resolve client ambivalences about change. Students learn about writing treatment plans and establishing working agreements or contracts, as well as about ongoing evaluation of their work together. Students are reminded to be flexible as prospects, situations, or resources change.

Chapters 9 and 10 focus on the skills of helping clients effect desired changes in feelings, ideas, and behaviors. Chapter 9 focuses on strategies and skills clinicians can use to help clients recognize, express, and manage feelings while gaining new perspective on their situation and future possibilities. We provide specific intervention strategies from the field of Positive Psychology to help clients focus on their positive emotions and well-being. We provide detailed material on developing hunches that may be offered to help clients see and feel things differently, and we urge clinicians to be aware of and careful about the levels of inference in their hunches. Chapter 10 stresses behavioral change and illustrates such skills as modeling, behavioral rehearsal, and reinforcement. Clinical case management roles and advocacy activities are also emphasized as crucial assets in helping clients improve their situations and opportunities.

Chapters 11 and 12 discuss advanced and thorny relational issues and challenges that can arise in work with clients. We address important issues, challenges, and clinical skills needed to work on the client–clinician relationship itself. Unlike other texts that discuss the relationship in-depth early on to set the stage for engagement of clients, we have purposely delayed detailed discussion of more complex relationship dynamics until learners have mastered some basic skills of engagement, exploration, hunching, and noticing nuances of process as the work unfolds. Chapter 11 integrates constructs from Relational-Cultural theory in discussing the relationship itself as a primary medium and force for growth and change. We provide many examples of relationship maintenance activities and problem resolution process in which clinicians own their own contributions to difficulties as these arise, and encourage client feedback about the clinician's focus, pace, and style of work. Chapter 12 focuses on boundary issues that arise when clinicians are asked to self-disclose, when activities outside the usual meeting place occasion unplanned contact with clients, or when limits must be set on inappropriate behaviors of clients or unethical behaviors of clinicians or agency personnel.

Chapter 13 reflects our appreciation of the ubiquity of crisis and trauma in the United States and around the world. This chapter differentiates types of crises, including the insidious trauma of racism and other forms of oppression. We discuss the ways we listen to, validate, and help to re-empower those affected by trauma, either directly or vicariously. We have a major new section on the special challenges of working with suicidal clients. We also discuss vicarious trauma in clinicians and other crisis responders, elaborating on steps we all can take to prevent vicarious trauma so that we remain psychologically and physically fit to carry out roles that ease others' recovery.

Chapter 14 prefigures the end of the course by walking students through the issues and tasks of endings and transitions in the work. We discuss the importance of including culturally determined ending rituals. Various kinds of breaks or planned holidays in the work are described, and client and clinician reactions to ending are elaborated on and illustrated through examples in the text and the video. Note is taken that, when brief interventions are planned from the outset, ending is always foreshadowed so that it feels like a goal rather than a loss or painful new step. We note that when family and cultural supports have been valued and included all along in interventions, these resources become important sources of ongoing support when the work ends.

Chapter 15 discusses the importance of self-care and lifelong learning. Supervision and peer and team collaborations are also emphasized as sources of lifelong learning. We end by discussing the many satisfactions of clinical work, as well as a number of professional needs, challenges, and requirements that learners will face as they move out of educational programs and into the complex "real world" of agency life and professional interactions and responsibilities with clients.

About the DVD

The DVD contains almost 180 minutes of illustrative video clips. Each chapter has companion video clips. Each topical segment is introduced with a brief explanation of its utility, followed by short clips of different clinicians illustrating either a problematic or an effective use of a skill or strategy. Watching and discussing the video segments stimulates interest in reading more about principles and clinician experiences in the text and in trying out ideas in class simulations and conversations with colleagues and instructors.

The video clips allow students to see real clinicians in action. Many people have asked us if the clinician's responses are scripted. They are not. All of the interviewers are seasoned clinicians who demonstrate a variety of different styles of skills used in response to client material. The clips of clinician group discussion of challenges in ethical and multicultural practice also lets students see seasoned colleagues spontaneously thinking aloud together about some very difficult issues in practice.

All of the participants reflect the diversity of clinicians and clients. The clinician discussion group and the six clinician–client pairs in the videos are from a wide variety of ethnic backgrounds and represent men and women of color and of different ages, abilities, socioeconomic status, sexual orientations, and interpersonal styles.

Video clips follow six clinician–client relationships and their work together from beginning to end. The clinicians use a range of practice principles and skills, and the client stories represent experiences that many students and practitioners work with in a wide variety of practice settings:

- An African American father dealing with conflict with his adolescent son
- An "out" gay man whose partner (not "out") is hospitalized following an accident
- An isolated, elderly Russian immigrant who has lost her grown daughter to cancer
- An Irish American teen in a residential setting developing the confidence and skills to return to community life
- An Asian American woman with mental illness working with her day treatment counselor on social anxieties mobilized at work
- A Latina woman who has been mugged and is now beset by past as well as present reactions to trauma

Clinician comments demonstrate process analysis and ownership of missteps. Clinicians in the DVD clips comment from time to time about what they did and how they felt about it. Students get to hear them discuss their thinking and responses as the work proceeds. Students also get to see that there is more than one "right" way to respond to a client. They learn that they will get to hone their own voice and style over time while working under supervision with a wide variety of clients.

The DVD clips can be used in class or at home. Students report that they enjoy reading and watching video clips at home and have also benefited greatly from watching individual clips in class, as instructors use these to illustrate concepts they are presenting. Home study and viewing have the advantage of freeing up blocks of class time from the watching of videos. This leaves more class time for questions and discussion of reading, text, and video examples, as well as challenges from the field. There is also more time for role-plays and other exercises that advance knowledge, skill application, and confidence.

About the Companion Website

The Companion Website includes over 60 self-exploration exercises and journaling experiences that heighten students' awareness of self and of others with whom students hope to work professionally. Over 60 essay questions then challenge students to go deeper in applying the theoretical understanding developed from readings, class discussions, and role-plays. Students can either store responses to questions in a notebook or journal for later discussion in class or submit them to the instructor over the Internet as part of an assignment.

The Website also contains a Glossary with definitions of the key terms at the end of each text chapter, along with flashcards created from the key terms and definitions. Other resources and recommendations are available on the Website as well.

About the Ancillaries

Instructor's Manual

The Instructor's Manual is available on the Instructor's Companion Website and in portable booklet form. It is filled with good ideas for teaching clinical theory and process and contains over 200 activities for use in class or as assignments for homework. For instructors new to clinical practice education, we suggest ways to structure time and to use oneself as a model to bring a spirit of collegiality to work with students in class. Each chapter begins with a brief summary of related text chapter content and an outline of text and exercise content. Outlines can be used to frame classroom sessions and to recall key concepts and their elaborative detail.

Test Bank

In response to requests from colleagues we have also developed a Test Bank of Multiple Choice and Short Answer Questions that can be used in conjunction with the suggested essays at the end of each chapter to create exams.

Acknowledgments

We would like to express our continuing appreciation to a number of people. We remain grateful to the talented clinicians who generously demonstrated their work in the six clinician–client pairs: Maryann Amodeo, Brenda Clarke, Betsy Groves, Joel Hencken, Terry McCandies, Jon Reusser, and Lourdes Rodríguez-Nogués. We are also very grateful for the participation of the seasoned clinician-educators who reflected together on the DVD about multiculturalism and ethics in professional work: Luz Lopez, Donna McLaughlin, Michael Melendez, and Mojdeh Rohani.

Many friends and colleagues have read the manuscript and given us feedback and advice. Former Wheaton student, now colleague, Molly Galdston provided invaluable assistance as we began our work on this new edition. The attention to detail she brought to helping us revise this edition is deeply appreciated. We thank Wheaton College colleagues Peony Fhagen-Smith, Ph.D., for her insightful comments and discussions on issues of race and identity and David Wulff, Ph.D., for sharing his numerous resources on religion and spirituality. Wheaton Faculty Secretary Barbara Curtis, with the able assistance of Jan Adie, took on the painstaking task of helping us check our references with grace and good humor. Margaret Gardner, reference librarian at Wheaton, was always there when we needed her. We thank Martin G. Evans, a volunteer reader for people with visual impairments, for his helpful comments. Finally, we are most grateful to all the students and colleagues who gave us permission to use their stories from the field and first-person accounts.

We extend thanks to the creative team at Brooks/Cole, Cengage: Seth Dobrin has been our very supportive editor for this fourth edition. He has been timely, resourceful, and responsive in shepherding us through the development of our text revision, DVD, Companion Website, and updated Instructor's Manual. Caryl Gorska for artistic and production support; Arwen Petty, assistant editor; Rachel McDonald, editorial assistant; Roberta Broyer, permissions editor; Judy Inouye, print/media buyer, and Julie Aguilar for her skill in creating our Companion Website. Thanks also to Daniel Nighting, our copy editor, for his steady feedback and to Mary Stone at Pre-PressPMG who walked us through the production process.

From Bianca Cody Murphy . . .

First and foremost I am indebted to my coauthor Carolyn for her good humor, creativity, stamina, and patience. I thank my partners at Newton Psychotherapy Associates—Priscilla Ellis, Sarah Greenberg, and Joan Berlin—who over 30 years of peer supervision have helped shape the way I practice. I am deeply grateful for the support of my colleagues in the psychology department at Wheaton College as I struggled through writing this edition while serving as our department chair. Finally, Sue Buerkel, my partner and soul mate, continues to be my harbor. Her love, support, and gourmet cooking sustain me.

From Carolyn Dillon . . .

I am so thankful for the support and good fun with family and with old friends Jim Sellers, Paulina Watson, Toni Tugenberg, Agnes Sector, Lisa Sutton, and Margot Kittredge. I am forever grateful to Boston University Social Work Deans Wilma Peebles Wilkins and Gail Steketee, who have so generously supported me over the many years of this project. It goes without saying that this long collaboration with Bianca Cody Murphy has been the opportunity of a lifetime. Through mutual support and feedback, we have integrated our complementary professional knowledge bases and abilities to elucidate values and ideas we both share. Thanks, all, for deeply enriching my life and purpose.

To the Reader

This is a text for both graduate and undergraduate students preparing to work in a variety of fields: social work, counseling, psychology, human services, criminal justice, psychiatric nursing, and a variety of other helping professions. We struggled to find a term to use in this book that would include all of these professionals: *Helper? Worker? Counselor?* After talking with colleagues, we realized that there is no single word that completely conveys the collaborative and strength-based work orientation that is so vital in today's complex and diverse practice settings. The terms *counselor* and *worker* seem discipline-based; and there are many helpers: formal and informal, trained and untrained. We decided to use the term *clinician* to describe the numerous professionals who are educated and skilled in helping and who are taught to be self-aware and purposeful in relationships with clients.

Throughout this book, you will find stories from the field (in italics) that reflect the experiences, interactions, and reflections of school counselors, outreach social workers, criminal justice workers, agency-based psychologists, private practice clinicians, crisis workers, milieu counselors, and day treatment staff. These stories are from real clinicians working in the field. Some reflect our own clinical experiences, but most come from colleagues and former students, who generously shared their experiences with us, and allowed us to share them with you. (Client privacy has been protected.)

Becoming a Professional

■ The Professionalizing of Helping

There have always been people who have helped others cope with difficulties or emotional distress. Culture has always influenced who helps, whom they help, and how they help. At different times and in different cultures, these traditional healers have been called shamans, elders, curanderos, healers, or sangomas (Stone, 1997). These people are perceived to have special gifts or talents, and have often received specialized education or training. They are skilled in helping people deal with problems in their lives (Torrey, 1972).

In the nineteenth and early twentieth century, new groups of helpers developed to assist people in distress. These included human service workers, counselors, social workers, psychologists, milieu therapists, psychiatric nurses, and psychiatrists. Although each of these disciplines has its own philosophy, mission, and emphasis, each requires highly specialized education to prepare these professionals to become effective helpers. As knowledge of human behavior and the social environment has advanced over the last 150 years, professional education has become more organized, scientific, and theory based, integrating learning in school with field-based internships or practicum. We refer to this new group of helpers as **professional clinicians.** (See note on page xxiv.)

A major purpose of clinical education was to develop expertise in helping. As a result, clinicians began to be seen (and to see themselves) as experts. For many, expert status conferred power and prestige and led to a privileging of the clinician's knowledge over that of clients. Employment in the helping professions and the development of clinical service agencies and counseling centers served to amplify position, status, and authority. The media, which both reflect and help create social realities, often portrayed confused clients seeking help from well-dressed, respected authorities, creating a dichotomy between the person needing help and the "wise helper." The licensing of clinicians further reinforced an aura of special wisdom and capability, since licensure requires years of formal preparation. It became easy for people to think of clients as empty vessels into which clinicians poured their special knowledge. Ironically, the use of arcane language and complex theory often made this knowledge less accessible to the very people with whom clinicians were trying to communicate.

Heavily influenced by advances in medicine, neurology, psychology, anthropology, and sociology, helping professionals created scientific procedures for data collection, intervention planning, and evaluation. Clinical education emphasized an observer's detachment and neutrality, with important exceptions. Freud occasionally analyzed friends and students (Roazen, 1992). Jane Addams lived in the settlement house among the poor immigrants with whom she worked (Addams, 1910). Because few services were available for African-American children, social services pioneer Janie Porter Barrett established the Locust St. Settlement for mistreated children in her own home (Barrett, 1926; Peebles Wilkins, 1995). But a gradually emerging emphasis on detachment and scientific objectivity contributed to clinicians' distancing themselves more and more from daily interactions with their clients.

Clinicians have also become both geographically and economically less accessible. As clinicians have become organized and professionalized, they have often moved out of homes, neighborhoods, and street corners and into offices and agencies where their help is shaped by time constraints, bureaucratic procedures, and the income requirements of agencies and clinicians (Iglehart & Becerra, 1995). Services are more concentrated in urban areas. Thus, those in rural areas and those without adequate transportation are often unable to access needed support. Today, many clinicians and practice settings attempt to overcome this distance and become more accessible through use of technology such as e-mail, Internet sites that provide resources, teleconferencing, and online support groups. However, Debra Parker-Oliver and George Demiris (2006) describe the digital divide between the rich and poor and note that the use of these technological advances may itself limit accessibility for low-income clients.

With the privatization of mental health services and the increase in managed care, clinicians may find their clinical decisions increasingly affected by their own or their agency's financial concerns and pressures. Agencies often require providers to serve more clients more rapidly and with fewer resources than in the past. Furthermore, a focus on finances has contributed to an atmosphere of entrepreneurial competition among the various disciplines for power, authority, and clientele. Finally, the ability to pay for services affects basic access to clinical help, as well as the type and amount of help that clients receive (Gorden & Kline, 1997). These financial issues can have a particularly negative effect on people from lower socioeconomic classes. However, it should be noted that financial accountability and oversight of care may have a positive effect on the quality of treatment.

As we noted earlier, Western medical models have a long history of explaining and treating emotional distress in physical or medical terms (Mezzich & Kleinman, 1996; Weick, 1983). Clinicians are often trained to diagnose pathology—to find what is wrong or broken and needs to be fixed. In mental health, the mandatory use of the *Diagnostic and Statistical Manual of Mental Disorders (DSM IV-TR)* (American Psychiatric Association, 2000), with its classifications of symptoms and disorders, exemplifies the emphasis on pathology. Both clinicians and clients may accustom themselves to focusing on problems and difficulties in the client's story and history to the near exclusion of strengths and successes, eliciting what family therapists David Epston and Michael White (1990) call "the problem-saturated narrative" (p. 19). Sometimes it may seem more important to diagnose than to relate. The word *clinical* itself reflects a medical orientation; it is derived from the Greek *klinike*, referring to the work of the physician at the sickbed.

The focus on the "sick individual" has sometimes separated people from their families and other natural helping networks. Clinical work has often focused on issues of individual autonomy and achievement, rather than on connection and collective action for social change. Furthermore, most models of helping, counseling, and psychotherapy were developed by and for White, middle-class, able-bodied, heterosexual males and may not be appropriate for most clients (Ellis & Murphy, 1994; Guadelupe & Lum, 2005; Perez, DeBord, & Bieschke, 2007; Stiver, 1991; Derald Sue & Sue, 2008).

As a result of these complex historical forces, what could be a special conversation between two or more people all too frequently becomes a ritualized and formal interview. At times, the voice and strength of the client may seem less important than the voice and strength of the professional.

In the past two decades, a strength-based approach has been developed and is widely used. Today, **clinical interviewing** is—or should be—a conversation characterized by respect and mutuality, by immediacy and warm presence, and by emphasis on strengths and potential. Because clinical interviewing is essentially relational, it requires ongoing attention to *how* things are said and done, as well as to *what* is said and done. The emphasis on the relationship is at the heart of the "different kind of talking" that is the clinical interview.

EXERCISE 1.1   Characteristics of Helpful People

Think about someone who has helped you in the past—a friend, teacher, neighbor, minister, or therapist. Make a list of some of the person's characteristics that you found particularly helpful. Compare your list with those of your colleagues. Of all the helpful characteristics on everyone's list, which ones do you find in yourself and which ones do you want to develop? In your journal, record specific ways in which you need to change to be a more helpful person. List specific steps you would need to take to make the changes.

After an extensive review of the literature, Barbara Okun (Okun & Kantrowitz, 2008) summarizes what she considers to be the "qualities, behaviors and knowledge of helpers [that] are most influential in affecting the behaviors, attitudes, and feelings of helpees" (p. 38): self-awareness, gender and cultural awareness, honesty, congruence, ability to communicate, knowledge, and ethical integrity.

While the focus of this book is on the development of professional skills as clinicians, we recognize the important role of traditional healers as well as the growing field of complementary medicine and indigenous helpers. **Complementary medicine** specialists, including acupuncturists, massage therapists, homeopaths, meditation and yoga teachers, and energy workers emphasize the harmonious integration of mind and body to achieve well-being.

Indigenous helpers include the gifted neighbors and community members to whom many people turn for advice, consolation, and concrete resources. Melvin Delgado (1997) writes about the importance of beauty parlors in Latino communities as nontraditional settings where mutual sharing and advice giving reduce the stigma of help seeking. "These settings are generally staffed by individuals who share the same ethnic, socioeconomic, and other key factors such as gender and religion as the patrons (maximizing psychological, geographical, and cultural access) and have a primary role that incorporates being a 'helper'" (p. 48). In a similar vein, Robert Taylor and his colleagues (Taylor, Ellison, Chatters, Levin, & Lincoln, 2000) describe the role of the Black church as one of the first places people in African-American communities turn for emotional support and concrete resources. Wahiba Abu-Ras and his colleagues (Abu-Ras, Gheith, & Cournos, 2008) discuss the imam's role in mental health promotion in the Muslim community.

■ The Clinical Interview: A Different Kind of Talking

Becoming a professional clinician can be seen as something that comes easily and naturally, a simple extension of familiar ways of caring and being that we have experienced our whole lives. Yet a clinical interview involves a kind of talking that is different from other conversations and informal helping relationships.

Purpose

Clinical interviewing is purposeful. It requires an intentional focus on the client's story, needs, and goals. This focus distinguishes it from friendly or casual conversation, in which people talk randomly about whatever they wish. Purpose and focus are always informed by assessment—the ongoing gathering of data and impressions that guide all aspects of the work. Clinicians need to stay very clear about the purpose of interviewing to avoid drifting from subject to subject in nonproductive ways. Specific purposes for clinical interviewing vary from client to client and from setting to setting. For example, the purpose may be to help a client cope with debilitating anxiety, to determine a client's eligibility for public assistance, or to help a child adjust to her parents' divorce.

Although there is a general purpose for the overall work together, there may be a number of specific goals for each session. Even if the goals are not explicitly stated, the clinician keeps them in mind. For example, the overall purpose of the work may be to help the client develop stable relationships, but, within a particular session, the goal may be to move into the history of how others in the family handle anger or to discuss why the client has canceled the last three sessions.

Although clinicians have additional reasons for clinical interviewing—to do our job, to earn money, to feel good about ourselves—the guiding purpose is to help clients. Interviewers agree to hold their primary aim, their service obligations to clients, over all other interests. This commitment to put clients' needs first is abrogated only in special situations when we are concerned about the imminent safety of clients or others.

Theory

Unlike casual conversation, clinical interviewing is informed by theory. **Theory** refers to a systematic set of principles used to understand and explain observable phenomena. There are numerous schools or models of counseling and psychotherapy, with over 400 counseling theories in North America alone (Prochaska & Norcross, 2007). Theory shapes the content and process of clinical interviews. The interviewer's theoretical stance affects the purpose and goals of the interview, as well as how the interviewer listens and responds to the client's story.

A confused or unclear theoretical stance can manifest itself in scattered focus or abrupt shifts in style, which are jarring for the client and can derail purposeful work. At the same time, it is important not to confuse having a theoretical base with orthodoxy. A rigid adherence to theory may impede the flexibility necessary to work with clients and their stories, and it may limit the imagination needed for new theories to evolve.

Your course and field learning will expose you to some widely used and empirically supported theories of counseling and psychotherapy, including cognitive, behavioral, psychodynamic, family systems, crisis intervention, and person-centered theories. Some models of psychotherapy focus more on specific types of skills than others. For example, behavioral therapists focus on helping people to unlearn maladaptive behaviors and to learn more productive ones (Bandura, 1969; Kazdin, 2001; Miltenberger, 2004). Cognitive therapists focus on teaching clients how to combat irrational thoughts (Beck, 1995; Ellis & MacLaren, 1998; Meichenbaum, 1996), while client-centered therapists maintain that empathy and relational skills are the central components necessary for therapeutic growth (Rogers, 1957). But all theoretical models require the application of basic interviewing and relational skills such as those we discuss in this text.

Most theories are thought to apply universally to everyone, but in fact many may not be applicable to the diverse people seeking help. Consequently, a number of writers have proposed theories of multicultural counseling and therapy that emphasize the interactive effects of ethnicity, culture, race, color, class, gender, sexual orientation, spirituality, ability, and age (Atkinson, 2004; Lum, 2007; Ponterotto, Casas, Suzuki, & Alexander, 2009; Derald Sue & Sue, 2008). Theories of multicultural counseling are designed to be integrated with traditional theories, not to replace them.

Scientific Base

Graduate clinical education often emphasizes what has been called the **scientist/practitioner model.** David Barlow and Mark Durand (2009) note that clinicians are consumers of science (studying the "latest scientific developments in their field"), evaluators of science ("evaluat[ing] their own assessments or treatment procedures to see if they work"), and creators of science ("conducting research . . . that produces new information") (p. 5).

Advances in brain imaging and biochemical analysis have helped us better understand the biological correlates of mental and emotional states. Important breakthroughs in neuroscience have led to new biological treatments of diseases such as deep brain stimulation to treat depression, bipolar disorder, and the auditory hallucinations in schizophrenia (Larson, 2008; Mayberg, Lozano, Voon, McNeely, Seminowicsz, Hanani et al., 2005).

Clinicians study and critically evaluate psychological, biological, and social science research to inform their practice. They also carry out evaluations of programs and procedures to keep improving the services rendered. Our practice informs our research and our research informs our practice.

Clinical practice is increasingly based on evidence from scientific research (APA Presidential Task Force on Evidence-Based Practice, 2006). Clinicians seek to provide clients with empirically supported treatments (EST) and methods that have been demonstrated to be effective with particular problems and populations (Chambless & Hollon, 1998; Chambless et al., 1998). Evidence-based practice (EBP) is a broader term used to describe practice that is based on the results of empirical, scientific research. We will discuss the issue of EBT and EST in more detail in Chapter 8. However, it is important to note that there is not much research on the applicability of empirically validated therapies to people from different cultures, nor has there been much empirical validation of culturally sensitive therapies (Atkinson, Bui, & Mori, 2001; Weaver, 2005). In addition, there are concerns about methodological limitations and the generalization of research results to a clinical population (Hunsley, 2007).

Structure

In addition to being purposeful and informed by theory, clinical interviews are structured. Both the specific interview and the overall process have a beginning, a middle, and an end, and each phase of the process has its own tasks and emphases. The first and continuing task is to make and sustain a warm, trustful, and collaborative relationship in which clients feel comfortable sharing and elaborating their stories. In the middle phase, clinicians and clients work together to develop new perspectives, skills, and resources from which change can evolve. In the last phase, the review and evaluation of the work and relationship occur, and plans for the future, including follow-up, are discussed.

A second kind of structure is the organization the clinician brings to the clinical interview. At times, clinicians may guide the conversation by the questions we ask, by the issues we respond to, by the subjects we introduce, or by the focus we keep. In addition, we establish rules and norms for behaviors, as well as boundaries around the relationship itself.

Time constraints also impose structure. Clinical interviewing is usually limited to a specified amount of time. The length of any individual meeting, as well as the number of meetings, is usually fixed, especially in **managed care** settings in which clients get a fixed number of visits for defined health or mental health problems. Time limits allow both clinicians and clients to know how much time is available to them for the work they do together. Because meeting time can be a scarce commodity today, it is usually regarded as sacrosanct and inviolable except in extreme circumstances. It should be noted that setting time limits on the length of the clinical interview and the helping relationship is a cultural artifact.

Contract

The participants in a clinical interview enter into a contract. The contract is a working agreement that specifies such things as the participants, purpose, goals, roles, expectations, techniques, time, structure, and cost of care. In evidence-based practice, the contract includes an agreement to carry out the systematic measurement of the client's functional levels. Our findings inform and guide subsequent goals, methods, and activities.

Contracts should be mutually developed so that participants are clear about their responsibilities and commitments, and they should be tailored to the client's style, needs, and language. The specific goals should be realistic and attainable, taking into account the stresses, strengths, and resources in the client's network. The more explicit the contract is, the better it is; the clearer the map is, the more likely the participants will arrive at the desired destination. Due to the shifting realities and resources in people's lives, contracts need to be flexible and subject to renegotiation.

Roles

Clinical interviews usually have two major prescribed roles: that of the client and that of the clinician. The client brings special knowledge of his or her own history and traditions, resources for growth and development, and particular strengths and coping skills. The clinician brings special knowledge of human behavior, psychological theory, systems theory, and communication skills.

The behavioral components of these roles are complex and varied, and they often overlap. People frequently think of the client as narrating the story while the clinician listens, sustains, and guides. However, in most interviews there is flexibility in behaviors, and, from moment to moment, either participant could be speaking or listening, guiding or following. Although the client is expected to do more of the talking, at times the clinician says more, as when sharing hunches, confronting client behaviors, educating about resources, or detailing necessary procedures. Regardless of participants' behaviors at any given moment, as clinicians we should always be cognizant of our responsibility to remain focused on the purpose and goals of the interview and on the client's needs. This principle applies whether we are trying to engage gang members on a street corner, listening to a new mother grieve the sudden loss of her baby, or taking an intake phone call from a lonely elderly man threatening to kill himself.

Neither the clinician's nor the client's role comes naturally to people; both clinicians and clients have to be educated about the expectations, responsibilities, and behaviors required by each role. You will learn about the requirements of your roles from academic study, field supervisors, and client feedback. Because clients may have had no experience with clinical interviews before they meet with you, it will be incumbent on you to orient them to roles, procedures, and expectations, inviting questions and feedback to minimize confusion or misunderstandings.

> *Whenever I begin to work with a new client, I spend part of the first interview talking about the nature of the clinical relationship. I have always liked the feminist therapy analogy that compares the clinician to a midwife. Therapy is explained as a process in which the client gives birth to new parts of herself. Like birth, the process is often painful but very exciting. I see myself as someone who has skills and training to assist her with the birthing process. I stress that I will work with her, sometimes comforting, sometimes supporting, sometimes encouraging as she gives birth[1]*

[1] Numerous first-person accounts from clinicians in the field are included in this text.

Labels

Labels and titles also distinguish clinical conversation from other forms of talking. A variety of labels may be used to describe the participants in a clinical interview. At times, the labels for clinicians designate a discipline: mental health counselor, psychologist, social worker, human service worker, criminal justice counselor, psychiatrist, pastoral counselor. At other times, labels are used to try to capture the roles and tasks of particular groups of clinicians: group facilitator, intake worker, pastoral counselor, case manager. And sometimes labels designate a specialization within a discipline: school counselor, neuropsychologist, geriatric social worker, forensic psychologist, clinical psychiatric nurse.

EXERCISE 1.2 By Any Other Name

Following is a list of terms used to describe the roles of a clinical interviewer. Each may have different meanings or nuances for different people. Apply each term to yourself, and, as you do so, notice any change in your feelings about or perception of yourself or your status as a helper. Record your observations in your journal. If you were a client, how would you feel seeing a professional with each of these labels?

interviewer	case manager
provider	shrink
therapist	life coach
clinician	change agent
counselor	helper
crisis worker	advocate
milieu therapist	analyst

Another category of labels is used to designate people with whom clinicians work: client, patient, member, resident, student, consumer, helpee. At times, the labels connote the setting; persons in a hospital may be called patients, and those in a halfway house may be referred to as residents. At other times, the labels reflect the customs of specific disciplines, agencies, or individuals.

I remember when many social workers in the fifties and sixties called their clients "patients," wishing to achieve a professional standing or recognition similar to that of psychiatrists and psychologists. A woman would come to the family service agency seeking housing and financial aid, but, in case conference, she would be described as "the patient." During the activist period of the seventies there was a shift to calling people "clients" to be more egalitarian. In the eighties, people with mental illness and their advocates asked that clients be referred to as "consumers," giving them more power, choice, and initiative in their relationships with governmental and service systems. With the advent of managed care and its medical model, I've noticed a resurgence in the use of the term "patients."

* * *

I've worked in a couple of day treatment programs for adults with developmental disabilities. In one, we called the participants "patients"; in another, "clients"; in another, "club members." I have lots of discussions with colleagues who object to my using the term "patient." They say it reflects a medical model that focuses on illness. They accuse me of being into power dynamics and suggest I call them "clients" instead. I like the word "patient" because for me it implies caring for the other.

Labels can be helpful in directing people toward specific disciplines, functions, or specialties, but they can be confusing: People with differing labels can all be performing the same roles or functions. The social worker, psychologist, and counselor may all provide counseling or psychotherapy. The client, the patient, the consumer, and the resident may all exhibit similar strengths and problems.

Labels can also obscure the fact that clinicians can have problems at the same time and of the same types as clients do. The distance between labels can appear great, whereas the actual distance between people and their narratives is less so. For example, a clinician may see a client during one hour and then, in the next hour, go to see his or her own therapist.

Labels may be used to express power, prestige, and status. They can also be used to distance, demean, and stereotype. How we connote ourselves and others has an impact on our relationship and interactions with them and on theirs with us. We need to guard against feelings of self-importance and unearned privilege that may be offensive to both clients and colleagues.

A Unique Relationship

Clinical interviewing engenders an intimacy between strangers. Even though the client and clinician have different roles, their unique relationship is like a fishbowl in which both regularly observe and experience the nuances of each other's behaviors and feelings. Just as we observe clients, clients observe us and note our subtle reactions. They observe when we seem focused and present and when we seem distracted and preoccupied. They notice what we attend to and emphasize and what we overlook and ignore. And just as clinicians may sit around and discuss clients in a team conference, clients often sit around and discuss clinicians' mannerisms and idiosyncrasies in great detail. Both clinicians and clients become known to each other in ways that are truly intimate, special, and rare.

Clinical interviewing occurs in the context of a relationship that involves a peculiar kind of mutuality. **Mutuality** refers to the fact that, although the interview focus is on the client's needs, the clinician is also affected by the give-and-take of the relationship. Both people inevitably grow and change through the give-and-take of an authentic and genuine relationship with each other (Jordan, 1991a). The peculiar part of this mutuality is that, while it is mutual, it is not equal. For example, it is chiefly the client who is regularly expected to reveal personal information in exquisite detail, while the clinician discloses personal information only on a very selective basis.

> *I often talk with clients about this "weird" relationship of therapy. Although clients may not know much about the facts of my personal life, and I usually know a lot about theirs, I still feel as though they know me in a very real and intimate way.*

Both the clinician and the client share responsibility for the process and the progress of the work. Yet because of our education, experience, and ethical and legal mandates, we are held accountable for its effectiveness and assume greater responsibility for the safety of the relationship. Furthermore, the relationship frequently entails an unspoken power imbalance due to the authority that many people vest in clinicians because of their professional licensing, status, roles, education, experience, and reputation as knowledgeable and caring people. This is particularly true when the client is mandated to attend sessions by a court or the criminal justice system. Clients may attribute a special authority to clinicians working in governmental, armed services, or law enforcement agencies such as courts, protective services, probation, or first responder teams. Finally, the client may literally be paying for the relationship, and the clinician is the one being paid.

> *I have had clients say, "I can't believe I have to pay someone to listen to me" or "I can't believe I have to pay to have a friend." I gently remind them that they're paying for my skills, not my friendship.*

Intentional Use of Self

We pay careful attention to the **intentional use of self** in the interview process. One of the paradoxes of clinical work is that clinicians are asked to be genuine, yet self-aware and deliberate at the same time (Rogers, 1980).

> *When I'm supervising students, they always ask how to decide when it's okay to be spontaneous and "real" and when it's not. It's one of the hardest things to teach and learn in clinical work. Even after I share my opinions and the theories behind them, students often act spontaneously, doing and saying things without much thought beforehand. They confuse being deliberate with being artificial. It takes a while to learn that one can be both genuine and deliberate.*

As much as possible, clinicians behave in considered or deliberate ways. Learning to be purposeful and goal-focused in your responses is one of the continuing challenges as you move from random and spontaneous chatting with clients and others, to saying or asking things for a clinical purpose. At times you may intentionally alter your style or behaviors to support client comfort and growth.

> *I am usually a very quiet, laid-back kind of counselor. I convey my attentiveness through eye contact, facial expression, and head nods. This usually works well with the clients I see at the clinic. When I was seeing Juan, I realized I had to change my style. He was legally blind and needed more verbal feedback and responsiveness from me.*

As clinicians, we also make very deliberate decisions about what we share about ourselves with clients. Personal sharing should occur only if the clinician believes that it forwards the goals of the work and only after careful consideration of its effect on the client. In Chapter 12, we will examine in greater depth issues surrounding personal sharing and disclosure.

Throughout the interview process, we also attend to our own actions and reactions. This attending to self is important for several reasons. First, we need to be aware of what our reactions may convey to clients, both intentionally and unintentionally. Second, the reactions that the client's story evokes in us may provide important information about responses the client may engender in others. Third, introspection increases our own self-knowledge, which is essential to the appropriate use of self in clinical interviewing. In addition, client stories or feelings may stir up the clinician's own old, unfinished business, signaling a need for further attention, perhaps through the clinician's own therapy. One of the most complex tasks that clinicians have to master is that of attending to many things simultaneously.

Listening on Multiple Levels

Any conversation takes place on several levels and has several forms of communication: verbal and nonverbal communication, overt and covert communication, content and process communication, and metacommunication—the messages about the message. In clinical interviewing, clinicians listen intently to all of these types and levels of communication. We listen to what clients say as well as to how they say it. We listen to our own inner process and the relationship process. And we listen to what is happening in the work and what is happening in the surrounding world.

Evaluation

Unlike most conversations, clinical interviewing involves evaluation. Clinicians examine their work session by session to assess the effectiveness of the specific focus, activities, techniques, and uses of self. Progress and process notes and audio and video recordings are all helpful. Clinicians review their work on a regular basis with supervisors and occasionally with outside consultants who have particular expertise.

Clinicians also engage clients in an ongoing evaluation of how things are going. Clinicians and clients can review the relationship and what has and has not been accomplished through either informal check-ins or by using formal progress and outcome measures. These activities allow the clinician and client to document whether measurable positive change is occurring. There is usually a process of formal evaluation at the end of the working relationship. Follow-up evaluations at specified periods after the work has ended can track how well gains from the work are being maintained. They may also remind the client of the clinician's ongoing concern and caring.

Informed by Ethics and Values

Unlike friendly conversation, clinical interviewing is governed by professional codes of ethics and by laws requiring or prohibiting specific clinician activities. Ethical codes stress the primacy of the service obligation to the client, confidentiality, integrity, and follow-through. They enjoin clinicians from practicing beyond our level of competence and prohibit sexual relationships between clinicians and clients. Chapter 2 provides more detailed discussion of ethics and ethical dilemmas.

EXERCISE 1.3 Your Values and Beliefs

Core values and beliefs are often learned from families and are strongly affected by culture and important reference groups. In your journal, record some of the guiding beliefs and values that are important to you. Do you anticipate that some professional values will challenge your personal beliefs?

Clinical interviews should reflect that we value the dignity and worth of all people. They should actively work to identify and eliminate ways of thinking, speaking, or acting that may reflect racism, classism, sexism, ableism, homophobia, religious discrimination, ageism, anti-immigrant bias, and other oppressive ideologies. We should convey nonjudgmental acceptance without necessarily approving of specific behaviors.

We believe that clinicians should do more than just think or behave ethically with clients. Ethical codes encourage us to take stands against social forces and institutions that impinge on clients' rights, health, and welfare. We should work in social and economic justice campaigns; fight to end discrimination on the basis of language, country of origin, and cultural practices; and work to change unjust laws and structures that are barriers to client well-being and achievement.

Multicultural Practice

The United States is increasingly pluralistic and multicultural. The rapidly changing demographics of the United States make it clear that the current Euro-American majority will soon be the numerical minority. Jeanne Slattery (2004) observes that "Euro-Americans are already in the minority in California, Hawaii, and New Mexico" (p. xxiii). Derald Wing Sue and David Sue (2008) note that this diversification of the United States is due to two factors: differential birth rates and immigration. Birth rates among Euro-Americans have declined, while those of other racial and ethnic groups have increased. There are also more documented immigrants, undocumented immigrants, and refugees than at any other time in U.S. history (Lum, 2004). As a nation, we are clearly becoming more mixed in terms of racial and ethnocultural group membership.

In our private lives, we are free to decide whether we want to interact with people who differ from us in significant ways or whether we want to carry out our lives mostly with people like ourselves. However, in our professional lives, human service workers regularly interview clients whose class, race, ethnicity, religion, age, language, ability, gender, living situations, cultural practices, values, and norms differ from our own. Note that we do not make assumptions about any clinician's identity. While there is not as much diversity as there should be among those entering and leading our professions (Malgady & Zayas, 2001), gains have been made, and we recognize that clinicians now can be from any country, language, and cultural group, as well as of any race, ethnic group, color, class, size, sexual orientation, spiritual affiliation, physical ability, and age.

Differences are not just limited to cultural differences. You will work with clients who differ from you in terms of age, race, culture, ability, class, gender, family form, sexual orientation, and religion. Knowledge about, experience with, and appreciation of the norms, styles, and strengths within these differences will help you attend to them earlier and more comfortably as you develop as a professional. We believe that only if we are knowledgeable about and sensitive to a wide range of cultural values, norms, and nuances can we hope to devise appropriate and effective clinical interventions in a global, multicultural society.

Clearly you must prepare yourself for multicultural practice: to meet knowledgeably and openly with clients having many cultures, religions, family forms, strengths and challenges, or migration stories (be it from one state, one country, or even one gender to another). Multicultural practice recognizes, respects, and responds with informed thoughtfulness to the variety of differences within and between people. It is an important feature of effective clinical relationships and work. We need to stay open to new learning and interpersonal experience, attentive to differences, building knowledge and skills, and engaging in ongoing self-reflection and dialogue with others different from ourselves.

Worldview

All clinical interviewing is embedded in a worldview—a system of values and beliefs—that shapes clinical work. A worldview usually has both explicit and implicit elements, both conscious and unconscious influences. We believe it is very important that clinicians use continuing education, supervision, and personal reflection to be aware of the assumptions guiding their professional practice and be able to articulate them clearly.

■ Our Worldview

Our own worldview is both **ecological** and **systemic.** Like all ecological and systemic practitioners, we recognize and appreciate the interactivity and interdependence of all living and nonliving things; we believe that there are biological, psychological, sociocultural, political, economic, spiritual, and environmental influences in what appear to be "individual" human behaviors or isolated family interactions (Bateson, 1972; Bronfenbrenner, 1979; Qin & Comstock, 2005; von Bertalanffy, 1968). We believe that people can best be understood in the context of the relationships, resources, and barriers to well-being in their lives. Furthermore, like many ecopsychologists, we believe human beings are affected not only by their relationships with others but also by their relationships with both the animate and inanimate environments (Roszak, Gomes, & Kanner, 1995). Therefore, we pay as much attention to the circumstances and the relationships of our clients, and to the effects of the larger world on them, as we do to their internal processes.

EXAMPLE

Mickey Riordan, a drug-abusing teenager, is arrested carrying a gun. In the subsequent court evaluation, it is learned that his mother is a prostitute doing prison time for heroin addiction and shoplifting. His father was killed a few years earlier in a drug raid. The boy lives with an aunt who works two jobs to support many extended kin; however, he often sleeps at friends' apartments, doing and selling drugs, and watching MTV. One could speculate that Mickey's behavior may result from his negative perceptions of self, which he has internalized because of the neglect and abandonment he has experienced at the hands of his adult caregivers. In addition, Mickey suffers from attention deficit disorder related to ingesting lead paint and being exposed to other environmental toxins dumped in his community, and he could be using drugs to calm his symptoms. Several local companies have moved their factories and supermarkets out of the community, leaving few jobs or career prospects in the town other than drug dealing. Furthermore, expanded military expenditures at a time of balanced budgets resulted in the closing of teen programs in his area so that his main opportunity for friendship is gang membership. The clinician working with Mickey needs to recognize all the factors that have an impact on him, including family, friendships, economic trends, corporate policies, political decisions, and environmental pollution.

In clinical interviews, we always listen for **reciprocal influences**—how every member of an interaction influences, and is influenced by, the others. Because of our belief in reciprocal influence, we do not believe that clinicians are "detached," "neutral," or "objective observers." Therefore, we pay special attention to how clients and clinicians influence and affect each other's behaviors in the course of their work together.

Our work is also influenced by the family systems concept of **circular causality** (Bateson, 1979). Events in complex systems often exist as both causes and effects of each other. Clinicians frequently see couples in which each partner blames the other for the troubles in their relationship. For example, one partner showers the other with affection, wishing to become more intimate. The other partner, feeling smothered and invaded, becomes unresponsive and withdrawn. The first partner, alarmed at the distancing, doubles his or her attention. This dance often goes on indefinitely, ending all too frequently in acrimonious debates about who is doing what to whom. In this example, the first partner may describe the interaction as follows: "My partner pulls away, so I have to chase after him to get close." The second partner may say, "My partner invades me, so I retreat." In trying to make sense of complex related behaviors, people tend to see behaviors as having starting points (causes) and stopping points (effects). However, the choice of a specific event as a starting or stopping point is arbitrary.

Furthermore, we recognize that systems are in constant flux, that life is not homeostatic, and that we are seeing the client at only one point in time. If we entered the relationship with a client at another point, we might see a different person. Clients often make contact with clinicians at a time of crisis, when they are stressed and burdened. What we see is only a snapshot of the person at that difficult moment in time. If we were to see that person at other times, in more supportive circumstances or in more empowered interaction with others, we might describe and respond to the person very differently.

> *Leslie was a very quiet, shy girl in my office. She was often quite teary and self-effacing. She had almost no self-confidence and was very soft-spoken. When I went to see her on the soccer field, I couldn't believe it was the same girl. She was so sure of herself: She gave orders to the other kids on her team; she laughed and yelled.*

Clients may show different aspects of themselves even within the same session. A client may talk about a parent in a regressed, childlike manner and then speak with authoritative confidence when discussing events at work.

We believe that there are **multiple realities,** or differing views about how things are, how they got that way, and how they ought to be. Clinicians need to be careful not to assume that their "reality," or point of view, is more correct or more meaningful than the client's. Each has knowledge and experience that informs and changes the other and the work, validating the strengths of both (Daniel, 2000; Jordan, 2004a).

We believe that all people's ideas are worthy of consideration and that silencing or excluding individuals or groups is the surest road to misunderstanding large segments of human experience. Moreover, clients are sometimes more attuned to both the hard realities and the natural supports of complex environments than clinicians are. Clinicians usually learn a great deal from client knowledge, experience, and perspective.

Experienced clinicians have long observed that, no matter how irrational things may seem to us as outside observers of others' lives, to the people living those lives, the "irrationality" may represent their best adaptation at the moment—a sensible way of negotiating daily life under oppressive circumstances. Clinicians must make continuing efforts to immerse themselves in the client's perspective rather than dragging the client into their own constructions of reality.

We are aware of the growing importance of spirituality in the lives of both clinicians and clients. Spiritual beliefs affect people's worldviews—how they make meaning, how they feel about themselves, and how they relate to other people and to the larger world. Spiritual practices can be an important part of a client's plan for change and a resource that can be called on to empower both the client and clinician (Canda & Furman, 1999; Hodge, 2003; Munk, 2005; Walsh, 1999).

Clients often seek clinical help when they are stuck because they have a limited perspective. One of the major goals of therapy is to help clients broaden their perspectives, to see things using different lenses, to construct new realities, or to reframe their situations. Indeed, we wish to foster in ourselves and in our clients a growing capacity to appreciate different and even competing perspectives.

> *I often tell clients that we don't have to agree and twin with each other, but we both need to listen with open minds. What appears off target one week may resonate clearly three weeks later. And this cuts both ways. A client may share an idea or an interpretation of an event different from my own, and while at first I may disagree, on reflection I come to see that interpretation as a very novel and helpful take on the situation, and I say that to the client.*

Our perspective is characterized by a deep and abiding belief in the capacity of human beings to grow and change in positive relationships and contexts that activate potentials and provide for the meeting of basic human needs. A **strengths perspective,** sometimes called a positive psychology approach, undergirds all effective clinical intervention. **Positive psychology** is concerned with well-being and optimal functioning, and "aims to broaden the focus . . . beyond suffering and its direct alleviation" (Duckworth, Steen, & Seligman, 2005, p. 629). Similarly, an **empowerment perspective** emphasizes the centrality of client participation and self-determination. Clients should be directly involved in the processes and outcomes which they believe are the most empowering for themselves (Boehm & Staples, 2004). Working within positive psychology, strengths, and empowerment perspectives, we try as frequently as possible to elicit, underscore, and utilize the often undervalued or unnoticed strengths with which clients have successfully addressed problems (Poulin, 2005; Saleebey, 2005; Wong, 2006).

Clients often report that professionals have asked them so often to recite what is *not* working that they forget to mention or to value what *has* worked. Clinicians' valuing of unsung acts of valor or achievement, no matter how small, can often fan a spark of hope. Noticing and validating strengths can bring new meaning to clients who have seen themselves (or who have been seen by others) as hopeless, incompetent, or of no importance.

In addition to helping clients gain new perspectives on their circumstances, clinicians may also work with clients to modify their circumstances. We may do so through direct advocacy, such as helping a client get welfare benefits, find day care, or gain access to a training program. We may also advocate for populations, such as when we work on getting legislation passed to fund school lunch programs, support the funding of community day programs for people with Alzheimer's disease, or testify regarding the need for programs for the homeless (Rappaport, 1987).

Finally, we believe that clinicians must work for social change. An old public health adage maintains that, instead of retrieving individual drowning victims one after the other from the river, we must go upriver to determine and eliminate the causes of the drowning. Part of our professional responsibility is to work for the health and mental health of our clients and to prevent conditions that contribute to disease and distress.

A **social justice perspective** informs our professional ethic of care. We believe that we have a social responsibility to work for a more equitable distribution of resources, rights, and opportunities for all people (Swenson, 1998). Clinicians must nourish structures and processes that encourage growth and development and oppose all forms of oppression and environmental degradation around the world.

Activism may be a part of our professional role, such as when we join with other clinicians to work for social change through organizations like Psychologists for Social Responsibility, Social Workers for Peace and Disarmament, Counselors for Social Justice, and The Public Interest Directorate of the American Psychological Association. At times, we may use our professional skills as volunteers in community agencies or in responding to national disasters.

Following the bombing of the Federal Building in Oklahoma, I was part of a team of clinicians who volunteered to work with child survivors and their families. As an expert on trauma in children, I was glad to offer my services. I always feel that it is important to do volunteer work using my clinical skills.

* * *

A couple of years ago, a group of friends and I began a series of support groups for people newly diagnosed with AIDS. Now we are using the same skills to help train peer leaders for a breast cancer support group. I can't tell you how much both experiences have enriched my life and my clinical work.

Our sense of social responsibility also involves personal activism, which leads us to organize, disseminate leaflets, and march. It takes us to state and national capitals to lobby, picket, and become leaders in political bodies that wield real power to effect large-scale change. It stimulates us to speak and write in the media and not only for scholarly meetings and journals.

I was part of a team that conducted research with families about the psychological effects of exposure to nuclear radiation. We interviewed atomic veterans who were exposed during the aboveground atomic testing in the United States. A couple of years later, I went with a group of mental health clinicians to the nuclear test site in Nevada to protest continued underground nuclear testing. We were subsequently arrested with hundreds of other protesters for trespassing on federal property.

■ Learning to Be a Professional

Many people decide to become clinicians because they have a strong desire to help others. Some pursue clinical education to advance into leadership roles where they are already employed or to gain new or advanced knowledge and skills as community organizers, activists, and social policy advocates. Gerald Corey and Marianne Schneider Corey (2007) suggest other goals—some conscious, some not—that move people toward clinical careers, including a desire to find and provide answers to problems, to learn more about themselves and their own problems, to make money as therapists, or to gain professional power, prestige, or status.

You may have decided to become a clinician because you have been told that you are a good listener and **natural helper,** who leaves people feeling understood and supported. You may be the "go-to" person for friends or family when problems arise. Perhaps you have prior experience as a community volunteer, Big Brother, Red Cross crisis worker, camp counselor, or hotline staffer. You may have experience in the mental health field, or you may be moving from a career in religious work, business, teaching, law, nursing, or an allied health profession. We all come with a set of strengths, skills, and natural helping styles.

Natural Style

Edward Neukrug and Alan Schwitzer (2006) note that natural helpers can be classified as natural "listeners, analyzers, problem solvers, or challengers" (p. 4). Those who are natural listeners are good at "active listening, empathic understanding, and rapport building" (p. 5). Analyzers are interested in understanding what causes problems for the client: They focus on "case conceptualization, diagnosis, and treatment planning" (p. 6). Problem solvers want to get things done; they "tend to be more directive, attempting to mobilize the person in need to make decisions, take action and decisively change behavior" (p. 6). Finally, challengers believe that they "can quickly push the client into seeing the world in a different manner, and will often confront clients through the use of questions, particularly 'why?' questions" (p. 7).

EXERCISE 1.4 Natural Style

In your journal, describe your own natural style. If others have commented on your helping style, what did they say? Discuss in class what you like about your style and what you might want to change or augment.

Growing from a natural helper into a professional clinician requires engaged interactive learning. Therefore, you can advance your learning best through work in relationships with others. Instructors, fellow students, colleagues, and clients will help you acquire and utilize knowledge and skills and shape your professional values, ethics, and attitudes.

The RE-VIEW PRACTICE Method

We have developed the **RE-VIEW PRACTICE Method** for acquiring and enhancing the skills of helping. The elements of the method build on and reinforce each other. The RE-VIEW acronym represents the key elements in becoming a more comfortable and informed professional:

- **R**ead about skills, their purpose, and intended effects.
- **E**xplore and discuss the skills in class.
- **V**iew instructors and other experienced clinicians employing the skills.
- **I**mplement the skills in video-recorded role-play exercises.
- **E**valuate your performance.
- **W**atch your video recording with others, giving and receiving feedback.

Read

Reading about clinical work is often a first step in formal education. You should read widely about different perspectives on clinical relationships and specific theories from the professional literature in social work, psychology, counseling, psychiatry, neuroscience, and nursing. We also encourage reading in sociology, anthropology, biology, economics, mind-body health, religious and spiritual practices, politics, literature, and history. Since you are dealing with the complexity of people from a variety of backgrounds, experiences, and social contexts, you should read about race, class, disability, sexual orientation, immigration, and gender and age discrimination so that you are well informed and can attend to differences and intragroup variations. We also suggest additional reading from popular literature to help you expand your knowledge base.

Also read about specific skills related to interviewing and helping. This book is designed to walk you through clinician–client work from preparation to ending, discussing the skills commonly used in each work phase and the complexity of issues that can arise in the clinical relationship. Cross-cultural and multicultural practice considerations and skills infuse text content.

Explore

Carefully evaluate what you read. Rather than just swallowing elegant or compelling theories in which practice is grounded, become a critical thinker. **Critical thinking** involves dividing theories into their conceptual constructs, assumptions, and hypotheses; understanding the history and context that inform these constructs; and evaluating their strengths, weaknesses, and practice implications (Mumm & Kersting, 1997).

Skill application is heightened as your instructor and classmates provide examples of how, when, with whom, and for what purposes a skill may be useful. Discussion and examples will help you apply skills in meaningful client-centered, nonjudgmental, culturally knowledgeable, and appropriate ways.

Clinical learning also demands self-examination and **introspection**—looking within yourself to appraise the nature, intensity, and meanings of feelings, thoughts, and dynamics that can affect your interviewing behaviors. Learn to articulate your values and beliefs, become aware of your use of self in relationships with clients, and uncover and correct misinformation and bias.

To help you transform accrued information and experience into a humbling yet empowering blend of reflective wisdom, common sense, and compassionate action, we have included a number of activities in the text and on the Companion Website. They contain critical thinking questions to help you reflect on readings and controversial issues, along with self-exploration exercises to bring to the surface your personal values and potential blind spots. Many of the activities can be done in class; others can be done at home. We suggest that you keep a journal of your clinical exercise experiences and reflections for discussion in class with instructors and colleagues.

View

An important aspect of learning about the structure, process, and skills of clinical work is to see interviewing in action. One way to accomplish this is to observe supervisors and other highly skilled clinicians at work. With the client's permission, you may be able to observe clinical work through a one-way mirror or sit in on a seasoned colleague's sessions. Another way to learn about clinical work is to experience clinical work first hand, as a client. Many students find personal counseling a useful experience in their own learning and growth. If you do not have the opportunity to observe clinical work as it occurs, many video recordings and films are available in which clinicians demonstrate skills informed by particular models of therapy.

While watching entire interviews is useful, we agree with Allen Ivey and his colleagues (Ivey, Ivey, & Zalaquett, 2010) that students learn best by studying "microskills"—the small-skill components of interviewing. The DVD accompanying this text contains clips of six clinicians from diverse backgrounds in clinical relationships with six diverse clients. The clips depict their work as it unfolds over periods as short as one day and as long as a couple of months. Each clip illustrates specific skills keyed to chapter content in the text. At times you will see more than one clinician using the same skill, to illustrate the different ways in which clinicians implement the same skill. In time you too will want to develop your own "voice" and way of implementing specific skills.

We believe it is important to observe as many clinicians as you can to see that clinicians all work somewhat differently, often while applying many similar guiding principles. We are pleased about the increasing number of video recordings and DVD clips available now showing a wide range of clinicians using an array of skills and working with a variety of clients. When we were in school, we watched videotapes that almost exclusively showed older White male gurus interviewing depressed White women—not at all representative of the diversity of colleagues and clients that we experienced in our internships.

Implement the Skills

Reading about and viewing skills in action are not sufficient. You must *do the work*. The best way to advance clinical understanding and skills is to work with clients and to get feedback from supervisors. As you begin your work with clients, you need other ways to learn and practice skills. Role-play sessions with students and colleagues can help you prepare for clinical work. If your school or internship site has a video lab or equipment, record your clinical interactions and view them alone or with others for learning purposes. As your skill and confidence grow, you will begin to develop your own informed style, voice, and way of using specific skills with different clients.

We present a number of role-play exercises in the text and on the Companion Website. Sometimes we present a situation for student "client" and "clinician" to play out. At other times the instructor may play a client with whom you can practice your skills.

Evaluate Performance Together

Continuous reflection on your work is crucial, no matter what stage or level you are at in your training or experience. One very sound way to evaluate and modify your professional style is to make yourself an open and honest recipient of other people's evaluations during your class and field education. Reviewing and rehearing what you said and did is often extremely revealing. Feedback from video recordings and direct observation helps us plan and guide further learning and skill development.

In internship case conference presentations, you will get to see senior staff sharing observations and recommendations about interactions that clinicians have had with their clients—why they might have done and said what they did and how to improve on the process. Classroom feedback from role-plays and video-recorded dialogues demonstrate how different instructors and classmates make evaluative comments and suggestions. From hearing how others express their feedback and by trying out feedback styles yourself as you comment on your classmates' role-play interactions, you become a better observer of yourself, developing self-observation language from what you have heard others say.

Process recordings constitute a wonderful way to reflect on clinical work. Of the many forms of **process recording,** we suggest writing a verbatim transcript of the interview (role-played or real) on one side of the paper. The other side can contain comments about the process—what you were intending to do, what you were thinking or feeling at a given point in the interview, and what you think the client was thinking or feeling. At the end of the recording, you can summarize new observations about yourself and the client from the interview experience, as well as what you wish you had done or said differently. You can also note questions for supervision and requests for specific help in skill building.

Watch

Reviewing your video and process recordings, both alone and in supervision, provides the opportunity for self-reflection and knowledge building. Observing your own work on video can provide guidance for personal growth because it reveals unhelpful reactions and behaviors in interviews, as well as bias or visible discomfort with certain clients.

Practice, Practice, Practice

The last part of the RE-VIEW PRACTICE Method is practice. While practice does not make you a perfect clinician, it makes you better and better. Learning to be a clinician is a lifelong process of knowledge acquisition and growth in self and skills. So you have to continue your professional development by reading, by practicing with many different clients and supervisors, and by giving and receiving feedback as you watch yourself and others at work, in self-aware and informed interactions with others (see Clip 1.1).

Instructors, fellow students, colleagues, and clients will help you in acquiring and utilizing knowledge and skills, as well as in shaping your professional values, ethics, and attitudes. Though becoming a professional is enjoyable and exciting, you will face many challenges as you begin the learning process.

CLIP 1.1
The RE-VIEW
PRACTICE
Method

EXERCISE 1.5 Lights, Camera, Action

Pair up with someone in class. Before you learn more about the skills of helping, video record yourself trying to have a helpful 10-minute role-play conversation with a peer. Notice how you feel as you watch yourself in the video. Save the recording so that you can see how you change and how you build on your basic strengths throughout the semester.

The Challenges Ahead

Moving from Spontaneous to Intentional

An inextricable part of becoming a clinician is learning to be aware of oneself, the client, the work, and the environment—all at the same time. Clinicians constantly observe, evaluate, and modify their clinical interactions to remain client-centered and goal-focused, and to know where the client is from moment to moment.

This planned use of self and skills requires restraint of some of our natural impulses and feelings. It can be difficult to feel genuine and intentional at the same time. Arnold Lazarus (1981) describes how a clinician friend of his wanted to become a therapist but was so intently focused on "acting like a therapist" that he lost his natural ability to help. Students often comment that they feel phony or awkward when they are thinking so much before they act. The challenge is to become comfortable as both an observant bystander and a genuine human being present in the moment.

Working Under a Microscope

The scrutiny of your knowledge, skills, and relational capacities by teachers, supervisors, and colleagues can be difficult. Trying out new skills while being observed can make beginning clinicians feel paralyzed and aware of every word and move. Many people describe this self-conscious shake-up in confidence and behaviors as they begin to receive supervisory and collegial feedback. You may experience unnecessary worry about whether you are as good as others who seem to have more knowledge, poise, comfort in self-revelation, and ease in role-play and case presentation or who just seem generally better suited for clinical work.

You may discover that your own ethnic or age group is not widely represented in the faculty, internship staff, and student body, and you may feel marginalized or expected to represent your reference group in discussions about diversity. You may be placed in a spotlight and feel self-conscious and even angry when colleagues turn to you expecting you to be the "expert" regarding some aspect of your identity or background.

You may come from a family or culture in which so much focus on yourself would be regarded as self-centered or grandiose, or you may be from a background where the scrutiny of your personal attributes, preparedness, and competence is considered intrusive and inappropriate. However, clinicians come to appreciate that reflecting on personal beliefs and practices and observing and being observed are essential to ensuring that they provide effective service to clients. Whereas students might look forward to a day of *less* study and observation, experienced clinicians often ask for *more*, not less, to get fresh perspectives on their work.

Learning That There Is No One "Right" Answer

Prochaska & Norcross (2007) noted that each of the 400 systems of psychotherapy they identified espoused its own epistemology as "effective and uniquely applicable" (p. 1). As you work with different supervisors or attend different classes, you will hear about many different approaches and sometimes contradictory beliefs about how to help others. Clinical work is rife with theoretical ambiguities and clashes over what constitutes best practice. You may feel some normal exasperation about the lack of one right answer or one way to resolve human problems. However, in time you will discover that patiently struggling with ambiguity may lead to new ideas and new approaches.

You will discover that, due to the great diversity of clients, what is helpful in conceptualizing and responding to one client may not be helpful with another client with similar problems. Furthermore, even when working with one client, you will discover many useful ways of responding to him or her, and each helpful response may lead you down a different path than you anticipated. Your professional education is designed to teach you how to evaluate and distinguish among the many useful ideas and applications in the context of specific cultures, individuals, families, groups, and situations.

Learning from Mistakes

Mistakes are part of all learning, but they can be disconcerting and embarrassing if you are used to doing most things well. Clinicians regularly reflect on their mistakes because mistakes are great teachers and can highlight areas for continued growth and improvement. In setting out in your clinical education, though, it takes trust to believe that instructors and supervisors have your interests at heart when they routinely critique your work. Always keep in mind that *critique* means to identify both the problematic and the positive and constructive aspects of your work.

Also helpful is hearing seasoned colleagues and mentors describing their own bloopers and realizing that mistakes will continue to occur throughout our careers. Seeing others talk comfortably and openly about their mistakes provides relief from secret fears that frequent mistakes make us inherently unsuited for clinical practice.

You may worry about handing in process recordings for practicum supervision because your supervisor will see that you have made the same mistakes that you made twice before and thought you were through making. But this worry is to be expected. "Once we accept mistakes as a human given and not just as personal flaws or too-daunting challenges, we can begin to normalize mistake making as part of a developmental learning curve in the counseling professions" (Dillon, 2003, p. 3).

Dealing with Strong Feelings

While studying to be a clinician, it is very likely that you will experience strong feelings. Clinical education is not just intellectual learning; it involves the heart as well as the mind. As you read in psychology, social work, and counseling, and as you begin to work with clients, you will hear painful stories and become immersed in human suffering. You may find yourself carrying feelings of sadness, anger, and pain about what you are studying and hearing. Some of what you are learning may touch sore spots or painful issues in your own life. Many of the issues that you discuss in class and that clients face may seem insurmountable because they are related to large-scale social injustice and require structural changes.

Though these feelings can help us understand something of what clients feel, at times your reactions may feel overwhelming and beyond your ability to contain and harness them constructively. Rather than suppressing or avoiding deep feelings, your challenge will be to learn to embrace them, modulate them, and learn from them. You will discover that others often share similar reactions. You can discuss these feelings with colleagues and supervisors to grow as a person and a professional. Clinicians who find that powerful feeling states continually disrupt their work with clients often use personal therapy for understanding and growth just as clients do.

EXERCISE 1.6 Challenges

What do you think will be the hardest part of learning to be a clinician? Will it be having people comment on your strengths and problem areas; giving feedback to other people; meeting new people; responding to people who are angry or sad or who have strong feelings; talking about subjects such as sex, money, and sexual orientation; working with a variety of people who are different from yourself; or something else? Discuss this question in small groups.

◼ Conclusion

Becoming a professional clinician is an extremely satisfying and challenging experience. You are starting a lifelong process of learning, interaction, self-observation, and feedback that will shape and reshape your knowledge and skills. In the process of learning to be a clinician, you will need to develop empathy, patience, a durable faith in people and process, the energy to work hard over time, respect for differences, a tolerance for ambiguities, and a sturdy, resilient self that collaborates well with others.

By now you are probably quite eager to start learning and practicing interviewing skills with clients. Each of the following chapters focuses on the specific skills used in helping relationships. It is time to start, and we start our work with clients even before we meet.

◼ Suggested Readings

We highly recommend the following books about the personal challenges of helping to complement your readings on skill development:

Baird, Brian N. (2007). *The internship, practicum, and field placement handbook: A guide for helping professionals* (5th Ed.). Upper Saddle River, NJ: Pearson.

Hill, Marcia. (2004). *Diary of a country therapist.* Binghamton, NY: Haworth.

Ram Dass & Gorman, Paul. (1985). *How can I help? Stories and reflections on service.* New York: Knopf.

The following texts provide good overviews of the major schools of clinical practice and counseling theory.

Corey, Gerald. (2009). *Theory and practice of counseling and psychotherapy* (8th Ed.). Belmont, CA: Wadsworth.

Prochaska, James O., & Norcross, John C. (2007). *Theories of psychotherapy: A transtheoretical approach.* Belmont, CA: Brooks/Cole.

For those interested in an overview of social justice and activism, we recommend the following:

Jacobson, Wendy B. (2001). Beyond therapy: Bringing social work back to human services reform. *Social Work, 46,* 51–61.

Kiselica, Mark S., & Robinson, Michelle. (2001). Bringing advocacy counseling to life: The history, issues, and human drama of social justice work in counseling. *Journal of Counseling and Development, 79,* 387–397.

Polack, Robert J. (2004). Social justice and the global economy: New challenges for social work in the 21st century. *Social Work, 49,* 281–290.

■ Self-Explorations

1. Give examples of people you know whose helping style you admire. Where do they fit in Neukrug and Schwitzer's taxonomy of natural styles?

2. Have you ever used acupuncture, herbal treatments, homeopathy, massage, meditation, or any other form of alternative or complementary medicine to help you cope with a physical or emotional problem? Which aspects were different and which were similar to traditional medical or psychological approaches? Why did you choose this type of help? Was it useful? Would you use this or another form of alternative help in the future? Why?

3. Has there been a time when after helping someone, you realized that he or she also had helped and changed you in unanticipated ways? What did that person say, do, or embody that helped you? How can that experience help you be a wiser helper in the future?

4. How do your family and friends feel about your decision to enter a helping profession? What reactions or comments of theirs show their support for your decision? What reactions or comments of theirs have challenged or questioned the wisdom of your decision?

5. Have you ever worked for social change or participated in social activism? Describe your original goals, as well as the short-term and long-term effects of this work on both you and the larger community.

6. Discuss instances in which you gave someone feedback about their performance of roles or skills in some undertaking (for example, work, sports, volunteering, trying out for a part). How forthright were you able to be in pointing out areas of performance that needed improvement? If you held back suggestions or criticism, why was that? How effective was your feedback in helping that person improve their performance?

7. When have you received feedback that helped you to improve role or skill performance? What aspect of the feedback was especially helpful to you? Discuss some feedback you received that was not helpful and explain why.

■ Essay Questions

1. There are many different types of helping professions: social work, counseling, human services, and psychology, to name just a few. What distinguishes each profession from the others? Visit the Websites for the National Association of Social Workers (www.socialworkers.org), the American Counseling Association (www.counseling.org), the American Psychological Association (www.apa.org), and the National Organization for Human Services (www.nationalhumanservices.org). For each, describe:

   a. The focus or mission of the profession.

   b. How this profession differs from the other helping professions whose Websites you visited.

   c. The education necessary to become a professional.

   d. How much this profession is respected and why.

2. Do you think clinical work is an art or a science? How much of a role do intuition and personal experience have in clinical work? How might clinical research inform clinical assessment and practice? Based on the material you have read, present thorough arguments on both sides and then draw your conclusion.

3. A "50-minute hour" is an arbitrary construction for the convenience of clinicians and agencies. Do you think clients can be expected to "turn it on" or "turn it off" every week at an appointed time? Discuss the pros and cons of scheduling in this way. Discuss how time-limited and scheduled interviews are culturally constructed.

4. Events in complex systems often exist as both a cause and an effect of each other. The authors give an example of the distancing and pursuing dance in a couple's relationship. Give another example that illustrates your understanding of circular causality in systems.

■ Key Terms

Circular causality

Clinical interviewing

Complementary medicine

Critical thinking

Ecological

Empowerment perspective

Indigenous helpers

Intentional use of self

Introspection

Managed care

Multiple realities

Mutuality

Natural helpers

Positive psychology

Process recording

Professional clinicians

Reciprocal influences

RE-VIEW PRACTICE Method

Scientist/practitioner model

Social justice perspective

Strengths perspective

Systemic

Theory

CHAPTER 2

Responsible Practice:
Cultural Awareness and Professional Ethics

In the last chapter we described a number of ways that clinical interviewing is different from informal or natural helping. In this chapter we focus on two key issues that are the bedrock of responsible practice: (1) attending to multiculturalism, difference, and diversity; and (2) working from a solid base of professional ethics. Following a review of salient issues and research findings regarding multiculturalism, racism, and identity formation, we discuss guidelines for multicultural practice. We then ask you to think about your own race, ethnicity, and identity and how these may both inform and complicate your work with clients. We introduce you to several important principles and standards of clinical practice ethics codes, asking you to clarify your own values and ethics and to think about potential ethical dilemmas you might face.

Please note that we do not limit our discussion of these important topics to one chapter. While this chapter is a general overview of issues and concerns, we infuse specific skills for addressing issues of culture, difference, and diversity, as well as skills you can use to implement your ethical stance when dilemmas and challenges arise in your work with clients, throughout the book.

EXERCISE 2.1 I Am What I Am

On a sheet of paper, write the phrase "I am . . ." on 10 different lines. Then go back and quickly complete each sentence with the first thing that comes to mind when you think "I am . . .".

Review your responses and note how many items refer to identity and how many are related to transient states like being hungry, tired, and the like.

Discuss your answers in small groups. Do others say things about themselves that you might also say about yourself? What can you learn about how you identify yourself?

Is there anything you "are" that you are ambivalent about writing down or discussing aloud?

In what circumstances do you think your answers might change?

■ Multiculturalism, Difference, and Diversity

Many professions use the term *multicultural* to describe the increasing diversity of the U.S. population in terms of race and ethnicity. **Culture** refers to a group's shared language, traditions, customs, rituals, history, and expectations of one another. **Ethnicity** refers to the classification of people based on their shared ancestry and culture. **Race** is "the classification of people based on geographic origin and shared physical characteristics like skin color, hair texture and facial features" (Parker & Chambers, 2005, p. 57). Doman Lum (2004) points out that *multiculturalism* implies that cultural groups in the United States now preserve their distinctive identities—their languages, beliefs, customs, and religions— and that "these distinctive practices represent enormous cultural wealth . . . [and] are a source of enrichment for society as a whole" (p. 3).

Race is a **social construct**—a concept invented by the needs, values, or beliefs of people in a society. Although the concept of race is socially constructed, people often behave as though there is something essential, innate, or biological about race and ethnicity. Some researchers who found racial differences in characteristics such as intelligence would attribute those differences to presumed genetic or cultural deficiencies of non-White people (for example, Hernstein & Murray, 1994; Jensen, 1969). However, scientists currently working on the Human Genome Project have shown that there are no real racial differences: "Research on human genome variation increasingly challenges the applicability of the term 'race' to human population groups, raising questions about the validity of inferences made about 'race' in the biomedical and scientific literature" (Royal & Dunstan, 2004, p. S5).

In previous decades, people who were different from the dominant European American ethnocultural groups in the United States were referred to as "ethnic minorities." "**Minority status** denoted a numerically smaller or politically powerless group in relation to a larger, controlling, and dominant majority. Whites were cast as the majority, whereas nonwhites were the minorities" (Lum, 2004, p. 3). However, Victor De La Cancela, Yvonne Jenkins, and Jean Lau Chin (1993) state that the term *minority*, used as a label to refer to populations of color, ignores the reality that Caucasians are the numerical minority globally. They go on to say that the use of the term *minority* has "oppressive connotations of disempowerment and poverty that are inappropriate and offensive in the context of African, Latino, Indigenous, and Asian ethnic groups who are becoming economically strong and sociopolitically organized" (p. 7).

> *I hate being referred to as "a minority." I'm Puerto Rican. Being called a "minority" makes me feel like people see me as "inferior." Aren't there more Puerto Ricans in New York City than Swedes? How come they aren't called a minority? People make all kinds of assumptions about minorities—like we're poor, deprived, and depraved.*

* * *

> *People call us Asians "the model minority." What the heck does that mean? We're the best of the worst?*

There is also a growing awareness that many people are **multiracial** and **multiethnic.** Not until the 2000 census were people able to check more than one box to identify their racial identity. In 2000, 2.4 percent (over 6.8 million people) checked more than one box to represent their race, but it is estimated that the number is much higher (Lum, 2004). When one considers multiethnic identity, the numbers are even higher. However, most people don't recognize or honor this complexity. Barack Obama is often referred to as the first "Black President" of the United States. In reality, he is biracial. In a similar vein, Tiger Woods is often referred to as a "Black golfer," based solely on his skin color. In reality, he is of mixed ancestry and is both multiracial and multiethnic. His mother is Thai, Chinese, and White. His father is Black, Native American, and Chinese (Shih & Sanchez, 2005).

> *I consider myself Black. My father is Black and my mother is Puerto Rican, but I somehow came out looking lily White. People always look at me strangely when I walk into the Black Student Association meetings.*

EXERCISE 2.2 Your Ethnocultural and Racial Background

In small groups, discuss your racial and ethnocultural background. How do your race and ethnicity influence your outlook on life—your values, attitudes, and behaviors? What are the racial and cultural backgrounds of members of your family? Are they the same as or different from yours? What factors make you feel positive about your race and ethnicity? Negative? Ambivalent?

Some argue that the concept of multiculturalism includes attention to more than ethnicity, race, and color. For example, Gilbert Herdt (1992) and Daniel Harris (1997) suggested that there is a gay culture with its own norms, language, rituals, and styles of communication.

Deaf activists describe a Deaf culture based on the use of American Sign Language (ASL) and the use of "vision instead of hearing for getting vital and incidental information" (Stokoe, 1989, p. 55). Padden (1989) uses an uppercase *D* to highlight Deaf people as a cultural group. Others assert that deafness is a culture and not a disability (Luey, Glass, & Elliot, 1995). Elizabeth DePoy and Stephen Gilson (2004) assert that thinking of people of varying abilities "as diverse rather than fitting within categories of 'normal' and 'not normal' is central" to a strengths approach in working with people with disabilities (p. 75).

> *I'd heard people use the phrase "Deaf Culture" before, but it wasn't until recently that I really got it. I was out on a Friday night in an area of town with lots of popular clubs. It was summer and as I came out of the bar I was in, I walked through a large group of deaf people—there must have been 200 or so at the outside tables and on the street in front of the club next door to the one I was in. They were all signing with each other animatedly and interacting in small groups of three or four. It was just like the scene I had left at the club, animated, happy, a bit sexually charged—only it was different. I never thought before about how people who are deaf socialize and date in large gatherings like that one, and it made me want to know more.*

Romel Mackelprang and Richard Salsgiver (1999) argue that there is a general culture of disability. Although recognizing that people with disabilities are heterogeneous in terms of class, gender, race, ethnicity, and sexual orientation and have a wide variety of disabilities (spinal cord injury, deafness, blindness), they suggest that the common oppression that people with disabilities experience helps to create a "disability culture with shared customs, traditions, and language" (p. 29). DePoy and Gilson (2004) report that there is limited empirical support for a "disability culture" but that "those who believe in such a culture assert that membership in it bestows identity, language, and position vis-à-vis other cultural groups" (p. 79).

Racial and Ethnic Identity

Identity is a term used to describe our self-conceptualizations. Identity can reflect how we see ourselves as individuals and how we see ourselves as part of a larger group or community. All identities are socially constructed, develop over time with input from a variety of contexts, and have many elements or aspects to them. Tracy Robinson (2005) contends that our identities are statused and have particular social meanings: "[I]n both subtle and blatant ways, people who hold membership in higher status groups are valued differently in society than those from lower status groups" (pp. 42–43).

Because of America's history of slavery, racism, and hate crimes against people of color, race has for a long time been a key component of identity for Americans. Janet Helms (1990) contends that racial identity "refers to a sense of group or collective identity based on one's perception that he or she shares a common racial heritage with a particular group" (p. 3).

The earliest work on racial identity development was conducted by William E. Cross, Jr. (1971, 1991; Cross & Vandiver, 2001). Cross described a six-stage process in which African Americans replace negative images (rooted in longtime contextual discrimination and oppression) with positive internal conceptions of themselves as members of a group. There have been a number of other models of racial identity development, largely based on Cross's work: American Indian identity development (Horse, 2001), African-American identity development (Cross & Fhagen-Smith, 2001), Latino identity development (Ferdman & Gallegos, 2001), Asian identity development (Kim, 2001), and multiracial identity development (Fhagen-Smith, 2003; Root, 1996, 2001; Wijeyesinghe, 2001).

Many people believe incorrectly that only people of color have a racial identity. White people often find it difficult to own or talk about their own race and the unearned privilege it often affords them (Daniel, 2000; Guadelupe & Lum, 2005; McIntosh, 1989; Sue, 2003).

Janet Helms (1985, 1990, 1995) has proposed a six-stage model of White racial identity development. Derald Wing Sue and David Sue (2008) note that Helms's model of White racial identity is important and valuable because it describes the "'defenses' [and] 'protective strategies,' or what Helms formally labels as 'information processing strategies' . . . which White people use to avoid or assuage anxiety and discomfort about issues of race" (p. 273). Some might suggest that Helms's model of White identity development is about coming to terms with one's privilege as a White person in the United States.

In the first stage, there may be little contact with people of color. The White person is not aware of his or her own race as such and may be oblivious to racism and its impact on others. The person may take what is often called a "colorblind" stance: *"I don't see a person's race as an issue—we are all members of the human race."*

In the second stage, disorientation and anxiety can occur as individuals realize that all people really are not treated equally. A self-reflective White person may feel guilt and shame due to a dawning awareness of the in-group privilege of Whiteness. The person may face unsettling dilemmas: *"I am not racist, but I don't want my daughter to marry a Black man." "I support the need for more diversity in our teachers, I know it is good for kids to have role models of people from different ethnic and racial backgrounds, but I don't think it is fair that I am passed over for a job because I'm a White man."*

In the third stage, to regain a psychological foothold, there is reaffirmation of race-based, distorted beliefs. The person may idealize attributes and achievements of White people, while devaluing other racial and ethnocultural groups and wondering why they cannot just be "like us." *"Yes, there are fewer people of color in management positions, but that isn't my fault. I've had to work for everything I have gotten. They just don't work hard enough. My father came over from Ireland with just the shirt on his back."*

In the fourth phase, White people who are self-reflective begin to "get it"—that there is racism, that it destructively affects non-Whites, and that they and their loved ones have participated in it. This awareness may be very intellectualized. There can be misguided "tolerance" and an at attempt "helping" people of color be—and have—more, "like us." *"I want to help you advance, so let me tell you how we do things here." "You need to tone down your emotions to get ahead."*

In the fifth stage, continued exposure to people of color, as well as exposure to injustices, brings about an earnest search for the meaning of racism in one's own history and current life. Zealotry in race-focused activism is not unusual as efforts are made to compensate for past denial, fear of losing White in-group acceptance, and racist acts. Gradually there is a wish for more and different experience with other cultures. *"Even though I don't like admitting it, I know that I benefit from racism and that, whether I intend to or not, I often act in unconsciously racist ways. It's hard work and it makes me uncomfortable, but I know I have to keep looking at and working on these issues."*

Eventually, in the sixth stage, White people who are motivated to do so consciously work with people of color to be antiracist, experiencing their commonalities with and differences from each other more comfortably and appreciatively. Individuals begin to use their own newly internalized ethical standards to define themselves and the world and to learn to relate, speak, and work publicly against oppression, even if it makes some White friends uncomfortable. *"I will continually speak out about injustices and oppressive acts when I see them and not leave people of color to bear the brunt of that responsibility. I will work with others to fight racism in myself, in others, and in our institutions and policies."*

The racial identity development of clinicians and clients has been a topic of much research (Kwan & Kwong-Liem, 2001; Vinson & Neimeyer, 2000). Renee Middleton and her colleagues conclude that "one factor that may influence multicultural counseling competency is the racial identity development of the practitioner" (Middleton et al., 2005, p. 444).

Difference

Difference and identity are not limited to racial or ethnocultural differences. Almost all of you will work with clients who differ from you in age, gender, family form, religion, class background, and other ways. Many of these differences are an important part of your own and your clients' identities. In their discussion of multiple oppressions, Amy Reynolds and Raechele Pope (1991) noted that people have multiple identities, not just one. Identities may include sexual orientation, age, socioeconomic class, educational level, job, marital or parenting status, important hobbies, and the like.

The **salience of identity** varies over time and circumstances. How you identify and feel about yourself may change depending on the situation. If you are the only person at work without children and people are discussing day care, your identity as a nonparent becomes more salient.

I am Irish on St. Patrick's Day and Italian when in Little Italy.

* * *

As a retiree, I like to be strong when doing yard work, but when riding the bus to town, I love it when younger people give me their seats.

* * *

I love being a biker. I love riding with my friends on the weekend, the camaraderie, and the road action. But lots of people think of bikers as criminals or "no-goods." I don't discuss the fact that I am a biker at work.

William E. Cross, Jr., Lakesha Smith, and Yasser Payne (2002) speak of the complexity of multiple identities:

Black persons with multi-culturally oriented identities may have as many as three or more attachment or bonding layers (e.g. an individual may be equally attached and bonded to her Blackness, her Puerto Ricanness, and her lesbian identity). This interconnectivity or multiplicity often leads such persons to see things as "connected", or as having connectivity potential, when others see only that which is singular, linear, monoracial, or monocultural (p. 101).

I look Black and people often assume I am. The other day at work we were talking about Passover and I mentioned I was having a Seder. One of my Jewish colleagues asked me when I converted—as if no Black people could be Jewish! I had to explain to him that my father was Black and my mother was Jewish.

Sharon Jones and Marylu McEwen (2000) have developed a conceptual model of **multiple dimensions of identity.** They suggest that we have *a core sense of personal identity* surrounded by intersecting circles that represent various identity dimensions contextualized within such influences as family background, sociocultural conditions, and opportunity systems (see Figure 2.1).

Diversity Within Groups and Invisible Differences

We need to recognize the complexity of people's multiple identities and the variations, permutations, and **diversity** that exist among members of the same group. For example, both clinician and client can be Cambodian, but one is a recent refugee from a poor farm village, while the other is from a wealthy family that came to the United States forty years ago. Clinician and client may both be middle-class professionals now, yet one comes from a working-class background. While both may be Native American, one is heterosexual and the other is gay.

Sometimes the differences between people are not readily apparent. For example, the client and clinician can have unseen and unspoken value differences. Both can be men, but men with different constructions of what it means to be a man. Both can be Catholic, yet each holds different, unexpressed beliefs about gay marriage and abortion. Whether the differences are cultural or not, visible or not, recognized or not, we can be sure that we

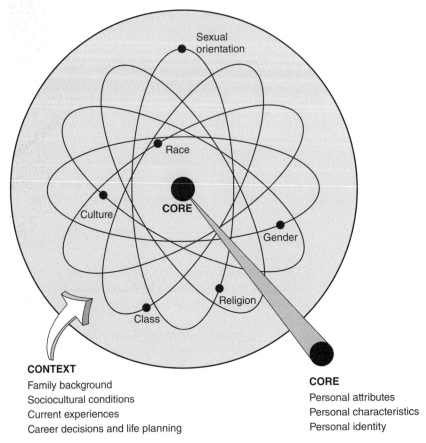

FIGURE 2.1   Model of Multiple Dimensions of Identity

Source: Reprinted with permission from the American College Personnel Association, One Dupont Circle, NW, Suite 300, at the National Center for Higher Education, Washington, DC 20036.

will all work with clients who are different from us and have different experiences, values, and beliefs than our own.

> *I was working with a lesbian woman. She was out and politically active. I had even seen her at a National Gay and Lesbian Task Force dinner. I assumed we shared a similar belief system. She was talking about gay marriage, and I was really surprised when she said that she didn't think gay people should adopt children.*

Prejudice, Discrimination, and Racism

A **stereotype** is a fixed, oversimplified image we have of members of a group. Stereotyping prevents us from seeing and appreciating both the full range of characteristics of, and the diversity within, the targeted group. Stereotypes very often lead to prejudice. **Prejudice** refers to either positive or negative bias, poorly informed opinions, or unjustified assumptions about individuals who belong to a certain group or fit into a particular category.

EXERCISE 2.3 Stereotypes

In groups of four, make a list of common stereotypes about people who are:

Native American	Arab
Black	Asian
White	Elderly
Latino	Gay
Jewish	Disabled

1. Next to each stereotype, note how much you agree with it using a scale of 1–10.
2. List positive, negative, or neutral aspects of each stereotype.
3. Prepare to discuss with the larger group where the stereotypes come from and how they get reinforced.
4. Think together about what you can do to try to overcome the stereotypes.

Prejudice often leads to discrimination. **Discrimination** is the unfair treatment of people because of prejudice regarding their class, gender, sexual orientation, age, size, ability, or racial, ethnic, or religious group membership. Prejudice is an attitude, whereas discrimination is a behavior. Many people around the world face prejudice and discrimination regularly. Color prejudice, gender bias, homophobia, and ethnic and religious discrimination are ubiquitous. Hate crimes, mosque and temple desecrations, and church burnings are vivid reminders of the problems that shadow and affect our interactions with each other. Globally, widespread political and interethnic violence precipitating mass migrations of refugees is further evidence of tensions and hatreds over differences and dominance. Thus the counseling help that people seek is often related to some form of oppression.

For example, clinicians may see lesbian women or gay men oppressed by homophobia or heterosexism. **Homophobia,** like racism, combines both prejudice and discrimination. Homophobia is hostility and hatred directed at gay men and lesbian women because of their sexual orientation. **Heterosexism** is "a world-view, a value system that prizes heterosexuality, assumes it is the only appropriate manifestation of love and sexuality, and devalues homosexualty and all that is not heterosexual" (Herek, 1986, p. 925).

Racism is the belief there are differences in human traits and capacities which are based on race and that these differences produce an inherent superiority of one race over another. We find it helpful to think of the distinction that James Jones makes between three kinds of racism: individual racism, institutional racism, and cultural racism. **Individual racism** is discriminatory behavior on the part of the individual. **Institutional racism** refers to social or governmental policies and structures that subordinate people of color. **Cultural racism** refers to the ways in which the cultures of people of color are denigrated and the culture of the dominant group is imposed on ethnic or racial minorities.

In discussing the behavior of individuals, Derald Wing Sue and his colleagues suggest that conscious, deliberate racial bigotry and oppression have evolved into a "more ambiguous and negative form that is more difficult to identify and acknowledge" (Sue et al., 2007, p. 272). **Aversive racism** is used to describe those who espouse egalitarian values, find racism offensive, and may be unaware of their own unconscious unintentional racist behaviors. These unintentional and often unconscious racist behaviors are called **racial microaggressions.** Sue and his colleagues describe three types of racial microaggressions: microassault, microinsult, and microinvalidation. Each devalues, offends, and injures its targets (Sue, et al., 2007; Sue et al., 2008).

Most clinicians, as indeed most people in the United States, may not consider themselves people who would engage in racist acts. Sue and colleagues (2007) maintain that "(n)early all interracial encounters are prone to the manifestation of racial microaggressions" (p. 284). Unintentional or aversive racism has the power to negatively affect the clinical relationship— whether the therapist is a person of color or the client is (Sue, et al., 2007; Sue et al., 2008). The *Surgeon General's Report on Mental Health: Culture, Race and Ethnicity* (U.S. Department of Health and Human Services, 2001) has hypothesized that clinicians' perceived racism, whether intentional or unintentional, may be one of the reasons for the low utilization of mental health services by African Americans, Native Americans, Asian Americans, and Latino/Hispanic Americans. Clearly we must become more aware of the potential effects on clinical work of racial microaggressions. We also need to protect against microaggressions based other variables including gender, sexual orientation, age, disability, and socioeconomic status.

Personal Dimensions of Identity

Patricia Arredondo and T. Glauner (1992) developed the Personal Dimensions of Identity (PDI) model, which examines how cultural, racial, and ethnic identities interact with other dimensions of diversity. The PDI consists of three dimensions:

1. *Dimension A* is a list of generalizable human characteristics—gender, culture, ethnicity, and language. Arredondo and her colleagues (Arredondo et al., 1996) view these characteristics as immutable and suggest that they are relatively fixed at birth.
2. *Dimension C* refers to the global contexts that affect the individual. These include the historical, political, sociocultural, and economic contexts in which we live and over which we have little control.

3. *Dimension B* may be a "consequence" of A and C and may result from the interaction between the "characteristics of the A Dimension and the major historical, political, sociocultural and economic legacies of the C Dimension" (Arredondo et al., 1996, p. 50). Dimension B includes such variables as educational background, geographic location, relationship status, work experience, and religion.

CLIP 2.1
The Clinician's
Identity and
Values

The PDI illustrates several premises: "a) that we are all multicultural individuals; b) that we all possess a personal, political and historical culture; c) that we are affected by sociocultural, political, environmental, historical events; and d) multiculuralism also intersects with multiple factors of human diversity" (Arredondo et al., 1996, p. 46). Thus, we agree with Paul Pedersen (1991) when he suggests that "the construct 'multicultural' becomes generic to all counseling relationships" (p. 7).

Multicultural Practice

As noted in Chapter 1, **multicultural practice** requires knowledge, empathy, and the ability to work with clients from a variety of backgrounds, customs and values. Research in progress will better define what have been called the **cultural competencies** needed for working with colleagues, clients, and community members different from ourselves.

EXERCISE 2.4 Multicultural Standards

In groups of four, make a list of standards that you think should guide multicultural practice. What specific steps would you need to take to make your clinical work more culturally responsible and responsive? Discuss your conclusions and guidelines with the whole class.

The professional organizations of those who work in human service and mental health all stress the need for clinicians to be aware of multicultural practice issues. The Association for Multicultural Counseling and Development has developed a list of *Multicultural Counseling Competencies,* which have been endorsed by the American Counseling Association (2002) (see Appendix 1). The National Association of Social Workers (NASW) has developed *Standards for Cultural Competence in Social Work Practice* (NASW, 2001), and the American Psychological Association has developed *Multicultural Guidelines on the Education and Training, Research, Practice and Organizational Change for Psychologists* (APA, 2002a).

Whether they call them standards, competencies, or guidelines, most researchers suggest that the following three dimensions be addressed in training helping professionals: attitudes and beliefs, knowledge, and skills for the sensitive implementation of interventions (Atkinson, 2004; Constantine & Sue,

2005; Devore & Schlesinger, 1996; Ivey, Ivey, & Zalaquett, 2010; Ponterotto, Casas, Suzuki, & Alexander, 2009; Robinson, 2005; Sue, Arredondo, & McDavis, 1992; Derald Sue & Sue, 2008). Multicultural guidelines include the following principles.

1. *As clinicians, we need to be aware of our own ethnic, gender, and cultural heritage.* We need to be aware of our negative and positive reactions to the values and traditions of other groups and of how our own cultural values affect our worldview. We can enhance our awareness only when we live, work, and make friendships with people different from ourselves—people with whom we can discuss our feelings and reactions and with whom we can exchange honest questions and feedback. These kinds of experiences are still too limited in the lives of many people and must be assiduously developed and nurtured. At the same time, it is important to recognize that we are responsible for our own learning and that we should not always depend on others who are different from ourselves to teach us what we should know about them.

2. *We need to acquire knowledge about the cultures and customs of the clients with whom we work.* We need to get information about the specific history and background of the cultural group; about family structures, communication patterns, gender roles, traditions, and values; about the impact of immigration; about the role of spirituality; and so on. We need to explore how culture and ethnicity affect help-seeking behaviors. We must attend to the effects of racism, stigmatization, and discrimination on our clients' daily lives.

3. *Finally, we need to use this self-awareness and knowledge to devise flexible strategies for intervention that are effective and congruent with our clients' values.* We must be aware of bias in research and assessment instruments, and we must design interventions and strategies that are appropriate and linguistically suitable.

EXERCISE 2.5 Matching

In groups of four, discuss the advantages and disadvantages of clinicians working with people who are similar and dissimilar to themselves. Discuss (1) the advantages of working with someone similar to themselves, (2) the disadvantages of working with someone similar to themselves, (3) the advantages of working with someone different from themselves, and (4) the disadvantages of working with someone different from themselves. Which would be hardest for you and why?

CLIP 2.2
Multicultural
Practice

To summarize, multicultural practice recognizes, respects, and responds with informed thoughtfulness to the variety of differences within and between people. It is an important feature of effective clinical relationships and work. We need to stay open to new learning and interpersonal experience, attentive to differences, building knowledge and skills, and engaging in ongoing self-reflection and dialogue with others different from ourselves.

■ Professional Ethics

Ethics is a branch of philosophy that deals with moral judgments and perceptions of right and wrong. A **professional code of ethics** establishes principles and standards of conduct that elucidate the values of a discipline or profession. *Principles* are values that are aspirational in nature, while *standards* consist of prescribed behaviors as well as proscribed conduct.

In our role as helping professionals, we are given a major responsibility: to fulfill the great trust that clients, their families, and society place in us. A major purpose of our codes of ethics is to protect the welfare of individuals and groups coming to us for help. Ethics codes also help us by clarifying our professional responsibilities and providing guidance about most of the situations we will face in our professional roles. Our codes inspire us to adopt high standards of behavior as we render complex and demanding services. Finally, they provide a framework for processing complaints about our professional behavior. Len Sperry (2007) writes that a code of ethics is "more than a set of rules and strategies to avoid legal liability and professional censure. Rather, it is a way of *being* in relationship to clients, supervisees, students, and colleagues that both promotes development and prevents harm" (p. xi).

Each professional clinical association has a published code of ethics: the National Organization of Human Services (NOHS, 1996), the American Counseling Association (ACA, 2005), the American Psychological Association (APA, 2002b), and the National Association of Social Workers (NASW, 1999). Membership in these professional organizations is voluntary, but usually a feature of membership is an agreement to become familiar with, and to abide by, the association's ethical code.

Our ethics codes incorporate and reflect carefully chosen societal values and aspirations that our professional organizations hope will serve as enduring benchmarks or **ethical principles** for practice rather than fleeting attitudes. For example, it is hard to imagine a human services ethics code without fundamental guidelines about practicing with respect for the dignity and worth of all people, ensuring the right of clients to participate fully and be well informed in intervention planning, and observing confidentiality in clinician–client conversations. These fundamental values have guided our professions for some time now, but other standards are newer, reflecting changes in society or addressing situations that practitioners had not faced previously. For example, new standards have been written that address the handling of electronic communication over the Internet. Ethics codes are thus updated periodically to incorporate more current wording or thinking, or new issues and value concerns emerging from academic research and professional practice venues.

Many codes of ethics begin with a statement of general principles that foreshadow the standards that follow. For example, NASW lists as overarching principles Service, Social Justice, Dignity and Worth of the Person, Importance of Human Relationships, Integrity, and Competence. These general statements are then followed by enumerated standards of conduct that are enforceable rules for professional conduct.

Ethical standards are quite specific. They detail preferred and pro-scribed conduct in the major domains of professional practice; for example, the APA has 89 standards of conduct. The clinician who violates ethical standards can be sanctioned by or expelled from the professional association. If the violation is referred to the state licensing board, the clinician may lose his or her license. A professional who violates a state or federal law may also be brought to court for criminal charges or face a civil hearing if a client sues for an ethical violation.

As noted, clinicians are also bound by federal and state laws. Each state develops its own laws to govern professionals and protect consumers. However, ethics codes sometimes hold the professional to a higher standard than the law. For example, Thomas Plante (1999) writes that, while it is illegal to have sex with clients in some states (but not others), such conduct is unethical in all states.

The ethics codes of the various professional associations differ depending on each profession's mission and goals. For example, the APA Code of Ethics has a lot to say about testing, because one of the defining characteristics of psychology is its roots in studying and measuring individual differences. However, most ethics codes address a number of general standards.

EXERCISE 2.6 Ethical Principles

Before reading further about ethical standards, divide into groups of four. Make a list of professional standards that you believe are essential principles for responsible clinical practice. Share your list with the whole class. Compare the list your class developed with the ethical principles of one or more of the professional associations mentioned in the text (adapted from Neukrug & Schwitzer, 2006).

Ethical Dilemmas

While the goal of ethical standards is to provide clear and specific direction, Neukrug and Schwitzer (2006) note that clinicians are often faced with **ethical dilemmas:** (a) sometimes two sections of an ethical code are at odds with each other; (b) agency or institutional policies conflict with an ethical code; (c) the law and an ethical code differ in their requirements; or (d) the clinician's moral values prevent compliance with an ethical code.

Ethics codes themselves often provide some guidance about steps to take to fulfill ethical obligations. For example, the NASW code states: "When such conflicts [as those cited] occur, social workers must make a responsible effort to resolve the conflict in a manner that is consistent with the values, principles, and standards expressed in this Code. If a reasonable resolution of the conflict does not appear possible, social workers should seek proper consultation before making a decision" (NASW, 1999).

Ethical Decision Making

Sometimes it is easy to decide what is "right" and "wrong" by conforming closely to ethical standards and code guidance statements. However, sometimes the decisions are more complicated. Ethical dilemmas often generate a conflict between a clinician's "tried and true" personal values and the profession's values and ethical obligations. Such dilemmas may involve choosing between two "rights" (for example, a client's right to self-determination and the professional obligation to protect her from self-harming). Ethical dilemmas often stir up anxiety, uncertainty, and ambivalence. Theorists have suggested a number of models to help professionals think about how to make a decision when faced with an ethical dilemma.

Ralph Dolgoff, Frank Loewenberg, and Donna Harrington (2009) describe an "ethical assessment screen" (p. 61) that can provide clinicians with a helpful first step in attempting to make an ethical decision (see Box 2.1).

While the ethical assessment screen focuses only on things the clinician can do, Gerald Corey, Marianne Schneider Corey, and Patrick Callanan (2007, p. 20) propose a seven-step model that involves the client in the process:

1. Recognizing a problem
2. Defining the problem (collaboration with the client is essential at this stage)
3. Developing solutions (with client)
4. Choosing a solution
5. Reviewing the process (with client) and rechoosing
6. Implementing and evaluating the solution (with client)
7. Continuing reflection

BOX 2.1 Ethical Assessment Screen

1. Identify the relevant professional values and ethics, your own relevant values, and any societal values relevant to this ethical dilemma.
2. What can you do to minimize conflicts between personal, societal, and professional values?
3. Identify alternative ethical options that you may take.
4. Which of the alternative ethical options will minimize conflicts between your client's, others', and society's rights, and protect to the greatest extent your clients' and others' rights and welfare, and society's rights and interests?
5. Which alternative action will be most efficient, effective, and ethical, as well as result in your doing the "least harm" possible?
6. Have you considered and weighed both short- and long-term ethical consequences?
7. Final check: Is the planned action impartial, generalizable, and justifiable?

Source: Dolgoff, Ralph, Loewenberg, Frank M., & Harrington, Donna (2009). Ethical decisions for social work practice (8th Ed). Belmont, CA: Brooks/Cole Cengage. page 61.

CLIP 2.3
Ethical Dilemmas

When you are faced with ethical dilemmas, we recommend that you consult with your supervisor or other senior colleagues. Consultation with experienced fellow professionals brings calm and thoughtful brainstorming to the review of the ethical issues and conflicts at hand. Consultation can also help in prioritizing issues that require decisions. Many state professional organizations can provide consultation with a professional or an ethics committee to assist you in thinking through decisions before acting.

In the following section, we discuss key ethical standards for clinicians and present some of the ethical dilemmas and questions that you may face in attempting to meet your profession's standards. This discussion is not intended to be all-inclusive or to replace your knowledge of your own professional organization's ethical code. Rather, we wish to highlight important principles and standards that our professions share and give you some examples of dilemmas that often arise in professional life. For each principle, we provide the specific standard as written into one or another of the professional organizations' ethical codes, so that you can experience alternately the conceptualizing language of each profession.

Professional Standards

Competence

> The following is a sample standard from the APA (2002b):
>
> STANDARD 2. COMPETENCE
>
> 2.01 Boundaries of Competence
>
> (a) Psychologists provide services, teach, and conduct research with populations and in areas only within the boundaries of their competence, based on their education, training, supervised experience, consultation, study, or professional experience.
>
> 2.03 Maintaining Competence
>
> Psychologists undertake ongoing efforts to develop and maintain their competence.

Clinicians strive to provide the highest quality service by developing and continually enhancing their knowledge and skills. To be competent in their roles, they must have appropriate education and experience. An important guiding principle for professional codes of ethics is to "do no harm."

Clinicians should not practice outside their area of expertise or beyond their level of competence, to protect consumers from poor or ill informed professional practices. Corey and his colleagues observe that "(e)ven though mental health professionals may not intend harm to clients, lack of competence is often a major contributing factor in harm done to clients" (Corey et al., 2007, p. 314). The authors then ask: "What are the boundaries of one's competence, and how do professionals know when they have exceeded them? How can practitioners determine whether they should accept a client when their experience and training might be questionable? What should be the minimal degree required for entry level professional counseling? To be competent to practice with a variety of client populations, does a counselor have to be both a generalist and a specialist?" (p. 315).

> *I don't know what it means to be competent. I was working at a clinic and they asked if I would meet with the family of a boy who is dying of cancer. I had only taken one course in the basics of counseling. I wasn't going to do therapy, I was just going to see if they needed any resources I could help them get. But the chances were that they were going to get into their son's condition and how that is affecting them. As a human being, how could I not respond with interest and ask more about how they are coping? How can you learn if you don't practice? But is it ethical to practice on real people?*

This student's question about competence and learning expresses a very common concern of students entering clinical education programs. Clinicians share this concern when they enter more complex and demanding settings than their education has prepared them for. Teachers, mentors, and supervisors, indeed, expect that students will learn "on" clients, but they also expect students to absorb knowledge quickly from class and field, as well as to deepen it through supervisory, client, and colleague feedback. Internship sites often have official standards for learning and practice provided by a discipline's national accrediting body. Your supervisor is responsible to make sure that clients are receiving competent care.

One way of measuring and indicating competence is professional certification and licensure. **Certification** is "a voluntary attempt by a group to promote a professional identity. Certification confirms that the practitioner has met a set of minimum standards established by the certification agency" (Corey et al., 2007, p. 338). These standards usually require hundreds of hours of clinical practice experience under the supervision of a similarly certified clinical supervisor, with additional requirements for continuing education. The National Organization for Human Services provides certification for human service providers who have graduated from an accredited undergraduate program and who have met standards similar to those just noted.

Social workers, psychologists, counselors, and marriage and family therapists must usually have a **professional license** in their states to practice clinically. Each state establishes its own unique set of criteria for licensing, including graduate education, specific course work (such as a course on ethics or on child sexual abuse), and a set number of supervised hours of clinical work (some while in graduate school and some following it). In addition, the candidate must pass a test to demonstrate knowledge of advanced practice concepts and methods. Corey et al. (2007) note that "(l)icensure is generally viewed as the most desirable form of legislative regulation of professional practice because it tends to highlight the uniqueness of an occupation and restricts both the use of the title and the practice of an occupation" (p. 338).

> *In my state, people can't legally say they are social workers unless they are licensed. Independent licensure indicates that you have demonstrated through supervised practice and formal examination the wisdom and competencies to practice safely and competently within agency structures or independently. Part of this wisdom is knowing when you need case consultation and where to find expert help.*

* * *

> *After graduation, I had to take a qualifying exam to receive licensure at the LCSW (Licensed Clinical Social Worker) level. I then worked two additional years (several thousand hours) under the supervision of a Licensed Independent Clinical Social Worker (LICSW). Finally, I had to pass a much more advanced exam in order to receive my LICSW licensure. I worked really hard to get that little "I" in there.*

Clinicians are ethically required to enhance their learning and develop new skills and competencies throughout their careers. Along the way, they are constantly informed by new research and creative ideas from the field that generate new methods and approaches (such as dialectical behavioral therapy, motivational interviewing, and mind-body wellness programs). It is their responsibility to keep abreast of changes in the field.

EXERCISE 2.7 Competence

In groups of four, discuss the following ethical dilemma:

Tara is a master's level social worker in a community mental health center in a small town in rural West Virginia. A man comes in with his son, who is depressed and said by the father to have been diagnosed with Tourette's Disorder. Tara knows a little about Tourette's and the complications its neurological tics can cause for the person, but she has never worked with anyone diagnosed with it. The nearest large hospital and counseling center is over 200 miles away, and the father says that, because of his work schedule, he cannot take his son there for help. He asks Tara to help him. What should she do?

The American Psychological Association has an ethics code standard that addresses working in an emergency to help people when the clinician does not have much or any real knowledge or experience with the particular kinds of problems they present. We may work with clients so that at least they are not denied all help, but only if we "make a reasonable effort to obtain the competence required by using relevant research, training, consultation, or study" (APA, 2002b). In this instance, Tara would seek immediate consultation with her supervisor or their team psychologist or psychiatrist to develop a plan of care that is best for the man and his son.

Informed Consent

The following is a sample standard from the ACA (2005):

ACA Standard A.2.a. Informed Consent

Clients have the freedom to choose whether to enter into or remain in a counseling relationship and need adequate information about the counseling process and the counselor. Counselors have an obligation to review in writing and verbally with clients the rights and responsibilities of both the counselor and the client. Informed consent is an ongoing part of the counseling process, and counselors appropriately document discussions of informed consent throughout the counseling relationship.

A.2.b. Types of Information Needed

Counselors explicitly explain to clients the nature of all services provided. They inform clients about issues such as, but not limited to, the following: the purposes, goals, techniques, procedures, limitations, potential risks, and benefits of services; the counselor's qualifications, credentials, and relevant experience; continuation of services upon the incapacitation or death of a counselor; and other pertinent information. Counselors take steps to ensure that clients understand the implications of diagnosis, the intended use of tests and reports, fees, and billing arrangements. Clients have the right to confidentiality and to be provided with an explanation of its limitations (including how supervisors and/or treatment team professionals are involved); to obtain clear information about their records; to participate in the ongoing counseling plans; and to refuse any services or modality change and to be advised of the consequences of such refusal.

Informed consent ensures that clients are fully informed about the benefits and risks of recommended interventions before they are implemented, and are made aware of optional approaches to those being offered in the moment. A key purpose of **informed consent** is to protect the right of clients to self-determination. It provides an opportunity for clients to raise questions about the clinician, the work, and potential outcomes. In most circumstances, clients have the right to refuse or terminate clinical work.

Jeffrey Hecker and Geoffrey Thorpe (2005) note that informed consent serves a number of functions. It empowers people by providing them with information that enables them to make wise decisions. It encourages conversation about realistic goals and objectives, and ways to meet them so that clients know what to expect. Informed consent not only protects the client; it may also protect clinicians from lawsuits on the part of disgruntled clients who feel harmed or misinformed by their provider.

Informed consent is an ongoing process, and involves finding a balance between telling too much or too little. After clinicians explain the nature of proposed procedures and their expected benefits and risks, the client is usually asked to read, sign, and date a form affirming a full explanation of procedures, the client's understanding of benefits and risks, and client's agreement to what is planned. If changes in plans or methods are proposed at any time during the intervention, a new informed consent process must precede them. Dolgoff and colleagues assert that "(a) person can be considered sufficiently informed to give consent only if he knows what will occur during the intervention or treatment, what the results of the intervention will be, and what will happen if he does not consent. He should know how much better (or worse) he will be if he agrees to the intervention than he will be if he does not agree. He should also have full knowledge about alternate options and their associated risks and benefits" (Dolgoff, Loewenberg, & Harrington, 2009, p. 90).

Thomas Grisso and Paul Applebaum (1998) believe that, to give informed consent, three conditions are necessary: (1) disclosure of information, (2) client competence to understand the discussion, and (3) voluntariness. Each condition raises a number of potential ethical concerns about informed consent. Other conditions discussed earlier are that the informed consent explanation and form be as brief and clear as possible, rendered verbally and in writing in the client's language, and readily accessible in case changes, questions, or issues arise.

In disclosing information, clinicians face two major questions: How accurate is the information? And how much should we disclose? The information we have is only as good as the research on which it is based, and some of that research may have serious limitations. This is especially important when discussing empirically supported treatments (ESTs). Research on the effects of a new treatment for substance abuse, for example, may only have been conducted with a limited sample (adult men) and may not apply to work with adolescents. Laboratory studies on the use of a new method to prevent wandering in people with Alzheimer's Disease may be promising, but are they valid when applied in a community-based program for elderly clients?

Clinicians need to decide whether to recommend treatments that to date have limited empirical support, yet have had some apparent success of which clinicians are aware anecdotally. These questions become especially salient when new, experimental treatments are available for use with a client for whom other interventions have not proved very helpful. Still, the clinician's mandate is to fully disclose what *is* known about the experimental intervention to date and what benefits and risks can be expected. This standard is clearly intended to prevent clinicians from hedging on information because they want to try out an intervention and from misleading prospective clients about the risks of interventions because they want to engage them in treatment.

Clinicians engage in thorough discussion with clients about proposed interventions in language that is easily understood. Ethical codes state that we must arrange for an interpreter to explain fully the possible risks and benefits of procedures in the primary language of the client if his or her primary language differs from the clinician's. Because of the awe and anxiety that people can sometimes feel in the presence of professional clinicians, they may need time to assimilate the information given to them and to digest its implications for their lives. But how much detail does the clinician need to give?

> *How thorough is thorough? I don't want to sound like one of those printouts you get with medication warnings: "Common side effects include hives, asthma, headaches, nose bleeds, rashes."*

* * *

> *I remember meeting with an anesthesiologist and going over my informed consent before surgery. He listed all the potential risks—including death. I remember thinking, "Do I need this surgery? Because if I don't, I am out of here. And if I do need it, I don't particularly want to hear everything that can go wrong. It would be good to hear about how it will help."*

Clients usually sign an informed consent form before beginning work with a clinician. If the client is not capable of giving informed consent (for example, a minor child or a person with dementia), a court-appointed legal guardian must give informed consent.

To give informed consent, the recipient needs to have the capacity to understand the information. Hecker and Thorpe (2005) suggest that when people come to see a clinician, they are often struggling with issues that can affect their ability to think clearly and make good decisions. For example, a woman may be seeking help from a human service worker about nursing home care for her mother. However, her distress about her mother's recent fall and her anxiety about having to move her away from her home may prevent her from fully hearing about all the possibilities available.

An interesting conflict about informed consent occurs for clinicians who participate in managed care programs. Corey et al. (2007) observe that "clients have a right to specific information regarding their treatment under managed care and the limitations of their treatment packages" (p. 158). They go on to say that managed care companies often have "gag clauses" that prohibit practitioners from sharing any negative information about managed care policies including options not covered by the plan (p. 158).

Marcia Hill (2004) describes some of the all-too-common difficulties clinicians can face with managed care companies:

> The client in this case was a man with overwhelming history of recent loss. To top it off, shortly after we started meeting, his wife left him, taking their only child. I had met with this client perhaps ten times by the time of the review, and the (managed care) reviewer said that we had to finish meeting within the next four sessions because, after all, this man was functioning and was able to go to work. (p. 205)

EXERCISE 2.8   Managed Care

Marianna Chesholm is a counselor who works full time in an adolescent drug program. In addition, she has a small private practice in which she sees two or three clients a week. Recently she has become frustrated with managed care companies that approve only three or four sessions at a time and that require her to spend hours each week talking with quality reviewers to obtain additional meetings. She is also concerned that sometimes the type of care that they approve for the client—such as group rather than individual counseling—is not always appropriate. She is considering removing herself from the managed care rolls but is concerned that doing so will limit her practice to people who have private insurance or who are rich enough to pay out of pocket. What should she do?

Multiple Relationships

> The following is a sample standard on multiple relationships from NOHS (1996):
>
> *Statement 6* Human service professionals are aware that in their relationships with clients power and status are unequal. Therefore they recognize that dual or **multiple relationships** may increase the risk of harm to, or exploitation of, clients, and may impair their professional judgment. However, in some communities and situations it may not be feasible to avoid social or other nonprofessional contact with clients. Human service professionals support the trust implicit in the helping relationship by avoiding dual relationships that may impair professional judgment, increase the risk of harm to clients or lead to exploitation.

Ethics codes caution clinicians against having multiple relationships with clients to protect both clients and the clinical relationship. When a clinician assumes more than one role with a client, it can confuse or hurt the client and the work-focused clinical relationship. While the clinical relationship is mutual, it is not equal. Professional status and helpful roles represent considerable power, both real and symbolic, to clients. That power may easily be abused, even if unintentionally. (We discussed this power differential and strategies for addressing it in Chapter 11).

Multiple relationships can occur when the clinician has more than one professional role with a client. Clinicians should not counsel coworkers, students, or others with whom they have a professional relationship. Nor should they hire clients in *their* professional role to do work for them. For example, hiring a client who is an electrician to do wiring in a clinician's home can cause a number of problems. The client may feel anxious about doing the work correctly, might not charge the clinician adequately for the services (to be nice or to show gratitude), or might even discover unwanted information about the clinician.

> *A female colleague of mine wanted to help a client who was very poor and needed money by having him do housework for her. When he saw the messy state of her home and how much picking up after her he had to do for low wages, he eventually quit working for her and quit seeing her for therapy, too. He had lost respect for her after seeing her as a real person.*

Multiple relationships can occur when there is both a personal and a professional role with a client. Clinicians should not see neighbors, friends, or relatives as clients. Good boundaries allow us to work with more objectivity and detachment than we could ever do with a friend or neighbor. Boundaries prevent clients from having to add the clinician's needs to their relational burdens. Relational ethics recommend maintaining the professional relationship as a special, boundaried, work-focused alliance. Carolyn Dillon (1999) has described the clinical relationship as one of the last Western professional venues in which we restrain our own needs and wishes for the sake of another.

Multiple relationships can occur when clients and clinicians socialize together. Clinicians do not usually socialize with clients outside the work setting. Clients can feel uncomfortable observing or being observed by their counselor at, for example, a small dinner party or outing. Clinicians may also feel uncomfortable. While clients may want to see the clinician in informal settings, doing so can confuse the nature of the professional relationship. While most social relationships are mutual, with personal information passing back and forth between the participants, the focus of clinicians' work is on the client and little of their personal information is usually shared.

Clinicians limit their relationships not just with clients but also with the people close to them. It might be inappropriate for a clinician to see a colleague's child in counseling or to hire a client's best friend as an attorney. At times we unknowingly find ourselves interacting with friends of clients. In a memorable scene in the TV series *The Sopranos*, Tony Soprano's psychiatrist, Dr. Melfi, sits through a dinner party in which her unknowing friends make fun of Tony Soprano's gaudy Mafia home next door. Tony, who has a crush on Dr. Melfi, watches forlornly from a window in his home while she seems to be having a wonderful time just out of reach. This episode reflects the kind of relational situations that can arise when social overlaps complicate clinical bonds.

Not all social interactions are prohibited. The American Psychological Association's ethical code notes that social interactions in some situations may be beneficial. For example, a clinician might attend a client's graduation or wedding, or the clinician and client might both be involved in a professional or community organization (APA, 2002b).

In any decisions affecting interactions with clients, we are aware and respectful of clients' needs and rights. We are also mindful of and responsive to cultural differences regarding boundaries.

C L I P 2.4
Multiple
Relationships

Prohibition of Sexual Relationships with Clients

> The following is a sample standard from the ACA (2005):
>
> Sexual or romantic counselor–client interactions or relationships with current clients, their romantic partners, or their family members are prohibited.

Ethics codes are very clear and unambiguous about one type of multiple relationships: Sexual or romantic relationships with current clients are strictly prohibited. Unfortunately, predatory clinicians may use their knowledge of clients' vulnerabilities to exploit their needs for love and closeness. Because of the serious potential for coercion, manipulation, and exploitation, sexual relationships between clinicians and clients are not only unethical but illegal in many states. While the prohibition of sexual or romantic relationships is one of the clearest standards and leaves little room for doubt or confusion, unfortunately the violation of this standard frequently brings clinicians before ethical committees and licensing boards (Pope & Vasquez, 2007). Clinician loneliness, self-interest, prejudice, ignorance, and personal distress can sometimes lead to these destructive violations (Knapp, Gottlieb, Berman, & Handelsman, 2007). The violation of this standard has hurt many clients, contributing to emotional breakdowns and even suicide. There have been numerous court judgments in favor of clients who have sued their clinicians for having sex with them. Clinicians are also enjoined from engaging in romantic or sexual relationships with important people in the client's life.

Clinicians should not have sex with former clients. The ACA says a romantic or sexual relationship should *never* occur within five years after the end of the professional relationship. The APA ethics code states that there should be at least a two-year interval. But this does not mean that the clinician can terminate counseling, wait a while, and then get involved with a client. The ethical codes state that sexual intimacy with former clients should not occur, "regardless of the interval *except in the most unusual circumstances*" (italics added).

If engaging in a sexual relationship even years after ending the professional relationship, the clinician must:

> bear the burden of demonstrating that there has been no exploitation, in light of all relevant factors, including (1) the amount of time that has passed since therapy terminated; (2) the nature, duration, and intensity of the therapy; (3) the circumstances of termination; (4) the client's/patient's personal history; (5) the client's/patient's current mental status; (6) the likelihood of adverse impact on the client/patient; and (7) any statements or actions made by the therapist during the course of therapy suggesting or inviting the possibility of a post-termination sexual or romantic relationship with the client/patient. (APA, 2002b)

Confidentiality

The following is a sample confidentiality standard from NASW (1999):

1.07 Privacy and Confidentiality

(a) Social workers should respect clients' right to privacy. Social workers should not solicit private information from clients unless it is essential to providing services or conducting social work evaluation or research. Once private information is shared, standards of confidentiality apply.

(b) Social workers may disclose confidential information when appropriate with valid consent from a client or a person legally authorized to consent on behalf of a client.

(c) Social workers should protect the confidentiality of all information obtained in the course of professional service, except for compelling professional reasons. The general expectation that social workers will keep information confidential does not apply when disclosure is necessary to prevent serious, foreseeable, and imminent harm to a client or other identifiable person. In all instances, social workers should disclose the least amount of confidential information necessary to achieve the desired purpose; only information that is directly relevant to the purpose for which the disclosure is made should be revealed.

The principle of confidentiality is intended to ensure the privacy of client–clinician communication. **Confidentiality** helps clients disclose to us information about intimate, sensitive, and—for them sometimes—shameful topics. They can feel safe to disclose more freely when they have established a trusting relationship with the clinician. Trust is enhanced when clients believe that we will be nonjudgmental and will not disclose anything without their express permission. Very few relationships afford such an opportunity to people, and it is a special aspect of clinical work that clients come to value enormously. Confidentiality is addressed not only by ethical codes but also by federal laws such as the Health Insurance Portability and Accountability Act (HIPAA) (see Chapter 3).

Clinicians may breach confidentiality "to prevent serious, foreseeable, and imminent harm to a client or other identifiable person" (ACA, 2005). In fact, helping professionals such as teachers, health care providers, and clinicians are legally mandated to break confidentiality if they determine that the following types of potential for harm exist: (1) The client is at risk for harming self or others, (2) children might be at risk of abuse or neglect, or (3) the abuse of elderly or disabled people is possible. Clinicians can also be compelled to testify in certain legal proceedings, such as at a custody hearing or when the clinician has conducted a court-ordered evaluation prior to trial.

If a client may be dangerous, clinicians have a duty to warn and to protect identifiable potential victims. In a precedent-setting case, a student at the counseling center at The University of California–Berkeley told his psychologist that he was going to kill a former girlfriend when she returned from Brazil. He did not name her, but she was easily identifiable. The clinician told his supervisor about the threat, then called the campus police. They took the student in for questioning but released him when he seemed rational. He eventually killed the woman, Tatiana Tarasoff. Her parents sued the therapist and the California Board of Regents. Eventually the California Supreme Court found in favor of the parents and said that it was not enough to notify the campus police; the psychologist had to warn the intended victim as well. The case of *Tarasoff v. Regents of the University of California* (1974, 1976) has been the basis for the ethical principle of **duty to warn.** The Tarasoff opinion affirmed that "(p)ublic policy favoring protection of the confidential character of patient-psychotherapist relationships must yield in instances in which disclosure is essential to avert danger to others; the protective privilege ends where the public peril begins" (Dolgoff et al., 2009, p. 95).

It is important to distinguish confidentiality from privileged communication. **Privileged communication** is the legal protection of confidentiality. Federal and state laws usually protect against forced disclosure during a legal proceeding of confidential information obtained from a **fiduciary relationship,** a relationship based on trust (such as those between doctor and patient, attorney and client, spouses, and psychotherapist and client). Laws about privileged communication vary from state to state and do not apply to all clinicians or in all circumstances. Review with your supervisor or team leaders both federal and state laws about privileged communication in any state in which you are to practice clinically.

If sued by a client, the clinician is allowed by law to terminate the therapy and use client materials relevant to his or her defense. Furthermore, insurance companies, quality assurance reviewers, or employers may require information before paying claims. However, in such cases, the clinician is careful to limit the amount of information disclosed, often reporting only the diagnosis and dates of service.

Some agencies have specific limits on confidentiality. Agency limits on confidentiality are different from the legal or ethical limits just discussed. For example, a school system may require clinicians to report all drug usage.

EXERCISE 2.9 Duty to Warn

Victor is seeing an HIV-affected client who is continuing to have unprotected sex with his girlfriend, who does not know about his diagnosis. The client is unwilling to reveal his HIV status, since he believes he was infected in a one-night stand with a prostitute. He fears his girlfriend would be devastated and would leave him if she knew about the prostitute.

In groups of four discuss what you think Victor should do in this situation. What are his options? Are you aware of any laws related to this dilemma? How did you finally arrive at your decision?

Client records are also confidential. The Health Insurance Portability and Accountability Act (HIPAA) limits how much information clinicians can share with others, due to mounting nationwide concerns that technology and the rising power of managed care corporations are leading to the too wide distribution of patient information in health care settings. The release of information to third parties requires informed consent. Clinicians cannot give information to others without the client's permission in writing.

The increasing use of computers and Internet services complicates the practice of confidentiality. Deborah Parker-Oliver and George Demiris (2006) note that information on computers is vulnerable to "hackers" who can get into clinicians' files. Furthermore, even after a file is deleted, there can be "hidden files (text residue) left behind" (p. 110).

While clinicians are limited in what they can share with others, remember that clients have a legal right to see and obtain a copy of their records, although a clinician's informal process notes are excluded. Knowing this, clinicians need to think carefully about what and how they write in client records. The NASW code standard 1.08 states:

> Clients should have "reasonable access" to information about them, and that social workers who are concerned that clients' access to their records could cause serious misunderstanding or harm to the client should provide assistance in interpreting the records and consultation with the client regarding the records. (NASW, 1999)

CLIP 2.5
Confidentiality

EXERCISE 2.10 Confidentiality

Darren, a 16-year-old high school junior, is sent to the school counselor's office because he was in a fight. During their meeting, Darren tells Mike, the school counselor, that he was not really in a fight. Two other students attacked him in the locker room because he is gay. Darren reveals that he just came out and is having sex with his boyfriend Henry, who is also a junior at the school. Darren does not want the counselor to tell his parents because he is sure they will throw him out of the house if they learn he is gay. The school says that all counselors must report student drug use or sexual activity to the school administration.

In groups of four, discuss the ethics code standards that would guide your thinking if you were the counselor. What personal values would guide you in thinking about this dilemma? Think further about your age now, your teen experiences, and how these would color your decision making. Remember that parents of minor children living at home usually have the right to access their children's school records, including information about any counseling of their child at the school.

Social Justice and Advocacy

The following are samples justice and advocacy standards from NOHS (1996):

Statement 10 Human service professionals are aware of local, state, and federal laws. They advocate for change in regulations and statutes when such legislation conflicts with ethical guidelines and/or client rights. Where laws are harmful to individuals, groups or communities, human service professionals consider the conflict between the values of obeying the law and the values of serving people and may decide to initiate social action.

Statement 11 Human service professionals keep informed about current social issues as they affect the client and the community. They share that information with clients, groups and community as part of their work.

Statement 12 Human service professionals understand the complex interaction between individuals, their families, the communities in which they live, and society.

Statement 13 Human service professionals act as advocates in addressing unmet client and community needs. Human service professionals provide a mechanism for identifying unmet client needs, calling attention to these needs, and assisting in planning and mobilizing to advocate for those needs at the local community level.

We have a responsibility to advocate for just and equitable public policy. Social justice principles and standards are written into ethics codes to remind clinicians that they should be advocates within the oppressive environments that many clients face every day. **Advocacy** occurs in a number of ways. Clinicians often engage in direct advocacy for a particular client, such as helping a client get welfare benefits, find affordable day care, or get into a training program. Clinicians also advocate for particular issues or populations: supporting funding of community day programs for people with Alzheimer's Disease, testifying about the need for programs for the homeless, or working for legislation to provide school lunch programs for children. On a broader level, we need to recognize the connection between public policy and the services we provide to individuals, groups, and families. We know that poverty, hunger, discrimination, poor housing, insufficient health care, lack of educational opportunities, insufficient day care resources, and unjust labor policies favoring some while restricting others—all affect the well-being of clients.

Professional organizations encourage activism. For example, social work programs require that their students take social welfare policy content; many also require that students participate in some form of community advocacy to prepare for the wider roles of the clinician in social change work. The APA's Public Policy Office is actively involved in many legislative and federal activities, meeting with members of Congress and their staffs, preparing background memos for congressional offices, organizing briefings, and working in coalitions with others. Professional ethical principles and standards suggest that we work as individuals, in groups, with communities, and with clients for political and social change to enhance the rights and well-being of all people.

Ethics and Online Interventions

Online counseling is growing exponentially, but so far, it is only lightly regulated by laws and rules that often vary from state to state. There are many legal ambiguities: Who will respond to an emergency if the client and clinician are states apart? Is a clinician licensed in one state legally able to provide services to a client in another? Is professional competence to provide face-to-face counseling the same as competence in online counseling? Midkiff and Wyatt (2008) note that verbal skill in counseling is not the same as skill in written communication. They suggest that state licensing boards may require continuing education units (CEUs) or coursework to demonstrate online competence. Clinicians must be knowledgeable about Internet communication modalities and stay up to date on encryption technology to ensure the privacy of transactions and stored data such as emails. Clinicians delivering online services have a professional responsibility to ensure the safety, rights, and well-being of their cyberclients (Fisher & Fried, 2003; Midkoff & Wyatt, 2008; Ragusea & VandeCreek, 2003).

Positive Psychology, Positive Ethics

CLIP 2.6
Words of Wisdom

Positive psychologists Mitchell Handelsman, Samuel Knapp, and Michael Gottlieb (2002) observe that ethics codes today focus too much on avoiding or punishing misconduct instead of promoting the highest standards of professional ethical conduct and the virtues of the work we do. They hope to develop professionals who prioritize moral values as compared with values tied more to self-interest and fears about lawsuits. They want learners to ask themselves self-reflective questions such as, What am I made of as a person? What qualities can I develop to enhance my ability to help others? How should I comport myself in professional life?

Handelsman and colleagues note that humility, prudence, respectfulness, integrity, benevolence, courage in the face of adversity, and persistence when distracted are positive professional virtues that can inform and guide practice. They suggest that such qualities constitute "moral character"—a way of being that, in addition to ethics codes, can help to guide decision-making in consultation with wise others when dilemmas and challenges arise. Clinicians should also be guided by "foundational ethical principles" including fidelity, beneficence, nonmalfeasance, justice, and respect for human rights and self-determination. Clinical educators should include more specific and positive ethics course work and case examples across the clinical practice curriculum. Continuing education courses in ethics should be mandatory and encourage critical thinking, caring, conscientiousness, and other virtuous behaviors in order to improve service and transform average clinicians into better ones. Self-reflection and self-care are critical in this process (Handelsman, Knapp, & Gottlieb, 2002).

■ Suggested Readings

The following are useful resources on multiculturalism, difference, and diversity:

DePoy, Elizabeth, & Gilson, Stephen French. (2004). *Rethinking disability: Principles for professional and social change.* Belmont, CA: Thomson-Brooks/Cole.

Lum, Doman. (2007). *Culturally competent practice: A framework for understanding diverse groups and justice issues* (3rd Ed.). Belmont, CA: Thomson-Brooks/Cole.

Perez, Ruperto, Debord, Kurt A., & Bieschke, Kathleen J. (2007). *Handbook of counseling and psychotherapy with lesbian, gay and bisexual clients.* Washington, DC: American Psychological Association.

Pedrotti, J.T., Edwards, L.M., & Lopez, S.J. (2008). Working with multiracial clients in therapy: Bridging theory, research, and practice. *Professional Psychology, 39,* 192–201.

Sue, Derald Wing, Capodilupo, Christina M., Torino, Gina C., Bucceri, Jennifer M., Holder, Aisha M. B., Nadal, Kevin L., & Esquilin, Marta. (2007). Racial microaggressions in everyday life: Implications for clinical practice. *American Psychologist, 62,* 271–286.

Sue, Derald Wing, & Sue, David. (2008). *Counseling the culturally diverse: Theory and practice* (5th Ed.). Hoboken, NJ: Wiley.

In addition, we believe everyone should read:

McIntosh, Peggy. (1989). White privilege: Unpacking the invisible knapsack. *Peace and Freedom* (July/August), pp. 10–12.

Sue, Derald Wing. (2003). *Overcoming our racism: The journey to liberation.* San Francisco, CA: Jossey-Bass.

The following are useful readings on ethics:

Barnett, Jeffrey E., Lazarus, Arnold A, Vasquez, Melba J. T., Moorhead-Slaughter, Olivia, and W. Brad Johnson. (2007). Boundary issues and multiple relationships: Fantasy and reality. *Professional Psychology: Research and Practice, 38,* 401–410.

Behnke, Stephen H., & Warner, Elizabeth. (2002). Confidentiality in the treatment of adolescents. *Monitor on Psychology, 33*(3). Retrieved September 24, 2009 from www.apa.org/monitor/mar02/confidentiality.html.

Corey, Gerald, Corey, Marianne Schneider, & Callanan, Patrick. (2007). Issues and ethics in the helping professions (7th Ed). Belmont, CA: Brooks/Cole-Cengage.

Dolgoff, Ralph, Loewenberg, Frank M., & Harrington, Donna (2009). *Ethical decisions for social work practice* (8th Ed.). Belmont, CA: Brooks/Cole/Cengage.

Handelsman, Mitchell M., Knapp, Samuel, & Gottlieb, Michael C. (2002). Positive ethics. In C. R. Snyder & Shane J. Lopez (Eds.). *Handbook of positive psychology* (pp. 731–750). New York: Oxford.

Knapp, S., & VandeCreek, L. (2008). When values of different cultures conflict: Ethical decision making in a multicultural context. *Professional Psychology, 39,* 660–666.

Luepker, Ellen. (2003). *Record keeping in psychotherapy and counseling: Protecting confidentiality in the professional relationship.* New York: Brunner-Routledge.

Midkiff, Donna M. & Wyatt, W. Joseph. (2008). Ethical issues in the provision of online mental health services (etherapy). *Journal of Technology and Human Services, 26,* 310–332.

■ Self-Explorations

1. We often take for granted our own assumptions, values, and ways of perceiving the world until we encounter people from another culture. Recall a time when you experienced "culture shock" by traveling to another part of the world or by interacting with someone from another culture and were surprised by some of your own assumptions. If you have not interacted with people from different cultures, think about a book or film in which you became aware of your own assumptions and discovered that they were not universal. A good book to read about the impact of cultural differences is *The Spirit Catches You and You Fall Down.*

2. Sometimes people find it difficult to have experiences with others who are different from themselves. What experiences have you had with people who are different from yourself? What did you learn from these experiences?

3. We can sometimes enlarge our experiences with people who are different from ourselves by volunteering in a homeless shelter or food pantry, working with people with AIDS, or attending a mosque, synagogue, or church different from our own. What kinds of activities can you engage in to broaden your experiences and friendships? What keeps you from undertaking such activities?

4. Discuss examples of unintentional racism or racial microaggressions that you have observed or experienced. Do you have examples of other types of microaggressions, such as those based on sexual orientation, gender, or socioeconomic class?

5. Identify someone who is different from you in a significant way (race, age, religion, sexual orientation) and from whom you have learned something about his or her culture or experiences. What specifically did you learn? What more would you like to know?

6. Read McIntosh's (1989) article on White privilege and Sue et al.'s (2008) article on racial microaggressions. (Both are in the Suggested Readings at the end of the chapter.) What do you see as the relationship between a lack of awareness of White privilege and the microaggression of invalidation?

7. Reflect on the people and institutions that contributed to your personal ethical stance prior to undertaking a clinical education. List your own bedrock guiding principles for everyday life, relationships, and work.

8. Describe a situation which you witnessed, or were part of, that challenged or brought into question your bedrock values or ethics. What effects did this experience have on your personal ethical development? Would you behave differently today? Why or why not?

■ Essay Questions

1. The APA, ACA, and NASW provide multicultural guidelines for working with diverse populations. Read some of the guidelines for culturally competent practice. How is culturally competent practice different from just good practice?

2. Do you think clinicians can be value free? Can clinicians be value neutral? How do you think clinicians should handle the issue of values in the clinical relationship?

3. Confidentiality has become much more complicated in the electronic age. Discuss the various ways that technological advances and managed care affect privacy and confidentiality. Can clinicians really offer confidentiality? What should clinicians do to ensure confidentiality?

4. Review the ethical codes of the APA, ACA, NASW, or NOHS. Discuss the limits of confidentiality when working with minors. An interesting article can be found at www.apa.org/monitor/mar02/confidentiality.html.

■ Key Terms

Advocacy	Individual racism
Aversive racism	Informed consent
Certification	Institutional racism
Confidentality	Minority status
Cultural competencies	Multicultural practice
Cultural racism	Multiethnic
Culture	Multiple dimensions of identity
Discrimination	Multiple relationships
Diversity	Multiracial
Duty to warn	Prejudice
Ethical dilemmas	Privileged communication
Ethical principles	Professional code of ethics
Ethical standards	Professional license
Ethics	Race
Ethnicity	Racial microaggressions
Fiduciary relationship	Racism
Heterosexism	Salience of identity
Homophobia	Social construct
Identity	Stereotype

CHAPTER 3

Getting Started

In this chapter, we talk about how clinicians prepare to meet with clients in a variety of settings and the expectations that both clinicians and clients may bring to their initial encounters. We also discuss ways to begin the clinical interview.

■ The Interview Environment

CLIP 3.1
Variety of Settings

Clinicians interview in a variety of settings. Since the location of the meeting and the physical surroundings affect the aura and process of an interview, it is incumbent on us as clinicians to be thoughtful in setting up our interview environments. Here we refer not simply to arranging an office, but to making every interview space welcoming and accessible to persons with disabilities. Ideally, interviewing environments should be located near the populations served, have office hours that accommodate clients' schedules, be near public transportation, offer child care, provide services in clients' native languages, and offer affordable services scaled to clients' income.

Creating a safe, quiet space for talking reflects an appreciation of the fact that people often share their stories more easily in an atmosphere of privacy and relative calm. Part of preparing for the interview is creating an atmosphere that is quiet and circumscribed enough to be conducive to reflecting and talking together. Such an environment can often be established more easily in office settings in which there is some degree of control over noise and intrusions. Whatever the environment, you should try to surround each unique situation with an invisible **bubble of calm** and focused attention.

The interview ambiance is portable and almost palpable, arising from the clinician's respectful, caring, and attuned presence. It can be experienced on a bus en route to a court hearing, in a kitchen with children and neighbors coming and going, and on a park bench outside a homeless shelter. With few exceptions, our steadiness and thoughtfulness regarding clients' needs and styles act as a containing and soothing environment, no matter the setting for the interview. Clients often experience the relationship as a respite and may describe to their clinicians how much they look forward to their time together, or what a "breather from the usual" this encounter is, or how safe and peaceful they feel with us—a unique experience for many. Janet Surrey (1991a) also views this unique feeling of safety and support as a source of enhanced client agency because relatedness stimulates confidence and initiative.

The Professional Office

Most people think interviews take place in an office, and clinicians may do a lot of thinking about office size, location, comfort, and accessibility. Much has been written about the effects on the interview process of office arrangement and decor, including the presence or absence of the clinician's personal belongings (Kadushin & Kadushin, 1997).

Few clinicians have the opportunity to create their own offices. Interns and clinicians pressed for space in community agencies may share office space and have little control over the physical environment in which they work. Whether we have control over our own office settings, work in an agency where we share space, or work in a cubicle, it is important that we take responsibility for the space in which we work.

> *I had been hired for a new clinic that admitted patients before the physical space was ready. I did counseling sessions in a hallway between two metal file cabinets for 4 weeks. Nervous about confidentiality, I hung a big cardboard sign on one of the drawers: "Counseling in progress. Keep a wide berth."*

We suggest the following guidelines for arranging office setup.

Offices should be private, soundproof, and as free of interruptions as possible. Unfortunately, even these basic requirements for privacy can be hard to meet.

When I was an intern, I was seeing a client at the community mental health center. Our offices were very small with no windows and it really felt like a rabbit warren. One major problem was that at times you could hear clients in other rooms. I remember sitting with a 20-year-old woman who had trouble expressing her feelings. We had been talking about her abusive mother when suddenly through the walls we heard the client next door screaming, "I hate her, I hate her." We both looked at each other, and my client said, "I guess she is mad at her mother." We both laughed. Later I talked at staff meeting about the problem and eventually we bought lots of those little sound machines to mask noise. That worked—for the most part.

Although you may sometimes feel powerless to affect the systems in which you are trained, perceptive interns have often brought about needed change by pointing out problems and working with clients and colleagues to resolve them.

Offices should be accessible to persons with disabilities. There should be ramps and accessible bathrooms. Offices should accommodate walkers, wheelchairs, and guide dogs. Federal law mandates accessibility in public settings, and professionals may have to work hard to ensure that private practice offices and smaller settings adhere to the guidelines.

Accessibility for people with disabilities is more than physical accommodation. Mackelprang and Salsgiver (1999) recommend a number of guiding principles for clinicians working with people with disabilities. These include maintaining a strengths perspective, recognizing that such clients are "different not deficient," and emphasizing self-determination. We can build all the ramps we want, but we are not truly accessible unless we are also sensitive to and knowledgeable about working with persons with disabilities.

Offices need to be flexible enough to allow both client and clinician a comfortable personal space. Most people have an invisible area around them that serves as a protective barrier. Intrusion into this **personal space** creates discomfort. Personal space varies from person to person, from culture to culture, and from situation to situation. People often have less need for personal space with a friend than with a stranger. Gender also plays a role; in Western cultures, men tend to leave more interpersonal space between themselves and male strangers than do women with female strangers (Harper, Wiens, & Matarazzo, 1978).

Cultural norms also dictate personal space (Leathers & Eaves, 2007). Ivey et al (2010) note that most North Americans seem to prefer a conversational space of about an arm's length. "(I)n some Arabic cultures, people prefer to talk at a distance of about 18 inches, a most uncomfortable distance for many Europeans. Arabs who experience the distance of Europeans may interpret such behavior as 'cold'" (Ivey et al 2010, p. 132). The British prefer greater distance than all three. Personal space is often influenced by power dynamics. Those in positions of relatively less power may have their personal space invaded by those with greater power. We try never to invade clients' personal space unless there is no option—for example, if jostled together while riding on a crowded subway, or if a client falls and we reach down to help him or her up, or if we have to assist in restraining someone whose behavior is escalating out of control.

Having movable chairs or furniture helps create a comfortable environment for both client and clinician. When there is a difference in comfort levels about personal space, the clinician should respect the client's needs. However, there are exceptions: The clinician who feels that the client's needs interfere with the ability to attend or to get work done may have to ask the client to move a little. In Chapter 11, we talk about other issues relating to physical contact and closeness.

In my private practice office, I have two chairs set up with about two and a half feet between them. One time I saw a client who pulled her chair up so close that our knees were touching. I pulled my chair back a little and she moved closer. I felt very uncomfortable with that much closeness. I wondered what it meant but did not feel like making a big deal about it yet. I had only just met her. I noted that she felt comfortable sitting very close and I said that made it hard for me to see her. I said I feel more comfortable with a little more distance between us. I stored the information away for future use.

Furniture arrangement should reflect equality and respect. Seating should be comfortable, yet not so comfortable that one is likely to fall asleep. The relative height and style of the seats, as well as their position in relationship to each other, should reflect the equality and respect of the client–clinician relationship. Clinicians should have a flexible office arrangement that can accommodate people in wheelchairs, those who use guide dogs, or people with other assistive devices. Although it is important to pay attention to the seating arrangements, remember that it is the sitter, not the seat, who communicates professionalism and respect.

I have a colleague who has one of those huge La-Z-Boy recliners for himself and a small folding chair for his clients. I've always wondered how the clients feel about that.

* * *

I was working with Karlene, a woman who was somewhat overweight. One day, my usual office was not available. We used another office that had comfortable chairs, but no couch, love seat, or chairs without arms. I didn't notice anything was wrong until she leaned back in her chair and the chair began to tip sideways. I commented on this and suggested that we move to an office with more comfortable seating. I only realized how tight the chair was when she struggled to get out of it. Even though she had been fairly open with me in the past, she said she would not have raised the issue of the chair if I had not brought it up. She cried as she talked about how bad it felt to live in a world where usual things (stores with turnstiles, movie theaters, and airplanes) were not accessible. She later shared that she had interviewed several therapists before deciding to see me. One of the factors that clinched her decision was the sturdy love seat in my office. The experience opened my eyes to the covert discrimination people experience when the world is not designed to be accessible to them.

* * *

The first time I worked with a woman in a wheelchair, I quickly removed the chair that normally is placed opposite mine in the office, assuming that she would place her wheelchair in that spot. I thought I was being sensitive. I didn't realize that she might prefer transferring out of her wheelchair to sit in an office chair until she told me. It also reminded me that I should be careful that the furniture in my office be solid and stable enough to support a transfer.

Many interviewers sit beside the desk, rather than behind it, so that the desk does not create a symbolic barrier. If the desk is placed against the wall and a chair is placed beside the desk, the client seated there can be invited to fill out information on the desktop or work side by side with the clinician on genograms, ecomaps, lifecharts, letters, or artwork. Some clinicians prefer a desk out of the way in a corner, with comfortable chairs placed in the main space of the office. Clinicians concerned about safety place their desks or chairs near the door so that they can exit quickly to summon help in the event of an emergency. If the interviewer has a preferred seat, it should be pointed out to clients while encouraging them to take any other seat they wish.

EXAMPLES

"Mrs. Lindahl, have a seat wherever you would like."

"Lawrence, feel free to sit on the sofa or any of the chairs."

"Janelle, I'll be sitting here; please take any of the other seats."

Clinicians seldom sit on a couch with a client because doing so may suggest a familiarity or informality that may be uncomfortable or inappropriate. In a home visit, however, sitting on a couch may be necessary and appropriate.

After working behind a desk in a regulation office setting, I devised a living room milieu for my private practice office. I associated the environment with a place for private, intimate talk and hoped my clients would too. I've set up my office with a large window behind me so clients can take a break from looking at me. It also gives a feeling of openness and airiness to the room.

With children, some teens, and some adults, casual seating on the floor may be used as long as clients seem comfort with this arrangement and there is a clinical reason for it. Children especially appreciate the clinician's willingness to "come down to their size" rather than looming over them. Family therapists, psychodramatists, relaxation trainers, and process group facilitators may all use floor seating from time to time.

Interviewing offices should be able to accommodate unexpected others who may accompany clients to the meeting. The clinician should know where extra chairs can be found if needed and where others may wait comfortably for the client if they are not to be part of the meeting. It goes without saying that attending to the needs of these others is also a way of demonstrating respect and caring to the client.

As in all clinical work, the interviewer considers the possible symbolic meanings of seating arrangements and behaviors, noting where the client, group, or family customarily chooses to sit in relation to each other and to the clinician. The choices may signal alliances, the degree of comfort with closeness and distance, cultural norms, or subtle shifts in relationships.

I can often tell what's happening in the midpoint of therapy by the chair the client takes. When we've gotten to the most psychologically affecting material, clients sometimes switch seats. Those needing more intimacy move closer to me; others needing more distance sit farther away.

No matter how the office is arranged, it is important to make sure that the client feels some flexibility in the office seating. You can indicate flexibility in a number of ways. One is by directly asking, after the client sits, "Is that okay?" Another is by remaining responsive to reasonable client requests for changes in arrangement.

I had brought a client into my office, which has two chairs and a couch in one area and a desk and chair in another. I told her to have a seat wherever she would like and she took a seat on the couch. I took a seat in one of the chairs and angled it a little to face the couch. I asked her my usual pro forma question: "Is that all right?" She responded by jumping off the couch and saying that she felt that the couch was much softer than it looked and that she felt like she sank into it. She said she was glad I had asked because she really didn't want to sit on the couch and felt uncomfortable about moving. She took the other chair and I turned my chair to face her more directly.

Office decor should be soothing, not distracting. Warm colors and soft lighting can help create a sense of caring, privacy, and intimacy. However, we are creating a professional environment, not a romantic setting. The lighting should be bright enough for people to see clearly. Try to create an environment that is not too "busy" or disorganized. Make sure that the interview space is not overly cluttered. Avoiding clutter applies to clinicians' desks as well. Having a desk that is relatively clear lets clients know that you have "made room" to see them. On the other hand, it has been suggested that having a messy desk might humanize the clinician in the client's eyes. Of course, we can never fully predict whether a client might find something in or about our offices uncomfortable or even offensive. Clients' reactions to our offices may provide us with important information and can be grist for the mill.

Individual clinicians may want to establish their own environments unless the setting or agency dictates or standardizes furnishings. Some clinicians like to display a few personal belongings or pictures of loved ones or pets. Others feel it is more appropriate to have a personally neutral office. Always anticipate the possible effects of displaying personal belongings, and be prepared to respond to questions these may elicit from clients or other visitors. Later in the chapter, we discuss safety issues related to the display of personal items and information.

Two relatively common pieces of office decor are a box of tissues and a clock. Some clinicians place the clock so that it is over the client's shoulder and they can unobtrusively note the time without distracting the client. We have found it useful to have the clock positioned in such a way that both the client and the clinician can easily see it. Sometimes it is helpful to have two clocks—one facing the client, the other facing the clinician—so that both can track time. Some clients feel more in control of the session if they know how much time is left, so that they are able to pace themselves. Others prefer not to see the clock because it reminds them of the arbitrary time limits on the session and on the clinical relationship. If you look at the clock frequently, clients may feel that you can't wait to get rid of them.

Clinicians who work with children or who do art therapy may display their clients' artwork in the office. Others may place presents from clients in the office. We discuss the implications of client gifts to clinicians in Chapter 12. Displaying gifts from clients raise a number of important questions: What will other clients think about the items? Will clients feel compelled to give the clinician similar presents? If the clinician is hanging one client's drawings, should all clients' drawings be hung? Would this be distracting to others? Where to draw the line?

Office decor should be appropriate to the types of clients we see and should reflect the cultures of the people with whom we work. For example, if we are seeing families and children, our offices should have toys and playthings. If we work with Mexican immigrants, we may want to have pictures or posters with Mexican themes. We must be careful about superficial or cosmetic fixes—displaying things just to make an impression. Clients can be put off by insensitive or inauthentic behaviors.

Try to experience what the office is like from the client's perspective. Sitting in all the available places in the office enables us to consider whether sunlight shines in the client's eyes, what is in the client's line of vision, and whether the chair is comfortable.

Always consider other needs of clients. Is a bathroom available to clients? Is it wheelchair accessible? What about drinking water? Can children play somewhere safely while their parents are being seen? Where can clients hang their coats? Is a phone available for client use? Are clients routinely asked at intake whether they need any special arrangements or accommodations to facilitate the interview process (e.g., child care, translator services, sign language interpretation, or ramp entrance)? Weaver (2005) notes that traditional Muslims pray several times a day, so that, out of respect, flexible scheduling should take these practices into account.

Make the best of the situation. Today clinicians often work in less than ideal circumstances. They may share small cubicles with many other people. They may have no privacy, no comfortable chairs, no office decor—not even a place to store their personal belongings. In those situations, you need to be as creative as possible. Arrange schedules so that you and each of your officemates have some time alone to meet with clients—for example, when others are at lunch or out of the office. You can bring in posters or plants from home to make the interviewer environment look nicer. You can see if other agencies, churches, or schools will give you space for private meetings with clients. Finally, you can join with colleagues to lobby administrators for more conducive environments for your work with clients.

When I was an intern, the office I had was awful. It was dark, had no windows, and had old broken-down furniture with graffiti on the desk. I went to the Christmas Tree Shop and bought some posters, a tablecloth to cover the desk, and two artificial plants. I even *found a poster of a field that was hung in a window frame so that it actually gave the impression of a window with a view. And all for $18.85!!*

* * *

We were so crowded at the mental health center that, with the director's approval, we asked the public library if they would give us a room in their basement where we could meet with clients. They ended up giving us two small rooms. Ironically, some of the people we worked with spent a good part of their day at the library anyway.

* * *

When I was a field supervisor for the school of social work, we placed a student in an Emergency Room. The only place they could find for her to write up her case notes was a small anteroom off the ER where they sometimes left the dead bodies until their families arrived. It was very upsetting for the student to write notes about her clients on a little table beside a gurney where a cadaver lay covered by a sheet, awaiting a family viewing. Several times she asked for a different space but staff said there was none. She called me, and the school decided that we could not use that setting for an internship anymore. When we told the ER we would not place students there under those conditions, they cleared a little space down the hall for the student to use.

EXERCISE 3.1 Field Visit

After securing permission to do so, visit a setting or agency where clinical interviews take place. Briefly sit in the waiting area and note what you would observe as a client. Go to one of the offices and sit in all the chairs. In your journal, make notes on what you see and learn. Be aware of privacy, lighting, furniture arrangement, décor, and so on. Do the agency and staff reflect the cultures of the diverse populations they serve? In what ways? Discuss your observations in class.

Out of the Office and Onto the Streets

Many clinicians do not see clients primarily in office settings, and many clients may not find an office setting comfortable or safe. To engage clients, we may conduct interviews in their home kitchens, in hospital rooms, on benches outside shelters, over coffee at fast-food restaurants, in prison visiting rooms, or in classrooms.

I got a call on intake at the mental health center from a family whose 17-year-old daughter had started to hear voices. My supervisor approved an in-home crisis evaluation to determine whether the girl could be sustained at home. I would be in touch with my supervisor by phone to determine the next steps once in the home. When I arrived, the daughter, dressed in a long wool coat, was fully immersed in a bathtub full of warm water, laughing and singing. She knew I was coming and invited me in "to see I'm just fine." Since she wouldn't leave the tub, I perched on the closed toilet seat and interviewed her there long enough to get a sense of her need for protection. Thus began a relationship that, following her 30-day hospitalization, continued for two and a half years.

Home Visits

There is a lot to learn about clients by meeting with them in their homes. People may behave very differently in their homes than they do in the office; they may be more comfortable, more outgoing—literally, more at home. Clinicians may be able to observe things about the client and his or her situation that are not readily visible in the office, thus expanding their perspective.

> *As a counseling intern at a suburban mental health clinic, I decided to do a home visit with the family of a 14-year-old adolescent I was seeing. When I arrived at the house, I noticed the striking contrast between the fortresslike outside (gate locked, curtains drawn, double locks on the door) and the absence of doors in any of the rooms inside the house. I began to wonder about family secrets and family boundaries. Later, my client revealed that she was sexually abused by her father.*

The home visitor often has a greater opportunity to meet the client's friends and family; see family pictures; note relationships with cherished pets and neighbors that the client may not think to mention in the office; and experience the way the client puts together, develops, and protects living space. Just as we attend carefully to the messages conveyed by our own office arrangements, we also note the environments and the messages they convey about clients and their situations. Culture, income levels, and personal taste all need to be taken into account before making inferences.

Home visits present a number of challenges to the clinician:

- *Clients may live in circumstances different from those of the interviewer—* some may be wealthy, others poor. A variety of factors such as poverty, exploitation, mental illness, and addiction can cause clients to live in inadequate or dilapidated housing lacking basic amenities. Large numbers of extended kin may have to live in two or three rooms. At the other extreme, clinicians visit the homes of wealthy clients living in opulence. Clinicians who visit the homes of people who hoard may interview in the midst of huge piles and be shocked by the client's living situation. Interviewers often work in alien and unfamiliar environments and may at times feel uncomfortable or intimidated.
- *The home is not a controlled environment,* nor is it set up to ensure privacy, flexibility, and comfort for interviews the way offices may be. Phone calls, kids waking from naps, elders calling out for help, visitors dropping by—all may seem like intrusions on the interview. We must remember that, as important as our work may seem to us, it is but a small part of many clients' hectic lives and may at times seem to them to be the least important thing they have to worry about.
- *From the client's perspective, the clinician may feel like the intruder, the outsider.* The clinician is the guest and may feel less in control of the environment or the agenda. In some situations, clients may not welcome the clinician and may want him or her to leave their homes. These factors may contribute to the unfortunate reluctance of many professionals to make home visits.

Tshanga, a 14-year-old isolated and depressed teen, was referred to family services by her mother "to see if you can find out why she is so sad." Since she would not come to see me, I made several home visits to try to engage her, but she would never let me inside the apartment. My supervisor made me go back for four weeks running and interview her standing outside, talking through the door and feeling ridiculous as neighbors passed in the hallway and stared at me as I talked to an invisible other. I did process recording on each of these visits, and my supervisor treated them like office visits, helping me focus on feelings, use humor, ask about school, inquire about boyfriends, and so on. At about the fifth week, Tshanga suddenly said she would let me come in today, but only if she were allowed to stand on the opposite side of the room. I was very receptive, and this is how our visits went the rest of the year.

- *Home visits may begin with greetings, social conversation, and sharing coffee or food.* Some clinicians may experience discomfort over the thought that during home visits they are not "doing the work" and are "just socializing." We believe that all these rituals are an integral part of the interview process and may contribute to the development of a positive working alliance. In many cultures, sharing food and informal conversation are an important part of social interaction.

Mrs. Lanzarone was not able to meet with me in the office because she had custody of her four grandchildren while her daughter was in prison for selling drugs. So I met with her weekly in the kitchen of her apartment, and I often held one of the kids in my lap while Mrs. L. cooked me Italian food for lunch. At first, I would come away from these sessions exhausted, which helped me understand what Mrs. L. was up against every day. Once I got used to it, I looked forward to our meetings and so did Mrs. L. She called this "Gramma's time."

Other Settings

In addition to home visits, interviews may occur in a variety of nonoffice settings. The workplace, the school cafeteria or playground, the shelter, the nursing home, the restaurant, the street corner, and the locked facility are all frequent sites of clinical interventions. Today's practitioners learn to move flexibly and comfortably among locales, tailoring interviewing strategies to the exigencies and advantages of nontraditional sites. For example, Janna Malamud Smith (2000) describes accommodating a client with asthma and agoraphobia by driving to her area, parking near her apartment, and interviewing her quite productively in the car.

Major challenges confronting clinicians when we work in a **borrowed environment** include the maintenance of confidentiality and focus, the intrusion of others with different roles and needs, and the pressure of time in an environment whose purposes can shift from moment to moment.

It was amazing how much we were able to do at the diner. Russell didn't want anyone in his small town to know that he had AIDS. He was afraid to come to the clinic, so we met at the Busy Bee diner in the next town. We could get a lot done as long as we found a corner table in the back, kept our voices low, and screened out all the hubbub around us by focusing intensely on our work.

It is crucial to remember that what we see in meetings with a client is only part of the larger picture—snapshots of a person's life at a particular time. To see clients in situations where they are interacting with others may broaden our perspective in unanticipated ways. The quiet teenager in the office may be very outgoing and funny in the playground. The woman suffering from major depression, tearful and seemingly paralyzed during therapy sessions, may still be functioning in superhuman ways in her leadership position at work. Whenever feasible, wise clinicians attempt to see clients in a variety of contexts to get a fuller picture of their strengths and issues. School counselors may observe students in classroom settings. Day treatment staff may observe clients in community meetings. Workers in an adolescent residential treatment center often make home visits to observe the teens interacting with their families. Carel Germain and Alex Gitterman (1996) use the term **lifespace interviews** to describe these informative in vivo transactions.

Back in the Office and Onto the Net

Clinicians are now able to provide clinical services over the Internet, sometimes called online counseling, etherapy, Internet counseling, cybercounseling, telehealth, or therap-e. These terms all refer to "delivery of therapeutic services over the Internet through a variety of delivery systems, including asynchronous email, chat-based messaging, discussion forums, closed circuit video conferencing, net guided interventions, virtual reality games, and Internet-based audio and video communication" (Finn & Schoech, 2008, p. 105).

"Sixty million Americans live in rural areas where health specialties or mental health services don't exist or are inadequate" (Winerman, 2006, p. 32). Telehealth programs have brought health and mental health care to a large number of clients with disabilities or health needs living in remote locations where healthcare and transportation are scarce or unaffordable. **Online counseling** is the term used to denote the provision of therapy or consultation via telephone, computer messaging, or teleconferencing.

Many clinicians have been reluctant to provide online counseling because of worries about privacy, safety, and quality of care. However, recent research has indicated that service provided at a distance by knowledgeable and caring providers who are comfortable using technology can be very effective (Barak, Hen, Boniel-Nissim, & Shapira, 2008; Rochlen, Zack, & Speyer, 2004). Brett Litz and colleagues found that Internet-based self-management treatment was very effective in treating armed service members who had post-traumatic stress disorder (PTSD) from either the Iraq War or the attack on the Pentagon on 9/11 (Litz, Engel, Bryant, & Papa, 2007). In fact, Medicare is now willing to reimburse practitioners for online counseling that meets specific standards related to quality and safety. Hopefully, increased funding of online technology will support the loan of computers or telecommunications equipment to those who are home-bound, live in isolated rural areas, or who do not have access to the technology because of its cost.

Goran, 33, who lives and works in a rural area, was depressed due to several recent losses. He wanted to see a therapist, but the nearest one was two hours away. Luckily, he heard about a clinic that was set up to do interactive videoconferencing in order to provide mental health services for clients in remote areas. He went to the first appointment in person and the therapist explained how they could work together using videoconferencing in place of face-to-face therapy in the office. Goran and the therapist discussed how the teleconference would work and he signed an informed consent form. He was shown how to use equipment loaned to him by the clinic that allowed him to have weekly videoconferencing therapy sessions with the clinician. He said that he felt comfortable working with the therapist in this way, and it saved him a lot of time and money. He doubted he would have gone for therapy if he had had to drive back and forth each time. He was surprised at how comfortable he felt after the first few sessions.

In this global age, people travel between countries on a regular basis. Army reservists are often sent abroad for three-month stints, workers can travel overseas regularly for business, and individuals may return to their countries of origin to visit family members. Videoconferencing, email, and other forms of online contact and services may help clients maintain continuity in their work with their clinicians when they travel.

Gail is a software engineer who travels twice a month to Japan and Germany. She regularly uses Skype to talk with and see her children while she is away. She and her therapist have arranged to use Skype occasionally for scheduled appointments when she travels and will not be able to see her therapist in the office for a long period of time.

Clients may seek support or information when they feel protected from visibility by the Web. For example, clients may feel more comfortable talking about body image issues online than they would face to face.

Guidelines for using technology to deliver services include the following:

1. Clinicians should receive professional training before attempting to use any form of online mental health services. While using online counseling may seem appealing, especially to those who have grown up in the age of Skype, chat rooms, and virtual reality, clinicians must be carefully trained in the skills of providing online services using ever-evolving technology. Some graduate schools are beginning to offer programs about online mental health service delivery, and there are an increasing number of continuing education programs on the topic.

2. Clinicians should familiarize themselves with their state's legal and ethical standards for online practice. Clinicians should be aware that their license may prohibit them from practicing across state lines. Anthony Ragusea and Leon VandeCreek (2003) discuss the ethical issues of online therapy via email, chat rooms, or interactive video.

3. Clinicians should be aware that confidentiality issues may be somewhat different when using technologies for treatment. Verbatim video recordings of sessions might become part of the client's record. Encryption programs can be used to protect online interactions, but they are not impenetrable. In addition, it may be more difficult to ensure confidentiality if the client is communicating offsite where others may walk into the room.

The specific challenges of conducting practice online are beyond the scope of this book. Marlene Maheu and her colleagues offer a thorough and excellent discussion of the complicated issues in using technology in practice (Maheu, Pullier, Wilhelm, McMenamin, & Brown-Connolly, 2005).

Safety

According to Susan Weinger (2001), the federal Occupational Safety and Health Administration (OSHA) announced in 1996 that "more assaults occur in health care and social service industries than in any other" (p. 3). Weinger cites research predicting that half of all human service workers will experience client violence at some point in their careers. Clients may have a history of violent behaviors, hear voices that tell them to harm others, or have episodes of uncontrollable anger. Clinicians need training in violence prevention as well as in how to respond to threats and acts of violence should they occur (Griffin, 1995; Jayaratne, Croxton, & Mattison, 2004).

> *I'll never forget the first time I heard about a clinician who was murdered. I was working at a community center when we received a call that a former colleague of ours had been shot by a client who had come to the clinic with a gun. He killed one psychologist and wounded another.*

As more and more clinicians conduct interviews in the community, they find themselves in situations in which they fear for their own safety.

> *When I was a counseling intern at an alternative high school, two of my students got into a fight and one, Doreen, had her arm slashed with a knife. After taking her to the hospital and dealing with the police who had been called, I brought Doreen home to her family. Her older sister ran into the bedroom and came out with a gun saying, "We have to kill that bitch who cut you." I was terrified.*

Clinicians need to feel relatively safe to be effective. When feeling personally at risk, they find it hard, if not impossible, to attend to clients and their needs. Clinicians who are too anxious to concentrate will not be able to help others. It is extremely important that you turn to supervisors, colleagues, or consultants when alarm bells go off about physical safety. Do not be embarrassed to ask for help before, during, or after critical incidents. In fact, many agencies have a formalized **critical incident review process**, in which staff members review incidents of threats or harm and plan strategies for managing such incidents in the future.

Home visits may present the clinician with special safety challenges. Weapons or drugs in the home, when coupled with simmering resentments and substance use, can present serious dangers to visiting clinicians. Sometimes a clinician may be asked to do a home visit to assess the impact of a family member's potential for violence. Patricia Spencer and Shari Munch (2003) recommend an **environmental assessment** of the neighborhood and residence to be visited. They encourage clinicians to determine which routes to the home are safest at various hours, whether and when gangs are active or drugs are sold in the area, and how area residents regard outreach workers. They further recommend that we be aware of who is at home, the possibility of weapons being present, and the location of exits so that a quick departure is available in case danger arises within or outside a residence.

> *I made a visit to a client recovering from an overdose in a hospital in a high-crime neighborhood. She had been a tough client, challenging me constantly, dismissing me as unable to understand her because of our differing backgrounds. When I walked into her hospital room, she was shocked to see me. "You're so little and you come all this way to see me?" she said. We visited for a while, and as I got up to leave, she said, "Now on your way to the subway, walk tall and put your hand in your pocket so they think you have a gun." I laughed but, believe me, I followed her advice. The next time I saw her, the hostility was gone.*

Clinicians should never touch or turn their backs on people whose escalating rage or fear might lead to an attack (Sheafor, Horejsi, & Horejsi, 1997). Avoid stepping into a dangerous fight between two or more people already out of control. Immediately call or run for help instead. Carl Tishler and colleagues suggest mirroring clients' body language "to communicate empathy for his or her current state and control of the situation. For example, sit with seated patients, stand with standing patients, and walk alongside pacing patients. A clinician who towers over seated patients conveys both intimidation and an unwillingness to learn about the patient's plight. Being seated while patients are standing makes the clinician vulnerable to violent attacks" (Tishler, Gordon, & Landry-Meyer, 2000, p. 36).

> *I didn't tell you what happened before I brought Doreen home and her sister pulled out the gun. I was the counselor in the classroom when another student, Yvette, pulled a knife on Doreen. I remember thinking, "I am the counselor—I should do something about this." I actually stood between the students and tried to talk Yvette into putting her knife away. All the while, Doreen was egging her on. I was lucky Yvette didn't use the knife on me to get to Doreen.*

With regard to physical safety, consider the following cautions:

- Avoid working alone in a building or isolated location, especially after dark. Brightly lit offices in otherwise darkened buildings can make both clinicians and clients vulnerable targets.
- Don't keep anything in your office that can be used as a weapon, such as statues or other heavy objects. Keep scissors, letter openers, and other sharp objects where clients can't easily access them.
- Don't reveal personal information that would allow a client to harm you or your family. For example, a family picture on your desk in which your child is in a school uniform might give a client information that could put your child at risk. Remove your name and address from any magazines you might bring in from home for the waiting room.
- Let someone at the agency know where you are headed when you leave for visits in the field.
- As a general rule, do not interview people who are intoxicated or who might have weapons.

- Carry a cell phone programmed to access emergency help instantly.
- When you are concerned about the degree of risk involved in a family visit, discuss with supervisors or consultants whether someone should accompany you.
- If you feel seriously endangered, leave the situation immediately and get help.

At my agency, people would be yelling all the time. We became somewhat oblivious to the sound of loud voices. We realized that if a clinician was in trouble and was calling out, no one would pay attention. We decided that we needed a code word that would alert us. We decided to use the word "conference."

No one can be completely safe. Clinicians and agencies have to decide what risks they are willing to assume. Agency protocols should stipulate that potentially risky home visits involving protective services and substance abuse be carried out by teams, not individuals (Jayaratne et al., 2004). It is essential that clinicians address these important practice issues with colleagues, supervisors, and agency or program administrators.

Today most schools, court settings, child protective services, and health settings have security guards posted at entrances or walking the corridors to respond to violent situations should they arise. In addition, agencies should have safety and escape plans in case dangerous incidents occur or clients threaten serious harm. Concealed alarms that signal trouble and coded language for signaling help can all avert harm to both staff and clients. Thomas Schwartz and Tricia Park (1999) describe educational programs for clinicians in psychiatric settings. Content should include readings on assessment and response to violent behaviors as well as clinician self-protection strategies. Important discussion topics include the causes of violence, the psychodynamics of aggression, and self-defense techniques. Laura Gately and Sally Stabb (2005) assert that violence prevention awareness and intervention strategies are not being adequately taught in clinical education programs. They believe that many settings can train staff and students in risk management using safety guidelines periodically issued by OSHA.

Clinicians also need to be concerned about the safety of their clients. Clients may be threatened with harm if they elect to share their stories with a professional. Undocumented immigrants may worry about deportation if they accept services. Battered wives may fear reprisals from spouses if they disclose their abuse. Mothers may fear losing custody of their children if they reveal their lesbianism. It makes little difference to people in crisis whether we are called psychologists, human service workers, counselors, or social workers if what we provide seems to offer more risk than gain. Even clients without such concerns may worry whether clinicians will really preserve confidentiality if pressure from others is used to try to obtain client information.

Some clients worry that they will be harmed by the clinicians themselves. Unfortunately, these concerns are sometimes justified. There has been a steady increase in the number of ethics complaints against clinicians due to sexual abuse, physical abuse, and financial exploitation (Pope & Vasquez, 2007; Reamer, 1995).

■ Even Before We Meet

It is human nature to anticipate what people and events will be like before engaging with them. Thinking about encounters in advance may reduce anxiety about the unknown and prepare us to cope with contingencies that may arise from contact with that which is unfamiliar. So, even before we meet, clinicians and clients alike develop expectations about each other and about the relationship.

Clinician Expectations

Exercise 3.2 helps you identify clinician expectations you may have about clients even before you meet them. Do the exercise, then continue reading.

EXERCISE 3.2 Anticipation

Write down in your journal the ideas that immediately come to mind about the following clients:

- Terry Mahoney is referred to the mental health clinic because of drug abuse.
- Domingo, a high school sophomore, is referred by his teacher because he is failing math.
- A young couple comes to you wanting to talk about the process of artificial insemination.
- Mrs. Giorgio is a 67-year-old woman whose husband has just died.
- Chang Yang is a 33-year-old Chinese immigrant accused of spouse abuse.

It is important to explore the sources of our expectations. Some expectations come from information about the client (such as the client's gender, age, ethnicity, or presenting problem). We refer to these factors as **client information variables.** In Exercise 3.3, see whether your expectations about each client change as information is added or altered. Complete that exercise before reading on.

EXERCISE 3.3 Changing Expectations

- Terry Mahoney is referred to the mental health clinic because of drug abuse. She is a 54-year-old social worker.
- Domingo, a high school sophomore, is referred by his teacher because he is failing math. He is 22 years old and is cognitively impaired.
- A young couple comes to you wanting to talk about the process of artificial insemination. They are lesbians who have been in a committed relationship for 7 years.

- Mrs. Giorgio is a 67-year-old woman whose husband has just died. They were married one year ago.
- Chang Yang is a 33-year-old Chinese immigrant accused of spouse abuse. Chang Yang is a woman.

What other variables might shape what you think about these clients? Note the similarities and differences in your reactions once you have additional information.

In answering the last question in Exercise 3.3, you may have focused on other attributes of the client, such as sexual orientation, class, race, ethnicity, family background, diagnosis, or appearance. Much of this information may precede the client into the office.

Very seldom do I see a client without having some information about him or her. Often it comes from a phone call with the client in which I learn a little about the reason for the meeting. Sometimes I receive information about the client from the referral source. I am frequently given a case file before I meet the client. I must admit that when I see a very thick case file, I worry that I've been given "a chronic client." I haven't even read any information, but I already have my preformed ideas.

Clinician Gestalt

Clinician preconceptions about clients based on client information variables are affected by what we like to think of as the **clinician gestalt.** As you may have already noted, it is not just the information about clients that shapes how clinicians respond to them; it is also the information interacting with our own values, beliefs, biases, professional knowledge, and past experiences. In turn, our values, beliefs, knowledge, and experiences are influenced by our educational, familial, and cultural backgrounds, including our race, gender, class, sexual orientation, ethnicity, age, and physical ability.

I remember my first week of internship at the community mental health center. I was assigned a "young divorced woman with two children coming to the clinic because she was depressed." My picture was of a woman who was 23, with kids about 2 and 4. I was so shocked when I went to the waiting room and found a 39-year-old woman! I was 27 at the time. I realized my supervisor, who is in her fifties, thought of the client as a young woman; but here she was older than I was. Before meeting her, I had pictured myself as older and wiser, even though I didn't have any children and was just starting out. Now here she was, and I was closer in age to her 20-year-old daughter than to her. Suddenly, I felt so nervous.

Furthermore, the characteristics of individuals and groups obtain meaning within larger social contexts, which include geography, historical period, and prevailing cultural norms. For example, the behavior of a woman who hears voices and talks back to them might have different meaning in different contexts. In sixteenth-century Europe, she may have been called a witch; in the twenty-first-century United States, she may be seen as having schizophrenia or as being "perfectly normal," depending on whether her behavior occurs on a subway in New York City or in a church where people routinely hear and respond to the voice of holy spirits.

EXERCISE 3.4 Clinician Gestalt

In your journal, identify the aspects of your own clinician gestalt that affect your reaction to or your preconceived ideas about the clients described in Exercises 3.5 and 3.6. These can include your beliefs, cultural heritage, past experiences, gender, class, race, ethnicity, age, sexual orientation, and ability in the larger social context in which you find yourself.

Diagnosis and Labeling

Another type of information that may precede a client into the office is a **diagnosis.** A diagnosis is not a description of a person; rather, it is a shorthand way of referring to a complex set of behaviors and characteristics. At times, diagnoses can be useful in facilitating communication between clinicians, which is essential for research and treatment planning. However, when we reduce the rich complexity of a person to a few behaviors, the diagnosis becomes a label.

Labeling is particularly pernicious because labels can predispose us to categorize people and react to them in formulaic ways. For example, some disability scholars believe that attribution of a disability status and the devaluation of certain diagnosed conditions undermine inclusion, civil rights, and the possibility of being thought of as diverse rather than "abnormal" (DePoy & Gilson, 2004). Sometimes labels cause us to see things, like symptoms, that are not there, and sometimes labels cause us *not* to see things, like strengths, that are there (Szasz, 1960).

In the now famous study conducted by David Rosenhan (1973), eight associates of the researcher acted as if they had a mental illness (schizophrenia) to get themselves admitted to various hospital psychiatric wards. Once admitted to the hospital, each of the mock patients behaved normally. The hospital staff, however, continued to see them as mentally ill, despite their protestations and even though they were no longer manifesting symptoms. Once they had been given a diagnosis—a label—their protestations were defined as further evidence of their mental illness. (Interestingly, the "real patients" on the units could tell that the researchers were not actually mentally ill and did not belong in the hospital.)

Certain diagnoses are particularly stigmatizing. **Stigma** refers to the negative assumptions and biases attached to people because of their membership in particular groups (Goffman, 1963). Judgments about people with particular diagnoses are culturally determined and can reflect the zeitgeist of the times, of the community, or of the agency. The diagnoses may frighten clinicians, constricting their openness and negatively impacting the interview process.

An elderly woman called the clinic asking for someone to come to the house and talk her son, who was diagnosed with schizophrenia, into coming out of a closet where he had been holed up for two days. I was on intake and went out with the on-call psychiatrist. I didn't want the doctor to see how anxious I was. I had seen the movie "Psycho" and thought we might be heading into a situation like that one. The man turned out to be a quiet, sad person who began to cry with relief when the doctor said he had come out to help him.

* * *

The three supervisors in day treatment told us that most of the women in the Daily Living Group were "borderlines" who would try to manipulate us because we were interns and didn't know any better. They explained the importance of setting firm limits on client behaviors and not giving "these people" extra attention if they did dramatic things. We were very anxious about starting the group and felt irritated with "these women" before we got to know them.

Diagnoses are usually determined after an extensive process of assessment, which may include observing, testing, interviewing, collecting historical data and life records, and conducting medical exams. Some of the people we see may not have been through an assessment process, but other clients come to us with an already established diagnosis.

EXERCISE 3.5 Diagnosis

In your journal, discuss the ways in which knowing the diagnosis of a client before you meet can be both helpful and problematic.

Preconceived Ideas and Clinical Intuition

Seasoned practitioners may refer to their preconceived ideas as **clinical intuition.** Clinical intuition entails much more than just preconceived ideas. The working hypotheses of the skilled practitioner are developed over time by comparing preconceived ideas and feelings with subsequent experience and learning. However, clinicians must always recognize that, at times, preconceived ideas and clinical intuition may interfere with their ability to be genuinely open to the client's story. In Chapter 8, we discuss the use of clinical intuition and hypothesis building in ongoing work with clients.

Client Expectations

Clients also bring a set of expectations about clinicians and the therapeutic process and environment. These expectations may come from the media, from previous experiences with mental health workers, from the reputation of the agency or setting, or from the information the clients have about the clinician.

The media often show exaggerated or stereotypical representations of "shrinks," social workers, and other counselors. These images are almost exclusively of White, able-bodied, middle-class individuals, like television's Dr. Melfi from *The Sopranos* or Dr. Paul Weston from *In Treatment*. They may expect the clinician to be helpful, but they may also be aware of sensational stories in the press that report clinicians' sexual and financial exploitation of clients.

Some clients may have had previous interactions with the mental health system. The man with schizophrenia who has seen nine other counselors at the day treatment program may come to see you with the expectation that you, just like the others before you, will be leaving soon. The woman who has received a psychiatric evaluation resulting in the loss of custody of her children may feel hostile and wary before meeting a new clinician. A Mexican-American family may be reluctant to seek help from the school counselor because, in previous encounters with other mental health clinicians, family members felt that the Anglo professionals were condescending and showed no respect for their strong family and community bonds.

Other clients may be reacting to information about the agency's reputation. For example, the factory worker seeking assistance about his troubled adolescent daughter may come to the Employee Assistance Program because his friends have told him that the people there are very helpful. A single mother may resist bringing her children to a homeless shelter because she has heard that it is dangerous.

Clients may also respond to clinician information variables that they know in advance. Knowing that the clinician is a man, a Latino, a social worker, or an intern may influence clients' preconceptions. Just like clinicians, clients react to information about the clinician, and their reactions are affected by their values, beliefs, and personal background in the larger social and cultural context. This is the **client gestalt.**

> When I was an intern, I was assigned to a White, middle-class woman in her forties who was a survivor of serious physical and sexual abuse. After we had worked together for five years and were in the process of terminating, she told me that when I walked into the waiting room on the first day, she almost walked out. She couldn't imagine how a young Black woman from what she guessed to be a working-class background (she was right) could be helpful to her. She said that she was glad she had stayed.

Cynthia Garcia Coll and colleagues suggest that, if an oppressed person meets with a therapist who appears to be from the oppressing group, the person is likely not to expect mutuality. Instead, he or she may experience a power differential, whether it is real or not, "as powerful as if it were real" (Garcia Coll, Cook-Nobles, & Surrey, 1997, p. 180).

EXERCISE 3.6 Client Expectations

Break up into small groups and discuss how you would feel if a client said that he or she did not want to work with you because you were too young or too inexperienced. How would you handle a client who said he had a preference for working with someone who was gay, heterosexual, Black, White, Latino, or Catholic? Does the client have a right to ask for a clinician with certain personal characteristics? What about requesting someone with specialized education or training?

Getting Ready

Students wonder about the reasoning behind the "50-minute hour"—why the clinical hour is often reduced to 45 or 50 minutes. We try to reserve a space between clients or engagements for a number of reasons: to jot down notes from the last meeting, to return phone calls, to consult with colleagues, to provide an intellectual and emotional space between the last experience and the one to come, to refresh ourselves between visits, and to prepare for meeting with the next client. Clinicians meeting with clients outside agency settings may use travel time for many of the same purposes.

Attending to Self

Before the actual meeting with the client, experienced clinicians prepare for the meeting in a number of helpful ways. They try to relax. Some take a short walk, some get a breath of fresh air, some stretch, and others meditate to get into a quiet state of readiness.

> *I realized after much trial and error that I could competently do five sessions in a row with 15-minute breaks in between. But I found at the end of the day I couldn't calm down fast enough to get to sleep. Now I do no more than three in a row at one time.*

> * * *

> *It took me a long time to realize that all the cups of coffee I was drinking to help me stay awake briefly stimulated me but then caused me to feel sleepy 15 to 20 minutes later. I had to learn to avoid caffeine, chocolate, and heavy meals before working with clients.*

Experienced clinicians also try to clear away any impinging thoughts or take care of any personal needs that may affect their ability to attend to the incoming client.

> *I had received a message from the clinic secretary that my son had called. He seldom called me at work, and I knew that if I didn't call him back, I would be sitting with my next Adult Children of Alcoholics (ACOA) group wondering what he wanted. I also knew that, if I called, I might be a minute or two late, and I had to decide whether I should keep my group waiting for two extra minutes or be distracted for the entire 90-minute group meeting. I returned his call.*

Thinking About the Client

In preparation for meeting with the client for the first time, clinicians should review the information available to them. This information may be in the form of client records; test results; referral forms; intake forms; comments from family, friends, or professionals; symptom checklists; and so on. Box 3.1 shows a sample intake form.

Some clinicians prefer not to have any information before meeting with the client for the first time. They would rather to see the client with fresh eyes so as not to be contaminated by colleagues' judgments. Others feel it is essential to read all the available material and develop hunches about where to go in the interview.

BOX 3.1   Sample Brief Intake Form

- Client name:
- Address and telephone:
- Who referred (self, others) and why:
- Presenting problem(s):
- Strengths and resources, including spiritual supports:
- Brief description of client and current situation:
- Previous history with service providers and outcome of contact:
- Any immediate crises or action needing to be taken:
- Insurance/payment information:
- Person to call in case of emergency:
- Recommendations:

Whenever possible, *the clinician should review all available materials before meeting the client.* Clients need to know that we have done our homework. If the clients have been asked questions, filled out complicated forms, or talked at length with an intake worker, they need to know that we care enough to make use of their information. This is indispensable preparation for a respectful encounter. At the same time, it is important that the clinician understand that these materials may contain omissions and distortions.

Clinicians should not rely solely on such material. We need to have an informed openness. We sustain this openness by not jumping to conclusions and by recognizing that clients may present themselves very differently in the interview situation, from moment to moment, from interview to interview, and from clinician to clinician. People usually react very differently to a person than to a questionnaire. They may reveal themselves more deeply within an unfolding relationship of trust and helpfulness than they do at the beginning of the relationship. Furthermore, a client's situation can change dramatically between intake and first session.

> *I was about to see a client whom the intake worker described as hostile, suspicious, and guarded. When I met with her, she seemed open, comfortable, and self-disclosing. Only later did I learn that she felt very uncomfortable talking with men. The intake worker was a man.*

Clinicians need to prepare for working with people from cultures different from their own. While being careful not to stereotype, you will need to gain extensive background knowledge about the cultures that may affect the client's beliefs and behaviors. According to Sam Chan and Evelyn Lee

(2004), "intercultural communication difficulties are not simply a matter of different languages, but of different thought patterns, different values, and different communication styles" (p. 271).

In addition to reading available client materials, *we often need to do extra reading and preparation.* For example, before seeing a client who has just surrendered a child for adoption, we may want to read material about birth mothers and the psychological sequelae of surrendering a child. Before meeting with a young transgendered male, we would be wise to read about issues of gender identity and the effects of rigid sex roles, homophobia, and transphobia.

Clinicians may also need to gather resources to share with the client as appropriate. It is often helpful to create a resource file that can be shared by others. Resource files may include lists of contacts in specific areas, community services for particular populations, or copies of articles from relevant professional literature. For example, to help a woman deal with her child's adoption, the clinician may want to know about any groups for birth mothers such as Concerned United Birthparents (CUB). When preparing to work with a lesbian woman new to the area, the clinician can identify lesbian support groups and relevant resources in the community and determine whether there is a gay/lesbian health center or faith communities that welcome lesbian women. Today, the clinician also can help clients find many helpful online resources.

Available information is used to help the clinician develop **anticipatory empathy.** Empathy is the ability to immerse oneself in another's experience and to imagine the feelings of that person in that situation. (We discuss empathy in more depth in Chapter 5.) Lawrence Shulman (2009) emphasizes a similar process, preparatory empathy, involving "tuning in" to get in touch with "the feelings, concerns and indirect cues about these that clients may bring to the helping encounter" (pp. 67–68). Judith Jordan (Miller, Jordan, Stiver, Walker, Surrey, & Eldridge, 2004) defines anticipatory empathy as thinking in advance of the meeting, about each client particularly, and about the impact our ways of being are likely to have on him or her. We then adjust our ways accordingly to express that empathy.

EXERCISE 3.7 Anticipatory Empathy

Client 1: Helena

Helena is a 39-year-old woman who is an active crack cocaine addict. To support her habit, she has been working as a prostitute. Her 6-month-old baby has just died of pneumonia. She has two other children, ages 2 and 3. You are the protective services worker who has been asked to assess whether the two children should be left in her care. Imagine Helena's experience and the feelings that might arise for her in this situation. What different feelings might she be experiencing about the death of her baby? What are some of the feelings she might have about her other children? What kind of feelings might she have about this upcoming meeting with you as her protective services worker?

Client 2: Jorge

Jorge is a 45-year-old man who has just lost his job in the defense industry. He has a wife with leukemia and two children—a boy, age 7, and a girl, age 9. He had worked for the plant as a bomb assembly expert for 15 years. He is seeing an employment counselor for help in getting a new job. Imagine Jorge's experience and the feelings that might arise for him in this situation. What pressures might he experience at this time in his life? What are some of the feelings he might have about his wife's leukemia? What feelings and anxieties might he have about losing his job? What expectations might Jorge have of the interview or of the interviewer?

Thinking About the Interview

Because of the many different reasons for interviewing and the different types of interviews, the following interview parameters can help organize thinking in preparation for meeting clients for the first time.

- What is the purpose of the interview? Why am I meeting with this client? Why do I think the client is meeting with me? How might the client's ideas about this meeting be different from mine? How much of the purpose is governed by the agency, by the insurance company or funding source, and by the client's or interviewer's own agenda?
- How might my culture and the client's culture affect the interview? How might they affect the development of our relationship?
- What are the time constraints on this interview? How long do we have to meet today?
- How long do we have to work together? Is this a time-limited or an open-ended contract?
- Are there any procedural requirements, such as forms to fill out, fees to negotiate, discussion of confidentiality, or permission releases?
- What are the desired outcomes of today's meeting?

Each of these questions is important in focusing the interview. For example, a clinician meeting with a client for a brief 10-minute session may spend little time exploring the details of the client's developmental history. In setting that requires many forms to be completed by the end of the interview, a clinician wants to be sure to gather all the information necessary to complete that task. If the purpose of the meeting is to evaluate a third grader's readiness for special education classes, a clinician may focus on the child's competencies and areas that need remediation.

Watchwords

In addition to thinking about the tasks of the interview, clinicians develop personal mantras, or **watchwords,** that are particularly important to keep in mind during the interview. These may be simple things, such as reminders about attending behaviors like "Keep good eye contact," "Relax," "Be honest when you don't know something," or "Stay focused."

As an interviewer becomes seasoned by experience, education, and supervision, these beginning reminders become second nature, replaced by watchwords about specific relational dynamics or complexities of interview techniques. For example, a clinician who has been working with a family for a while may have to remind herself before the next interview: "You know how anxious you get when this family argues. Remember to stay out of the fray." Approaching an interview with a client who is slow to speak, a clinician may say to himself, "Her mother puts words in her mouth, so leave some pauses for her to initiate talking."

Watchwords usually develop out of supervision, from reading the professional literature, from direct observation of colleagues at work, and from client feedback about a clinician's demeanor or approach. They are used to promote careful attentiveness and responsiveness, rather than to admonish or punish.

> *As a new interviewer, I always felt that I needed to talk or do something when pauses or uncertainties arose in the interview. I still remember a piece of advice a supervisor gave me when I first started out: "When in doubt, butt out."*

But sometimes words are not necessary. An image can replace words as a mantra.

> *Sometimes as I prepare to see a client for the first time, I imagine that, as I'm sitting in the room with the client, my team is sitting behind me with their hands on my shoulder. That helps me remember that I'm not alone in the work that I'm doing.*

Although we have been talking about how clinicians prepare for the first meeting with a client, the process of getting ready—attending to ourselves, to the client, and to the interview—should occur before all interviews.

Preparing for subsequent interviews differs little from preparing for the first one: The goals are to create as calm an interview space and state of mind as possible, screening out intrusions and preparing for the client by attuning to his or her particular style, circumstances, and focal content of prior sessions. Notes about previous meetings are reviewed, attending to themes, emphases, or notable interview exchanges that may need revisiting in the next or subsequent sessions. Careful attention is given to the ongoing process and to the clinician–client relationship (see Chapters 10 and 11).

CLIP 3.2
Getting Ready

■ Greeting and Welcoming

The interview begins when the clinician greets the client. Clients may have preconceived ideas before meeting the clinician. Later, they may say that they had strong positive or negative feelings about the clinician based on the clinician's manner of speaking when making an appointment by phone or on the promptness with which the clinician responded to an urgent walk-in request to be seen. They may even base their reactions on their accumulated feelings about helping professionals in general.

The Setting as Representative

The work setting or agency is the first thing clients see. Clinicians should spend time conferring with colleagues about how to create a warm and welcoming entry and waiting area appropriate for clients of different cultures. When possible, reading materials, pictures, and background music should reflect the local diversity of tastes and interests.

While waiting, clients may have the opportunity to observe clinicians as they interact with colleagues and other clients. These observations may color a client's feelings about the agency and the staff. Thus, it is important that staff members be aware of their demeanor and behavior at all times. The time spent in waiting areas also allows clients a first impression of the degree to which the staff and setting are or are not representative of their own ethnicity, culture, and language group. Staff, forms, and public waiting areas can be intimidating. Clients can feel exposed to public view while waiting, which can add to their distress.

Public waiting areas present unique problems for the interviewer in maintaining professionalism and confidentiality. While most clinicians enter the waiting area and call out the client's name, clinicians should be aware that this may compromise confidentiality. An alternative might be for clinicians to announce their own names, rather than the client's. For example, a clinician announces, "I'm Kalana Johnson—is someone waiting to see me?"

What's in a Name?

Styles of address differ from culture to culture, locale to locale, and person to person. In some agencies, informality dictates that clients and staff alike are called by first names; in others, more formality and hierarchy are observed. We recommend that clinicians use clients' formal titles and last names until they say otherwise. At the outset of contact, clients and clinicians should discuss the names by which each prefers to be addressed. Hilary Weaver (2005) notes that this avoids the imposition of power inherent in our deciding what to call people.

> *In my internship at an outpatient unit, we were taught to call our clients by their last names, like Mrs. Huggins or Mr. Ward, as a sign of respect. So I was shocked when I transferred to another outpatient unit and heard my supervisor call her adult client "Billy." She explained that this was the way they did things there. She said it reflected a more laid-back, intimate style. Now I notice that I sometimes call people by their first names, and sometimes by their last. It depends on the situation and what the client and I work out together.*

* * *

> *As a geriatric social worker, I have heard many complaints from older women patients who resent being called by their first names by people who don't know them. One woman told me: "It felt disrespectful when, the first time we met, this young boy half my age asked, 'How are you, Bernice?' He didn't ask me what I wanted to be called. I got him back. I said, 'Not bad, Tom.' I read his name from his name badge. He was surprised that I called him by his first name. He was the doctor and wasn't used to this."*

Some clients may anglicize their first or family names because they feel that they may be too difficult for others to pronounce, to avoid discrimination based on ethnicity, or to "fit in" with the mainstream culture. Clinicians should always take the time to learn the pronunciation of clients' names. First and family names have different meanings in different cultures.

> In most Asian countries, women keep their own family surname when they marry, even though they may often be referred to as the "mother of X" or the "wife of X" in their mother tongue. Do not assume, therefore, that the wife of Mr. "X" will be Mrs. X. You will also find that some women have encountered so much confusion on the part of U.S. government agencies or other social agencies that they have started using their husbands' last names. And even if an Asian woman does use her husband's name, the therapist should find out if it is a true choice or just a way of avoiding lengthy explanations to agency personnel. For example, you could say, "I know you use Mrs. 'X' with your son's teachers but your own name is Mrs. 'Y.' Which would you prefer me to use?" (Chao, 1992, p. 167)

CLIP 3.3
Greeting and
Welcoming

Christine Chao goes on to state, "Refugees have given up everything they once knew; unless it is their choice, they should not be made to give up their names" (1992, p. 168). No one should be made to give up his or her name. Regardless of the formality or informality of the culture or setting, it is important for the clinician to be respectful of clients' wishes. Clients' preferences should dictate how they are addressed.

■ Opening Lines

Wherever the interview takes place—in the office, at home, on the street, or online—there are a number of helpful ways to begin. Factors that influence the opening style include the meeting location, the people present, the motivation of all participants, the purpose of the meeting, and the time available. Cultural styles are also important to take into account. Some clients may need a more informal period of social exchange at the beginning of the interview to assess the clinician's skill and authenticity, whereas others may prefer a more formal expert-consultee approach (Lum, 2004).

Chao (1992) notes that:

> in Asian families the father can experience a treatment referral as a personal assault on his authority and therefore resist it. Understanding this dictates a careful response: "I meet with fathers the way one head of state meets with another head of state; the ruler has been forced to seek help and must be treated with respect and dignity. . . . I tell the father something about the families of which I am a member, . . . where I obtained my degree, what my training was, where I have worked. . . . I let the father know that he is the expert in terms of his culture and his country of origin. . . . Granted, his kingdom is in trouble, perhaps his subjects are rebelling, but he is still "king" and that position, with all of its responsibilities and stresses, must be acknowledged. I am an ambassador with whom he can consult for possible solutions. I am the guest in his kingdom. (pp. 175–176)

EXERCISE 3.8 Opening Lines

You are a counseling intern at a community mental health center. You're about to meet Rich Navic, a 44-year-old depressed man about whom you have no other information. In your journal, write four or five opening lines you might use with him.

Participants, Roles, Tasks, and Time

After a friendly greeting, the interviewer usually begins by acknowledging the names and roles of all present and reviewing either the initial request for help or the reason for the interview. We should use clear language, avoid professional jargon, and clarify our role by giving examples of the types of help provided. Many clients may not know that, in addition to counseling, many clinicians can also provide testing and evaluation. We may serve as teachers and trainers, advocates for services, links to other staff, conflict mediators, and so on.

Clarify the amount of time available for the initial meeting, as well as the total number of sessions available to the client, so that participants can ready themselves psychologically for time-sensitive conversation. Usually, these issues are all briefly addressed in the first moments of the interview. How a clinician begins the interview may reflect a number of factors, including values, personal style, intent, or goals. Sometimes clinicians begin in a certain way because a supervisor has advised them to or an agency research protocol mandates certain clinician statements at the beginning of a research study.

EXAMPLES OF OPENING LINES

"I'm the social work intern on the team, Ngo Diap. I meet with all patients' families to find out how the transplant process has affected everyone. We know how hard and complicated it can be. I also want to talk with you about how to manage when Tim comes home. We have 40 minutes to meet today, and, if you want to, we can meet for two more sessions before Tim's discharge. I can also help arrange for visiting nurse services and home physical therapy when Tim comes home. You might also be interested in our Wednesday night family group. I could tell you about that later, if you like."

"I understand you wanted to speak to someone about your divorce. I'm a counseling intern here at the center, and I'd be happy to meet with you to see whether I could be of assistance. We have 50 minutes to meet today."

"Thank you for letting me come out to see you, Señora Ramirez. As I said over the phone, I'm the psychologist at Centro Hispano Well-Baby Clinic and I wanted to talk with you about getting Carmelita ready to go to preschool. If it's okay with you, I can stay for about 45 minutes."

Confidentiality and Its Limits

The **Health Insurance Portability and Accountability Act (HIPAA)** protects the privacy of those receiving health and mental health services. HIPAA requires that clinicians provide clients with a notice of privacy practices about the use and disclosure of protected health information (PHI), which must be signed by the client before the work begins. It is important that the client understands the notice of privacy. Clinicians should encourage clients to raise any questions they have about HIPAA and confidentiality at anytime. Appendix 1 contains a sample handout statement that directly addresses confidentiality and its limits.

EXAMPLES OF CONFIDENTIALITY STATEMENTS

"Mrs. Franz, I know that you have read and signed our Notice of Privacy but I just wanted to remind you that our conversation today is private. However, counselors are mandated to disclose information if they feel that the client is a danger to herself or others. I also know that your insurance company is going to want to know your diagnosis and the number and length of visits. Do you have any questions about the Notice of Privacy?"

"Most people think that what they tell a social worker is totally confidential. However, we are evaluating your family to decide if your son should live with you or your husband after the divorce. Since we have been asked to do this evaluation for the court, you should know that whatever you tell me can be shared with the judge and with the other lawyers involved in the case. I know this is all in the privacy form you signed but I just wanted to make sure that this specific situation is clear to you."

"Julie, an exception to the confidentiality of our meeting is that, as an intern, I review with my supervisor my conversations with clients to make sure I'm giving you the very best service. Do you have any questions about what I've said about confidentiality?"

The Internet and other technological developments complicate issues of confidentiality (Fisher & Fried, 2003; Luepker, 2003; Ragusea & VandeCreek,

2003). Email and cell phone conversations between clinicians and clients and between professionals provide quick and easy access and are rapidly taking the place of phone conversations, but they are not secure. Advances in health informatics and practice management systems can allow patient records to be centrally located and available to all of the person's health care providers. Both Presidents Bush and Obama have pushed for health information technology systems or **electronic medical records (EMR),** which would allow access to consumers, providers, insurers, and hospitals. Legislation of electronic medical records needs to ensure the privacy of these records. Katherine Nordal, the executive director of professional practice of the American Psychological Association, notes that "maintaining privacy will be central to ensuring success of these electronic medical records since without strong protections, people may not seek the . . . services they need" (2009, p. 53).

These organizational and technological changes, together with the demands of managed care companies, create new privacy and confidentiality challenges. Clinicians should not only work within agencies and professional organizations to establish and review policy and procedures to protect client information, but also inform clients that there is no absolute guarantee of privacy or confidentiality in the electronic age.

Client Rights and Responsibilities

Many agencies and clinicians have developed a list of **client rights** and responsibilities, such as the right to see one's records upon request; the right to receive information about the range of available treatments; the right to be treated with respect; and the right to be informed fully and accurately about the procedures, benefits, and possible risks. Frequently, information regarding confidentiality and clients' rights is posted in waiting areas or is available as handouts. However, the clinician should review these issues directly with clients to be sure they are understood. Box 3.2 contains a sample client rights statement. Appendix II includes a statement of client rights about Protected Health Information mandated by HIPAA. A more inclusive list of client rights appears in Box 3.2.

Focal Opening Lines

Focal opening lines offer an initial framework, or a set of guidelines that are especially helpful when clients are new to talking with a professional or when they are feeling confused, overwhelmed, or scattered. These guidelines lend structure to the process without foreclosing client contributions to the direction of the interview. Structure and guidance are also crucial when time is limited and therefore focus and roles need to be developed without delay.

BOX 3.2 Client Rights

Part of our obligation to our clients is to inform you of the principles of care and your rights as a client of our agency:

- As a person served by this agency, you have the right to a high standard of care.
- You have the right to be treated with courtesy, respect, and dignity.
- You have the right to receive interpreter services to assist in understanding and fully participating in the services offered. If we cannot provide such service, we will make every effort to refer you to a provider who speaks your language or an agency that has interpreters who speak it.
- You should be informed about various services offered and the process by which the decision is reached as to which of these services is/are most helpful to you.
- You may request at any time to know who is responsible for the program that is providing you service and how he/she may be contacted.
- You have the right to ask about the relevant qualifications of the people who are helping you.
- You have the right to review your record. You may exercise this right by providing a written request to review your record, together with your reasons, to the director of the program that is providing you with services.
- You and your clinician should review your treatment plan periodically. You have the right to ask your clinician or the program director for a reevaluation or consultation by another clinician. This may be at your own expense.
- If a medication is prescribed by a physician, you should be informed as to what the medication is, why it is being prescribed, what it is expected to change, and its common side effects.
- If research is being conducted or any experimental procedure is being recommended, you will be informed before being involved in any such study-procedure. You have the right to refuse to participate in any research without jeopardizing your care here. Your written consent must be given before you would be included in any research or experimental procedure.
- If you wish to be referred to another agency or to a private practitioner, we will make every effort to refer you to the most appropriate resources.
- You have the right to receive an explanation of the basis by which your fee is set and to ask for a reevaluation of your fee. You have a right to a copy of the bills or statement of charges submitted to any third party.
- You have the right to receive care in a place free of architectural barriers if you have a limiting physical condition.

_____   _____
Client's Signature   Date

_____   _____
Witness's Signature   Date

_____ Client given copy but did not sign.

_____ Rights explained but client not given copy because

_____

EXAMPLES OF FOCAL OPENING LINES

For the opening lines in the preceding examples, after the routine introductions stating (1) names and roles, (2) the reason for the meeting, and (3) the time available, the clinician may use focal opening lines such as the following:

"Let's review the plans for Tim's return home."

"Tell me about the circumstances that led to the divorce."

"Let's talk about how Carmelita feels about starting preschool."

Even when you have prepared a focal opening line, it is important to remain flexible and ready to respond to the unexpected. Always be open to clients' needs and to making culturally appropriate accommodations.

EXAMPLE OF FLEXIBILITY AND ACCOMMODATION

Clinician: Are you Larry Kwan?

Client: Yes.

Clinician: I'm Gaylord Dunes, the social worker from the New Horizons work training program. I've come to the hospital to meet with you today to discuss what our program can offer you after you leave here. If you want, we can meet down the hall where it's quiet. Then you can tell me what you think and ask any questions about the program.

Client: My brother and uncle are coming to pick me up for my weekend pass at home. Can they listen, too? They are out of work also, and our family is suffering from this.

Clinician [recognizing the importance of family in Asian cultures]: Of course, we can all meet together. I have from 9:00 to 10:00 free to talk with you and them. Let me just tell the nurse where we'll be so that your family can join us. Maybe there's more I can help with besides employment.

Nondirective Opening Lines

Nondirective opening lines provide less information, leaving the client a greater opportunity to set the agenda, pace, focus, and tone. Using nondirective opening lines, the clinician begins with introductions, including names and roles, the reason for meeting, and the time available, then provides only minimal prompting to get things started.

EXAMPLES OF NONDIRECTIVE OPENING LINES

"I believe you asked to see one of the social workers this morning."

"Where should we start?"

"What would be most helpful to talk about?"

These nondirective openings provide an immediate opportunity to assess client skills in organizing, communicating, and relating to both the clinician and the tasks at hand. However, if we find that the client is unable to respond to nondirective openings, we may need to provide more focus and structure.

Opening Lines Help Set the Tone

In addition to communicating information, opening lines convey a tone that can have lasting effects on the relationship. Opening lines can communicate warmth, indifference, welcome, aversion, hierarchy, disorganization, comfort, or fear. Sometimes the same opening line may have different meanings for two different clients or to the same client at different times. In Chapter 4, we discuss how tone is conveyed by means other than just words; in Chapters 10 and 11, we talk about the clinical relationship and its important elements and dynamics.

CLIP 3.4
Opening Lines

EXERCISE 3.9 Noting Tone

Go back to Exercise 3.9. Review the opening lines you wrote in your journal for Rich Navic.

Were they focal or nondirective?

What tone do you think you conveyed?

What would you change about your opening lines at this point and why?

■ Conclusion

Clinical interviewing can occur in a variety of settings. No matter where the interview takes place, we should carefully prepare for the meeting, getting both the environment and ourselves ready for the encounter. How we greet the client and begin the interview can set the tone for future work. Once initial contact is made, clinicians use a number of basic skills to establish an empathic relationship to help the client tell his or her story and begin the process of problem solving. The next chapter elaborates the basic skills of attending and accurate listening, skills that are essential to all good clinical interviewing.

■ Suggested Readings

Important resources on the uses, risks, and benefits of technology in clinical work include:

Maheu, Marlene, Pullier, Myron L., Wilheim, Frank H., McMenamin, Joseph P., & Brown-Connolly, Nancy E. (2005). *The mental health provider and the new technologies: A handbook for practice.* Mahwah, NJ: Erlbaum.

Parker-Oliver, Debra, & Dimiris, George. (2006). Social work informatics: A new specialty. *Social Work 51,* 127–134.

Ragusea, Anthony S. & VandeCreek, Leon, V. (2003). Suggestions for the ethical practice of online psychotherapy. *Psychotherapy: Theory Research Practice, Training, 40,* 94–102.

The *Journal of Technology in Human Services* has a special volume (Volume 26) devoted to the use of technology in clinical practice.

Clinician safety is addressed in:

Spencer, Patricia C. & Munch, Shari. (2003). Client violence toward social workers: The role of management in community mental health programs. *Social Work, 48,* 532–544.

Weinger, Susan. (2001). *Security risk: Preventing client violence against social workers.* Washington, DC: National Association of Social Workers Press.

Critiques of the use of labels and diagnoses appear in the following sources:

Caplan, Paula. (1995). *They say you're crazy: How the world's most powerful psychiatrists decide who's normal.* Reading, MA: Addison-Wesley.

Kutchins, Herb, & Kirk, Stuart. (1997). *Making us crazy: DSM: The psychiatric bible and the creation of mental disorder.* NY: Free Press.

For a thorough discussion of HIPAA:

Barnett, Jeffrey E., Wise, Erica H., Johnson-Greene, Doug, & Bucky, Steven F. (2007). Informed consent: Too much of a good thing or not enough? *Professional Psychology: Research and Practice 38,* 179–186.

Benefield, Hope, Ashkanazi, Glenn, & Rozensky, Ronald H. (2006). Communication and recods: HIPAA issues when working in health care settings. *Professional Psychology, Research and Practice, 37,* 273–277.

■ Self-Explorations

1. Which aspects of your nature and presence may make it easy for you to maintain a "bubble of calm" around the interview process? Which may make it harder? Are there environmental or client factors that can jar your calm?

2. Recall that people coming to see clinicians often feel like "strangers in a strange land." Have you ever visited a place or country where the norms, language, customs, and ways of managing time were very different from your own? How did you feel? Which differences pleased or engaged you and which did not?

3. The next time you are in a social situation, be aware of people's personal space preferences. Notice what happens when you move very close to a person. Record the other person's reactions. Then record how you feel when others come very close to you or cross into your personal space. How is your need for personal space influenced by your family and culture?

4. Remember a time when someone called you by your first name and it felt strange to you. In what circumstances do you like to be called by your first name? When do you prefer to be called Mr. or Ms.? What other appellations may be appropriate (e.g., Señor, Madam, Reverend)? Do you have a nickname? Who calls you by that name? In what circumstances do you like to be called by your nickname? When would it feel odd? Think about the professionals with whom you interact. Notice what they call you and what you call them. What did you learn from your observations? In the future, when would you call clients by their first names and when would you call them by their last names or titles? Would you ever call clients by their nicknames?

■ Essay Questions

1. Many people would agree with the statement that clinicians should refuse to work in situations where they feel unsafe. If clinicians refuse to go into situations in which they feel unsafe, how will the people who must live in those situations ever get clinical help when they need it? Discuss this question with the class.

2. Client rights are easy to grasp, but what are "client responsibilities" in clinical work? How do clients find out what their responsibilities are?

3. On the one hand, we have a professional responsibility to get as much information as possible. On the other, we have a growing awareness that many people around the world find it difficult or offensive to reveal intimate or personal information to a stranger. As practitioners, what factors do we need to consider when trying to balance gathering information with respecting people's discomfort in sharing highly personal information?

4. Review Appendix II and then discuss under what conditions a clinician might decide that giving a client a copy of the psychotherapy notes might cause harm to the client. How could the clinician reconcile this decision with the professional principle of client empowerment, and the importance of quality and trust in the clinical relationship?

5. Discuss the pros and cons of focal versus nondirective opening lines.

■ Key Terms

Anticipatory empathy

Borrowed environment

Bubble of calm

Client gestalt

Client information variables

Client rights

Clinical intuition

Clinician gestalt

Critical incident review process

Diagnosis

Electronic medical records

Environmental assessment

Focal opening lines

HIPAA

Labeling

Lifespace interview

Nondirective opening lines

Online counseling

Personal space

Stigma

Watchwords

CHAPTER 4

Attending and Listening

■ Interviews

Interviews are a specific form of conversation, and, like all conversations, they are mutual. Both parties have a stake in the outcome and the influence of each on the other contributes to growth in each. Indeed, dictionary definitions of *interview* include "sight shared by two people" and "a mutual view."

Interviews have many layers of meaning and influence, only some of them apparent to participant-observers. Nowhere is this more true than in cross-cultural communication. If we have learned anything from clinical experience, it is that there are always multiple realities. Individuals speak, listen, and make meaning from their own unique perspectives. Two people may share the same experience, and yet each perceives it uniquely. Individual experience and meaning are mediated by such things as age, race, socioeconomic class, gender, culture, ethnicity, sexual orientation, spiritual and political structures and beliefs, geographic locale, the era one lives in, and individual and societal ideologies. Two people may share similar backgrounds, values, or belief systems, yet experience and interpret things differently because they differ in other important respects.

Therefore, as you go about the task of attending and listening, you need to remember that there are few if any fixed truths or realities, apart from the inevitability of birth and death. Knowledge, beliefs, and practices inevitably change with the passage of time and through the transformative influences of various cultures and groups on each other. Thus, we always consider and value multiple perspectives even though they make our task of attending and listening more complex.

In this chapter we focus on attending to verbal and nonverbal content, to the affect that they may signify, and to emergent themes and patterns. In later chapters, we discuss how participants in an interview mutually affect each other.

■ Focused Attending

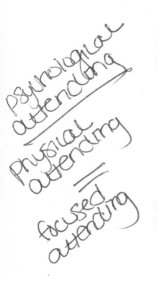

Clinicians need to create an ambiance of focused attention in which meaningful communication can occur. We attend in order to listen; we listen in order to understand. Understanding contributes to empathy, and empathy engenders a readiness to respond and an opening up of oneself to a mutual process rather than a top-down interaction. Thus, focused attending is an essential component of the therapeutic process, consisting of psychological attending and physical attending.

Psychological Attending

The bubble-of-calm attentiveness that the clinician brings to each interview is the result of (a) psychological readiness and openness to the client and (b) the clinician's commitment to creating an environment in which other people feel as welcome, appreciated, cared about, and heard as possible. **Psychological attending** involves putting aside personal distractions, worries, and self-concerns to give center stage to the client's story. We think of psychological attending as setting up radar to receive the signals the client is sending.

Psychological attending requires both discipline and flexibility. The client's story and demeanor inevitably arouse responses in the clinician that can distract attention from the client's experience. These "blips" on the radar screen need to be noted. As discussed in Chapter 11, the clinician's reactions to the client's story provide important information and should not simply be dismissed as interference.

Physical Attending

The **posture of attention** is the physical manifestation—literally, the embodiment—of the clinician's interest in and openness to the client, the story, the relationship, and the work to be done together. It readies the interviewer to listen.

Gerard Egan (2010) describes the components of **physical attending** using the acronym **SOLER:**

S—sit squarely
O—open posture
L—lean forward
E—eye contact
R—relax

EXERCISE 4.1   Physical Attending

This beginning in-class exercise is designed to help you practice basic clinical skills, to allow you to get to know your fellow students, and to begin to develop a relationship with each other. Therefore, you are asked to talk about yourself.

In class, divide into groups of four, with each student assigned role A, B, C, or D. Student A talks to student B about his or her day, why he or she is in the class, or why he or she wants to be a clinician. Student B practices attending behaviors, while students C and D observe and make notes about student B's attending behaviors. If possible, video record the interaction and, after getting feedback from students C and D, watch the video together. Rotate roles until each student has had the opportunity to be both the speaker and the attending listener. Do not worry about what you say; just focus on your physical behaviors.

Record your thoughts about the exercise in your journal. What did you discover about yourself? Note how comfortable or uncomfortable you felt both when you gave attention and when you received it, as well as when you were an observer.

The clinician adopts a posture of attention to communicate presence, interest, and close following. In a society characterized by rushing and preoccupation, this type of attention can be a unique experience. For many clients, such attending feels reassuring, caring, and desirable. For others, however, this close attention between strangers may feel inappropriate, invasive, or threatening.

> *My first job was at a family agency where I was taught the importance of eye contact. When I moved on to work with clients with persistent mental illness, my supervisor told me my gaze was too direct and "hot" for clients with low tolerance for contact and that I needed to learn to look away and down briefly, without seeming to drift from the subject. I found this one of the hardest things I ever had to learn.*

Furthermore, attending behaviors are **culture bound**. What is considered attentive in one culture might be offensive in another. For example, Weaver (2005) asserts that "eye contact is disrespectful in some Latino, Native American, and Asian cultures" (p. 42), especially in the presence of people perceived as authority figures. We cannot emphasize enough the importance of getting to know the expressive nuances of the cultures and people with whom we work. Before you get to know clients more fully, avoid describing them in records or meetings as having "poor or no eye contact" or "poor relating skills." We need to learn from our clients which cultural or family practices and taboos may be operative when being interviewed by a professional who, from the client's perspective, is "not one of us."

> *I was conducting an in-service training for teachers in the local grammar school. One of the Irish Catholic teachers was talking about how disrespectful and stubborn the Vietnamese students were. I asked her to give me an example, and she said: "They never look at me when I talk to them. Even when I tell them to pay attention, they sullenly look away." The Vietnamese interpreter, who was part of the training, came to see me and told me that for a Vietnamese child to look an adult in the eyes is "like an American child sticking his tongue out at an adult."*

It may seem easy to apply Egan's SOLER skills in an office. But because clinical interviewing may take place in a variety of nonoffice contexts, clinicians have to think about how to adapt a posture of attending in those settings. A clinician accompanying a client in a car, bus, or taxi is usually sitting side by side with the client. In such circumstances, a useful way to attend is to look where the client is looking so as to join the client's perspective or position, heightening a sense of connection. In such crowded, side-by-side situations, there may be jostling together and body contact, which may feel uncomfortable. However, remember the *R* in SOLER: to relax and not let the unanticipated create anxiety that distracts us from focused attending. We talk more about issues concerning physical contact in Chapter 12.

In a home visit, the client may move around, carrying out tasks while sharing information and feelings. For example, in visiting with a young mother with children at home, we may interview in the kitchen while the mother makes formula, folds laundry, or attends to a child's needs. In such situations, the clinician's comfortable repose acts as a pivot for the client's moving about and often has a calming or settling effect. When a client feels more comfortable pacing about, entering and leaving the room, or attending to the needs of young children, the clinician's stable presence remains a constant in good attending.

> *I used to interview Janice, a young woman with schizophrenia, in a tiny office on the inpatient unit. She was often not comfortable in close proximity, but I didn't want to talk with her in the dayroom, where others could overhear. I would see her in that little office, but in a different way than I was used to. I would just remain comfortably seated while she paced, walking in and out of the room. Eventually, she would relax some and sit down with me briefly. I was surprised by how much she was able to share with me in this sporadic way.*

In group work, family, or team meetings, the interviewer faces the additional challenge of attending to more than one person at the same time. In interview situations with multiple participants, the key is flexible attentiveness. On occasion, the clinician may pan the group, not making extensive or specific eye contact with any one individual. At other times, the clinician may make sequential eye contact with each individual or focus on specific members. It is important that we convey continuous interest in each person by making periodic eye contact with each, even if it is not returned. In a group that may include women whose cultures forbid female eye contact outside the family, the clinician might, in circular fashion, pan the floor in front of each woman's place, so that each feels uniquely noticed and valued.

Clients also have a posture of attention. Their attending or nonattending behaviors affect clinicians in much the same way that clinicians' behaviors affect clients. In our experience, clinicians are more likely to attend to a client who attends to them in an open and welcoming way. It is not unusual for clinicians to become more anxious, stiff, or self-conscious in the presence of a client they feel is demonstrating hostility, indifference, or nonattending behaviors. Again, we always need to be careful about misinterpreting client behaviors.

EXERCISE 4.2 Nonattending

Ask a friend to have a conversation with you, and video record it if you can. After a minute or two of talking, purposefully withdraw your attention. You might look away, look at your watch, cross your arms, or tap your foot. Notice what happens to the conversation. If you record the conversation, watch the video together. Ask your friend what it felt like when you stopped attending.

There is no one right way to attend. Over time, clinicians learn to communicate attentiveness without rigidly adhering to behavioral guidelines. For example, we can cross our legs, look away, close our eyes, or lean back and still be conveying attentiveness. Moreover, as we get to know our clients better, we adapt our physical attending to their nuances and changing needs.

A few years ago, I was working with Oscar, a man who had difficulty talking in therapy. He suffered abuse as a child and was unable to share feelings, fearing that if he expressed them, they would not be validated by the clinician. We talked about this and brainstormed how he could feel more comfortable talking with me. In one session, he shared that he thought he might be able to talk to me if I didn't look at him. We tried different ways of arranging things. When I turned my chair around, Oscar could talk more freely, but he missed my facial expressions, and I had a hard time hearing exactly what he was saying. Through trial and error, we discovered that, if I just closed my eyes, he was able to open up and share feelings he had never shared before. I think it was the act of letting myself be vulnerable that made it safe enough for him to take a chance. With my eyes closed, I felt less secure and found that I had to trust him in a new and challenging way. Emotionally, I joined him in the process of taking a risk, while never leaving my essential role as the therapist. I also discovered that, without visual distraction, I could tune in to his words in a more deliberate and focused way.

Some clinicians believe that clearing the mind is a prerequisite for physical attending. Others believe that assuming a posture of physical attending helps clear the mind. In our view, psychological and physical attending

CLIP 4.1
Attending

are exquisitely intertwined and continuously resonating with one another: Psychological attending enhances physical attending, which enhances psychological attending, and so on. However, always pay attention to the client's reactions to your attending behaviors, since these reactions may be worth exploring in the future.

■ Clinical Listening

A major task in any interview situation is to listen. Clinical listening is more complicated than just hearing the client's words. **Clinical listening** requires focused attention and alertness to everything going on in the interview and in the relationship. Clinical listening means that we attend to both verbal and nonverbal communication, listening to what clients say, how they say it, and how they feel about what they say. We also listen to what clients *don't* say. We listen for emerging themes and patterns, both during an individual interview and over time. In addition, we listen to the relationship that develops with the client. Equally important, we listen to our own inner process.

What we listen to—and are able to hear—is shaped by our own experiences, our family, our culture, the media, and the zeitgeist of the time. That is why, when a group observes an interview and discusses what happened, each person has a slightly different take. Supervision, process recording, and video recording are extremely important to clinical learning because they often pick up what we do not hear or notice.

> I remember talking with my supervisor about a client. She asked how the client handled her abortion. I had no idea where this came from. I didn't hear the client say she had an abortion. Then we listened to the tape together, and my supervisor pointed out that the client had said she "had a termination."

What the clinician hears may not be what the client intended. The client may unintentionally reveal something, or the clinician may misinterpret the client's meaning. Factors that contribute to inaccuracies or distortions in listening include a lack of knowledge or experience; cultural or other bias; defensive filters; clinician inattention, anxiety, distraction, or hearing impairment; misinterpretations of another language; and countertransference. We elaborate on these factors in Chapter 5.

Nonverbal Communication

People often think of an interview as the words spoken between two or more people. However, research by Birdwhistell (1970) suggested that as much as 65 percent of what is communicated is nonverbal. **Nonverbal communication** includes physical appearance, body posture, gestures, movements, and facial expressions and the aura or "air" that each person brings to an encounter (Knapp & Hall, 2009). Clinicians need to be extremely careful not to misperceive the client's nonverbal communication because it can be easily misinterpreted.

A helpful practice is to observe the nonverbal communication and later check in with the client about its meaning. In online counseling (especially by email), nonverbals are not visible. Participants may use "emoticons" to illustrate their reactions as the interactions unfold (Midkiff & Wyatt, 2008).

EXERCISE 4.3 Noting Nonverbal Information

Break up into groups of four. Focus on person A (who remains silent) and record what information you have about person A that is communicated nonverbally. Compare and contrast your lists. What did you observe? What was the person communicating to you? What were the similarities and differences in what you each observed? How would you interpret what you observed? Note that you are making assumptions that can only be confirmed or corrected later by person A.

Sue and Sue (2008) note that research has shown that African Americans tend to communicate more nonverbally than White people and to trust nonverbal communication more than verbal communication as a true representation of a person's thoughts and feelings. "African Americans are better able to read nonverbal messages (high context) than are their White counterparts and . . . they rely less on verbalizations than on nonverbal communication to make a point. Whites, on the other hand, . . . need greater verbal elaborations to get a point across" (D. W. Sue et al., 1996, as quoted in Derald Sue and Sue, 2008, p. 92).

EXERCISE 4.4 Video Recording a Conversation

Make a 5-minute video recording in which you have a conversation with a colleague. You can talk about yourselves, about your work, or about the experiences of the day. Watch the video once with your colleague with the sound on. Note your nonverbal behavior. Watch the video a second time, without the sound, and again note your nonverbal communication. Did you notice different things? Record in your journal what you learn.

Appearance

When we meet someone for the first time, we often make assumptions about gender, race, ethnicity, age, sexual orientation, and class based solely on physical appearance. However, these assumptions may or may not be accurate. Race and ethnicity are social constructions, not absolute characteristics, and people are often multiracial and multiethnic (Renn, 2007; Root, 2001; Wijeyesinghe, 2001). Within constructed categories, individuals differ from each other in special ways and, as Robin Cook-Nobles notes, "we are not unidimensional" (Garcia Coll, Cook-Nobles, & Surrey, 1997, p. 186).

Clinicians often use physical appearance, style of dress, demeanor, and hygiene as indicators of clients' functioning, including the ability to care for themselves. Many intake forms have traditionally included dress, manner, and bearing as important diagnostic information. Of course, taking into account personal taste, cultural styles, and the economic realities of clients' lives is always important. A person without a coat during a midwinter snowstorm might be demonstrating disorganization and poor judgment—or might be unable to afford a coat, or was just unprepared for an unexpected storm.

Body Posture

The body often reveals a lot about mental and emotional states. When people are depressed, they may slouch or walk with their shoulders hunched. When people are happy, they may stand erect and have a "spring in their step." The connection between body and feeling states has been a topic of great interest in both the psychological and medical fields (Benson & Klipper, 1976; Borysenko, 1987; Lowen, 1975). Will Schutz (1967) notes that the connection between body and feelings is captured in North American colloquialisms such as "lump in the throat," "butterflies in the stomach," "hair-raising," "green with envy," "pain in the neck," and "heartsick."

Other cultures also note the connection between mind and body through their choice of words. Jeffery Scott Mio, Lori A. Barker, and Jaydee Tumambing (2009) note that while "individuals from Latino and Mediterranean cultures may complain of 'nerves' and headaches, those from Middle Eastern cultures may complain of 'problems of the heart,' and Asians may talk about weaknesss, tiredness, or 'imbalance'" (p. 243). Clinicians must carefully attend to physical complaints, according them their rightful place in the clinical encounter.

> *I was working with a Vietnamese woman who had recently come to the United States. She came to see me complaining of headaches and wanting to know how to get rid of them. Being Vietnamese American myself, I knew that her headaches were a way of her telling me about the emotional pain she felt. I told her that I often got headaches when I was worried about my family, and she began to talk about what kinds of things were going on in her head that may have been causing her pain.*

Clinicians should pay attention to the range and fluidity of their clients' body motion. As we get to know our clients, we can observe how they may be feeling from the way they use their bodies. If the presence of disease or disability limits the client's range of motion or use of the body, the clinician, of course, is sensitive to other nuances of expression.

Gestures

Many people gesture when they communicate. People may tap their feet, flail their arms, shrug their shoulders, clench their fists, or wring their hands. Everyone has a unique style of gesturing, and the clinician needs to become familiar with each client's style and learn what each client's particular gestures express.

Whenever Kerry was nervous, she would jiggle her hands by her chair. Tori would play with the top button of her blouse, whereas Rob would rub his left wrist with his right thumb, and Concetta would stare up at the clock as though wishing the time to hurry by.

In addition, we need to be aware that gestures have different meanings in different cultures. Chan and Lee (2004) describe "friendly" North American gestures that can have very unpleasant meaning for some people from Asian cultures:

The American gesture for "come here" (using the pointing finger with the hand raised and palm inward) is a hostile, aggressive gesture among Southeast Asians or is the manner in which one beckons dogs, lower animals, or an "inferior" person. Similarly, the crossing of the index and middle fingers as a gesture for "good luck," the "V" sign to indicate "peace." The "OK" sign (with curled thumbs and forefinger), or the thumbs up signal all potentially constitute obscene gestures with sexual connotations for Southeast Asians, as well as many other ethnic/national groups. (Axtell, 1991)", (Chan & Lee, 2004, p. 273).

Facial Expression

Participants in conversations tend to pay a lot of attention to the face and facial expressions. People may smile, frown, wrinkle their foreheads, raise their eyebrows, or purse their lips at particular moments in the conversation. Again, we are careful not to overgeneralize or make culturally inappropriate interpretations. For example, Chan and Lee (2004) note:

In general, the value that is placed on control of emotional expressions contributes to a demeanor among selected Asian groups that is often interpreted by Eurocentric individuals as "flat," "stoic," "enigmatic," or even "inscrutable." Koreans, for example, in keeping with the national character of the "Land of the Morning Calm," may present with a demeanor referred to as my-po-jung (lack of facial expression). Casual smiling and direct eye contact when greeting or interacting with strangers is considered inappropriate (p. 273).

From his research on the expressive styles of various cultures, Doman Lum (2004) finds that many clients feeling despair or anger due to oppression and economic hardship may mask or armor themselves with a flat facial expression in early clinical encounters, defending against feelings of vulnerability. Facial expression may soften and flex as the client experiences respect and mutuality with the clinician.

Clinicians should also be alert to sudden changes in facial coloration or the stress-induced development of hives or facial tics.

A co-therapist and I were seeing a heterosexual couple. At the end of the interview, my colleague expressed concern about the wife's emotional state. I hadn't noticed anything particular, so I asked why he was concerned. He said that her arm broke out in hives when we were talking about how they handled anger in the family. Because of where I was seated, I had missed the blotches, which he spotted.

Eyes—"the windows to the soul"—may tear with sadness, widen with surprise, or narrow with suspicion. Eyes can also reflect organic problems; for example, pupil dilation may signal a tumor or drug use. People convey a lot with their eyes, which may be one reason that they sometimes close their eyes or look down and away so as not to reveal their inner experiences. While clinicians often put a lot of significance on eye contact, noting when it is made or broken, we noted earlier that meaning attributed to eye contact is culture bound. For example, Teresa La Fromboise and colleagues recount the Navajo myth about a monster called He-Who-Kills-With-His-Eyes, which they believe "teaches Navajo children to avert their eyes to avoid bringing harm to others" (La Fromboise, Berman, & Sohi, 1994, p. 32).

Some physical conditions can significantly impact bodily posture, gestures, facial expressions, and eye contact. The body movements and functions of some persons with disabilities or who are on certain types of medication are not always voluntary and should not be misconstrued as nonverbal communication. Sometimes it is hard for clinicians to remain focused and at ease in the presence of involuntary body movements or some forms of physical disability. This lack of comfort is easily recognized by clients.

> *Andrew was a client who had cerebral palsy. I felt very uncomfortable with his jerky movements. I didn't know whether to ask him directly about his condition because I didn't want to make him feel uncomfortable. Ten minutes into the interview, he asked, "Is my shaking distracting? I do it all the time, but more so when I am tired. Usually, I can control it better, but between being tired and somewhat nervous about being here, I know I am shaking like an earthquake."*

Clinician Nonverbal Communication

Clinicians also communicate nonverbally through dress, manner, bearing, facial expression, eye contact, gestures, and so on. Clinicians always need to be self-aware in interviews with clients. For example, the way the clinician dresses can convey respect to the client. It is important to determine whether head coverings are required if we are meeting a client at a church, temple, or mosque. In many cultures, a clinician wearing a tank top, short skirt, or flip-flops to an interview might be considered disrespectful to the client.

Perhaps because of early abuse or trauma and because of the perceived power inherent in the clinician's role, many clients may be highly sensitized to nonverbal changes in demeanor. They scan us all the time to see whether we prove to be safe, caring, comfortable, and attentive to them as unique and special. A continuing task of clinical learning is to increase awareness of what we might be conveying at any given moment. We should think about what we want to communicate nonverbally and, whenever we can, have ourselves video recorded in clinical interactions to increase awareness of our styles and mannerisms.

> *I remember the first time I ever watched myself on videotape. I was shocked to discover that, throughout the entire interview, I kept nodding my head. I looked like one of those dolls you see in the back of a car, whose head keeps bobbing up and down on a spring. I still have to work on only nodding occasionally.*

Our facial expressions are often a focus of client attention. While we may be paying attention to our gross body movements (posture, gestures, and head nods), it may be harder to be aware of the subtleties of our facial expressions.

EXERCISE 4.5 Facing the Camera

Break up into pairs and have a 10-minute conversation. You may talk about any topic that you wish. For the first 5 minutes, person A is the "face" and the camera focuses on a close-up of person A's face. For the second 5 minutes, the camera focuses on person B's face. After making the video, watch it with two other colleagues and get feedback about your facial expressions. What did you learn about yourself and about others?

CLIP 4.2
Nonverbal
Communication

When looking at your facial expressions in Exercise 4.5, you become aware of one facial expression at a time. However, when interacting with others, facial expressions are constantly changing. You may smile to convey happiness; however, you may be unaware that you also smile when you are nervous. It is therefore helpful to look at your facial expressions in video recorded conversations. You may not always be conscious of shifts in expression or of the meaning that other people may attribute to your facial expressions.

Verbal Communication

Much of what happens in the interview consists of what the client says and what the clinician says. The clinician listens to both the words the client says and how she or he says them. It is amazing how difficult it can be to recall exactly what another person has said. This is why some clinicians jot down main themes and comments right after each interview in order to retain as much information as possible in informal clinician notes that are not included in the clinical record. We will discuss the clinical record in more detail in Chapter 7.

EXERCISE 4.6 Repeat After Me

Break up into groups of four and assign roles A, B, C, and D. Person A is the speaker and person B is the "parrot." Persons C and D attempt to record verbatim what person A says so that they can correct person B's accuracy. Recording the conversation will give you much more accuracy.

Person A begins by saying one sentence. Person B repeats the sentence exactly, using the formula "You said '. . . .'" Persons C and D report on the accuracy and then watch the video to check it. Since clients seldom talk in single sentences, person A then says two additional sentences, which person B parrots. Finally, person A says three additional sentences that person B attempts to parrot. This is harder than it seems. By watching the video, you can see how much you miss when someone talks to you. Discuss what factors may get in the way of your ability to remember.

Of course, clinicians do not often parrot a client's exact words. We must, however, pay careful attention to the specific words that clients use, because the words may have special and crucial meanings to explore further.

I remember working with a female client who told me about a disagreement she had had with her husband. I said, "So you and Jacques had an argument about money." She said, "No, we had a fight." When I asked her to clarify, she explained that they had come to physical blows. For her, argument implied disagreement, whereas fight implied physical contact. I learned to listen carefully for when she used the word argument and when she used the word fight.

Just as words can be a vehicle of communication, they can also be barriers. Clients (and clinicians) can use a barrage of words to distract others from topics they wish to avoid. They can also use specialized language or in-group jargon to distance themselves or demean others. Beginning clinicians often feel as though they have to pretend that they understand what the client has said, even when they do not. (This can also happen in supervision or team meetings, when others are using jargon or expressing "superior" knowledge.) Beginners often hope that, if they just wait and listen, they will catch on. By doing so, they may make faulty assumptions. Even when they honestly think they understand the words clients are using, they may be wrong.

In a supervision class, a student from Romania reported a conversation she had with a British patient from a nearby state hospital. The patient told the student that he got "really pissed" the night before. Because she was unfamiliar with American colloquialisms, she asked him what he meant by "pissed." Since I'd read the student's journal and knew what the patient had answered, I asked the other members of the class what they thought he meant. They all assumed he meant he was angry. I then asked the student; she reported that the patient said it meant he had gotten very drunk. In this instance, the student's unfamiliarity with American jargon gave her the permission to ask what the client meant. If she'd understood jargon better, she might not have asked and thus might have misunderstood the client's words.

Before reading any further, do Exercise 4.7.

EXERCISE 4.7 What Are You Trying to Say?

Define each of the following italicized terms or phrases:

1. Katie was wearing *knickers*.
2. The project will be finished *at the end of the day*.
3. A business indicates that there is *a backlog* at its warehouse.
4. At a meeting, one of the participants suggested *tabling the item*.
5. A friend of yours tells you that, when she meets her boyfriend, she will *fill him in*.
6. A friend of yours tells you that his presentation *bombed*.
7. John was really *pissed*.

The purpose of this exercise is to demonstrate that, although the same terms or idioms may be used in different cultures, they can have different meanings.

1. America: knee-length trousers
   Britain: women's underpants
2. America: usually taken literally, the end of the working day
   Britain: whenever it gets done—an open-ended finish time
3. America: a list or orders waiting to be filled
   Britain: an overstocked inventory
4. America: put the discussion off until another time
   Britain: discuss the item immediately
5. America: that she will elaborate, clarify, or tell him
   Britain: that she will hit him over the head
6. America: a failure
   Britain: a success
7. America: angry or upset
   Britain: drunk

From: Hill, G. William, IV. (1998) *Activities and Videos for Teaching Cross-Cultural Issues in Psychology.* Retrieved from www.lemoyne.edu/OTRP/otrpresources/otrp_ccissues.html#activities.

Paralinguistic Cues

How clients (and clinicians) say things is as important as *what* they say. **Paralinguistic cues**—the tone and pitch of voice, rate of speech, emphasis, stuttering, sighing, and other vocalizations—are crucial elements of verbal conversation (Hall, 1959). There are cultural differences in paralinguistic communications. For example, Terry Tafoya (1989) discusses the sociolinguistic concept of "pause time" and notes that Native Americans often leave a longer space between the ending of one person's statement and the beginning of another's.

EXERCISE 4.8 Paralinguistic Cues

Practice saying the following sentences with different tones, speed, emphasis, and other paralinguistic cues. Demonstrate how the same words can convey different meanings.

Are there any other solutions to this problem?

Tomorrow is Christmas.

Mrs. Jorgensen wants me to come to school tomorrow morning at 7 A.M.

Exercise 4.5 helped you see how you look to clients. Ivey and colleagues (2010) offer a similar exercise (presented here in Exercise 4.9) in getting feedback about how you sound.

EXERCISE 4.9   Vocal Qualities

Use a video or audio recorder for this class exercise. Divide into groups of four. One person becomes the speaker, who tells the others a 2-minute story in a normal tone of voice. With their eyes closed, the others listen for vocal qualities, noting their reactions to the speaker's volume, speech rate, and regional or ethnic accent. The group then provides feedback. Rotate roles until everyone has been the speaker and received feedback. In your journal, record what you have learned.

(Adapted from Ivey et al., 2010).

Silence

Silence is a form of communication, not just a blank space between periods of speech. Clinicians attend to silence, noting when it occurs, its frequency or patterning, and any affective coloration that may accompany it. For example, a client may fall silent after talking about the death of his mother. Another client may be silent because she does not know how to proceed. A third client may sit silently because of a lack of trust. Sometimes silence is simply a sign of respect or a signal that the client is waiting for the clinician to speak. Often, clues about the meaning of silence may be gleaned from the content immediately preceding the silence and the nonverbal communication that may occur during or after it.

Silence may have very different cultural meanings. In North American cultures, a long silence may be a sign of tension or discomfort. However, Virginia-Shirin Sharifzadeh (2004) notes:

> In most Middle Eastern cultures, social interaction and connectedness take precedence over the need for privacy. . . . Whereas for many Americans privacy requires actual physical distance, many Arabs, for example, achieve it by becoming silent and temporarily tuning out in a crowd (Safedi & Valentine, 1985). Such silence and tuning out may be interpreted as rude or as daydreaming by many Americans. (pp. 395–396)

In male-dominant cultures around the world, women and girls may be expected to remain silent until an authority figure instructs them to speak briefly on a designated subject. In a therapeutic encounter with women socialized in this way, the client may silently await our guidance before responding in a guarded way, intending not to offend the clinician—or her own cultural tradition.

Metacommunication

Metacommunication refers to the nonverbal cues, such as tone of voice, gestures, body language, and facial expressions, that either affirm or negate what is said verbally. Metacommunication conveys messages about the message, as well as messages about the relationship between the communicators (Bateson, Jackson, & Weakland, 1963). Clinicians attend to the relationship between verbal and nonverbal cues and to changes in the client's style of communication. Sometimes verbal, nonverbal, and paralinguistic cues are concordant, as when an angry person says "I'm mad!" in a loud voice while hitting the table with his or her fist. Sometimes they are discordant, as when a client timidly says in a low voice while looking away, "I know I can get that job." Clinicians need to look for how verbal and nonverbal cues do or do not match, paying careful attention to discrepancies, because these may signal ambivalence or important areas for further exploration. A mother may roll her eyes while thanking her daughter for help. Some clinicians think that the nonverbal aspect of communication is more important than the verbal component—that nonverbal communications reveal the client's true feelings. We think that clinicians should take note of any discrepancies, whatever their form, without making too facile an interpretation.

It is also important to note any changes in the style or manner of communication (such as when a usually animated speaker becomes quiet and soft-spoken or when a client who is usually very attentive looks away a lot). Taking careful note of nuances and alterations of style applies to clinicians' communications also.

As noted previously, metacommunication may be interpreted differently in every culture. For example, we might interpret a client's sudden eye twitch when recalling a loss as a sign of suppressed grief, but a Native American shaman might interpret it as the presence of a powerful spirit guide signalling the client to stop looking at the loss and focus back on the good that the deceased did in the community.

EXERCISE 4.10 Communication Discrepancies

Two people go to the center of the room to talk about what it is like to try to make friends when they are all newcomers to a training program. Half the class takes notes on person A and the other half on person B, noting their verbal and nonverbal behaviors and whether they are concordant or discordant. Share your observations with each other. Note the variations in what observers report.

■ Listening to Clients' Stories

Clinicians listen to verbal and nonverbal communications. But what are we listening for? We listen for the behaviors, feelings, thoughts, context, and meanings that constitute the client's story. We also listen to how clients punctuate their stories, emphasize or highlight content and themes, and remember or forget things they shared earlier.

Behaviors

Behaviors are the actions people take in their lives in response to other people, ideas, impulses, feelings, events, or outside stimuli. Clinicians listen for behaviors that are effective and that promote connection with others, as well as for those that *appear* to be self-defeating. (We say "appear" because, early in the work with someone, we do not know what purposes client behaviors may be serving for themselves or for their families or larger systems.) We listen for the extent to which behaviors are impulsive or well thought out and the degree to which they are elective or driven by inner compulsions, organic factors, external demands, or other people. We also listen for how flexible or rigid behaviors are, as well as how rational or irrational they appear to be in the client's situation. We note the effects that people's behaviors have on each other.

We need to make sure that we accurately understand the meaning of the client's behavior. It is easy to make faulty interpretations of the client's behavior, particularly when our cultural background is different from the client's. For example, a clinician might regard a client's tearing at her clothes and falling to the floor upon news of a death in her family as out-of-control behavior, whereas her family would regard her actions as a culturally appropriate form of grieving.

Feelings or Affect

Clinicians listen for the variety and range of feelings (e.g., sadness, surprise, anger, happiness, anxiety), noting the frequency of each feeling state and which feelings seem to predominate. We listen for the behaviors clients use to express their feelings (e.g., whether anger is expressed through sulking, silence, withdrawing, hitting, threatening, self-harming, throwing objects, or direct angry statements). We listen to discern whether clients can modulate their feelings or whether they feel overwhelmed by them. As noted earlier, expressive styles differ among cultures, families, and locales, and prevailing group norms may dictate that members not express strong personal feelings or conflicts in public or with outsiders. Such expressions might be interpreted as rude, shameful, weak, or aberrant.

Thoughts and Cognitive Style

Clinicians listen for clients' thoughts and cognitive style. We listen to what clients think about—people, things, events, or feelings. We listen for the degree to which clients seem to think about their inner lives, external events, or their connections with others. We listen for the degree to which their thoughts are positive and hopeful or negative and pessimistic. We also listen to how they think and how they handle new thoughts or conflicting ideas. Is the thinking flexible? Is it organized and rational? Do thoughts jump from one topic to another? Does the client feel obsessed by particular thoughts? Does the client think concretely or abstractly? Can the client express thoughts openly and directly?

Context

Clinicians listen for the context in which their clients' stories take place. The immediate context consists of the client's personal circumstances: current living arrangements, family and social relationships, economic status, personal history, health, and the particulars of daily life. For example, it is important that the clinician know that a woman's mother was just diagnosed with Alzheimer's Disease, which might contribute to her feeling of depression. In another instance, a White clinician must try to appreciate that racial discrimination and being passed over for a promotion could contribute significantly to the suspiciousness and distrust shown by an African-American client.

The immediate context is always embedded in a larger systems context, including economic, social, political, and religious forces and institutions and even global relationships and developments. For example, a woman may be sad and anxious because she lost her job (her immediate context). She lost her job because she could not get reliable day care and often had to leave work to take care of her 2-year-old daughter (the immediate context). One of the reasons she could not find reliable day care was that, as a result of increased defense spending, Congress had to cut federal subsidies to day care providers so that now fewer providers are in her neighborhood (larger systems context).

> A number of years ago, I was working with a family in which the parents reported that their daughter was having nightmares about nuclear war. Although my first instinct was to wonder about what "wars" were happening in her "nuclear" family, I also had to consider the fact that she had just seen the movie The Day After, a dramatic representation of the consequences of nuclear war.

Similarly, the immediate context can affect larger systems. The woman who lost her job, for example, could organize her neighbors and colleagues (the immediate context) to write Congress to get federal funding for day care programs reinstated (the larger systems context). We listen to how the immediate and larger systems contexts of our clients' lives resonate with and mutually influence each other.

Meaning

Clinicians must listen for how clients interpret or make sense of their situations, feelings, behaviors, and thoughts. How do they understand the way things have evolved in their lives? How do they understand current events? For example, what meaning does a wife attribute to her husband's working late three or four nights a week? Does it mean he is working hard to provide for her and the children? Does it mean she has lost her attractiveness? Does it mean his boss is overly demanding? Does it mean he is having an affair? Does it mean he is afraid of being replaced by a younger, less highly paid staff member unless he overperforms?

Clinicians listen to whether clients are open to alternative meanings and whether they can hold multiple perspectives simultaneously. For example, can a father understand that, although his attention to his son's schoolwork each night means (to him) that he cares, to his son the father's inquiries may mean that he is being critical? Clearly, the components of stories are neither discrete nor static. Thoughts, feelings, behaviors, relationships, events, and meanings constantly interweave and influence each other, and clinicians are always listening for the interactions and influences.

Emphasis

Different theoretical models emphasize different components of the client's story. Behaviorists emphasize behaviors, their triggers, and their reinforcing consequences. Psychodynamic theorists focus on client developmental history and relational dynamics. Cognitive theorists focus on thoughts as precipitants of feelings and behaviors. Existential and narrative theorists emphasize clients' meaning making. Expressive theorists focus on feelings. Systemic and family theorists pay great attention to the context of behaviors and relationships.

Agencies often oblige clinicians to use information-gathering tools and formats that may shape what they attend to and listen for. For example, evaluation forms for brief treatment increasingly focus on behaviors and behavior change and their reverberating influences.

> At the mental health center, my supervisors were always asking me about how my clients felt and how they expressed their feelings in different situations by saying things like, "So how did she feel about that?" When I went to work at a health maintenance organization (HMO), my supervisor asked about behaviors a lot more: "What did he do then?" "Is this a pattern or a one-time thing?" I noticed a subtle change in what I focused on with clients. At the mental health center, my clients used to go through boxes of Kleenex; now I notice that my clients hardly use any!

It is not just theories, agencies, or trends that influence how we listen to the different components of the client's story. We sometimes listen more for behaviors, sometimes more for feelings, sometimes more for events. At other times, we listen more for meanings and emphasis. This flexibility is natural and essential, and it should be guided by client priorities and goals.

EXERCISE 4.11 Listening to the Story

Break up into groups of four. Assign roles A, B, C, and D. If possible, video or audio record the conversations. Person A is the first speaker and person B the first listener. Persons C and D are the first observers. The speaker talks to the listener for 2 minutes and describes an event in his or her life. The listener responds to the speaker in any way he or she chooses. Observers take notes on what the speaker is communicating. It might be helpful to divide a sheet of paper into five columns to record your observations about context, thoughts, feelings, behaviors, and meanings.

After 2 minutes, the listener tries to report what the speaker said about his or her context, thoughts, feelings, behaviors, and meanings. The speaker may correct the listener, and the observers can point out omissions.

Watch the video and compare your observations to what actually happened. Take 2 minutes to debrief, noting what kinds of things were easier to hear and remember. Rotate roles until everyone has had a chance to be speaker and listener. Record in your journal what you learned.

CLIP 4.3
Verbal
Communication

It is important to remember the client's story—both the general message and the details and nuances. We listen carefully to remember what clients have shared with us. We listen to understand, and, with the help of supervision, we use this understanding to develop appropriate focus, empathy, hunches, and plans. Because clients tell us so much in a short period of time, process notes and audio or video recordings are useful for remembering and reflecting on what the client has shared.

■ Listening for Themes and Patterns

People's lives develop rich meaning and complexity, which at times can be organized into themes and patterns. Because the themes and patterns often reflect some of the client's central organizing schemas, clinicians must attend to them as they emerge both in the client's story and in the clinical relationship. Repeating themes and patterns often signal topics important to explore further.

Themes

Themes are repeated sets of ideas and beliefs. They may be expressed directly and with awareness ("There I go again, blaming myself"). However, they often emerge indirectly and without conscious recognition, as when a client describes a persecuting sibling in one session, a persecuting lover in another, a persecuting employer in another, and annoyance at the clinician for "running the show" in yet another. Clinicians commonly encounter client themes of loss, betrayal, oppression, injustice, hopelessness, and despair, as well as companion themes of courage, persistence, survival, and resistance to oppression.

> *For almost 6 months, I had been working with Johann on problems with self-control at work. It took me that long to realize that in almost every session, he would mention alcohol. For example, he would say: "Last night a couple of us went out for drinks"; "The other day we put away a couple of martinis at lunch"; or in describing a picnic at work, he said, "We polished off a keg of beer."*

EXERCISE 4.12 Say It Again, Sam

Samuel is a 33-year-old Russian immigrant to the United States who lives in a small town in Ohio. He is meeting with a female counselor to discuss employment opportunities. At the beginning of the interview, while talking about work, Sam said that a person who speaks poor English has no chance of advancement in his current job. Later, while discussing his childhood, he said that he never had any of the advantages of his older brothers, who were bigger and stronger than he. As the session was ending, he said that he was sure that the woman clinician did not like him because he was a man. How would you describe the underlying theme of this interview? How would you convey it to Samuel?

Patterns

Patterns are repeated behavioral or affective sequences. Like themes, patterns may have a great impact on clients' daily lives, and clients may be aware or unaware of them. Some common patterns observed in client stories include the avoidance of intimacy, frequent angry outbursts, crying when anxious, addiction to substances or people, and picking inappropriate partners. Other patterns include choosing loyal friends, asserting oneself in adversity, protecting vulnerable others, and using spiritual resources.

> *Jack Henry came to the job center because he had lost his job. This was the fifth job he had lost in 12 years. It turns out that he always gets in conflict with his boss and he eventually leaves in a huff.*

The clinician should pay careful attention to themes and patterns that come up during the interview. Sometimes a theme or pattern emerges across a series of interviews, or it may be something the clinician notes during specific interviews or things that the client reveals over time. Some of the patterns are nonverbal.

> *I noticed that Becky always got teary when she spoke of her mother but seemed strangely cold and intellectualized when she described her father.*

Observing themes and patterns is just a first step. We discuss how to use themes and patterns to help people see, feel, and do things differently in Chapters 9 and 10. We also discuss how to comment on themes and patterns within the clinical relationship in Chapter 11.

Themes and patterns can also emerge from clinicians. One clinician may have a tendency to focus on anger rather than on sadness (as a theme), whereas another may start jiggling his foot when anyone talks about sex (a pattern). Clients can observe these themes and patterns in us just as we do in them. Supervision and feedback are important in developing greater self-awareness, which can inform our behavior in the interview.

CLIP 4.4
Themes and
Patterns

Dana said, "You always look so uptight when I describe seeing Lynn. It makes me not want to tell you when I see her."

* * *

Sonia told me that she could always tell when our time was about to be up because I would reach for my appointment book while she was still talking.

◼ Listening to the Relationship

Clinical conversation is much more than words exchanged and feelings shared. The nature of the relationship in which the story unfolds is crucial to its evolution. The maintenance of a positive, supportive relationship is thus a clinical goal in and of itself. We therefore pay careful attention to what happens within the clinical relationship and listen for the thoughts, feelings, and reactions that the interview may arouse in both ourselves and the client.

So there I was—leaning forward, sustaining eye contact, being aware of transference and countertransference, reflecting themes and parallels, trying to respond with sensitivity in my words and tone . . . So there I was trying not to freak out. I have wanted to be a therapist since I was 10 years old. I used to think they just sat back in cozy, expensive chairs and said nice things for 50 minutes a few times a day. I was really wrong. I had a taste of what was ahead, but I had to remind myself I was only just beginning.

In Chapter 11, we discuss the complicated relationship dynamics and the skills used to address them. In the next chapter, however, we discuss the initial development and continuing maintenance of the relationship through clinical support and empathy.

◼ Bridging Linguistic Differences

In addition to dealing with how cultural filters affect the ways in which clinicians and clients listen to each other, a specific challenge is trying to bridge linguistic differences when the clinician and client do not share the same primary language.

Talking in a Nonnative Language

"In the context of a world of greater mobility and where there are so many refugees, there is probably no practitioner anywhere in the world who will not at sometime have to confront the issue of language differences in mental health work" (Swartz, 1998, p. 35). The APA Guidelines for Providers of Psychological Services to Ethnic, Linguistic, and Culturally Diverse Populations (APA, 1990) suggest that "psychologists interact in the language requested by the client and, if this is not feasible, make an appropriate referral" (p. 6). However, clinical work is often conducted in a language other than the client's primary language. For example, a Mexican client with a rudimentary knowledge of English may be asked to speak in English with an Anglo clinician or even with a Mexican-American clinician raised in the United States whose primary language is English. Communicating complex experiences or emotionally charged issues in a second language can be extremely difficult, especially when talking about things that occurred before the second language was learned.

> *I remember that when Mercedes and I would talk about things in her childhood, she would often slip into Spanish. At times, she would speak in English, talking about how she missed her mother and father. When I asked her to "say it in Spanish," she said, "Yo extraño a mi mami y papi" and burst into tears.*

It can be particularly productive to ask the client to say a particular word in his or her own native language—words that may carry significant meaning and affect.

> *I have a friend from Puerto Rico who is a very visible, out lesbian. She gives talks around the country about being lesbian. However, she has told me that she isn't "out in Spanish." The word used to denote lesbians in Spanish carries with it such a negative connotation that she can never say it. So she has never come out to her parents, who speak only Spanish.*

Sometimes neither the clinician nor the client is speaking in his or her native language. This can happen when neither speaks the other's language, but both have some facility in a third language. Some impatience, frustration, or misunderstandings may result.

The Use of Interpreters in Clinical Work

Although it is best if the clinician and client speak the same native language, this is not always possible. The clinical practice field is not representative of the many cultural and language groups of the people served. Most clinicians speak only one language and do not consider the development of bilingual or multilingual language proficiency as a relevant part of their clinical education or competency of a clinician (Swartz, 1998). Therefore, it is frequently necessary to work with an **interpreter** when doing clinical interviews.

No matter how good the client's use of a nonnative language appears to be, whenever the language of the clinician is not the client's native language, we should offer the services of an interpreter. An interpreter may be particularly important if the clinician is providing new, stressful, or technical information, such as assessment results, or discussing a medical procedure (Joe & Malach, 2004).

Interpreters enable effective cross-cultural communication by converting one spoken language into another or by converting spoken communication into sign language. **American Sign Language (ASL) interpreters** use a combination of signing, finger spelling, and body language to convey meaning and tone. "Some interpreters specialize in **oral interpreting** for deaf or hard of hearing people who lip-read instead of sign. Other specialties include **tactile signing,** which is interpreting for people who are blind as well as deaf by making manual signs into a person's hands; cued speech; and signing exact English." (Bureau of Labor Statistics, 2008, p. 2)

Interpreters convey the meaning of concepts and ideas, cultural references, and any colloquialisms that cannot simply be interpreted by replacing the word in one language with its equivalent in another. The job of an interpreter is to manage all of this without altering or modifying the meaning or tone of what is said (BLS, 2008).

Leslie Swartz identifies four different interpreter roles. The "invisible interpreter" interprets the words of the client to the clinician and vice versa in a style where the words in one language are simply replaced with the equivalents in another. The "interpreter as culture broker" explains the client's behaviors and their meanings in their cultural context. The "interpreter as junior partner" often has had training in the mental health field and offers opinions and observations about the client's behavior that are incorporated into the work. The "interpreter as advocate" empowers the client, who does not speak the dominant language and is therefore in a less powerful position, and helps the client get needed resources (Swartz, 1998).

Amodeo, Grigg-Saito, and Robb (1997) suggest that collaborations between clinicians, clients, and interpreters can result in capacity building for all three members of the relationship. The clinician's ability to listen to and understand the client accurately is enhanced by having an interpreter. Interpreters can perceive and intuit subtle dynamics that the clinician may miss. Clinicians become more knowledgeable about community values, beliefs, and communication styles. Interpreters can also be astute observers of content and process and can provide helpful feedback to the clinician that informs and enhances the work.

> *I've learned a lot from working with our interpreter, Martine. She has taught me so much about Haitian culture. Getting to know her and learning from our interactions together has helped me understand my clients better.*

Interpreters help clients to communicate, and they can provide a sense of connection and support for the client. Clients who feel better understood and helped may be more willing to seek assistance from the agency.

Finally, interpreters may benefit from learning "more about medicine, mental health, substance abuse, or social service, and about the ways that health and illness are treated in the United States" (Amodeo, Grigg-Saito, & Robb, 1997, p. 78). Interpreters who work closely with clinicians may find they have a natural aptitude for helping and may continue their education to become providers themselves.

Challenges of the Interpreted Interview

The interpreted interview introduces "the additional complexities of a three person relationship" (La Framboise, Berman, & Sohi, 1994, p. 53). This is further complicated by the fact that "two of the people in this triangle can-not communicate with each other" (Swartz, 1998, p. 30). The clinician may feel sidelined while watching the interaction between the client and the inter-preter, especially if they appear to be more engaged with each other than with the clinician. The client may feel there is an alliance between the interpreter and the clinician—an alliance from which the client may feel excluded.

The interpreted interview can interfere with customary pacing and flow in the interview. Since there needs to be time and space in the conversation for the work of the interpreter, the interview may require more time. The interpreted interview has unique potential for errors or bias. Like clinicians, trained interpreters may have biases or cultural styles that inhibit them from accurately interpreting either the clinician's or the client's comments (Lynch, 2004). Vasquez and Javier (1991, cited by Swartz, 1998, p. 39–40) have described a number of errors that can be made by interpreters (see Box 4.1).

BOX 4.1

According to Vasquez and Javier (1991), the most common mistakes made by interpreters include:

1. *Omission*—occurs when the interpreter leaves out part or all of a message sent by one ot the people speaking. This can happen especially when there is a large amount of content in the interview and the interpreter starts leaving out parts of what has been said.
2. *Addition*—occurs when the interpreter adds to what the speaker has said, often to clarify matters or to make the interview flow more smoothly or politely. This can be a problem es-pecially when the interviewer has specific questions or instructions for the client but these are added to by the interpreter and the interviewer does not know this is happening. It can invalidate any assessment of intellectual functioning, for example.
3. *Condensation*—is a very common problem, where the interpreter summarizes what has been said according to the interpreter's own views as to what is important in the interview. These views may differ significantly from those of both the interviewer and the client. Every clinician who has worked with an interpreter when neither has been properly prepared will have had the experience of the interpreter and the client having a long conversation and this being interpreted to the clinician as "He says 'no'".
4. *Substitution*—occurs where the interpreter replaces what has been said by something which has not been said. It may be difficult to believe that this happens, and it may also be tempting to be very angry with interpreters who do this, but in fact every social conver-sation we have involves our making assumptions about other people, and interpreters are just acting on a process that happens in discussions anyway.
5. *Role exchange*—occurs when the interpreter takes over the role of interviewer and substi-tutes the interviewer's questions with those of his own. Problems in this area will of course depend on the nature of the role the clinician and the interpreter believe the interpreter should have—if the clinician's model for correct interpreter practice differs from that of the interpreter, there will almost inevitably be role problems.

But as Swartz (1998) notes, problems with interpretation are not necessarily problems with interpreters. Clinician may not be adequately trained to work effectively with interpreters, and interpreters may be devalued in the setting. Furthermore, it is the nature of interpretation that there is not a single equivalent word for each spoken word in a different language, making a "perfect" interpretation impossible. "What is needed is a method of interpreting, which serves the clinical purpose as well as it can" (Swartz, 1998, p. 41).

Guidelines for the Use of Interpreters

Whenever possible, family members or others with dual relationships or vested interests should not be used as interpreters because overlapping relationships may affect the validity and reliability of the translation or curtail frank expression of information and feelings.

> *I had a bad experience with an interpreter, which makes me very aware of how carefully you have to prepare before working together with a client. The hospital was attempting to provide counseling support to an unmarried Portuguese teen who had just delivered a baby. Since no one on the staff spoke Portuguese, a Portuguese-speaking priest was invited to serve as an interpreter. I asked the priest to explain to the girl the services that were available to her in the community. He spoke to her briefly and then she burst into tears. I asked the priest why the girl was crying, and he said he felt it was important to begin by reminding the girl that she had committed a mortal sin for which she must ask God's forgiveness.*

Don't ask a staff person, student, or intern who is bilingual, but is not paid as an interpreter, to step into that role as needed. Pamela Hays (2008) notes that "this is another way in which people of minority cultures are expected to do extra work while the dominant culture fails to educate itself" (p. 121).

Use professional interpreters. Professional interpreters must be fluent in both languages, and are often certified by their professional organization. There are a number of different tests that allow interpreters to demonstrate their proficiency. Some professional interpreters have a college degree in a specialty area such as biology or psychology that would prepare them to work in a medical or clinical setting. Such subject matter expertise would be particularly helpful when the interpreter is in what Swartz (1998) calls the "junior colleague" role.

Be sure that the interpreter is fluent in the specific dialect that will be spoken in the interview. For example, although most people in Thailand speak Thai, those in northern region of Thailand speak Isan, a dialect of the Lao language spoken in Laos. If the interpreter is fluent in Tai but not Isan, communication becomes more difficult.

Have a pre-interview meeting. Lynch (2004) and Wong (1987, cited in La Framboise et al., 1994) recommend that the clinician meet with an interpreter in "a pre-interview session to build a relationship of trust and to plan the objectives of the interview, the topics to be covered. The clinician and the interpreter should discuss the preferred style of interpretation, whether it be word for word, summarizing or cultural interpretation" (p. 53). The clinician can discuss the expectations and goals for the interview. Familiarize the interpreter with specific terms that will be used. The interpreter can inform the clinician about the specific culture and any cultural issues that the clinician should be aware of—for example, whether or not direct eye contact should be made.

Hays (2008) suggests learning about the interpreter's background during this pre-interview meeting. That will help to increase rapport and demonstrate respect for the interpreter as a colleague. During the pre-interview meeting, the interpreter can inform the clinician about "any cultural, social class or political differences that could inhibit the interpreter's work with a particular client" (Sundberg & Sue, 1989, cited in Hays, 2008, p. 119). Hays recalls:

> When I consulted with the leaders of a particular Vietnamese community in which I was going to work, I was advised that there were two main political groups and that if I hired an interpreter who was even loosely connected to one, I should also hire another who was not, because people aligned with one group would not work with an interpreter who was aligned with another. (Hays, 2008, p. 119)

Schedule extra time for the interpreted interview or appropriately adjust your agenda and goals for the meeting to accommodate the time it takes to conduct an interpreted interview. Most interviews are conducted using consecutive interpretation rather than simultaneous interpretation. In **consecutive interpretation,** one party speaks, the interpreter conveys what was said, then the other party speaks, followed by the interpreter. Both the clinician and client need to leave space after speaking so that the interpreter can work. **Simultaneous interpretation,** where the interpreter speaks as one of the parties is speaking, rarely occurs in clinical interviews. Simultaneous interpretation, like that used in the United Nations or in meetings of heads of state, is so stressful that the interpreter can usually only do this work for 20 minutes at a time.

Directly address confidentiality with all three participants present. Clients may worry about confidentiality if there is another person in the room. It can be helpful to have each person sign a confidentiality form so that the client sees that both the interpreter and the clinician are bound by the same rules.

Directly address the client and look at the client, not the interpreter. All communication should be in the voice of the speaker. For example, if the client says "I am too tired to work," the interpreter says "I am too tired to work," not "She says she is too tired to work." Chairs should be arranged so that the clinician and client can face each other but also so that both can see the interpreter.

Check in with both the client and interpreter about the process. Since the interpreted interview is more complex, it is important to ask both of the other participants how the interview is going from their perspective: Is it going too fast? Does the client feel okay about the interpreted interview?

Meet with the interpreter after the interview. Get feedback from the interpreter. Are there issues that we are not addressing that we should? Has the interpreter noticed anything that the clinician should know? Give the interpreter feedback. Discuss the style and pacing of their collaboration.

Allow the interpreter to ask any questions they may have about what has transpired.

Remember that the interpreter is not a machine. Just like the clinician, the interpreter may have reactions to what has been discussed. Allow time to debrief.

Using Easily Understood Language

Clinicians should use language that clients from many backgrounds and regions can understand. We may see clients who, although newly immigrated, speak English as a second or third language. These clients may not need interpreters, but we must speak clearly and remember that our southern, Asian-American, or Bostonian accents may not be easy to understand. Be careful not to use jargon, slang, idioms, or abbreviations.

> *Mra Sabai had recently emigrated from rural Myanmar. She had studied English in school when Myanmar was called Burma and was a British colony. However, she was confused when the social worker said Mra Sabai could wait until the cows came home before DSS would help her. She didn't have any cows. What was DSS anyway? Mra Sabai figured it must be some dairy organization.*
>
> * * *
>
> *Evianne recently left Romania. He wondered what the counselor meant when he suggested he go "the whole nine yards." A yard is about the same length as a meter; he knew that. But what was significant about that particular length?*

■ Conclusion

Clinical work requires careful listening and an accurate perception of what is being transmitted by clients. We carefully attend to the client, listening to verbal and nonverbal communication and paralinguistic cues. We note behaviors, feelings, themes, and patterns as they emerge in the interview, alert for idiosyncratic, cultural, and locale-specific meanings. Through listening, the relationship develops and the story unfolds. We educate ourselves about effective work with interpreters and advocate for having interpreters on staff or on call. As we discuss in the next chapter, accurate listening is not enough. For effective change to occur, support and empathy are essential.

■ Suggested Readings

A novel that is helpful in understanding communication difficulties in cross-cultural contexts is:

Fadiman, Anne. (1997). *The spirit catches you and you fall down.* New York: Farrar, Straus & Giroux.

Nonverbal communication is addressed in:

Knapp, M. L. & Hall, Judith A. (2009). *Nonverbal communication in human interaction* (7th Ed.). Belmont, CA: Wadsworth.

Leathers, Dale & Eaves, Michael. (2008). *Successful nonverbal communication: Principals and applications* (4th Ed.). Hoboken, NJ: Wiley.

The following address working with linguistic differences and interpreters:

Amodeo, Maryann, Grigg-Saito, Dorcas, & Robb, Nancy. (1997). Working with foreign language interpreters: Guidelines for substance abuse clinicians and human service practitioners. *Social Work, 15,* 75–97.

Lynch, Eleanor W. (2004). Developing cross-cultural competence. In Lynch, E. W. & Hanson, M. (Eds.). *Developing cross-cultural competence: A guide for working with children and their families* (3rd Ed.). (pp. 41–77). Baltimore, MD: Brookes.

Swartz, Leslie. (1998). Language diversity and mental health care. In L. Swartz, (Ed.). *Culture and mental health: A South African view.* (Chapter 2, pp. 25–51). New York: Oxford.

■ Self-Explorations

1. Spend 5 minutes in front of a mirror acquainting yourself with the subtleties of your facial expressions. Relax your face completely, noting what your face looks and feels like when you are completely at rest. See how it looks and feels when you are happy, when you are unhappy, when you want to look inquisitive, or when you show disapproval. Record what you learned by observing your facial expressions.

2. Think about people in your life who are "bad" listeners. What do they do that indicates to you that they're not listening? How do you respond when they act that way? Are you aware of times when you are a "bad" listener? Explain.

3. Do you pay more attention to what people say or to what people do? How do you reconcile inconsistencies between what a person says and how he or she says it? How might this affect your work with clients?

4. People hold tension in different parts of their bodies (for example, a clenched jaw, shoulder and neck pain, stomach aches). Where do you experience tension? It is important to identify your own tension centers so that you can use signals from these areas to alert you to personal reactions arising in the interview situation.

5. Have you noticed any ways in which you manifest anxiety when interviewing (for instance, foot jiggling, pen tapping, perspiring, shifting around in seat, losing track of what's being said)? What might clients think when they see you doing these things?

■ **Essay Questions**

1. What is meant by nonverbal and paralinguistic cues? How are they important to the clinician? What are some nonverbal cues that a clinician can give unintentionally to a client?

2. List the five components of physical attending and note other things that clinicians can do to show that they are listening to their clients.

3. People from different cultures may use silence for different purposes. Describe as many reasons as you can why clients may be silent.

4. Discuss the challenges of using interpreters when working with people who do not speak the same language as the clinician. How can these challenges best be overcome? What advice would you have for a clinician who needs to work with an interpreter? What advice would you give to the interpreter?

■ **Key Terms**

ASL interpreters

Clinical listening

Consecutive interpretation

Culture bound

Interpreter

Metacommunication

Nonverbal communication

Oral interpretation

Paralinguistic cues

Patterns

Physical attending

Posture of attention

Psychological attending

Silence

Simultaneous interpretation

SOLER

Tactile signing

Themes

CHAPTER 5

Support and Empathy: A Sustaining Presence

■ A Supportive Presence

A supportive presence is crucial to the development of a trusting relationship in which meaningful conversation can occur. The clinician's caring and support cannot be communicated solely through attending and listening. It is also consciously communicated by sensitively timed and orchestrated words, gestures, behaviors, and emotional responses—all of which, together, communicate an active presence and wish to help.

Warmth and Caring

Clinicians must genuinely care about clients and their well-being. It is only common sense that clients will respond more readily to interviewers who are warm and caring than to those who come across as bureaucrats, technicians, or "cold fish." Warmth and caring are often conveyed with a smile, a cordial handshake at the beginning of the interview, close attention to what is being expressed or felt, and the use of appropriate facial expressions and gestures. Some individuals may prefer a detached and distant clinician, but even they usually like to believe that the clinician has some feeling of care for them. More frequently, people rate warmth and caring extremely high when asked to list attributes they would like in a potential clinician, mentor, or adviser (Lambert & Barley, 2002; Rogers, 1958).

Clinicians may find it difficult to decide how to show caring. On the one hand, we do not want to appear too detached and professional. On the other hand, if we are too saccharine or "touchy-feely," clients may feel put off.

One of the things I notice when I am teaching first-year social work students is what I call their "singsong" tone. They often say things like "Oh-h-h, I am so-o-o-o-o sorry to hear that." It reminds me of the behavior and tone of voice often used with small children and older people. That's why I like to have students hear themselves on tape. It also helps if they can sit in on colleagues' interviews to hear how different clinicians "really" sound when they're speaking with clients.

Warmth and caring are relational processes. These feelings do not arise in a vacuum, but are elicited by thinking about or interacting with other people, animals, music, nature, and the spiritual. To see how you look when attempting to demonstrate warmth and caring, look in a mirror or watch yourself on video.

EXERCISE 5.1 Conveying Warmth and Caring

In class, break up into groups of four. Take turns being the speaker, the responder, and two observers. The speaker tells a story about him- or herself while the responder practices conveying warmth and caring. Observers note the specific behaviors that they think convey warmth and caring. The list can include things like facial expressions, postures, comments, and tone of voice. The observers also make note of any lapses in warmth. If possible, video record yourselves so that you can observe yourself doing the things you do to communicate warmth and caring. Note that each person may experience and manifest warmth and caring in different ways. In your journal, record what you have learned.

Acceptance

Another important element of sustaining presence is acceptance. Clinicians must be able to appreciate and affirm clients as people without necessarily condoning specific behaviors that might be harmful to themselves or to others. Carl Rogers (1958) refers to this kind of acceptance as **unconditional positive regard.** To accept clients as people sounds deceptively simple, but it can be quite difficult when client behaviors either go against societal laws or norms or are in radical conflict with our own professional and personal values or preferred styles of behavior.

Societal Norms

Societal norms are widely held standards of conduct to which all members of a society are expected to adhere. Norms usually dictate what is acceptable and what is not—what the powerful majority in a society defines as right and sanctioned or wrong and forbidden. Norms are often codified into laws; for example, most societies have laws that prohibit incest, murder, and theft. Usually norms prescribe gender roles, dress, bearing, and speech, and they distinguish what is acceptable in public from what is to be confined to private life.

Clinicians often see clients who have sought out or been referred for help because they have violated social norms or taboos. Sometimes they have broken the law. More often people come because others may believe that their behaviors, although not illegal, violate social norms (e.g., the woman who yells and talks to herself in the subway or the man who prefers to wear women's clothes). People may also consult with a professional when they experience a conflict with social norms, such as the man who is struggling with his sexual attractions toward men.

Some norms endure, whereas others change over time. Dress and gender roles have changed dramatically since the 1950s. People from one age group may cling to norms that may seem outdated to those in other age groups. An older man may think it polite to open the door for women, whereas a young feminist woman may be insulted, believing that he thinks women are weak and need help. Sometimes there is a contradiction between what society prescribes as a standard or norm and what actually happens. In the United States, two-parent families are held up as the norm, but this country actually has one of the highest rates of divorce and single-parent families in the western hemisphere. Millions are spent on the war on drugs, while millions are also spent on government subsidies and research grants to the alcohol and tobacco industries.

Every culture defines its own norms. Most societies around the world today, including the United States, are pluralistic—that is, composed of many diverse cultures. Problems can arise when differing cultural norms conflict, especially when one group has more socioeconomic and political power than another. For example, many Native Americans believe in the power of the dead and may attribute misfortunes to the actions of ghosts or spirits, some of whom they may claim to see. A naive or misinformed clinician may interpret these beliefs and reported experiences as delusions or hallucinations.

> An intern reported that the team psychiatrist on the inpatient unit told her to tell a father that he should dress more appropriately when visiting his adolescent daughter. The psychiatrist said that the father was "dressing in a seductive manner with his shirt unbuttoned and gold chains calling attention to his hairy chest." The intern, an Italian American woman, felt this behavior was not seductive but rather represented an Italian father's way of dressing up for a Sunday visit.

Traditional norms in Haiti and several other Caribbean islands may prescribe corporal punishment as an appropriate response to a child's misbehavior and as a sign of caring and concern, whereas in the United States the same kind of hitting might be called child abuse. Lillian Comas-Diaz (personal communication, 1996) states that, although corporal punishment may be acceptable in one's country of origin, the parent living in the United States must be educated about the possible consequences of that practice in the United States.

Finally, while working to improve our understanding of diverse cultures and their norms, we need to be careful that we do not mistake behaviors due to cultural influence with those that may be due to illness, addiction, antisocial stance, or individual style. We also need to be aware of **culture-bound syndromes**—that is, "recurrent, locality-specific patterns of aberrant behavior and troubling experience that may or may not be linked to a particular DSM-IV-TR diagnostic category" (APA, 2000, p. 898).

Personal Values

Individual values are cherished beliefs that develop in the context of family and sociocultural influences. Clinicians may value anything from personal autonomy to personal hygiene and can find themselves dismayed or offended by clients who do not share their value systems. We need to be aware of our values and how they influence responses in ways that may leave clients feeling unaccepted. We must be dedicated to being nonjudgmental—unconditionally accepting people for who they are without necessarily accepting all their behaviors. The clinician's nonjudgmental stance leaves clients free to confide openly and honestly without fear of rejection, shaming, or reprisal.

David Hodge (2003) argues that helping professionals such as social workers and other clinicians have developed a widely shared liberal worldview and set of moral values different from those of the working and middle classes from which many clients come. "The literature suggests that conservative populations that are disproportionately working class are, in aggregate, cognizant of the discrepancy in values . . . and believe that social workers do not understand or respect their values, and are hesitant to receive service" (p. 11). Our ethics require us to respect the dignity and worth of all people and to behave in ways that affirm that respect, regardless of differences in personal values.

EXERCISE 5.2 Personal Values

Think of a time when you found your personal values challenged. Think of a time when your personal values changed. Record each story in your journal. What did you learn about yourself and about others from these experiences? Then, think of a time when you felt forced to go along with values you did not respect. Reflect on that experience and how you might deal with the situation differently now. Why?

As we work with clients and are exposed to diverse situations and beliefs, we often find our values challenged and changed. A side benefit of clinical work is that our perspective is enlarged so that we both see and appreciate more of the world beyond our own perspective. We stretch and grow through exposure to differences.

> *I used to see the halfway house as a way station where people were supposed to get it together and then move on. After many years of watching dozens of people with mental illness bounce back to the hospital after leaving transitional living programs, I came to realize that, for many isolated people, long-term communal living may be the end goal rather than a "halfway" achievement.*

* * *

> *Eileen, a 48-year-old woman who had always lived with her family, was discussing whether to move out and get her own apartment. I saw her desire to live alone as a healthy one. I didn't even recognize that living independently was a personal value of mine; I thought it was a sign of "mental health." I believed that adult women should be able to separate from their families to develop autonomy. It wasn't until I talked with a colleague that I realized I had to be careful not to let my values influence our discussion.*

At other times, we may have cherished values confirmed by the similar beliefs and experiences of clients from diverse cultures, reminding us of the larger universal community of shared human values. At such intersections of shared experience and values, mutuality is often experienced more easily and visibly without the clinician and client thinking of themselves as identical.

EXERCISE 5.3 Clients I Might Find Hard to Accept

Following is a list of clients with different characteristics. In your journal, rank-order them from the easiest to the hardest for you to accept. Discuss what made each one easy or hard for you to accept. In class, discuss in small groups what kinds of clients you would have a hard time accepting and what steps you might take to become more accepting.

Woman having an abortion

Mother who is drug addicted

Client who hates professionals

Client who yells in the session when angry

Religious zealot

Husband who is abusing his wife

Transsexual female

Person who is a bully

Clergyperson sexually involved with a parishioner he or she is counseling about loneliness

Man who makes racist statements

Person who is very critical

Adolescent male who is gay

Stylistic Differences

Everyone has a personal style—individual habits and preferences expressed in interactions with others. Personal style is often mediated by culture, gender, race, ethnicity, class and economic opportunity, age, sexual orientation, and geographical region. When feeling misunderstood, one angry person raises his or her voice, whereas another bursts into tears. One client may appear stoic, whereas another seems to plead for help constantly. One client waves a pen while talking, whereas another sits rigidly without moving for the entire session.

As you develop professionally, you may find yourself more or less responsive to particular client styles, looking forward to meetings with certain clients and dreading meetings with others.

> *Usually, I can be accepting of most of my clients' behaviors, but Maddie's whiny tone really grated on me. I had to use every trick in the book to remind myself of her pain so as to stay attentive to her story and not just shout, "Stop whining!" Joanne, an intelligent and competent teacher, spent most of the session time asking my opinion of family and life issues, rather than giving her own. I found this extremely annoying as I knew it to be unnecessary, given her capacity to figure things out. But I came to appreciate that, in her family, one never gave an opinion in front of an authority figure—that would be considered disrespectful. It took a while for her to perceive our situation as different and exempt from her family's rules.*

Clinicians also have unique personal styles and preferences. Some are formal and businesslike; others are relaxed and down-to-earth. Some retain a serious demeanor with clients; others take a lighter touch. Some readily reveal themselves to clients; others prefer to present a "blank screen." The important point about the personal styles of clinicians and clients is not that they match perfectly but that they are not so discordant as to constantly distract from the focus of the work or be offensive.

It is the clinician's responsibility, not the client's, to try to make the interviewing ambiance as harmonious and supportive to the client as possible. An uncomfortable presence or judgmental attitude makes for uncomfortable relating and working, and it can wordlessly signal lack of respect, empathy, and attunement to the needs of others. Lambert and Barley (2002) state that hundreds of studies over 60 years of empirical research on psychotherapy outcomes have found that "some therapists are better than others at contributing to positive client outcome. Clients characterize such therapists as more understanding and accepting, empathic, warm, and supportive. They engage in fewer negative behaviors such as blaming, ignoring, or rejecting" (p. 26). The clinicians' interpersonal skills have been shown to be a predictor of clinical success (Anderson, Ogles, Patterson, Lambert, & Vermeersch, 2009; Norcross, 2002a).

Norms, values, and personal styles are all interrelated, and sorting out one from another can be hard. Supervision can help you explore your attitudes and values so that you can learn to be accepting of clients even if you do not accept a particular behavior. Although the development of openness, respect for differences, and true acceptance of others is a lifelong task, it is also a clinician's ethical responsibility.

Clinical Repose

The clinician's anchored and relaxed presence acts as an island of calm and allows the client to stay self-focused without being distracted by the clinician's needs or anxieties. This repose is central to supportive presence. It provides a clear but unobtrusive **holding environment** for the work and the relationship. Clients come to know that they can count on the clinician to remain centered and steady regardless of events and developments. Even in the face of the unexpected, clinicians try to remain as calm and reliable as possible. The clinical environment is portable and can be constructed almost anywhere to establish safe and supportive conversation. **Clinical repose** is developed with experience and tends to relax, reassure, and open others to the clinical process because it gives them confidence in the helper's reliability. This repose is expressed by a relaxed, open posture and gaze, along with a calm, confident manner.

In learning how to create a supportive presence, students often complain that they lose their natural warmth and spontaneity; they feel that the restraints imposed by other-centeredness make them self-conscious and interfere with their natural responsiveness. At first, their newly adopted professional tone or detachment may cause loved ones to say, "Quit therapizing me!" With time, experience, and good supervision, clinicians are able to combine informed awareness and appropriate self-control with genuine warmth, caring, and acceptance in a way that feels increasingly comfortable and natural.

EXERCISE 5.4 Clinical Repose

In small groups, discuss any ways in which your clinical presence is different from your manner when you are just being yourself in your private life. Note any thing that disrupts your clinical repose. How can you work to enhance your repose and presence? In thinking about repose and presence, what have you learned about yourself? Is your clinical presence beginning to alter the way you carry yourself in your private life? Have people commented on that?

Genuineness

To be effective, support has to be genuine—sincere and free from pretense or hypocrisy. As one of his six necessary and sufficient conditions for change, Carl Rogers (1957) speaks about "genuineness or congruence." By **congruence,** Rogers means that "the therapist is willing to express and be open about any persistent feelings that exist in the relationship. It means avoiding the temptation to hide behind a mask of professionalism" (Rogers & Sanford, 1985, p. 1379). Barbara Okun writes about the need for clinicians to be honest: Clinicians "can communicate honesty by being open with clients, by answering questions to the best of their ability, and by admitting mistakes or lack of knowledge" (Okun & Kantrowitz, 2008, p. 40).

While attempting to communicate a supportive presence, clinicians need to avoid fake smiles, counterfeit approval, and false reassurance (e.g., "Don't worry—things will get better"). Many clients can spot faking easily because they have often been manipulated by the pretenses of others. They may not comment because they need the approval or services that the clinician can offer. Perceptions of inauthenticity undermine confidence in the clinician and impede the development of a trusting relationship.

There is a difference between genuineness and total honesty. A wise French saying, *"Toute la verité n'est pas bonne à dire,"* translates as "The whole truth is not always good to say." To create a supportive presence, we need to be selective, always considering the impact that our remarks and behaviors have on our clients. Subsequently, we do not always say everything we think, but we should think about everything we say. And what we do say, we have to mean. As clinicians, we are always "in role." Although we have to be ourselves, authentic in our role rather than hiding behind it, we also have to be deliberate. For example, we might think that a diagnosis of a particular kind of cancer puts a client at high risk of dying, but we would not say so. The goal is to accompany the client in the moment of his or her experience, not to be a wizard or mind reader.

Availability

Clinicians further support clients by making ourselves easily available. We need to be physically and psychologically accessible. As discussed in Chapter 3, clinicians indicate a willingness to join and work with clients by setting up offices that are welcoming, having hours that fit with clients' needs, being available by phone, and being flexible in setting the frequency and length of sessions. In addition, we demonstrate availability by being culturally responsive and by attempting to provide services in the language of the client's choice. In sum, every effort is made to reduce feelings of distance or alienation.

As a social worker in the rehabilitation hospital, I needed to meet with the children of Rachel, a woman in our hospital recovering from a serious stroke. I'd been seeing one daughter each week for 30 minutes or so to provide support as she began to screen nursing homes and come to terms with her mother's chronic disability. When two more daughters became involved, I began to meet with everyone together, including Rachel, for an hour. I had to switch our meeting time to the early evening to accommodate their work and home schedules. I planned our meetings for Wednesdays so that it would be easy for them to stay for the stroke education group that met on Wednesday nights.

A number of factors constrain the amount of time that clinicians can see clients face to face, such as the client's busy schedule, financial and insurance limitations, and long-distance travel. Clinicians need to be flexible in finding additional ways to be available to clients. We can now do so in person; by phone and cell phone, email, letter, or fax; by Skype or videoconferencing; and through encrypted Internet Website exchanges. An example from a recently developed telehealth program illustrates this kind of meaningful flexibility in getting services to clients who otherwise are unable to reach them easily. Dawn McCarty and Catherine Clancy (2002) report that South Carolina has only one psychiatrist fluent in American Sign Language. Videoconferencing has linked her with several mental health centers across the state at given times. She uses sign language in assessing client needs and strengths, recommends follow-up treatments, and, as needed, prescribes medications for people all over the state who are deaf or hearing impaired.

It is important to discuss with clients the easiest ways to reach us. Some people check their email several times a day and others only once a week. Unanswered calls for help pose both therapeutic and liability problems. However, the use of cell phones, fax machines, and computers presents the clinician with the difficult challenge of ensuring confidentiality. These forms of communication are accessible by others, and therefore sensitive material should not be transmitted by these means unless the client has provided written permission.

At times in the relationship, the clinician may offer the client more opportunities for contact, such as when the client is going through a particularly difficult time or when the clinician or client believes that the client can make productive use of additional contact. Proposed increases in contact should be reviewed with supervisors in advance because they can have unforeseen consequences. Most clients respond favorably to a goodwill offer of additional visits or "other times you can reach me." Some clients, however, can abuse the availability, experience it as seductive interest on the part of the clinician, feel too dependent after additional calls or visits, or think the clinician sees him or her as exceptionally needed. The clinician has to note the use the client makes of the added contacts and respond accordingly by discussing any untoward effects of this extension of self and role.

In emergencies or to support clients under duress, clinicians may accompany clients to emergency rooms, court proceedings, hospital admissions, school evaluation meetings, and other places. In Chapter 10, we discuss accompanying clients as a form of clinician influence. Visiting incarcerated clients can also be supportive under well thought-out conditions. We always try to consult with supervisors or senior colleagues on the implications of activities with clients outside the usual scope of the work.

> *I visited Maureen in jail two days after she stabbed her husband in front of her two boys. I knew she would be beside herself with guilt and shame, and possibly suicidal. She was also new to the area and had no friends. My supervisor suggested I take her some personal items like a comb, brush, lotion, and some magazines to pass the time. She could not believe I would come "to such a place to see a person like me." I also went to their court hearing and then out to lunch in the neighborhood with her and her husband after he dropped the charges. The agency provided the money for all of these services, seeing it as building the family's view of themselves as "mattering." We really began our deeper family work after that. No one had ever given them the time of day.*

Many other services and arrangements can be set up to support clients between interviews to diminish feelings of isolation or vulnerability. The clinician can establish a safety net that includes family members, friends, on-call staff or hotlines, brief inpatient hospital stays, attendance at Alcoholics Anonymous (AA) or Narcotics Anonymous (NA) meetings, day treatment, sheltered work, respite care, and the like. Positive attitudes of network providers, a readiness to help, the availability of interpreters as needed, affordable transportation, and well coordinated schedules all make a difference as to whether "supports" feel truly supportive or not.

Validation of the Client's Story

Validation occurs when we endorse and appreciate the realities of the client's story. The clinical encounter may be the first opportunity people have had to feel that their stories are moving and believable and that the details ring true to a witness.

Universalizing is another supporting and validating technique, used to undercut a client's sense of isolation or differentness. In universalizing, we frame our response in such a way as to locate the client as one of a universe of people sharing similar feelings, experiences, or opinions.

EXAMPLES OF UNIVERSALIZING

"A lot of other people share that feeling."

"Who wouldn't be nervous in a dark parking lot late at night!"

"Most working moms like yourself have the same fear you do about being laid off or losing their benefits if they take a maternity leave."

"Join the crowd."

Universalizing is not always useful. Some clients may need to feel unique in their experiences or perceptions—the only specialness they may have known. Such clients may respond to universalizing with irritation or disappointment, communicating a feeling that the interviewer just does not understand their unique situation. Others may have experienced aloneness, alienation, or differentness for so long that simple reassurances from the clinician about the commonality of their experiences are insufficient to break up their core sense of alienation. To them, the clinician may appear naive or inattentive to their deep levels of distress. As with all techniques, we watch carefully for the client's response, note it, and explore it further, if necessary. It is paradox of clinical work that clients can feel unique and special while at the same time appreciating that others are in similar situations and experiencing similar feelings.

Identifying and Affirming Strengths

CLIP 5.2
Affirming Client
Strengths

Clinicians who hold strengths perspective recognize clients' courage or persistence in working toward goals. Recognition and confirmation can build self-esteem and initiative. Clients often come to see that the strengths used in one situation are often transferable to other seemingly insurmountable crises of the moment, making problems seem more resolvable. Identifying and affirming client strengths further the development of a supportive presence. Clients often feel invisible, marginalized, and powerless. Affirming clients' strengths helps them to feel recognized, increases their sense of belonging or "mattering," and enhances their personal efficacy. As clinicians we can usually validate client strengths more effectively when we are aware of and secure in our own strengths and can appreciate the importance of self-validation.

EXAMPLES OF STRENGTHS PERSPECTIVE RESPONSES BY CLINICIANS

"It's amazing how much you got done with almost no support."

"You said you 'ran out' on every relationship you ever had, but you've come to see me for three months straight now, and this is a relationship. This relationship counts; it's a very important exception to your stated pattern, and it suggests to me that you do not in fact run out on every relationship. Maybe we could take a look at when relationships work for you and when they don't."

"I notice you whizzed right over the statement that, for the first time, when you felt like drinking this week, you increased your AA attendance. That was such an important step. I'd like to hear more about how you made that change happen."

"You say you're embarrassed to talk to me over and over again about your job achievements, but I like to hear about them. I think it's wonderful that things are working out for you now, and, frankly, I think you deserve a little more support for your successes than is out there for you right now."

Provision of Concrete Supports

Clinicians in both agency and private practice often demonstrate support for clients by helping them access needed services. Professional attention to the deleterious effects of poverty, economic dislocation, and institutionalized bias has increased clinicians' appreciation of the importance of providing for the basic human needs of individuals and families. These needs include food, clothing, shelter, adequate financial support, transportation, pathways to and financial support for education or training, and access to opportunities for recreation and affiliation.

Abraham Maslow (1968) outlined a hierarchy of human needs with concrete needs at its foundation. He postulated that, unless these basic human needs are met, people understandably do not develop much beyond the level of profound despair and so may not feel able to take action on their own behalf. It is unrealistic, if not cruel, to ask desperate people to sit around reflecting on their psychological lives and perspectives. In our crisis intervention discussion in Chapter 13, you will learn that following disasters, the first thing interventionists do is attend to immediate concrete needs—getting large numbers of people safe, clothed, fed, housed, reconnected, and sheltered from further harm. Counseling comes later.

Providing needed resources can be a critical factor in building trust and in developing a therapeutic alliance. Clients often experience us as more respectful of their struggles when we actively help them obtain needed services, such as food stamps, housing, referrals to job training, some respite from the long-term care of relatives, and so on. We may be perceived as more appreciative of the exigencies of daily life and the bureaucratic snares that often await the person seeking services. A caution is that, although clinicians may at times directly provide needed services or resources, clients' resourcefulness is best developed when they learn how to exercise their own knowledge and skills on behalf of themselves and their loved ones. We agree with the wise saying that, if you give a hungry person a fish, he or she will eat for a day, but if you teach that person to fish, he or she can eat for a lifetime—if there are fish!

Clinicians are ill advised to impulsively offer concrete help if such offers are motivated by rescue fantasies, the wish to be liked, or a client's demands. Such moves frequently backfire, leaving all parties feeling used or betrayed. Lending money (as opposed to helping the client obtain funds) is also an unwise clinician practice, as is giving rides in personal vehicles (because of the risk of injury to the client if there is an accident or if a client who is suicidal or psychotic jumps out into traffic).

Advocacy

Another very important kind of support, intrinsic to the work clinicians do with people, is advocacy for client rights and opportunities. **Advocacy** takes place when clinicians join with others in political activities and movements in the community to achieve increased rights, protections, access, and opportunities for all people, including but not limited to our clients. As advocates, we also inform agencies or practice groups of important services or amenities that are not available to clients. Clinicians need to work together with colleagues and community groups to improve the conditions within which services are delivered. Advocacy also occurs when clinicians struggle with insurance companies or other payers to get the proper amount and kinds of services for clients. All of these activities have the potential to heighten client morale and hopefulness and to energize the clinical work.

■ Empathy

Supportive presence is good for starters, but it is not enough to carry the clinical process forward from its beginnings of cordiality, interest, and openness. The clinical relationship cannot move forward without empathy—the ability to immerse oneself in another's experience without losing one's own sense of self.

Some theorists make the distinction between perspective taking and empathy. Grit Hein and Tania Singer (2008) refer to cognitive **perspective taking** as "the ability to understand intentions, desires, (and) beliefs of another person, resulting from (cognitively) reasoning about the other's state" (p. 154). By contrast, they refer to empathy as "an affective state, caused by sharing of the emotions or sensory states of another person" (p. 154). However, when we speak of clinical empathy, we mean both the ability to take the perspective of the client and the ability to share the emotional states of our clients.

Empathy requires that the clinician see and experience the world from the client's subjective perspective while maintaining the perspective of an outside observer. It thus requires a constant oscillation between observing the client, feeling and thinking as if one *were* the client, and then feeling and thinking *about* the client's experience. In addition to what it contributes to a supportive presence, empathy provides the clinician with important human experience and information on which to base hunches that inform future clinical work.

Paul Pedersen and colleagues (Pedersen, Crethar, & Carlson, 2008) propose an expanded view of empathy—**inclusive cultural empathy.** They believe that all human beings are shaped over the years by our parents and many "culture teachers" who instill a variety of cultural beliefs, practices, and ways of relating. We are influenced by our multiple identities in a variety of cultures. Each culture teacher asserts that his or her cultural ways are "the best" ways.

Thus the clinician and client come together as two complex culture bearers who have both similar and different interpretations and expectations of how to relate and how to understand and resolve the problems for which the client is seeking help. The clinician's empathy must incorporate exploration of and respect for the client's various cultural influences as well as a recognition of his or her own. We like to think of inclusive cultural empathy as the ability to put on night vision goggles so that the clinician can see all of the cultural teachers and people who influence the client and those who influence the clinician. This complexity distinguishes Inclusive Cultural Empathy (ICE) from traditional theories or ideas of empathy.

Researchers using functional magnetic resonance imaging (fMRI) have found that different neural networks are activated in perspective taking and empathy.

As Jean Decety and colleagues (Decety, Michalska & Akitsuki, 2008) note: "When we attend to other people in pain, the neural circuits underpinning the processing of first-hand experience of pain are activated in the observer" (p. 2607).

CLIP 5.3
Empathy

Empathy is a complex process that is often misunderstood. The following clarifications may be helpful:

1. Empathy is not sympathy. Sympathy is what I feel *toward* you; empathy is what I feel as you.
2. Empathy is much more than just putting oneself in the other person's shoes. Empathy requires a shift of perspective. It is not what I would experience *as me* in your shoes; empathy is what I experience *as you* in your shoes.
3. Empathy requires a constant shifting between my experiencing *as you* what you feel and my being able to think *as me* about your experience.

EXERCISE 5.5 Experiencing Empathy

In your journal, record a time when someone really understood you, when they seemed to know exactly what you were feeling—a time when you felt someone's empathy. In class, describe the experience to your colleagues. How do you think that person knew so much about what you were feeling?

Empathy and Human Development

The ability to empathize is innate. Numerous neuropsychological studies have shown that even as children, people respond physiologically to the pain of others (Decety et al., 2008; Eisenberg, Spinrad, & Sadovsky, 2006). But we know that not all people are able to take the perspective of others or demonstrate empathy. Disturbances in empathy during childhood or through later life stresses and losses can impede or distort the formation of the very mirror neurons that activate empathic behavior (Neuman et al., 2009).

Jean Baker Miller and colleagues at the Wellesley College Stone Center have written about the development of empathy and mutuality in relationships (Jordan, Kaplan, Miller, Stiver, & Surrey, 1991). They suggest that empathy is developed through mutually engaging exchanges that begin in infancy. Infants and children experience pleasure when they feel they are being accurately seen and heard by their caregivers. They internalize and practice the engaging skills of observing and feeling with others. They receive feedback and praise in relation to the accuracy of their empathic responses, reinforcing their pleasure and increasing their attempts at empathy. Likewise, their caregivers feel and show similar pleasure when on the receiving end of the child's budding caretaking behaviors or when delighting in the child's playing nurse, Mommy, or helper.

> *My 3-year-old daughter noticed that I was sad and she patted my back and said, "Mommy, you're sad today. . . . Do you want my teddy bear?" I said, "Yes, sweetie. I am sad. You are a very good girl to try to take care of Mommy."*

The accuracy and appropriateness of joining with the experiences of others are fine-tuned over time. Basically, one learns empathy by experiencing empathy, by being on the receiving end of empathy. The experience of being accurately seen and heard by another has few equals. Those who have been denied or shortchanged in their experience of empathy *from* others often show little or tenuous empathy *for* others. Those who have been overwhelmed by requests for empathic caregiving may manifest "compassion fatigue"—an emotional tiredness from caring that can lead to emotional detachment and avoidance of people in need (Figley, 1995). In either situation, people may be less likely to reveal themselves to or care much about others.

Moreover, members of oppressed groups may generously empathize with each other but maintain emotional distance as protective armor when with outsiders—including clinicians—who are viewed as members of a subordinating group or culture (Walker & Rosen, 2004).

Developing Clinical Empathy

Empathy is a developmental process that can be consciously fostered and strengthened in adulthood in a number of ways. To think and feel as another person, we need to have a lot of experience with others, and we need to learn about the range of reactions that people have to various situations.

Judith Jordan (2004b) speaks of this developmental process as gaining relational awareness—awareness of what a relationship both provides and requires. We can gain this knowledge by enriching and expanding our own life experiences and by learning about human diversity through experiences with others who are different from us. This learning won't take place simply by reading, having classroom discussions, or watching films. It must be accomplished by becoming neighbors, workmates, and friends with people from different cultures and socioeconomic classes.

Empathy often leads to activisim. Sharon Freedberg (2007) describes empathy as the fuel for coming to care about and act in the wider world to help improve conditions for others.

A simple and useful technique in establishing empathy with another person is the psychodramatic process of getting into role—taking on the physical and psychological characteristics of the other (Moreno, 1946). We assume the other's posture, manner, tone, and intentions, as well as the dynamics of his or her personal history, family, and cultural experiences.

EXERCISE 5.6 Becoming the Other

Think of an important person in your life, perhaps a member of your family. Get into the role of that person. (For example, let's assume you have taken the role of your sister, Jen, although, of course, you can take the role of anyone you want.) Now, tell the group your name. (In the instructions, we use "Jen," but you can play anyone.) Assume the body posture, tone, and manner of Jen. What are you wearing? Jen, think about how you look, dress, feel, and speak. Remember your history, family, and culture. Give a brief monologue about yourself to the group,

Jen, and then let the group interview you in role for 5 minutes to learn more about you. Video record the monologue.

Group members help each stay in role by using the role name. (For example, "Jen, how do you feel about . . . ?" or "Jen, is that how you speak?" or "Is that how you hold your body, Jen?") While you are in role, group members may ask you questions about how you feel about current social issues, what is important in your life, or about the relationship between the person you are role-playing and you (e.g., between Jen and her sister).

After completing your role-play, talk with the group about the experience. Watch the video together. In your journal, record what you learned about the other person when you took the role. Did you learn anything about yourself? Did you learn anything about your relationship with the person?

Exercise 5.6 may have been easy because you are familiar with the person you were asked to play. You have a history of interaction and a wealth of information about the person on which to draw. Similarly, as clinicians, we need basic background information about the people we work with to build empathy, because empathy is a relational process and cannot occur in a vacuum.

EXERCISE 5.7 Information Builds Empathy

Play Leti. Notice that you cannot do it without some basic information about Leti that helps you get into her role. Write down what kinds of information you would want to have to empathize with her. Compare the information you want about Leti with the information that others might want to know. Note the different kinds of information people seek. You might want to know her age, ethnicity, living situation, and other important circumstances before even trying to empathize. Discuss with others the things that help you, personally, empathize with someone and the things that make empathizing harder for you. Record your reactions in your journal.

One of the tasks of the initial interview—indeed, of all interviews—is to gather necessary and relevant information (to be detailed in Chapters 6 and 7). Sometimes gathering information is easy: from an intake form; the initial telephone call; or comments from friends, family members, or referring persons. Many times, clients themselves readily provide continuing information with which we can identify and which we can use to empathize. When clients are silent or do not talk easily, we still use the empathic process by imagining ourselves as the other to understand why they are expressing themselves through silence rather than through speech. Shulman (2009) regards silence as an important form of communication and speaks of "reaching inside silence" as an important technique in expressing empathy and reengaging the client in verbal exchange.

Students often ask, "How can I be empathic with people whose experiences I've never had and can scarcely relate to?" (Examples could be pregnancy, imprisonment, or the death of a child.) To be empathic, we need to both broaden our knowledge of the wide range of human experience and, quite simply, open our hearts.

Clinicians strengthen empathy by trying it out with many different kinds of people and getting differential feedback from them regarding the accuracy and timeliness of our empathic responses. Under the pressures of school or work, it is often easier to socialize with people whose backgrounds and experiences are similar to your own. However, push yourself beyond the familiar and expand the network of those with whom you interact. Social activism in various communities is a great way to meet new people and become familiar with beliefs, values, and experiences different from your own. In-class exercises and group assignments are also designed to enhance your knowledge of other people's experiences and perspectives. Ideally, in the process, you increase your capacity for empathy with a widening range of people in varying situations.

> *As a southerner, I had been taught that Catholics were under rigid papal control and that, if Kennedy were elected president, he would be taking orders directly from the Pope. I laugh now to think how incredibly naive this was. It wasn't until I came to social work school and actually became friends with a number of Catholics that I realized that many of these new friends were freer from religious strictures than I was as a southern Methodist. It was also the first time I befriended people of color and worked with people from the inner city. My ideas changed so much as we all shared our stories in role-plays, over lunch, and hanging out after work.*

While nothing beats relating, reading the professional literature and attending conferences are other ways to become better acquainted with the conditions and experiences of many different people. Professional reading can be augmented with novels, plays, autobiographies, and the like. Educational and commercial films, videos, plays, and documentaries offer additional opportunities for learning. For example, the films *Hoop Dreams* and *Crash* may be useful for developing empathy with some inner-city families, while the films *Philadelphia* and *Yesterday* may help people grasp the struggles and challenges of some men and women living with AIDS.

EXERCISE 5.8 Expanding Your Capacity for Empathy

This week, read or watch something you think will expand your capacity for empathy. It could be a story about a person with a mental illness, a family from a different culture, or someone struggling with an issue with which you are unfamiliar or uncomfortable. Record in your journal why you chose the topic and what you experienced and learned from it. Also discuss what it would be like for you to be *in* this situation, rather than reading about it or watching it.

You can also broaden your human experiences by volunteering in the community: working at a meal site, senior center, or homeless shelter; helping with a neighborhood campaign for better schools or voter registration; marching for an end to domestic violence; or joining candlelight vigils. All this constitutes the expanded role of the clinician in working for peace, justice, equity, and basic rights for all

> *I did my master's thesis on working with people who were dying. However, it wasn't until many years later, when I volunteered at AIDS Action Committee, that I had any idea of what it might be like to face my own death. Meeting each week with men who had just discovered that they had a life-threatening illness made me much more sensitive to the issues and feelings around death and dying. I moved from "knowing" to "experiencing."*

EXERCISE 5.9 Empathy Role-Plays

Take the role of each of the people described in the following vignettes.

You are Janelle, a 23-year-old African American mother of two children who has moved to a new neighborhood.

You are Kieran, an Irish Catholic college junior, and you have just been told that you have been cut from the Notre Dame football team.

You are Kim Soong, a 16-year-old adopted daughter from Korea, and your parents just told you they are getting a divorce.

You are Frankie, a 78-year-old widower, and your daughter told you it would be best for you to live in a nursing home.

You are Rosalie, a woman being stalked by her boyfriend.

In your journal, discuss the following: What helped you get into each role? Did you have similar experiences on which to draw? What information and experiences were helpful in taking on each role? Which role was hardest to get into and why?

In Exercise 5.9, you may have noticed that it was easier to get into some roles than others. It is often harder to get into a role in which we have to take on negative or uncomfortable feelings (e.g., fear, shame) or an identity discredited by others (e.g., gay, welfare recipient, drug user).

Empathy can also be difficult if the client's experiences arouse some unfinished business or personally charged issues for the clinician. Clients often notice when clinicians tighten up or detour around personally charged issues.

> *When my client began expressing her sadness about her mother's death, I noticed that I did not want to feel her sadness. Prior to the interview, I had just been at the hospital visiting with a good friend dying of cancer. The moment my client cried, I actually stood up and said, "Please go ahead; don't let me interrupt. I just have to shut the window; it's freezing in here." When I returned to my seat, she changed the subject without skipping a beat.*

A major challenge in empathizing is maintaining self-awareness and centeredness while "feeling as" the other and communicating that feeling effectively. We need to be able to distinguish the client's feelings and experiences from our own. While attempting to be empathic, clinicians need to guard against projection and overidentification with clients. In **projection,** clinicians disavow and repress their own unpleasant or taboo feelings, then attribute the feelings to clients ("I'm not angry—*she* is."). In **overidentification,** clinicians emphasize the similarities between themselves and clients, and minimize or deny things that would reveal unsettling differences between them. Whereas empathy takes us *toward* client experience, projection and overidentification take us *away* from it, as our defenses arise to protect us from our own inner anxieties about the relationship.

Communicating Empathy in the Relationship

We move from *feeling* empathic to *being* empathic by converting our perceptions, feelings, and intuitions into postures, gestures, sounds, words, and behaviors. The basic methods we use to communicate support and empathy include supportive sounds, mirroring, and empathic echo. These methods incorporate two important components. First, the clinician is the caring other who offers supportive responses as the client reveals his or her story. Second, the clinician is the empathic other who reflects back content, affect, themes, and patterns in the client's story from the client's perspective.

Supportive Sounds

We demonstrate our presence and close attention by making periodic use of **supportive sounds,** such as "ohhh," "mm-hmm," "uh-huh," "yes," "ah," and "I see." These brief utterances mark our active involvement in the client's narrative and are often gently interjected during long narrations by the client. They indicate to the client that we are listening and following the story closely, and they can encourage the client to continue talking.

EXAMPLES OF SUPPORTIVE SOUNDS

Client: It hurt so much when I was dismissed like that.

Clinician: Awww . . .

Client: I didn't want to give my boss the pleasure of seeing me cry.

Clinician: Mmm . . .

Client: I have some ideas about what to do next, though.

Clinician: Good. I'd like to hear them.

Since responses must be genuine to be effective; we make every effort to avoid speaking in a repetitive, hackneyed, or singsong manner. In the preceding example, a minimal response suffices to show caring and presence while keeping the clinician out of the way of the story so that the *client's* voice is exercised and validated.

> *One of the first times I listened to myself on tape, I noticed that I kept saying "right" to the client. It wasn't that I was agreeing with her; it was my way of saying "uh-huh." I realized the danger of using that phrase when she said, "My husband is a pain in the ass," and I said, "Right." I suddenly worried that she would go home and tell her husband that her counselor agreed that he was a pain in the ass!*

Mirroring

Mirroring is a physical form of reflection. In mirroring, the clinician matches the client's posture, facial expression, and gestures. For example, if the client is leaning forward, the clinician may also lean forward; if the client is frowning, the clinician may also frown. Mirroring helps us develop empathy for the client's perspective, and it communicates that we are closely following and are "where the client is." We are always careful not to mimic the client or interfere with the natural flow of productive conversation. Imitating or copying the client's every movement can make the client self-conscious and distract attention from the whole person and the emerging details of the story. Mirroring thus involves art as well as technique, and it is a matter of nuance and subtle responding.

As rapport and **synchrony** build between interviewer and client, their postures often become more congruent. Kadushin & Kadushin (1997) note that the client can also unconsciously begin to parallel the clinician's posture, tone, and nonverbals. Clinicians can use this knowledge about synchrony to shape interviewee behaviors by using relaxed posture and comfortable gaze to calm and soothe an overexcited client or by using exuberant facial expressions and gestures to energize someone about a hard-won success.

EXERCISE 5.10 Mirroring

Watch any ongoing conversation between two people and note how the participants begin to mirror each other nonverbally. Is the synchrony present from the outset? If not, how long does it take to set in, and what forms does it take?

Empathic Echo

Empathic echo refers to a verbal reflection of the client's story—that is, behaviors, thoughts, affect, and meanings in context. For purposes of theoretical discussion, clinicians often distinguish between content and affect, although the two are always interacting at some level. **Reflection of content**

involves making statements that accurately represent the client's statements about behaviors, thoughts, and interactions. It can also entail making statements regarding the context or situation in which the client's story is embedded. **Reflection of affect** consists of making statements about the feelings that may wrap around or suffuse the client's content.

Gerard Egan (2010) differentiates between basic and advanced empathy. Basic empathy is the skill of joining the client's perspective and is similar to our concept of the empathic echo. The clinician attempts to reflect content and affect that are the most crucial to the client. The goal of reflection in the empathic echo is to have the client experience the clinician as joining his or her perspective. In Chapter 8, you will learn that reflection techniques are central to motivational interviewing, a set of strategies designed to help clients resolve ambivalences about changing (Miller & Rollnick, 2002).

In **advanced empathy,** the clinician reflects the meaning beneath the surface of the client's awareness. Egan (2010) notes that skilled helpers listen intently to clients "for the message behind the message" and attempt to see clearly what clients only half say or hint at (pp. 227–228). We agree with Egan that one can reflect content and affect for reasons other than to convey basic empathy. As we discuss in later chapters, the clinician can choose to reflect some parts of content or affect to increase clients' awareness of patterns and themes, to confront, to explore, or simply to move the conversation ahead.

Empathic reflection of content.   Reflection of content may seem simple, but it is a lot harder than it sounds, and it involves clinical judgment. The interviewer has to decide whether speaking is appropriate at the moment and, if so, whether to reflect the words themselves or their presumed meanings. We do not always use the same words as the client; more often, we paraphrase what the client has said using similar words and phrases that ideally convey the same meaning.

EXAMPLES OF REFLECTION OF CONTENT

Client: I had my one-year anniversary at AA.

Clinician A [using the same words]: You had your one-year anniversary in AA.

Clinician B [using different words]: You haven't had a drink in a long time.

A risk in using words other than those of the client is that the clinician may choose words that do not convey the same meaning as the client intended. In the preceding example, Clinician B's view that one year is a long time might not correspond with the client's perspective. For the client, the one-year anniversary may be small compared to his cousin's 22 years of sobriety. Also, having one year in AA does not necessarily mean that the client has not had a drink in a year.

Linguistic differences can also complicate accurate reflection. Roger Fisher, William Ury, and Bruce Patton (1991) tell the following story that exemplifies the difficulties:

> The Persian word "compromise" apparently lacks the positive meaning in English of "a midway solution both sides can live with" but has only a negative meaning as in "our integrity was compromised." Similarly the word "mediator" in Persian suggests "meddler," someone who is barging in uninvited. In early 1980, UN Secretary General Waldheim flew to Iran to seek the release of American hostages. His efforts were seriously set back when Iranian television broadcast in Persian a remark he reportedly made on his arrival in Tehran: "I have come as a mediator to work out a compromise." (p. 33)

Reflecting content is further complicated by the fact that people tend to talk in paragraphs, conveying several ideas at once. Human communication is multilayered, and the clinician is constantly making judgments about which of the many pieces of shared content is the most important to reflect at the moment. At different times in the interview or in the working relationship, we reflect and emphasize different pieces of client content to challenge, to help expand awareness, or to develop new perspectives on problems. At this point, we are using reflection as part of the empathic echo; because we are trying only to demonstrate empathy and support, we need to reflect what we believe the *client* sees as the crucial content. Other content is stored for future consideration.

EXAMPLE

Client: I had a terrible day. The bus was late, my daughter was sick, and the boss yelled at me for being late for work again.

There are six pieces of content that could be reflected following this client's statement:

1. Terrible day
2. Late bus
3. Sick daughter
4. Late for work
5. Not the first time late for work
6. Boss yelling

The clinician is free to reflect any of these pieces of content, and three different clinicians might all choose different reflections, depending on the stance or focus each wants to sustain.

EXAMPLES

Clinician A: Your daughter was sick, the bus was late, and you were yelled at by your boss for being late again. It was a terrible day.

Clinician B: You had a terrible day.

Clinician C: What a lot of things to cope with in one day!

Clinician A decides to reflect all of what the client said, to acknowledge hearing it while leaving the conversation leadership to the client. Although this may be useful in letting the client know that the clinician heard all that was said and simply wishes the client to continue, just repeating everything the client says time after time can feel tedious and meaningless to both client and clinician. Too many repetitions can dull the liveliness of spontaneity and make the clinical conversation feel too far removed from ordinary exchange. Rarely does anyone just repeat back what someone else has said.

Clinician B notes to herself that the client was late for work "again," which may be an important piece of information to pick up on later, especially if it signals a pattern undermining the client's achievement of stated goals. However, since she is attempting an empathic echo, she reflects what seems most crucial to the client in the moment of this encounter: the "terrible day." She stores the information about being late for work, the boss's yelling, and the daughter's illness, perhaps to make use of them later. Clinician B uses the *first* piece of content because in this instance she feels that it captures the gestalt of the entire communication. At other times, clinicians reflect the *last* piece of content in clients' narratives, just as an encouragement for clients to go further.

Clinician C's response is a summary comment, using words that are different from those of the client. Such a response is an attempt to reflect content *and* tone so as to express and build empathy.

EXERCISE 5.11 Empathic Reflection of Content

Read the following client statements. List the pieces of content—the different ideas—in each statement. Which pieces might you reflect to show empathy or support for the client? Reflect the content in two ways:

1. By using the client's own words

2. By paraphrasing the content or meaning of what the client said

Client A: I am trying to choose between a career with the military or with the police. The military will give me a chance to see the world and experience other cultures. I can also get my B.A. degree for free. But my father and my uncles are all cops.

Client B: I just found out that my aunt is having her kidney removed. My uncle is 86 and is really worried about her. He has high blood pressure and diabetes. I have to find out about nursing care for both of them.

Client C: The kids at school are picking on me. I am the only girl in the shop class. We have to make a model for a tool shed, and no one will be my partner. If I can't get a partner, I'll fail.

Note that you are only reading this and that your experience of the exchange might be different if you actually heard the client's statements, replete with nonverbal, paralinguistic, and metacommunication clues.

Now, instead of reading each statement to yourself, pair up with a colleague and take turns making each statement. Note differences in tone, emphasis, speech rate, and other paralinguistic cues as the speaker and the content change.

Empathic reflection of affect.   Clients can tell us directly how they feel, as when they say, "I'm so proud . . . ," or "I am scared," or "I am so sad that. . . ." Sometimes, though, the words clients use to describe their feelings are ambiguous—for example, "I was upset that I got fired." The term "upset" could mean that the client was sad, worried, angry, embarrassed, or any number of things that we can only imagine unless the client elaborates.

Often the clinician is left to guess what the client feels, combining prior knowledge of the client's habitual patterns and the literal words spoken with the accompanying tone, emphasis, facial and body movements, or feelings. We need to develop a capacity to recognize when feelings are arising, to discern one feeling state from another, and to decide when and when not to focus on them. We also need to familiarize ourselves with the variety of ways in which clients express feelings, coming to appreciate local, cultural, and idiosyncratic styles and influences.

EXAMPLE

Client: I'm so pissed off at my brother for telling my mom I'm pregnant, when I wanted to tell her myself.

Clinician A: You're pregnant and your brother told your mother.

Clinician B: You're mad at your brother. He betrayed your confidence and that hurt.

Clinician C: You're disappointed that you didn't get to tell your mother you're pregnant.

Clinician A decided to reflect content only. She noted two pieces of content: that the client was pregnant and that her brother told her mother.

She did not reflect the client's feeling, perhaps because of how the client expressed herself: "pissed off." The clinician may have felt uncomfortable reflecting that term or uncomfortable about getting more anger into the room by focusing on it. Other clinicians might feel that, unless the angry feelings are acknowledged and validated, attempts to focus intellectually on content will not get very far because the client is "so pissed off."

Clinician B reflected that the client was angry and hurt. Note that this clinician used the words "mad" and "hurt" to reflect the client's feeling. Clients may at times use words that we feel uncomfortable reflecting. We have found that it is wiser not to fake comfort; it works better for us to paraphrase the client than to use terms we are not comfortable with. For example, adolescents can use extreme language for purposes of group belongingness or to test or shock adults. Clinicians may try to assume this style and end up seeming and sounding phony.

Clinician C did not reflect the feeling that the client directly expressed—anger. She reflected what she felt the client might also be feeling—disappointment. Even when clients directly express feelings, clinicians attempting empathy may pursue other feelings that, although unspoken, may also be crucial to the client's perspective in the moment.

Each of the preceding reflections takes the conversation in a different direction. Clinician B's response might lead to a focus on the client's relationship with her brother, whereas Clinician C's might lead to concerns about talking with her mother. All the approaches have merit, and all are attempts at empathy.

EXERCISE 5.12 Empathic Reflection of Affect

Go back to Exercise 5.11. Describe the different feelings that might go along with the content of each client's statement. Which feelings might you reflect to show empathy or support for the client? Reflect the affect in two different ways. Again, note the additional clues to intent and meaning when you *hear* communication rather than read it.

The empathic echo is more than simply an echo of specific words or feelings. In reflecting either content or affect, clinicians carefully attempt to reflect the way clients understand or make meaning of their situations, feelings, behaviors, or thoughts. We thus reflect not only *what* is said but also *how* it is said—its tone, its coloration, and the metacommunication and paralinguistic cues (described in Chapter 4). We use the empathic echo for several reasons: to show we are listening, to increase the client's feeling of being attended to closely, and to increase the client's feeling of being understood. The empathic echo allows the client to correct any misconceptions the clinician may have.

Empathic Failures

CLIP 5.4
Empathic Failures

Empathic failures occur when clinicians miss the boat and reflect the wrong content, feeling, or meaning. At other times, we may drift from the moment and miss a very important theme or feeling altogether, all the while appearing to listen and nod attentively. Clients often notice when clinicians drift away, and they may signal their awareness by asking, "Now, where was I?" or "What was I talking about when I got off there?"—as though *they* were lost, not us! Another empathic mistake interviewers sometimes make is to confuse one client's story with another's and make a remark about an event or loved one unrelated to the client, hurting the client's feelings. The client may think, "I'm indistinguishable from all the others."

Dillon (2003) has identified many ways that clinicians can make empathic mistakes:

- *Boilerplate empathy.* The clinician uses singsong or stockpiled and overused empathic statements that sound as though they were learned from TV sitcoms rather than from supervisors: "I feel your pain," "Oh, my!" "I see what you're saying."
- *Piling it on.* The clinician makes empathic comments or sounds after almost every client statement. The comments are too numerous, too exaggerated, too childlike in tone, or so repetitious that they feel inauthentic: "Wow," "Awful," "No way," "Oooh," "I feel so bad for you," "Geeee," "You must have felt terrible."
- *Getting the facts wrong.* The clinician says, "This is the anniversary of your brother's suicide . . . an important day." The client says, "No, that was last month."
- *Trivializing via excessive universalizing.* The clinician can make the client feel that a uniquely painful situation is being trivialized as just one of a hundred similar instances: "Lots of people feel that way." "You're not alone." "I know lots of women who have lost their husbands."
- *Mistaking personal sharing for empathy.* The clinician shares an experience similar to the client's with the intention of empathizing, but takes the focus away from the client's story: "I've been there myself." "That happened to me and I know how you must feel." "When my father died, I . . ."
- *No clinician response.* The clinician who is not following closely may miss important moments when an empathic response is sorely needed. The absence of a response at a crucial moment (for example, the clinician simply says "Hmmm" or leaves a silence) can be experienced as a lack of interest.

There is an increased likelihood of empathic misses when the client and clinician come from different ethnic or sociocultural backgrounds (Comas-Diaz & Jacobsen, 1991; Derald Sue & Sue, 2008). Even within the same cultural or ethnic group, people can act on faulty assumptions or generalizations. Empathic failures can also occur when the clinician overidentifies with or idealizes the client or feels some antipathy toward the client. In addition, empathic misses may occur when the client is particularly difficult or when the client demeans, attacks, or sabotages the clinician.

Psychodynamic theorists postulate a process called **countertransference,** in which the clinician unconsciously sees the client as representative of an important figure from the past and behaves toward the client as though the client *were* that person. Countertransference distortion negatively affects the clinician's ability to be empathic because empathy requires the ability to accurately perceive and join with the client's perspective. We discuss the psychodynamic concepts of transference and countertransference in greater detail in Chapter 11.

Clinicians should make use of detailed process recordings, video and audio recordings, supervision, and role-play with colleagues to become aware of, understand, and ideally to change personal feelings, beliefs, and reactions that interfere with empathy and caring.

Group supervision is very useful in the mutual sharing and spotting of overidentifications, scapegoating, aversions, and other behaviors that negatively affect clinician empathy. Personal therapy is highly recommended when clinicians continue to have problems with caring, sustainment, and empathy. Those continuing to have serious difficulties with empathy over time may need to conclude that clinical work is not a suitable undertaking for them.

Learning from Empathic Failures

Even when our reflections of content and affect are misguided or wrong, attending to the errors can be extremely important in modeling for clients that mistakes can occur without destroying relationships. Both client and clinician are reminded that the important step in maintaining connection is not the perfection of the participants but the work of sorting things out together in a mutually trusting and accepting bond.

Mutuality is heightened when the client gets to educate and correct the clinician about what was actually said or what is happening between them. The customary power imbalance in clinical work is somewhat mitigated through this two-way feedback. We listen for empathic failures, acknowledge them with grace, and thank clients for their patience, reactions, and feedback as we correct our course.

EXAMPLE OF EMPATHIC FAILURE AND CORRECTION

Client: My child has gone off to college. It's really a change in my life.

Clinician: You must feel very sad now that your last child has left home.

Client: Not really. I actually feel relieved to finally have time to spend on myself.

Clinician: So you don't feel sad. You feel relieved, and perhaps excited, that there are new opportunities for you.

Client: Yeah, it *is* very exciting.

I was seeing a client who had been abruptly let go from her company during a downsizing. She said she was incredibly anxious. I started to reflect how worried she must be about economic issues—how she would pay the rent, where she would get a new job, etc. We spent almost the whole session talking about that. The next week, she came in and said that what really had been bothering her was how other people would perceive her. I had missed the point of her anxiety. I immediately acknowledged that I had been thinking that she was worried about money when she was worried about something else. At first, I felt bad. Later, my supervisor pointed out that it was great that she corrected me. I didn't have to be perfect. I had created an atmosphere where she felt comfortable telling me when I was wrong. We really were a team working together. I was trying and she was helping me really understand her.

■ Conclusion

In this chapter, we reviewed two basic elements that sustain clinical work: support and empathy. We communicate support through a reliable clinical presence that provides genuine warmth, caring, acceptance, and validation and that affirms client strengths. We also demonstrate support by being available, by providing concrete services, and by advocating with and for clients.

Empathy is the ability to join the perspective and experience of the client— to feel *with and as* the client while maintaining the position of a centered, observing, and communicating other. Clinical empathy can be expressed through supportive sounds, mirroring, and empathic reflection of content and affect. However, as we saw in the clinical examples, clinicians may not be empathic, and attempts at empathy may fail. The conscientious clinician uses every opportunity to develop and sustain the clinical relationship. By applying our empathic skills socially and globally, we can align ourselves with disadvantaged and oppressed people and join with other activists in attempting to change the awful conditions in which so many people live.

In the next chapter, we discuss methods clinicians use to help clients further elaborate their stories and experience their strengths.

■ Suggested Readings

This is a classic work on the helping relationship:

Rogers, Carl. (1957). The necessary and sufficient conditions of therapeutic personality change. *Journal of Consulting Psychology, 21,* 95–103.

There are a number of excellent works on the process and complications of empathy, including the following:

Coleman, Daniel. (2000). The therapeutic alliance in multicultural practice. *Psychoanalytic Social Work, 7,* 65–90.

Comas-Diaz, Lillian, & Jacobsen, Frederick M. (1991). Ethnocultural transference and countertransference in the therapeutic dyad. *American Journal of Orthopsychiatry, 61,* 392–402.

Jordan, Judith V. (1991b). Empathy and self-boundaries. In Judith V. Jordan, Alexandra G. Kaplan, Jean Baker Miller, Irene P. Stiver, & Janet L. Surrey (Eds.), *Women's growth in connection: Writings from the Stone Center* (pp. 67–80). New York: Guilford Press.

Neumann, Melanie, Bensing, Jozien, Mercer, Stewart, Ernstmann, Nicole, Ommen, Oliver, & Pfaff, Holger. (2009). Analyzing the "nature" and "specific effectiveness" of clinical empathy: A theoretical overview and contribution towards a theory-based research agenda. *Patient Education and Counseling, 74,* 339–346.

Pedersen, Paul B., Crethar, Hugh C., & Carlson, Jon. (2008). *Inclusive cultural empathy: Making relationships central in counseling and psychotherapy.* Washington, DC: American Psychological Association.

Robb, Christina (2007). *This changes everything: The relational revolution in psychology.* New York: Picador-Ferrar, Straus & Giroux.

■ Self-Explorations

1. What are your thoughts about physical touching in the clinical relationship? How has touching been handled in your family? Are people physically affectionate? How about outside your family? Do people pat each other on the back, hug hello, touch each other in sympathy or in humorous exchanges? Is your culture a "touchy" culture? Do friends touch each other? What about strangers?

2. Make a list of your personal strengths. How important are they to you? How did you learn that each was a strength? Was writing down your strengths easy or hard to do? What familial and cultural messages came up for you as you thought about your own strengths?

3. Sometimes it is hard for the clinician to be fully present with the client and attend to his or her story because of uncomfortable feelings that arise when discussing certain subjects. Do any topics make you uncomfortable or cause you to have difficulty being empathic? What are they? Why are they difficult for you?

■ Essay Questions

1. What are the advantages and disadvantages of clinicians working with people who are similar and dissimilar to themselves? What are (1) the advantages of working with someone similar, (2) the disadvantages of working with someone similar, (3) the advantages of working with someone different, and (4) the disadvantages of working with someone different? Which would be hardest for you and why?

2. Discuss some of the things that may get in the way of a clinician's acceptance of a client. What kinds of things should clinicians do when they find it hard to be supportive of a client?

3. Empathy is key to the development of the clinical relationship. Define *empathy* and discuss the three components of empathy described in the text.

4. Do you think it is permissible under any circumstance to lend a client money, offer a client a ride, or cosign a document for a client? When and why? What might be the potential downside of offering such concrete support?

5. Discuss the factors that should be taken into account when deciding whether to extend extra time, appointments, or phone calls to clients. Do you have any examples from your own experiences of "going beyond the usual" with a client?

■ Key Terms

Advanced empathy	Overidentification
Advocacy	Perspective taking
Clinical repose	Projection
Congruence	Reflection of affect
Countertransference	Reflection of content
Culture-bound syndromes	Societal norms
Empathic echo	Supportive sounds
Empathic failures	Synchrony
Empathy	Unconditional positive regard
Holding environment	Universalizing
Inclusive cultural empathy	Validation
Mirroring	

CHAPTER 6

Exploration and Elaboration

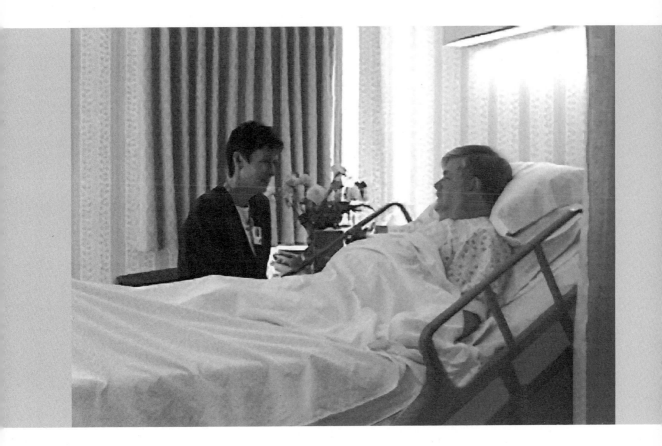

Supportive ambiance and empathy alone are not sufficient to help clients grasp their situations and bring about the changes they desire in themselves or in their lives. In the following chapters, we explore a variety of ways clinicians work together with clients to create change: using exploration, developing hunches and new perspectives, changing old behaviors and learning new ones, using the clinical relationship as a venue for change, and moving to action. In this chapter, we discuss how clinicians can deepen the level of conversation by helping clients explore and elaborate on their stories.

◼ Levels of Exploration and Elaboration

Few narratives, especially ones shared with a relative stranger, emerge full-blown all on their own. In addition to creating a supportive relationship, safe space, and congenial tone, the clinician uses the techniques and strategies of exploration and elaboration to elicit and expand on the story. In **exploration** the clinician gathers initial information through the use of questions, prompts, and probes. In **elaboration** the clinician encourages the client to expand on and enrich the details of the story.

Exploration and elaboration help both clinicians and clients. They help clinicians gather new information, clarify ambiguities or uncertainties, raise new issues, and attain a deeper and more accurate understanding of the client. They help clients expand their stories, note and elucidate their meanings, and develop new perspectives. Exploration and elaboration are important to every aspect of clinical work. They are central to the assessment process as clinicians clarify and prioritize presenting problems and assets. However, exploration and elaboration are not limited to the assessment phase; they are also crucial in establishing working agreements and in planning and implementing interventions.

Arnold Lazarus (1981) was the first to describe the layers, or circles, of personal territory. He suggested that people keep their most private thoughts in an inner circle, shared with few others. Dusty Miller (1996) further proposes that the interview conversation itself has outer, middle, and inner layers or circles. The *outer circle* houses the opening—sometimes surface—exploratory conversation between people who are just getting to know each other. Outer circle exploration occurs early in the interview, as the client is assessing the clinician's trustworthiness, respectfulness, and reliability. The goals of this outer level of exploration are to develop knowledge of the presenting situation and to establish a relationship of trust and collaboration by talking about subjects that do not push the client too quickly into forbidden or overly distressing topics. It focuses on clarifying the reasons for referral, eliciting the strengths and vulnerabilities of the client and his or her systems, fleshing out client demographics, and spelling out interviewer–client roles and agreements on how to proceed.

The *middle circle* houses a more revealing exploration of deeper-level content, conflicts, and feelings as the relationship develops and both the client and the interviewer feel themselves on more secure ground. A shift to the middle circle involves more focused exploration, which may elicit more painful detail, reflection, and affect. Here the clinician may begin to raise topics not yet broached or elaborated on by the client. Whereas the earlier focus often tends to be more about information, middle circle exploration usually elicits more complicated feelings and meanings. Often, more is shared about significant or previously undisclosed behavior patterns, relationship issues, and situation dynamics.

The *inner circle* houses feelings and content about frightening, taboo, or shame-bound areas. This level of exploration brings people into areas of the story that may have been previously unshared with others or that may have been unknown even to the clients themselves. At this level of conversation, clients often discover things about themselves and their relationships with others about which they previously have been unaware. Often a good deal of embarrassment, reluctance, hesitation, and confusion is manifest at this level. Only after trust and talking are well established do most people risk the maximum exposure of the inner circle.

The following examples demonstrate outer, middle, and inner circles of conversation in response to clinician probes. Although the clinician's questions and the client's responses all move from outer to inner circles, often the client's responses have more to do with where the participants are in the interview or in the relationship than with the specific questions the clinician asks. Family and cultural norms about sharing personal information or material that might shame the client also affect the client's willingness to disclose information (Chan & Lee, 2004; Sharifzadeh, 2004).

EXAMPLES

Outer Circle Talk

Clinician: Can you tell me something about your work?

Client: I work as a painter for a large painting company. I'm the supervisor for a crew of four. I like the outdoor activity and being my own boss.

Middle Circle Talk

Clinician: You mentioned things you like . . . are there things you don't like?

Client: Well, I find it hard to be the boss sometimes. I'm not really comfortable telling people what to do. I hate it when someone screws up and I have to get after them.

Inner Circle Talk

Clinician: Where do you think this "hating to get after people" comes from?

Client: I always hated being bossed around myself. I was the youngest boy in the family, and my four older brothers were always on my case. I guess I feel that I never want to come across as a bully and make people feel as bad as I did. I never thought about that before. . . . It's weird how something that happened when I was a kid could affect me at work today.

Levels of conversation and exploration are not discrete, and they do not appear in neat sequences, one right after the other. More often, clinicians and clients subtly shift between levels within each interview and from interview to interview. Most interviews begin at the outer circle to "warm up" participants to further exploration and discussion and then move, when they are comfortable, to deeper levels of elaboration. Inner circles of communication usually are not reached until a level of trust has been established between the participants. It is not unusual for clinical interviews to stay at the outer and middle circles for several sessions. In fact, some clinical relationships stay almost entirely at the outer and middle circles and still get very important work done. In addition, a client may be able to work at inner circle levels on topic A, but only outer circle levels on topic B.

The depth and intensity of exploration should always be guided by the clinician's awareness of cultural norms, customs, and taboos. Lum notes Ramon Valle's (1980) suggestion that clinicians spend some start-up time in friendly conversation, or *platica,* when working with Latino clients:

> Latinos are accustomed to mutual extended discussion, which is a recognized form of relationship building. "Platica" stresses mutuality and reciprocity, meaning an open and free exchange of information between two parties. Helper-initiated friendly conversation about the weather, humorous incidents, or recent activities sets the stage for development of a relationship. (Lum, 2004, p. 153)

During times of crisis, when the time available is limited or the need for prompt intervention is urgent, both clinicians and clients may move rapidly to inner circle conversation without necessarily building the relationship first. Such accelerated exploration often occurs in mandated protective service evaluations; for example, a child's insufficiently explained burns, an elderly woman's black eye and broken arm, or the delusion of a person with mental illness that he is flying between buildings may all be cause for more direct, persistent exploration to protect people from further harm.

Other clients may also move quickly to inner circle conversation, believing that this is what "therapy" is all about and pushing ahead without sufficient awareness of the impact that too much self-disclosure may have on them. At some point in their careers, almost all clinicians have seen the results of rushing into inner circle conversation: overwhelmed clients canceling for a period of time or never coming back, feeling too exposed. We need to be aware that, while frequently the goal of clinical work may be to deepen the level of conversation, deepening is only one goal among many. An equally important goal is to maintain the safety of the clinical experience so that clients do not feel overwhelmed by revealing too much too soon. Usually, we also try to move the conversation to the middle or outer circles before the interview ends, so that clients are not left feeling overwhelmed or exposed as they return to their community roles and responsibilities.

> A mentor told me never to do emotional surgery on people if what they needed was a transfusion, and never to do emotional surgery in the session without leaving enough time to suture the client back up before leaving, so they don't go out alone and have an emotional bleed with no tourniquet in sight.

It is important to note that beginning clinicians often confuse "going deep" with succeeding as an interviewer. In reality, good clinical interviewing can occur even when the interview does not move beyond the outer circle of conversation. The purpose and goals of the contact, as well as the time and resources available, usually have a great influence on the level and duration of clinical conversations. Success is most often measured by the realization of agreed-upon aims and goals, not by the number of painful subjects covered. Indeed, the thoughtful clinician tries to introduce momentary **intervals of respite** into intense exploratory conversation, carefully helping clients move back and forth between deep immersion and more detached review. Respite protects the client from being overwhelmed and allows the clinician to check in with the client to ensure that the process feels okay to continue.

> *Lupe came into the Rape Crisis Center for her second interview after being assaulted at her high school homecoming party. This time she did not hold back and talked for almost 20 minutes straight, graphically describing the attack, and with a whole lot of crying. This was a different girl than I saw last time, and I think she would have cried and talked the whole time if I hadn't stopped her. At about 20 minutes, I asked if we could stop for a minute so she could catch her breath and check in with me about how it was to share all this with me. First she cried quietly for a time. Then she let out a huge sigh. She held herself and rocked a little. I said we could take our time; there was lots of time for the story to come out. She said she wasn't used to talking so much and apologized for "making me listen to all this." I said this is what we're here for, so women can speak out in safety. She nodded and leaned back against the wall. She said she didn't know what she would have done without this place. In a bit, she described a nightmare no one else wanted to hear.*

The rest of this chapter focuses on techniques clinicians can use to help clients explore or elaborate their stories and move, when appropriate, between conversational levels or circles.

■ Techniques of Exploration and Elaboration

A number of techniques can be used in exploration and elaboration. The most useful are questions, prompts, silence, reflection (including underlining and summarizing), refocusing, and initiating new topics.

Questions and Questioning

Asking questions is one of the most reliable and effective techniques for gathering information, deepening discussion, or broadening focus. Clinicians ask questions about:

- The client's thoughts, feelings, behaviors, and relationships.
- The client's strengths and resources.
- The client's cultural identities, beliefs about help seeking and about what causes problems and how they may be resolved.
- Other people in the client's life (what the client reports that other people feel, think, or do).
- The client's circumstances and the larger social contexts within which the client interacts, with attention to any effects of discrimination, bias, or other forms of oppression.
- The client's reactions to the clinician, to experiences in the clinical relationship and the agency, and to former counseling or other services received.

In general, interviewers routinely ask more questions in the engagement and assessment phases of work than later on. The aim is to elicit a working sketch of the story and its participants, as well as their strengths, resources, and stressors, as guides for more immediate decision making and planning. The use of many questions early on is particularly prevalent in managed care settings and brief treatment work, in which engagement, assessment, planning, and intervention all occur in the first contact. Historically, detailed early questioning has also characterized crisis intervention work, such as protective service evaluations and emergency room interviews (see Chapter 12). A lot of gentle questioning often occurs in initial contacts with clients who present for help but have difficulty expressing themselves.

Asking questions may seem to the novice interviewer an easy, even routine, matter. In reality, asking appropriate and timely questions is one of the hardest clinical skills to master. Good questioning requires sensitivity to where the client is; exquisite timing as to the fit between the question, the moment, and the people present; and conscious self-containment to avoid asking numerous tangential questions that may readily come to mind.

Beginning interviewers frequently either ask too many questions (to fill out mandatory forms or because they do not yet know what else to do) or ask too few (because they feel intrusive in asking or feel embarrassed to go more deeply into sensitive or forbidden areas). They can also delve too soon into personal questions before a relationship is established or cultural norms about self-disclosure are clarified, thus appearing disrespectful or rude.

Attitudes toward questioning are often influenced by family and cultural norms and taboos. For example, clients and clinicians both may have been taught that asking personal questions is prying. Again, it is essential that clinicians become familiar not only with the communication norms and styles of the many different cultural and social groups with which we work, but also our own. Hilary Weaver (2005) notes that Native American clients may feel more comfortable and responsive if the clinician demonstrates cultural sensitivity and uses self-disclosure before asking personal questions. Many cultures still educate members not to share feelings with outsiders, not to discuss conflicts outside the family, and not to disclose in-group information that could damage group members or weaken group cohesion (Derald Sue & Sue, 2008; Dwairy, 2009).

Our own attitudes toward questioning are similarly influenced by our upbringing, education, and life experiences. Clinical theories vary regarding the importance of questioning, and some mentors and supervisors encourage active exploration by the clinician, whereas others do not.

General Principles Regarding the Use of Questioning

1. **Questions should be intentional.**   Clinicians should know why they are asking what they are asking. Clinical questions always have to have a purpose, and we should always be aware of the possible effects that each question might have on the client.

2. **Clients should know why questions are being asked and how the answers will be used.**   Joe and Malach (2004) suggest that clinicians convey clearly to clients why particular questions will be asked, what the nature of these

questions will be, and how answers to them will be helpful in designing appropriate services. They also believe clinicians should invite clients' questions about them or any aspect of the process. Clients should be told that they are free to consult with family members before answering questions. Joe and Malach's discussion of practice principles is for use with Native Americans, but we believe that their advice is widely applicable to respectful work with all clients. In addition, we like to tell clients that they can decline to answer any question that does not feel right to them.

3. *Clinicians need to be sensitive to cultural attitudes toward questioning.* Every culture, and most families, inculcate norms regarding who can ask what, of whom, in what order, and which questions should be asked only in private or without certain members present. It is imperative that clinicians develop cultural sensitivity and competence in asking questions regarding such subjects as race, class, sex, money, religious beliefs and practices, serious illnesses, addictions, and family violence. Barbara Okun and her colleagues (Okun, Fried, & Okun, 1999) observe that North Americans are used to "telling it all, exploring it all" even with relative strangers, while many of the world's cultures find this diving-in style shockingly intrusive. Because members of the family or culture are the most expert interpreters of their own meaning systems, they should be asked directly about preferred customs and styles in providing the needed information to outsiders such as clinicians.

4. *Questions should be well timed.* Clinicians should know why they are asking what they are asking *now*—at this particular time in the interview. The clinician must think about whether it is possible to get the same information by another means that will not disrupt client flow; often it is simply a matter of waiting for the client to disclose more information.

5. *Too much questioning makes the clinician the director.* Gentle guidance and data-gathering questions are inevitable in emergencies and in initial sessions with clients not used to clinical work. As the work evolves, the clinician wants the client's thinking and voice to strengthen through maximum encouragement, participation, expression, and initiation of topic or focus. Too many clinician initiatives lessen this potential for strengthening.

6. *Questions can interrupt concentration.* Although questions are often necessary and helpful, every question, no matter how well intended, interrupts the natural flow of the client's narrative. If the client is already elaborating useful detail, avoid intruding because you have been wanting to ask something. Instead, continue to attend and wait for a natural break. Few things are more maddening than attempting to tell something to another person and being constantly interrupted by questions that throw the narrator off track.

7. *Flexibility in data gathering is essential.* Sometimes clinicians are forced to ask lots of questions immediately to get the information necessary to make decisions by the end of the meeting. Even in such a situation, we may alter a planned agenda if the client sits down and bursts into tears, comes in and starts shouting, or describes an impending crisis or a personal success. Usually, we explore briefly what is happening rather than abruptly refocusing the conversation to get the planned questions asked.

Data gathering to fill out required forms should come only after showing concern and support for the client, and a data-gathering agenda should always give precedence to situational or psychological emergencies. Clients are more likely to broaden or deepen their stories when they feel calm, safe, and understood. However, we realize that in fast paced medical or mental health settings, filling out numerous forms in order to ensure services can sideline or delay a person-situation focus.

> *I had to ask a woman to complete insurance forms even though she was sobbing because she had just learned she had kidney failure. A doctor was breathing down my neck because no further services could be delivered until the paperwork was done.*

In such situations, the clinician might say "I know we don't know each other well and it's hard to answer a lot of questions right off the bat. But this paperwork is required for agency services and insurance purposes and we have to get it done today. It can get a little tedious, so please try to bear with me. However, we can take a break if you need to—just let me know."

8. *Good questions can be supportive and therapeutic, as well as useful for gathering data.*   Questioning can serve many purposes: to help the client expand the story, to gain new perspectives, to provide more information, or to clarify ambiguity for the clinician. Questions can also be used to support or underline client strengths or to reflect empathy. For example, "How have you managed so much at once?" is both a real question and an affirmation of client strength. "You are showing remarkable courage. What helps you hold up through this long court process?" performs a validating function, as does a question such as "You mean there's even more that's happened to you?"

9. *Difficult questions should be introduced carefully.*   Kadushin and Kadushin (1997) suggest that the impact of difficult questions can be mitigated by the use of prefaces or lead-ins that help clients save face, that "universalize problems," or that "raise a client's self-esteem in preparation for dealing with a question which is apt to be self-deflating" (p. 261). For example, you might preface a question by saying: "So many moms have told me they feel alone and pushed to the wall when they strike out at their children. What were you feeling before you hit Kendra Lee?"

10. *Too little questioning can make for drift or leave the client at a loss for direction.*   Although an interview can be conducted without the clinician asking a single question, sometimes we may need to help a new, unfocused, or disorganized client by asking gentle questions in plain language, designed to keep things on track when the client starts to wander. A new client may start to talk about her worries about being a mother for the first time, then describe a new mother she saw on TV, then talk about how much cable TV costs, and then talk about the things she watches on cable in the evening when the baby is asleep. Although none of these subjects is "bad" and all are pieces of information about the client and her experience, the goals of the session determine to what degree the clinician reintroduces the original topic by gently asking questions that redirect the client to it.

Clinicians may also need to ask questions for purposes of clarification or to get more information. Too little questioning can occur when the clinician thinks personal questions are becoming too intrusive or does not want the client to feel pushed too soon to reveal difficult material. At other times, we may not ask questions for fear of seeming unempathic ("If I ask a question, she'll think I haven't been following closely and have forgotten her details"). Sometimes the clinician's own unresolved issues may prevent the timely exploration of personally sensitive material.

> *My supervisor urged me and urged me, but I just could not ask that lady more details about her divorce right then, and I wasn't ready to have my supervisor or others at work know I was splitting up with my wife then, in much the same way my client was split- ting up with her husband. I would go into each session with a plan to ask Ms. Morales more about what had happened, and somehow, the time would just zoom by and it would be the end of the session and I hadn't asked her.*

11. *Follow-up questions are often necessary.* Clinicians need to stay with a line of inquiry long enough to mine it sufficiently for details about content, meaning, or feelings. Sometimes we should ask more follow-up questions regarding something the client has said, but we do not. Sometimes clinicians feel they should know the answer or may have been told the answer before and are embarrassed not to have remembered it. Sometimes they are embar- rassed to ask clients what they mean, fearing to appear ignorant when in the not-knowing position.

12. *Clinician questions can be both verbal and nonverbal.* Raising an eye- brow, cocking one's head, responding wide-eyed to statements—these and many other lighthearted responses of the clinician can act as questions to which the client can respond immediately and with goodwill. Such clinician responses represent a warmer, less formal style of probing, and they are best used in the context of a solidly established working relationship. Otherwise clients new to counseling might feel teased or made fun of by facial gestures that they are not familiar with or that may be culturally inappropriate.

13. *Answers to questions can be both verbal and nonverbal.* Clinicians need to listen to both the verbal and nonverbal answers of clients. Sometimes there are discrepancies between the verbal and the nonverbal. Any discrepancies in clients' answers are stored away as potentially important pieces of informa- tion for possible future exploration. We also listen for discrepancies between clients' stated intentions (e.g., "I'm going to AA every night next week") and their actual behaviors, which can be known only over time, through explora- tion (e.g., "I only got there once").

14. *Clinicians need to attend to apparent patterns and themes that emerge in client answers to questions.* For example, the repeated exclamation "Am I stupid or what?!" following descriptions of habitual behaviors definitely should be explored further. So should statements like "There I go again" and "I can't believe I let that happen!"

15. *Clinicians need to be aware of what they are not asking.* Clients often notice clinician patterns just as we notice theirs. They often note—sometimes subliminally—which topics we do not ask about (such as racial and cultural differences, sex, money, or violence). It is not unusual for clients to protect us by not bringing up subjects about which we have shown uneasiness or

embarrassment. It is all too easy for us to say that clients are not talking about certain issues, only to discover through examination of process recordings or video recordings of sessions that *we* are not asking about the issues.

16. ***Questions can be used as defenses or weapons by both clinician and client.*** Questions can be used to diminish or shame the other so that the questioner feels more powerful. The following are examples of hostile questions that are not seeking the answer they appear to solicit.

"What is the point of all this?"

"Is this really what we're here to talk about?"

"Haven't you asked me that enough times?"

"Are you finished yet?"

"You mean you don't know after all this time what the Twelve Steps are?"

Closed-Ended and Open-Ended Questions

Questions can be closed-ended or open-ended. **Closed-ended questions** are the more focal of the two types and can usually be answered with a word or two, after which the client characteristically ceases talking and waits for the next question from the clinician. Closed-ended questions often begin with interrogatives such as "do you," "are you," or "have you" and hint at what the interviewer expects the response to be. In contrast, **open-ended questions** give the client more opportunity or flexibility in responding and elaborating. Because open-ended questions keep the client in the driver's seat of the conversation, we usually prefer them. These questions often begin with interrogatives like "what" or "how," but not necessarily.

EXAMPLES

Closed-ended: Do you live alone?

Open-ended: What is your living situation?

Closed-ended: Did that make you sad?

Open-ended: How did you feel about that?

Closed-ended: Did you hit him back?

Open-ended: What did you do then?
                What happened then?

In the last question, two different open-ended questions are offered. While both allow the client to elaborate the story of being hit by another person, the first is more directive in that it focuses specifically on the *client* and what he or she *did* in response. The second question is more nondirective and allows the client to proceed in any direction. The client could say what he or she did, what he or she felt, or what someone else did or felt.

EXERCISE 6.1 Opening Up Closed-Ended Questions

In small groups, take each of the following questions and think of several other ways you could phrase it as an open-ended question.

"Did that make you feel guilty?"

"Would you stay put or run if he threatened you?"

"Is our work together a help to you?"

"Are those tears telling me you are sad?"

"Are you relieved to have her gone?"

Problems with closed-ended questions. The use of closed-ended questions introduces a number of problems. First, these questions give the client little opportunity or encouragement to expand on the theme at hand because they often suggest single-word answers such as "yes," "maybe," or "no." Second, with closed-ended questions (as well as too many questions in a row), the clinician keeps the initiative, disempowering the client, who may quickly be conditioned to expect to answer just one question and passively await the next. Reducing the client to the role of mere respondent may inadvertently replicate the experience of far too many clients who historically have been made to feel that they are the objects rather than the subjects of their own lives and stories. Further, by establishing the clinician as expert, closed-ended questions may set up the expectation that, given the answers to the questions, we will be able to solve the client's problem.

Moreover, closed-ended questions often suggest the answer the interviewer expects or prefers—for example, "Did that make you mad?" "Was that when he hung up?" "Are you nervous about our meeting?" The client who sees the interviewer's preference within the question may feel worried about differing with the clinician's point of view or feel irritated by the clinician's "mind reading." In the preceding example, the question "Did you hit him back?" could convey to the client that hitting back is what the clinician thinks the client would or should have done when hit.

At times, though, clinicians *need* to use closed-ended questions. Such questions are essential when agency routine or necessity requires that the clinician get a great deal of information in a very short time to determine immediate eligibility for needed services. We may go through a symptom checklist ("Do you have any sleep problems?"), a benefits enrollment form ("Do you have other sources of income we haven't covered?"), or an emergency room family history ("Has anyone in your family had problems with alcohol?"). Also, closed-ended questions can be imperative in establishing clear assessment understanding ("Are you thinking of hurting yourself?").

Furthermore, if someone is rambling agitatedly or is getting out of control with fear or confusion, a series of organizing closed-ended questions often provides much-needed structure and calming.

EXAMPLE OF PURPOSEFUL QUESTIONS

Closed-Ended Questions

Clinician: Do you have a place to sleep tonight, Aaron?

Client: No, no! Do I look like I have any place?

Clinician: Is there anyone I can call to let know you're okay?

Client: Nobody. I don't want nobody to know . . .

Clinician: Do you have any money to buy dinner?

Client: No . . . I'm flat out.

Clinician: If you're hungry, I can get you a voucher for a cafeteria meal.

Client [relaxes and sits back]: Okay . . . I could stand something hot for a change. Could somebody go with me, though? This is my first time here . . .

Clinician: Can you sit here with me while I make a couple of calls to find a shelter bed for you? Then I can go with you to the cafeteria.

Client: Yep . . .

EXERCISE 6.2 Interviewing Using Questions

Divide into teams of three. Person A is the interviewer, person B the interviewee, and person C the observer. The interviewer asks the interviewee about his or her day. The observer notes all the questions and reviews them to see how many were open-ended and how many were closed-ended. Switch roles. This time the interviewer uses only closed-ended questions. In the final round, switch roles again and use only open-ended questions. Discuss anything from this exercise that you want to keep in mind when asking questions. Record what you learned in your journal.

Tried-and-True Questions

Certain questions remain useful over many decades of experience. Easily and directly, they just seem to get at the things we need to know to assess, plan, and act wisely in our clinical roles.

EXAMPLES OF TRIED-AND-TRUE QUESTIONS

Reason for coming: What brings you here to see me?

Timing of request: Why are you seeking help now?

Anticipation of the experience: How did you think I might help?

Client as the driver: What would you like to accomplish today?

Client as the driver: Where would you like to begin?

Elaboration of person-situation information: Can you tell me more about your situation?

Support network: Who else is available as a support or help in this?

Situation dynamics: Who, if anyone, is making things more complicated just now?

Previous experience with professionals: Have you ever spoken with a professional before? If so, how did it go?

Elaboration: Are there other things you haven't mentioned yet that would be important for me to know?

Concretizing the desired outcome: What will we look for to know that the changes you want have actually taken place?

Exploring the influence of others on participation: What do people say about your coming to talk with me?

Checking-in: What's it like for you to be talking about these things with me?

Checking-in: Is the work moving in the way you hoped it would?

Checking-in: How does the work we're doing compare with what you thought it would be like?

Checking-in: Is the pace we're going at okay for you?

Checking-in: Would you let me know if, at any time, we go too fast or get into things you're not comfortable talking about?

Clarifying: Does what I'm saying make sense?

Not knowing: Could you put that in other words so I can understand it better?

Elaboration: Can you say more about that?

Problematic Types of Questions

"Why" questions can be problematic because they often sound judgmental—and they often are. "Why did you do that?" may leave the client feeling defensive. "Why do you feel that way?" can leave clients wondering if their feelings are strange or unnatural. Although at times asking clients to think about motives for their behaviors or feelings might be helpful, we have found that "why" questions rarely work. We prefer to use phrases such as, "What do you make of that?" or "What do you think caused it?" or "As you look back, what do you think was going on?"

Pseudoquestions are often directives or commands disguised as questions. For example, a parent who says, "Are you going to do your homework now?" really means "It's time to do your homework." A clinician who begins a session with the question, "Did you want to pick up where we left off last time?" is actually saying, "Let's pick up where we left off last time."

Double questions occur when we ask the client to respond to more than one question at a time. A confused look on the client's face often indicates uncertainty as to which question to address. Double and even triple questions are not unusual in the interviews of newcomers to clinical work, and occasionally these forms of questions show up in the work of experienced clinicians as well.

EXAMPLES OF DOUBLE QUESTIONS

Clinician A: Tell me about your week. How are the kids doing in school? What's going on at work?

Clinician B: So, are you feeling more depressed? Are you having fights?

Tangential questions veer from the main topic, taking side roads without good reason. These occur when the clinician either is curious about an unrelated detail or does not have a clear focus or direction in mind. The clinician who goes off on too many tangents can create an aura of hopping around aimlessly or of being superficial.

EXAMPLES OF TANGENTIAL QUESTIONS

Client A: I've had the hardest day! We're putting out a new computer program, and everybody was so stressed out.

Clinician A: What kind of computer program is it?

Client B: My mother's new boyfriend moved in with us last week. I don't like him very much.

Clinician B: What day did he move in?

Ratatat questioning barrages the client with one rapid-fire question after another. The questions often impart pressure and do not leave time for in-depth exploration. They may all be on one topic, or they may shift from topic to topic so that no subject is pursued long enough to develop any real depth or meaning. Again, the tone of the meeting is one of superficiality; it seems to lack a clear direction or interest on the clinician's part.

EXAMPLE OF RATATAT QUESTIONING

Note that these ratatat questions are all closed-ended as well.

Clinician: Where did you go to high school?

Client: Sacred Heart.

Clinician: When was that?

Client: Sixty-three.

Clinician: Was it a big school?

Client: Pretty big. I was . . .

Clinician: Did you date while you were there?

Client: Not really.

Clinician: And after that, did you date . . . later on, I mean?

I told my supervisee that I thought she was covering so many subjects in her interviews that it didn't give clients enough time to really get into anything in depth. She didn't agree, so I asked her to videotape her next client session and then watch the interview with a tablet handy so she could count up the number of new subjects introduced by her questions. She was astonished to find that she had asked 37 questions in 45 minutes and had covered a wide array of subjects. She was surprised by both the number of questions she asked and the number of topics introduced.

EXERCISE 6.3 Asking Hard Questions

Break up into small groups and list topics that you personally find difficult to explore. Practice asking the other members of your group two questions about one of your least comfortable topics, those that you would find hard to ask a client. Give each other feedback to assist in reconstructing questions or style so that the questions come across more comfortably. Did your questions elicit what you anticipated? Record what you learned in your journal.

Prompts

Prompts are brief responses by the clinician that encourage the client to continue with the story or to add to what has been said. Prompts are often given in the form of questions or brief utterances that pick up on the client's last remarks. Prompts are meant to be minimal and to signal the clinician's close following of the story and interest in details. Some clients respond well to prompts; others may prefer that the clinician just sit quietly and listen unobtrusively.

Silence

The clinician's judicious use of silence can help the client explore and elaborate. Although silence can be uncomfortable for both the clinician and the client, sometimes the best way to encourage clients to tell their story is simply to leave room for it to unfold. Clients may use silences to reflect on what has been said, to make choices about where to take the story next, or to experience reactions to what is happening in the moment. Sometimes they may simply not know what to do or say next. If the clinician is too quick or too active in ending a silence, clients—especially those whose experience has already undermined initiative—may be conditioned to sit and wait for the clinician to direct the process.

The meaning of silence and comfort with silence are culturally based. Chan and Lee (2004) note that "in most cultures throughout the world, individuals *start* talking when they have to; Americans, instead, tend to *stop* talking when they have to" (p. 272). Sharifzadeh (2004) notes that, for those from Middle Eastern cultures, "what is left unsaid is as important as what is said" (p. 405).

Reflection

In addition to helping build empathy (see Chapter 4), reflection can also be used in exploration and elaboration. It can be used as a probe to encourage the client to explore a specific area further. Reflection avoids the problems of too much questioning. Rather than asking a direct question, the clinician can indicate a line of inquiry by reflecting back a specific part of the content or affect in the client's story, thus encouraging continued discussion. Carl Rogers, the founder of person-centered counseling, was a master at using reflection, prompts, and silences to help his clients elaborate and expand on their stories.

Client: You know, I'm not feeling bad for a man of fifty. I have my health, an okay relationship with my wife—although she wouldn't agree. My best buddy just died, but I still hang out with a great group of guys. We go bowling every Friday.

Clinician A: You're feeling that your relationship with your wife is "okay," but you don't think she'd agree.

Clinician B: Your best friend just recently died.

In the **dot-dot-dot reflection** technique, the clinician simply repeats back the last thing said and hangs it, unfinished, in midair for the client to complete. Dot-dot-dot is a very useful technique in any conversation when the client loses track for a moment. It is an unfinished sentence of reflection that, if written out, would appear as triple dots (. . .) indicating an invitation to complete the sentence.

EXAMPLES OF DOT-DOT-DOT REFLECTION

"You came home, fed the puppies, and then you . . ."

"You were saying that after you got your GED, you would . . ."

"First we talk about Glen; then we . . .

Underlining is a special form of reflection. The clinician underscores important content or experience by the strategic use of verbal or nonverbal emphasis. This emphasis is often rendered through tone of voice, facial expression, or emphatic gesture.

EXAMPLES OF UNDERLINING

"So you *did* talk to your partner after all."

"You felt *angry* that your sister didn't lend you the money."

"But I *want* you to give me feedback on this work."

In **summarizing,** the clinician pulls together the major ideas, themes, or patterns that have just been discussed and reflects them to the client. Summarizing is a form of reflection in which the clinician sums up in condensed form what has just been discussed. In pure reflection, we usually repeat only one thing the client has just said. In summarizing, we usually reflect many ideas or themes. During the interview, summarizing can be used as a prompt to help the client further elaborate the story. At the end of the interview, summarizing can be used for closure.

EXAMPLE OF SUMMARIZING

Client: I don't know whether to adopt a baby from China or to wait on this list and try to get an American child. It could be years and I'm not getting any younger.

Clinician: Mm-hmm . . .

Client: My parents want me to wait for an American child. They say you never know the kind of experience a baby might have in overseas orphanages. You could be in for a lot of medical expenses.

Clinician: So they want you to wait?

Client: Yeah, but my friends are even worse. They say I shouldn't wait or I will be too old to handle a child. As it is, I'll be sixty by the time the child graduates from college.

Clinician: I see.

Client: Well, there are going to be layoffs at work, and some of my colleagues keep telling me I should be worried that I will lose my maternity benefits.

Clinician [summarizing]: So it sounds as if a lot of people have ideas about what you should do—your parents, your friends, and the women at work.

Client: Yeah, and what's important is that *I* figure out what *I* want.

CLIP 6.1
Questions,
Prompts, and
Probes

EXERCISE 6.4 Using Reflection Techniques to Explore

In small groups, experience what it is like to interview without using any questions. Each person uses only reflection techniques: prompts, dot-dot-dot, underlining, and summarizing. In the large group, discuss any advantages and disadvantages of using no questions when interviewing.

Refocusing

When the client has left a specific topic or theme that the clinician deems important, the clinician can use the technique of **refocusing:** returning the client to a desired topic by gently inserting it into the conversation again.

Sometimes clinicians interject when the client takes a breath, but sometimes we may just have to gently intrude upon a long stream of conversation in which no breaks are apparent.

In fast-paced managed care environments emphasizing brief clinical interventions, the need for highly focused interviewing assumes increasing importance. The clinical conversation focuses on the stated objectives of the interview. Comfort with refocusing assists in this effort, and this comfort can be developed only by using the technique under supervision. The following interjections can be useful in refocusing.

EXAMPLES OF REFOCUSING

"I'm wondering if we can get back to the topic of . . . ."

"Getting back to the requirements of your probation, do you have to . . . ?"

"Earlier we were talking about . . . ."

"Forgive me for interrupting, but I'm not clear what this has to do with our work on your sobriety."

"How is that related to the issue of . . . ?"

"Let's continue with what we were talking about earlier."

"Excuse me, but our time's almost up, and we haven't designed the next steps you wanted to map out today."

CLIP 6.2
Refocusing

Initiating New Topics

At times, clinicians follow the client. At other times, our acquired knowledge of human behavior and person-in-situation dynamics suggests potentially fruitful areas for further exploration not yet introduced by the client. The art of exploration involves learning (a) when to follow and just accompany the client on the journey unfolding and (b) when to introduce and explore new areas.

EXAMPLES OF INTRODUCING NEW TOPICS

"I realize I don't know anything about your relationships with your siblings."

"We haven't talked about how you handle your anger."

"We've discussed your home life but not much about work. Could we talk some about that today?"

■ Important Factors in Effective Exploration and Elaboration

Good exploration concerns itself with many complex issues. While seeming so easy at the outset, effective exploration calls for good timing. The clinician must also be sensitive to the client's tolerance level for both the topic and the depth of exploration, to the client's cognitive capacity and expressive style, and to the state of the clinical relationship. We need to accumulate knowledge of the many ways to encourage and elicit a story: how to use tried-and-true methods of exploration; how to ask questions in the client's language and style; how to maintain a "not-knowing perspective"; how to cushion intensive exploration with sustaining techniques; and how to appreciate and respond to client reluctance. Finally, we need to know when to stop pressing for more.

Sensitive Timing

Why am I asking this particular thing, at this particular moment, in the visit or the work?

Every clinician has had the experience of asking something that gets no response, that gets a look of puzzlement, or that goes over like a lead balloon. Typically, we say after the meeting, "I wish I had waited until the client brought that up herself" or "I wish I hadn't interrupted him with that question, which wasn't as important as what he was saying—it really threw him off."

Timing has to do with *what* and *how much to ask, when to ask it,* and *whom to ask.* Part of developing a timing instinct has to do with noticing how different people react to exploration and noticing which behaviors of the interviewer seem to broaden or deepen the conversation instead of shutting it down or causing undue discomfort. The sharing of personal information is framed and timed differently for everyone and is very much shaped by family and cultural norms and taboos. Chan and Lee (2004) speak of the need of Korean families to save face, maintaining the dignity, honor, and self-respect of the individual. "One must anticipate that a family member . . . will be reluctant to initially reveal 'vital' information if this will cause loss of face (Kim, 1996). The helping professional is cautioned against venturing into a frank discussion of specific problem areas too quickly" (p. 280).

Timing has to be considered in each interview, as well as across the sequence of all interviews. It is important to note from first contact how readily and under what circumstances clients share personal information and how accurately and realistically the story seems to be unfolding. Many clients indicate right away, by opening up or closing down, how they feel about questions and probing, and they signal what topics are easier or harder for them to explore. Their behavioral cues assist the clinician's judgments about the timing and dosage of further inquiry. Indeed, the cues can be used to focus further tentative exploration, as when, for example, the clinician might note that the client looks down and blushes anytime dating or sex is mentioned. The client may then elect to say more, to look down and blush again, or simply to stare at the clinician and await her lead. Each of the responses is useful new information.

An important challenge for the clinician is to notice the client's patterns and styles of responding to exploration and to watch carefully for what evolves *following* an exploration. A spontaneous deepening of conversation often indicates growing trust and readiness to share at a more personal level. More deepening or opening up of content or feelings often signals to the clinician that the timing is right to risk middle circle and inner circle exploration. The clinician has to attend carefully to the client's response to any question or probe, to be ready to pick up on the response, or just to store it away. Respect for a client's need to ebb and flow is imperative. No one is "on" all the time in clinical work—neither the clinician nor the client. Sometimes clients signal problems with the clinician's timing by saying things like, "You don't usually push me on stuff like this—you usually let me take my time. Why are you pushing me today?"

Even when trust and safety are well established and evidenced by increased client participation levels, certain material always proves relatively difficult to elicit and develop. Just which material proves difficult varies from person to person, culture to culture, and locale to locale. Again, clinicians should watch what evolves once exploration begins. Clients often manifest unreadiness to proceed with further exploration by protesting the need for it, questioning or criticizing the questioner, demeaning the topic, changing the subject, or abruptly cutting the session short.

> I remember Junior just getting up and walking out without a word when I brought up his wife's charging him with incest and asked his reaction to the charges. Later, he told me by phone that he found the question "shocking and disgusting" and that if that is what I think of him, then he would like to work with someone else in the program.

The State of the Clinical Relationship

> *Is the relationship strong and trusting enough to bear the questions I'm about to ask? Knowing this client, what is the most respectful way to explore this material?*

The level of trust and comfort between clinician and client greatly determines the timing and the substance of exploration. In a good working alliance, all that may be required for exploration is a supportive, empathic milieu and some initial broad questions that set the framework of the meetings. The client takes it from there, in his own style, at her own pace. But people new to each other have to feel each other out, testing for comfort and safety. For example, a lesbian client might not come out to her clinician until the latter has demonstrated trustworthiness and acceptance. The clinical encounter is a fishbowl in which both parties become known to each other in conscious and unconscious ways: the former by listening and watching, the latter by intuitive "radar" honed over years of human interaction. As we have seen, safe and sound work together gradually builds trust, ease, and synchrony.

Every relationship, however, has its ups and downs, and no less so the relationship between clinicians and clients. Clients may at any time balk or react to exploration in unaccustomed ways, perhaps because of increased outside stress or illness, unexpected behaviors on the part of the clinician, or misinterpretation of the clinician's intentions. New topics may suddenly reveal to both client and clinician an unexpected level of sensitivity, apprehension, or shame. Similarly, we may balk at material brought up by the client, leaving both parties feeling awkward and uncomfortable. No conversation just rolls along without stumbling points.

The ongoing work of a good relationship is first to acknowledge stumbling points and then sort through them together. Rough spots are not a disaster. In fact, they offer possibilities for relationship building and the deepening of conversation. The clinician may want to say simply, "Something's just happened. Let's stop a minute and talk about it. I think it's important not to just let it go by." Here the clinician demonstrates the value of examining the moment and models the skill of addressing things directly with great caring (see Chapter 11). Since clients seldom bring up perceived problems in the clinical relationship, Lambert and Barley (2002) believe that, early in the contact, "it is for therapists to inform clients that dialogue about the therapy relationship is a vital part of therapy and that expressions of negative feelings are allowed and appreciated" (p. 27).

The Client's Readiness to Explore Charged Areas

Will the material I am about to pursue make things better or worse for the client? If worse, whose interests are served by this inquiry?

As clinical conversations develop, all decisions about exploring charged areas are based on the cumulative assessment of the client's capacities, vulnerabilities, and tolerance for varied content and affects. Our overriding intent is to do nothing to harm or needlessly intrude on the client. For example, a time of increased client stress is not the preferred time to go on fishing expeditions into painful areas, stirring up themes or feelings that only add to the stress already besetting the client. Clinicians should be thinking about what is in the client's best interest at any given moment, weighing the appropriate challenge of new learning against its emotional price.

We prefer the gradual introduction of deeper-level exploration, carefully monitoring and often discussing the client's reactions to advancing exploration. We understand that both clients and clinicians can be traumatized by the detailed recounting of overwhelming stories (McCann & Pearlman, 1990), and we proceed carefully, always asking at the outset of each new session how the client experienced the last session, both right after the session and during the time since. Coping levels and resources (or the lack of them) give us important clues as to client readiness and capacity to continue exploring.

The Client's Cognitive Capacity and Expressive Style

Can I put this in her metaphor or language? How would he say it to me if our positions were reversed?

The kind of exploration and elaboration we do also depends on the client's intelligence, educational level, and cognitive capacities, including the accuracy of perception, reality testing, judgment, logic, abstract and concrete thinking, use of fantasy, insight, and general quickness of mind. Cognitive capacity can be affected by a lack of adequate nourishment, stimulation, soothing, and modeling; trauma; limited educational opportunity; and messages from others that thinking is dangerous. It can also be affected by stress levels, tiredness, biological dysfunction, and mood.

Always trying to "be where the client is," the clinician tries to frame prompts, reflections, and questions in a style that follows that of the client, insofar as this feels natural and appropriate to the participants. We generally try to avoid jargon and esoteric language, although we have sat in many meetings in which professionals seem to need to use such language to assert power or expertise. Some terminology may become so common among clinicians that we are not even aware that it is jargon. Still, we try to keep language immediate, simple, encouraging, and respectful of each client's style.

Using the client's **metaphor** (a word or phrase that stands for another similar concept) creates a sense of close following and respect for the way the client frames the world. Sometimes we purposely want to praise the client's special metaphors as a way of making things very clear or as being a real gift that not everyone has. At other times, we listen for frequently used metaphors (e.g., "This is part of my journey," "I'm digging myself in deeper," or "I'm in a stew") and, without noting them out loud, simply use them in the conversation.

> *When my client Glen talks about failing at work, he'll say, "I'm on the highway and I'm going fine, but I don't know which exit to get off. What if I get off at the wrong exit? How would I find my way back to the highway?" He constantly uses such metaphors, and I think this tends to work against him sometimes. I follow along with his metaphors for a while, but eventually I start talking more concretely about what interests him, his previous jobs, etc. I think Glen uses metaphors as a way of distancing himself from problems so he doesn't have to deal with them directly.*

Sometimes clients bring in expressions or wise sayings from within their particular cultures that we later salt back into the conversation because we like the way the saying sums things up.

> *A client talking about how little she has left from her check after paying bills suddenly lit up when remembering a funny saying that her mother, also poor, had used on the kids to lighten things up when they carried on about wanting a bike or a new dress or an ice cream. She would say "If we had ham, we could have ham and eggs—if we had eggs." She was delighted when I used this saying (with a smile) in responding to her request for more time because she had come late that day due to doing her nails, and she had seen people lined up outside to see me to get approvals for taxi rides home.*

EXAMPLES OF METAPHORS

"Do you have to take *this* much baggage on your journey?"

"If I were going to dig myself out, I might start by . . . ."

"Tell me more about the vegetables in this particular stew . . . ."

Marwan Dwairy (2009) notes that "the language of traditional people is typically full of metaphors, representing their experience through cultural symbols, idioms, and proverbs" (p. 201). He suggests that Arab and Muslim clients specifically "may profit from metaphor therapy because the Qur'an is written in a metaphoric language and the Arabic language makes ample use of metaphors" (p. 201).

Informed and Respectful Process

Am I maintaining a deliberate, informed, and respectful stance in my explorations with all clients?

Educational and class differences can negatively affect the language that clinicians use with and about clients while exploring and elaborating the story. At times, we have noticed colleagues using pomp, jargon, or flourish in the presence of clients who are famous or wealthy and talking down to poorly educated or nonnative speakers. Furthermore, many clinicians seem to feel that it is all right to ask poor or disempowered people anything, while at the same time they may feel extremely uncomfortable and apologetic probing the lives of the rich and famous.

Clinicians may also make mistaken assumptions about groups of people and not explore things as frankly as they should. For example, they may not ask a lesbian woman if she is having safe sex, ask a "good Catholic girl" if she ever had an abortion, or ask a longtime widow in her seventies if she thinks of dating again.

Maintaining the Not-Knowing Position

I'm not really sure what he meant by that; I need to ask about it.

There's a lot about this situation that needs clearing up. I need to explore further before I come to so many conclusions.

I haven't asked about subject x for a long time. I should ask, to see if anything has changed since we last talked about it.

A **not-knowing perspective** has two important aspects: (1) it is okay not to know, and (2) clients often know more than we do about the realities of their experience.

New learners often think they need to show that they know a lot to retain credibility with clients, but comfort with not knowing is absolutely essential for eliciting the client's story. When we do not adequately grasp clients' situations, they often say things like, "I'm not sure you really get what I mean" or "See what I'm saying?"

Surprisingly, to elicit more information, saying "I don't understand" is often more useful than saying "I understand" or "Yes, I know." Such responses from a clinician can be interpreted by clients to mean "enough said," whereas "I'm not sure I understand what you mean" invites the speaker to elaborate, even in different words. We can have brilliant hunches, but we never really understand things until clients spell them out more fully. Even then, clients may add material later that gives completely new meanings to situations or events. No matter how much we think we understand, we must always remember that clients are, and will always remain, the experts on their own lives.

Bjorn Blom (2009) suggests that clinicians need to act like anthropologists who deliberately "un-know" what they have learned so as to get a fresh perspective as they observe and listen, instead of incorporating and imposing assumptions that can be incorrect and biased. Blom believes that clients can be more empowered when they can tell their stories in their own way, less constricted by structured interview questions. He urges two practices to help us see when and how we impose our views and cultural norms on clients. The first is **introspection,** looking for our own bias and controlling behaviors. The second he calls **extrospection,** wherein we stand away and watch ourselves in action with clients to see where the power in the interview is, and adjust ourselves as needed so that the power stays with the clients.

Sustaining Techniques to Cushion Intensive Exploration

What can I do or say at intervals so that the inquiry feels less intrusive and the client feels less vulnerable?

Clinicians try to ensure that feelings of relief and support outweigh any potential feelings of vulnerability or threat from overexposure of personal information. **Sustaining techniques** offer clients support as they open their stories to deeper exploration and elaboration. **Checking-in** is a sustaining technique in which the clinician is really asking how things feel or seem to the client after a period of exploring. Check-ins emphasize to the clinician the importance of the client's feelings, observations, and participation generally. They are like the periodic reading of the road map together or the joint taking of the temperature of the interview. "What's this like for you?" and "How are you doing with this?" are two standard ways of checking in. Another is, "Have we talked enough about this for now? Should we give it a rest for today?"

Another sustaining technique during elaboration work is **crediting client strengths,** especially those shown in sharing the story and unfolding its layers in spite of any pain or risk involved. As long as the clinician is authentic in giving the credit, it can take almost any form; for example, "It takes courage to do what you're doing." or "You have an amazing ability to connect with people."

Slowdowns can also be sustaining. They are the verbal equivalent of tapping the brakes and are often framed in such a way as to reduce the speed of the interview: "Take your time now; there's no rush." "You needn't rush this. Give yourself the time you need." Here the clinician models patience and carefulness with self, which is novel for many clients.

Validation of the difficulty of disclosure can also feel sustaining: "This is hard, and I respect your willingness to do it." At other times, we might say, "You've talked about some really painful things today, and I can appreciate the exhaustion from it that you're describing."

Appreciating and Using Resistance

I need to view the client's responses to my inquiry as her best means of protecting herself and her loyalty systems at the moment. The main thing the client is "resisting" is having familiar things taken away or tinkered with in ways that do not yet feel safe. I had best slow down or change course.

Seemingly sensible exploration sometimes hits a stone wall of silence, protest, denial of relevance, or refusal to respond. Refusals to follow the clinician's leads or suggestions are referred to as **resistance.** Resistance to clinician questions should not be seen as a negative trait of the client. Clinicians should appreciate clients' needs to protect themselves from questions that might create more distress or a threat to their sense of stability. Resistance may signal a need for caution. (In psychodynamic theory, the term *resistance* refers to the unconscious defenses against the emergence of painful or forbidden material.) We discuss resistance in more detail in Chapter 8.

When the client balks at further elaboration, the clinician can honor and reframe the balking as sensible: "I think you're absolutely right to stop here for now. It's good to see you being careful of yourself and not just plunging into topics because I suggest them. I don't think we should continue with this topic right now, and I want you to keep on waving me off of anything like this that seems absurd or hurtful." Again, this technique works only when we believe what we are saying. Another response to balking is simply to say something like, "I can see that what I asked doesn't feel right to you; can we stop a minute and talk about it?" This is an example of examining the moment, a skill discussed in Chapter 11.

Enough Is Enough

I need to let this line of questioning or exploration go—at least for now.

Sometimes when clients balk, it may be wise to go down another path or to try exploring with different words on another day or when they signal readiness by introducing a topic akin to the one refused earlier. Sometimes clinicians get "on a mission" and pursue a hunch or an agenda, unable to let go. Such persistence may be required as part of a mandated protective role; for example, when the clinician has reason to fear for the client's safety.

It may also arise from the clinician's own needs to be right, to prove a hunch, or to please a supervisor who is pushing for material about which the client is not forthcoming.

CLIP 6.3
Sustaining
Techniques

Interns and beginning clinicians are especially vulnerable to pressure from supervisors and consultants to go after information that, in face-to-face contacts with clients, may be impossible or unwise to obtain. Pressuring clients usually makes no sense, feels very unempathic, and often ends in power struggles, cancellations, and the termination of work. Sometimes it ends with the client going to the agency director and requesting another clinician. Recognize when enough is enough, let go, and move on unless there is imminent risk of harm to the client or to others.

A final point: Clinicians clearly influence the conversation by the areas we choose to explore, by the topics to which we respond and do not respond, and by how we frame exploration or elaboration probes. Good clinical work requires a constant monitoring of our behaviors—our acts of commission and omission and our attempts to understand these actions. Process recordings, clinical notes, and the use of audio and video recording help us monitor our use of influence so that we can use it intentionally and appropriately, not only in exploration and elaboration but throughout all clinical work.

■ Conclusion

Exploration and elaboration help the client put ideas and feelings into words so that assets and problems are clarified in ways that make goal setting, planning, and problem solving possible. Information gathered and hunches evolved are distilled into the purpose and focus of working together. Questions, prompts, silence, reflection, refocusing, and initiating new topics are important skills in exploration. Sustaining, watchfulness, and sensitive timing all cushion the sometimes painful process of elaborating the story.

In Chapters 7 and 8, we see how exploration and data gathering in assessment inform the selection of goals and the work of contracting and evaluation. We discuss the ways in which periodic evaluations of process and progress are used to keep the work on track toward the achievement of agreed-upon objectives.

■ Suggested Readings

Anderson, Harlene, & Goolishian, Harry. (1992). The client is the expert: A not-knowing approach to therapy. In S. McNamee & Kenneth Gergen (Eds.), *Therapy as a social construction* (pp. 25–39). Newbury Park, CA: Sage.

Dwairy, Marwan. (2009). Culture analysis and metaphor with Arab-Muslim clients. *Journal of Clinical Psychology, 65,* 199–209.

Saleebey, Dennis (Ed.). (2005). *The strengths perspective in social work practice* (4th Ed.). Upper Saddle River, NJ: Pearson.

■ Self-Explorations

1. Remember a time when someone was asking you about something that you did not want to discuss. What was the topic? How did you feel? In what ways did you indicate that you either did not want to talk about it at all or that you did not want to talk about it further?

2. Think about a time when a friend raised a personal matter that he or she seemed uncomfortable discussing. How did you encourage the person to talk with you? Did you ask direct questions? Did you talk about yourself in a similar situation, hoping he or she would feel more comfortable? Did you change the topic? What did you learn about yourself through this experience?

3. Did your family or culture impose restrictions on the types of questions or topics you could ask other people about? For example, "You shouldn't ask people about their income"? Were there secrets or pseudosecrets in your family that you were not supposed to ask about?

■ Essay Questions

1. Clinicians can help clients elaborate their stories in many other ways than just asking questions. Describe four additional techniques that can be used to aid in exploration.

2. List several kinds of questions that this chapter suggested that you *not* use. For each kind, describe its potential problematic effects on the client and the interview.

3. What are some of the pros and cons of asking open-ended questions? Under what circumstances is it appropriate to ask closed-ended questions?

4. Discuss five principles of effective exploration.

■ Key Terms

Checking-in	Prompts
Closed-ended questions	Pseudoquestions
Crediting client strengths	Ratatat questioning
Dot-dot-dot reflection	Refocusing
Double questions	Resistance
Elaboration	Slowdowns
Exploration	Summarizing
Extrospection	Sustaining techniques
Intervals of respite	Tangential questions
Introspection	Timing
Metaphor	Underlining
Not-knowing perspective	Validation of the difficulty of disclosure
Open-ended questions	

CHAPTER 7

Assessment, Formulation, and Goal Setting

A hospital social worker meeting with a family around a health crisis, an outreach worker talking to a teen mother on the street, a high school counselor working with a teen who is suicidal—all must begin with (a) an assessment, (b) a formulation and conceptualization of the issues, and (c) a collaborative setting of clear, specific goals. Only then can clinicians and clients develop an intervention or treatment plan. Throughout this work, the clinician and client are also continuously engaged in building their relationship.

■ Assessment

We use the skills of exploration and elaboration to help us assess and make sense of the client's story. Assessment involves gathering and analyzing information about the client, the story to date, and the contextual or larger system influences affecting the client and the story. Doman Lum (2004) notes that "(a)ssessment comes from the root 'asset,' which is an item of value or a resource owned" (p. 219). Thus, a critical aspect of assessment is to work with clients to identify their valuable assets.

Levels of Assessment

Six classic questions are often used by interviewers to organize the assessment agenda: *Who? What? Where? Why? When? How?* These questions can be used at two levels.

The first level concerns the **process of the assessment** itself. We start with the "why" of assessment because it often predicts "whom" and "how" the clinician assesses.

Why has the client come, or why was the client referred? Why am I doing this assessment?

Who is "the client"? (The client could be a person, family, group, organization, or larger system.) Who should be involved in the assessment process? Who made the referral?

What do I want to know? What information should I gather? What cultural considerations should inform assessment and planning with this client?

How can the client be actively involved in designing the assessment process? How should we gather the information? What methods will be most useful in getting the information?

Where should the initial assessment take place: in the office, home, street, shelter?

When will the client and I have enough understanding to begin to plan and contract?

At the second level, the answers to these questions form the **content of the assessment.** At this level the questions are asked in a different order:

Who are the main participants in the successes and problems of the people or systems being assessed?

What are the presenting problems, strengths, resources, and needs in this system? What are the potential barriers? What incentives for change can be identified? What will change look like when it is achieved?

Where do the successes and problems most often manifest themselves, and where will effective interventions most likely occur?

Why is the client presenting at this time, and why would the client be interested in continuing beyond the initial meeting?

When did major influencing events take place, and when did the problems begin? When did the problems reach the level of precipitating a contact with professionals? When in the client's life am I entering the story?

How can I, the client, and others help at this time? How can I adapt so that the relationship and the work feel helpful, safe, and comfortable to each unique client?

We agree with David Sue and Diane Sue (2008) that in order to be culturally responsive, assessment should be collaborative and contextual.

By directly asking the client the following questions, the clinician can gain a better understanding of the client's perspective on the issues involved, including spiritual and/or cultural explanations of the causes and the client's belief system about ways to intervene:

"What do you think is causing your problem?"

"Why do you think is this happening to you?"

"What have you done to treat this condition?"

"How has this condition affected your life?"

(David Sue & Diane Sue, 2008, pp. 62, 64).

Formal Clinical Assessment

Clinicians are often asked to do formal, reasonably structured assessments of individuals for the purpose of diagnosis, treatment planning, or research to determine eligibility for specialized services such as disability assistance payments, residential placement, or inpatient treatment. In formal assessments, we start with what problems, needs, or issues are motivating the client (or others) to seek help.

We evaluate the person's overall functioning, exploring current and past behaviors, strengths, relationships, cognitions, affect, and contextual influences. We explore the person's physical health and well-being, including medications and their effects. We assess for potential substance abuse. We explore for current and past social barriers to well-being and achievement, as well as other stressors. We attempt to understand how these are affected by the client's race, culture, ethnicity, class, gender and sexual orientation, age, abilities, spirituality, and family developmental history and background. Compton, Galaway, and Cournoyer (2005); Hepworth, Rooney, Dewberry Rooney, Strom-Gottfried, and Larsen (2010); and Lum (2004) provide in-depth discussions of formal assessment with clients from a variety of cultures. Box 7.1 contains a Sample Assessment Outline.

Formal assessments are often repeated both during and at the conclusion of clinical work as part of the evaluation. In evaluation, we examine the effectiveness of interventions and may suggest steps to maintain gains in the future.

Clinical assessment need not be limited to individuals. We routinely conduct family assessments in which we evaluate the structures, roles, communication, and overall functioning of the family as a whole, as well as the more-specific transactions between family members. A clinician may also assess the dynamics of a classroom, an activity group, a neighborhood gang following a member's death, and so on. At the macro level, professionals also assess agencies, institutions, organizational structures, and forces in the wider community—even systems of ideas and related behaviors, such as classism, sexism, and racism. See Netting, Kettner, and McMurtry (2008) for a more-thorough discussion of macro-level assessment.

B O X 7.1 Outline for Assessment

---

1. **Identifying and demographic information**
   Name, age, gender
   Sexual orientation
   Relationship status
   Religion
   Cultural or racial identities
   Employment, education, training
   Economic status, including problems or needs

2. **Presenting problem or concern**
   Current
   History
   Past treatment

3. **Strengths and resources**
   Coping mechanisms
   Social supports, including friends, cultural, and community networks
   Cultural and spiritual beliefs and practices
   Motivation and readiness for change

4. **Background**
   Family history
   Significant developmental events
   Effects of race, culture, sexual orientation, age, class, immigration, and other influences

5. **Biopsychosocial stressors**
   Previous
   Current or continuing

6. **Psychological functioning**
   Behavioral observations
   Cognitive or intellectual capacity and skills
   Emotional/affective state and self-regulation

7. **Health and biological factors**
   Physical health
   Disability
   Medications
   Substance use, abuse, and dependence
   Wellness activities (exercise, yoga, meditation, etc.)

8. **Test results**
   Intelligence
   Neuropsychological
   Psychological

9. **DSM IV-TR diagnosis (all five axes)**

10. **Formulation or conceptualization**

Assessing for Strengths

All too often, clinical assessment focuses on individual problems, shortcomings, and weaknesses. Good assessment requires that we assess the client's strengths and coping mechanisms as well. Positive psychologists challenge us to have a more "holistic conceptualization of mental health that includes not just mental illness but also optimal functioning and human flourishing" (Wong, 2006, p. 134). Wong (2006) points out that clinicians and clients can capitalize on these identified strengths by using them to create change more quickly.

Pamela Hays (2008) suggests that clinicians specifically assess for **cultural strengths** and supports at the individual, interpersonal, and environmental levels. Cultural strengths at the individual level might include pride in one's position and achievements within one's specific culture, involvement in religious or spiritual practices, and the use of culture-specific coping mechanisms such as the Buddhist acceptance of suffering as an integral part of life. Interpersonal strengths can include regular participation in cultural rituals and/or celebrations. In Brazilian families, the strong identification with, and attachment and loyalty to, one's family; familial interdependence; the extended family; cooperative and prosocial tendencies; and a collective orientation have been identified as cultural strengths (Carol, Koller, Raffaelli, & de Guzman, 2007, pp. 335–336). Environmental supports can come from the client's physical and natural environment. For example, "(c)lients of rural origin or Indigenous heritage may find involvement with or nearness to animals, plants, mountains, and bodies of water to be important sources of spiritual strength [C.T. Sutton and Broken Nose, 1996]" (Hays, 2008, p. 124).

Assessing for Barriers to Growth and Development

As a part of ongoing assessment from an ecological perspective, clinicians must continuously listen for overt and covert barriers to the realization of clients' potentials. For many years, clinical assessment focused almost exclusively on the intrapersonal—the individual's characteristics, behavioral patterns, and intrapsychic dynamics. Now, most clinicians prominently focus assessment on the interpersonal and the systemic. We ask about intrapersonal, interpersonal, and societal forces that may hinder the client's problem-solving abilities, growth, and development. It is essential that the clinician consider the impact of such larger social forces as poverty, language barriers, racism, sexism, ableism, and other systems of oppression (DePoy & Gilson, 2004; David Sue & Sue, 2008; Weaver, 2005).

> *In training, when I saw the documentary True Colors, I realized for the first time the way that racism affects the daily interactions of African Americans in the United States. Watching two men (paired for similarities on education, age, dress, social skills) as they spent a week in a Midwestern town doing exactly the same things revealed how the fact that one was Black and the other White affected every aspect of their daily lives—from walking into a department store to browse, to renting an apartment.*

For example, a good assessment may uncover instances where people were persecuted due to their political beliefs. Without important assessment focus on the traumatic experiences of political oppression, a clinician would be missing a vital aspect of their functioning and distress.

Integrating Spiritual and Religious Questions into Assessment

Millions of people around the world use spiritual and/or religious experience and affiliations for guidance, support, and social connection. Researchers have noted the enormous support people find in relationships with a God, Goddess, or guiding spirit; with pastors, rabbis, imams, and spiritual healers; and with faith communities (Abu-Ras, Gheith & Cournos, 2008; Faver, 2004; Haight, 1998; Hodge, 2006; Richards & Bergin, 2000; Taylor et al., 2000).

The empirical literature on the association between well-being and both spirituality and religion is generally supportive regarding the beneficial effects of both (Lewis & Cruise, 2006; van Dierendonck & Mohan, 2006). From their review of the literature, Stephen Joseph, Alex Linley, and John Maltby (2006) conclude that "possible mechanisms for the relationship between religion and well-being are found in the mediating roles of increased social relationships and purpose in life" (p. 2). Catherine Faver (2004) believes that "recognizing and strengthening our relatedness to other people and perspectives and to sources of meaning and purpose beyond the self produce joy and vitality, which sustain the capacity to care for others and the world" (pp. 242–243).

At the same time, many agency assessment forms and protocols contain no reference to or questions about a client's religious experience and beliefs about or use of spiritual resources in coping with stress and enriching their lives. By not bringing spiritual beliefs into assessment and practice, clinicians may seem to be signaling that these are not important or appropriate topics in counseling. In actuality, culturally appropriate assessments always include questions about both cultural and religious beliefs, practices, and preferred styles of caregiver behavior. For example, Hodge (2005a) has found that many Muslims don't want to receive medical care from providers of the opposite sex unless a member of the client's sex is present .

A good spiritual assessment might turn up instances in which clients have been wounded or excluded by faith communities. Some may have been sexually abused by religious or spiritual leaders and feel so ashamed and confused about it that they keep these matters private for a long time. Gay, lesbian, and gender-variant people have often been shunned by communities of faith and have developed their own spiritual fellowships.

Clinicians can ask one or two simple assessment questions regarding client spirituality, thus demonstrating respect for spirituality as a potentially renewing and connecting force. Clients often will signal whether they do or do not want to continue this line of exploration.

EXAMPLES

"Do you have any spiritual or religious practices or beliefs that are comforting for you?"

"Are you actively involved in a temple, a church, a mosque, or any other faith community? What has this membership meant to you?"

"Is there a special place where you walk or sit to connect with nature or the universe or to get a feeling of acceptance and belongingness?"

"Are there readings, sayings, songs, art, or poems that lift your spirit when you feel like giving up?"

"Do you meditate, pray, or use rituals of any kind to connect you with a force beyond yourself?"

"Are you undergoing any kind of spiritual crises at this time? If so, what sort?"

These questions should not be thrown at the client in a linear, rat-a-tat fashion. We usually ask them when we are exploring strengths and achievements, or we can simply ask them as space arises, when clients are talking about how hard and hopeless life seems at times or when they are describing the support they experience in daily life. Sometimes clients initiate a discussion of spirituality by mentioning religious or spiritual support they've received. Other clients may talk about the way they may have been oppressed or exploited by religious beliefs, leaders, or institutions.

Not all clients will find these questions helpful. Some may not have any religious or spiritual affiliations or beliefs, and others may be reluctant to discuss this information with a professional. Still others may ask, "What does this have to do with what I am here for?"

I was asking Rip about strengths and successes in his life because so far, he had only mentioned the problems and stresses. As a part of this inquiry, I asked him if he ever used prayer or meditation to lift his spirits. He replied sarcastically: "I never touch the stuff . . . please don't start on that, I had it stuffed down my throat my whole childhood." Without getting defensive, I simply said that I make it a practice now to ask people if they are spiritual because so many people all over the world call on a higher power or use other spiritual activities when feeling down, but we professionals rarely ask them about these important practices or encourage their use. Rip said he didn't mind me asking about it. He then talked with more feeling about a harsh childhood in which the aunt who raised him was always saying how God would punish him for this or that behavior. He couldn't wait to get away from such a God and is not eager to go back! I appreciated that and asked him tell me more about his "getaway" at 18 . . . a source of pride.

David Hodge (2005b) has developed a "spiritual assessment toolbox" to identify "spiritual assets . . . [that can help to provide] effective, culturally sensitive services while concurrently providing a forum to explore spiritual strengths that might be used to ameliorate problems or cope with difficulties" (p. 314). His toolbox includes spiritual histories, lifemaps, genograms, ecomaps, and ecograms.

Methods of Assessment

Formal clinical assessment uses a variety of methods, including:

1. **Assessment interviews** such as client self-reports and the clinician's experience in the interview, interviews with family members, and interviews with relevant others. Assessment interviews may be unstructured, semistructured, or structured. **Unstructured interviews** allow the clinician to follow the lead of the client. **Semistructured interviews** may provide a list of content areas that the clinician should cover in the assessment interview. **Structured interviews** consist of a set of standardized questions to be asked in a specific order. Whitson (2009) notes that interviews can be used for both diagnostic and descriptive purposes. An example of a structured interview for the purpose of diagnosis is the Structured Interview for Axis I DSM-IV-TR Disorders (SCID-1) (First, Spitzer, Gibbon, & Williams, 1997).

2. **Observation** in a lab, natural settings, or lifespace. Clinicians may observe client behaviors in either naturalistic or controlled environments. Clinicians often make **informal observations** of the client's behavior in the interview or natural or lifespace setting. For example, a halfway house counselor may observe the social interactions of a depressed woman living in the house. Observations can also be formal and structured. For example, the clinician may formally observe the behavior of a child in the classroom or observe the client playing in the schoolyard. In **formal observations,** the clinician clearly defines the target behavior, its antecedents, and its consequences. "Observation is an assessment tool; therefore, it should be evaluated in the same manner that we evaluate other assessment tools (examining the reliability and validity of our observations)" (Whitson, 2009, p. 242).

3. **Testing** includes intelligence tests, personality tests, symptom checklists, and neuropsychological and other medical tests. Many clinicians use standardized assessment tests and instruments to help them better understand their clients. Testing instruments should have both reliability and validity. Assessment instruments can include symptom checklists such as the Symptom Checklist (SCL-90) or the Brief Symptom Inventory (BSI). Clinicians may also use personality tests such as the Minnesota Multiphasic Personality Inventory 2 (MMPI-2), which looks at patterns of personality and emotional disorder. Projective tests such as the Rorschach test and the Thematic Apperception Test (TAT), both based on the psychodynamic concept of the unconscious, provide clients with unstructured stimuli to which they respond. Clinicians can use neuropsychological tests such as the Luria-Nebraska Neuropsychological Battery (LNNB), the Bender Visual-Motor Gestalt Test, and the Mini-Mental Status Exam to assess client cognitive and perceptual performance.

Clinicians also can use tests to help clients understand their skills and strengths. The Myers-Briggs Type Indicator (MBTI) examines preferences in the ways in which people perceive and make judgments. There are special tests for use in career counseling, including interest inventories and aptitude tests. Positive psychologists suggest using the VIA Inventory of Character Strengths (VIA-IS), an online questionnaire clients can complete in 30 minutes, immediately receiving feedback about their "signature-strengths" (Peterson, Park, & Seligman, 2006).

Testing presents a number of challenges. It is often regarded by clients as a pass or fail activity, so many clients may be reluctant to participate. Tests are often culturally biased. Hays (2008) asserts that "most standardized tests originate from a European American worldview that permeates procedural norms in the research and development of such instruments" (p. 130). She notes that sometimes tests are "restandardized" on a population that is more representative of the population at large. Such restandardization may lead to deletion or modification of test items. Another solution to the problem of cultural bias in tests is the development of culture-specific instruments such as "the Hispanic Stress Inventory (Cervantes, Padilla, & Salgado de Snyder, 1990), the Vietnamese Depression Scale (Kinzie et al., 1982), and some of the instruments described in the Handbook of Tests and Measurements for Black Populations (R. L. Jones, 1996)" (Hays, 2008, p. 131).

4. **Review of life records.** Clinicians can review the life records—records of clients' previous treatments, their school records, and other written documents including previous test reports. It is important that the clinician discuss these reports with the client and avoid giving them too much credibility. They may not necessarily provide an accurate reflection of the client in the past and may not provide a valid picture of the client as he or she is now.

Clinicians need to explain their methods of assessment and have clients sign detailed informed consent forms for any procedures or assessment activities to be undertaken. Because of confidentiality requirements and HIPAA regulations, they should obtain permission releases for any relevant information to be obtained from others.

Technology-Assisted Assessment

Many assessment tests can be taken online and quickly scored using computers, providing both the client and clinician with immediate feedback. Observational and interview data can also be analyzed using technology. Computer-assisted assessment tools can help clinicians and clients measure change. Clients can complete an online assessment measure before the clinical work starts (baseline), during the work together, and at the end of the work (post-treatment). These measurements can be used in evaluation. The measurements allow the clinician and client to monitor the client's progress, make adjustments where necessary to forward the work, and provide empirical evidence of change when used in evaluation.

Assessment Interviewing Techniques

As discussed in detail in Chapter 6, the techniques of exploration and elaboration are particularly useful in assessment interviewing. These techniques include questioning, prompting, probing, reflecting, summarizing, underlining, refocusing, and initiating new topics.

While most clients come to professional encounters expecting to answer questions, reveal information, and share ideas about their situations, many have no idea of how the process of disclosure and exploration actually *feels*. They may have impressions from others or from the media, but, just like us, they have to carefully feel their way into the process of making themselves known as they become more comfortable with us.

In so doing, they may feel pressured to consider the feelings of significant others who have a stake—spoken or unspoken—in the process. What is revealed during the assessment process may have major consequences and can affect relationships, economic supports, living situations, custody rights, and future prospects of all kinds. No wonder, then, that apprehension and caution can manifest themselves during exploration.

Krishna Guadalupe and Doman Lum (2005) note that, in work with Latino families, rapport building is very important before beginning to probe with assessment questions (p. 373). The same point applies to working with people with Asian roots (Chan & Lee, 2004), with clients from the Middle East (Sharifzadeh, 2004), and with Native American clients (Joe & Malach, 2004; Weaver, 2005).

Sustaining techniques are crucial to assessment to ease the way (see Chapter 6). For example, assessment may proceed smoothly until the clinician asks for permission to send off for records from a psychiatric hospitalization. A client might respond by saying, "So you think I'm mental, too?" This kind of reaction can signal sensitivity to what the clinician thinks or to being judged, a stigma left over from the experience of mental illness, or a concern about what the record will reveal. At this point, the clinician might stop to explore what meanings the client attaches to the request for hospital records, giving the client a chance to express concerns or even perhaps to share past experience in which having a hospital record worked against him or her. Sympathetic appreciation of the concern, as well as universalizing the fear of stigma and negative consequences, might be very sustaining.

EXAMPLE

Client: So you think I'm mental, too?

Clinician: People sometimes worry that, once someone learns of their hospitalization, they will be viewed as mentally ill, rather than as a person who has a mental illness.

It is important to educate the client about the process. For example, a young child (referred for counseling because of his distractibility and impulsivity in the classroom) might be embarrassed to have his play therapist, an admired psychologist, observe him in the classroom as part of the assessment process, worrying about being seen at the most problematic times. The clinician might spend a few moments exploring the child's sensitivity and his attendant fantasies of what would occur during the visit. Then some time might be spent educating the boy about the usefulness of assessment, of getting to see firsthand how things are for him in the class, and exploring the things that might be making it hard for him to focus and learn.

Similarly, before including testing in the assessment process, a clinician would educate the client about the tests and about the nature, purpose, and process of the testing situation and then elicit client reactions to all of these information.

Another useful technique is to encourage the client to assess the clinician as part of the assessment process. Usually in assessments, the clinician asks clients many questions, which can leave them feeling as though they are "in the hot seat." Reminding clients that they are also evaluating the clinician can heighten the sense of collaboration and shared responsibility.

> *Sometimes during an assessment interview, I will say to the client: "I've gotten to ask you a lot of questions. Is there anything you would like to ask me?"*

* * *

> *Clients often ask about my training or about what I think will happen in our work. Sometimes they ask if I think I can help them. If they don't ask anything, I might say, "Sometimes clients want to know if I've had any experience with the kind of problems they're bringing in."*

* * *

> *When I am going to do an assessment observation in a classroom, I often let the child come behind the one-way mirror and watch me as I interact with some of the kids. I say to them, "You can watch me, and then I'll watch you . . . and then let's talk about what we see."*

All Interviewing Requires Assessment

Formal assessment procedures are most frequently required in hospitals, outpatient mental health clinics, and forensic and protective services evaluations, but many clinicians work in situations or settings that do not require formal assessment protocols. No matter how the setting or task is, clinicians must always do some kind of assessment before planning and acting in concert with or on behalf of clients. Street outreach workers may not use a formal standardized test, but they do assess client strengths, problems, styles of interaction, and even cognitive abilities. As noted in Chapter 4, the clinician is also always listening for content, affect, themes and patterns, and contextual influences in the client's story. As clinicians come to appreciate the importance of understanding before responding, assessment becomes second nature.

As a social worker, I am always thinking about the "person-in-situation" context. Even when friends ask for advice, I find myself asking all sorts of questions as they talk. I am trying to figure out all kinds of things in their "surround" or environment that might be influencing the situation.

Principles of Assessment

1. *Assessment is an objective and an outcome of initial conversation, as well as an ongoing process guiding clinical interchange.* It begins immediately when people meet, and it is continuously threaded into ongoing interchanges as the story deepens and broadens. The more we know, the more we want to ask or understand. Moreover, people and their situations change fluidly over time; little remains fixed. Knowing this, we realize that situations and dynamics always merit reexamination along the way because information, people, activities, relationships, and contexts all can change.

2. *A full assessment includes evaluation of the clinician, the relationship, the appropriate services, the surround, and the interface among all of these elements.* For example, the clinician may ask, "Is this the agency or setting that can provide the best resources for this particular client?" We also continuously assess the motivation of the clinician and the agency to make sure that they are persisting, advocating, and caring about the people they are committed to help.

3. *Assessment should be reliable.* **Reliability** refers to assessment consistency. When applied to testing, reliability means that the score a person obtains on a particular test should be consistent even if the test is given by different testers or administered at different times **(test-retest reliability).** But reliability is important in all parts of assessment, including observation and diagnosis. "**Interrater reliability** refers to the level of agreement between two observers rating the same behaviors. . . . **Diagnostic reliability** refers to the level of agreement between two or more diagnosticians about whether individuals meet criteria for psychiatric (or other) diagnoses and which diagnosis is primary" (Hecker & Thorpe, 2005, p. 548).

4. *Assessment should be valid.* **Validity** refers to accuracy—how well the assessment measures what it intends to measure. Does the assessment give us an accurate picture of the individual? Assessment tools that were developed and normed on a specific population (for example, European-American men) may not be valid for use with a person who is from a different population (for example, an Asian-American woman).

5. *Assessment should be culturally responsive.* Both the methods used and the areas explored should be sensitive to cultural differences. Derald Sue and Sue (2008) note that "Euro-American counselors tend to view their client's problems as residing within the individual rather than society. . . . Many minorities accept the importance of individual contributions to the problem but they also give great weight to systemic or societal factors that may adversely affect their lives" (p. 180). The clinician should assess not just the individual client but also the effects of oppression, racism, bilingualism,

ethnic identity conflicts, and other social conditions. The clinician should also look for strengths and supports that come from the client's culture.

In working with immigrant families, Elaine Congress's (2004) **culturagram** (Figure 7.1) illustrates the complexities of family culture. Its matrix shows the interwoven influences of important family variables such as the language spoken at home, health beliefs, and contacts with cultural institutions for support. The clinician should ask about all of these influences during interviews over time rather than barraging the client with them all at once. Client reflections on these influences in daily life often weave together a narrative of coping via empowering connections and traditions.

6. *The more methods and strategies used to assess, the more balanced the understanding we are likely to develop.*   When feasible, we like to observe—or at least ask in detail about—functioning across many domains. The woman who stays with a batterer and does not currently appear to be able to protect herself or her children from harm may be a leader in her church's women's group or a helpful suicide hotline responder. Perhaps we do not think to ask what she does in her free time because we have already assumed she

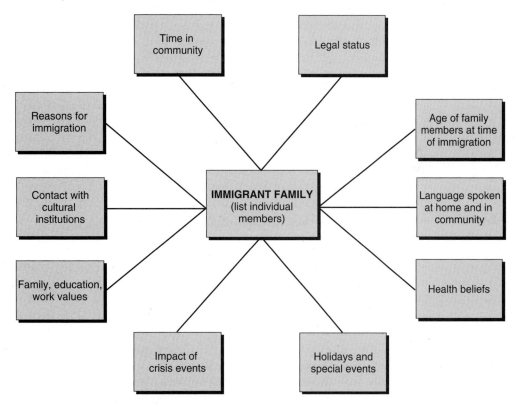

FIGURE 7.1 Culturagram

Source: Congress, Elaine. (2004). Cultural and ethical issues in working with culturally diverse patients and their families: The use of culturagram to promote cultural competent practice in health care settings. *Social Work in Health Care, 39,* p. 253.

does not have any. By the same token, observing an adult at a neighborhood meeting or in a home visit, or observing a child in a gym or in a classroom, may provide much more clarity about skills and limitations than office interaction ever would.

Test information may provide us with new insight into the cognitive strengths of clients so that we may plan our intervention to fit their cognitive style. A physical exam could reveal diabetes, which might be one alternative explanation for the symptoms that the client defines as "anxiety attacks." Brain scans can now reveal in great detail possible problems in brain tissue, chemistry, or functioning that could enrich and potentially alter our assessment conclusions about "dysfunctional behaviors" in people of all ages.

Several helpful tools are available to capture and reflect client experience, relationships, and themes or patterns. The **genogram** reflects multigenerational family relationships and patterns (Gerson, McGoldrick, & Petry, 2008). The **ecomap** reflects clients' social networks and the nature and extent of reciprocity in relationships with significant others. The **life chart** provides a birth-to-present time line of dates and ages at which major life experiences with others impacted the client positively or negatively.

Jeanne Slattery (2004) has devised a "strength-based genogram" to complement traditional genograms that tend to focus on problems, losses, and conflicts. The **strength-based genogram** clarifies intergenerational models and sources of individual and family assets and accomplishments. An important feature of many immigrant families' assessment narratives is the travails and triumphs in their migrations from distant homelands and family networks. Clinicians too rushed to elicit the details of these heroic stories miss a great opportunity to validate client strengths for use another day. The strength-based genogram can be used with individuals, groups, and families. Concentrating on strengths in visual form reminds people of their meaningful histories and assets and the many possibilities that these suggest.

EXERCISE 7.1 Your Strength-Based Genogram

Construct your own strength-based genogram based on Slattery's model. Bring your genogram to class. Discuss what effect an intense reflection on strengths and connections had on you. How have your family's strengths contributed to who you are today?

---

7. *Multiple perspectives help in assessment.*   We cannot always include as many participants in the assessment process as we would like, but we do understand as clinicians that the more perspectives we include, the greater the likelihood is of adding new dimensions to our understanding. Events are experienced differently by all parties to them; each puts an interesting spin on the story and, in doing so, fleshes it out usefully. Often we make the mistake

of limiting the number of people in the room for purposes of control, focus, or expediency. Remember that we often sacrifice information and valuable relationships for control.

I'd never met with a family before, and I found seeing the parents and their five children awesome. The dad had had a heart attack, and the mom was depressed thinking that he looked older and more tired and might die suddenly. The adolescent kids seemed a little sullen and critical of him for "making Mom wait on you hand and foot." There was a little 4-year-old who ran around the room distracting everyone, so for two or three meetings I had her play outside with the secretary. My supervisor suggested I bring the little girl back in next meeting, and this time ask her what she thought of daddy being sick at home. She looked straight at me and blurted out, "Daddy squished our brother." Mom tried to silence her and looked so uncomfortable. I asked, "How?" She looked at dad, who paled, but said it was okay. Mom then told me that 10 years before, dad had come home for lunch and, in backing out of the driveway to return to work, he ran over and killed their 2-year-old. Mom said it broke everyone's heart. No one knew what to say next . . . me either.

8. ***What is observed is altered by the presence of the observer and the activities of observation* (Maturana, 1978; von Foerster, 1981).** The interviewer has to keep in mind the influence that he or she has on the behaviors of clients and the reciprocal influence they have on him or her.

We were doing interviews on videotape for a research study. Children were observed for two weeks by two different evaluators. When Randy was in the room with Bonita, she was active, made eye contact, and explored the room. On those days when Susie was with her, Bonita sat down in a corner and didn't make eye contact. Needless to say, Randy and Susie each had very different evaluations of Bonita. We also observed that Susie was less active with Bonita than she was when we observed her with other children. We really got a sense of what our teacher meant when she talked about "reciprocal influence."

9. ***Clinicians can be drawn into or "inducted" into systems they are assessing.*** Becoming a participant in the system can undercut the clinician's capacity to see, experience, and accurately report it to outsiders or to colleagues. A blurring of roles can occur when clinicians overidentify with client systems, have strong needs to rescue, or get caught up in unwitting reenactments of old, unresolved scenarios of their own.

A couple of years ago, I was supervising a student, Nadine, at the Department of Family and Children's Services. When one of her clients came to the agency, I thought I could smell alcohol on the client. It became obvious to me that the student was ignoring the fact that the mother was drinking again. When I pointed it out to Nadine and questioned her about why she thought she missed it, she said that she probably didn't see it because she was hoping that the kids would have some stability. If the mother was drinking again, the kids would be sent to separate foster care families. Nadine, just like the kids, really wanted to believe that this time the mother would succeed in sobriety. I thought it was possible that Nadine might have also come from a family where the kids were taught to pretend parents weren't drinking when they actually were.

10. ***Where we carry out our assessments influences the kinds of data we gather.*** People are often much more comfortable in their natural settings than in office or agency settings. On their own ground, they may be more

comfortable and open. On the other hand, people threatened in their own environments may relax in an agency, where they feel safe and protected.

11. ***Remember that we are seeing the client only at one particular moment in time.*** At that moment, we are seeing but one frame of an entire movie. The clinician needs to remember that the client who today looks well put together may have been very distressed 5 years ago, 5 months ago, or 5 days ago. The client who is struggling to get an entry-level job today may have been a physicist in his country of origin the year before. Therefore, it is helpful to make sure that we obtain as much information as possible about the whole story to date.

> *When I started working for the state, I had to go 20 weeks without pay because of civil service complications. I was new in the area, without resources, and it was suggested I apply for temporary public assistance, which I reluctantly did. The intake social worker was incredulous that I was a social worker with a masters degree needing public assistance. I could see she didn't believe me by the frown on her face. I gave her the name of the financial director at my agency to validate my application. She called and got the facts while I sat there. At no time did she show one ounce of care for my plight. I got food stamps and left feeling very embarrassed. It left me very much more understanding of how clients feel judged by clinicians, as though low income is always their fault.*

Furthermore, clinicians usually meet clients at a highly stressed time. Because seeking assistance from strangers can be stressful and can cause clients to regress from previously higher levels of functioning, they can present their stories with more urgency, anxiety, and disorganization than we might see under different conditions. Were we to enter the story at a different time or see the client at a less-stressed point in life, we might gain a different perspective.

> *When I was working in a detox setting, we were encouraged not to give alcoholics a personality diagnosis until they had been abstinent for a year or so because their functioning could look so much healthier once they were off drugs for a while.*

* * *

> *When I next worked in physical rehab, an elderly woman with hallucinations and without family available came into the hospital unable to offer a coherent story. It looked as if she would be transferred out to a state hospital locked unit. However, a caring nurse asked me to look in her record from the referring hospital to see if there was anything else that would explain her mental state. When I got to the medications section of the record, I saw that the woman had been on big doses of antidepressant prior to coming, but these were abruptly discontinued in our hospital. When the psychiatrist heard this, he said that sudden withdrawal from antidepressant meds often causes brief psychotic symptoms. When he put her right back on the antidepressant, her psychotic behavior abated quickly. The chart review also revealed that she had been a senior seamstress for almost 50 years and was nicknamed "Golden Fingers" for her dexterity. She had always lived independently before her diabetic complications and leg amputation. She proved to be very spunky and affable in rehab and in planning for eventual discharge. She had a long-time taxi driver friend who worked with the team and found her an accessible first-floor apartment in her old neighborhood. People had mistaken her confusion for a permanent impairment. So had she.*

12. *The "assessor" is also being assessed by the client,* whose estimation of the clinician greatly affects what the client shares.

> *Lara was a 19-year-old single mother of a 1-year-old son in our Transitional Living Program. She was usually cast as a shy "outsider," and people wondered why she was so shy. One day, as we were hanging out in the kitchen, she told me that she had been attracted to women for a couple of years and that she was afraid that other mothers would find out. She was worried that people might think she was an unfit mother. I thought, "No wonder she's so quiet. She's scared." I asked her what made her tell me. She said she had been watching the way I interacted with the other mothers and I seemed to be pretty open to different things.*

13. *Research informs clinical assessment,* just as it does clinical practice. The clinician uses empirically validated research data on human behavior to inform assessment. For example, the clinician who is familiar with research showing that the lack of economic resources often prompts women to stay in battering situations will ask abused women about their financial supports and potential for generating income. The clinician who knows that people who suffer from depression often have, among other symptoms, fitful sleep, and early morning awakening will include questions about any changes in sleep patterns.

14. *Real understanding involves more than data gathering,* for it brings the heart as well as the mind to bear, and it involves the intuition as well as the intellect. Intuition is a "sixth sense" combination of autonomic bodily reactions, perceptions, and insights gained through experience.

> *As a social work instructor, it is often hard to explain to students how to hone intuition and the sensing of things that cannot be rationally explained or aren't empirically derived. I often describe it as getting a "flavor of" something or "having an internal beeper go off." I don't want to just have students learn to "listen to their gut," but, on the other hand, if we don't pay attention to it at times, we can really miss important clues for further assessment. Sometimes it involves goose bumps on the arms, a "funny feeling" in the chest or gut, hair standing up on the back of my neck, or a welling up of things I can't name but that I feel are for sure at work in the room or in the person's life. Sometimes I think this ability to "sense" things is a gift that one is born with and can't just be implanted. But I do believe that intuition is nurtured and validated through clinical experience and life experience in general.*

■ Conceptualization or Formulation of Assessment Findings

Data gathering is an important part of assessment, but a second and equally important part of assessment is how we pull all the data together into a practical and meaningful guide for work.

> *On my first job, I hoped to impress my supervisor, a friendly psychiatrist, by handing in a seven-page assessment before supervision so he could see how much information I had gathered about my first client. He started off by saying that I sure had gathered a lot of information and that he just had one question: "So what?" He explained amiably that my assessment had nothing in it to make sense of the woman's request for counseling, to*

help us understand her described symptoms better. He said that the "so what?" question is short for "so, what's going on here beyond the obvious, and how might we help?" He went on to help me add that "meaning making" piece to my assessment skills.

The integration and analysis of assessment data is called **case conceptualization** or case formulation. The **formulation** condenses and attributes meaning to all the rich data emerging from the assessment process. It reflects the clinician's interpretations of what the facts imply about past and current functioning of the client system at hand and about future potentials, issues, and dynamics within and between people and their related systems. In formulation or conceptualization work, we look for participants, themes, patterns, and dynamics in the client's story. A formulation often provides tentative prognostic statements regarding expectations for the short, medium, and long term of any work to follow. It usually outlines important implications for intervention suggested by assessment findings and hypotheses, and it contains recommendations for the treatment plan and interventions. While formulation may include a Diagnostic and Statistical Manual (DSM) diagnosis, a meaningful formulation is much more than the diagnosis alone. It includes recognitions of client strengths and coping mechanisms; motivation and readiness; and community, cultural, spiritual, and social supports.

We attempt to understand the story in the context of the client's ethnicity, race, culture, class, gender, sexual orientation, age, economic situation, risk factors, and unique background. We weave in any observed effects of discrimination. We hypothesize about the impact of all these factors on the client's beliefs, moods, behaviors, relational interactions, and readiness for change. Strengths are highlighted as assets to be tapped and emphasized in the work to come. Pieces of information gathered begin to be assembled like a big picture puzzle of tentative hunches, interpretations, and conclusions.

In many settings, **multidisciplinary team** meeting time is set aside for case conceptualization. These team formulations benefit from the collaboration of a number of clinical colleagues with specialized knowledge, skills, and biopsychosocial perspectives to assist in better understanding the client.

When I was working at the mental health center we had to have team consultation after every intake. A psychologist might administer personality tests, a neurologist might provide information about MRI results, a social worker might report on a family assessment. Even if only one person conducted the assessment, it was essential that three out of the four disciplines—social worker, psychologist, psychiatrist, psychiatric nurse—be represented at the meeting so that a variety of perspectives could be included in the case formulation. At the end of the team meeting, a formal assessment/formulation report was placed in the client's file.

Clinical social work educator and researcher Cassandra Clay (personal communication, 2006) describes two different clinician stances for assessment and formulation work. First we have to "get up close" in assessment, using empathy, facilitative questions, and support, to elicit intimate client assessment information. Then in formulation work, we have to "stand back to get the bigger picture," using moderate detachment, intellect, and informed clinical judgment, to tease out interpretations and implications.

Good formulations require **clinical judgment** to select appropriately from many theoretical explanatory models to try to explain the phenomena observed in clients, their stories, and their interactions with the clinician and others. The theory or theories we select shape what we do in the assessment and formulation process: the persons included in the assessment process; the kinds of questions asked and information emphasized or minimized; the way the purpose, goals, and methods of assessment and intervention are spelled out with the client; the language used in conceptualizing the data gathered; and the specific goals and plans for the work.

For example, to try to understand and interpret the situation and behaviors of Mickey Riordan (the client we discussed in Chapter 1, see page 15) we incorporated knowledge from psychodynamic, family systems, social systems, political, class, and biological theories. That example contained both assessment and formulation statements. We noted that psychodynamic and family theories might attribute Mickey's problem behaviors to individual developmental stressors, family breakdown, and neighborhood violence, when other factors, including federal policy and environmental hazards, might also contribute. Again, it is crucial to know what theoretical and cultural lenses we are looking through when we assess, interpret, and speculate about clients' lives and stories, which are extremely complex and contextualized in multiple layers of overt and covert influence.

Levels of Inference

When clinicians like the ones evaluating Mickey Riordan develop their formulations, they are making inferences based on the information they have at a given point in time. Michael Nietzel and colleagues (Nietzel, Bernstein, Kramer, & Milich, 2003) offer an informative discussion of the **levels of inference** clinicians may use when making hypotheses.

Clinicians who use low levels of inference stay close to the data and do not make major leaps away from the known facts. For example, Helga complains of trouble sleeping through the night. A clinician using low levels of inference might suggest that something was worrying Helga. Clinicians who use moderate levels of inference often base hunches on known correlations between one behavior and another. For example, a clinician using moderate levels of inference might infer that Helga is depressed, knowing that sleep disturbance is often correlated with depression. Clinicians using high levels of inference see the behavior as a sign of some deeper issue or meaning interpreted through the lens of a preferred theoretical model. Such clinicians might hypothesize that Helga was a victim of sexual abuse in her family and that the abuse occurred at night, leaving her hypervigilant at night, thus disturbing her sleep.

Nietzel and colleagues (2003) further suggest that the level of inference is closely related to the clinician's theoretical orientation. Behavioral and humanistic therapists often use low or moderate levels of inference; psychodynamic theorists may use moderate to high levels. High levels of inference can be risky, because they are often based on intuition, personal experience, and speculation. The greater the speculation is, the higher the level of inference becomes. We need to be extremely careful about sharing hunches that are highly speculative in nature. Because of the power invested in professional pronouncements, clinicians can worry or mislead clients who trust such statements more than their own experience. Furthermore, speculations developed on the experience of a clinician in one culture can seem off base to a client from another culture.

In developing a formulation, we draw inferences from the raw data obtained during the assessment process. Separating data from inference takes practice. A clinician might note that Lorenzo's IQ test score is 80 and might infer that he has borderline intellectual functioning, when actually on the test day he was stressed out by neighborhood violence, had not slept much all night, and could not think clearly—circumstances not elicited in assessment. A clinician might observe that Mahdia slurred her speech during the initial meeting and infer that she was intoxicated, when it turns out she has had a stroke that is affecting her speech. A clinician might notice that in a family intake the father speaks loudly, interrupts others, and answers questions addressed to other family members, and then he might infer that the father is authoritarian, not understanding that he is behaving as fathers are supposed to behave in his culture.

Making a clear distinction between data and interpretation is important because, as human beings, we can be subject to mistaking our own strongly held opinions and impressions for "facts," thereby misunderstanding clients and their actual situations, triggers, motives, potentials, and assets. For purposes of clarity and accuracy, clinicians have to record the specific data underpinning each inference they have drawn, rather than recording just the inferences themselves. In effect, we need to practice evidence-based thinking.

EXERCISE 7.2 Moving from Data to Inference

A number of pieces of data follow. What kinds of inferences can you draw from them? What is a low-level inference? What is a high-level inference? On what do you base your inference? Discuss your answers in the class.

Jenny is depressed.

Alijah scored 108 on an IQ test.

Holly is 28, and she cuts herself on her arm with a razor.

Sam and Irma have been married for 30 years.

Jim has been stopped for speeding 10 times.

Madela is 23 and has night terrors.

Formal DSM Diagnosis

Health and mental health settings may require that the formulation include a **formal diagnosis.** The **Diagnostic and Statistical Manual (DSM),** developed by the American Psychiatric Association, is currently utilized in the United States and in many other countries to diagnose mental disorders. Another internationally recognized diagnostic classification system is the World Health Organization's **International Classification of Diseases (ICD).** The purpose of having a diagnostic classification system is to provide clinicians from a variety of disciplines with a framework and a common language for assessment, formulation, treatment planning, and research.

The DSM-IV-TR defines a **mental disorder** as a behavioral or psychological syndrome (groups of associated features) that is associated with (a) emotional distress, (b) impaired functioning or disability, or (c) a behavior that puts the person at risk of pain, suffering, disability, death, or loss of freedom. The DSM definition of mental disorders excludes expected or culturally sanctioned responses to a stressful event such as the loss of a loved one. The DSM also excludes "deviant behavior (e.g. political, religious or sexual)" and "conflicts that are primarily between the individual and society" (American Psychiatric Association, 2000).

The DSM contains over 300 clinical syndromes or diagnoses of mental disorders, each with a list of specific symptom criteria that must be met before the diagnosis can be given. The manual attempts to categorize symptoms into discrete, research-informed diagnostic entities in an effort to discriminate one condition or disorder from another with the goal of developing increased reliability and communication, among clinicians, and more-effective case formulation, research, and treatment planning. However, a diagnostic system is descriptive, not explanatory. It describes a cluster of symptoms; it does not explain their origins, nor does it discuss treatment approaches. For example, the criteria for a Major Depressive Episode are listed in Box 7.2.

The manual also includes a section, "V Codes," for conditions or states that are not mental disorders but instead may contribute to, exacerbate, or co-occur with major mental disorders or in reaction to destabilizing social conditions. These are also classified on Axis 1 if they are the principle focus of attention. These V codes include bereavement, academic or occupational problems, religious or spiritual problems, and problems of abuse and neglect. Among the newer V Code categories is that of "Relational Disorders"—couple, family, group, or parenting problems, unsettling or harmful enough to cause people to seek or accept assessment and intervention services.

The DSM is a **multiaxial diagnostic system** that attempts to provide more information than just a diagnosis. The five axes or "domains of human experience" are described in Box 7.3.

Some Critiques of DSM

Proponents of strengths, empowerment, and positive psychology perspectives wisely continue to argue caution about reducing people to their symptoms and problems—a process that can stigmatize and mislead,

B O X 7.2 DSM-IV-TR Criteria for a Major Depressive Episode

A. Five or more of the following symptoms have been present during the same 2-week period and represent a change from previous functioning; at least one of the symptoms is either (1) depressed mood, or (2) loss of interest or pleasure.

  1. Depressed mood most of the day, nearly every day as indicated either by subjective report (for example, feels sad or empty) or observation made by others (for example, appears tearful). Note: in children and adolescents, can be irritable mood.

  2. Markedly diminished interest or pleasure in all, or almost all, activities of the day, nearly every day.

  3. Significant weight loss when not dieting or weight gain (for example, a change of more than 5 percent of body weight in a month), or decrease or increase in appetite nearly every day. Note: in children, consider failure to make expected weight gains.

  4. Insomnia or hypersomnia nearly every day.

  5. Psychomotor agitation or retardation nearly every day (observable by others).

  6. Fatigue or loss of energy nearly every day.

  7. Feelings of worthlessness or excessive or inappropriate guilt nearly every day (not merely self reproach or guilt about being sick).

  8. Diminished ability to think or concentrate, or indecisiveness, nearly every day.

  9. Recurrent thoughts of death (not just fear of dying), or recurrent suicidal ideation without a specific plan, or a suicide attempt or a specific plan for committing suicide.

Source: Reprinted with permission from the Diagnostic and Statistical Manual of Mental Disorders, Fourth Edition, Text Revision. (Copyright 2000). American Psychiatric Association.

B O X 7.3 DSM AXES

Axis I: Clinical Syndromes and Other Conditions That May Be a Focus of Clinical Attention—includes all diagnoses (except those listed in Axis II) or other conditions such as academic problems

Axis II: Personality Disorders or Mental Retardation—chronic long-term conditions

Axis III: General Medical Conditions—that are important to understanding the diagnosis and treatment or that may have a role in causing the disorder

Axis IV: Psychosocial and Environmental Problems—problems that may affect diagnosis and treatment

Axis V: Global Assessment of Functioning—rating on a scale of 1–100 of how well the person is currently functioning and may also include the highest level of functioning during the past year.

because people are always so much more than their symptoms (Caplan, 1995; Kutchins & Kirk, 1997). Dennis Saleebey (2001) proposes a Diagnostic Strengths Manual with categories whose descriptive "symptoms" are each something the client does well each day. Advanced clinical practice, psychopathology, and abnormal psychology courses present opportunities to learn much more about understanding and applying DSM and ICD diagnostic frameworks and about arguments for and against the use of symptom-based frameworks (Kutchins & Kirk, 1995; Williams & Spitzer, 1995).

People of color, new immigrants, gays, lesbians, people who are gender nonconforming, people with severe mental illness, and people who are homeless are among the many people who have been the object of negative, inaccurate, or stigmatizing formulations and diagnoses applied by professionals due to misinformation and lack of experience (Ault & Brzuzy, 2009: Mezzich & Kleinman, 1996; Derald Sue & Sue, 2008; White Kress, Eriksen, Rayle, & Ford, 2005). Research studies of the past 20 years also revealed that White clinicians across many different settings have diagnosed clients of color as having more pathology and poorer prognoses than White people with identical demographics and functional profiles (Baker, 2001; Rollock & Gordon, 2000; Snowden & Cheung, 1990).

There is an extensive controversy about whether DSM diagnoses should be applied cross-culturally. Two important perspectives about the relationship between culture and psychopathology are **cultural universalism** and **cultural relativism.** According to Joanne Thakker and Tony Ward (1998), "(u)niversalists emphasize the Western biomedical framework to find similarities across cultures" (p. 507). On the other hand, relativists assume that culture has a significant impact on mental disorders and that, if cultures vary, there will be differences in psychopathology. "Relativists assert that diagnostic categories are essentially abstractions or constructions used to explain psychiatric phenomena within the context of Western culture. . . . Hence they are necessarily limited in their capacity to explain such phenomena in diverse settings" (Thakker & Ward, 1998, p. 508).

Because of frequent cross-cultural misunderstandings and misinterpretations when diagnosing people from other cultures, the DSM (APA, 2000) includes a list of **culture-bound syndromes.** These syndromes are behaviors that are considered abnormal in some cultures but are rare or unheard of in others. In addition, a Cultural Formulation section provides a list and brief discussion of some cultural issues to consider before diagnosing "disorders" in people from cultures different from that of the person making the diagnosis. The **cultural formulation** includes the cultural identity of the individual, cultural explanations of the individual's illness, and cultural elements of the relationship between the individual and the clinician (Thakker & Ward, 1998).

Reformulation and Reconceptualization

The formulation is subject to continuous review and change as we learn more, over time, about clients and their situations. As assessment continues over time, we may gain new information that requires readjusting our initial conceptualization. As client feelings of comfort and safety increase, support-ive clinicians with good listening and elaboration skills often elicit more in-formation, feelings, and details. Our awareness of the tentative nature of our most sacrosanct interpretations and conclusions keeps us humble and open to new understanding, leading to a *re*formulation or *re*conceptualization.

Shifts in information, inferences, and interpretations should be written in the client's record and communicated verbally with involved colleagues. For example, if your colleagues thought that a teen's bulimia might be fueled by her perfectionism, and you have since learned that her parents were sud-denly divorcing without warning at the same time as her younger sister was diagnosed with leukemia and their prized pet died of old age, you should share that information with them.

Lum (2004) notes that many new immigrants and people of color with numerous experiences of racist and classist oppression may approach White clinicians with wariness and distrust—wearing a protective psychologi-cal mask or armor. Their lack of affect may cause clinicians to misdiagnose them as depressed, bored, or uninterested. Such clients, suspicious of what might be done with their information, might not disclose much so that the clinician's "big picture" is inaccurate. If upon the establishment of a trusting relationship new information is revealed, understandings about the client need to be reconceptualized, and the treatment plan may need to be altered. Similarly, if the clinician becomes aware of cultural or other biases that in-fluenced the original formulation, the case formulation and, sometimes, the approach may need to be adjusted in light of new understanding.

> Hospital staff asked me to assess a 93-year-old African American woman with pneu-monia, Miss E., whom they described as "noncompliant," resistant to getting well, and probably needing a nursing home to ensure her nutrition and self-care. The patient was refusing meals and existing on tea and toast in the early morning and at dinnertime.
>
> When I went to assess the patient, I found her to be annoyed, engaging, and talk-ative. She proudly stated that she had reached her age by taking only tea and buttered toast and an occasional meal with family and friends. All of her family and most of her friends had by now died from heart attacks and strokes she attributed to "eating too much." She also explained that she has regular visits from the neighborhood health clinic's home health staff. All of this was validated by her church pastor, who visited a day or two later and was "a great fan of Miss E's." After my report back to the staff, they had a better understanding of her. They no longer saw her as resistant and noncompliant and they stopped trying to force her to eat. They recognized that she had faithful support in the community and agreed that she probably would not need a nursing home.

■ Assessment Summaries or Psychological Reports

We conclude the assessment process by writing an intake report, also known as an **assessment summary** or **psychological report,** in which we summarize assessment findings and case conceptualization. Most licensed agencies, man-aged care programs, and insurance companies require such an assessment re-port before treatment planning can begin and then require briefer treatment summaries and progress reports at intervals to make judgments about the accuracy of case formulation and the benefits (or lack thereof) of the intervention.

Reports must be accurately and clearly written, avoiding jargon as well as speculation or inference for which there is little or weak evidence. For example, to describe a teen as "acting out" is not helpful. Terms like *acting out* too often connote a "bad" teen who is breaking rules or insulting staff. The clinician should describe the specific behavior in a particular setting and hypothesize possible triggers and consequences contributing to and maintaining it. Clinicians need to understand behavior in the context of its social antecedents and consequences.

Assessment reports usually include identifying and demographic information about the client, along with name, age, gender, sexual orientation, relationship status, and occupation. The report then includes presenting problems or concerns: the reasons for the referral or the reasons the client sought help from the clinician and the history of the presenting issues (how long problems were in development, when and how the problems began, and the nature of their development over time). If the client has seen other providers for help in the past, previous treatment and its effects are summarized.

The report describes the client's background: family developmental history (including family strengths), significant childhood events, meaningful migration stories, cultural and larger systems' influences and issues, biopsychosocial stressors, and oppressive forces affecting functioning. A description of a client's overall functioning often includes relational and other behavioral observations, cognitive and intellectual levels and skills, and emotional and affective state and self-regulation. The results of mental status exams or other psychological, intellectual, or neuropsychological tests are included. The report also describes health or biological conditions that may be related to the presenting problem, including medical history and medications and their effects. Also important is any history of substance or drug use, abuse, or dependence (Amodeo & Jones, 1997). Most psychological reports require a DSM diagnosis on all five axes.

The written report culminates in a brief formulation or conceptualization. However, the report should not be exclusively problem focused, because everyone has strengths, and tapping and enhancing strengths and social resources are important goals of any intervention. Strengths and resources include personal abilities and talents; resilience and coping mechanisms; the motivation and capacity to work for change; social and spiritual support networks; and agencies and services available in the client's geographic area. The assessment report becomes part of the clinical record, which we will describe in detail later in this chapter.

CLIP 7.1
Assessment and Formulation

Communicating Assessment Findings

Both during and upon completion of an assessment, we discuss our findings and conclusions with the client. This includes sharing with the client the results of any tests or information obtained through interviews with others and reviews of life records or any other material or experience with the client. In sharing this information, we are careful to note and validate the client's strengths, normal developmental issues and challenges, and other areas for potential work.

Communication should be direct, stated in plain language, and interspersed as needed with support and empathic comments. The clinician seeks feedback from the client, listening for thoughts and reactions that may differ from those of the clinician and exploring these further. Discussion of the assessment process and findings supports the working alliance as clients and clinicians prepare to set up goals and contracts for their work together.

We believe that it can be helpful to have friends or family members present for the discussion of assessment findings. Writing about Native American families, Joe and Malach (2004) suggest that "when an entire family is included, communication should be directed to the entire group" (p. 129), showing respect for all, unless the family requests another style of communication. At times we may also include in this discussion a local healer, herbalist, spiritual guide, or other figure when we are certain that the client is contemplating using their services in addition to, or instead of, ours. These are usually highly respected members of the client's community and deserve our respect and inclusion as well. Especially when medications may be recommended, it is important to communicate well with other nonmedical care providers who may be administering treatments that may trigger risky side effects when combined with Western medications.

However, in working with some matriarchal and patriarchal families, it may be important to direct comments to the elders in the group, signaling respect for cultural traditions. Again, cultural awareness and judgment are required. If uncertain about conversational protocol within a given culture, the clinician should ask the presenting client as to whom comments and questions should be addressed.

Clinicians are often uncertain about whether to share a DSM diagnosis. Many authors have written about the stigma of labeling and the problem of self-fulfilling prophecies (Caplan, 1995; Rosenhan, 1973; Torrey, 1972). Some clinicians prefer not to discuss the diagnosis because much of the formal DSM nomenclature ("cyclothymia," "schizoaffective disorder") can be scary or off-putting, and the focus of the moment is on pathology and dysfunction rather than on strengths and possibilities.

However, clients do have a right to ask for their diagnosis. Many have reported feeling very relieved finally to have a name for their experiences. Once a condition or set of experiences is named, clients and family members can obtain more information about "the disorder" from the Internet, public libraries, and other resources such as self-help groups. Clients may be relieved to discover that what seem to be strange and unique feelings or behavioral patterns are actually also experienced by others with whom they now can consult for advice and support.

The clinician should discuss diagnoses and related interventions in clear, easily understood language. A reflective comment, such as "You seem to prefer being alone most of the time to interacting with people," is more respectful and meaningful than, "You have what we call schizoid personality." Even more meaningful is a follow-up question such as "How do you react to what we have said?"

The Clinical Record

Assessment data (including the reason the person has come for help, any test results, and social and medical history), formulation (including diagnosis and goals for the work), and treatment plans (including progress towards goals) are all part of the **clinical record.** The clinical record also includes any forms completed by the client (including HIPAA documents and permission releases), reports received from other providers, and any reports about the client that are sent to anyone else, including reports to insurance carriers (Bersoff, 2008).

The purpose of the clinical record is "to (a) provide good care; (b) assist collaborating professionals in delivery of care; (c) ensure continuity of professional services in case of the (provider's) injury, disability, or death or with a change of provider; (d) provide for supervision or training if relevant; (e) provide documentation required for reimbursement or required administratively under contracts or laws; (f) effectively document any decision making, especially in high-risk situations; and (g) allow the (provider) to effectively answer a legal or regulatory complaint." (APA, 2007, p. 995).

It is important that the clinical record be accurate, clearly written, and free of jargon. It should be updated after each client contact. The amount of information needs to be detailed enough to be useful, yet as minimal as possible to protect client privacy. Some agencies, hospitals, and prisons may mandate what is included in the client's record and how things like the treatment plan should be updated. Box 7.4 contains the type of information that may be included in the client's record.

HIPAA requires that the clinician's psychotherapy notes not be part of the client's record. "'Psychotherapy notes' means notes recorded (in any medium) by a health care provider who is a mental health professional documenting or analyzing the contents of conversation during a private counseling session or a group, joint, or family counseling session" (United States Department of Health and Human Services, 2009).

The confidentiality of the clinical record must be ensured. For those clinicians who are subject to Heath Insurance Portability and Accountability Act of 1996, HIPAA rules and security standards must be followed. The clinician must be sure that anyone who comes in contact with the client's record, including agency or office staff and billing personnel, be trained how to handle confidential client information. The record itself should be secured in a location where it is safe from loss or damage. Electronic records should be encrypted, archived, and stored offsite. The clinical record should be kept for a period of 7 years after the end of the work to allow for reasonable future access if needed (NASW, 1999; APA, 2002b).

As noted in Chapter 2, both our ethical codes and HIPAA regulations mandate that clients can have access to their clinical record upon request. If a client requests to see his or her record, the clinician should discuss with

BOX 7.4 The Clinical Record

Information in the client's file:

- Identifying data (e.g., name, client ID number)
- Contact information (e.g., phone number, address, next of kin)
- Fees and billing information
- Where appropriate, guardianship or conservatorship status
- Documentation of informed consent or assent for treatment (Ethics Code, Standard 3.10)
- Documentation of waivers of confidentiality and authorization or consent for release of information (Ethics Code, Standard 4.05)
- Documentation of any mandated disclosure of confidential information (e.g., report of child abuse, release secondary to a court order)
- Presenting complaint, diagnosis, or basis for request for services
- Plan for services, updated as appropriate (e.g., treatment plan, supervision plan, intervention schedule, community interventions, consultation contracts)
- Health and developmental history

For each substantive contact with a client:

- Date of service and duration of session
- Types of services (e.g., consultation, assessment, treatment, training)
- Nature of professional intervention or contact (e.g., treatment modalities, referral, letters, e-mail, phone contacts)
- Formal or informal assessment of client status

The record may also include other specific information, depending upon the circumstances:

- Client responses or reactions to professional interventions
- Current risk factors in relation to dangerousness to self or others
- Other treatment modalities employed, such as medication or biofeedback treatment
- Emergency interventions (e.g., specially scheduled sessions, hospitalizations)
- Plans for future interventions
- Information describing the qualitative aspects of the professional– client interaction
- Prognosis
- Assessment or summary data (e.g., psychological testing, structured interviews, behavioral ratings, client behavior logs)
- Consultations with or referrals to other professionals
- Case-related telephone, mail, and email contacts
- Relevant cultural and sociopolitical factors

Source: American Psychological Association. (2007). Record Keeping Guidelines. *American Psychologist, 62,* 993–1004.

the client the reason for the request before providing a copy of the record. According to HIPAA regulations, clients do not have access to psychotherapy notes, but they may ask to see them. NASW recommends that clinicians should "limit clients' access to their records, or portions of their records, only in exceptional circumstances, when there is compelling evidence that such access would cause serious harm to the client. Both clients' requests and the rationale for withholding some or all of the record should be documented in clients' files" (NASW, 1999, Standard 1.08). In those circumstances, the clinician can provide the client with a written summary of the record or send the record to another provider or the client's attorney.

■ Goal Setting

Desired Outcomes

Goals express the desired outcomes of the working relationship agreed upon by the clinician and client. Many human service professionals working in schools or other settings are required to use formalized methods to assess change and progress toward goals. As often as possible, goals should include **desired outcomes** that are observable and measurable and that can be used in assessing the effectiveness of interventions.

EXAMPLE

Goal Outcomes   To improve self-esteem and self-efficacy.

Client will be able to express opinions and give feedback to others.

Client will tolerate praise and positive feedback.

Client will make more positive statements about self.

Client will demonstrate increased eye contact with others.

Client will identify positive talents and strengths about self.

Client will increase the frequency of speaking with confidence in social situations.

Client will report a decreased fear of rejection.

Client will increase statements of self-acceptance.

Goals are informed by images of how clinicians and clients would like things to be in the future, and they can be either short term or long term.

Short-term goals can be accomplished relatively quickly, whereas **long-term goals** may take more time. Clinicians can ask clients about their goals by asking future-oriented questions such as:

- "How would you like things to be different?"
- "What are your goals for our work together?"
- "If our work is successful, what will be changed for you?"
- "How will things look when they are the way you want them to be?"
- "Which of your attributes would you like other people to notice more?"

Also ask clients what is working for them and what they would like to keep.

EXAMPLE

Clinician: You said you often feel alone. Are there things you do that make you feel less "out of it"?

Client: No . . . um, well, at the gym when I'm working out, I feel better.

Clinician: What is it about working out that helps?

Client: I don't know. I get out of myself, I guess.

Clinician: Anything else about the gym?

Client: I guess I'm with people. I talk to the other guys some days. I don't feel so alone.

Clinician: So could we say that a goal of yours might be to go to the gym more often?

Specific and Concrete

Goals flow from assessment findings, and they have to be specific and concrete to provide clear directions for ensuing work together. Clinicians often ask questions such as:

- "What specific things would be different if you were to achieve your goal?"
- "How will we know when we have achieved the goals you want?"

Sometimes clients come in with very concrete and specific goals: "I want to score 10 points better in my basketball games" or "Can you help me get into the Jobs Program?" Often, however, they come in with goals that are abstract or are generally stated: "I want to feel better." The clinician then needs to help them be more specific and eventually formulate more-concrete goals.

EXAMPLE OF HELPING CLIENTS SET CONCRETE GOALS

Clinician: If our work is successful, what will be different about your son?

Client: Davey won't be so depressed.

Clinician: What will show us that Davey isn't so depressed?

Client: He'll smile more.

Clinician: What else will you notice?

Client: He'll play with friends after school instead of just hanging out at home alone.

EXERCISE 7.3 Turning Abstract Goals into Concrete Goals

In your journal, record goals that you have for yourself. Turn these general goals into specific, concrete goals with measurable outcomes.

Partializing and Prioritizing Goals

Clinicians help clients partialize goals; we help clients break major goals down into component parts called **objectives.** Each goal may have many objectives. For example, recovery from alcoholism is a broad goal within which there may be a number of specific objectives: to recognize and own a problem with drinking, to attend AA meetings, to develop friendships with people who are sober, and to live in a stable environment. We have to help clients take broad goals and **partialize,** that is, break them down into component parts. In doing so, we take vague or general concepts like "feeling more independent" and identify their defining components so that each can be addressed in the order of its priority in problem resolution.

EXAMPLE OF PARTIALIZING GOALS

Clinician: What goals do you think we should have for our work together?

Client: I want to be more independent.

Clinician: How would that look?

Client: I'd have my own place, my own spending money and schedule.

Clinician: What kinds of things would need to happen for you to be more independent?

Client: I would have to improve my English and get a job.

Often clinicians and clients can see problems as so enormous and lacking in definition that they can feel burdened and overwhelmed. A feeling of hopelessness can suffuse the work. By breaking goals down into concrete objectives and talking about them in simple everyday language, tasks can seem much more achievable, and clients can feel much more hopeful.

EXERCISE 7.4 Partializing

The following is a list of goals that clients might have for their work with a clinician. Partialize them into smaller objectives. In your journal, write down the broad goal, and for each goal, make a list of component objectives. Discuss your list with your fellow students in the class.

Freydia is a 27-year-old mother who has been using crack cocaine for 4 years. Her children, ages 7 and 9, have been removed from her care by Child Protective Services and are currently living with her mother. Freydia comes to the drug program saying, "I want to get my children back."

Thomas, a 20-year-old college sophomore, drops out of school. He has just been diagnosed with schizophrenia. His mother has brought him to the day center saying she hopes that "somehow he will be able to get back to college."

Rad is a 49-year-old refugee from Bosnia. He was an engineer in Sarajevo, but now he cleans buildings at night. He does not speak English well. He wants to get certified as an engineer and get a job so he can bring his family to the United States.

We help the client **prioritize** goals and objectives, ranking them in the order of their urgency or importance. The ranking of priorities has to take into account the client's capacity and motivation to work on the selected tasks during and between visits, the likelihood that achieving the objectives will have positive consequences, and the availability of resources required to achieve the objectives.

When feasible, we prioritize a relatively easy goal or objective so that the client can experience mastery, which fuels further efforts. Every effort is made to stage the work so that, when possible, small successes build on one another.

EXAMPLE OF PRIORITIZING OBJECTIVES

Clinician: What would be your first step in becoming more independent?

Client: Get a job first, I guess; then I can pay my bills.

Clinician: What kinds of things would you have to do to get a job?

Client: Well, I would have to go out on interviews.

Clinician: Are there steps you would need to take before that?

Client: Well, first, I guess I would have to start search for jobs that are available.

Clinician: How can you find out about jobs?

Client: I can read the want ads in the paper. I'd have to start buying the paper first. I can also look online.

Priority setting is also affected by the needs and feelings of others in the client's family or social system. Different **stakeholders** may have different goals. For example, Davey's mother wants him to smile more. Davey may want his parents to stop fighting, or he may want his mother to be less concerned about whether he smiles. The parents of Thomas, the young man with schizophrenia, may stipulate that he can live at home only if he stops smoking in the house. Giving up smoking may not be Thomas's goal, but, since he needs to live at home, realistically he has to change his priorities and accommodate his parents' wishes; perhaps all can agree that Thomas can smoke on the back steps. It may even turn out that this "smoking" issue masks other fears regarding his condition.

The **demands** of the larger society can also intrude on priority setting. Freydia, the woman who wishes her children back, might see getting sober and getting work training as priorities. However, in a conversation with the clinician, Freydia realizes that she is going to include a mandated 6-week parenting course in her priorities.

EXERCISE 7.5 Prioritizing

Go back to Exercise 7.3 in your journal. List the strengths and resources that will help you meet the specific goals. Then prioritize the specific goals and objectives. In the class, share your goals, objectives, and priorities. Remember to set priorities that:

CLIP 7.2
Developing Goals

- You want.
- Are attainable.
- Are in accord with the resources available.

■ Conclusion

Assessment, formulation, and goal setting help clinicians and clients make plans to work together for change. This work includes developing treatment plans. Such plans may include specific interventions and strategies for change, as well as contracts identifying who, when, where, and how the work of change will be done. Intervention or treatment plans also include an evaluation of whether and how much change has occurred. Throughout this process, clinicians should always provide facts to substantiate hypotheses, observations, conclusions, and recommendations, since many people have been harmed by clinician and diagnostic bias and interventions based on cultural prejudice or ignorance.

■ Suggested Readings

American Psychological Association. (2007). Record keeping guidelines. *American Psychologist, 62*, 993–1004.

Hays, Pamela. (2008). *Addressing cultural complexities in practice: Assessment, diagnosis, and therapy* (2nd Ed.). Washington, DC: American Psychological Association.

McGoldrick, Monica, Gerson, Randy, & Petry, Sueli. (2008). *Genograms: Assessment and intervention.* New York: Norton.

Peterson, Christopher, Park, Nansook, & Seligman, Martin. (2006). Strengths of character and recovery. *Journal of Positive Psychology, 1*, 17–26.

Whitson, Susan. (2009). *Principles and applications of assessment in counseling* (3rd Ed.). Belmont, CA: Brooks/Cole-Cengage.

Good critiques of the DSM-IV include:

Caplan, Paula. (1995). *They say you're crazy: How the world's most powerful psychiatrists decide who's normal.* Reading, MA: Addison-Wesley.

Kutchins, Herb, & Kirk, Stuart. (1997). *Making us crazy: DSM: The psychiatric bible and the creation of mental disorder.* New York: Free Press.

Thakker, Joanne, & Ward, Tony. (1998). Culture and classification: The cross-cultural application of the DSM-IV. *Clinical Psychology Review, 18*, 501–529.

White Kress, Victoria, Eriksen, Karen, Rayle, Dixon, Andrea, & Ford, Stephanie J. W. (2005). The DSM-IV-TR and cultures: Considerations for counselors. *Journal of Counseling and Development, 83*, 97–105.

■ Self-Explorations

1. Recall a time when you underwent a type of assessment to receive a service or enter a program. What aspects of the assessment process were comfortable and routine, and what provoked anxiety for you?

2. Have you ever been labeled in a positive way, for example, as a "good athlete," "Dean's List student," or "student leader"? What were the labels? Describe their effects on you. Have you ever received an unsettling or stigmatizing label, for example, "slow learner," "class clown," "low life," or "dumb blonde"? What were the labels? Describe their effects on you.

3. Have you or anyone in your family ever received a DSM diagnosis? What were the positive and/or negative effects of having received the diagnosis?

■ Essay Questions

1. What are the sources of and methods for collecting assessment data? What are the strengths and weaknesses of each method?

2. Discuss issues of reliability and validity. What do you think clinicians can do to improve both the reliability and validity of assessment interviews?

3. Explain the purpose of gathering spiritual or religious information in assessment and how that information may enhance or inform sessions, planning, and intervention.

4. What factors can negatively affect a clinician's ability to make accurate inferences about a client from assessment data? List and describe three potential biases in clinical inference.

5. Read the suggested readings by Paula Caplan (1995) or Kutchins and Kirk (1995 or 1997). Then discuss the strengths and weaknesses of the DSM-IV-TR.

■ Key Terms

Assessment interviews

Assessment summary

Case conceptualization

Clinical judgment

Clinical record

Content of the assessment

Culturagram

Cultural formulation

Cultural relativism

Cultural strengths

Cultural universalism

Culture-bound syndromes

Desired outcomes

Diagnostic reliability

DSM (Diagnostic and Statistical Manual)

Ecomap

Formal diagnosis

Formal observation

Formulation

Genogram

Goals

ICD (International Classification of Diseases)

Informal observation

Interrater reliability

Levels of inference

Life chart

Life records

Long-term goals

Mental disorder

Multiaxial diagnostic system

Multidisciplinary team

Objectives

Observation

Partialize

Prioritize

Process of the assessment

Psychological report

Reliability

Review of life records

Semistructured interviews

Short-term goals

Stakeholders

Strength-based genogram

Structured interviews

Testing

Test-retest reliability

Unstructured interviews

Validity

CHAPTER 8

Planning for and Evaluating Change

Through the initial assessment and case conceptualization process, the idea of "getting help" now begins to take on form and meaning. People begin to realize that, contrary to expectations, help and change are not prepackaged procedures or supplies that the professional "delivers." Instead, the work is collaborative: a supportive, participatory, and dynamic process that clinician and client must coevolve using their own vision, capacities, determination, and resources. Clients realize that they may need to make changes in their familiar ways of thinking, feeling, relating, and behaving.

Clinicians realize that they, too, need to make changes in response to the specific style, pace, assets, and needs of each client. They need to be flexible and willing to adapt familiar approaches so that each client feels more empowered and at ease in the work ahead. Both clinician and client prepare for the time, energy, and personal commitment required to plan and to carry out effective work together.

During goal setting and treatment planning work, clients realize more clearly than before how promising and helpful the work of change can be.

At the same time, they realize that this work may involve some pain and the relinquishing of long-familiar habits and relationships. Resulting ambivalences can lead to hesitation and mixed feelings about proceeding. Awareness of the ways in which the process of change unfolds can help clients and those working with them anticipate what may lie ahead.

■ Preparing for Change

Stages of Change

After reviewing and comparing several hundred therapeutic models, Prochaska, Norcross, & DiClemente (1994) noted common components of effective change strategies as well as stages, or phases, of change. They assert that "over 45 percent of clients drop out of psychotherapy prematurely, since treatments too often don't match the stage clients are in" (p. 16). They identified six still-relevant stages of change (pp. 38–50) and suggest specific activities that can help in each stage.

1. *Pre-Contemplation.* People minimize and rationalize their problem behaviors, attributing them to fate, family, and social influences, or to genetics. Pre-contemplation is often found in court-mandated referrals and in clients pressured by significant others to "get help or else."

Advice giving, lecturing, and moralizing almost never work with individuals who are not ready to take ownership of behaviors that others see clearly and experience as harmful. Remembering from time to time that it is human to ignore or deny painful realities helps us to remain patient with people who persist in justifying self-defeating behaviors. Also remember that at least the client has come to see you—perhaps a gutsy first step, no matter how ambivalent or reluctant his or her presentation.

Sometimes pre-contemplators can be helped by empathizing with the fix they are in and sympathetically naming possible unsettling consequences if their habits persist. If clients feel accepted for who they are rather than judged for who they are not, they are likely to be more receptive to the information that professionals can provide about the complex nature and multiple causes of problems, the painful consequences of continued behaviors, and examples of strategies and programs that have educated and supported others under similar pressure to change.

At the same time that we want to show support and understanding of the client's anxiety about change, it is important not to become an "enabling helper." That term describes clinicians and client partners or allies who may be tempted to collude with clients' rationalizations of problems because they fear the client's anger or rejection if they address problems directly and forthrightly.

Matilda said it wasn't a big deal that she kept losing every job. She said employers have always discriminated against her because she is overweight—she's not the "eye candy" that male bosses like to have around. I realized she was 2 years out of college and had already lost three or four jobs in short order. She was not able to discuss any other things that might have brought trouble on herself. She said she'd only come to see a counselor because she lives at home and her parents put pressure on her to come. I didn't want to make her feel bad about herself, so I didn't push the job topic this time.

* * *

My supervisor told me I wasn't helping Jax by just listening to all of his excuses about why he can't get to school on time, since his mother always gives him a ride to the corner down the street from the school. My supervisor reminded me that Jax had a history of drug use and that he might be meeting up with his old crowd briefly before school. This could put him at risk for using again. She told me to ask him about this possibility but I couldn't do it right away—it just seemed like he would resent me for not trusting or believing him. I wanted to make a relationship with him first by being nonjudgmental— then I could ask him.

2. ***Contemplation.***   In this stage, the client experiences a dawning aware-ness of a need for change—but simultaneously does and does not want to change. This ambivalence is manifested in hopeful anticipation mixed with doubt or retreat. We can help clients by encouraging the open dis-cussion of problems and prospects with friends or in social groups, where others are sharing similar stories and detailing strategies that helped them face themselves and their problems and initiate change. Prochaska, Norcross, and DiClemente (1994) also encourage educating clients about anteced-ents and consequences of their habitual behaviors so that they can avoid or minimize time spent in relationships or environment that trigger these behaviors.

Clients can be helped to develop and use self-monitoring tools (jour-nals or tracking sheets) and discuss ways to deal with daily temptations and triggers. In-session visualization exercises help clients positively imag-ine and describe themselves and how their lives will be different in the future, when problematic habits no longer control them. Teaching clients to give themselves positive self-talk for owning behaviors and embarking on change helps them maintain their self-observation and self-restraint in this early phase.

Because of his threats to harm her after she left him, LeQuan's wife had taken out a restraining order against him. Referred to our Court Clinic for anger management work, he explained to me that his religion was firmly against violence, and he was ashamed of punching his wife and hitting his kids with a belt when they did anything wrong. As I asked more questions about his current daily life, I learned that he is a respected mechanic and supervisor of younger trainees at the large, busy repair shop where he works. Initially I had us focus on his solid work history, crediting his achievements. He said he would never threaten or punch anyone at work, so he wondered why he does that at home. We first worked on a couple of calming and diverting strategies (counting to ten, listening to easy jazz on his iPod, walking his dog Remy). He began to think about returning to karate classes that had always helped him blow off steam and feel more confident. He mentioned talking with a church elder, but that elder had shamed him for being so hard on his wife and kids, so that didn't feel helpful. He did think he could ride motorbikes more with work friends to stay busy and feel good with other guys. But as he got more active with others and comfortable with me, he would recount times still when he would "cruise the wife's place" on his bike, which he knew was a no-no. But he came to talk to me about this, closer to the event, which was a sign of growth. He would continue to get mad, though less so and for shorter periods of time.

3. *Preparation.*　In this stage the client establishes goals for change, outlines small steps, and even sets a time for start-up. This stage is characterized by swings between impulsive leaps forward and slips backward into problematic behaviors. Clinicians can offer support if clients feel embarrassed or have doubts about continuing. Highlighting past successes is helpful in fueling hope and initiative. We can ask clients to tell others about their intended efforts so that they can elicit continuing social support and check-ins from others.

We can also ask clients to recall people they know or have heard of who have experienced the drastic consequences of hurtful patterns (for example, someone who died of alcohol-related cirrhosis), then acknowledge and honor their grit and determination in facing problems head-on and using their self-commitment to change rather than give up. Joining a relevant mutual aid group adds support and coping information during the early stressful period of initiating change behaviors.

Anson didn't agree with his male partner's assessment of him as having a drinking problem. Instead, he always laughed and joked at parties about being Irish and loving to "push a few back" in order to lighten up and have fun in a crowd. He came to the counseling center because of recent problems sleeping the night through and hoping we might give him some medication to help with sleep. When I learned in the evaluation that he was having rich dinners late and consuming four or five drinks before and during them, I asked if he would at least give some thought that too much food and drink were part of the sleep problem. He was willing to take home some literature I routinely hand out to older men about weight and heart problems, Type II diabetes, and alcohol and aging. He told me the next visit that he and his partner were both thinking about going to an open AA meeting but wanted to find one outside their area, which might take a little time. I said I was glad to hear it and would look forward to hearing how it went.

4. *Action.*　At this stage the person's planned actions for change proceed more evenly. Goals and steps are kept small and manageable.

We help clients focus on the benefits derived from new behaviors and the lessons they are learning from mastering the inevitable rough spots. Clients need to understand that the temptation to return to familiar habits is normal. They can also predetermine small rewards to give themselves for positive change behaviors. (In subsequent chapters, we discuss specific tools, strategies, and techniques that can help clients substitute new thoughts, feelings, and behaviors for old ones.)

Louellen had low esteem after years of being teased unmercifully because of her weight. Though a good partner, mom, and line nursing supervisor, she had never risen higher in nursing management because she was terrified of rejection if she applied for leadership jobs for which she was fully prepared by now. She came to see me for interviewing skill coaching and confidence building. We very quickly developed homework exercises that included affirming self-talk as well as imagined interviews, noting down for discussion with me the points at which things would start to get tough in her mind. We would use her notations to replay these tough spots in our sessions, practicing other things to say and do instead of peeling away into self-chastising. She brought in two of her daughter's puppets so we could script interview scenarios using them to rehearse. She began to look and feel much happier, and without telling me, applied for a position she saw in the paper. To her chagrin, her application didn't even garner a response, triggering a temporary "I told you so" feeling. Reassured by me that we all have interviewing hits and misses, she tried again, but first went to see a nursing recruiter. I felt certain this would land her several prospects, and before long, she had two good choices to work with.

5. *Behavior maintenance.*   Additional support and coping tips are gained from joining support or recovery groups and from getting a sponsor or special friend to talk with during crises or lapses. People may change some relationships and environments to support continued growth. For example, people with drug or alcohol problems may replace old "using" buddies with clean and sober friends who share their motivation and readiness to change.

Clinicians can provide encouragement and praise while helping clients remain aware of temptations. We can review why these changes have been made so that clients do not forget why they took this hard work on in the first place.

Charlesie keeps attending and speaking at AA after 15 years of sobriety. She recognizes that both the other attendees and the process of reflection and mutual aid keep her humble and focused on living one day at a time. She retains an older female sponsor whom she can call should special problems arise—and they do from time to time. I'm seeing her just now because her daughter died a few months ago in a plane crash, and this terrible loss reminded her of the loss of her mother in an auto accident when Charlesie was just a young teen. I told her that these losses were terrible, and that coming in to grieve was just the right step to take for herself at this time.

6. *Recycling.*   Change usually involves two steps forward, one step back, because growth is a spiraling rather than a linear process. People may return to the pre-contemplative or maintenance stages often, to reflect and plan, sometimes resuming work at higher levels.

Prochaska, Norcross, and DiClemente (1994) urge people to remember that one lapse is not a relapse and that lapses are human. Advise clients to work each stage one step at a time and to remember that the most lasting change takes months and sometimes years. All change work has its ups and downs, and it is crucial that you remain hopeful and encouraging when clients feel like giving up on themselves. They often later describe how much this belief in them kept them going.

Charlesie came back to see me several years later after her father died of cirrhosis due to a long history of alcohol abuse. She realized that she had some unfinished business that she hadn't confided the first time. It was her drunk dad, and not her distracted mom, who was driving when the car accident killed her mom but not her dad. She hated him for a long time after that and often wished him dead. Now that he is, she feels guilty and is also sad once again about the loss of her mom and her daughter. She recalled me as a good listener, very important now because her whole family is gone now except her. I invited her to start in, in any fashion she wanted to.

Reframing "Resistance" to Change

We know that some clients drop out of the work early on, even during or just after the assessment, realizing that more is required than they are interested in or can commit to at present. Others may agree to planned work, but with ambivalence, self-doubt, or trepidation about consequences. For many years, practitioners have described lack of motivation, noncompliance, and resistance as major obstacles to change. Whereas these terms were once used to describe the client, we now recognize that environmental and clinician/agency factors greatly affect a client's attitudes toward the work.

Stone Center proponents of Relational-Cultural Theory believe that resistance is relational (Comstock, 2004). They suggest that regarding resistance as a flaw in the client overlooks the fact that difficulties in the relationship are often "products of relational disconnections and empathic failures" (p. 91). They believe that "movement out of disconnection requires looking at what both the client *and* the therapist bring to the relationship at any particular point" (p. 91). Sometimes cultural differences between counselor and client can cause a client to disconnect or drop out of the intervention without explanation.

Peter De Jong and Insoo Kim Berg (2001) urge clinicians to remember from a strengths perspective that all clients have competencies to be elicited as fuel for change work. Any apparent "resistance" may mean that a clinician hasn't found the right way to join with the client's perspective yet, and signals a need for the clinician to ask more not-knowing questions about what the client just said, then reflect the client's answer back, rather than educating or confronting him or her about being "resistant."

In addition to relational factors, contextual factors affect continuance. Agency policies, procedures, staff, and location may seem too far removed from a client's experience, language, and comfort zone. Stresses at home and the lack of resources (including transportation and child care) can affect attendance and follow-through. The cost of treatment and medications can be beyond many clients' means. The timing of suggested meetings, when planned around clinicians' availability and schedules, can interfere with other important obligations. Loved ones, feeling threatened by the intended changes, may discourage following through on sessions and planned work. Unexpected local crises and agency cutbacks can also undermine or end planned work.

Building Motivation to Change

William Miller and Stephen Rollnick (2002) define motivation as an interpersonal process, the product of interactions between two people. They point out that clients who appear unmotivated at a given time or with a given clinician or program may go on to change behaviors in the future, given the proper moment, circumstances, advice, and support. Instead of focusing on the presence or absence in clients of motivation or noncompliance with treatment, they suggest **motivational interviewing** (MI) strategies to enhance client participation.

Miller and Rollnick (2002) believe that all human change involves ambivalence and that it should be no surprise to clinicians that, when we lean on clients to change in the ways we think best for them, they respond with numerous justifications for keeping things as they are. Clinicians can demonstrate client-centered empathy in motivational interviewing in which the therapist's acceptance of a client's reluctance to change infuses the work with a nonjudgmental and collaborative spirit (Burke, Arkowitz, & Menchola, 2003). There are two factors that influence a client's readiness to change: how important the particular change is to the client, and the client's confidence in making the desired changes (Burke et al., 2003).

Techniques for Resolving Ambivalence About Change

Miller and Rollnick (2002) have conducted a number of empirical studies on motivational interviewing. They have found several techniques effective in resolving ambivalence regarding change:

- *Using the decisional balance sheet.* A major technique to help people move toward change is the **decisional balance sheet** (see Box 8.1), which can help in beliefs clarification and decision making. The client describes

---

BOX 8.1 Decisional Balance Sheet

Continue to Drink as Before		Abstain from Alcohol	
Benefits	Costs	Benefits	Costs
Helps me relax	Could lose my family	Less family conflict	I enjoy getting high
Enjoy drinking with friends	Bad example for my children	More time with my children	What to do about my friends
	Damaging my health	Feel better physically	How to deal with stress
	Spending too much money	Helps with money problems	
	Impairing my mental ability		
	Might lose my job		
	Wasting my time/life		

Source: From *Motivational Interviewing: Preparing people for change,* 2nd Ed. by William R. Miller & Stephen Rollnick (2002, p. 16). © 2002 Guilford Press. Reprinted with permission of Guilford Press.

the costs and the benefits of keeping things as they are and the costs and benefits of changing. As the client then reflects on each belief listed, the clinician empathizes with how hard it is to feel two ways about something so important, mirroring the feelings and thoughts the client shares on examining the pros and cons.

- *Reflecting back to clients an approximation of what they have just said* is another frequently used technique that keeps them in charge of puzzling out how to proceed when seesawing toward and away from change action. This reflective process makes them the drivers of the process and deciders of what they wish to do. Clinician reflection often encourages clients to go deeper in their self-reflection, continually sifting through the benefits and costs of staying the same and stirring things up in very productive ways.

- *Creating and amplifying the discrepancy between present behavior and the client's broader goals and values.*   Clients experience such a discrepancy when we help them contrast what they listed as the cons of staying the same and the benefits of changing, or when they compare the benefits of staying the same and of changing. The eventual dissonance created by these comparisons can bring about a gradual reduction in ambivalence and some movement toward change.

- *Rolling with the resistance.*   "The counselor does not impose new views or goals; rather, the person is invited to consider new information and is offered new perspectives. 'Take what you want and leave the rest' is the permissive kind of advice that pervades this approach" (Miller & Rollnick, 2002, p. 40). Holly Swartz and colleagues (2007) affirm that the stance of the clinician should be that of a student learning more about the client's troubles, beliefs, values, and assets so that the client's stance becomes that of the teacher. They believe that in the same respectful manner, the therapist should also ask clients' permission before giving suggestions or providing information, and then ask what clients thought about what was posed.

- *Turning the question back to clients* for further comments (rather than answering it or musing on it) is another technique that respects and patiently draws out the insights and capacities of clients, involving them as active fellow problem solvers.

- *Expressing our faith and confidence in the client's ability to make the desired changes supports self-efficacy.*   Miller and Rollnick (2002) suggest that the gap between present behavior and the desired future behaviors is crucial to keep in mind: The greater the gap is, the greater our efforts must be to understand and support clients so that discouragement and defeatism do not derail their aspirations and activities.

Since the clinician does not take sides in clients' internal debates about what they might gain or lose in changing and in staying the same, they have no one to "resist" but themselves. Clients who highly value self-determination have only themselves to argue with, and the argument can become tiresome after a period of seesawing back and forth.

Miller and Rollnick (2002) remind us that a lot of change takes place without any assistance from professionals or programs. In the past, "recovery" was called a **"spontaneous remission"** of symptoms, as though it were the symptoms which acted by going away. However, the human resilience and determination that so often spur improvement and other changes could be readily observed in survivors of 9/11; of the British subway terrorist bombings; of hurricanes Katrina and Ike; after the South Asian and African tsunamis; and following massive earthquakes in China, Turkey, and Pakistan. These disasters provide inspiring examples of how people from all walks of life can effect change by working together when professionals and institutions provide little or no help.

■ Intervention or Treatment Plans

Assessment and case conceptualization lead to intervention or treatment plans. The word *treatment* is most often used in medical and mental health settings, and *intervention* in community based settings. In some settings these plans are called service plans to avoid use of the word *treatment*, which implies that a client has an illness, when in actuality most of his or her problems may be rooted in socioeconomic and cultural stresses.

Intervention plans or **treatment plans** spell out agreed-upon goals for the work to come and the people, methods, and resources proposed to achieve the goals. Neukrieg and Schwitzer (2006) describe the treatment plan as a "road map [and] tool by which clinicians put their case conceptualization and theoretical perspectives into action" (p. 224). Plans usually include a number of topics (see Box 8.2), starting with overarching goals and including more specific goals and objectives for the work. It specifies the participants in the work and their specific roles and responsibilities.

BOX 8.2 Treatment Plans

- Goals
- Participants
- Modalities
- Techniques and strategies
- Logistics
- Other services and resources
- Advocacy
- Evaluation

The core of the plan elaborates the specific methods and techniques to be used to accomplish each goal. Included also is the modality or combination of modalities that are to be utilized (individual, family, or group). The plan should address important logistics: where the work will take place; the expected length and number of sessions; expected cost; and other important contingencies, such as transportation, child care, available space, and the like. We also have an ethical obligation to discuss potential risks or adverse effects that clients may experience as part of their work for change. Clients can give informed consent only if they are aware of the potential downsides to the proposed work.

A meaningful plan must also acknowledge any constraints that managed care or agency mission and policies place on plans and goals. For example, Mark Young (2005) notes that, in many managed care and agency settings, the client may be seen for only 6 to 10 sessions. Economic restraints call for creative planning ahead, making explicit how ancillary services and supports are to be arranged—and by whom—when brief contacts end even though clients may still have pressing needs. We appreciate that, in addition to counseling, many other services and resources can be helpful to clients, no matter how extensive our work with them. The plan should be explicit about other services and resources to be utilized—for example, AA attendance, an exercise program or meditation class, a study group, a GED prep class at a nearby school, or court-ordered weekly check-ins with a probation officer.

Since client problems are often a product of environmental factors and oppressive systems, we believe that some plans may recommend interventions such as political activism or work for social justice such as fighting for a change in minimum wage laws or working to ensure school programs for the children of undocumented immigrants. Both clients and clinicians can engage in these activities to address systemic issues and to change oppressive systems affecting clients and their attainment of goals.

Sonia's 11-year-old son Elias had been killed in a random act of violence in her neighborhood. He was sitting on the stoop when gang members started attacking each other with guns and he was caught in the crossfire and killed. Sonia was dealing with her grief about his death and her feelings of hopelessness and powerlessness about the future. At another point she said that she hoped no one else would have to experience what she did. The clinician knew about an antigun rally that was happening in the city and asked her if she thought she would be willing to attend the rally as part of their work together. She and the clinician put attendance at the rally into her plan for their work together. (Sonia not only went to the meeting, she ended up speaking passionately about the need for gun control and had many people thanking her for the actions she had taken to curb the violence in their city.)

Plans should also include statements about how—by whom, at what intervals, and with what procedures—progress toward goal achievement will be measured and evaluated. All plans should be articulated in clear and specific language that is plainly understood by clients. Some clinicians find it helpful to review or utilize standardized planning guides in order to write the plans succinctly and specifically.

Choosing Strategies and Interventions

How do we choose among the wide variety of strategies, interventions, or techniques that can be included in a treatment plan? Some clinicians base their decisions on a theory of counseling or psychotherapy or on empirically validated methods. Others are eclectic in their choice of theory, selecting what they believe to be effective methods from various theories or weaving empirically validated methods into their preferred theoretical model. Whatever the guiding theories, all treatment plans must be crafted to give full consideration to the unique capacities, supports, and needs of each client and situation.

Theories of Counseling and Psychotherapy

Theoretical models of counseling and therapy are usually taught at advanced levels of clinical education, where students learn theory in class, then practice applying it in their supervised internships and bring issues and challenges from the field back to class for further discussion. You may be familiar with some widely used theoretical models, including psychodynamic, behavioral, cognitive, humanistic, positive psychology, and family systems models. Recall from Chapter 1 that Prochaska and Norcross (2007) identified over 400 different models of therapy in North America alone, each one touting its unique ability to inform and promote change.

In the past, clinicians from a particular theoretical school usually developed a relatively generalizable treatment plan based chiefly on their theoretical orientation. This plan would be utilized with a wide variety of clients, problems, and situations. For example, clinicians using analytically informed psychodynamic theory believed that client symptoms resulted from repressed unconscious conflicts from early childhood or adolescent development. Therefore, the goal of therapy was to help make these conflicts conscious in order to resolve or rework them. The preferred modality was individual therapy. The clinical stance was that of providing a rather blank slate onto which clients could project their unresolved anxieties and conflicts from relationships with past significant others. Techniques might include free association and the analysis of client transferences, defenses, fantasies, resistance, dreams, and slips of the tongue. Meetings might occur two to five times a week, and the work could last for years.

Some clinicians still predominantly utilize one theoretical model and adhere to the guiding principles and strategies spelled out in that model with little variance. These colleagues often describe themselves according to the model they are using: as cognitive therapists, as dialectical-behavioral therapists, as family systems therapists, as holistic therapists, as interpersonal therapists, as solution-focused therapists, and the like.

In using theory to guide plans and interventions, all clinicians need to guard against culturally biased assumptions that could convert a theoretical lens into a cultural blinder. Sue and Sue (2003) describe a clinician working with an African-American man who could not find a job and wanted help with job search skills. The clinician reported: "Using a humanistic existential approach, I reflected his feelings, paraphrased his thoughts, and summarized his dilemma. This did not seem to immediately help" (p. 63). No wonder! The client was seeking information and advice about how to look for a job. The clinician had his own preferred approach down, and he was going to use it regardless of the client's expectations, preferred help seeking and relating style with professionals, and specific issues and requests.

Evidence-Based Practice

A great deal of empirical evidence about the effectiveness of certain therapeutic models and techniques in use with specific conditions (anxiety, depression, eating disorders, shyness) has emerged in the clinical practice research literature over the past two decades (Norcross, Beutler, & Levant, 2006). In addition, dozens of empirical research studies have validated the clinical relationship as a central factor in intervention effectiveness, regardless of the type of intervention (Anderson, Ogles, Patterson, Lambert & Vermeersch, 2009; Neumann et al., 2009). **Evidence-based practice** (EBP) is the general term used to describe "clinical practice that is informed by evidence about interventions, clinical expertise, and patient needs, values, and preferences and their integration into decision making about individual care" (Kazdin, 2008, p. 147).

One aspect of evidence-based practice has been a growing reliance on **empirically supported treatments** (ESTs) in intervention planning (Lebow, 2006). Empirically supported therapies are "clearly specified psychological treatments shown to be efficacious in controlled research with a delineated population" (Chambless & Hollon, 1998, p. 7). For example, a clinician who is working with an anxious client is likely familiar with research demonstrating that cognitive techniques are useful in reducing generalized anxiety (Clark & Beck, 2009). Accordingly, cognitive therapy would be a significant part of the treatment plan. In some circumstances, clinicians using EST procedures follow a **treatment manual** that spells out step-by-step instructions and techniques to resolve a particular set of problems.

Manualized treatments require prior instruction in the careful use of their strategies, language, and techniques and regular supervision to keep the therapist on track in the use of the specified methods. Some practitioner-researchers believe that the application of manual-based interventions leaves much to be desired (Goldfried & Eubanks-Carter, 2004; Westen, Novotony, & Thompson-Brenner, 2004).

Most EST research is conducted with **randomized clinical trials** (RCTs) with a relatively homogeneous sample of participants (Hunsley & Lee, 2007). Thus it may not be generalizable to clients of ages, genders, races, or cultures differing from the sample population studied. Furthermore, the criteria for participation in an RTC study may be overly selective and not reflect the realities of most clients. For example, in a study of a treatment for obsessive-compulsive disorder, the sample may be limited to only those clients who have no other co-occurring diagnoses. While this allows for control of the study, it may not be applicable in a clinical setting where many people with obsessive-compulsive disorder may also have depression. It is also important to remember that most studies are **nomothetic**—they give us answers about a group of individuals in general—whereas clinical work is **idiographic**—it focuses on one specific individual.

Since many managed care organizations are beginning to sanction only empirically supported treatment modalities that are reimbursable by insurers, some argue that, unfortunately, this restriction of treatment options may result in insurance companies, not clinicians and clients, deciding the treatment plan.

Eclecticism

Research has shown that most practitioners today are **eclectic** (Prochaska & Norcross, 2007). They incorporate more than one theoretical perspective into their clinical work because of the utility of concepts and methods gleaned from a variety of theoretical models. For example, psychodynamic therapists may incorporate a number of family therapy principles and techniques, inviting family members and friends to occasional sessions in which systemic exploration may assist all in achieving better understanding and communication. Cognitive techniques for working on distorted ideas and misinterpretations of events to effect changes in mood are also more widely used by clinicians of many persuasions. Clinicians have an ethical responsibility to provide detailed information about their theoretical orientation, what assessment strategies and interventions they offer, what they do not offer, and how the work often unfolds.

Eclecticism requires knowledge and experience. A *New Yorker* cartoon portrays a therapist saying "I am eclectic. I take a little from Freud, a little from Jung, and a little from my Uncle Harry, who is a very wise man." However, clinicians who are eclectic often have a guiding or foundation theory into which they incorporate demonstrably useful techniques from other theoretical models. Many beginning clinicians say they are eclectic because they know a little bit about a lot and wish to apply numerous theories at once in their work with clients. "Loose eclecticism"—using whatever ideas feel right or comfortable for the clinician but which have not been well validated for use with clients—differs from a considered application of different methods in which one has been educated over time and under excellent supervision.

> *I learned about "miracle questions" at a solution-focused therapy conference and was taken with the optimism and future possibilities they appeared to generate in clients. So the next week I found myself using miracle questions with all my clients. In my interview with a depressed woman that week, I asked brightly: "What if you woke up tomorrow and a miracle had happened while you slept, and things were changed in the very way you wanted them to be . . . how would they be different?" Then she said in a serious tone, "So you're predicting I'll always wake up tomorrow"—and she began to describe her suicidal thoughts.*

The judicious use of methods from more than one theoretical approach can be quite useful. However, our planning decisions should be based on the client's needs, style, culture, and preferences, not on something that we think is interesting or exciting to do or that is rigidly imposed to control cost of care. Derald Sue and Sue (2008) affirm that, when working with clients from different backgrounds or cultures than our own, we have to be flexible and eclectic, drawing from established strategies and techniques while incorporating new culturally appropriate interventions.

Treatment Plans Should Be Jointly Constructed

We must fully engage clients as active participants in the design of any treatment or intervention plan, employing their own vision and other strengths as partners in the work to come. Their active involvement in planning also tends to keep it grounded in the realities of their capacities and readiness as well as the competing situational demands in their lives. Active involvement also helps build and sustain co-ownership of the design and implementation of plans, as well as their redesign if they prove less workable than originally anticipated. Prochaska and Norcross (2007) affirm that people attempting change are more likely to change if they feel they have some choice in the matter as well as choice among several change strategies.

Once assessment and goal setting have taken place, many clinicians write up formal plans in which the specific long-term and short-term goals and objectives are prioritized and specific interventions are laid out. Such plans become a part of the intervention record and they may be changed as significant new information comes in.

> *Gina's doctor referred her for counseling for depression and anxiety following a recent diagnosis of breast cancer. Since our cancer center also offers a support group for newly diagnosed women, our initial plan was for her to see me to work on her depression, and then attend the group for support. After attending two group sessions, Gina said that attending the group did not feel "supportive" to her. She found herself getting anxious and upset when she heard other women's experiences. The group just seemed to increase her depression. After some discussion, we changed the treatment plan. Instead of attending the group, she would read some of the many books that had been written about women coping with cancer and the positives that came out of the cancer experience for them.*

■ Contracting

Contracting involves the development of working agreements among clinicians, clients, and any significant others vital to the realization of the goals and objectives. In general, **contracts:**

- Enumerate the goals.
- Describe the roles and responsibilities of all involved parties.
- Include the interventions and methods to be used to attain the goals.

- Describe the frequency, duration, and length of the meetings, and, if applicable, the costs and payment arrangements.
- Include the means for evaluating the work or measuring progress toward the specified goals.
- Include a provision for how the contract can be renegotiated.
- Discuss the consequences of failure of either party to carry out their agreed-upon responsibilities, as well as how to handle unanticipated complications.

Although contracts can be informal or formal, clinicians are increasingly moving to more formalized contracting arrangements based on treatment plans. **Formal contracts** are highly specific and concrete in order to clarify responsibilities and minimize drift and ambiguity. They enable both client and clinician to judge whether they are accomplishing what is intended. Formal contracts are often written, and they may list each goal and its component objectives, specifying particular tasks and anticipated time lines for achievement of each objective. This form of contracting is intended to lead to more structured **treatment by objectives.**

Issues in Contracting

1. *There are individual session contracts as well as overall contracts.* The clinician and client may agree during the session to focus on certain subjects and to table others. Or they may agree at the end of one session that next week's meeting should include all of the children and be held at the homeless shelter so that the clinician can better appreciate the conditions under which the family is struggling to maintain itself.

2. *Contracts should be mutually constructed.* Both client and clinician should participate in developing the contract, each contributing ideas and preferences as to what should be done and how. Each should be able to specify what is expected from the other.

It has been suggested that some Asian, Latino, Native American, and Middle Eastern clients prefer a contracting process in which the "expert" clinician directs the process and develops the plan, telling the client the steps to take to resolve their difficulties. If the clinician attempts to establish a more mutually constructed contract, the client may regard the clinician as weak or ineffectual (Lum, 2004; Derald Sue and Sue, 2008).

At times the client may not want or may not be able to be an equal participant in the construction of the contract. For example, the involuntary client (e.g., a man who is forced to see a probation officer) may not have many choices about the contract; he may be told whom he has to see and what he has to work on. In negotiating the contract, the clinician can try to give the client room to negotiate something, such as the time of the meeting. Contracting can be prefaced with the idea that almost everyone has things to talk about or hope for (De Jong & Berg, 2001), and, since the client is obliged to attend, why not use the time to work on something the client is interested in or concerned about?

When working with members from oppressed groups, we recognize that the client may be feeling fearful or powerless and so may be unable to negotiate a contract but instead simply agrees with whatever the clinician suggests. In such situations the clinicians can help clients recall times when they had small successes and accomplishments, using these to help clients remember their creativity and power.

3. *Contracts should include all stakeholders whenever possible.*   Others significant in the client's life may be involved in the process, and so may other service providers who have a stake in the desired outcomes. Wise clinicians make sure that all these others are included in the contract in some way. If not, clinicians may lose significant input, misattribute problems, weaken alliances, or cause others to impede the implementation of the contract. In constructing a contract with a young teen mother who lives at home, for example, the clinician should involve the family in order to support them and to be sure that they will be able to provide the teen with transportation to the center. The adjustment counselor who wants to set up a behavioral program for a hyperactive child should make sure that not only the classroom teacher but also the principal, the school, and the family sign on.

4. *Contracts should be specific.*   The more specific the contract is, the more able the parties are to determine whether they are carrying out their roles and moving toward the specified goals. If some steps (for example, "maintain sobriety") must be taken before others can be taken, they should be spelled out in the contract.

> In the adolescent drug treatment program, the kids have specific behavior contracts that are determined each morning at a group meeting. The goals are written up and posted in the dining room. Privileges such as watching TV or playing basketball are earned by achievement of these daily goals. The kids also contract to attend daily group therapy and family meetings weekly.

5. *Contracts require informed consent.*   Clients need to be aware of the potential risks and benefits of the work. The woman who is coming to the clinic because she is depressed should be informed that, when people change their behavior and become less depressed, their relationships with others are often affected. Her partner, friends, and family may begin to respond to her differently, and she may want to make other changes in her life. This could be seen as either a benefit or a risk. Optional treatments and their benefits and risks should also be discussed with her.

In addition, clients need to know what other options and resources are available to them to meet their desired outcomes. The couple who is seeing a counselor about marital difficulties should also be informed about other resources, such as pastoral counseling, couples groups, or marital enrichment groups, which they may choose instead of, or in addition to, counseling. Options and resources are very important when counseling lesbian, gay, and transgendered clients new to the area or in the process of coming out. You can work to link them with relevant resource centers, social and support groups, health providers, and welcoming and supportive religious or spiritual organizations. Similarly, you can also help isolated or silenced people of color, newly arrived immigrants, and disaster survivors from other locales link up with cultural centers, ethnic mutual aid organizations, health and mental health resources, and work and educational opportunities where they can access other people who are familiar with their customs, languages, and preferred practices.

At times, when working with children or with adults who are not able to give informed consent because of cognitive impairment or mental illness, the clinician is both legally and ethically bound to get consent from legally authorized guardians. However, even in these instances, the clinician should explain the contract to the client in as clear and detailed a way as possible. Often a friend, guardian, relative, or interpreter can assist in conveying meaning in ways helpful to the client.

6. *Contracts should be flexible.*   In the early days of formal, written human services contracts, Brett Seabury wrote of the dynamic nature of contracting, recognizing that people, resources, and situations change (Garvin & Seabury, 1997; Seabury, 1976). The clinician and client should be flexible and willing to renegotiate the contract in response to changing circumstances, emerging information, or client growth.

> *Gemma and I had a contract that we would work for 12 sessions to help her control her angry outbursts in the classroom. After five meetings, she seemed to really be managing this well. We talked about what we should do with the remaining sessions and decided that she would like to work on becoming less shy. I decided to continue to meet with Gemma even though she had accomplished the original task. Gemma enjoyed our meetings and would be disappointed if they stopped before scheduled. I thought that to end now would not reinforce Gemma's hard work and that it might even result in more angry outbursts on Gemma's part in order to continue our relationship.*

7. *Contracts should be realistic.*   Contracts must take into account the resources, capacities, motivation, and opportunities that people and agencies have to meet the contract requirements. Setting up a contract in which a teen mother is expected to come to the agency twice a week for parenting group meetings is unrealistic unless the agency is sure that transportation is available and child care is provided.

> *Max resisted having a regularly scheduled weekly appointment, feeling he had been locked into something he couldn't control. So at the end of each session, I'd ask, "Would you like to come again?" We would wind up with the same appointment each week. It was unrealistic for me to expect him to commit to a long-term relationship.*

8. *Contracts should be upheld.*   For example, if the contract contains a specific prohibition against using substances while in the homeless shelter, the shelter worker needs to stand firm, even if it means refusing shelter to the client for the night. In such a circumstance, caring clinicians can offer the client detox or a referral to a "wet" shelter—one that houses those who are actively drunk or on drugs.

9. *Contracts should avoid built-in problems.*   Charles Garvin and Brett Seabury (1997) discuss three problems with contracting and treatment plans—hidden agendas, corrupt contracts, and sabotage. Contracts can include **hidden agendas**—secret aims of the clinician that are unexpressed to the client. The clinician may believe these goals will greatly improve the client's situation or functioning, but he or she fears that the client will balk at them and hopes that the power of the relationship will later make the goals possible to pursue openly. Hidden agendas often doom the work, since "it is close to impossible . . . to change people against their will, especially when they recognize that they have been deceived" (p. 165).

Corrupt contracts occur when multiple service providers, working separately, make different agreements with clients, or clients with them, without all of the parties realizing that different goals or methods have been agreed upon. A client may tell a probation officer that she is attending a weekly support group for former sex workers, while telling the group's leader that her mandated attendance at an AIDS support meeting prevents her from attending the sex workers group more than once every other week. Because the group leader and probation officer are not communicating, the treatment plans established with the client are unauthentic for all practical purposes, and the client will attend no meetings whatsoever as a result.

Sabotage can occur when one member of a treatment team encourages a client to act out against the plan because he or she does not believe in the goals and plans the team has established. For example, a counselor might feel sorry for a client and identify with his wish for more freedom. She might help him secretly go off the unit for the day while supposedly working in the laundry because she feels the limits imposed on the particular client are unjust or inappropriate.

10. *Contracts can be changed if they prove unworkable.*   Sometimes the hopeful plans of enthusiastic clinicians and clients far exceed the time and resources actually available, and they must be revised. Realistic revisions are preferable to pressuring clients to do things that changing circumstances or resources prevent them from doing. Under pressure, clients may feel disappointed in themselves and fear disappointing the clinician too. Compromises or postponements—and sometimes accepting that the planned work is finished—may be necessary to "be where the client is."

Wrenn and I worked hard together to find public funds to pay for her junior college education so that she could realize her dream of becoming a paralegal. Then, unexpectedly, she got pregnant again "by accident" and was unable to go on with her education. She put off telling me because she expected me to be mad after all that work. I wasn't mad, but in my heart I couldn't help wishing she could have followed her dream. I said that maybe she could just take an evening course. She smiled sadly and said that, with work and childcare for her toddler, those paralegal days were pretty much over. She wanted to continue seeing me to discuss whether she might find a way to set up a childcare center in her home, and I agreed.

Holding clients to contracts is one of the hardest things for beginning clinicians to do because they are highly motivated to help others and may feel reluctant to say "no" or apply limits. Many have reported in supervision that they fear losing the client if they do not bend the rules or look the other way. Other clinicians fear the anger of clients when they remain firm in the face of challenges to agreements made in the client's best interest.

We, too, need to be held to our part of the contract. Arriving late, canceling appointments, forgetting tasks between meetings, and not providing agreed-upon resources or services are violations of the contract that should be addressed. Clients may have a difficult time in confronting us about our failures to meet our part of the contract.

Regular review of the contract allows both clinicians and clients to comment on adherence or missteps. Compton, Galaway, and Cournoyer (2005) refer to such reviews as "fidelity checking" to see whether planned steps of change are actually taking place and, if so, to what extent. Fidelity checks can help us keep our commitments to clients and confront them when they, too, have trouble following through with agreed-upon tasks and steps.

EXERCISE 8.1 Contracting

CLIP 8.1
Establishing a
Contract

In class, role-play the scenarios in Exercise 7.4 (Freydia, Thomas, and Rad). Negotiate written contracts that follow the principles outlined in this chapter. Decide who should be involved in your contract and make sure that it is specific, mutually constructed, flexible, and realistic. Include a section on informed consent. Think of any circumstances that might require you to adjust or adapt the contract. Role-play the renegotiation.

■ Evaluation

Many people confuse the terms *evaluation* and *assessment*. We assess clients and their situations. Then we plan our work together. Finally, we evaluate that work to determine its effectiveness. As we noted in Chapter 1, **evaluation** is an ongoing part of all clinical work. We should examine our work session by session to determine the effectiveness of the specific focus, techniques, or uses of self. Progress and process notes, weekly assessment measures and scales, audiocassettes, and videos are all helpful in this process.

We review our work on a regular basis with supervisors or with outside consultants who have particular areas of expertise. In addition, agencies or insurers often require monthly progress reports or quarterly summaries for management to oversee the extent, nature, and quality of care. In some settings, these evaluation reports are required even more frequently. Computer programs and tools for tracking information and progress are facilitating the evaluation process. At the same time, there is concern that the increasing mechanization of the process may negatively affect the clinical relationship.

Common Elements in Evaluation

Measurement of progress and effectiveness takes differing forms, but instruments or procedures usually have some common elements.

- *There is an assessment of baseline functioning,* enumerating strengths as well as patterns or problems targeted for change. On this functional baseline, change goals are developed, contracts made, and hoped-for outcomes evaluated.
- *Some form of progress measurement is used consistently.*   This can include informal discussion of the work and its effects, the periodic readministration of original assessment measures, or the use of other evaluative measures, such as a symptom checklist like the Beck Depression Inventory (BDI-II) that tracks specific behaviors or feeling states over time.
- *The measurement of progress often occurs at specified intervals and certainly at the end of the contracted work together.*   Finally, there is a process of evaluation at the end of the working relationship. Clinician and client may use formal outcome measures or simply review the relationship, the work, and what has been accomplished. As managed care and quality assurance become more prevalent, clinicians are more frequently asked to demonstrate the effectiveness of their interventions.
- *There can be periodic follow-up evaluations* to see whether gains or changes have been maintained or further services are needed. When initially contracting for work, clients are informed that there will be follow-up. Many may find it reassuring that the agency and clinician care enough about them to check on how they are doing later on.

Principles of Evaluation

The questions to ask in assessment before intervention are very similar to the questions in evaluation after intervention. These include the who, what, when, where, and how issues that can complicate the evaluation of progress, the outcomes, and the postintervention maintenance of well-being.

- *Evaluation is influenced by who does the evaluating.*   A risk in evaluation is that clinicians, for motives of self-preservation, may be biased toward finding positive changes and outcomes. Clients can also be inaccurate reporters because they have invested time, energy, and money in the work and quite understandably want to believe that they and their situations have changed for the better. They may also wish to please or reward their clinicians by putting a positive spin on developments and by suppressing questions or doubts. Outside observer-evaluators, including family members, may also be differently motivated to see positive or negative results, depending on the effects of outcomes on them. For all of these reasons, it seems most efficacious to use multiple reporters in the evaluation process.
- *Evaluation should focus not only on problems but also on the strengths of clients and their related systems.*   Naturally, evaluations focus on changes in the frequency and duration of the problems targeted for intervention.

A principle of positive psychology is that growth and well-being, not simply the elimination of problems, should be an outcome of clinical work. Just as in assessment, evaluation must also focus on the frequency with which previously identified strengths and resources are used and new strengths and resources are developed.

- *Evaluation should utilize a number of evaluation methods.* Clinicians often utilize standardized tests and self-reports, such as logs and journals, to help clients monitor the effectiveness of their work together. Sometimes direct observation is possible. For example, if a teacher wants a child to be less aggressive with other students or to engage with more people in interactions, an objective observer can actually record the change in behavior frequency before, during, and after an intervention aimed at behavior change.

- *Whenever possible, evaluation should occur in real-life settings.* Clients can make changes that are observable in the clinical setting but not necessarily generalize or translate them to broader areas in their lives. For example, a client may learn to be more assertive in the office or even in the classroom, but not in the playground or at home. The clinician who evaluates the work solely by looking at assertive behavior in the classroom might consider the intervention successful, whereas the clinician who looks at behavior in many settings may report a mixed picture, pointing the way toward specific further work.

- *A follow-up evaluation should be conducted.* Follow-up evaluation can occur one month, two months, or even years after the intervention. Follow-up enables the clinician and client to reevaluate the long-term effectiveness of the work. At times, follow-up evaluations can serve as "booster shots" to the original work, helping clients remember and continue to build on the positive outcomes of their work.

EXERCISE 8.2 Evaluation

Using the cases from Exercise 7.4 (Freydia, Thomas, and Rad), describe the methods you would use to evaluate the effectiveness of your work together. Address the who, what, when, where, and how of evaluation.

■ Conclusion

Planning for and evaluating change is an important part of all clinical work. In preparing and planning for change, we work with clients to construct clear and realistic contracts and to measure progress and outcomes using a variety of reporters and procedures. In designing interventions, we rely on knowledge and theoretical orientation; experience with the clients; assessment of the client's motivation, capacity, and resources; and a sense of the time and professional resources available. We also utilize the professional literature and the findings from clinical efficacy studies that examine and compare various intervention outcomes for specific problems and populations.

Regardless of theoretical orientation or the specific intervention strategies planned, clinicians use a number of the same skills in working with clients. In subsequent chapters, we discuss many of the specific skills and relational processes that clinicians use to help clients think, feel and behave differently—and to achieve their goals.

■ Suggested Readings

Amodeo, Maryann, & Jones, L. Kay. (1998). Using the AOD cultural framework to view alcohol and drug issues through various cultural lenses. *Journal of Social Work Education, 34,* 387–399.

Cournoyer, Barry R. (2004). *The evidence-based social work skills book.* Boston: Allyn & Bacon.

De Jong, Peter & Berg, Insoo Kim (2001). Co-constructing cooperation with mandated clients. *Social Work, 46,* 361–374.

Miller, William R. and Rollnick, Stephen. (2002). *Motivational interviewing: Preparing people for change* (2nd Ed.). New York: Guilford.

Good readings on evidence-based practice and ESTs include:

APA Presidential Task Force on Evidence-Based Practice. (2006). Evidence-based practice in psychology. *American Psychologist, 61,* 271–285.

Hunsley, J. (2007). Addressing key challenges in evidence-based practice in psychology. *Professional Psychology, 38,* 113–121.

Kazdin, Alan E. (2008). Evidence-based treatment and practice: New opportunities to bridge clinical research and practice, enhance the knowledge base, and improve patient care. *American Psychologist, 63,* 146–159.

Norcross, John C., Beutler, L. E., & Levant, R. F. (Eds.). (2006). *Evidence-based practices in mental health: Debate and dialogue on the fundamental questions.* Washington, DC: American Psychological Association.

■ Self-Explorations

1. Develop a decisional balance sheet for a problem you are struggling with. Be sure to be clear about the pros and cons of each side of the dilemma.

2. Recall a time when you decided to make a change and took steps toward it, but then felt sorry that you did. Once you regretted it, what, if anything, did you do then?

3. Have you ever found yourself urging or leaning on friends or family members to change when they were not ready, willing, or able to do so? What were the sources of your zeal? Looking back, what would you do differently now?

■ Essay Questions

1. List some obvious benefits of evaluating outcomes. Discuss three or four cautions when setting out to evaluate outcomes.

2. What are some of the benefits and limitations of evidence-based practice?

3. Some clinicians use assessment tools (such as the BDI-II or the Symptom Checklist) in the interview to measure progress or outcomes. Discuss the positive and negative effects that their use might have on the interview process or on the relationship.

4. Discuss the criteria for a good evaluation report.

■ Key Terms

Contracts	Intervention plan
Corrupt contracts	Motivational interviewing
Decisional balance sheet	Nomothetic
Eclectic	Randomized clinical trials
Empirically supported treatments	Sabotage
Evaluation	Spontaneous remission
Evidence-based practice	Treatment by objectives
Formal contracts	Treatment manual
Hidden agendas	Treatment plan
Idiographic	

CHAPTER 9

Gaining New Perspectives: Helping Clients Feel and See Things Differently

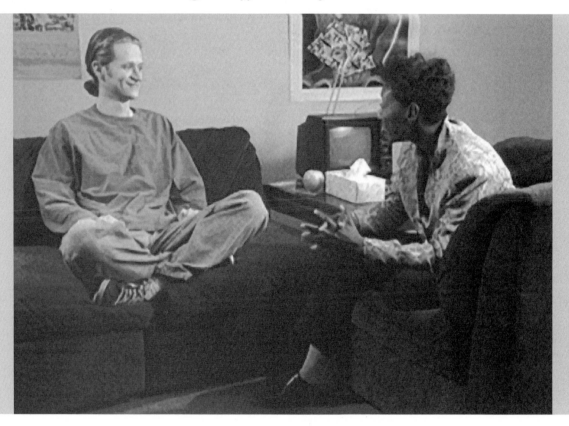

While utilizing a variety of guiding theoretical and practice models, clinicians often draw from a fund of basic counseling skills in implementing interventions with clients. In this chapter, we elaborate on skills commonly used to help clients feel better and develop new perspectives. Developing new perspectives often alters feeling states, and working with feelings often alters perspectives. Distressing thoughts and feelings are often so intertwined that they play off of and feed into each other in powerful ways. Jean Baker Miller and Irene Stiver of the Stone Center use the term **"feeling-thinking"** to describe these interlocking and mutually interacting bundles, believing that "all thoughts are accompanied by emotions and all emotions have a thought content" (1997, p. 212).

■ Working with Feelings

Clients often come to see clinicians because of feelings of sadness, anxiety, anger, and hopelessness, or because they are overwhelmed by unusually strong feelings:

"I can't seem to handle my anger."
"I feel so sad all the time."
"I am so easily frightened."

Some clients directly express feelings related to important events, relationships, and conditions in their lives. Others describe emotional distress signaling them that something is wrong, yet when asked for clarification, they cannot be more specific about the feeling or about feelings they lump together as "distress."

"I don't know what's wrong, I just don't feel right."

Some come in and recount painful stories without any accompanying feelings, as though numb. Others come in with feelings known to them but wait until some trust is established before sharing them even superficially. Still others come in describing distressing patterns and themes, unaware that unresolved feelings from past events could be affecting current thinking, feeling, and behaviors.

> *Evan came to the counseling center for help because he felt stuck. Evan described himself as cranky a lot of the time and always getting involved with "women who criticize me for the least little thing." He was a talented artist, but drifted from job to job: "I can't seem to settle in and succeed at anything."*
>
> *As we talked about his life, Evan told me that 15 years ago, after he had just received his driver's license, he was in a terrible accident. An SUV driven by an intoxicated man suddenly crossed into his lane. Evan swerved sharply to avoid a head-on crash, but in doing so, crashed into a nearby traffic signpost. His best friend was thrown through the windshield and died instantly.*
>
> *He was aware that something was wrong, but he wasn't yet aware that feelings of guilt and the distorted idea that he didn't deserve happiness because of the accident might be contributing to his current difficulties.*

Evidence-Based Treatment

Several empirically validated and widely used treatments were developed with specific goals of helping clients learn to identify and manage feelings. Medication is an empirically validated form of treatment that is often used to augment the effectiveness of other treatments.

Cognitive Behavioral Therapy (CBT)

CBT maintains that that distorted thinking or faulty information processing is at the root of many of the problems that people present (Beck, 2005). Aaron Beck, the founder of CBT, emphasized the influence of what he called the

negative cognitive triad: view of self ("I'm a loser"); view of the world ("My people never get a real break"); and view of prospects for the future ("My jail time will always keep me from succeeding"). The best way to alter feeling states and behaviors is to change the ideas or thoughts that precede and "drive" them. CBT has had substantial empirical validation for over three decades and is now applied effectively across a wide variety of settings, problems, and populations (Beck, 2005). Many clinicians today incorporate some cognitive techniques into their practice because of the way they clarify for and educate clients about the self-undermining beliefs and attitudes that affect their emotions and behaviors. However, Hays notes that the empirical basis regarding cross-cultural application of CBT is "sparse" (2008, p. 5).

To challenge the client's distorted thinking, the clinician asks the client to describe the situations in which negative feelings arise. The client is asked to describe his or her thoughts about these situations. The clinician and client then list central distorted cognitions; automatic thoughts; exaggerated, self-defeating, all-or-nothing cognitive schemas; and misinterpretations. They target these thoughts for change, and the client agrees to do homework as well as in-office work to restructure these cognitions into more encouraging and empowering thoughts. Clients are urged to see their thoughts as hypotheses to be tested out instead of ideas written in stone. Clients can be asked to keep a log at home in which they list triggering situations and events, the thoughts these stimulated, and the feelings that arose. The client is also asked to dispute these thoughts and to bring the log to the next session.

Hays (2008) cautions that challenging the validity of the client's beliefs "may be risky" (p. 199) when the clinician and client come from different cultures. "A safer approach is to avoid the questions of rationality and validity altogether and focus on a collaborative exploration of the 'helpfulness' (i.e., usefulness) of a thought" (p. 199).

It is important when working with CBT not to overemphasize the cognitive or internal part of the problem. Clinicians must always explore the social, environmental, and cultural contributions to clients' problems (Hays, 2008; David Sue & Sue, 2008). "Ellis (2000a) acknowledges the necessity of not only working to change an individual's musts and demands, but also the importance of assisting clients in their fight against an 'unfair and irrational system'" (David Sue & Sue, 2008, p. 197).

Dialectical Behavioral Treatment (DBT)

Marsha Linehan and colleagues developed **Dialectical Behavioral Treatment** (DBT) as a specially tailored cognitive-behavioral program for people whose powerful, poorly regulated feeling states and self-destructive impulses make life hard for themselves and for people around them (Heard & Linehan, 1994; Linehan et al., 2006). Although the DBT skills training manual has been translated into Spanish, David Sue and Diane Sue (2008) note that they are not aware of any empirical studies about the effectiveness of DBT with ethnic minorities.

DBT programs are noted for their self-calming, self-rewarding, self-distracting, and self-assertion strategies and formats, and their measured steps toward efficacy. The therapy is a structured, manualized, step-by-step group learning process in which clients are helped to support each other while better grasping the complex roots of their self-harming thoughts and often dramatic feeling responses to stresses or disappointments. Through discussion of coping strategies and calming procedures modeled by specially trained group leaders, group members come to accept themselves for who they are and construct more appealing daily lives with more pleasing activities and validating relationships in them. DBT clinicians also note that medications and hospitalization to protect against self-harm are also available to restore a balance of self-containment and self-expression.

Interpersonal Therapy (IPT)

Interpersonal Therapy (IPT) is a brief, 16–20 week process developed in the 1980s by Myrna Weissman, Gerald Klerman, and associates to help clients express and contextualize the feelings associated with major depressive disorders (Weissman, Markowitz, & Klerman, 2007). They believed that psychological disorders always take place in social/interpersonal contexts and that a brief, specific therapeutic focus on resolving or reworking clients' current, here-and-now interpersonal problems, losses, and transitions relieves depression more quickly than long-term therapy does. Clients may recontract for another series of sessions after an interval in which they try out new behaviors.

The clinician and client focus on a current relationship or situation in which there is a loss or transition. IPT clinicians emphasizes the importance of eliciting, validating, and empathizing with sad and angry feelings rather than avoiding them for fear that the client might be overwhelmed by them. Clinician and client engage in role-plays to develop relational skills and practice new behaviors. IPT has been empirically validated in numerous treatment-outcome comparison studies as an effective brief treatment for mood disorders with ethnically diverse populations (Blanco, Clougherty, Lipsitz, Mufson, & Weissman, 2006; de Mello, de Jesus Mari, Bacaltchuk, Verdelli & Neugebauer, 2005; Henrichsen, 2008; Weissman, Markowitz, & Klerman, 2007).

Positive Psychology Interventions (PPIs)

Unlike DBT and IPT (which focus on coping with and exploring negative feelings), **positive psychology interventions** focus on a client's positive traits, emotions, and activities. Empirical research has shown that PPIs enhance feelings of well-being and happiness by building and expanding the client's positive emotions, engagement with others, and capacity to lead a meaningful life (Frederickson, 2009; Lyubomirsky, 2007; Seligman, 2002).

Barbara Frederickson (2001) has developed and tested a "broaden and build theory" in regard to the developmental effects of positive emotions.

Her research has shown that "positive emotions broaden the scope of attention and cognition, thereby facilitating the building of personal resources and initiating upward spirals toward increasing emotional well-being" (Burns et al., 2008, p. 360). Furthermore, "clinicians who induce positive emotions (e.g. by asking clients to think about their 'best times') or who time skill-based interventions to correspond to patients' naturally occurring positive moods may increase the chances that patients will more rapidly and fully learn therapy-based skills" (Burns et al., 2008, p. 369).

Direct Exploration of Feelings

Familiar open-ended questions help in eliciting client feelings. Questions such as "What are you feeling as I explain this?" and "What did you feel when that happened?" help clients focus on their reactions. Questions that probe for a little more detail might include "Did you have other feelings besides shock when Baptiste hit your daughter?" or "Who are you most comfortable sharing those feelings with?" If feelings have been openly shared, we might then ask: "Shall we stay with your feelings a bit longer, or get back to what you were saying?" Encouragement to continue can be provided through minimal empathic sounds and prompts: "Yes . . ." or "Good . . ." or "Just let the feelings come." or "Try not to fight your natural feelings."

It is important not to judge or criticize the expression of feelings. Clients often stop and ask, "Is this okay for me to say?" or "Are you sure you don't mind my saying how mad I am at the director of this place?" Sometimes during moments of tearfulness they may look down or away. The clinician can universalize about the hesitation that so many people feel when sharing their feelings more deeply with a relative stranger and then appreciate aloud the client's willingness to take this risk. Validating and normalizing human feelings can help relieve embarrassment or concerns about being strange or odd that people can experience when describing their emotions or feeling patterns.

Sometimes when clients have shared a lot in one session, we check in with them in the next visit about how it was for them to share those feelings. We attempt to avoid overwhelming clients with too much feeling exploration.

Clients often experience relief through the expression of feelings as long as such expression or ventilation is modulated and under control. As discussed in Chapter 13, research on trauma and crisis interventions over the past 15 years has revealed that, when clients are shocked and overwhelmed in the immediate aftermath of disaster and trauma, intense exploration of their feelings can further destabilize them (Herman, 1997; Knight, 2009; van der Kolk & van der Hart, 1991). But even if the client is not in crisis, we need to think carefully about the potential negative effects of feeling exploration in terms of timing and dosage.

I was working with a woman whose mother was dying of cancer. She would talk a lot about how much time it took to take care of her mother and the day-to-day logistics of taking her to the hospital for treatment, arranging visiting nurses, feeding and bathing her mother, going on drugstore runs for supplies, etc. When I asked her about how she felt, her response was, "I don't have time to feel." I wondered if, in fact, that was true—perhaps she was afraid that her feelings of sadness, resentment, pain, and loss would overwhelm her and interfere with her ability to do all that she needed to do to take care of her mother.

As always, the clinician should be aware of the culture of the client and how it might influence feeling expression. For example, Japanese culture values stoicism and avoidance of negative outcomes in social interactions and the maintenance of social harmony. A clinician inviting emotional expression from a Japanese client might be experienced as disrespectful of the client's cultural values (Ehrenreich, Fairholme, Buzzella, Ellard, & Barlow, 2007). Combat troops may hide their feelings for fear of being viewed as weak within a military culture that emphasizes stoicism.

The assessment process with clients usually reveals whether they are open to—and can bear—direct exploration of feelings or whether more indirect expression is warranted. Clients can also change their perspective about feeling expression. As trust builds, some may come to appreciate the opportunity to explore feelings. At other times, clients may become uncomfortable with their strong expression of feelings, or they may start to feel disloyal to their family or culture in sharing strong feelings with a stranger.

Indirect Exploration of Feelings

Sometimes clients who are not used to expressing feelings directly respond spontaneously when presented with stories illustrating situations like their own, in which someone else is having feelings. These situations often facilitate an emotional identification by the client with someone in the story, stimulating a spontaneous sharing of the client's own feelings as he or she relates to personally relevant elements of the story. The following is an example of indirect exploration:

When I was a volunteer at the rape crisis center, Darlia came for help. Although she came to the center, she didn't want to talk about being raped. We have a number of books in our library that describe how people coped with being raped and one day I noticed she was reading Maya Angelou's I Know Why the Caged Bird Sings. In the book, Angelou gives an account of her own rape and how she was mute for a year or more following the assault. Darlia started to cry as she was reading and when I stopped by her chair, she told me how much it saddened her to think that a woman as strong and outspoken as Angelou had felt silenced and embarrassed about being raped. It led us to a great discussion about how other women might feel about being assaulted.

Discrimination of One Feeling from Another

People sometimes cry when they are mad and respond irritably when sad. They may be awash with feelings that they lack words to describe. Clients often benefit from learning to recognize and describe their distinct feelings. For many, this feeling of clarity is a revitalizing first step in authentic self-acknowledgment and self-assertion. Clinicians and clients can review together the range of feelings and expressive styles manifested in literature, music, and life. Then we move from the general to the particular, asking clients to monitor themselves for authentic reactions to people and events in their lives, becoming more familiar with exactly what they feel, when, and with whom. Discussion of various feeling responses in sessions can foster client reflection on evocative interactions as they are happening. This kind of feeling discrimination not only helps clients realize and appreciate the richness of their own feeling life, it also helps them become more aware of which particular people, events, and situations trigger specific feelings and which do not.

If culturally appropriate, we can provide journal exercises as homework in which clients monitor, name, and comment on their daily feelings and then bring their findings and observations in for discussion. Sometimes clients see movies or hear songs that inspire feeling reflections in them, and these are fertile sources for client work on recognizing, naming, and beginning to express and enjoy feelings. Some clients may write poetry or songs to express their feelings and share these with their clinicians. The important goal is for clients to recognize and honor their real feelings, whether deciding to express them or not. A side benefit of these activities is the development of a new habit of personal reflection that can be a first step toward political awareness and positive action steps.

While we want to help clients name and discriminate their feelings, it is important that we do not tell them what they are feeling. If we mistakenly attempt to speak for or second-guess them, they might respond by saying, "I am mad, so please don't try to tell me that what I'm 'really' feeling is sad."

Managing and Containing Negative Feelings

In contrast to people who believe in keeping feelings private, some people express their feelings excessively or impulsively without much regard for context or their impact on others. They may storm out of a meeting when they disagree with their employer or burst into tears at the slightest frustration. They may become demanding of attention when feeling needy, or repeatedly yell in a frightening way when overtired. Others may feel overwhelmed by feelings of sadness, anger, or anxiety.

Clinicians can use a number of cognitive and behavioral techniques to help clients manage or contain feelings.

- *Identifying emotional triggers.*   **Triggers** are the people, circumstances, ideas, and events that stimulate emotional reactions. AA and other recovery programs teach clients how to become aware of triggering situations and remain calm and intentional in order to avoid escalating. Clinicians may also ask clients to list the people and situations that most upset them or get them going in a worrisome way. We can discuss ways to avoid or minimize time spent in triggering situations, and help clients learn strategies for staying calm when in such situations. Clients learn that they can have both clear and strong feelings without letting them rise to their boiling points—the points at which they lose control.

- *Using scaling questions.*   Peter De Jong and Scott Miller (1995) recommend teaching clients how to use **scaling questions** to estimate the extent of their emotional arousal on a scale of 1 to 10. Using 0 to describe having no feelings about a situation and 10 to represent total escalation, clients learn to recognize the degree of feeling stimulated by each situation. If the baseline rating with a certain triggering person is a 9, then a goal is to begin to lower reactivity by a point or two, using strategies such as calming procedures, walking away, or changing the subject. Scaling talk is easily learned and actually enjoyed in its use, because it keeps the client aware, situation to situation, of both progress and slips backward. Both kinds of behavior provide important subjects for discussion. Moreover, when we are not present, clients can still evaluate their feelings: "Boy, that was a '3' with my landlady—down 2 points, and about a '7.5' with my 'ex'—worse than I expected." These informal reports help reinforce the strategies that *are* working to contain and soothe.

- *Developing a personal "stop" strategy.*   Often clients who rapidly escalate need other people to restrain or help calm them down, which is difficult for everyone involved. An early activity with these clients is to help them recognize when they are starting to escalate emotionally and to teach them how to interrupt the escalation with a "Stop!" or "Cut it out!" command they say to themselves. Some prefer to picture immediately a brightly colored stop sign. Others learn to picture the word "Stop!" or "Don't!" in their minds. The goal is to find a short command and use it the moment they feel themselves reaching their personal boiling point.

- *Walking away.*   Two important skills in containing and deescalating are learning to detour around or walk away from triggering people and situations if feelings continue to escalate. Rehearsal of detouring and walking away helps prepare clients before the inevitable upsetting situations arise. Some of the hardest clinical situations are those in which clients start to practice walking away exactly as encouraged by the clinician. Then suddenly, the person from whom they are trying to distance gives pursuit and tries to drag them back into a risky quarrel or activity. We try to help clients deal with such provocations by constructing in-session role-plays in which the clinician models for the client how not to turn back into the risky situation. Then the clinician plays the provocateur in order to see if the client can walk away, and if not, why not. If the provocateur is physically threatening, the client learns not simply to walk away, but to flee as quickly as possible and call for help.

- *Changing the channel.*   Distraction strategies help people switch their minds from painful thoughts and feelings to more calm and pleasing ones. When distressed, clients are encouraged to do something they like that leaves them feeling calmed, proud, and able to think of themselves as much more than a set of problems. Baths, reading, listening to music, calling a friend to book time together, playing with a pet, shopping in a favorite store, cooking favorite foods—all such activities have the potential to soothe and affirm. "Turning the page" and "changing the channel" are other names for actions taken to switch quickly from emotional escalation to activities that affirm self-worth.

- *Self-calming strategies.* A number of strategies can be useful to help clients control and contain strong feelings. Self-calming strategies such as refocusing the mind on a peaceful place, or imagining oneself walking by a river accompanied by a wise guide, come from Buddhist mindfulness practices. Many clients already know how to use positive self-calming strategies but often forget to or don't make the time to. If encouraged, they might exercise to work off steam, attend support groups that reinforce self-containment, pray or chant, listen to quieting music, or watch a TV program that makes them laugh. Clients can also learn relaxation techniques, self-talk, or self-coaching ("You'll get through this, you always do, so calm down" or "Cool your jets!").
- *Medication.* In some instances, medication may be useful to help people cope with overwhelming feelings. People with mood problems should be evaluated medically for possible use of medication in addition to counseling. Numerous well-controlled comparison studies since the 1980s have demonstrated that a combination of medication and counseling focused on enhancing self-efficacy and coping resources is highly effective in reducing depressive and other mood symptoms (Frank, Novick, & Kupfer, 2005; Nemeroff, 2008; Otto, Smits, & Reese, 2005). The clinician has to stay in close contact with the medical staff overseeing the use of medications, so that all helpers are aware of developments and reactions and are aware of potential side effects.

EXERCISE 9.1 Handling Strong Feelings

What do you do to handle strong feelings when you are upset? In groups of three or four, share the various methods you use. Did you learn any new methods from your colleagues?

People sometimes use alcohol and other substances to contain feelings or blunt affect. Substance use and abuse can be an important hidden contributor to the inability of some clients to rein in or modulate moods (Hanson & Gutheil, 2004). Initial and continuing assessment should include direct inquiry about the frequency and amount of drinking and other drug use. Clients may be reluctant to disclose the actual amount of their substance use because of dependence, denial, embarrassment, or a wish to continue to use substances in spite of their negative effects on functioning. Clinicians are particularly inclined to miss the importance of alcohol use in the elderly. Meredith Hanson and Irene Gutheil (2004) cite studies revealing that some professional caregivers don't believe that older people have substance abuse problems. Others think older people are entitled to pleasure from drinking since they've worked hard in their lives and deserve to do what they want. We recommend that you take advanced coursework in substance abuse assessment and treatment because of the number of people whose lives are affected by substance-related problems.

Creating and Enhancing Positive Feelings

Clinicians can use a number of techniques in maximizing focus on clients' achievements, virtuous traits, beneficial coping strategies, and progressive steps towards engagement with others in a meaningful life (Fredrickson, 2009; Lyubomirsky, 2007; Seligman, 2002).

- *Regularly eliciting success stories from the client's past.* We mentioned in Chapter 3 that many people are so used to clinicians focusing on problems to be solved that clients don't spontaneously share anything about their strengths and successes. The technique of actively eliciting successes keeps the spotlight on things the client has done well, contributed to, been a happy part of, or achieved. Some people may feel that success talk is equivalent to bragging, of which they disapprove. The clinician reframes these successes as important memories to build on. The client might be able to make similar things happen in the present.
- *Recalling "Three Good Things."* Often people troubled by events or situations are so focused on these troubles that they forget to see and appreciate the good things within or around them. Positive psychologists have suggested that clinicians can help alter this focus on the unhappy by asking clients to write down **three good things** that went well in the day for a week (Seligman, Steen, Park, & Peterson, 2005). Then they are asked to reflect on their own role in the three good things: what they may have done or said that contributed to the good things happening. Empirical research has demonstrated that this activity can increase happiness and decrease depressive symptoms for up to 6 months (Seligman, Steen, Park, & Peterson, 2005; Sheldon & Lyubomirsky, 2004.)
- *Encouraging positive relationships.* Depressed people often blame themselves for not "getting well" or for complaining, and expect everyone to be alienated by their despair. They often tend either to isolate themselves or to hang out with other depressed people who "understand" their misery. Clinicians can try to elicit any memories clients have, from earlier points in their life, of fun times with friends, neighbors, special relatives, or pets. The client is then asked about what his or her contribution was to these happy relationships, and what they could try to do now to create happy ties with others. Sometimes the clinician or the agency can help link clients with support or hobby groups where friendships might be sprouted little by little. Some isolated individuals might need some social skills modeling for how to reconnect a little bit at a time.
- *Asking the client to commit random acts of kindness.* For many people, good feelings are derived from virtue-based acts. Sonja Lyubomirsky

(2007) has shown that positive feelings can come to people who engage in "**random acts of kindness.**" The client can be asked to make a list of 15 acts of kindness that he or she could easily do (give some money to a person who is begging, put money in a parking meter that has expired, call an elderly person to check on their well-being, volunteer to do the dishes, etc). The client can be asked to commit some of these acts each week and note how they feel after doing them.

- *Constructing positivity portfolios.*   Barbara Fredrickson (2009) has developed the concept of increasing good feelings by constructing personal **positivity portfolios.** Clients can create a separate portfolio for each of the emotions of joy, gratitude, serenity, interest, hope, pride, amusement, inspiration, awe, and love. A joy portfolio, for example, can include things like cards, poems, pictures, and sayings that the client finds joyful or uplifting. The portfolio is carried with the person so that he or she can look at it at the first twinge of a down moment to prevent a downward slide by focusing on the pluses in his or her life. Fredrickson has suggested that people can carry them in their iPhones. (Clinicians, too, might benefit from some iPhone uplift when tired or stressed!)

- *Encourage communing with nature.*   Ecopsychologists describe the pacifying and uplifting effects of sojourns in public parks, time spent by rivers, ponds, lakes, and waterfalls, walks on sunny beaches, and the like. Visits to nature preserves remind us of our oneness with all living things, and inspire not only good feelings but a sense of well-being and happiness (Burns, 2005).

Clinician Reactions to Client Feelings

As fellow human beings empathizing with clients, we are often deeply moved by their lives and stories. Feelings of pleasure, sadness, worry, disappointment, tenderness, irritation, and fear are not at all unusual as we work with the strengths, problems, and prospects of many people.

> *When a 9-year-old who was legally blind began to cry about her "differentness" from other kids, and I had seen how delightful and creative she was in the playroom, I felt tears well up and come down my cheeks.*

* * *

> *I felt so much happiness when Kiki got her dream job that the two of us, walking down the school corridor, stopped and jumped up and down with shared joy and excitement for her.*

* * *

> *Suleima's story stayed with me for days. She had crossed the desert with her kids and made it to safety. All of that courage and achievement, and here she is now, abused regularly by her American boyfriend. What a hand Fate deals some people.*

Students sometimes worry that being professional and intentional means that these human reactions are now inappropriate. In our experience, these natural reactions are important signals to clients of our humanity and of our ability to join closely with their experiences and feelings. Indeed, Jean Baker Miller and Irene Stiver (1997) assert that one of the most powerful growth-inducing moments in clinical work is when a client sees that he or she is actually able to affect or move the clinician. Our feelings also make rich topics for supervision and consultation because, while having them is normal, being selective about how, when, and with whom to express them involves a combination of knowledge, timing, relational sensitivity, and caution (Walsh, 2009).

Also, how we register and express our reactions may not be compatible with the client's normative ways, either because of individual variance or cultural norms.

> *Counselor:* Youn, you are not expressing anything about the death of your Grandmother, and I know she has been a huge support for you.
>
> *Youn:* When it is a person's "time," we are respectful of that and of a good life lived. Also, I am relieved to see her out of pain. I believe she may return, and that we will see each other again. I miss her, but I feel at peace, too. I light sticks for her each night to show my love and reverence.

Cautions When Working with Feelings

Working with feelings is an educational objective that many students anticipate eagerly. This work turns out to be some of the most complex work we do, and it can both free people up when done skillfully, and set them back when we blunder. We suggest the following guidelines as you develop and try to apply your new knowledge.

- Learn about different cultural norms for sharing emotions with professional or cultural "outsiders."
- Do not explore for too much too soon.
- Notice whether the client's story flowers and deepens or tightens up and suddenly refocuses after intense feeling expression.
- Acknowledge small growth steps in identifying and expressing feelings.
- Note your own reactions to client feelings and reflect on their various sources.
- Discuss in supervision any lingering discomforts you feel in reaction to client feelings.
- Be ready to provide support and empathy when clients are upset.

Maureen Walker of the Stone Center (2004) writes of the vulnerability that some clinicians feel when they increase their authentic responsiveness to clients' feelings and situations. Walker observes that "the implicit message in many traditional training settings is that therapist vulnerability is evidence of therapist ineptitude" (pp. 12–13). In contrast, Walker urges clinicians to use their accruing relational knowledge "to relate to the client in active and alive ways, experiencing him- or herself more as a real person-therapist than as a therapist-impersonator" (2004, pp. 12–13). Linda Schiller (2007) reports from a relational theory-based group's experiences: "Some of the most powerful moments for them in the group process occurred when the worker shared an affective response to their contributions or stories. Several members stated, 'I loved how you were real with us. It made me feel that you didn't hold yourself above us, and I really felt seen, for perhaps the first time, in this group'" (p. 23). An ongoing goal of clinical education is to develop and sustain self-awareness about our reactions to clients' emotional states.

■ Gaining New Perspectives

When people come for counseling help, they often feel stuck. They may experience or view things in fixed or seemingly immutable ways and feel distressed or hopeless, seeing few options to their situation or perspective.

> *As a boy from a poor part of a large city, Shane thought he had only two options open to him if he was going to "get somewhere": be an athlete or join the army. The idea of completing high school and college was really foreign to him, since no one he was close to ever had done those things. His nickname for me was "Big Dreamer."*

Others may hold tenaciously to a view that feels right to them, and their limited ability to see alternatives may be problematic in helping them approach the future differently.

> *Angie came from three generations of women who married alcoholic men who beat them when drunk. The women had all stayed in their marriages, believing that "marriage is for life." All of their children had needed counseling for depression or substance abuse, and, when I talked with Angie in detox, she was getting ready to return home to Dougie, an active alcoholic. She hoped that her own sobriety would act as an example for Dougie and that by sticking by him she would influence him to go with her to AA. She said: "I've got to think of Dougie; I can't just think of myself."*

One of our major clinical tasks is to help clients develop new perspectives or envision other potentials that may maximize strengths or effect change. **Perspective** refers to viewpoint: the position you take as you envision yourself, others, and the world. If you change where you stand, things can look quite different. For example, a tree looks very different to you when you are flying over it than it does when you are lying beneath it. Similarly, an alcoholic home can look different to its members than it does to an outside observer, who may focus chiefly on symptoms rather than on the connections between people or on time-honored intergenerational, cultural, or gender norms. In both instances, stance and context affect perspective and vision.

We frequently work with clients to assist in the development of new dimensions to their understanding—other possibilities that may not have been presented to them, that they may not have previously considered, or that they may have been afraid of entertaining. **Reframing** is the general term applied to a group of skills that clinicians use to help clients gain new perspective. Using reframing, clinicians can help clients to gently shift their ways of thinking about a situation, opening up new possibilities and potential solutions.

> *A teen client told me that she was having a hard time with her father her because he nagged her. Every night when he got home from work he asked her, "Have you done your homework?" She was hardworking and thought that her father didn't appreciate how hard she really worked. She would often complain "Doesn't he trust me?" I suggested that perhaps her father's behavior could be seen as a sign of caring and a wish for her to do well. Her father was extremely hardworking himself and only got home from work late at night after she had already done her homework. Maybe he was asking her because he wanted to be a good father and connect with her. She agreed and added that she knew he felt very guilty about the hours he worked.*

When clients can safely begin to see things from new perspectives, they often begin to feel or act differently; they may even feel and act for the first time in many years. Having a multiplicity of perspectives gives clients options from which they may choose those that they find to be most useful to them. Some need help to change to more positive and hopeful perspectives regarding themselves, their prospects, and potentials. Others need help facing harsh realities and discovering resources of which they were previously unaware. Our simple encouragement of them to explore, express, examine, challenge, and try out a range of ideas and feelings can itself be novel and inspiring.

Accentuate the Positive

As just noted, people seeking help often describe themselves as "a loser," "sick," or "hopeless" in reaction to ideas they have taken in from others regarding themselves or their situations. These views may be expressed directly, or they may lurk beneath an exterior of bravado or mock acceptance.

> *I ran a group for young adults with schizophrenia, and one night I asked them what music best represented the way they felt about themselves. One young man said that the Beatles' song "Nowhere Man" was the song that he identified with. Another responded sadly, "Fool on the Hill."*

Highlight and Commend Client Efficacy

While recognizing and appreciating a client's perspective, we have to maintain a positive outlook and convey it actively to the client. We *do not* mean ignoring or minimizing the client's very real pain by making simplistic statements like, "Let's look on the brighter side." Rather, we mean that, after empathizing with the client's experience of "being nowhere," we try, when the moment is right, to elicit or highlight instances of efficacy or agency, with special attention to the abilities that the client may not recognize or may trivialize as irrelevant.

De Jong and Miller (1995) recommend the use of exception questions and coping questions to focus on client strengths. **Exception questions** ask about situations or days in which "the problems" have not happened: Who or which things helped, or were different at that moment, that improved the situation? When can those very people and things be brought together again in order to experience positive differences again? What has been learned in those exceptional moments that might be transferred to similar moments and challenges?

Coping questions focus clients on how they have gotten where they are today, given the chronic adversity of their circumstances: "How have you managed [or survived], given all that you're up against?" The client usually notes something that keeps them going when they think all is finished: kids, prayer, a cousin who counts on them. We can then explore these activities or relationships to emphasize their power in the client's life.

Transferability of Skills

We believe in teaching **transferability of skills** in a way that builds a sense of competence and hope. We suggest that what works in situation A could well work in situations B and C.

> *Zarita was down on herself for "being out of control" at home with anxious obsessions that drove her husband crazy. We explored her work as a clerk-magistrate at the court, where she had been through every imaginable thing with unflappable cool: bomb scares, threats to her life from convicted felons, unexpected fights erupting in court, and so on. My anxiety went sky high as I heard her examples from court, and I shared this with her. She explained that her family had always put huge importance on dignity and self-control in public. At home, though, both parents yelled at each other and at the kids, would slam doors, cry—"the works." I said I could appreciate more where these two sides of her came from: the "cool and collected one" in court and the "out of control one" at home. She had never appreciated how in control of her reactions she was at work and was very pleased to see it. "But how," she asked, "can I bring the collected one home?" We went on to identify the skills she used in court to calm herself ("count to 10" or "take deep breaths") and then visualized an upsetting scene at home in which she could practice using the same skills.*

Construct Positive Future Visions

We also accentuate the positive when we help clients construct positive visions of their future lives and selves. Steve de Shazer notes that we can use language to construct a positive reality for clients. "Sentences are constructed in such a way as to create an alternative future. For example, 'When the problem is solved, what will you be doing differently?' . . . instead of 'if' [it is solved] . . ." (cited in Koob, 2003, p. 135).

Steve de Shazer and Insoo Kim Berg, the founders of Solution Focused Brief Therapy (SFBT), have developed the **miracle question** to help clients gain new perspectives on their problems and focus on the positive desired goal rather than just on what is "wrong." De Shazer suggests the clinician say the following:

> "I have a strange, perhaps unusual question, a question that takes some imagination. Suppose . . . after we finish here, you go home tonight, watch TV, do your usual chores, etc., and then go to bed and to sleep. . . . And, while you are sleeping, a miracle happens . . . And the problems that brought you here are solved, just like that! . . . But, this happens while you are sleeping, so you cannot know that it has happened. . . . What will be different that will indicate that the problem is resolved . . . How will your best friend discover that this miracle has happened to you?" (1988, p. 5).

Conceptualizing how the subsequently changed reactions of others might affect the client in turn is helpful. De Shazer notes: "When the client imagines feeling better in a wide range of situations involving various other people, then he or she can make the switch from 'I am able to imagine I feel better' to 'I am able to imagine that I am better'" (de Shazer, n.d.).

Act as a Positive Mirror

We seek out and reflect an alternative view of the client—a technique we refer to as acting as a **positive mirror.** We reflect and credit small achievements the client may have overlooked or undervalued, emphasizing positive connections that clients may already have in their lives.

Beginning clinicians can be tempted to give false reassurance to assuage the client's pain ("Everything will be fine" or "I'm sure that if we work on this, we can make things better for you"). They may not readily understand why this type of reassurance is false because they are urged to maintain and share an optimistic viewpoint with clients. By false reassurance, we simply mean that, given the complexities of everyday life and the changing nature of people and situations, we cannot predict either the future or the utility of imagined interventions.

Use Appropriately Timed Hopefulness

Rosy expectations may be unbelievable to despairing clients. Such expectations may be incorrect or inappropriate for the moment or situation at hand, especially with clients from families or neighborhoods where poverty, violence, and a lack of opportunity and support appear unremitting. What is required instead is the complex skill of communicating appropriately timed hopefulness while maintaining empathy for the pain, injustice, or stuckness of the moment. We usually empathize in the moment and then later quietly shift to some potential in the person or situation.

> *Stevie was a 20-year-old mother of two girls who had just been denied custody of them because she had hit them while she was drunk. She said she now had a record of child abuse that would likely be checked every time she went for child care jobs, and child care was the thing she always thought she could do best for a living. I asked how it was for her to think that what she'd loved best might be out of her reach in some instances now.*

> *I said it sounded like she'd felt alone and down for so long that it must seem futile to hope for anything. She blew off some more anger and then started to cry and said, "I might as well just give up." I said I could see why she would feel that way and that it was an awful feeling to want her girls and her work back, and yet to want to give up sometimes. She nodded.*

Build on Here-and-Now Connections

To be effective, clinicians have to build on here-and-now connections and achievements to help clients develop realistic hopes for a more positive future. This future image may not be totally or even primarily positive, but it is important that clients identify **islands of possibility** that serve to fuel hope for the work. Stevie's story continues:

> *After things had subsided a bit, I reminded Stevie that she had told me earlier of wanting to complete her night school diploma and try for LPN training. This seemed to me within reach while the kids were still in foster care, and I said so. I then said that I had seen other folks like herself get some support and ideas from talking with me like we've done today. I told her that I would love to see her try it, to see if it added anything to help her think through the times she feels so lost and alone. It might not, but on the other hand, what if it did? Stevie said she would consider it, but the main thing she wanted today was to find out if she could visit her two girls in foster care on their birthdays. I asked how she wanted to go about finding out. First she asked if I would call ("Who wants to talk to a con?"). Then she laughed and said, reaching for the phone, "If I can call my sister a million times a day to ask if she's seen my boyfriend, I can work the phone to ask about my kids. If I can't use the phone, how am I ever going to get an LPN job?"*

Creating Alternative Perspectives

Sometimes clients have been exposed to only one way of thinking about things, and their thinking reflects that one way and little else. They may be aware of alternative views but are manifesting loyalty to family, cultural, or religious precepts by adhering inflexibly to a perspective, even though it is not proving useful to them in attempting to resolve tensions or problems at hand. At other times, if clients have been dominated or silenced, they may simply hold on to a perspective to enjoy a rare opportunity to affirm their own way of thinking. Moreover, some clients feel threatened by alternative perspectives that may feel unfamiliar or risky.

At times, we introduce **alternative perspectives** to broaden clients' sense of possibilities, to heighten and encourage a spirit of curiosity and exploration, or to counter the automatic thinking that we all tend to do under stress. Clients may have a variety of reactions to the introduction of novel explanations or ways of thinking about people and situations. Although some welcome new points of view and feel stimulated by them, not everyone is delighted to explore ideas different from their own.

> *Takis and I had met a few times to talk about his experience in hospice. In about our fourth meeting, I asked him if he had any faith or any belief in anything beyond himself*

that he could call on to help him through this time. He looked at me with a good deal of sarcasm and said he hoped I was not going to introduce "some kind of spiritual crap" into his quiet little corner here. He said he was raised strictly in the church but had been an atheist for a long time.

* * *

Polly Mae had been talking about what a loser her mother was. She was an alcoholic who had spent most of Polly's life in and out of the hospital. Polly hated having such a poor role model and disidentified with her mother. At one point, I noted that at times her mother really seemed to have a way with people. Polly at first said this made her afraid I would be on her mother's side and would be taken in by her like everyone else. After a minute or two, she said, "You know, she was good at 'working' people. I think I have a little of her skill, but I hope I put it to better use."

There are many ways to introduce or stimulate new perspectives. Some are things that the clinician and client can do together during the session. Others are suggestions for things that the client can do between meetings.

Questioning and Brainstorming to Elicit New Perspectives

Clinicians can help clients elucidate new perspectives simply by asking questions such as:

"How else could we see that?"
"Can you think of any other ways to explain this?"
"What other kinds of things could be going on?"

Sometimes a simple technique of listing alternative explanations or possibilities is useful. The clinician and client can **brainstorm** together, making a list of numerous alternative explanations, sometimes recording them on a flowchart. No idea is evaluated or judged; each is simply put on the table or chart. Then the clinician and client can review the list to see if any of them are useful.

Using Role-Plays to Expand Perspective

Role-plays are a useful technique with many applications. In Chapter 4, we discussed using role-plays to help the clinician gain empathy for the client. In the next chapter, we discuss using role-play techniques to help clients do things differently. Role-plays can also be used in a number of ways to help clients gain new perspectives.

- *Take the other side.*   The clinician may take a position that plays out the other side of an issue, struggle, or ambivalence: "Ayman, you said that you'll never find another job now that you are in a wheelchair, but there are lots of jobs I could imagine for you." When the clinician plays the other side, the risk is that the client gets into a "stuck opposer" role, rejecting any alternative the clinician presents. On the other hand, clinicians must be aware that some clients quickly defer to what they perceive to be the superior knowledge of the clinician. One way to avoid such dilemmas is to reverse things and have the client take the other side: "Ayman, I know that right now it seems impossible for you to think of being able to get another job. If you could take the other side for a moment—pretend you are an optimistic champion of people with disabilities—what kinds of things might you say to a guy who thinks he'll never get another job because he's in a wheelchair?"

- *Take the role of the other.*   When talking about a relationship, people are often so wed to their own point of view that they have a hard time appreciating another's perspective. Role-playing the other can help clients broaden their views of a relationship and offer new insights about another person. We might give the following instruction: "Jeremy, we've been talking a lot about your take on your relationship with your brother Hugh. Let's try having you play Hugh for a moment so you can get some insight into how he might see things. Sit in the chair over there. When you do, you become Hugh." (Client moves to other chair.) We can then interview "Hugh," asking such things as "How do you feel as Hugh?" and "Hugh, what do you think about Jeremy?"
- *Play the outside observer.*   Clients sometimes get a better perspective if they feel removed from the situation. The clinician can help clients see things from a different angle by asking them to bystand the situation: "If you were an outsider viewing this situation from afar, what different ideas might you have about what is going on? Or if you were reading a novel about these people, how would you understand their story? Would you have any observations about the central characters?"

Using Video to Expand Perspective

One useful way of helping clients take the observer role to get new perspectives is by video recording the process as they interact with family or group members or with the clinician. Client and clinician can watch the video together and discuss new ideas that may emerge or things they might have missed during the interview. Clients can also take videos home and review them to see if they gain any new perspectives while literally observing themselves. We ask the client to make notes on personal observations and reactions that can be addressed during the next meeting. These new perspectives may include observations about the clinician and the relationship, as well as about the client or the current focus of their work together.

Encouraging Contact with Others

Contact with other people can assist clients in redefining themselves and their stories. Clients can be encouraged to open themselves to the novel, often liberating ideas of others by joining self-help groups such as AA, Parents Anonymous, and Breast Cancer Support. In communities of color, an advocacy organization, an African American church, an Asian neighborhood or family improvement association, or a tribal council can all provide opportunities for clients to think about their problems and issues in new ways and gain greater perspective in the presence of new and energizing ideas. We often see rapid changes in thinking following group participation. Clients can move from lonely, discouraged isolation to heightened hopefulness and self-acceptance. Hope and self-regard almost invariably lead to thinking more imaginatively and energetically about life situations and possibilities.

Developing New Metaphors

Another way of helping clients create alternative perspectives is to help them in **developing new metaphors**. George Burns (2007) notes that in the original Greek, *metaphor* means "to carry something across" or "to transfer," and that in communication, it refers to carrying one image or concept across to another as a creative expression or healing representation. As an example, he cites the following effectively chilling metaphor from Aristotle: "His vulture eyes followed their every move." Burns discusses a 1994 study by Ferrara that found an average of three metaphors per 100 words in a single hour of therapy (p. 4). Burns believes that metaphors "open our eyes [a metaphor] to new ideas and possibilities" (p. 4), and he highlights the importance of listening for and sometimes reflecting back the metaphors that clients use to express their assets, characteristics, experiences, hopes, and anxieties.

Richard Kopp (1995) defines metaphors as "mirrors reflecting our inner images of self, life, and others" (p. xiii). He believes that cultures, families, social groups, and individuals structure reality through the use of guiding images (metaphors), and, by helping clients change the negative or powerless metaphors that structure their versions of reality, we can help them move rapidly toward positive change. He gives an example of a woman who was helped through questioning to shift from describing her husband as an out-of-control locomotive and herself as a tunnel to describing herself as a "derailer" of locomotives. Kopp is discussing his theory of "metaphor therapy." We believe that the skill of helping clients develop new metaphors can be used by all clinicians to help clients broaden their perspectives.

> *Marisol said that trying to date in this country was like swimming with sharks. We talked at length about the risks of dating strange men in a big city. She was used to scuba diving in her country, so I compared our meetings to scuba lessons where she could identify the safety equipment she needs and she could enjoy the coral reefs (club scene) while learning to tell the beautiful fish from the predators.*

Culturally responsive clinicians are aware of the rich metaphoric traditions of the clients with whom we work and can use these metaphors in helping clients enlarge their perspectives. Those working with Native American clients, for example, may make use of some of their traditional stories.

A note of caution: Just as we need to be certain that our clients understand the meaning of our words, we have to be particularly careful that they understand the meaning of our metaphors.

The other day the clinic director called me into his office to discuss a complaint he had received about me from a family I was seeing. I was surprised that the family had complained because I thought we were doing well. The family had told the director that I showed them no respect. They told the director that as far as I was concerned, their son's problems "could just go up in smoke." When I thought about it, I realized that during our last meeting I had suggested that "we put Frankie's problems on the back burner for a while" while we focused on some other issue in the family. "Putting something on the back burner" to them meant "letting it go up in smoke."

Using Spiritual Practices

Clients sometimes mention spontaneously that they pray, chant, meditate, or envision conversation with a god, goddess, powerful spirit, or universal presence when feeling lost or defeated and needing to reestablish a hopeful perspective. They may also seek guidance from a religious figure whose presence and advice they find renewing. Clinicians ask about, honor, and utilize spiritual assessment and validation techniques when working with clients for whom spirituality has a central place in resilience and well-being.

Wahiba Abu-Ras and colleagues (Abu-Ras et al., 2008) describe the importance of religion and spirituality in providing a framework for dealing with emotional hardships. Traditional Islamic teachings exhort Muslims to resolve inner conflicts through acts of devotion that include prayer, fasting, repentance, and recitation of the Qur'an to bring about healing. "While on this journey [of spiritual development], a person passes through periods of self-doubt, self-accusation, and self-acceptance to reach the pure self and, finally, the ultimate peaceful self" (p. 161). Some imams have successfully facilitated this change in perspective and feeling states by combining elements of psychodynamic, cognitive, and behavioral therapies.

CLIP 9.1
Developing New
Perspectives

Developing Working Hypotheses or Hunches

Clinicians also help clients develop new perspectives by sharing ideas or hunches about content, affect, themes and patterns, or relationship dynamics of which they may be unaware. **Hunches** are informed guesses, or working hypotheses, about the client and his or her situation.

As discussed in Chapter 5, Gerard Egan (2010) coined the term **advanced empathy** to describe the process of hypothesizing from experience with the client. For Egan, hunches are based on empathy with the client about themes or feelings the client may not yet have verbalized or even understood. Shulman (2009) refers to this process as "tuning in . . . to hear the client's indirect cues" (p. 68). Following the work of Theodor Reik (1948), others have referred to the activity of hypothesizing by means of empathy as "listening with the third ear." Although we like to think of developing working hypotheses and hunches as trying to understand the unspoken, we must remember that, until the client confirms or disconfirms our hunches, we are at risk of misunderstanding or misattributing meaning. Our hunches must always be tentative, awaiting the client's affirmation or denial.

As noted, we often refer to hunches as intuition, and some clinicians talk about "getting this feeling" when they are with someone, experiencing their intuition as a sensory or visceral event. We believe that clinical intuition and hunches are actually derived from a number of sources:

1. *Clinical theory or research.* The clinician may have a hunch that the client who has recently lost a loved one due to death may be having trouble sleeping, based on research demonstrating a correlation between grief and sleeping problems. The clinician who is trained in psychoanalytic theory may have a hunch that a person with a snake phobia may have repressed unconscious conflict with her father, whereas a cognitive-behavioral therapist might posit a conditioned association between a snake and an anxiety state.

2. *Clinical experience in general.* The intern working with the client who has recently lost a loved one might have a hunch, based on accumulated practice wisdom, that the client may react sensitively to the intern's announcement of an upcoming vacation because this is another loss of support at a hard time.

3. *Clinical experience with the specific client.* As the clinician gains information and understanding about the client and his or her situation, hunches develop more easily. The guesses are informed by the clinician's growing knowledge of the client's idiosyncrasies, of the themes and patterns in the client's story, and of information gleaned from the clinical relationship itself.

4. *Knowledge about larger social issues,* including political and socioeconomic conditions that might have an impact on the client. The clinician might consider that health care policies that limit hospital stays for new mothers might increase the anxiety of the pregnant woman who is about to give birth for the first time. Or, if a clinician knows from a TV news alert that war has suddenly broken out again in a refugee client's homeland, that clinician might have a hunch that she should mention the war when the client first comes in, express concern, and explore its impact on and implications for the client and her family.

5. *Personal experience and beliefs.* The clinician who is in recovery from alcoholism may be more alert to clues indicating alcoholism than would other clinicians for whom alcoholism is a more distant issue.

6. *Reading between the lines.* The clinician may develop hunches about things that are unspoken but seem implicit in the client's story.

EXAMPLE: WALLY

Wally is a 60-year-old computer programmer who has had four sessions with the Employee Assistance Program (EAP) counselor of the computer company where he has worked with moderate success for the past 20 years. The company is downsizing and is offering faithful employees like Wally an adequate early retirement package if they leave within a month. If they opt to stay on board, they have to move with the company to one of two distant states, with no clarity about future security. Wally wants to move and even seems excited about it, but he reports that his wife does not want to move. She said that, if he does not want to retire, he should just get another job in the community where they currently live. He states that his two sons are in computer businesses in nearby towns and seem settled here with their families. His youngest son has just had his third child, and his oldest son has two young infants. His wife, Evelyn, is a paralegal who can probably get work anywhere, but she prefers to stay near the boys and the five grandchildren. The EAP counselor has offered to have a meeting with Wally and his wife to talk about the options, but Wally has said he would rather not bring Evelyn.

Some Hunches About Wally

Hunch 1: Wally seems willing to sacrifice family ties for job security.

Hunch 2: The reason Wally is asking to be seen alone is that he may have a secret that he has not shared with his wife or children. Furthermore, he may be coming to see the counselor about the secret under the guise of asking for help about his job situation.

Hunch 3: Wally is depressed and wants to make a change to feel better.

Hunch 4: Wally feels that he has no choice and must move if he wants to continue working.

Hunch 5: Wally is attempting to protect his wife by not including her in the counseling sessions.

Hunch 6: Wally would welcome the opportunity to put distance between the couple and their children and grandchildren.

Discussion

Hunch 1: Based on theory. The clinician is familiar with life-cycle theory, as well as with recent literature on gender differences. She has learned that men in Wally's age cohort frequently use work achievement as a way of obtaining meaning and purpose, whereas women frequently use family and other relational connections as a way of developing a sense of self-worth. The clinician thinks that Wally's concerns about premature retirement are causing him to sacrifice family ties for job security, in direct conflict with Evelyn's wishes to be near family.

Hunch 2: Based on clinical experience. The counselor has worked with many couples over the years and has noticed that a partner asking to meet with the counselor alone often subsequently discloses a secret in the absence of the other partner.

Hunch 3: Based on established client patterns. Wally has reported that in the past he has often used what the clinician thinks of as "geographic cures"—moving far away from a conflict in the vain hope that such a move will resolve everything. When Wally got out of high school, he said he wanted to get away from the small town where he was born and "start fresh." He had previously reported that, when his young son was having difficulty in school, Wally moved the family to another town "to give him a clean slate." Perhaps Wally is looking to move to make a change that he hopes will help him feel better.

Hunch 4: Based on knowledge of social conditions. The clinician has seen many reports that men in their sixties are unlikely to find another good job when they are laid off. She knows that there have been many plant and company closings in the surrounding area. She thinks that Wally may feel that his only chance of staying employed is to move.

Hunch 5: Based on the clinician's personal experience. The clinician comes from a traditional Polish working-class family and has noticed that in her community the men often do not talk about financial or work issues in front of their wives to protect them. She has often heard the phrase, "We don't want to worry the women and children." Knowing that Wally is Polish, she thinks that his desire to meet alone may have to do with traditional Polish working-class values.

Hunch 6: Based on reading between the lines. Wally has occasionally talked about his wife's involvement with the grandchildren. In previous conversations, he has said things like: "She's always over there"; "Now that the babies take so much of her time . . ."; and "When she finally gets home. . . ." The clinician has stored away all of these phrases, thinking they might indicate that Wally is feeling left out or jealous over the amount of time his wife is spending with the children and grandchildren.

EXERCISE 9.2 Hunches

Develop a number of hunches about the clients in the following vignettes. What is the basis of your hunch (theory, experience, knowledge about social conditions, or other factors)?

Leah is a 13-year-old runaway living on the streets with a group of three other teens. They show up at the food kitchen occasionally, where a counselor has talked with Leah about the possibility of coming back into school and maybe into foster care. Leah actually seems interested in school. She tells the counselor: "I might like to finish school. I was good at it, but there's no way I'm living in another family. I've been on my own too long and I don't want to take orders from anybody. Besides, my friends need me. We do okay."

Arturo is a 34-year-old musician making his living playing in a small quartet that performs at functions like weddings and bar mitzvahs. He is seeing an employment counselor about career training: "I don't know, I guess I should get a real job. I'm 34 and it doesn't look like I'll make it as a classical musician. My wife says it's time for me to quit fooling around. I love what I do, but there's no future in it."

Huston, age 49, has just been released from jail, where he served 11 years for child sexual assault. He's meeting with his probation officer: "Man, I'm uptight about living outside. It's kind of scary after all these years. I have no family left; my only friends are the guys I met in the slammer."

Kimsoo, age 44, came to the United States to undertake religious studies and to become the first female minister in her village back home. After being here for 4 years, she is experiencing a number of conflicts about returning to Korea: "I feel really torn. I always thought I wanted to be a minister, and my family and church are counting on me. But things here are so different from back home. Plus, I didn't expect to get involved with an American the way I have."

Improving Hypothesis-Building Capacity

Intuitions, hunches, and feelings provide rich data for supervision and the enhancement of clinical listening and responding abilities. With experience, these processes can be used in sessions with clients as material for work. Clinicians can consciously develop and improve hypothesis-building capacities in the following ways:

- Value your intuitions, speculations, and sensory responses, and make them explicit for further analysis.
- Review your ideas and reactions with supervisors and consultants, exploring many possible alternative views of what the data might mean.
- Attempt to predict from your hunches and guesses what may happen in ensuing sessions, so as to be able to test your thinking against what actually transpires.
- Keep revising your impressions in supervisory discussion because people, events, and transactions keep changing.

Sharing Hunches

There are a number of guidelines for how to share hunches with clients:
Offer hunches tentatively. Because our hunches are only informed guesses, we must be careful how we present them to clients. We thus offer hunches tentatively, sharing ideas provisionally, as questions or as possibilities rather than certainties:

"Could it be that . . . ?"
"Perhaps . . ."
"I wonder if . . ."
"Is there a chance that . . . ?"

Avoid the pitfall of assumed brilliance.   Clinicians need to avoid the pitfall of assumed brilliance, a state of mind that leaves us thinking that our hunches absolutely have to be shared because they are so wise and may have immense effect on the conversation. Some clients may need to have an authority tell them things and may agree all too readily with the clinician's every hunch, subordinating their own judgment to the clinician's.

On the other hand, clients might reject a clinician's hunch, even though there is merit in it, because they are reacting against the clinician or because they are not yet ready to make the connection that the clinician has made. It requires a great deal of skill to know when to let go of a hunch and when to store it away. We can come back to an issue later if we feel the client is readier to hear it or deal with it, or we may conclude that we were off base in our speculation.

During my third meeting with Graciela, I remember thinking that the trouble she was having with her roommate seemed to be like two sisters fighting over who was most loved. I had a hunch that her relationship with her roommate might be evoking some of the competitive feelings she might have had with her sister. When I mentioned this to her, she said: "You psychologists are all alike . . . always trying to read something into things. I can't believe you could actually be so stereotypic. I thought you were really getting to know me. How could you be so wrong?" I felt stupid and naive. I remember it took me a long time before I was willing to take a risk and share a hunch again.

* * *

When I first broached the subject with him, Mustafa rejected the idea that the reason he might not be applying for jobs as an electrician in Boston was because he was fearful of entering a "White-dominated trade." He said he just knew there weren't any jobs. A couple of weeks later, he said he had been thinking about it and that he now felt that some of his reluctance was about being a Muslim among all those "Irish Catholic guys."

Well-timed and sensitively shared hunches can help clients develop new perspectives. Sharing hunches also models for clients the process of looking for alternative meanings or possibilities in their thoughts, feelings, or actions.

Share hunches in a way that makes clients think they came up with them. Clinicians can share their hypotheses in a number of ways. We can directly share a hunch using an "I" statement. Often, however, because we want clients to experience a sense of efficacy and to develop their own voices, we may share a hypothesis in such a way that the client feels it came from him or her. In the following example, note the differential responses of the client. With Clinician A, the client attributes the wisdom to the clinician. With Clinician B, the client assumes ownership of the idea.

EXAMPLES

Carrie and Jana have been a couple for two years. They are often fighting but seem to keep getting back together. The clinician, aware of their family histories, has a hunch that they do not stay separated because each of them is afraid of living on her own.

> *Clinician A:* Looks to me like both of you may have some fears of separating. (Clinician directly shares her hunch.)
>
> *Client:* Yes, you are right. I think we might.
>
> *Clinician B:* Sounds like you're saying that both she and you might be afraid of separating. (Clinician B is also sharing a hunch but does so in such a way that the client feels that it came from her.)
>
> *Client:* Yes, I do think so.

Sharing an inaccurate hunch is okay. Always remember that a hunch can be wrong and that sharing an inaccurate hunch is okay. The hunch may help clients clarify an issue or clarify their own perspective as separate from the clinician's. When we offer a hunch in a tentative or provisional way, it encourages clients to correct or amplify it. Clinician tentativeness is expressed in tone and language. It is fine to share a hunch directly, as Clinician A does in the example, but she could also have shared it by saying, "Could it be that . . . ?" or "Have you considered the possibility that . . . ?" These questions make it easier for clients to think about whether the clinician's hunches are accurate.

EXERCISE 9.3 Sharing Hunches

Go back to Exercise 9.2 and frame a response in which you share your hunch with the client. If possible, video record your response and play it back. What do you notice?

Encouraging Client Hypothesizing

Hunches often come from clients themselves, sometimes well before the clinician ever thinks of the material offered in the hunch. Some clients are more "psychologically minded" than others: They do a great deal of speculating on the meanings and motivations within events and relationships and readily develop their own working hypotheses.

Be conscious of how this reflective capacity can be nourished and developed. We can emphasize the importance of thinking about meanings and interrelationships and encourage clients to develop their own working hypotheses by frequently asking what clients think about things or how they understand situations. Clients can be helped to search out their own hunches if the clinician uses appropriate prompts, such as:

"Let's stop for a moment and think about this."
"How could we understand this?"
"What's your take on this?"
"What are your thoughts about this?"
"What might be some different ways to think about this?"

Reinforce constructive introspection.   Clients occasionally share their ideas or thoughts or offer insights about things. Clinicians can reinforce clients' constructive introspection by responding positively:

"What an interesting idea."
"So you're trying to figure out where this might come from. Good work!"
"It's so important that you're coming up with these insights."

Leave silence for pondering.   Another way to encourage clients to respect and develop their own hunches is through a purposeful use of silence—silence for pondering. After the client says something or shares a story, we intentionally leave a brief period of silence, assuming a pensive expression to indicate that we are thinking about implications or contemplating meanings. Here we model for clients the importance of taking time to think things out rather than responding glibly or moving on too quickly. Sitting with silence is natural for some clinicians, but others may have to consciously develop it so that clients can be left sufficient space to gather and plumb their own thoughts.

Leaving room.   Related to the purposeful use of reflective silence is leaving plenty of room in the conversation for clients to muse on and share their own hunches. As clinicians, we can come to value the sound of our own voices and wisdom too much, too readily offering our personal hunches instead of gently urging clients to risk developing their own. Clinicians may pay lip service to the principle of empowerment by always asking the client to speak first, but, when the client does not respond quickly enough, we may too quickly chime in with our own ideas or hunches.

Know when to "hold 'em."   Clinicians must decide how, when, with whom, and to what extent to share hunches. Such decisions are often a matter of judging how quickly and comfortably clients can correct clinician statements when necessary, especially given the authority that both clients and clinicians tend to attribute to clinician insight and wisdom. We do not and should not always share our hunches. Keep in mind that we wait for more information with which to validate or invalidate speculations and that we give high priority to opening up opportunities for clients to author their own narratives. Before sharing any hunch, be sure to ask yourself what effects the hunch might have and be prepared to take responsibility for any negative fallout.

> *I remember being in supervision with a young psychology intern who was always sharing his "ideas about what's going on" with the client. He intended to be helpful and was often confused when his clients stopped coming to see him or complained that they felt he was judgmental.*

Beginning practitioners often mistakenly define the helping process as the imparting of wisdom, and worry excessively about not conveying enough to clients to appear competent and helpful. While there is great merit in developing knowledge and skills in hypothesis building, clinicians have to learn to refrain from sharing their own ideas too quickly.

A friend of mine who is a rock climber (and therapist) shared a quote with me from Rebuffat (1965) about guides that I think captures an aspect of clinical helping, too: "With the inevitable repetition of the same ascents, the work of the guide could become tedious, but the guide is not just a machine to climb slopes of ice and walls of rock, to know the weather and the route. He does not climb for himself: He opens the gates of his mountain for his companion. He knows that such and such a climb is interesting, that this particular area is as delicate as a piece of lacework, he knows at which turn there is, suddenly, a wonderful view. He says nothing, but his reward comes with the smile of his companion when he sees it."

Sometimes clients may not want to develop their own hunches, expecting the clinician to come up with explanations and answers. Weaver (2005) notes that Asian-American families may expect an authoritative approach from a clinician and quick symptom relief without losing face through self-disclosure. "Communication . . . tends to flow downward from superior to subordinate, often in the form of directives" (p. 180). Sam Chan and Evelyn Lee (2004) cite two Chinese proverbs illustrating inhibition in the presence of an authority figure: "The nail that raises its head is hammered down" and "The taller the tree, the more wind it attracts" (p. 281).

It may be tempting to leap in, particularly if we feel that the client's journey is one we know well and can speculate on in helpful ways. Although it may at times be helpful, and even necessary, for the clinician to share hunches and hypotheses, it is important that clients develop and utilize these skills themselves whenever possible. In this way, they develop skills that they can use long after the clinical relationship ends.

CLIP 9.2
Sharing Hunches

Making Observations About Stuck Patterns

We can help clients enlarge their perspective by making observations about stuck patterns of thinking, feeling, or behaving that seem to get in the way of the client's goals. Sometimes the client is unaware of these patterns, and we gently suggest them in the form of a tentative hunch. For example, a client feels strongly that she will be judged harshly for speaking her mind and, as a result, does not speak up in most situations. The clinician may observe how the client's resultant silence has prevented her from moving up in her job in a company that rewards verbal initiatives. He might offer his observation in the form of a hunch: "I notice something interesting about you. Because you're afraid you'll be criticized, you remain silent and then, ironically, you often get criticized for not speaking up." If the client agrees with the hunch about a pattern holding her back, she might respond with comments such as, "I never realized I did that before" or "I never thought of it from that perspective."

Reflecting Discrepancies

As noted in our discussion of motivational interviewing in Chapter 7, while listening to clients' stories we pay attention to discrepancies or inconsistencies. Among other things, **discrepancies** can manifest as inconsistencies between two statements, between thoughts and feelings, between intentions and actual behaviors, and between verbal and nonverbal communication. It is very human to be unaware of our discrepancies until they are brought to our attention, and they often illuminate struggles, ambivalences, or conflicts we are not quite ready to resolve. Clients are often unaware of their own contradictions or inconsistencies. Clinicians may point out discrepancies to clients to help them examine the several sides of an issue or reaction, so that they can proceed in the work with new perspectives and with more information and clarity about themselves, their situation, and how the mind works when divided about things.

Clinicians try to note discrepancies as they arise. We may then choose to reflect the discrepancy directly, develop unspoken hunches based on observed inconsistencies, or wait to see if a pattern develops that would make a hunch more compelling. Some clinicians refer to pointing out discrepancies as *challenging* the client (Egan, 2010), and others call it *confronting* (Ivey et al., 2010; Kadushin & Kadushin, 1997; Okun & Kantrowitz, 2008). We believe that **reflecting discrepancies** can serve many functions, depending on the intent of the clinician and the impact on the client. The clinician may *intend* to clarify; the client may *feel* challenged or confronted.

The techniques that clinicians use to point out discrepancies are many and varied. Some common techniques include:

1. *Reflect the discrepancy.*
   "While you described your sadness, you were smiling."
   "You've said that you like school, and you've said that you hate being a student."
2. *The "on the one hand . . . on the other hand" technique.*
   "On the one hand, you say that you really like your job; on the other, you are always late for work."
3. *Name it directly.*
   "I sense an inconsistency here."
   "I hear two things at once."
   "You seem to be of two minds about this."
4. *The "help me understand" technique.*
   "You say that you and your brother don't get along but that you are looking forward to visiting him. Help me understand how these two fit together."

EXERCISE 9.4 Helping Clients See Discrepancies

Divide into groups of three. Using the following examples, role-play various ways of pointing out the discrepancy to the client. Assume the roles of clinician, client, and observer/commentator. Note how it feels to be the client and how you respond to different ways of having discrepancies pointed out to you.

Nancy, age 55, is talking to an EAP counselor because her boss has said she must: "I don't have a problem with drinking and I don't know why people say I do. Sure, I have a few. Who doesn't? They say it affects my work, but, hey,

I give them a good morning's work. Sometimes I have a few drinks with lunch, but that's no big deal. My boyfriend says he doesn't like how I act in public. Half the stuff he accuses me of I don't remember. I'm just having a good time, so what's his beef?"

Marcel, age 30, a recent widower, says he wants to find a new mother for his young children. He's been going to every church singles event for the last 6 months. He is talking to his pastor: "I miss Gabrielle so much. It's only been 7 months since she died. She was a rare find. I can't imagine anyone taking Gabrielle's place, but the kids really need a woman's touch."

CLIP 9.3
Identifying
Discrepancies

Education or Information Sharing

In clinical work, education and **information sharing** refer to introducing new concepts or information the client may be unaware of as another means of widening possibilities or extending opportunity. Information can be liberating. The abused single mother who is afraid of losing custody of her children if she seeks safety in a homeless shelter, the male teenager who is attracted to other males, and the lonely widower who has few social contacts can all benefit from information and resources.

Information sharing usually occurs in situations in which clients are unaware of resources or of their rights in a particular situation. Clinicians frequently provide information about transportation, respite care, funding sources, training opportunities, elder resources, child care, and preventive health care services. In addition, clinicians need to inform clients about legal rights or protective services. Information sharing may be accomplished in several ways.

Helping Clients Identify Sources of Information

We can directly ask whether the client knows where to get the needed information.

"Do you know where you can get information about TMJ [temporal mandibular joint disease]?"
"How would you find out about the legal rights of lesbian mothers?"
"Do you know about mutual aid groups for anorexia in your area?"

Such questions can help the client delineate what information is needed and how to go about getting it. Some clients are able to identify the sources of information and obtain it for themselves. Clients' confidence and resourcefulness are often increased by successfully seeking out their own information, and success at this task can reinforce skills that are useful in the process of locating other needed resources and networks.

Providing Materials

Some clinicians, especially those who work in specialized services, have resources and materials readily available for use by clients. A clinician who works in a drug treatment program might have pamphlets about HIV/AIDS prevention. Someone who works in a hospital with people who have had spinal cord injury might have brochures from health care companies about home health equipment. Some clinicians have bulletin boards where they post information about mutual aid groups or other supportive services that might be of interest to clients. Clinicians can consider posting specialized information and resources on the Internet. It is important that your agency have important informational materials translated into each of the languages spoken by the populations you serve. If the agency is too underfunded to afford these translations, staff, interns, and clients can create joint fundraising campaigns to fund this important work.

Bibliotherapy is a form of intervention in which the clinician refers clients to specific readings, sometimes lending clients the books. Remember, though, that some clients can't read in their own languages; others can't read English or other languages in which helpful materials are published. We can try to give clients audiotapes or videos in their own languages for their use at home (e.g., relaxation tapes or conference tapes on subjects that would be instructional and supportive for clients).

Web resources and educational Websites may also be suggested. Before you recommend any Web resources it is important that you make sure that the information is from a reputable source. Alert clients that material they find on the Web may not be accurate.

Today there are also therapy-related Websites, blogs, and chat rooms where various therapeutic models are explained and discussed, with comments from ostensible clients explaining how helped they have been by a therapist or a particular intervention. On the Web, clients may also receive solace, peer support, and directions for locating clinical programs or therapists for various problems. State and federal health and mental health Websites also provide a great deal of helpful information about prevention activities and treatments for various disorders. Again, these resources can be most helpful if made available in a variety of languages.

Directly Imparting Information

Clinicians who have the expertise may at times give clients information directly. The clinician working with a couple who has decided to adopt may directly share information about what to expect during the prescreening interview with the agency social worker, informing the couple that the interviewer often asks to see the room where the child will sleep. The clinician working with a client who is phobic about HIV may reassure him that he cannot become HIV infected through kissing or hugging.

Clients can be very appreciative of the clinician's imparting of information, which can serve as a shortcut when people are especially busy and already stressed. However, when providing information, we should be careful not to have clients see us as "the expert" or "the one with all the know-how." Harry Aponte (1994) aptly observed that the mission of providers "is to serve, not to colonize" (p. 11). Giving direct information can tempt some clients to come back any time they have a question instead of exercising their own resourcefulness. Teaching people how to get needed answers gives them confidence and skills they can use forever.

Finally, when providing information, clinicians should be careful that the client does not feel pushed toward or into a particular stance or service. For example, if the clinician gives a pregnant 13-year-old information about abortion but not about adoption, she and her parent or guardian may feel that the clinician has tried to guide her in a specific direction.

Accompanying Clients in Seeking Information

Sometimes we may accompany the client who is attempting to get information, offering to go with the client to lend support. At other times, the client may ask the clinician to come along. In some clinical settings, going with clients to obtain information and services is a valued, routine function; in others, it is an exceptional occurrence. Supervisors can help you think carefully about the pros and cons of accompanying the client or of going with one client but not with another.

> *I was working with a client who was dying from bone cancer. He was interested in getting information about dying at home. He asked if I would go with him to a meeting with the people from the local hospice because he was afraid he wouldn't be able to remember what was said and he wanted my help in processing the information and figuring out what to do. I was glad to go with him, and it gave me a chance to meet people in his potential helping network and learn more myself about what they could offer.*

Sharing Information Through Self-Disclosure

Through the selective and judicious sharing of personal information, clinicians can sometimes provide clients with helpful information. For example, with a client about to undergo abdominal surgery and deciding how soon to return to work, the clinician might share that she had similar surgery and felt tired in the afternoons for more than one month after surgery. Information sharing through self-disclosure is often based on learning from life experience and is meant to convey empathy as well as information. Lesbian, gay, and transgendered clients often benefit enormously from having providers who have "been down that road" themselves and who can share both optimistic and cautionary advice and coping strategies.

When sharing information through self-disclosure, we try to be brief and avoid sounding either condescending or self-righteous. Before self-disclosing, we always pay attention to where the client is and to the impact of sharing. Some clients see the disclosure as informative, some may be pleased to know more about the clinician, and others may find that the self-disclosure moves them away from their own issues. In the previous example, the client may find that she is now worrying about the clinician's health, subsequently asking more about the clinician's surgery instead of focusing on her own concerns about surgery. One risk of sharing information through self-disclosure is that the client may feel pressured to act in the way that the clinician did; one benefit is that such sharing may strengthen the mutuality of the relationship. We discuss self-disclosure more fully in Chapter 11.

CLIP 9.4
Sharing
Information

EXERCISE 9.5 Sharing Information with Clients

In small groups, come up with a number of issues about which you might feel comfortable sharing potentially useful information through self-disclosure. Role-play and video record scenarios, rotating the roles of client and clinician. Discuss the impact that your sharing information in this way has on the client. Try sharing the same information with the client using the other techniques suggested. Watch the role-plays and notice the different effects on your client of conveying the same information in different ways.

Introducing New Topics

Clinicians always attend to the whole shape of their contacts with clients. Attention is paid to what is being focused on across a series of contacts, not just during each interview. Is the focus too scattered or too limited? Are there repeating or stuck themes or themes that may be digressing from material not yet covered, thus limiting the client's and clinician's perspectives?

Clients may work intensely on certain situations, relationships, or themes but never touch on others. Preoccupation with particular stressors or persistent problems is understandable, yet at times it can prove unproductive because the same subjects are discussed over and over without leading anywhere. At other times, clients and clinicians can unwittingly stay narrowly focused to avoid painful or taboo areas. Shulman (2009) regards such conversation as creating an "illusion of work" (p. 153).

In any event, sometimes the clinician has to raise new areas for exploration, to fill out the picture. Introducing new perspectives can help clients enlarge their view of self and context, especially when things have been omitted from a story because the client does not think these topics matter. Sometimes focusing on a new area highlights the strengths of a client or situation.

> *Lonny and Carla fought like cats and dogs in the office. You name it, they argued about it. Then they would proclaim, "See? All we know how to do is fight." It seemed that there was nothing to hold them together. I realized that we'd been talking, and they'd been arguing, about everything—money, time, sex—but they never talked about their children. When I asked about the kids, their whole demeanor changed. They softened; they agreed with and appreciated each other as parents. The whole feeling in the room changed, and I felt the first glimmer of hope for this couple. Here was something about their "team" to build on.*

New topics need not be introduced abruptly. The clinician usually waits for an appropriate opening—even just a pause for breath—and then gently introduces the new topic.

"We haven't talked much about . . ."
"I'm curious to know more about . . ."
"I realize I don't know anything about . . ."
"We've talked a lot about . . . but not about . . ."
"While we're on that subject . . ."

■ Working for Social Change

Social forces, including the attitudes of others, account for much of our clients' distress. Far too many people are left feeling that they *are* problems, rather than that they *have* problems, which are often due to socioeconomic and political factors beyond their control. As clinicians, we recognize that, in addition to helping clients gain new perspectives, sometimes the best intervention is to work to change the attitudes and beliefs of others and to change larger systems and institutions, especially those that limit opportunities for others.

I was a school counselor who was seeing a couple of high school students who identified themselves as gay. As these two young men talked about their experiences, it became clear that a lot of the stress they felt was in response to the attitudes that some of their teachers seemed to have toward them. I realized that, to help the students, I also had to work with the teachers. I offered an in-service for teachers in which I used a number of techniques including stories by several lesbian/gay/bisexual students about the extent of the pain they experienced in being either ignored or attacked. I shared information about the development of sexual orientation, and I had the teachers role-play scenarios in which they had to experience the plight of lesbian, gay, and bisexual students. Some of the teachers said that the workshop raised some issues that they had never thought about. The students later reported that they felt that some teachers were showing a little more sensitivity after that.

* * *

One of my classmates in social work school was in a wheelchair because of multiple sclerosis. She wanted us to perceive more fully how many barriers there are to mobility in the supposedly enlightened environment of a university. She had several of us experience what it was like to be in a wheelchair for half a day. Because the entrance ramp was blocked by bicycles chained to it, I had to be carried into the building by strangers happening by. Then I had to try to make it across the street in the wheelchair at a stoplight that changed so fast that I couldn't get across. I asked for help from passersby, who would stare at me and walk right on by. Others offered help when I didn't want or ask for it. I returned to the meeting room exasperated and really full of ideas about what should happen differently for people in wheelchairs. We were all quite shocked that we'd never really appreciated what they go through. That one day really shifted my perspective about barriers to access.

Workshops, community training, and media presentations all can help change the perspectives of others and may have an indirect effect on clients with whom we work. As clinicians, we work for social change on behalf of clients. Sometimes clinicians can even find appropriate ways to be present in the same political or social action campaigns and protests as their clients, such as Walk for Hunger, Take Back the Night, or Save Darfur campaigns or political marches for civil or human rights. These shared events affirm our common humanity and strengths. Robert Polack (2004) notes that with the globalization of the economy and the impoverished state of 20 percent of the world's citizens, there are enormous opportunities for both clinicians and clients to become involved in global justice work.

EXERCISE 9.6 Broadening the Views of Others

In small groups, make a list of commonly held social attitudes, such as racism, classism, heterosexism, ableism, that you believe may have a negative impact on your clients. Choose one of the problematic attitudes and design a public education campaign around it. What techniques will you use to help people alter or broaden their perspectives? Describe persons or institutions that you believe are likely to respond favorably or unfavorably to your efforts.

■ Conclusion

In this chapter, we reviewed a number of action strategies and techniques that can help clients develop new perspectives and feel things differently. We noted that it is hard to overestimate the power that develops in clients from learning to name, talk about, and stand up for their own ideas and feelings in the presence of a validating and encouraging other. We also affirmed the power of religion, spirituality, and support groups in clients' efforts to effect positive and enduring changes.

Often this work requires that we, too, develop new perspectives and become more aware of our own feeling reactions. As clinicians, we can broaden our own views and expand our range of feelings using the same techniques that have proven useful in helping clients develop new perspectives. Bystanding, brainstorming, observing and working out our own discrepancies, role-playing the part of the other, gathering new information through continuing education, and looking for and changing stuck patterns in ourselves are all ways we can expand our knowledge and responsiveness.

■ Suggested Readings

There are a number of highly readable self-helps books:

Borysenko, Joan & Dveirin, Gordon. (2006). *Say yes to change: Essential wisdom for your journey.* Carlsbad, CA: Hay House.

Burns, David D. (1999). *The feeling good handbook.* New York: Plume-Penguin.

Kabat-Zinn, Jon. (1994). *Wherever you go, there you are: Mindfulness meditation in everyday life.* New York: Hyperion.

The following provide useful information for clinicians about working with thoughts and feelings:

Beck, Judith. (1995). *Cognitive therapy: Basics and beyond.* New York: Guilford.

Burns, George (Ed.). (2007). *Healing with stories: Your casebook collection for using therapeutic metaphors.* New York: Wiley.

Dwairy, Marwan. (2002). Psychotherapy in competition with culture: A case study of an Arab woman. *Clinical Case Studies, 1,* 254–267.

Fredrickson, Barbara L. (2001). The role of positive emotions in positive psychology: The broaden-and-build theory of positive emotions. *American Psychologist, 56,* 218–226.

Padesky, Christine & Greenberger, Dennis. (1995). *Mind over mood: Change how you feel by changing the way you think.* New York: Guilford.

The following readings offer provocative insights on complications in clinicians' efforts to empower others:

Everett, Joyce, Homstead, Kerry, & Drisko, James. (2007). Frontline worker perceptions of empowerment process in community-based agencies. *Social Work, 52,* 161–170.

Rose, Stephen M. (2000). Reflections on empowerment-based practice. *Social Work, 45,* 403–412.

Yan, Miu Chung. (2008). Exploring cultural tensions in cross-cultural social work practice. *Social Work, 53,* 317–328.

■ Self-Explorations

1. When you were growing up, what messages did you get from your family, culture, or religion about how you should or should not show feelings? Were certain feelings more acceptable than others? Did you conform to these messages? How do these messages affect your ideas about feeling expression now?

2. How good are you at dealing with confrontations? Do you avoid directly confronting people? Do you feel comfortable in doing so? How did people handle confrontation in your family and culture? Are you more likely to go too far or to be too polite? Too harsh and direct or too avoidant and cautious? (Adapted from Young & Chromy [2005].)

3. Think of a time when you were "stuck" or in a rut. What things did you find helpful in getting a new perspective?

4. How do you react when someone around you expresses intense emotions? Would you be comfortable with clients who have and express strong emotional reactions?

■ Essay Questions

1. People often say it is good to express their feelings. When is it useful to help clients contain their feelings? Describe some of the strategies or techniques clinicians can use to help clients manage or contain their feelings.

2. Describe strategies that clinicians can use to help clients accentuate the positive.

3. Do you think it is unprofessional for a clinician to show emotional reactions with a client? What are the cautions and benefits of clinicians sharing feelings with clients?

4. It is sometimes easier to give clients information than to help them find the information for themselves. If you have the needed information readily available, is it "phony" or just making more work for clients if they have to get information themselves? Discuss some reasons why clinicians might encourage clients to seek information. What are some potential problems of directly imparting information to the client?

5. Describe some of the sources from which clinicians develop hypotheses, and discuss some of the pros and cons of offering a hypothesis to a client.

■ Key Terms

Advanced empathy

Alternative perspectives

Bibliotherapy

Brainstorm

Coping questions

Developing new metaphors

Dialectical Behavioral Treatment

Discrepancies

Exception questions

Feeling-thinking

Hunches

Information sharing

Interpersonal Therapy

Islands of possibility

Miracle question

Negative cognitive triad

Perspective

Positive mirror

Positive Psychology Interventions

Positivity portfolios

Random acts of kindness

Reflecting discrepancies

Reframing

Scaling questions

Three Good Things

Transferability of skills

Triggers

CHAPTER 10

Changing Behaviors: Helping Clients Do Things Differently

Sometimes people come to see clinicians because they want to change patterns of behavior that are not working for them or because they want to learn new skills and new behaviors. Clarinda wants to find new ways of handling her anger rather than yelling. Howard, diagnosed with obsessive-compulsive disorder, wants to learn how to control his compulsive hand washing. Estrella wants to learn how to be more assertive at work. Pete wants to develop better study habits. Liam wants to learn the skills he needs to live on his own as an adult with mental retardation.

Sometimes clients come for practical information about how to do things. Bernice wants to know how to adopt a child as a single woman. Yves wants his boys to get green cards so they can help support the extended family. Lana wants a referral to the Reach to Recovery program in her area.

Clients may come to see a clinician because other people are concerned about their behaviors. Chet is referred by his teacher to the school counselor because he calls out in a disruptive way in class. Gilbert is sent by the court to see an alcohol abuse counselor after being convicted for driving while intoxicated. Gladdie is taken to see a neighborhood clinic counselor by her children, who are concerned that she has scarcely left the house since the death of her husband.

Sometimes clients may not be coming to do things differently. Although not initially seeking to change behavior, the client comes to realize that the presenting problem is connected with behaviors that might need to be changed or replaced with new skills. Francesca comes complaining that she is depressed and unhappy. In talking with the psychologist, she discovers that, if she did some things differently (e.g., getting together with others even when she does not feel like it), she might begin to feel better. Selina comes to see a social worker about her boyfriend's abuse of her. In talking with the social worker, Selina realizes that her children have been affected by her boyfriend's violent behavior, and she then wants to learn how to talk to them about it. In due time, she decides to end her relationship with her boyfriend and asks how to get a restraining order.

A clinician often helps clients focus on changing personal behaviors. It is also important to work to change patterns of behavior in the larger society. Frederick came to see a pastoral counselor about his plan to volunteer to help reconstruct some of the southern Black churches destroyed by arsonists and about his fears about personal safety. Shusei is taking a course on conflict resolution at the local mental health center because she wants to serve as a volunteer mediator in family court. After Selina is successful in moving away from her relationship with her abusive boyfriend, she decides that she wants to help other women overcome what she refers to as *marianismo* (the female counterpart of *machismo*), which she believes contributes to Latina women's willingness to put up with violence from men. She sets up a local educational program and eventually becomes a national spokesperson for Latina women. Damien attended the 1996 Million Man March in Washington, D.C., to rally men of color to action, and ever since that experience, he reports a heightened sense of belonging, power, and responsibility. Just as he committed to being actively involved in parenting his son, he is now looking forward to being a strong family role model for his grandchildren. Sometimes working on behavior change leads to social action, as it did for Selina. At other times, social action can lead to personal behavior change, as it did for Damien.

■ Ripples in a Stream

As clients change their behaviors, learn new skills, or accomplish practical tasks, many aspects of their lives are affected. Not only behavior, but also perspective, emotions and feeling states, self-concept, and achievement levels may all change, because all are interrelated. Sometimes people ask: "Does changing one's perceptions change one's behaviors, or vice versa?" "Does changing one's behavior change one's mood, or vice versa?" or "Does insight change behavior, or vice versa?" Which occurs first does not matter as much as that something occurs, for we know that change in any domain has a ripple effect on all others.

People often find that, when they do things differently, they see and feel things differently. As clients learn to do things differently, their perspectives about themselves—how they envision their potential and place—changes. Successful achievement and connection with others, even in small amounts, can often counteract hopelessness. By achievement, we do not mean scaling life's Mount Everests or winning important posts in government; rather, achievement is finally doing those things in daily life that clients had wished to do but that had seemed impossible. Achievement could mean making just one friend or speaking up for the first time.

As behaviors change, so do relationships. Doing things differently affects not only the client's own behavior, but also the behaviors of others with whom the client relates. Working for social change affects the individual's perspective, mood, self-concept, worldview, and activities, but it also affects large groups of others and perhaps society as a whole. African American men like Damien coming together in Washington, D.C., for the Million Man March triggered a much needed nationwide soul searching and commentary regarding persistent discrimination based on race, class, and gender. The march also stimulated a number of organizations to stand up more forthrightly for societal change and antiracism work.

In Chapter 9, we discussed techniques used to help clients see and feel things differently. In this chapter, we focus on techniques that can help clients *do* things differently, building on many principles discussed in previous chapters.

■ Exploring What the Client Is Doing "Right"

To help clients learn new behaviors and skills, it is crucial to elicit client strengths, minor triumphs, and successful adaptive strategies and activities, no matter how small. A natural tendency in clinical work is to focus on what clients want to do differently, especially when using a time-limited or problem-solving approach. However, we recognize the importance of emphasizing what is already working for clients, what clients like, what they want to preserve and expand, as well as what they want to change. It helps to underscore the idea that clients' successes came about not by magic or fate, but through hard work, persistence, and a successful connection with others who care and help.

> *Denny came to see me because he was having difficulties at work. His company was going through a period of retrenchment. There were a lot of layoffs. He had been given more responsibilities since there were fewer people to get tasks done. He felt overwhelmed and was impatient and irritable at home. As we talked, I asked him what he felt good about at work. He spoke of how he was, in fact, pleased with many of the new responsibilities he was being given. He said, with some pride, that it was because his boss knew that he could get things done. He had in the past and would do so now.*

Similarly, we explore with clients any problem-solving skills they have learned from struggling, coping, and mastering challenges in the past, emphasizing that these skills can be used to resolve current problems too. Many people undervalue their former experiences because of past mistakes and failures that continue to haunt their thinking. When we see this happening, we emphasize the transferability of skills and behaviors, underscoring as assets those effective behaviors and skills that are already in the client's repertoire.

> *Alphonse said that, in struggling with his alcoholism, he learned how to relinquish battles over things he cannot change, and now he tries to focus effort on that which he can do something about. This helps him be more patient with his rather rigid supervisor, instead of butting heads with her all the time.*

* * *

> *Jobeth learned from raising three teens alone that she has more strength than she ever thought and that, if she just takes one thing at a time, she can get through many challenges without being overwhelmed.*

* * *

> *Trish said she learned from the protective services worker how to count to 10 and leave the room before hitting her children. Now she recognizes that counting to 10 and cooling off in another room are also good ways of avoiding angry confrontations with her landlady.*

Historically, clinicians have given too little credit to the substantial support their clients might derive (or have been deriving) from spiritual or religious beliefs. Some have been slow to recognize that spiritual beliefs and belongingness can give a sense of purpose and worth to embattled or isolated individuals and groups. For example, from her research in communities of color, Wendy Haight (1998) describes "spiritual socialization" as a protective factor in children's healthy development (p. 213). She found that such socialization provides youth with core experiences of acceptance, dignity, and worth that can counteract stigma and oppression.

Similarly, Melvin Delgado (2007), Robert Taylor and colleagues (2000), and Wahiba Abu-Ras and colleagues (2008) discuss the crucial role that **faith-based organizations** play in providing the hope, spiritual and social support, advice, and consolation through which large numbers of underserved people find self-respect and empowerment to counter experiences of marginalization and stigmatization. In addition, these organizations are neighborhood-based, easily accessed, and usually provide services and activities from early morning to late evening.

> *Madelena said that when her husband was killed in a tank explosion in Iraq, the first thing she did was run to her mother's and grieve with her and two aunts. The second thing was to meet with her priest and say a rosary for her husband. She has joined a group for widows sponsored by her church.*

* * *

> *Chip was in training to be a firefighter and was talking about how anxious he felt when he had to go into a burning building. I knew that he had participated in the Gulf War and I asked him if he felt a similar fear then. He said he did. I asked what he did to enable*

CLIP   10.1
Identifying
Exceptions

him to get through it. Chip said that in the Gulf War he learned to pray when under fire. I asked if he could use this now. He was surprised, saying he didn't think counselors believed in things like praying. I said that I do and that I was glad if it comforts him. He said that he doesn't tell his buddies, but when he's in a bad fire and is afraid, he prays silently in his head for himself and the others involved.

◼ Helping Clients Own Their Part in Things

Now and then, most of us manifest the human tendency to perceive that the causes of our difficulties lie in others or in forces beyond our control. Many people go about their daily lives unaware of their motivations, of particular triggers of happy or sad feelings, of others' effects on them, or of possible ways their histories might be shaping what they say and do. Clients learning to do things differently have to learn to assume responsibility for personal behaviors that may be contributing to problems. At the same time, they also learn to credit themselves for behaviors that result in successful change.

◼ Identifying Behaviors to Change and New Skills to Learn

To help clients do things differently, the clinician helps them identify behaviors, relationships, and tasks they wish to work on or new skills they need or want to learn.

A number of guidelines facilitate this process:

1. *Clinicians help clients be as concrete and specific as possible in describing what they want to do differently—their goals and motivation for change.* Remember that the clearer the clinician's and client's views are of the desired objectives and possible strategies for attaining them, the more likely they are to accomplish them. As we noted in Chapter 9, it helps to develop clear images or metaphors of what the change will look like, so that clinician and client will know when they have achieved it.

2. *Clinicians help clients identify contexts in which the behavior occurs and encourage them to examine when, with whom, and under what circumstances the targeted behaviors occur.* An awareness of the circumstances in which the behavior occurs can help the clinician and client think about appropriate interventions. Behavior is never separate from its context.

Jason was referred to the psychologist for his aggressive behavior with younger children at the residential treatment center. Upon exploration, the psychologist discovered that this behavior was pretty much limited to the residential program and that Jason did not seem to have this difficulty with younger children at school.

3. *Clinicians help clients identify precipitating events and triggers, or easily pushed emotional "buttons," that seem to set off a habitual behavior pattern or sequence.* Sometimes these triggers and sequences are so deeply imbedded and out of awareness that the clinician must patiently retrace with the client circumstances or interactions that precede unhappy moods, behaviors, or preoccupations that the client cannot explain. The clinician has

to do detective work with the client to discover and understand the precipitants of the behavior. Bringing into awareness information and understandings previously split off from conscious memory is referred to as **insight development.** Insight can help clients understand and change their behaviors as well as their feeling states and relationships with others.

> *Every time Paul's wife asks him if he has stopped for a drink after work, he gets angry and slams the door, goes to the basement workshop, and stays there fuming until after everyone is in bed.*

* * *

> *Annmarie noticed that she was most likely to be short-tempered with her children when one of them says something about missing their father.*

EXAMPLE

Client: I've been acting very short-tempered all week. On Wednesday, I was in an especially foul mood. I was kind of grumpy with everyone that day.

Clinician: Were there any particular things that happened that day?

Client: No. It was an ordinary day.

Clinician: What were your thoughts or feelings on waking?

Client: Nothing special that I can recall.

Clinician: How about events or people the evening before?

Client: Nope; watched TV, went to bed seemingly okay.

Clinician: Anything on TV that distressed you?

Client: No . . . cop shows, news.

Clinician: Was there anything about this day of the week or date that had any significance for you?

Client: [Hesitates.] Now that I think about it. There *were* a lot of ads on TV for Father's Day . . .

Clinician: Hmmmm. Father's Day is coming up. Might you be missing your father at this time?

Client: I never think about him. . . . [Then she begins to cry.] My mother always told me that it was best if we just got on with our lives: "There's no sense crying over spilt milk." I guess I felt that she was so hurt about my father's death that I shouldn't even miss him, since that would hurt her, too.

---

4. *Clinicians and clients work together to identify the consequences of the current behavior.*   **Consequences** are responses or contexts that reinforce or encourage the behavior, as well as things that serve as disincentives (reasons the client wants to change the behavior). We also explore the effects of the

behavior on others, because the reactions of other people in the client's life are likely to impact the planned work and may serve as encouragers or discouragers of change.

> *Ricardo was referred to the teen shelter counselor because he kept running away. I kept looking to find out what was happening right before he would run away—to see if there was something that triggered his behavior. It took a while for me to ask what the consequences were of his running away. He told me that, when he runs away, it is the only time his parents talk to each other anymore. He said, "Sometimes they even come to get me together."*

5. *Clinicians work with clients to identify exceptions to stated problematic behaviors or behavioral sequences.* We listen for "I always" and "I never" statements and then gently challenge them and search for exceptions that represent client strengths. For example, regular visits with the clinician may be used as an exception to the avowal, "I can never make and keep a relationship." It will be important for clients to try to build up more exceptions like these in their daily lives to act as encouragements. We can also explore the possibility that the unwanted behavior does not occur with the same frequency or intensity in some contexts. Then we can encourage clients to frequent those contexts or develop new ones like those to experience more pleasure and less frustration.

EXAMPLE

Client: I never seem to be able to finish things on time. Everybody says that about me, too. I just can't meet deadlines.

Clinician: I could swear you told me when we first met that you had done okay in boot camp—and in fact met your girlfriend at squad leader camp. Did I get that wrong? You must have been doing okay to be chosen as a squad leader.

Client: But that's different. That was the Army. If you screw up there, you lose pay, time off, stuff like that. You can't be late with things there.

Clinician: Since you say you are invariably late, how come you weren't late with stuff then?

Client: Hmmm . . . let me think a minute. Well . . . there were rules and codes that you followed; it was real plain what you had to do and what would happen if you didn't. It was not confusing at all.

Clinician: So then it helped to have things spelled out clearly, have a specified timetable, and be shown how.

Client: I didn't think about it like that. I just followed the rules and did okay. As a matter of fact, I hated to leave the service, but the pay was so low I couldn't support a family on it.

Clinician: I wonder if there are other jobs we could think of where there would be those kinds of codes or instructions that would make it clearer and easier to meet deadlines.

---

6. *It is often useful to ask clients to think about what specific skills or behavioral sequences they would need to learn to do things differently.* The desired goals can be broken up into simpler component skill and behavioral parts so that they seem more ordinary, sensible, and achievable. If the client does not know what steps or skills are required, the clinician can help to identify specific behavioral sequences, checking out the client's comfort level with the suggested steps, and fine-tuning them as they go along.

For example, the social worker who is working to help Lincoln live on his own might help him list the specific behaviors he needs to learn to achieve his goal: wake up on time, attend to his personal care, set up and use a money management system with family or staff, learn to do his own shopping a step at a time, learn and master bus fares and routes, find out specifics of sheltered work opportunities, and so on. Here we are using the same partializing and prioritizing skills that are applicable to the goal-setting and contracting phase of work.

7. *Clinicians and clients identify the resources that provide support and backup for this difficult work.*   Doing things differently can be hard. The client's preexisting skills can be resources, as can other people who may support the client in making the change. If the client has few resources or is under a great deal of stress, it may not be a good time to attempt to make a change. Helping clients improve their situation (for example, getting a green card, getting good permanent housing) may be necessary before they can effect other kinds of behavior change.

As clients talk about how they wish to do things differently, the clinician must assess how realistic their hopes are. An old joke captures the spirit of this exploration very well:

Patient: Doctor, will I be able to play the flute after my hand surgery?

Doctor: Only if you were able to play it before.

We constantly engage in reality checks of (a) the client's *capacity* to change, (b) the client's *motivation* to change, and (c) the *opportunity, time, and resources* to make the desired behavioral change. Because each of these factors may change over time, the clinician and client must periodically reexamine the appropriateness of their behavioral goals. Sometimes both the client and the clinician have to let go, at least temporarily, of overly ambitious expectations and goals.

EXERCISE 10.1 Identifying Behaviors to Change

Think of three problematic behaviors that you would like to change in yourself. Be as concrete and specific as possible. In what contexts does each behavior occur? Note any precipitants or triggers that set off the unwanted behaviors. What are the current consequences of each behavior? What reinforces each behavior, and what makes you want to change it? What specific skills or behavioral sequences would you need to learn to change the behavior? What resources do you have for making the change? After looking at all three behaviors, choose the easiest one to work on this week. (This is a first step in prioritizing targets for change.) We will come back to this behavior in a later exercise.

■ Normalizing Ambivalence

When discussing motivational interviewing in Chapter 8, we noted that all of us experience some anxiety and mixed feelings about changing because there is no change without loss. Artists ask, "Will my art be ruined by therapy?" Clients ask, "Will the worker take my kids away when she hears how I really behave sometimes?" Clinical interns ask, "Will I lose my spontaneity and humanness if I take on the kind of discipline that my supervisors demonstrate?"

Often we forewarn clients that some **ambivalence** is likely to arise as the work proceeds. From time to time they may feel pulled by simultaneously opposing ideas, feelings, or impulses: "I want/don't want to change," "I do/don't trust this clinical social worker," or "I will be able to attain my goals/I am pretty hopeless." We should expect pendulum swings in both directions. Mixed feelings often manifest themselves in behaviors such as lateness to meetings, abrupt endings, and sudden struggles with the clinician that are difficult to fathom.

Often people do not adequately anticipate the sense of loss they experience in giving up old ways, even though at times it feels exciting to contemplate or experience the change. Just as we do when contracting with clients initially, we normalize ambivalence and note that sometimes behaviors are like old friends, and they have to be honored and mourned before moving on to the new ones. We can also sympathize, noting that giving up the familiar for the unfamiliar is never easy, because it means giving up some control over our lives as we open them up to others' scrutiny, feedback, and potential influence.

■ Behavioral Techniques for Helping People Change What They Do

Many of the techniques discussed in previous chapters to help clients see and feel things differently can help clients *do* things differently as well.

Setting Priorities

In Chapters 7 and 8, we noted that when talking about goals and contracts for clinical work, you should help clients prioritize the many things that they would like to do differently. Clinicians help clients set the tasks that they will work on in a reasonable, realistically achievable sequence. Small step-by-step successes then provide the impetus for moving forward with behavior change work.

Step by Step

When working for behavior change, clinicians and clients can move slowly through a series of steps sequenced from the easiest to the most difficult. We often find that specific objectives require new behaviors and specific skills. Chapter 7 demonstrated how objectives can be broken down into smaller, more readily achievable steps and their component parts through the work of partializing.

Taletha, a shy teen, wanted to work with her school counselor on how to make friends because she was lonely and doubted that anyone would pick her as a friend. She didn't talk to the other girls at school. When she was in a group of girls, she said she felt really self-conscious. She couldn't imagine what to say and thought that the other girls all thought she was stupid. This made her even more anxious and less willing to talk. Therefore, she never went out with the team after games.

The counselor suggested they think about starting small by working toward making one friend. They detailed the things Taletha would have to do to make a friend. As they worked together, the counselor noted and commented that Taletha often looked down and away instead of at her while they talked, and she muffled or fumbled her words when nervous. Taletha agreed to practice a number of times making eye contact and exchanging comments with the counselor to improve her confidence in her social skills.

The counselor went to one of the high school basketball games and noticed that Taletha was quite a good player. When she was on the court, she seemed confident and she certainly was able to make eye contact with her opponents—often staring them down as she drove past them.

Taletha identified "a candidate for friendship" and spelled out the steps of approach: volunteer for the same team in gym, begin to make eye contact and exchange greetings, ask for help with a basketball technique, and so on.

The counselor, borrowing from the way Taletha said she "psyched herself up" for a game, taught Taletha some techniques that she could use to counter her negative self-talk by "psyching herself up."

Obviously, Taletha's counselor attempted to break the large task of establishing new friends into small, more readily achievable component parts. Behavioral therapists use the term **shaping** to refer to the process of breaking a task into its component parts and then rewarding small steps—successive approximations—to the desired behavior.

EXERCISE 10.2 Component Parts

Using the following chart, continue the process with Taletha of breaking down behaviors into their component parts. Are there other components that you would want to work on with her? Would you do anything differently from the counselor in the scenario?

Desired Behavior	*Component Parts*	*Subcomponents*
Make new friends	1. Improve self-esteem.	1a. Practice positive self-talk.
		1b. Talk about prior social successes.
		1c. Discuss other things she feels good about.
	2. List possible new friends on the team.	2a. Pick a person likely to be most responsive.
		2b. Discuss approach strategies.
	3. Prepare.	3a. Practice eye contact with the clinician.
		3b. Practice opening lines.
	4. Approach the new person during a team practice break.	4a. Use the opening lines.
		4b. Continue with small talk.
		4c. Use silent self-talk to keep going.
	5. Anticipate the team trip.	5a. Save babysitting money for the trip.
		5b. Discuss the details of the trip with her parents.
		5c. Ask the new friend if they can sit together on bus.

CLIP 10.2
Partializing
Behaviors

EXERCISE 10.3 Identifying and Prioritizing New Behaviors and Their Components

Which new skills would you have to learn in order to attain the new behavior you identified for change work in Exercise 10.1? Break these new skills down into smaller component parts. Now, prioritize the three new behaviors so that you work first on the easiest behavior to change, then the second easiest, then the third.

Exposure Therapies

Many clients seek help to change their avoidance behaviors—for example, avoiding crowds or social gatherings, or refusing to drive or fly. **Exposure therapy** techniques help clients overcome their avoidance behaviors by exposing them to specifically identified anxiety-provoking stimuli with the goal of eliminating anxiety through habituation. Exposure can be done in imagination, in real life (*in vivo*), or using virtual reality technologies.

A commonly used exposure technique is **systematic desensitization.** Systematic desensitization is based on the behavioral theory of **reciprocal inhibition** (Wolpe, 1958)—inhibiting one response (anxiety) by the occurrence of another response (relaxation) that is mutually incompatible with it. With the help of the clinician, the client creates an **anxiety hierarchy** rating frightening stimuli on a scale of 1 to 100. For example, a person with a fear of flying may rate seeing a plane overhead as a 3, driving to the airport as 35, getting on a plane as 60, etc. The clinician teaches the client relaxation techniques. In the beginning of the session, the clinician asks the client to use the relaxation technique until the client reports no anxiety. Then the clinician gradually exposes the client to each of the anxiety-producing situations, moving from one to the next only after the client has mastered the anxiety at the previous level. Now, this exposure can be done in imagination, in real life (*in vivo*), or using virtual reality or Second Life technologies. Because fear cannot exist with relaxation, the fear is thus extinguished and the client is able to engage in activities and behaviors previously avoided.

Virtual Reality Exposure Therapy (VRET) was developed as an "*in vivo*-like" exposure treatment to immerse severely anxious or traumatized clients in a computer-generated virtual environment relevant to each client's particular anxiety stimuli (Parsons & Rizzo, 2008). For example, someone who avoids going to the grocery store because of fear of crowds would first get practice in a preferred calming strategy and get used to refocusing to calm immediately at moments of anxiety. Then, using VRET technology—very similar to Wii virtual game activities—he or she would move forward to be exposed gradually to the sights, smells, and sounds of a virtual grocery store beginning at the front entrance and carriage racks.

VRET allows for more careful control and monitoring than either *in vivo* or imaginal exposure (Rizzo et al., 2009). Measurements of baseline and rising anxiety levels are recorded electronically throughout the exposure, to prevent too-intense anxiety states that could affect blood pressure and heart functioning. The clinician has her or his own parallel technology for viewing and accessing every aspect of the client's exposure behavior and experience, and can stop or alter the exposure at any time. As with Wii, the treatment technology updates itself constantly in response to the user's movements within a virtual environment specifically set to trigger the particular anxiety for which the client is in treatment. Alessandra Gorini and Giuseppe Riva (2008) note that "different companies have developed complete VR systems for the treatment of common anxiety disorders and specific phobias, such as: fear of heights, fear of flying, driving phobias, social phobia, fear of public speaking, fear of spiders, panic disorder, and post-traumatic stress disorder (PTSD)" (p. 217). Many traumatized veterans are being successfully treated for anxiety symptoms through empirically-validated VRET treatments (Rizzo et al., 2009).

Modeling

A good way for clients to learn new skills or to change behaviors is to watch other people acting in the desired way. **Modeling** is based on the behavioral principle that people learn new behaviors, attitudes, values, or feelings by observing others (Bandura, 1976). They are more likely to imitate the behavior of the model if they feel that the model is similar to themselves or is a respected authority figure or celebrity. TV commercials and advertising campaigns are often based on using a model's influence to get people to behave in certain ways. People are also more likely to imitate the behavior of the model if they see the model being successful and reinforced for the behavior. The behavior must also be desirable to the client.

Clients need to be encouraged to find their own style or way of being, rather than just imitating the model's behavior. Students in a workshop on nonviolent conflict resolution might watch a video in which they observe other students demonstrating the technique. Yet students must be encouraged not just to parrot what they have seen, but to modify those behaviors to fit their own style. As you continue to observe clinical mentors and models, you, too, need to slightly modify the behaviors you observe so that you can truly "own" and internalize them.

Clinicians are important models, whether or not we intend to be. For example, if the client wants to learn how to be more direct, we can help by modeling directness in the relationship itself. We also model by sharing our own experiences with a particular way of doing things. However, clinicians have to be judicious in self-disclosure. We must always remember the power and authority inherent in the clinical role. Clients may feel that they have to behave exactly as we do, believing that "the clinician knows best." It is important that the client and clinician acknowledge that there are usually many ways to handle a situation and that trial-and-error practice is how we all learn and refine new skills, depending on their effects from situation to situation.

Clients can find other models by joining groups or workshops with others who share a common interest in learning similar skills. Self-help groups are based on the premise of **mutual aid,** in which participants offer caring and encouragement while providing support and close attention to each other (Shulman, 2009). AA meetings, Widow-to-Widow programs, and religious groups are examples of ongoing groups providing opportunities for clients to observe and practice new behaviors in response to modeling from others who engage or inspire them (Schiller, 2007).

Books, films, commercial videos, and Internet offerings can also help clients learn new ways to be and do. Suggesting that a client read about someone with whom he or she can identify may provide a model for behavioral change as well as offering specific information about steps that can be taken toward the desired change. For example, a young mother can profit from a book or TV show about a woman similar to herself who details how she mastered adversity and went on to establish her own day care center or Neighborhood Crime Watch group.

Rehearsing New Behaviors or Skills

Behavioral rehearsal allows clients to practice new behaviors or skills in the safety of the clinical relationship. Behavioral rehearsal usually takes some of the anticipatory anxiety out of future events. It also gives clients a chance to master behavioral skills by identifying the ones needed and trying them out with the clinician's feedback and encouragement. Then they try out the behaviors in the actual situation with more ease and confidence than would have been possible without the rehearsal. Rehearsal of new behaviors, such as being more direct, is widely used in **assertiveness training** groups. Clients wishing to become more confident and assertive observe the ways in which the leader and other models assert themselves in various challenging interactions. They then practice self-assertion skills in the group and receive praise for successful assertions. Many clients need help strengthening their voices and advocating for rights and services. Prochaska and Norcross (2007) state, however, that clinicians wishing to model assertiveness for their clients "need to be effectively assertive individuals" themselves (p. 271).

In another form of rehearsal, the clinician and client can **role-play** scenarios or interactions in which the client can practice the new behavior, with the clinician and client working collaboratively. They may exchange roles in the scenario, allowing the clinician to model the desired behavior, or the clinician might play the "other" with whom the client attempts the new behavior. Both clinician and client provide feedback to each other, practicing and fine-tuning potential interactions.

If possible, video the role-play and have the client watch it and comment on it. Filming allows clients to observe and critique themselves, commenting on both what works and what does not. Such self-observation can contribute to the building of self-awareness and insight. This work comports with the major premise of our RE-VIEW PRACTICE Method: Interns and clients learn new behaviors most easily when they can (a) see the behaviors enacted by an experienced other, (b) rehearse them, (c) practice them in real-life settings, (d) observe themselves enacting the behaviors, and (e) share their experiences with others for further discussion and reinforcement to fine-tune their behaviors.

In **imaginal rehearsal,** clients rehearse new behaviors mentally, pretending that they are acting in desired ways. Many of us rehearse things mentally to prepare for anticipated events or situations. Carrying around new positive images of themselves as having worked out a plan of action for challenging situations can help clients build confidence as a side benefit of behavioral rehearsal.

Eventually, the goal is to have the client move from rehearsal in the clinical setting to trying the behavior out in real life. Clients can be encouraged to try the new behavior gradually, starting out in small ways or safe settings. They may practice the new behavior in a group therapy setting or try it with people with whom it is easy to take risks. Remember that behaviors learned in a clinical setting are often harder to execute in the real world, where many complications can arise and reinforcement may be poor or nonexistent. For example, the woman who learns to be more assertive and to express her opinions may find that, even though this behavior is reinforced in school settings, it is frowned upon and even punished in her family.

I was working with a client who was very shy. She said that she often felt uninvolved or like she was standing outside of the conversation when she was in social situations. We talked about what specific things she could do that might help her feel more a part of the conversation. She decided that she could reflect back what the person just said and ask questions as a way to begin to engage. We practiced these skills in the office for a while, with me playing a friend. She said that she would like to try these skills at the next big party. I suggested that she try it one night at dinner with her partner so that she could practice in a safe environment and get some feedback.

EXERCISE 10.4 Practicing New Behaviors

Think of a situation in which you would like to try out a new behavior. It might be the behavior you identified in Exercise 10.1 or a different one. In groups of three, identify a behavior that you would like to practice. Using role-plays, rehearse the new behavior, getting and giving feedback from others.

Use of Reinforcement

Behavioral theory asserts that people tend to act in ways that have been reinforced. **Reinforcers** are consequences or events that occur after a behavior and that increase the probability of the behavior occurring again in the future. We can make use of behavioral knowledge by exploring with clients how they are reinforced for current behaviors, as well as what might be desirable reinforcement for new behaviors (Pryor, 1984).

Allysa reports that smoking has always made her feel calmer and that this effect reinforced her smoking.

* * *

Nick always got attention from the teacher when he clowned around. (Although the teacher was yelling at Nick, he liked the attention.)

* * *

Carol said that she would buy a new CD if she lost 10 pounds.

What is reinforcing to one person may not be reinforcing to another. Telling a child that if she is good she can have a lollipop works only if the child likes lollipops. Therefore, when working with a client and using reinforcement, remember that, to be effective, reinforcers must be valued by clients and established by them.

I was working as a counselor in an alternative school program for adolescents with poor impulse control. One of the students, Damar, refused to sit at the table when the teacher requested that he do so. I decided that I would try to get him to change his disruptive behavior using a reinforcement program. I knew that the student had to determine what would be the best reinforcer. When I sat down with Damar and asked what reward he would want for complying with the teacher's request, he said, "Sex or drugs." Well, need-less to say, these were not things we could use as reinforcers. We eventually negotiated that he would be reinforced by being able to sit in "the teacher's chair"—one with wheels. Eventually, Damar wheeled himself closer and closer to the table and stayed there.

A specific method of using reinforcement is the **contingency contract.** Contingencies are elements of a contract on which the successful attainment of goals depends. Contingency contracts are clearly articulated agreements that say to a client, "If you do this, then you will get that" or "If you do this, then you will lose that." These contracts are frequently used in halfway houses, group homes, school settings, and involuntary detention centers.

In working with Steven and his family about his temper outbursts at home, the human service worker helped them decide what kinds of rewards Steven would get for specified behaviors and from whom. They also set up a list of privileges he would have to give up if he engaged in certain identified problematic behaviors.

I have my own sort of contingency contract. I tell myself that for every 10 papers I grade I can get a reward—a cookie and a cup of tea.

Residential settings often employ a **token economy,** a specific kind of contingency contract in which the client actually earns tokens or points for desired behavior and pays tokens for misbehavior. Tokens can be used to buy a desired reinforcer in designated amounts. For example, a teen may trade tokens for a trip to see a movie or a baseball game or to play video games an extra half hour after supper. Teaching clients about reinforcement and helping them define their own reinforcements are useful ways of helping them learn how to do things differently with feelings of satisfaction.

Homework

Homework consists of specific behavioral assignments, such as keeping a behavioral log, practicing meditation, going to a meeting, trying to express feelings more directly, recording times when one has self-defeating ideas, and the like. Any purposeful activity that the client plans to carry out between sessions can also be called homework. Homework can be assigned by the clinician, or mutually developed by the client and clinician.

Homework often involves other people. A sister may agree to accompany a woman who has agoraphobia to the supermarket to encourage her and help her use her calming techniques when she feels panicky. The parents of a 10-year-old might be involved in reinforcing his desired behavior of studying for one hour after school each night. A friend may role-play a prospective employer in a behavioral rehearsal for a job interview.

Behavior change affects others, whether they are involved in homework or not. The clinician and client need to identify the people in the client's life who may be affected by the client's changes. Because these stakeholders are needed to support the anticipated behavioral changes, clinicians often meet with them to provide education about what helps, reinforcement for their own participation, and support for their efforts to help the client change. Sometimes other people or larger systems are obstructing the work. In that event, the clinician may need to shift the work to engaging the people and systems and trying to agree on goals and roles.

Archie was a 48-year-old man with a developmental disability whose aging parents called the agency because they were worried about what would happen to him when they died. I began to meet with Archie and attempted to teach him some skills that he would need for living in a group home: doing his laundry, making his bed, cooking his own meals. One day I suggested that Archie practice making his bed each day for the next week and that he tell me how well he did. When I questioned him the next week, he said he didn't make his bed at all. He said that his mother would come in each morning and remake it for him, telling him that he wasn't able to learn how.

I decided to meet with Archie's parents and encourage them to let Archie do things for himself, even if they weren't done perfectly. Otherwise, he would never learn how to be independent. Unless they taught him basic daily living skills now, upon their deaths his helplessness might affect the kind of living conditions he would be able to qualify for. His parents were afraid of losing the roles they had played with him for many years; their care of him was their main activity. I helped them redefine their role as teaching him new things. As Archie and I continued our work, I would occasionally meet with his parents to support them in their roles as Archie's teachers.

Using Direct Influence to Help Clients Do Things Differently

We can sometimes help clients change their behaviors by **using direct influence.** Because of the power inherent in the professional role, this kind of professional activity obviously increases pressure on clients to behave in given ways, and many clinicians do not like to exert such influence because it can feel manipulative, coercive, and contrary to our ethical mandates to ensure clients' maximum self-determination.

However, we may choose to use the power of our role because it is part of a theoretical orientation in which being directive is legitimized. Sometimes we make use of our influence because we believe that clients or their dependents will be adversely affected if certain behaviors recur or if certain actions are not taken. Or we may put our weight behind behaviors or actions when the client refuses to act and we think a specified action will significantly improve the client's life (for example, make a job application to bring in desperately needed income or get needed health care when a medical condition is life-threatening).

The use of direct influence is often mediated by race, class, status, culture, age, and philosophical and religious principles. Sue and Sue (2008) believe that the culturally responsive clinician must recognize that some clients may expect and prefer that a clinician tell them what is wrong and what to do. We noted in Chapter 9 that some Native American and Asian people accustomed to following the orders of traditional healers may prefer that the clinician give advice and directives. Clinical approaches that are based on Western concepts of client autonomy, independence, and self-discovery may not be useful. At the same time, clinicians must carefully understand the power dynamics of working with clients, particularly those who have been oppressed and marginalized and who consequently feel compelled to go along with whatever the clinician and other authority figures suggest.

The following techniques demonstrate a variety of ways in which clinicians use influence to promote behavior, from the least to the most use of clinician influence.

- *Offering suggestions.* At times, the clinician may give suggestions to clients about how to behave in a situation. Advice giving is usually avoided unless people and situations are very stuck, because it presents the clinician as the knower and the client as the recipient, which is something we try assiduously to avoid. Because clients should feel responsible for their own behaviors the clinician frequently gives advice in a tentative way, asking clients what they think about the suggestion.

  "Perhaps if you tried. . . . Do you think that might be helpful?"
  "I have a suggestion, let's see what you think about it. . . ."
  "I was wondering if you could. . . . Might that work?"

- *Giving directives.* At times, the clinician may directly tell clients what they need to do. For example, the milieu therapist may tell Justin that he must keep his pants zipped. The psychologist on inpatient service may tell Doris that she cannot hit other patients. The social worker may tell a mother that she must attend a job skills training program if she is to continue receiving public assistance.

  Ivey and colleagues (2010) note that, when giving directives, the clinician must be clear and concise, check out whether the directive was understood, and then determine its impact on the client. In giving directives, the clinician is particularly careful to convey respect and caring for the client. Using directives too frequently can backfire, leaving clients feeling either blamed or controlled, although as noted above, some clients may see the clinician who uses directives as caring, while the clinician who does not may be viewed as neither caring nor helpful.

- *Accompanying the client.* Clinicians might accompany clients to meetings or to agencies that are important to their well-being. We may go with a client to a crucial legal hearing if our presence facilitates testimony. We may accompany a client to appeal what seems an unfair rejection of application for benefits, when verbal appeals by phone have failed for unclear reasons. We might go with a shy immigrant mother to register her children for nursery school or arrange to give a teen client a ride to his first Alateen meeting.

  Accompanying clients can have many results. Clients can feel incredibly supported by the presence of the clinician. In addition, accompanying clients may help them follow through with an intended behavior because it is hard to wiggle out of something with the clinician right there. When accompanying clients, it is important to check in with them. The clinician might ask, "How is it to have me here?" We might also check in again during the next scheduled meeting: "Looking back, was having me go with you the right decision?"

- *Representing the client.* Barry Cournoyer (2005) discusses the skill of representing the client with others, using clinician authority to broker services that the client has not been able to obtain alone. For example, a clinician may ask for a meeting with officials from the housing authority to convey a client's desperate situation and help the client get priority housing.

- *Calling on authorities to enforce a behavior change.* At times, we have to involve others in helping the client change behavior. For example, the mother who is abusing her child may not be able to stop without outside intervention. Clinicians are required by law to report cases of suspected abuse or neglect of children, older people, or people with disabilities.

> *I'll never forget the first time I had to file a 51A [a report of suspected child abuse]. I was working with Kathy, a young mother who had a 2-year-old daughter. I had observed how the daughter cringed if the mother made any moves toward her. I also knew that the mother was under a great deal of stress and said that at times she was so annoyed with her "selfish" daughter. I informed Kathy that I knew she didn't want to hurt her child and that she was trying to be a really good parent, but it was difficult with so many pressures on her. I told her that I was going to try to get her some help by calling in the Department of Social Services. I hoped that they would do an evaluation and help her get the resources she needed to take care of her child and to avoid hurting her. Kathy was angry at me and asked if DSS would take her daughter away from her. I said that I hoped they wouldn't but that, if they did, I hoped that she would be able to get her back really soon.*

> *They didn't remove her daughter, but they did offer her some respite care, and she became eligible for job training. I was really scared about what this would do to my relationship with Kathy, but I think she really felt my caring, and the fact that the Department of Social Services didn't remove her child made it easier. We continued our work together. I am not sure what would have happened if they had taken her daughter away, but I would hope that we still could have found a way to continue our work.*

- *Warning the client that the relationship will be terminated unless the client meets certain conditions.* Sometimes there are behavioral conditions that must be met for the clinical relationship to continue. Some teen residences require that members be sober to continue living in the house. A clinician may say that she will terminate the clinical relationship if a client does not follow through on an agreed-upon behavior change. An outpatient clinic may have a policy that clients who cut themselves will not be allowed to continue as outpatients. A social worker may assert that she will not continue to meet with a client individually unless the client attends the group therapy session every day.

> *I was seeing a client with bipolar disorder who was not taking his medication. His behavior was becoming more manic. I was stuck with a dilemma. I wanted to tell him I couldn't work with him unless he took his medication but I was also afraid that if I stopped seeing him, there wouldn't be much hope he would take his meds.*

As harsh as they may seem, requirements can serve as an impetus for change. In modeling the expectations, structure, and seriousness of purpose in our work together, requirements may succeed where other methods have failed. Such strategies are controversial, however. Some clinicians worry that such terminations may leave the client stranded without crucial structure and support. Others caution that clinicians are acting out their frustration or anger with the client, often simply reenacting unresolved power struggles from the clinician's and client's earlier lives. Warnings and terminations should never be carried out without considerable conversation with clients beforehand and only under the most thorough supervision.

CLIP   10.3
Using Direct
Influence

EXERCISE 10.5 When All Else Fails

Would you terminate a clinical relationship with a client under certain circumstances? Make a list and discuss the pros and cons of this strategy with your fellow students in class.

Addressing Behavioral Balking

A client sometimes starts to work on a behavior targeted for change (for example, keeping a journal on binge eating) and then suddenly "forgets" either her journal, the correct time of the appointment, or the appointment itself. She might say that this happened because the bus came late or she needed to take work home and had no time to write in the journal. In another instance, a clinician might not show up for supervision, saying that he had so much on his mind that he forgot. Sometimes clients do not do what they agreed to do in order to signal that we are pushing in the wrong direction or imposing rules that seem unjust. Sometimes they need to take a breather or a rest from the work of behavior change.

At other times, the clinician may inadvertently push the work too fast or too deeply, stirring up more anxiety than the client can tolerate. This anxiety may be verbalized, but it can also emerge in behaviors. Cancellations, lateness, forgetting, getting off track, becoming defensive about the return of old nonproductive patterns—all can signal discomfort, a need for a breather, or a reluctance to proceed due to fears of losing more than one may gain by changing behaviors, contexts, or relationships.

At such times, we might simply share the hunch that perhaps the client is feeling divided about proceeding for reasons that need airing and sorting through together. We might reach out by phone or visit someone who has suddenly canceled or dropped out, to process the disconnect. Our main goal is to get things on the table unambiguously so as to clarify and ventilate attitudes or conflicts that are stalling further work together. Part of the disconnect may be due to us or our ways of working, so we must stay open to these possibilities and explore them. In addition, we need to consider that changing realities in the client's situations may contribute to this change in commitment.

CLIP   10.4
Addressing
Behavioral
Balking

Validating, Commending, and Celebrating Accomplishments

Clinicians should recognize, validate, and celebrate clients' achievements in changing old behaviors and learning new skills. Validation can be an important social reinforcer, encouraging the client to continue the work. In some settings, there are specific rituals that recognize client achievements. In AA groups, for example, clients are given a chip for one year of sobriety. In halfway houses, clients might be "promoted" to a new level of responsibility and freedom based on their upholding their part of a contingency contract. A clinician might share cake and coffee with a client to celebrate his or her hard-earned success in getting a job after years on welfare.

EXERCISE 10.6 Your Own Behavior Change

Go back to the behavior you chose to work on this week. What techniques would you use to change that behavior? With two colleagues in class, work on changing your behavior. Keep a record of what techniques you used and how effective they were. Did you encounter resistance in yourself as you tried to change? Continue to work on changing the behavior using different techniques until you are successful. Plan a way to celebrate your success.

◼ Conclusion

We believe that both clinicians and clients can be helped to learn new ideas and new behaviors by clearly identifying what is to be mastered and breaking it down into tasks and steps that utilize specific skills. These steps and skills are most readily learned from clear, consistent, and encouraging models with whom there can be good-natured exchanges in the process of rehearsing new behaviors. Planned reinforcers help stoke our persistence, just as they do for clients who are trying to master new ideas, insights, and skills. Interviewing skills are best learned in relationships with others who are prepared and motivated to give informed feedback. Self-observation through journaling, video recording, and feedback from others help refine skills.

We believe that learning through connection, collegial exchanges, shared risks, and mutual aid are all reinforcements for new learning. These principles underpin all clinical work, including work with clients in crisis, which we discuss in the next chapter.

◼ Suggested Readings

Blanco, Carlos, Clougherty, Kathleen, Lipsitz, Joshua, Mufson, Laura, & Weissman, Myrna. (2006). Homework in interpersonal psychotherapy (IPT): Rationale and practice. *Journal of Psychotherapy Integration, 16,* 201–218.

DeAngelis, Tori. (2009). Virtual healing. *Monitor on Psychology, 40*(8), 36–40.

Gorini, Alessandra & Riva, Giuseppe. (2008). Virtual reality in anxiety disorders: The past and the future. *Expert Review Neurotherapeutics, 8,* 215–233.

Prochaska, James O., Norcross, John C., & DiClemente, Carlo C. (1994). *Changing for good.* New York: Morrow.

■ Self-Explorations

1. Think of a behavior that you have learned from someone else's modeling. Who was the model? What did you see him or her do? What were the consequences of the model's behavior? What made that behavior desirable to you? How did you modify the behavior you observed to make it your own? What reinforced the changes you made to be more like the model?

2. You have been engaging in behavioral rehearsals throughout this class as you have practiced interviewing skills in role-plays with your fellow students. What kinds of feedback have been most useful to you? What kinds have been less useful and why?

3. Have you ever participated in a contingency contract or similar situation in which reinforcements (for example, tokens, stars, stickers, prizes, or money) were awarded, contingent upon your behavior? How did you feel about that? Do you ever give yourself rewards for particular behaviors? What is their effect?

4. How does it feel for you to be helping clients change things that you yourself have not yet changed but need to? What goes on for you internally when the client's change work surpasses what you personally have been able to do about a needed change of your own?

■ Essay Questions

1. From your reading, list guidelines for helping clients identify behaviors to change and new skills to learn.

2. What do we mean by the "transferability of skills" in clinical work? What helps clients achieve it? Did you yourself come to professional education with any skills that you can see yourself transferring positively into clinical practice techniques for use with clients? Have you had to alter any aspect of your old skill usage in the process of professionalization? Discuss these questions.

3. Discuss the benefits and risks of behavioral modification programs. If you have worked in or observed such a program, describe what you experienced as well as any aspects that created concern for you.

4. From your reading of this chapter, list the numerous techniques clinicians use to help clients change their behaviors. Discuss the pros and cons of each technique.

5. With which change techniques are you the most familiar and comfortable at this point in your learning? Discuss any techniques you would feel less comfortable using, and explain why.

6. In the course of our helping them change, clients often give us feedback about our ways, expectations, or statements, and these can have a positive reshaping effect on our professional development. Have you had such reshaping feedback from a client? What happened, and how did you alter yourself accordingly? Were there any difficulties in doing so?

■ Key Terms

Ambivalence

Anxiety hierarchy

Assertiveness training

Behavioral rehearsal

Consequences

Contingency contract

Exposure Therapy

Faith-based organizations

Homework

Imaginal rehearsal

Insight development

Modeling

Mutual aid

Reciprocal inhibition

Reinforcers

Role-play

Shaping

Systematic desensitization

Token economy

Using direct influence

Virtual Reality Exposure Therapy (VRET)

CHAPTER 11

The Clinical Relationship: Issues and Dynamics

◼ A Unique Relationship

A client once said to me, "This is the strangest relationship I've ever known. I trust, love, and reveal myself deeply to someone I barely know."

A clinical relationship can be one of the most important and memorable relationships in a person's life, for both client and clinician. Its power and meaning for people are evidenced by its widespread appearance in popular culture as the subject of numerous jokes and cartoons and as a topic in novels and films. Many people come to count on the professional clinical relationship as a source of support, reflection, information, and activity for meaningful change. The qualities of nonjudgmental acceptance, confidentiality, client-centeredness, and purposefulness render the clinical relationship a unique experience in most people's lives. It feels almost too good to be true, and, for most people, it takes some getting used to.

The clinical relationship not only provides a context in which change can occur; it is often the means *by* which change occurs. Many years of research and numerous empirical studies have shown that the therapeutic relationship is central to effective intervention. From their review of empirical research on psychotherapy outcomes, Michael Lambert and Dean Barley conclude that "(m)easures of therapeutic relationship variables consistently correlate more highly with client outcomes than specialized therapy techniques" (2002, p. 26).

The clinical relationship can be used as an interpersonal laboratory in which developments and issues arising within the relationship can be worked on *in vivo* to bring about change. Miller and Stiver (1997) suggest that **mutual empathy** is at the core of human development and of all effective work with people, whether with individuals, families, groups, or communities. They assert that mutual empathy in the clinical relationship leads to **mutual empowerment** in both clients and clinicians.

Miller and Stiver (1997) assert that mutual empathy and feeling moved by each other's behaviors and reactions within the work combine with honest process observations and feedback to stimulate mutual growth in clinicians and clients in five ways:

1. *Increased zest and vitality are experienced from the energizing effect of emotional joining.*
2. *Capacity to act is increased by the awareness of one's positive contributions to the ongoing relationship and process.*
3. *Knowledge is enhanced regarding the ways in which relationships can develop.*
4. *The participants' sense of worth increases due to each other's recognition and validation.*
5. *Pleasure in this particular relationship creates a desire for more connection in a gradually widening circle of growth-fostering relationships.*

Developing skills for relational work with clients requires knowledge of common human dynamics and of the relational preferences and patterns of many different cultures. This skill development also requires great self-awareness on the part of clinicians. Clients' lives and stories are precious. Our responsibility for their protection and safety in clinical work includes observing and adjusting our own thoughts, feelings, behaviors, and intentions so that we stay client-centered and purposeful in our professional use of self.

Relational tending is one of the hardest skills we have to learn in life as well as in clinical work. It requires accurately spotting and verbally addressing our mistakes in relationships with clients and others, and then working out together any hurts these mistakes cause. Ongoing self-observation and relational tending are aimed at minimizing the effects on the clinical relationship of clinicians' unresolved issues, personal biases, need for control, and blind spots.

We believe that the development of awareness, knowledge, and skills for tending the relationship is one of the most difficult yet satisfying aspects of clinical education. Beginning clinicians often think that because they are nice people or have had so many good relationships, the relational aspect of work with clients should come easily. You may be surprised to discover how complicated the relationship can become in the course of purposeful work together. The clinician and the client enter into a relationship to work on a task or accomplish designated goals, yet almost inevitably, they also attend to some aspect of their relationship as their work together unfolds.

Most newcomers to clinical work are unaccustomed to the degree of attention to process that is required in clinical interviewing: the noticing and retaining of detail and nuance; the reflecting on meanings; the repeated self-exploration and adjustment in response to client needs; and the complex art of interweaving purposeful self-restraint and self-expression. The beginning clinician takes on the enormous task of learning how to attend to self, other(s), and the process of the relationship, while simultaneously focusing on the purpose and goals that gave rise to the relationship in the first place. There is, in short, much to learn.

In previous chapters, we have focused on many of the skills the clinician uses in the process of interviewing and problem solving. This chapter discusses some special issues in the clinical relationship and elucidates skills useful in addressing these issues as they arise.

■ Relationship Dynamics: The Real and the Symbolic

It is important that we attend to our reactions to clients, since these reactions often provide important information for further consideration. In addition, we pay careful attention to clients' reactions to us. The reactions of client and clinician to each other are dynamic and interactive. Some theorists attempt to distinguish between the "real," in-the-moment encounter between the two people and the "symbolic" relationship—referred to in psychodynamic theory as the transference and countertransference relationship (Coleman, 2000). The following discussion of the related psychodynamic concepts of transference and countertransference may be helpful in understanding traditional psychodynamic principles regarding these processes and their importance in therapeutic relationships.

Transference

In psychodynamic theory, **transference** is the unconscious process by which early unresolved relational dynamics or conflicts are unwittingly displaced or "transferred" onto the current relationship with the clinician and then re-enacted or expressed as though appropriate or "real" in the moment. It is crucial to remember that transference is an unconscious process and that, when individuals are caught up in it, they are unaware of its distorting influence on their thoughts, feelings, and behaviors in the moment. Remembering this helps us to be more understanding, patient, and less reactive to what would otherwise seem to be irrational or unwarranted behaviors in clients, ourselves, or others.

Psychodynamic theorists postulate both positive and negative transference as expected features of helping relationships. Both positive and negative transference can mobilize unresolved developmental issues for clients and clinicians alike regarding dependence, competence, authority, closeness, trust, and tender and sexual feelings. In **positive transference,** the client idealizes the clinician and may experience him or her as incomparably wise, caring, and helpful. When not extreme, such idealizations are thought to fuel the early stages of most human attachments and to sustain relationships through times of hardship and disappointment.

My supervisor told me that a teen client of mine seemed to be viewing me as a "kindly grandfather," even though I was a 26-year-old woman. She noted from an earlier process recording how the boy had fished and hunted with his grandfather, the only positive figure in his grade school years. Now he is frequently asking me to do things with him, things he used to love doing with his granddad.

Psychodynamic clinicians believe that positive transference helps sustain the **working alliance** in spite of mistakes and disagreements. In the clinical relationship, clients may be unconsciously expressing unsatisfied longings for a wise, caring, and safe helper, from whom to gain soothing and strength for the work at hand. Unfortunately, positive transference can also lend itself to exploitation by unprincipled practitioners, since it tends to blind clients to their clinicians' manipulations and its halo effect can make clinicians seem far more caring and wise than they actually may be.

In **negative transference,** the client is thought to unconsciously express or act out in the moment old, unhappy, stuck scenarios with the clinician as though the clinician were actually the exploiter, the abandoner, the molester, or the punisher who has harmed the client in the past. A client may misinterpret what the clinician says or does, may mishear words, or may mistake benign clinician behaviors as uncaring, exploitative, intentionally mean, or belittling. The inherent messages are frequently "You don't really care" or "You hurt me just like X did"—charges that reflect the antithesis of clinical purpose. Negative transference can be hard to tolerate, especially when we are doing our utmost to be available, supportive, and helpful while under attack. It can drive a wedge between the client and clinician unless the latter is conscientious in getting continued supervision to assist in the management of reactions and of clinical process with the client.

At times, a clinician's manner or style may inadvertently approximate that of someone harmful to the client in the past. Furthermore, clients may even seem as though they are actually trying to get the clinician to harm them—for example, by flirting with or asking the clinician to socialize with them, by offering gifts or bribes, by menacing the clinician, or by openly violating laws the clinician is mandated to uphold. Many trauma theorists believe that severely abused individuals may unwittingly re-enact behaviors from harmful relationships in the past (Chu, 1991; van der Kolk & van der Hart, 1991).

Ethnocultural Transference and Countertransference

Lillian Comas-Diaz and Frederick Jacobsen (1991) speak of **ethnocultural transference,** in which previous inter- or intraethnic cultural experiences are unconsciously displaced onto the clinical relationship. Hays (2008) notes that "(t)he reactions of clients and therapists to one another (transference and countertransference) often reflect cross-cultural relationships, conflicts, and power imbalances in the real world" (p. 83).

Such a reaction might manifest in a number of ways: A client might be overly compliant or demonstrate mistrust and suspiciousness toward the clinician. Similarly, a clinician might overexplore cultural issues to the detriment of meeting client needs; might deny differences, failing to spot them as salient in the moment; or might communicate pity, guilt, or aggression around ethnocultural issues.

Hierarchical Transference

Lillian Comas-Diaz and Beverly Greene (1994) believe that, in response to clinician authority, many poor female clients with histories of being subordinated may manifest **hierarchical transference**—feeling powerless and helpless in the relationship. Such feelings need to be noted and worked through as an empowering aspect of relational work. Of course, hierarchical transference can occur with all people, not just poor women.

Countertransference

Freud coined the term **countertransference** to describe the clinician's unconscious reactions to the client. Clinicians today are asked to scrutinize the relational process regularly for countertransference because it can occur in situations that replicate unresolved scenarios from the clinician's past. For example, the normally accepting clinician above might begin to loathe or dread meeting with the relentlessly critical client. On reflection, he comes to see that, because of his own early experience of harsh criticism from his perfectionist father, he is taking the client's criticism personally and is resenting the client for it, as though at this moment he were back in the room with his own father. This realization, developed in discussions with his supervisor, helps him relax with the client and explore the latter's critical barrages more empathically.

Beyond Transference: A Feminist Therapy Perspective

Feminist therapist Laura Brown (1994) suggests that the symbolic relationship between clinician and client is more than and different from transference as it is typically described:

> The therapist is not simply defined as a neutral screen upon which internal reality is projected by a client; thus, the client's end of the symbolic exchange is not simply a distortion of the therapist based upon the client's prior experiences. Nor are all the passionate responses of therapist to client and client to therapist defined as necessarily derived from disruptive or disturbed elements in each person's past. . . . In addition, the participants' collective pasts and their positions as members of communities that may have met, touched, and even clashed apart from their individual experiences will inform how they symbolically experience one another. (p. 98)

This is particularly true when the clinician and the client are from different cultural groups. The client's reaction to the clinician may be "less related to the client's feelings about her parents than to the client's daily experience of the [clinician's] culture" (Hays, 2008, p. 79).

We agree that the clinical relationship is multilayered, complex, and mutually influencing. We think of the clinical relationship as both real and symbolic and as evolving over time as participants influence each other and gradually enhance their relational understanding and skills together.

Clinician Self-Reflection on the Relationship

The following questions may prove helpful as you regularly reflect on possible symbolic reactions with clients:

- Why am I reacting with this particular client in a way that is unusual for me?
- What buttons might this client be pushing in me?
- What buttons might I be pushing in this client?
- What do critical (seductive, bossy, self-centered, demanding, etc.) people stir up in me?
- Are my reactions to this client (or client story) being displaced from another life experience?
- Can I identify a pattern of reacting to certain types of people in characteristic ways that are not purposeful for the work or helpful to the client?
- Do I think of some clients often and of others almost never? If so, why is that?
- Am I favoring some clients over others? On what evidence am I basing that concern?
- Could my client and I be in some sort of diversionary process in which our sudden focus on our relationship is, unwittingly, for the purpose of avoiding some other topic neither of us is comfortable addressing at the moment?
- Am I regularly reviewing my work with all my clients or only with some?
- Is personal reflection enough to change my reactions, or do I need supervision or personal therapy to assist me in professionalizing my responses with clients?

It is essential to engage in regular personal reflection and conscientious work in supervision to better understand the dynamics of the clinician–client relationship (Walsh, 2009). Because relationship dynamics have been a central focus of psychodynamic therapy, that focus is often misunderstood by beginning clinicians as the "real meat" of all clinical work. Not only do many of today's time-sensitive working agreements preclude such a focus, but working with the symbolic requires regular process supervision by a highly skilled and thoughtful clinical mentor who is accomplished in this complex work. By no means should inexperienced practitioners simply launch impulsively into speculation with clients on possible past-to-present links underlying behaviors in a session. After reviewing written or recorded process recordings over time, supervisors can help you decide if it is useful to undertake any work with clients on symbolic relationship issues and, if so, how to undertake it with proper timing, sensitivity, and clarity.

■ Relationship as Foreground or Background

At times, the relationship serves as the background for clinical work, providing a safety net or holding environment for the work of sustainment or change. At other times, the relationship becomes the foreground, the focus of the work itself. A number of factors determine how the relationship is defined and the extent to which it is purposefully made the foreground or background of the work.

1. *The clinician's theoretical orientation usually suggests what kind of relational activity, style, intensity, and focus constitute an effective and purposeful use of relationship.* Psychodynamic theory, for example, emphasizes the importance of directly addressing the dynamics of the relationship when the client seems to be re-enacting unconscious conflicts with significant others in his or her past (transference). The clinician uses interpretations of clinician–client dynamics to help the client "work through the transference."

Behaviorally oriented clinicians may see clinician–client interaction chiefly as providing information about the client's repertoire of effective or maladaptive behaviors. They may directly use the relationship as a means for rehearsing interpersonal skills or modeling the management of future scenarios. Time-limited Interpersonal therapists don't usually focus on the relationship; their primary focus is on the client's relationships and situational losses in the world and on building coping skills to deal with these losses or changes. Almost all theorists suggest directly focusing on the here-and-now clinical relationship when problems arise that affect the work—for example, when there is direct conflict or when the client cancels without explanation.

2. *Ethnocultural norms for relationships—including relationships with professionals—are important influences on how and when the clinical relationship will be foreground or background.* There may be no equivalent for client–clinician relationships in many cultures so that, at the beginning and periodically thereafter, a respectful negotiation of relational roles and expectations is necessary. For example, in some cultures, a social worker is an agent of the state who provides food, money, and housing only. A counselor might be expected to be a wise person who listens to problems and then unilaterally pronounces advice or solutions. Negative comments by the client on the helping process might be conceived of as unthinkable. Focusing on the relationship itself might feel rude or inappropriate. Again, it is important that we ask our clients how they frame the help-seeking process and roles, as well as how they view a professional relationship and its importance or unimportance (Derald Sue & Sue, 2008; Weaver, 2005).

Sharing food and personal talk during a session are important elements of building rapport with many clients. In that sense, these are very much foreground relationship considerations, even though the relationship and its dynamics per se are rarely an explicit focus of the work.

3. *The use and management of the relationship are affected by the clinical goals, the client's capacity and motivation, the role of the clinician, and time parameters.* The clinical relationship may be a less direct focus of attention in settings or roles in which clinicians see many people briefly to provide practical information, concrete problem solving, moral support, and mobilization of resources. The dynamics of the clinical relationship are more frequently a focus of discussion when the clinician's primary purpose is to provide longer term counseling or therapy.

4. *The stage of the relationship or of the interview process affects decisions about the use of the relationship.* In initial or brief encounters, the clinician's primary relational tasks are to be warm, attentive, empathically attuned, responsive, and focused with the client on mutually determined goals for the meetings. As trust and safe experience build, the clinician may focus with greater frequency on the relationship itself to provide feedback, conflict resolution, self-disclosure, and intentional relational skill rehearsal. Later, as the work together draws to a close, developments in the relationship can be used as familiar examples of what happens in relationships and of how awareness and skills can be learned with caring others through thoughtful interchange and feedback.

5. *Factors in the client and the clinician also affect the use of the relationship in clinical work.* Clients' cognitive and emotional capacities, their relationship norms and histories, and their comfort with intimacy and self-exploration all affect the degree to which relationship dynamics can be productively addressed. Clinician factors that can influence the use of the relationship include education and skill, openness to insight and client feedback, and willingness to adjust oneself to the relational protocols and comfort levels of a wide variety of clients. We have affirmed our belief in client and clinician as coevolvers of the story, but we also believe that the clinician remains practically responsible for knowing when, how, and to what extent to make direct and appropriate use of the relationship in the clinical interview. At the same time, the client is encouraged from the outset to air any clinician–client relationship questions or issues for discussion, rather than pretending all is well.

■ Directly Addressing the Relationship Process

The clinician may directly address the relationship process for a number of reasons.

1. *To provide the client with the necessary information about what to expect in the clinical relationship at the beginning of work.*

Example

A clinician at the college counseling center clarifies with the client the roles, responsibilities, and conditions of the working relationship: what the client can expect from the clinician and the setting, and what is expected of the client. The clinician discusses confidentiality and its limits so that the client knows under what circumstances the clinician might have to report information disclosed. She explains informed consent procedures and invites the client's comments, reactions, or questions about the nature of their relationship.

2. *To help clients accomplish designated tasks.*

Example

A clinician who, as an intake worker, sees a woman once to evaluate her eligibility for food stamps might not normally focus direct attention on the relationship dynamics. However, if the client's style of angry demandingness with the clinician is so disruptive that it might derail the application process at the food stamp office, the clinician shares her own reaction to the behavior and inquires briefly into possible outside sources of the anger to determine if other kinds of intervention are indicated. If not, she alerts the client to the probable effect that the client's anger may have on staff at the food stamp office. She then very briefly explores other ways the client might express her needs and get them met.

3. *To help clients expand their relational competencies—the skills necessary to develop and maintain relationships with others.*

Example

A clinician working in a group home with clients who are focusing on loneliness or failed relationships makes reference to ways in which the clinician experiences the clients. The clinician then helps the clients explore their reactions to him with the aim of enhancing their interpersonal awareness and feedback skills.

4. *To address problems or issues in the relationship that need to be addressed.*

Examples

A counselor who notices that a talkative parolee suddenly has nothing to say this week wonders aloud about whether his silence has anything to do with the relationship between them.

After announcing a planned vacation, the psychologist spends some time talking with the client about how she feels about this interruption in their work together.

The milieu therapist suggests that the resident and clinician should talk about why things do not seem to be moving in their work together.

A rehab counselor on an inpatient psychiatric service interrupts her explanation of a job application process when she feels that the client's anger and frustration are making him feel unsafe.

A client sees her hospital social worker at the Gay Pride March. In the next session, the worker explores with the client her reactions to seeing him in the march and discovering that he is gay. The social worker asks whether and how this knowledge might affect their working relationship.

The drug counselor whose client has given her an expensive present for Christmas discusses with her client the meaning of the present in their relationship and their work together.

5. *To summarize the work and affirm gains as the relationship is ending.*

Example

At the end of their 6 months of working together, an employee assistance counselor invites the employee to reflect with him on the nature of their work. He talks with her about his perceptions of her, requests that she share with him her perspective on their work together, and they talk about how they both have been affected by it. They talk about the outcomes of the work and evaluate what they have achieved together.

In addressing the relationship process, the clinician may use the skills of *(a) examining the moment, (b) processing the overall process, and (c) exploring indirect or parallel references to the relationship.*

Examining the Moment

At times, the clinician will use the skill of **examining the moment**—addressing what is happening in the clinician–client relationship at a given moment in time. This me-and-you-in-the-here-and-now work usually aims at gaining greater understanding of dynamics, of highlighting a repeating dynamic, or of working through tensions or feelings apparent at that moment in the interview. Egan (2010) refers to this skill as **immediacy.** Examining the moment can be particularly useful when something unexpected happens, when some outside event impinges on the relationship, and when the clinician or client notices something out of the ordinary.

When examining the moment, clinicians have a choice of focus. The focus can be on the client: "I notice this or that about you right now." This centering on a client experience or behavior is a way of building the client's self-awareness and modeling the safe, direct expression of feelings.

E X A M P L E

Clinician: Althea, let's stop a minute. I noticed that, just now, when I asked you about your son, you crossed your arms and started to kick your leg. What was going on for you just then?

> *Client:* I guess I felt like you didn't believe what I just told you.
>
> *Clinician:* Can you help me see what I did or said to leave you feeling that way?

Examining the moment may be used to focus on the relationship itself: "I'm noticing this or that right now about the relationship between us." Such a focus models noting and responding to the nuances of communication and builds skills in tending a relationship. This is particularly important if there appear to be unexplored feelings and issues—an "elephant in the room"—that might undermine the relationship.

EXAMPLE

> *Clinician:* Things feel so tense here today.
>
> *Client:* [Silence]
>
> *Clinician:* This doesn't feel like our usual way of working together. What do you make of it?
>
> *Client:* I have something to tell you, but I don't know how.

Examining the moment can be used to focus on the clinician's own feelings and reactions: "I'm noticing this or that about myself in relation to you right now." Sometimes this focus is used to model either comfortably revealing oneself or expectable reactions to what is being discussed. It can be important for clients to know that they have an impact on the clinician, which can foster a sense of empowerment.

EXAMPLE

> *Clinician:* You weren't looking at me when you told me the story of being in the hospital with Jeddie, so I wanted you to know that your account brought tears to my eyes.
>
> *Client:* I'm sorry to make you cry. Nobody likes to hear about the death of a child.
>
> *Clinician:* Please don't apologize. It's so sad, but I'm very glad that you are talking with me about it, and I'm moved by your story and your bravery.

When examining the moment is used to share the clinician's discomfort with the client's behavior, it has to be undertaken very cautiously. Clinicians must carefully monitor their own responses and discuss them with a supervisor before disclosing them to the client. In an emergency situation, however, the use of self-disclosure might be necessary to maintain safety in the moment. Therefore, all clinicians must discuss with their supervisors how they would handle a situation in which they felt unsafe, in case such a situation arises.

EXAMPLE

Clinician: You're scaring me with this shouting and threatening, Knox, and I can't listen and react well when I'm scared. Please sit down with me now and try to calm down so we can keep talking about what's happened.

Examining the moment can be used not only to help the client explore what is currently happening in the relationship, but also as a source of feedback that may have implications for other areas in the client's life.

EXAMPLE

Client: When will I ever have a boyfriend? I feel so-o-o-o awful. Everyone else has had a lover but me. I feel like I just crawl across the ground while everyone else is up and running. It's not fair. My life is awful. [Whining]

Clinician: Sounds like you feel really disappointed that this hasn't happened for you. [Clinician thinks to herself: "She is bright, healthy, financially okay—her life could be so much worse, especially compared to the woman I just saw who is poor and dying of cancer, with two young kids and nobody to take care of them."]

Client: Yeah, when Stephanie [a best friend] got raped, I went to visit her in the hospital and I thought, "Look, she's got her friends and family here, her boyfriend sent her flowers, she's got everything . . . it's not fair."

Clinician: Might you have been feeling a little jealous of all she seemed to have?

Client: Yeah . . . she even had sex! [Referring to the rape]

Clinician: [Feeling appalled by the client's response, the clinician decides to share her reaction to help the client understand something about the effects of her behavior.] Just now when you were talking about how awful you felt about not having a lover, I found myself thinking: "Gee—this situation is not all that bad." I was startled by my thinking that. . . . it's just not the way I usually respond when a person is hurting. Your pain is very real, so I had to ask myself why I'm having thoughts like that. Then I thought, "Well, maybe it's the way she described her situation so dramatically: 'It's so-o-o awful, I crawl across the ground.'" When you said that you were jealous of your girlfriend who had been raped, I think I found it hard to be supportive of you. I know that you must feel bad about what happened to her and I am sure that you recognize how awful it was for her. It was hard to hear your pain without reacting to the way you phrased it.

Client: Hmmm . . .

Clinician: I've a hunch you could be feeling that no one appreciates how bad you feel. People saw your friend's pain and gathered around her. . . . Even I took her part in my thoughts. No one seems to hear you.

Client: No one seems to care—everyone acts like I don't have anything to complain about.

Clinician: I wonder if sometimes other people might be responding to you as I did. Instead of giving you their care and support, they seem to minimize your pain—perhaps because of the way you express it?

Miller and Stiver (1997) describe a **central relational paradox** observed in clinical relationships. People who are repeatedly silenced or invalidated may try to connect by holding back important parts of their experience and feelings for fear that disclosure may end the connection. For example, when feeling disappointed or misunderstood by the clinician, such clients may pretend everything is fine or may change the subject if asked for their reactions to specific clinician behaviors. Miller and Stiver affirm the courage it takes for these clients to become more authentic in a relationship of trust and caring.

While the clinician has the responsibility to monitor what is happening in the relationship and make use of important moments, the client is also likely to comment occasionally on what is going on in the moment. Such noticing by the client gives the clinician an opportunity to reinforce the client's ability to tend to relationships—an important skill in all relationships and one for which clients may receive little validation or thanks in their daily lives.

EXAMPLES

Client A: Can we stop for a moment? I just wanted to tell you how nervous I felt when you just said that you will be out of town next week.

Clinician: I'm glad you stopped us to talk about this. Please say more about what happened for you when I said that.

* * *

> *Client B:* You look uptight. Do you need a minute?
>
> *Clinician:* I'm sorry to take your time with this . . . I guess I am worried. When I came in the front door, my cat had dripped blood in the entryway, and I have her on my mind a little. I just cleaned up before you rang the bell.
>
> *Client B:* Do you need to take five minutes to go check on the cat? I have my crossword puzzle from traveling on the bus.
>
> *Clinician:* Thanks, I'll just be a minute. Let's make up the time on the other end if that's okay.
>
> *Client B:* It's okay. I have a cat and I would be just as worried if she were sick.

It is the fortunate clinician who has a client willing to acknowledge when a statement or behavior of the clinician has a negative or worrisome impact. We need to appreciate a client's strength in giving such direct feedback, recognizing that, in many cultures, one does not criticize a "helper" or "wise person."

EXAMPLE

> *Client:* I don't know how to tell you this, but I feel really uncomfortable when you walk me to the door. I get the feeling that you're afraid I won't leave.
>
> *Clinician:* I had no idea you felt like that. Thanks for telling me. Let's talk some more about your concerns.

Honest acknowledgment of in-the-moment process events can be unique for both clinician and client because many of us have been taught to skirt around interpersonal tensions or blunders should they arise in social conversations (Miller & Stiver, 1997). It takes courage for both clients and workers to stay in connection when experiencing conflict with each other and to own their contributions to difficulties when they arise (Jordan, 1990).

> *Aldana said I could dish it out in the group but not take it. This was a really uncomfortable thing for me to hear, even though I could feel myself blush every time she or other members gave me feedback that was other than positive. I always thanked people for the feedback, but then kept reacting to it visibly. I hadn't known much "good criticism" in the foster home I grew up in, and, thanks to these women, I came to realize how much corrective feedback felt like criticism from the foster home. My supervisor had already suggested something similar in supervision, so when it came up in the group, too, I got myself a therapist to talk with about my reactions and my history.*

EXERCISE 11.1 Examining the Moment

In small groups, practice the skill of examining the moment with clients in the following scenarios. Think of as many ways to express yourselves as you can.

Jermaine, an excellent 19-year-old college basketball player, has come to see the campus counselor to mull over whether to graduate or to drop out now and join a pro team. As you comment on how hard the decision is and review potential options, he begins to glaze over and stare out the window.

Cookie, a depressed, often silent 14-year-old, comes into the session looking unusually bright and animated, although not saying anything.

Edgar, an 80-year-old man seeking to have his wife arrested for physically abusing him, frowns and huffs as you explain that there needs to be a home investigation before further action can be taken.

CLIP 11.1

Examining the Moment

When you have completed the exercise, talk together in a large group about the usefulness and the complications of examining the moment.

Processing the Overall Process

At times, clinicians **process the process**—discussing the overall course of the relationship with clients. The clinician may do this to point out a theme or pattern, whether positive or negative, in the relationship and to trace its development backward over the course of the work so far. The clinician may sum up in broad strokes developments or achievements of note.

EXAMPLE

Clinician: You know, Van, it's amazing how you've hung in with this relationship in spite of all your fears of people taking control of you. We had our moments back there when you thought I was trying to make you join that group.

Client: Yeah, I just didn't want to be in any group, and you kept pushing it on me. A few times I thought of quitting.

Clinician: Yes, and it was important—so different for you—that you could say you'd rather see me alone because you needed the privacy.

Client: I thought you'd be mad.

We can also invite the client to process the process with an invitation to examine it, such as "Could we look at how things have been going in the relationship these last six weeks?" The client may be able to respond to such an invitation easily, may require more time or support, or may not be able to make process observations. Clinicians support all reasonable client efforts to make process comments because it is important for them to develop the skill of observing and commenting on relational processes. In addition, clients may not be used to people "telling it like it is" in relationships or receiving critical feedback gratefully (because of its power to alter clinician behaviors productively).

We can help the client anticipate possible problems in other relationships in the future if the relational behavior exhibited in the clinical relationship is enacted with others.

EXAMPLE

Clinician: During our work together, I've noticed how quickly you interrupt me if you feel that I am going to say something appreciative about you. You will often stop me before I can give you a compliment, or you belittle what you've done. For example, last week when I said that you were very generous to have volunteered to work overtime over the Jewish holidays, you said, "Anyone would have done the same thing."

Client: Yeah, I get embarrassed when someone tells me I do something well.

Clinician: I can imagine that other people notice your discomfort and then don't tell you about their positive perceptions of you. One of the results is that you often feel that you don't get much feedback.

Client: I just get so embarrassed.

Clinician: That might be a problem in the new job you're taking, since you have to have quarterly reviews with your supervisor. Can we talk a little about that embarrassment? Maybe I can help you with that.

The clinician can use overall process comments to strengthen client awareness regarding the process of relationship building. Surrey (1991b) believes that the mutual empowerment from honest relational feedback and tending leads to greater relational **"response-ability"**—a growing appreciation of what relationships mean and require and how to remain faithful to them when it is not always easy to do so.

EXAMPLE

Clinician: One of the things I appreciate most about you is the way that you have of stepping back and looking at what is going on in our relationship. You've often helped to focus our attention on things that we should be talking about—things that sometimes I hadn't thought about. I think that that must be what makes your friends appreciate you so much.

EXERCISE 11.2 Processing the Process

In small groups, practice the skill of processing the process with the clients in the following vignettes.

CLIP 11.2
Processing the Process

Olandra always pressures for advice, but then responds with "Yes, but . . ." to everything the clinician suggests.

Kenny has been skipping every second or third session, saying he "just forgot."

Jerri has been great at going out and trying things, no matter how hard, and keeps at it, even though feeling discouraged at times.

Exploring Indirect References to the Relationship

The clinician always listens for parallel patterns or themes in the client's comments. For example, sometimes after clients lose someone to death, they find themselves losing keys, gloves, and so on. In **exploring indirect references** to the relationship, the clinician wonders whether the client may be responding to issues or feelings arising in the clinical relationship.

EXAMPLE

Client: I am so tired of people asking me questions. My mother-in-law keeps asking me how I'm doing and I'm sick of her nosing around in my business.

Clinician: Is that how you feel with me sometimes?

Client: Well, now that you mention it . . . I know that I am here to talk about how I feel about my sister's accusations of sexual abuse by my father, but sometimes I just want to forget about it. When I see you each week, it is a constant reminder.

Clinician: So at times it feels like I'm pushing you to think about things you would rather forget?

Client: I guess I would be worrying about it anyway, but it's easier to think that, if I weren't seeing you and you weren't asking me questions, I wouldn't think about it at all.

In the preceding example, the clinician addresses a reference to something outside the relationship (reactions to questions by the client's mother-in-law) to see whether it parallels anything that might be going on in the clinical relationship (reactions to the clinician's questions). Conversely, a clinician could explore things going on *inside* the clinical relationship that may relate to relationships or events outside it.

EXAMPLE

Clinician: You'd rather not have to think about it at all.

Client: I find myself getting mad at you.

Clinician: It feels like I'm making you do something you don't want to do.

Client: I don't want to be mad at my father . . . that's really what I'm feeling. How could he do that—how could he force her?

In this example, the clinician intentionally chose her words, recognizing that they parallel how the client may feel about her father "making" her sister do things she "didn't want to do." This kind of attention to parallel themes requires very careful monitoring and is part of the careful attention paid to relationship issues.

CLIP 11.3
Addressing Indirect References

Cautions About Addressing the Relationship Process

Clinician genuineness in thought and feeling expression can model a more open way of being that builds relationships. For example, we can show sadness about a loss, irritation at repeated insults from a client, surprise at being accused of not doing something. We can spell out mistakes we think we made with the client, apologizing for them and inquiring about their impact. We can patiently encourage the client to go more deeply into reactions while affirming the risk people often feel in self-revelation. We can also specify feedback from clients that has changed our way of thinking and working, thanking them for the courage to speak up. As often as is appropriate, we try not to pretend in relation, because this inauthenticity only repeats what many clients have already experienced over and over again.

There can be complications in examining the moment, processing the process, or reflecting on indirect references to the relationship. No matter how useful it feels to us, focusing on the relationship displaces other topics or work at hand. We have to compare the expected benefit with the cost of such a focus: Will the time the discussion takes truly forward the agreed-upon work? Furthermore, being noticed in such detail may prove too intense for some clients (just as it does for some clinicians) who are more comfortable simply focusing on agreed-upon goals or tasks.

Examining what is happening in the moment, in the process, and in indirect references to the relationship is an ongoing part of our thinking.

However, it does not have to be made manifest with clients for good clinical work to happen. In fact, a problem can arise when clinicians overvalue focusing on the moment, either processing the process or examining indirect references to the relationship so frequently that the exchange risks becoming a "Woody Allen" type of parody of clinical conversation. In addition, if the content of the work is painful or uncomfortable for the client or the clinician, either may be tempted to divert the focus to the relationship to avoid discomfort with the content. The clinical relationship should never be the center of the universe.

■ Addressing Issues of Difference, Power, and Influence

Addressing Client–Clinician Differences

In Chapter 1, we talked about race, class, gender, culture, sexual orientation, age, physical ability, and other differentiating attributions and their implications for the clinical relationship. Differences are often fraught with concerns about dignity, respect, power, voice, the honoring of valued strengths and traditions, and the right to determine one's own fate as often as possible.

Very often it is appropriate to put issues of difference on the table right away to demonstrate the clinician's awareness of widespread concerns about such differences and willingness to tackle difficult subjects. At other times, a clinician may wait until remarks or behaviors suggest that a discussion of differences is indicated. We may address the issues in a number of ways.

1. *Examining the moment.* Clinicians may use their skill in examining the moment to directly address differences between the client and themselves. This is most easily done when the subject comes up, often in response to the clinician's naiveté or lack of knowledge.

EXAMPLE

The clinician is Catholic and the client is Jewish:

Client: My sister suggested that I join a havurah.

Clinician: A hurrah?

Client: No, a havurah.

Clinician: Tell me more about that.

Client: [Client explains the havurah.]

Clinician: What was it like for you that I didn't know about a havurah?

Client: I wouldn't expect you to know.

Clinician: You know, this helps me remember that we haven't talked about what it means for you to see someone who isn't Jewish—that's such an important part of your identity.

Sometimes a clinician raises the issue of difference to open channels of communication when the client has signaled a reaction to difference. Taking time out to examine things in the moment often strengthens the alliance and signals to the client that everything is grist for the mill of examination and sorting through. Clinicians need to develop both understanding and composure, since clients' behaviors and statements around differences can sometimes make it hard to remain empathic and nonjudgmental.

E X A M P L E

The counselor is Black and the client is White:

Clinician: I noticed that when you walked in and saw me, your jaw dropped.

Client: Uh . . . I was surprised you were a man. I thought with the name "Lacy," you would be a woman.

Clinician: Some of my White clients have told me that initially they reacted to my being African American. They say they worried I couldn't help them the way a White person could.

Client: People actually said that to you? Didn't that hurt your feelings?

Clinician: As a matter of fact, I think it's really important that people be able to speak their minds here so that we can talk about things and try to work them out together. Counseling doesn't work too well if people sit on things they feel strongly about.

Client: Well . . . to tell you the truth, you're the first Black professional I ever got help from. I don't know how it will be.

Clinician: How what will be?

Client: How it will be to tell my friends at the mill that I have a Black psychologist.

Clinician: Could you say more about your concerns?

---

2. *Commenting on a client's indirect reference to the relationship.*   Clients often lack experience in confronting differences and realizing that differences have an impact on relationships of all kinds, including the clinical one. They may address differences only obliquely, but this gives the attentive clinician an opportunity to make the latent manifest.

E X A M P L E

This is an exchange between a woman in a battered women's shelter and a male human services worker:

Client: You'll never again find me anywhere near a man for long.

Clinician: Since I'm a man, let's take a minute to see how it is for you to be talking with me. Sometimes clients feel they have to take whomever they get as a counselor, but that's not true here. I want to make sure you're in the best situation for you.

Client: I do hold back. You'd hate me if you knew what was on my mind half the time.

Clinician: I am so glad you let me know about holding back, although I'm not surprised, given what guys have done to you. I'd like to hear more about what you've been thinking, if you feel okay telling me.

Client: I've thought of asking for a woman to talk to.

Clinician: What are your thoughts about that?

EXAMPLE

The social worker is White Euro–American, the client is Black Jamaican:

Client: I hate those White folk at work who keep saying that they wish they could have dreads like mine.

Clinician: What do you hate?

Client: The way they pick some stupid part of me like my hair to talk about. I feel like their pet sometimes.

Clinician: I'm sorry that happened to you. Do those feelings ever come up between you and me?

---

3. *The clinician introduces the difference into the conversation.* If the client does not offer, the clinician often brings the subject up because clients may fear the consequences of broaching differences with a clinician. This is especially true if the clinician is a member of a group that the client thinks of as powerful and potentially harmful or about whom the client has strong antipathies or feelings from past experience. It is essential to explore the relational and political implications of differences, because they are often intertwined with issues of racism, class privilege, power, and inequality that need to be recognized and discussed.

EXAMPLE

The clinician is male and straight; the client is lesbian:

Clinician: Darcy, we have never talked about the fact that I'm straight and you're lesbian.

Client: It never seemed to come up since I was just talking about work and stuff.

Clinician: A lesbian woman might feel that her sexual orientation does affect how people react to her at work. I was wondering if you had any thoughts about that.

Clinician Power and Influence

Closely related to client–clinician differences are issues of power and influence. Clinicians do have real power: We are not simply benign, caring others. In reality, a professional whose assessments, reports, or testimony contribute to life-affecting custody determinations or judicial proceedings has real state-sanctioned power to which clients may understandably respond with anxiety, uncertainty, and defensiveness. Relationships benefit when this clinician power is addressed directly and with respect for client feelings about it.

Sometimes, directly or indirectly, the client brings up the subject of the clinician's power. In such instances, it is important to attend to the underlying messages and intensity of affect attached to the client's communications.

EXAMPLES

"You could get my kids back for me if you really wanted to—just like that!"

"You people think you know everything and can make other people do anything you want with your psychological tricks."

"I don't like you to look in my eyes; it makes me feel like you're trying to read my mind."

"You can go on vacation whenever you feel like it, but I have to get the approval of the whole team, my parents, the school. Would you like it?"

"You're the doctor—you tell me!"

"I liked you because I could tell right away that you knew what I was feeling without me really having to tell you."

"Well, I suppose you are going to go right out of here and report me. So go ahead; I'm not afraid of inquisitors."

The clinician responds to such statements with empathy, acknowledging a power differential in the clinical relationship and perhaps asking the client what it is like to think of the clinician as having more power. For some people, to see the clinician as powerful can be unpleasant; for others, it can be reassuring. The clinician explores both sides of the client's reactions, as well as past experiences with people who may have exploited power over the client.

EXAMPLES

Client A: You could get me my kids back if you wanted to.

Clinician: What's it like to think I have that kind of power and am not using it for you?

Client A: I feel mad about it sometimes.

Clinician: I would feel mad, too, if I thought somebody could help me but wasn't. When you're mad with me about it, what thoughts come to mind?

Client A: I picture you talking secretly to my family worker and telling her I'm not fit to have my own kids.

Clinician: Oh . . . this helps me begin to understand why you seem so tense with me sometimes.

* * *

Client B: So go on and report me; I'm not afraid of inquisitors.

Clinician: Am I sounding like an inquisitor?

Client B: You got that right.

Clinician: That's not what I ever meant to sound like . . . you've had so much meddling in your affairs over the years. Can you help me do a better job here? Can you show me how I sounded?

Client B: You said three weeks ago that you have to report any intended crimes, and today I said I felt like knocking Max's block off.

Clinician: It could be hard to trust me if you're worried I'm going to think of the angry things you say here as crimes. Where did you get the idea that your angry thoughts are crimes?

In addition to real authority invested in certain clinical roles, clinicians often have **symbolic power**—the power, expertise, and influence attributed to them by clients. They also have the power that comes from the different activities of clinicians and clients, such as who keeps notes on whom, who sets the schedule, who sits in the waiting room, who pays for the visit, who sets the boundaries, and so on. At times, the clinician elects to address this symbolic power directly, as when the client attributes any good things that occur in the work to the clinician's knowledge and skills rather than to his or her own hard work.

EXAMPLE

Client: Thanks to you I can now get my kids back, get some child care, and go get that high school equivalency offered at the school up the street.

Clinician: Thanks to me? Mostly what I did was encourage and believe in you. You're the one who did the hard work every day of the last year and a half. You went to the meetings, you worked with the homebuilders, you met with the protective worker, and you got counseling with Esteban.

Clients may also blame all their misfortunes on the clinician's interventions or mere presence in their lives. This premise, too, can be addressed as it arises in client statements such as, "My last worker had real good luck getting me jobs; you must not have the kind of connections she did."

As discussed in Chapter 9, sometimes clinicians assert or address the use of their power or influence with the client to set limits or to move work forward in a particular way. When intentionally choosing to use direct influence, it is important to attend to the resulting effects on the client and on the relationship.

EXAMPLE

Clinician: Last week, I said that you had to go to five AA meetings a week in order for us to continue working together. I wanted to check in with you first thing today to see how that sat with you.

Our ethical stance can also be novel for clients who are used to seeing people with power exploit it for their own gain. Worker ethics may be tested time and again to see if they hold up.

Curtis saw me smoking not far from a sign that said "No smoking." He asked me if it would be okay if he went up to the neighborhood bar and just had one beer, since he'd been clean of all street drugs for almost five weeks now. I asked him if this request could be connected to my smoking where I wasn't supposed to. He grinned and said that what's good for the goose should be good for the gander. I realized I was living in a fishbowl here where the things I did and said could really matter, so I said that I had a saying to match his: Two wrongs don't make a right. He laughed. I said I regretted smoking in the house, and that even one wrong is wrong. He asked me if I wanted to go shoot some baskets now, and I said I did. On the way, he said solemnly that smoking could be dangerous to my health. I was affected by his worry, realizing that I simply hadn't stopped to think through the impact of my behavior on him and our other clients. I honestly hadn't realized either that a resident would actually care that much if I lived or died.

EXERCISE 11.3 Power

In your journal, record your answers to the following questions.

Have you seen a professional use power over a client?

What were the circumstances?

What were the effects?

Have you ever used the power of your professional role with a client?

What were the circumstances?

What were the effects?

Client Power and Influence

One of the goals of the clinical relationship is to help clients feel and experience their own power in the world. Since the clinical relationship acts as a microcosm of human experience in the world, clinicians can help clients experience and assert more power by recognizing, examining, and increasing the client's power in the clinical relationship itself.

Clients actually have many different kinds of power in the relationship. They can approve or disapprove of clinician responses, activities, and ideas. They can continue or drop out whenever they wish, even if mandated (they can elect to take the consequences rather than see a clinician, and many do). They can pay or refuse to pay for the relationship, and they can keep clinicians and agencies waiting for payment by not filling out or mailing in the necessary forms. They can complain to agency heads and boards, to local and state elected officials, and through letters to newspapers or appearances in the media. They can say complimentary or disparaging things about the clinician to other clients and professionals without speaking directly to the clinician, and they can sue the clinician for perceived damages if they feel harmed by the care given.

Clinicians can be awed by clients who have socially perceived status and power, particularly the rich and famous—the VIPs. Rules and limits can be stretched in ways that do not help such clients cope with ordinary frustrations. In addition, we can fail to be as searching in our exploration or as frank in our feedback as we might with non-VIPs. Often only senior personnel are allowed to interact with "important" clients, so beginning clinicians rarely have an opportunity to learn about how to deal with the entitlement or very real vulnerabilities of these clients. Confidentiality can also be violated when clinicians cannot resist boasting about a famous person who was seen at their agency.

> *A wealthy elderly man came into rehab for physical therapy for serious injuries from a fall while intoxicated. His wife would sneak bottles of liquor into him in her knitting bag. He would come to afternoon physical therapy sessions somewhat high. The wife was a very impressive person. Her brother had donated a lot of money to the hospital, and no one wanted to confront her about bringing in liquor.*

Regardless of social status, all clients have very real power in the clinical relationship. Just as clients may be deeply affected by their interactions with clinicians, so, too, are clinicians often deeply moved and changed by interactions with clients. Just as we may help clients "see and do things differently," so do clients affect how we perceive things, feel things, and act.

Our ways of viewing and experiencing the world can be radically changed by our experience with them, and almost every clinician's empathy, listening skills, and capacity to respond quickly have been improved by client feedback. Although clinical supervision often focuses on the things clinicians are doing helpfully, it can focus just as often on verbal or nonverbal signals from clients that the clinician missed, detoured around, or dismissed as not important.

While we bring clinical skills and expertise to the relationship, clients bring their own self-knowledge and expertise. Although the roles in the clinical relationship are not equal, the clinical relationship is an egalitarian relationship in that we try to develop and maintain equal respect and value, even though there are differences in roles and responsibilities. The goal is to help the client achieve more power, both in the relationship and in the world (Brown, 1994). However, Julie Mencher (Eldridge, Mencher, & Slater, 1997) asserts that the asymmetries of power in the clinician–client relationship disqualify it from being the egalitarian relationship we say it is and wish it could be.

Overvaluing the Power and Influence of the Clinical Relationship

As clinicians, we can put so much stock in ourselves, our skills, and our theories that we overvalue the clinical relationship and what it can achieve. We can even begin to believe that events and realities in the client's life should be subordinate to the clinical work and relationship. A client's tardiness or sudden absences may automatically be interpreted as related to the client–clinician relationship dynamics, when we know that children really do get sick at the last minute and buses actually do run late sometimes. We try to avoid putting clients in the position of feeling guilty about their behaviors in the relationship because this relationship, while meaningful, is only one of the important forces in their busy lives. The more connections they have with others, the more this is likely to be true.

> *A psychiatrist told my friend that, if her parents who lived in England should die suddenly, she should plan not to spend more than a few days in England or it would interfere with the "level of caring" in their work together.*

* * *

> *My client, a really poor single mom, called to say she needed to miss a week because it was three days until her next check and, if she spent the money for bus fare, she wouldn't be able to buy peanut butter and jelly to keep the kids fed the next few days. My supervisor told me "Anybody can afford $1.00 for the bus." Later I came to know better.*

Beginning clinicians can also undervalue the power and meaning of their relationships with clients. They may rebuff praise when it would be good for the client to give it and experience the meaning of that to the clinician. They may minimize the importance of what they say with clients or the importance of clients' lateness or absences. They may skim over learning, as though clinical education was just more courses to be gotten through. Striking some balance, it is probably fair to say that this unique relationship is very important to many people but is not the be-all and end-all that some professionals wish it were.

Aversions to Clients

Dislike of a client is one of the hardest things to recognize, own, and talk about with a supervisor because of our blinders and our guiding ethical principle of nonjudgmental and unconditional acceptance of all people. Dislike can sometimes be triggered by unconscious countertransference (reacting to a client as though he or she were a person in the past who was disliked). However, dislike can also be a product of prejudice, bias, and stereotyping by the clinician.

When aversive reactions remain unspoken and unresolved, clients can be left with a clinician who may never come to like or respect them. Clients are thus stuck—sometimes for a long time—with someone with whom they may never experience growth-producing mutual empowerment, described by Miller and Stiver (1997) as an enormous unheralded benefit of clinical encounters. It helps to recall that we can all be hard to like sometimes, yet can still find common ground and goals for respectful work together. Supervisory review of aversions when they arise can greatly assist in understanding and resolving them for purposes of growth in both clinician and client.

Virtual Relationships

Millions of Americans live in rural areas where health specialties and mental health services either don't exist or are inadequate (Winerman, 2006). A shortage of professional clinicians and services in rural areas has hastened the establishment of online counseling.

In addition, some clients may prefer the advantages of online counseling, which include clients working at their own pace on exercises or questions from the clinician, a reduction in the stigma of going to see an office-based clinician, time savings for all involved, and greater access to help for people with disabilities, including hearing problems. Clients may benefit from these distance interactions if the modality and the persona of the clinician are a good enough fit from the client's perspective (Cuijpers, van Straten, & Andersson, 2008).

Although clinicians may worry that the relationship suffers when they are not in face-to-face contact, advances in technology, including videoconferencing, enable the establishment of effective clinical relationships. The same relational skills discussed earlier apply in technology-based clinical relationships. However, there are special requirements when using videoconferencing. The clinician needs to be trained in videoconferencing technology so as to be at home with the technology and able to appear warm, caring, and confident on camera. Nonverbal cues may be distorted or lost due to poor technological quality, so the clinician may need to be more active in inquiring about client reactions as the conversation unfolds.

Research comparing the quality of the clinical alliance in online versus face-to-face relationships has shown little or no difference, especially when online clients are already comfortable with computer interactions (Knaevelsrud & Maerker, 2006; Murphy, Paranass, Mitchell, Hallett, Cayley, & Seagram, 2009). Even clients who engaged in a typed online clinical relationship and who had no visual contact with the clinician reported that over a course of weeks it began to feel like a face-to-face encounter. Clients report feeling they are able to reveal their true selves on the Internet and that they have "close online relationships" (Bargh, McKenna, & Fitzsimons, 2002).

■ Conclusion

The clinical relationship provides not only the context in which change can occur but also the means by which change occurs. As a real human relationship, it provides the client and the clinician with the opportunity to develop relational competencies, including how to tend and discuss process in a relationship, how to resolve interactional problems when they arise, and how to increase respect and mutuality in a relationship with another.

Although each of the parties in the relationship has preferences as to how much relational focus there should be in the work together, the clinician is charged with the fiduciary responsibility of ensuring that the relationship is safe, effective, and appropriately centered on the client's needs. This responsibility holds from start to finish, whether the relationship develops *in vivo* or is media-based.

In Chapter 12, we will address how the clinician deals with the disclosure of personal information and other specific boundary issues that can arise in clinical relationships.

■ Suggested Readings

The following books provide an excellent discussion of issues of power and influence in the clinical relationship:

Brown, Laura. (1994). In *Subversive dialogues: Theory in feminist therapy.* New York: Basic Books. See The Relationship in Feminist Therapy (Chapter 4).

Norcross, John C. (Ed.). (2002b). *Psychotherapy relationships that work: Therapist contributions and responsiveness to patients.* New York: Oxford University Press. See chapter on empirically supported relationships.

Walker, Maureen, & Rosen, Wendy B. (Eds.). (2004). *How connections heal: Stories from relational-cultural therapy.* New York: Guilford.

Relationship issues in online therapy are addressed in:

Bargh, J. A., McKenna, K. Y. A., & Fitzsimons, G. M. (2002). Can you see the real me? Activation and expression of the 'true self' on the Internet. *Journal of Social Issues, 58,* 33–48.

■ Self-Explorations

1. Have you ever met someone and, without knowing much about the person, had a strong initial reaction (positive or negative), but later, as you got to know the person, changed your initial reaction? Do you think that your initial reaction may have been due to some sort of transference on your part? Discuss.

2. How comfortable are you interacting with people from a financial or socioeconomic class group different from your own? Have class differences ever caused you to feel less at ease and competent than you usually do? Discuss.

3. Think about a time in your life when you had real power over someone. How did you feel about that power? Compare this with a time when someone attributed symbolic power to you. How did you feel about that attribution?

4. How comfortable are you in communicating using the Internet? Have you ever used Skype or any other forms of videoconferencing? How does it compare to in-person conversations? If you haven't used these technologies, what is holding you back?

■ Essay Questions

1. What is meant by transference? Briefly explain how the ethnocultural and feminist approaches differ from psychodynamic theories regarding this concept. What do you think about the concept of transference? Have you ever experienced or observed transference in action? Describe.

2. Briefly describe two methods that clinicians can use to directly address relationship process with clients. How are these methods different? Discuss the challenges of each. Write out a client–clinician dialogue illustrating your use of each of the methods in action.

3. From your reading, discuss the five types of growth and change that mutual empathy stimulates in both clients and clinicians.

4. Detail the ways in which the various clinicians you watched on the DVD manifested warmth, empathy, and caring. In your view, was any clinician more—or less—successful in showing empathy? Why?

5. Discuss some pros and cons of online clinical relationships.

■ Key Terms

Central relational paradox

Countertransference

Ethnocultural transference

Examining the moment

Exploring indirect references

Hierarchical transference

Immediacy

Mutual empathy

Mutual empowerment

Negative transference

Positive transference

Process the process

Relational tending

Response-ability

Symbolic power

Transference

Working alliance

CHAPTER 12

The Clinical Relationship: Addressing Self-Disclosure and Other Boundary Issues

Professional boundaries are the lines of demarcation between clinician and client as they come together in a work-focused relationship. Theoretical models may describe in some detail what they construe to be the ideal arrangements, behaviors, and operating procedures in a professional clinical relationship. Professions, agencies, institutions, and individual states have standards of practice or ethics and regulatory codes defining the dimensions of a professional relationship and describing the behaviors and practices that are and are not permitted between professional and client.

Traditionally observed boundaries in the clinical relationship have included the following understandings: The relationship remains centered on the client's work needs, not on the clinician's needs. The contract itself acts as a sort of boundary around the conversation, suggesting focus and direction for the work and minimizing drift. Specific time constraints on the number and length of meetings provide further structure. Planned contacts outside the office should be for the express purpose of forwarding

337

contracted clinical work, not to develop other forms of relationship. The clinical relationship, while friendly in tone, is to be maintained as a working alliance, not as a friendship and not as a prelude to a friendship. Unavoidable outside contacts are discussed in-session to resolve potential complicating effects on the clinical relationship and on other people.

In smaller communities and less formal neighborhood service settings, outside contact as neighbors or fellow participants in community activities is expected and usually regarded as normal and not a complication of clinical work, as long as clinician conduct is guided by professional norms and values. Laura Kessler and Charles Waehler (2005) assert that the cultural realities and values of rural and deaf communities—interdependence and a preference for "insiders"—may be similar to those of LGBT communities, whose tight-knit nature makes multiple relationships between clinicians and clients unavoidable. Moreover, working with a clinician role model who knows first-hand about the joys and challenges of the minority experience can be a relieving side benefit of such alliances, so long as the work focus remains clear.

Sexual contact between clients and clinicians is strictly prohibited by professional codes of ethics and is punishable by law in many states. These traditions and ethical standards are common to most service professions today, to ensure the well-being of clients and to protect both the public and the professions from unscrupulous providers.

In the last chapter, we explored some of the situations in which the relationship becomes foreground, and we elucidated skills useful in addressing issues that arise in the relationship process itself. Boundary issues frequently arise that also might require the clinical relationship to become foreground. In this chapter, we focus on boundary issues including (1) disclosure of personal information about the clinician, (2) confidentiality issues, (3) limits on conversation, (4) out-of-office contacts, (5) requests for more time, (6) legally mandated boundary intrusions, (7) gift giving and receiving, (8) touch, (9) sexual attraction, and (10) limit setting.

■ Disclosure of Personal Information About the Clinician

Clients may obtain information about clinicians in a number of ways:

1. The clinician may choose to share personal information with the client, who can also receive information from others about the clinician.
2. The client may unwittingly discover something about the clinician from a public source, perhaps by reading a newspaper report that the clinician had an automobile accident or got married. The client may see the clinician on TV or during a community service project or an activist demonstration.
3. The client may ask the clinician personal questions.
4. The client may purposefully seek out information about the clinician from other sources, such as the Internet.

Self-Disclosure

Self-disclosure refers to the clinician's sharing of demographic information or personal experience with the client. You may have heard that clinician self-disclosure is always frowned upon as narcissistic or disruptive, but we believe that judicious self-disclosure can help develop trust, especially for clients who are not comfortable with what may seem like artificial distance and anonymity. Melba Vasquez (2005) notes that information is a form of power, and that receiving information from and about us gives clients more power in the relationship than they would otherwise have with less transparent clinicians. She observes that shared clinician information also allows clients to reciprocate empathy with us from time to time (an empowering feature of relational tending discussed in Chapter 11). Vasquez notes that feminist therapists of the 1970s and 1980s were among the first to provide guidelines for periodic, well-thought-out self-disclosure to reduce the power differential in therapeutic relationships.

Self-disclosure can be used in many ways as an element of other skills:

1. *Information sharing.*   In an example in Chapter 9, the clinician is working with a client who is about to undergo abdominal surgery and who is not sure when she will be able to return to work. The clinician, who also has had abdominal surgery, shares the information that she personally was tired for about six weeks but gradually got her old energy back.
2. *Modeling.*   In Chapter 10, we talked about how the clinician can help clients do things differently by modeling new behaviors and skills, one form of which is self-disclosure: "When I was studying for the licensing exam, I found that one thing that worked for me was to set aside two hours every morning before everyone else got up."
3. *Empathy building.*   In Chapter 5, we discussed how judicious self-disclosure could help the client feel joined with and understood: "I've been thinking about all the things you may be feeling right now. I myself was divorced earlier in life and I know it can trigger a lot of feelings."
4. *Examining the moment.*   As discussed in Chapter 11, when addressing what is happening in the relationship at the moment, the clinician can reveal what he or she is thinking as a form of feedback: "As you were talking about how you had to take care of your brother, I found that I was feeling sad— you were such a little girl and there was no one taking care of *you*."

Self-disclosure can be particularly important when working with members of oppressed or isolated groups. Derald Sue and Sue (2008) believe that "a culturally diverse client may not open up (self-disclose) until you, the helping professional, self-disclose first. Thus, to many minority clients, a therapist who expresses his or her thoughts and feelings may be better received in a counseling situation" (pp. 179–180). Clinicians may elicit more trust if they use some self-disclosure and demonstrate cultural sensitivity before asking Native American clients personal questions (Weaver, 2005). In some cultures, people only discuss business after a warm-up period of social exchange (Chang, Scott, & Decker, 2009).

Many Asians believe that it is improper to talk with strangers (Weijun Zhang, cited in Ivey & Ivey, 2007, pp. 192–193) and that they should discuss their problems only with family members. Thus, the clinician is often assigned an honorary kinship role and is referred to as aunt, uncle, or elder brother or sister (Lum, 2004). Lum also notes that many cultural groups have relationship protocols that guide intergenerational, interpersonal, and intercultural exchanges. All of these situations require that clinicians be flexible in disclosing personal information to their clients.

From their research on client preferences regarding therapist self-disclosures, Craig Cashwell, Julia Scherbakova, and Tammy Cashwell (2003) found that both Caucasian and African American respondents preferred some counselor self-disclosure, especially when the counselor's ethnicity was different from their own. These researchers suggest that clinicians use a brief trial self-disclosure in the first session, carefully noting whether clients signal interest or disinterest in the information. A main point in self-disclosure is that clients should experience it as a client-centered sharing rather than a clinician-centered or irrelevant diversion from the work. We should pay careful attention to verbal and nonverbal signals from the client about any brief self-disclosure, and explore those signals before moving on.

Whenever and for whatever reasons we consider using self-disclosure, we should begin by asking ourselves the following questions:

- Why am I considering self-disclosure around this issue?
- Why am I using self-disclosure at this moment?
- Is it in the client's best interest?
- Is there any way I could accomplish the same goal without using self-disclosure?
- What are the potential effects on the client of my self-disclosure?
- How might this help our relationship? What possible negative effects might it have?
- Am I sure that I am not doing this to meet my own needs at the expense of the client?
- How will I feel if the client tells other people what I have disclosed? (Remember the paradox of confidentiality: While the clinician may not discuss the client, the client is completely free to disclose information about the clinician to anyone, anywhere, at any time. It is wise to remember that clinician disclosures can have long lives in the community.)

It is important to evaluate the effects of self-disclosure and directly check in with the client about the information revealed. We recommend personal reflection on the following questions following self-disclosure:

- How did the client make sense of what I have shared?
- Did the client have feelings about or reactions to what I disclosed?
- Is there any sign that the self-disclosure is affecting the relationship or the work focus?
- Did the disclosure have the intended effect?

- Have I asked the client what it was like for him or her to have me share that information?
- If I had to do it over again, would I disclose in the same way, change the way I disclosed, or not disclose at all?

EXERCISE 12.1 Self-Disclosure

In small groups, discuss the pros and cons of sharing personal information, and discuss the differences between offering the information and being asked questions. In what ways do you think this kind of sharing is similar or different for clients? How do clients come to know clinicians without actually hearing much specific information about us?

Disclosure by Others

Clients may learn something about the clinician because it is revealed accidentally or by others.

EXAMPLES

A client may see a clinician attending an AA meeting.

A client may learn that a clinician has breast cancer when he learns that she will be speaking as a breast cancer survivor at a public hearing on funding for cancer research.

A client may discover that her daughter is working in the same law firm as the clinician's gay male partner and that they are considering adopting a child.

As with intentional self-disclosure, the clinician must evaluate what effects the information might have on the client and then directly address these with the client. In addition, the clinician might explore what it was like for the client to learn the information indirectly or from someone else.

EXAMPLES

Clinician A: Todd, we haven't talked about what it was like for you to learn that I was a member of AA.

* * *

Client B: My friend Ginger told me that you will be talking at the breast cancer rally.

Clinician B: and . . . ?

Client B: Well . . .

Clinician B: Do you know what I will be talking about? [To determine if the client has the information that the clinician has had breast cancer already.]

Client B: No.

Clinician B: [Clinician decides that she had better tell the client directly.] I have had breast cancer, and I will be speaking at the rally about the need for more funding.

Client B: Oh.

Clinician B: What's it like for you to learn that about me?

Client B: I'm glad you're an activist.

Clinician B: And what's it like for you to hear I have had breast cancer?

Client B: I guess it scares me. I didn't know you were sick.

Clinician B: [Deciding to share more information to alleviate the client's fear.] I had a very small tumor removed two years ago, and I have been fine since then. My prognosis is excellent.

Client B: I'm glad to hear that.

Clinician B: [Letting client know it's okay to talk about it.] Given your history of people who have left you by dying, I can see how this might raise some strong feelings for you. I want you to feel comfortable talking to me about those feelings as they come up for you. Let's go back and talk more about your being scared.

* * *

Clinician C: I just found out that your daughter Carrie is working at the same law firm as my partner, Len.

Client C: Yeah. That's something, huh?

Clinician C: That kind of puts you in an interesting position. You may be finding out things about me that I haven't told you and that you haven't asked.

Client C: Yeah.

Clinician C: I hope that you will feel comfortable talking to me about anything that comes up for you. I am confident that we can handle it together. Has anything come up that you want to mention?

Client C: Well, now that you mention it, Carrie said that she was going to a baby shower for Len.

Clinician C: Yes, Len and I are adopting a son. What was it like for you to find out this information from someone else?

Client C: It's odd because I think I know you so well, and yet here is this important thing that's happening in your life and you hadn't told me.

Responding to Personal Questions

Sometimes clients ask personal questions: How old are you? Are you married? Have you ever had an abortion? Whether the clinician chooses to answer depends on a number of factors, including cultural considerations, theoretical orientation, personal comfort in sharing information, the state of the relationship and the focus of the moment, agency preferences or policies, and the anticipated effects on the client. Feminist therapists, for example, often use judicious self-disclosure to try to reduce unequal power in the relationship.

Clinicians think carefully about the effects of both answering and not answering client questions. Not answering is a traditional psychodynamic strategy, designed to allow the client to project any anxieties, frustrations, or fantasies onto the "blank screen" of the clinician, indicating earlier unconscious issues that might need to be recognized and explored. Clinicians may not respond to personal questions in order to encourage the client to search for other possible meanings or motivations in their questions. Many colleagues today simply answer questions they are comfortable with without taking up much of the client's time, and then bring the focus back to the client. This is done without leaving the client feeling criticized for asking. Usually the intent of a comfortable answer to a personal question is to demonstrate being at ease with oneself in a professional role and to show respect for the client's curiosity and cultural norms for relating. Curiosity about the clinician is also natural when clients are being asked constantly to disclose personal information and feelings to a professional they barely know.

EXAMPLES

> "Rather than spending more of your time on *me,* could we get back to what you were saying just before that question? You seemed worried."
>
> "Let's get back to *you* now. That's the most important focus."
>
> "You get so little time just to focus on *you* . . . shall we get back to why you're thinking about dropping your nurses' aide training program?"

Disclosures are always a subject for continuing review. Sometimes clients say they are glad or relieved to hear things, but later they share more complex reactions of which they were not initially aware. Similarly, a clinician may sometimes feel that disclosure is right and comfortable but at other times feel overexposed or prodded to reveal more than he or she is comfortable with.

Sometimes clinicians do not want to answer a client's direct question. It takes skill and finesse not to answer a direct question without leaving the client feeling embarrassed and rejected. We have found that it is often helpful to reflect back to the client what the underlying purpose of the question might be and to address that—or simply explain why we are not answering.

EXAMPLES

Client A: [During a first interview.] I was wondering how old you are.

Clinician A (Example 1): Might you be wondering if I have enough experience to work with you on the issues you've mentioned?

Clinician A (Example 2): I am wondering what reasons you might have for asking me my age. [To stimulate exploration by the client of the meanings behind the question.]

* * *

Client B: I don't know much about you. Are you married? Lesbian? Where do you live? Do you have kids?

Clinician B: It's natural that you would want to know more "facts" of my life. Therapy is an unusual relationship that in some ways is imbalanced. I know a lot about you and the facts of your life, while you know very little about mine. However, I do think that in one sense you know me quite well. Over the last four weeks, you have gotten a sense of me in a very real and genuine way, even though some of those facts might be missing. Do you know what I mean?

* * *

Client C: Last week, when you told me you were pregnant, you asked me if I had any reactions. I didn't then, but now I do have a question.

Clinician C: Okay . . .

Client C: Are you going to put the baby in child care?

Clinician C: Could you also be wondering if I will still be working with you or putting you in someone else's care?

Client C: Hmmm . . . I never thought of that. Maybe I am.

Sometimes the clinician chooses not to answer the question but wants to explore the client's fantasies about the clinician. These fantasies may provide useful information about how the client sees and experiences things.

EXAMPLE

Client: [Office is in clinician's home.] Do you live here by yourself or what? I didn't mean to pry . . . just curious about it.

Clinician: What thoughts have you had about it?

Client: Not many. Just wondered.

Clinician: I'm interested in what you imagined.

CLIP 12.1
Information About
the Clinician

EXERCISE 12.2 Responding to Personal Questions

In teams of three or four, role-play a client and clinician. Have the client ask the clinician personal questions. In the role of the clinician, practice different ways of responding. Note how you feel when the client asks you a question. Observers take notes on what occurs. If possible, video record the role-plays. As you watch the video, note both your verbal and nonverbal behavior in response to the client's questions. Discuss with your team what you have observed.

■ Confidentiality

We mentioned earlier that at the beginning of the relationship, the clinician discusses with the client confidentiality and its limitations. Now, we explore exactly how to address directly issues of confidentiality and their impact on the relationship as they arise.

EXAMPLES

Clinician A: Delma, I wanted to let you know that I have just received a request from your insurance company to fill out a form about our work together.

Client A: Oh yeah, I remember you said you might have to do that.

Clinician A: Let me tell you what they are asking and what I will say. [The clinician goes on to describe what information is requested and what information he will provide.] Do you have any questions about it?

Client A: No, I think that's okay.

Clinician A: If you have any concerns about it, please let me know.

Client A: Well, will you tell them what I told you about my brother? [Client had disclosed that her brother was a drug addict.]

Clinician A: I don't have to reveal that information at all.

Client A: Good, I was worried he might get fired.

* * *

Client B: I just saw someone from my church in your waiting room.

Clinician B: What was that like for you?

Client B: I don't want her to know that I'm coming here.

Clinician B: Tell me what you're worried about.

Client B: I don't want her to know my business.

Clinician B: What do you think she might think about your being here?

Client B: [Responds with her fears.]

CLIP 12.2
Confidentiality as
a Boundary Issue

Clinician B: [Clinician explores the client's concerns and then reaffirms the confidentiality.] It's true she will know that you are here and she may have her fantasies about why, but no one here will say anything about what you and I talk about. Have you had problems in the past with someone seeing you get help?

■ Limits on Clinical Conversations

In addition to the boundaries (confidentiality, time) *around* the entire clinician–client conversation, there are boundaries *within* the conversation, including (1) the focus that structures, concentrates, and clarifies the conversation and (2) any existing proscriptions against certain topics of conversation in particular settings.

The Focused Conversation

The clinician helps the client stay focused on the topic at hand to avoid getting sidetracked by other issues the client may raise. For example, if a client and an employment counselor contract specifically to work on job skills, but the client continually brings up concerns about his relationship with his son, the clinician may either (1) explore the issue in more detail to see if there is a possible connection between the client's concerns and the issue they have contracted to work on or (2) help the client refocus on the task at hand but consider talking with a family specialist about parent-child concerns. Unless the ongoing agreement is to talk about anything that arises for the client, the clinician usually tries to help the client stay focused to make the most of their time together.

EXAMPLE

Clinician: Luis, I know you're worried about your relationship with your son, but we had agreed that your need to work is so urgent that right now our main job is to help you figure out how to get ready for tomorrow's interview. I hear your worries about Luisito, though, so let's get you hooked up with one of our family life counselors as soon as we end today to talk about your relationship with your boy. I feel that it's important today to stay on course with our work.

The Proscribed Conversation

Proscribed conversation occurs when an agency prohibits clinicians from discussing certain topics with clients. At some faith-based agencies, for example, the social worker may be prohibited from discussing abortion as one of the options for an adult woman who is facing an unwanted pregnancy. A high school counselor may be told that, because of a vote by the school board, she is not permitted to discuss issues of sexual orientation with any of the students. State and federally funded counseling programs may also forbid focusing on activities such as educating women about family planning alternatives.

EXERCISE 12.3 Restricted Conversations

In small groups, discuss whether you believe that an agency has a right to restrict the topics of conversation between a clinician and client. Under what circumstances? How would you handle a situation if the agency you worked for proscribed an area of clinical conversation?

When clinicians are prohibited from discussing certain issues or carrying out specific activities, at minimum we must clearly articulate the limits on conversation to the client and offer a referral to an appropriate professional if the client would like further assistance. Local volunteer and faith-based organizations have often been established for the specific purpose of assisting those whom professionals are restricted from helping. The process of helping people get the help they need from someone else should be suffused with the same acceptance, empathy, and caring we demonstrate with any client. Particularly important is the need to offer the referral in a manner that does not suggest that the issues clients want to discuss or the services they need are somehow bad, wrong, or taboo.

EXAMPLES

Clinician A: Nancy, this is a Catholic family agency, and I am not permitted to talk with you about abortion as an option for handling this pregnancy. If you want to consider that, I can refer you to a counselor I know at Family Planning who can explore that alternative with you.

* * *

Clinician B: Thomas, it sounds like you are thinking you might be gay. I am glad you were able to come to me about this. Unfortunately, the policy in our town doesn't allow school counselors to talk about issues of sexual orientation with students. But I know a great youth worker in town who has had lots of experience talking with kids about gay issues. I can refer you to him if you'd like. I want to be sure you understand that my not being able to work with you on this has nothing to do with how I feel about the subject or about you.

EXERCISE 12.4 Restricted Conversation Role-Play

In teams of four, role-play the following scenarios, in which you are prohibited from discussing certain topics with clients. Discuss the ethical issues that such a prohibition might raise for you. How would you handle a situation in which you disagreed with the stated policy of the agency for which you worked? In your discussion, remember the ethical principle of upholding contractual agreements with employer agencies, as well as working for the best interests of your client. Record your reactions in your journal, and prepare to discuss them in class.

As a high school guidance counselor in a Catholic school, you are forbidden to join students who have asked you to march with them in the local Gay Pride March.

A 27-year-old mother who is receiving welfare assistance asks if you think it is okay that she is working two nights a week as a waitress and not reporting the income to the government. She says that she couldn't pay for food and heat if she didn't have this little extra income.

A managed care plan prohibits you from discussing with your clients your view that their son needs to be in a day treatment program, which the plan has rejected as too costly.

■ Out-of-Office Contacts

Not all clinicians see their clients in offices. However, we use the phrase *out-of-office contact* to refer to times when the clinician sees clients in settings outside their normal meeting place.

Planned Contact Outside the Office

Contact outside of the normal meeting place may be a planned part of the work together. Planned out-of-office contacts include home, hospital, and institutional visits. These places may be the normal settings for meetings—the hospital social worker routinely sees her clients in their hospital rooms—or they may constitute an unusual event, as when the counselor who usually meets with a client at the clinic suggests a home visit. The clinician might also accompany someone to an AA meeting, go with someone to the welfare office, or drive a client to the battered women's shelter. These types of activities are clearly related to easing the way for the client to get needed services.

Some clinicians may attend commitment or marriage ceremonies, christenings, graduations, healing services, or funerals. Sometimes they provide a supportive presence for lonely or isolated people. At other times, they may join with family and friends to help celebrate or honor an occasion that marks special achievements related to the aims of clinical contact.

EXERCISE 12.5 I Do . . . or Maybe Not

In your journal, record your thoughts about whether you might attend a client's wedding. Under what circumstances, if any, would you do so? What factors would go into your decision? What might be the advantages of your attendance? The disadvantages? Discuss your responses in class. What watchwords might guide your behaviors while there?

In the situation in Exercise 12.5, the clinician bases the decision on whether to see the client outside the normal meeting place by thinking about whether it furthers the work they are doing together. Sometimes clients ask to see us in other situations, but we usually do not enter into activities and relationships with clients outside the office without compelling professional reasons to do so. Though a friendly tone may characterize the working relationship, the clinical relationship is not a friendship. Putting some boundaries around the relationship clarifies its work purpose and focus and removes from the client the onus of trying to guess how far the relationship can be taken or what motivates the clinician's attention and caring. Another purpose of boundaries is to prevent lonely or unprincipled clinicians from preying in various ways on lonely, vulnerable clients.

> *I remember when I was working at the group home, I went with the residents to see a movie as part of their recreational activity. For me, it was work; for them, it was fun. One of the residents asked me if I would go to the movies with him the next week when he was out on a pass. I had to explain the difference that when I went with the group, it was part of my role as a resident counselor. I wasn't just going out with the group as a friend.*

When a client asks to see us in a setting other than the normal meeting place, we need to carefully consider the request and discuss it with a supervisor. If the decision is not to go, we should support the client while clearly articulating the reason for the refusal.

EXAMPLE

A clinician has helped the client cope with depression so serious that she had lost a job as an accountant as a result of it. Over the last six months, they discussed the client's desire to open her own accounting office. She had been discussing how excited she was about having a party to celebrate her "return to the real world."

Client: I want to ask you if you would come to my office warming.

Clinician: How were you picturing it would be with me there?

Client: You've been so important to my improvement. I guess I want you to see what I've made of myself.

Clinician: It's really a celebration for you of overcoming your depression as well as of opening the office.

Client: That's why I want you there.

Clinician: It's nice that you want to include me. I, too, share your excitement in being able to go back to work—and to set up your own office at that. You have every right to feel proud.

Client: I know. Thanks, I do feel proud.

Clinician: Unfortunately, I won't be able to come. I don't see clients outside the office. Maybe we could celebrate your success here. I will, however, be thinking about you that day. Would you like to bring in pictures of your office?

Client: Yeah, I'd like to bring in pictures of the party, too.

Clinician: Great.

When meeting purposefully with clients outside the customary meeting place, it is important to be careful that roles are clear and that boundaries, though flexible, are still well defined.

EXAMPLE

The client is a teenager who dropped out of high school. He has met with the youth worker regularly over the last three years. They have worked together to help him get back into an alternative school program, and, after many difficulties, the client is going to graduate.

Client: So—you gonna come to my graduation?

Clinician: I'd be happy to be there.

Client: We're gonna have one big party after.

Clinician: Well, I'll be at the ceremony, but I won't be coming to the party.

Client: Why not, man?

Clinician: We've spent a lot of time working together to get to this day. I am delighted that you did it, and I want to be there to celebrate your success, so I'll be at the school. But I'm your counselor, and counselors don't usually go to parties with their clients.

Client: Why not?

Clinician: Well, that's one of the ethical rules that guide our relationships with clients. It's part of what makes it different from other relationships that you have in your life. A little distance helps me think more clearly about the people I work with. That may be one of the things that helps us work so well together.

Client: So what are you gonna do, stay in the back of the auditorium?

Clinician: Well, how should we handle this? I'd be happy to meet your mom and your aunt or anyone else right after the ceremony if you want to introduce me, but you don't need to.

Client: Yeah, I want you to meet them.

Clinician: Well, let's talk about how we can do that and what it'll be like.

We must always think about the implications of our presence for clients and directly address the topic with them, particularly when there is a change in setting. However, we believe it is always important to explore the client's reactions to the clinician's encounters with other people or places in the client's life. The clinician might ask questions such as:

"How was it for you, my coming to your home to meet with you last week?"
"How was it for you when I met your sister?"
"What was it like for you when I went with you to the hospice?"
"Now that you're seeing me in the clinic instead of in the shelter, how does it feel?"

EXERCISE 12.6 Outside Contact

Outside contact can be complicated, as clinicians sometimes have flexible interviewing strategies, such as talking with a client at a coffee shop where conditions are less formal or having a meal with a family in their home. What, then, would be the difference if clinicians and clients went to the movies, if it gives the clients good feelings about themselves? Would you think it is ethical? Record your response in your journal and then discuss this topic in class.

Unplanned Contact

Sometimes the clinician and client happen to see each other outside their normal meeting place. A clinician may see a client at a party, on the street, or in the bank. These **unplanned contacts** are not part of the work together, but they should be briefly addressed in the relationship.

EXAMPLE

Clinician: Bumping into you at the market was the first time we've seen each other outside the office.

Client: Yeah . . . I didn't know what to say.

> *Clinician:* I thought we handled it well by just saying "Hi." Have you had any other thoughts about it?
>
> *Client:* No. Now I know that if we bump into each other again, we can just say "Hi" and move on.
>
> *Clinician:* That would be fine. We can also talk in our session about anything that comes up for you if we meet.

Because it is always possible that clinicians and clients may have unplanned out-of-office contact, clinicians should ask clients in advance how they would like to handle such contact. In some cultures, people might feel honored to introduce the clinician to family and friends. On the other hand, some clients might be embarrassed and might not want the clinician to acknowledge them.

> *I routinely discuss with clients how we want to handle the situation if we see each other outside the office. Some clients would like me to say "Hi, how are you?" and move on. Others would prefer that I ignore them so they are not in the position of having to explain to friends who I am or how they know me.*

We must put clients' needs first and try to avoid specific situations where clients might be uncomfortable in our presence. Some clinicians believe they should avoid any contact with clients outside the office, even if the client is okay with it. This belief may be derived from their theoretical perspectives or their wish to keep their work and private lives separate.

> *A couple of times, I have had to leave a small party or even a restaurant because I knew a client was there and that she would feel uncomfortable seeing me dancing, talking, or socializing with others.*

* * *

> *I live in a very small town, and I have to be careful about what dinner invitations I accept. Twice in the past year, I have been invited to a dinner where a client of mine would have been present. I have learned to ask the host who is coming, and if a client is, I find an excuse not to attend.*

Sometimes clinicians cannot avoid interacting with their clients outside the clinical relationship.

> *I live in a village of 1,750 people and bump into my clients everywhere—market, gas station, beauty shop, gym. There's one Catholic church, and we attend it pretty often at the same time. I have to be extremely careful in protecting confidentiality, but there is no way I could not have contact outside. Once people see I don't tell their stuff, we relax about it.*

* * *

> *When I walk through campus, I often bump into students I have seen in the counseling center. I don't initiate contact or conversation with a client outside the office. I take my cue from the client. If he or she says "Hi," I will say "Hi" back. Some clients readily say*

"Hi" in front of their friends, some ignore me completely, and others acknowledge with a nod of the head or eye contact that no one else will notice. And then, of course, I'll check in about our contact at the next session.

Without the client's permission, the clinician may not reveal anything about the nature of his or her relationship with the client. If we bump into someone we have worked with and a friend asks who it is or how we know him or her, we have to find a way to answer that does not disclose the clinical relationship. We have used the following responses:

"I know her from town."
"Just someone I know."
"We've known each other for a while."
"I know her through work."

These vague responses can feel awkward, but it is crucial to maintain client confidentiality.

CLIP 12.3
Out-of-Office
Contacts

I've told people I know that if we're walking along and I suddenly turn my back on them and don't introduce them, just walk ahead and I'll catch up. In one funny instance, a charming teen client of mine saw me walking in the square, followed me, and jumped out of the bushes, doing a little song and dance. My friend and I laughed, and I just said, "Go ahead and I'll catch up in a minute." My client said, "He's cute . . . is that your main squeeze?" I just laughed and asked what she was up to. She filled me in briefly, and let me go on. What can you do? A clinician's friends learn not to ask when things like this happen.

■ Addressing Requests for More Clinical Time

Clients sometimes ask for more time than has been agreed to. They may ask for extra meetings, phone calls, or extensions of the length of regularly scheduled meetings. Clients who request more time may be upset, anxious, in need of anchoring contact or assessment, or they may even be testing the clinician's caring by pushing on the limits of the relationship. The clinician's response should be flexible, and it depends on a number of factors:

1. *The clinician's practice framework shapes the response.* For example, clinicians using a brief treatment framework might confine all contact to the given sessions and encourage clients to hold material until the next session. Crisis intervention specialists might be available 24 hours a day for a given number of weeks or months. Many clinicians use a combination of variable personal availability and local emergency resources to provide a ready response to reasonable client requests for more time.

2. *The agency's rules and procedures regarding coverage for clients' needs govern the clinician's decisions about offering extra time.* For example, some have emergency services that they prefer clients use outside scheduled appointments; others do not wish staff to take client calls at home.

3. *The clinician's assessment of the client's agenda, capacities, needs, and availability of other supports influences the response to requests for more time.*

Clinicians carefully assess how requests for more time do or do not seem to complement the agreed-upon goals for client functioning and growth. Extending time to some clients is a necessary lifeline in crisis, but for others it can be an invitation to exploit the clinician or to undercut their own new strengths. Only when the clinician and client have experience with each other can they determine what is truly in the best interest of the client's functioning, and the decisions may vary from time to time. The degree of seriousness of an emergency arising in the client's situation also determines the appropriate response.

4. *The clinician's response also depends on the amount of time and energy he or she can reasonably devote to requests for extra time, particularly after hours and between sessions that are booked one after another.* Clinicians sometimes develop "calling times"—specific times for telephoning during the day or evening—whose limits clients are asked to respect so that clinicians can renew themselves.

Whether or not we agree to requests for extra time or phone contact, we must carefully address the meaning for the particular client of both the request and the response. Any change in the originally agreed-upon contract needs to be carefully considered. Upholding reasonable conditions and limits may help clients get the work done more efficiently and, for clients with a poor sense of boundaries and time, may assist in the internalization of structure. There are times when clinicians may give clients more time, especially in a crisis situation or if the client is at risk of self-harm. We discuss the need for this flexibility in Chapter 13.

Time constraints are one of the unusual aspects of the clinical relationship, and they differentiate it from many other types of relationships with which clients are familiar. Holding to set times leaves the clinician time for work with many clients; it also structures the work so that clinician and client are less likely to exhaust themselves with too much data, analysis, or emotional intensity. But this clinical sense of time may be at variance with that of clients. As Tafoya (1989) noted, "Many native languages do not measure time in standard units. The Sioux language has no translatable equivalents for words like late, waiting, or time. The term 'Indian time,' often interpreted as being late, in fact refers to doing something when 'it [the time] is right'" (cited in La Fromboise et al., 1994, p. 33). Derald Sue and Sue (2008) believe that clinicians' adherence to a 50-minute hour and exact schedules may put them at odds with non-Western clients whose traditions regarding meetings are not so time-bound.

Changing the rules suddenly, while perhaps necessary in serious emergencies, can confuse clients. For example, regularly extending the session for extra time and then suddenly ending on time may leave clients feeling that they have lost something special or have done something wrong.

EXAMPLES

Client A: Could you see me every other day? I'm so panicky. . . . I don't think I can make it through the days.

Clinician A: I can hear how rough things feel to you just now and I'd like to hear more. I am not going to be able to see you more often, but let's see if we can find other supports for you.

* * *

Client B: Can I have your number in case I get depressed over the weekend?

Clinician B: What kinds of things are you worried about? [After the clinician explores in depth what the client's concerns are and ways the client might handle it—like calling friends, going out, using positive self-talk—he might say the following.] Yolanda, I don't accept calls at home, but if you feel it's an emergency and you feel you need to talk to one of our staff, we have on-call workers you can reach by phone, 24 hours a day. If you want, I will tell them that you might call.

Clients may not ask for additional contact in advance. They may just call the clinician or appear at the agency for unscheduled meetings.

EXAMPLE

Client: I got your number from the phone book and I hope it's okay that I'm calling. I couldn't wait until our next appointment to tell you that Gordon said I shouldn't call him at work anymore. I'm so mad and I just didn't feel like waiting until Tuesday to tell you.

Clinician: I am sorry to hear that you are having such a hard time, but it's pretty late. I don't usually take calls at home, but I want to make sure you're okay.

Client: I'm fine. I just wanted to tell you.

Clinician: Okay. We can talk more about what happened on Tuesday.

If clinicians agree to see a client for extra sessions or to receive calls at home, at some point they must clarify any time limits on this service. They should also clarify who is available to the client when the clinician is not.

EXAMPLES

Clinician A: Pietro, I can talk with you for 10 minutes on Wednesday morning, but we have to stop at 11:00 sharp. Can you do that?

* * *

Clinician B: Francis, we can have an extra half-hour meeting this week, but we won't be able to do that on a regular basis.

Like everything else we do, providing extra time or contact requires careful consideration. Extra contact can be justified as appropriate support for clients under unusual stress, but it can also undermine client resourcefulness if the client does not attempt to seek other sources of support. In addition, the clinician can sometimes feel helpful and even heroic providing extra contact but may feel resentful at other times, thus sending clients mixed messages about what is okay.

■ Legally Mandated Boundary Intrusions

Joseph Walsh (2009) discusses mandated boundary "intrusions" in which protective service workers become intruders who, by court order, enter client residences against the client's will to protect or rescue vulnerable or ill members from abuse or neglect. These boundary crossings usually occur only after outreach to try to help the family through provision of intensive supportive services or if there is an indication that someone is at risk of immediate harm. While they are often life-saving and positively redirecting for the family, these mandated boundary crossings into people's homes do reveal a sanctioned imbalance of power in certain client–clinician relationships, and can leave clinicians feeling ambivalent about these activities because of our historic emphasis on client self-determination and empowerment.

■ Gift Giving and Receiving

Sometimes clients give clinicians gifts. Gifts may represent messages about the relationship, and it can be useful to explore what clients were thinking and feeling when they thought of giving the clinician a gift, how they picked the gift, and how they pictured the clinician reacting when the gift was presented. It is not unusual for clients to give clinicians gifts they wish they could have for themselves. In the case of someone who has been taught throughout life to do things for others in order to earn love, the clinician may help the client more by discussing the gift and asking the client to keep it than by accepting it. On the other hand, some people may try to control clinicians by showering us with gifts, and others may be uncomfortable either giving or receiving presents.

The acceptance of a small gift (a Hanukkah card, flowers in thanks for special help) is often appropriate and respectful of the client's need to honor the relationship and its meaning. In such circumstances, the clinician thanks the client for the thoughtfulness and responds with courtesy— tasting an edible treat only if the client will share it or putting the flowers in water. The use or placement of the gift should not make other clients feel they are expected to give gifts as well. A clinician may accept small tokens from some clients and not from others, and all responses should be carefully thought out and based on the client's specific needs (Brown & Transgrud, 2008).

Sometimes clinicians do not accept gifts. Regarding **gifts as symbolic messages** about dynamics in the clinical relationship, the clinician may talk about the meanings and intentions behind gifts rather than accepting them. In these instances, the refusal has to be couched in a respectful and plausible discussion of the reasons for declining the gift.

> *A client gave me "an Easter present" of a gold crucifix right when she was the maddest at me. I said she seemed to be mad (she was glowering and seething), so I wondered why she would want to give me something. She asked whether I was going to give it back, and I said that, to me, the important thing was to understand what she was mad about. She said she wasn't mad. She looked at the crucifix, then at me, and said, "I guess I was picturing you on the cross in a lot of pain, so you could finally feel like I do." I wondered if she was feeling that I didn't appreciate her pain, and she said she didn't think I did.*

Clinicians try not to accept expensive gifts so as not to get caught up in anything seductive or anything that compromises their clinical judgment by making them feel somehow beholden. Yet sometimes we can reinforce a client's faltering sense of self-worth by simply accepting the gift and appreciating the client's thoughtfulness.

> *When I was leaving the agency, a client brought me a gift. She was poor and I didn't want to take a gift from her. I said that I knew she appreciated our work together and that I would always remember her. I wasn't sure if I should take the gift, but because she begged me to take it in thanks for our work, I decided that I should at least open it. It was a pen with my name on it, and so I decided that I couldn't give it back to her. I told her that I would always remember her for the specialness of herself—even without the gift.*

It is important to think about the client's culture and how that may affect the meaning of your refusal to accept a gift. In many cultures, a gift is always given to thank another person for services rendered or to show respect for another. Rejecting a gift might be taken as evidence of extreme disrespect for another's way of being (Barnett, Lazarus, Vasquez, Moorhead-Slaughter, & Johnson, 2007). However, repeated gifts should be explored. For example, a client who regularly brings in "surprises" like coffee or donuts may unwittingly be repeating the relational pattern that was reinforced throughout her life—that of serving, feeding, or pleasing powerful others. Rather than ignoring such gifts, it is helpful to explore the meaning of the gift-giving pattern.

> *An Irish client of mine, the caretaking oldest of 11 children, always knocked herself out at the holidays baking cakes and cookies for others. Earlier in life she had been in a convent, where she baked for the pleasure of others. This was a woman who asked for nothing and who got scarcely anything from others—something we were working to improve. Lo and behold, at Christmas, she brought me a huge pudding that she'd stayed up all night to make. She mentioned that, after our meeting, she was going home to bake some more of these for cousins. When I refused the pudding for the sake of helping her to see her self-abnegating pattern, she burst into tears and got very mad with me. These were unpleasant, yet very important, feelings to get on the table. She was able to grasp the point I was trying to make with her, and came to value a long-forbidden thought that it was okay to do for herself sometimes, and not just for other people. The next Christmas she sent me*

a note of relief and gratitude that she wasn't baking for many people any more and it relieved her of so much pressure.

Clinicians need to be aware of their own reactions to receiving gifts. A clinician's discomfort and uncertainty about what to say or do when given a gift by a client can interfere with thinking about the gift's possible meanings and with responding appropriately (Brown & Transgrud, 2008).

Supervisors can help beginning clinicians frame a variety of responses to gifts deemed inappropriate. Often, simple statements can be effective.

EXAMPLES

"I appreciate your thoughtfulness in bringing me this coffee, but I want this to be a place where you can finally get for yourself and give to just you."

"I get plenty from the work with you without your having to bring me anything else."

"I like to think of this as a relationship where you can finally take instead of give for a change. Could you stand that kind of switch, do you think? It would be interesting to see what happens."

"Staff aren't allowed to accept gifts, but if you feel you want to say thanks for the work we do here, donations to the Tiny Tots program can be left with the secretary."

EXERCISE 12.7 Gift Role-Play

In groups of three or four, make up scenarios in which a client brings a gift to the clinician. Role-play different ways of handling the situation and, if possible, video record them. Under what conditions did you feel comfortable accepting a gift? Under what conditions did you think it would be unwise? How did you address the issues with the client? What did you learn from watching each other and from watching the video?

Sometimes the clinician gives the client a gift. A gift may serve as a symbol—something that the client can keep with him or her as a symbol of the connection with the clinician.

When I was to be away for surgery, a client who'd had a lot of losses in her life gave me a soothing tape to play during the post-op period. She said she knew she couldn't visit me in the hospital, but she wanted to "be there," to do something to help me as I had helped her. When she later left for a six-week trip to Asia, I in turn gave her a tape of soothing music to play, saying I would be thinking of her, wishing her a safe journey, and picturing her having a great, relaxing time with her friends.

■ Use of Touch

Whether and how to engage in touch with clients remains an important issue in clinical relationships, and is influenced by clients' and clinicians' cultural beliefs and preferences, as well as differing clinical theoretical orientations. Gabrielle Syme (2006) notes that all civilizations use some form of touch when meeting, whether with a handshake, a hug, a bow, or a quick kiss on the cheek. She believes that "the majority of people know when touch is inappropriate and erotic and appropriate and non-erotic" (p. 66) and that taboos about touch in clinical practice "are odd because the 'laying on of hands' is part of the ancient art of healing" (p. 66). In fact, touch is also an important element in many religious and spiritual rituals as well as in energy-based and mind-body therapies today (Gallo, 2002).

However, touch has also been used by exploitative clinicians as a prelude to sexual intimacy. This is why touching a particular client has to be thought out in advance with a supervisor and applied with great thoughtfulness and care. Clients who have been subjected to traumatizing experiences of touch may both repel and desire touch—may long for a clinician's hug and then be horrified by it. Others welcome a quick opening or closing hug and feel comforted by it. Some settings or agencies may forbid all physical contact between clinicians and clients. Others may have "good touch" as part of their mission to help both child and adult clients experience safe contact. Your supervisor can help you assess each client and think about whether and how touch may or may not play a role in the relationship.

Ken Pope and Patricia Keith-Spiegel (2008) warn that everyday acts can have an unintentional impact in the clinician–client relationship. "We help a client take off a heavy winter coat, meaning only to be polite and helpful, unaware that the client may experience our stepping close, touching, and removing an article of clothing as unwanted, intrusive, disrespectful, or even frightening and seductive" (p. 644). Clinicians who have any physical contact with clients should be aware of their own liability in addition to the client's well-being and protection.

■ Sexual Attraction

Sexual attractions can occur in the intimacy of the clinical relationship. A client can be attracted to a clinician, and a clinician can be attracted to a client. Syme (2006) documents numerous instances throughout the history of psychotherapy in which clinicians have entered into sexual relationships with clients. However, romantic or sexual interaction between client and clinician is strictly forbidden by the ethical codes of all of the helping professions, and is a criminal offense in a number of states.

If a client expresses romantic feelings or directs inappropriate sexual behaviors toward you, you should always consult with a supervisor before addressing the issue in the relationship. On rare occasions, the client may become sexually assertive, gazing at the clinician's breasts or genitals while talking, rubbing against the clinician provocatively on entering or exiting the room, or attempting other forms of physical contact such as surprise kisses or hugs. Clients frequently exhibit these behaviors when they have grown up in an atmosphere of inappropriate sexualized intimacy and violence or when they doubt their attractiveness and urgently need it validated. Other inappropriate client behaviors include suggestive stories, offensive sexual jokes, holding a handshake too long, or winking (Hartl, Zeiss, Marino, Zeiss, Regev, & Leontis, 2008).

A clinician who feels sexual attraction toward a client should discuss it with a supervisor rather than mentioning it to the client. Gerald Schamess (1999) believes that attractions in therapy are frequent, human, and some of the least discussed experiences in professional practice. He underscores the importance of open discussion with supervisors to develop understanding and skill in managing such attractions.

Clinicians may respond to a client's sexual attraction in any number of ways. How and why we choose a particular response is beyond the scope of this chapter. Suffice it to say that the issue is complex and depends on a number of factors, which include theoretical orientation, the clinician's understanding of the client and what the sexual attraction may represent, the type of work the client and clinician are engaged in, and how the client raises the issue. Clinicians should also consider the possibility that maybe their own behaviors, including dress and deportment, are stimulating the client's sexual feelings.

The following are some relevant practice principles when sexual feelings arise:

1. ***The clinician can explore the client's sexual attraction and related fantasies.*** Some clinicians believe that this exploration provides useful information about the client's dynamics and is therefore appropriate for their work together. The skills of exploration and elaboration are used to obtain more information about the attraction the client has expressed.

EXAMPLES

Client A: I had a weird dream about you last night. We were having sex. It's so embarrassing.

Clinician A: I am glad that you told me about it. Counseling is an intimate experience in which lots of feelings can arise, including sexual ones. Would you feel comfortable telling me more about the dream, and let's see if we can understand this better?

* * *

Clinician B: Lauren, I notice that right now you are leaning forward toying with the top two buttons of your blouse in a way some people might describe as seductive. Let's talk about it.

> *Client B:* [Straightens out skirt and sits back.] I wasn't aware of it. But I have to admit, I do find you sexy.
>
> *Clinician B:* Sometimes when people feel close to their counselors, they can start to feel attracted to them, especially if they learned as kids that sex often comes with closeness.
>
> *Client B:* Wow, so I'm just like a textbook "patient" . . .
>
> *Clinician B:* Did I leave you feeling that way?
>
> *Client B:* I wasn't asking you for a date. I just said I think you are sexy. No big deal.
>
> *Clinician B:* This isn't easy to talk about, I know, but it could help us understand how you get into sexual relationships with people without really knowing them and then get hurt.
>
> *Client B:* Do you mean that maybe I come on to people without being aware of it?
>
> *Clinician B:* Do you think that could be so?

---

2. ***The clinician can reassure the client about how commonly tender and sexual feelings arise in situations of intense personal sharing.*** Clients often report feeling attraction to clinicians because of the intimacy of the clinical relationship. They may feel frightened or confused by these feelings, especially if they have experienced sexual abuse at the hands of intimates or have come from strict religious backgrounds that expected sexual feelings to be suppressed.

3. ***The clinician can refocus the conversation on the contracted work.*** Sometimes clients may raise sexual feelings as a distraction from the work at hand if the work is too difficult for them at the moment.

4. ***The clinician can let the client know that he or she would never act on romantic or sexual feelings.*** Whether the clinician explores the issue in more detail, reassures the client about the commonness of the experience, or refocuses the conversation back to the topic, it is always important to clearly state the boundaries so that there is no confusion.

5. ***The clinician should carefully document any discussion of sexual feelings, both for review in supervision and as a protection against future misinterpretation by clients or others.*** Your supervisor will suggest language you are to use to document such discussions in order to protect you from any later claims of malfeasance. Moreover, when working on a clinical team, it is important that colleagues see in the record that the topic of sexual feelings has been broached by the client, so that the team can try together to understand what may be triggering such feelings.

6. ***It is wise to have a general conversation with a supervisor about how to handle sexual attractions.*** It is important to be prepared since we can never predict whether, when, and with whom romantic feelings or sexual attraction will come up in our work (Walsh, 2009).

In the preceding example, the clinician explored feelings appearing in the moment as they may relate to other experiences in the client's life. He also reassured her that such experiences are common in clinical work. He affirmed safe boundaries that would allow them to talk about feelings without acting on them. This very capacity to feel, examine, and discuss things *without acting on them* is a goal of both good clinical learning and sound clinical practice. Paradoxically, some clients who fear closeness may actually cross boundaries to distance the clinician, whose repulsion they fully anticipate. For other clients, sexualized encounters may be a cultural or gender norm on which the client is acting at the moment. Following supervisory review of the behavior, the clinician may be helped to directly address it and its inappropriateness to the professional relationship. As with most boundary issues, the clinician can follow up by exploring the meaning of the behavior from the client's perspective and experience.

EXAMPLES

Clinician A: I've noticed that, when we talk, you often seem to be staring at my breasts. That makes me uncomfortable, and I wonder if you could try making eye contact with me or looking someplace else instead. Am I the first woman to mention this?

* * *

Clinician B: Birch, when you leave the room, you always lay your hand on my back as you go out. I'd rather you not do that, but I'm also interested in what that's about for you?

Directly addressing sexualized behaviors can help clients begin to develop boundaries appropriate to the context of clinical working environments. At the same time, we must be professional in our own dress, manner, language, and tone so that we do not elicit the very behaviors we then confront.

EXERCISE 12.8 Talking About Attraction

In small groups, take turns role-playing a client either talking about or manifesting sexual attraction. Practice how you would respond to the client without acting. Talk with your team about how to do that in a way that neither demeans the client nor encourages the fantasies or behaviors.

■ Limit Setting

Beginning clinicians may mistakenly feel that the principles of acceptance and nonjudgmentalism prevent our ever acting in ways that limit the client's freedom or cause unpleasant feelings. They may ask whether **limit setting** on client behaviors is a clinician-centered rather than a client-centered activity. We believe that it is both. Clinicians cannot work productively in an atmosphere that threatens their fundamental sense of comfort and well-being, and clients can usually read rather accurately a clinician's negative reactions to things they do. Limit setting is also important for client growth. Letting clients persist in demeaning or offensive behaviors gives them a confusing double message about what we think is appropriate in relationships, and it models the kind of denial or trivializing of abuse that many clients have already experienced too much of. Limit setting helps clients learn self-containment, an important developmental step in human relationships.

■ Self-Reflection on Boundary Issues

All clinicians will experience boundary issues now and then throughout their careers. It is never too soon or too late to begin reflecting on issues presented in this chapter, for as Pope and Keith-Spiegel (2008) wisely note:

> All of us can—and do—make mistakes about boundary decisions and other aspects of our work, overlook something important, work from a limited perspective, reach conclusions that are wrong, hold tight to a cherished belief that is misguided. An important part of our work is questioning ourselves, asking "What if I am wrong about this? Is there something I am overlooking? Could there be another way of understanding this situation?" Could there be a more creative, effective way of responding? . . . Nothing can be placed off limits for this questioning. (p. 641)

■ Conclusion

In this chapter, we have discussed the importance of appropriate yet flexible boundaries in maintaining a warm, trustworthy relationship in which participants can count on each other for integrity and respect. We have provided numerous examples of establishing limits with clients about such things as time, topics of conversation, privacy of the clinician, and sexual behaviors to maintain clear and comfortable boundaries in the clinical relationship. When setting these limits, the clinician unfailingly conveys respect and caring for the client.

We believe that the process of establishing, tending, and maintaining the clinical relationship contributes fundamentally to helping clients change. This relationship not only provides a context in which change can occur, but it is often the means by which change occurs in the client and in the clinician.

Learning to care about, tend, and authentically participate in a relationship builds skills that benefit both clinicians and clients in their future connections and work with others. Ironically, the relationship itself can become so important that, while it often reinforces change efforts, it can also inhibit them. It can feel so rare and so good that the participants may unwittingly slow down change to postpone losing this very special relationship because work is completed and the relationship ends.

In Chapter 13, we will discuss what clinicians do in crisis intervention and the effects this work can have on those who frequently carry it out.

■ Suggested Readings

There are a number of excellent readings on multiple relationships and sexual attractions in clinical work:

Barnett, Jeffrey E., Lazarus, Arnold, A., Vasquez, Melba J. T., Moorhead-Slaughter, Olivia, & Johnson, W. Brad. (2007). Boundary issues and multiple relationships: Fantasy and reality. *Professional Psychology: Research and Practice, 38,* 401–410.

Bridges, Nancy. (2005). *Moving beyond the comfort zone in psychotherapy.* Lanham, MD: Jason Aronson.

Brown, Chris, & Trangsrud, Heather B. (2008). Factors associated with acceptance and decline of client gift giving. *Professional Psychology, 39,* 505–511.

Hartl, Tamara L., Zeiss, Robert A., Marino, Catherine M., Zeiss, Antonette M., Regev, Lisa G., & Leontis, Arrie. (2008). Clients' sexually inappropriate behaviors directed toward clinicians: Conceptualization and management. *Professional Psychology, 39,* 674–681.

Lazarus, Arnold, & Zur, Ofur. (2002). *Dual relationships and psychotherapy.* New York: Springer.

Pope, Kenneth S., & Keith-Spiegel, Patricia. (2008). A practical approach to boundaries in psychotherapy: Making decisions, bypassing blunders, and mending fences. *Journal of Clinical Psychology, 64,* 638–652.

Schamess, Gerald. (1999). Therapeutic love and its permutations. *Clinical Social Work Journal, 27,* 9–26.

Syme, Gabrielle. (2006). Fetters or freedom: Dual relationships in counseling. *International Journal for the Advancement of Counselling, 28,* 57–69.

The following are useful readings on self-disclosure:

Cashwell, Craig S., Scherbakova, Julia, & Cashwell, Tammy H. (2003). Effect of client and counselor ethnicity on preference for counselor disclosure. *Journal of Counseling and Development, 81*(2), 196–202.

Goldstein, Eda. (1997). To tell or not to tell: The disclosure of events in the therapist's life to the patient. *Clinical Social Work Journal, 25,* 41–57.

Pope, Kenneth S., Sonne, Janet L., & Greene, Beverly. (2006). *What therapists don't talk about and why: Understanding taboos that hurt us and our clients.* Washington, DC: American Psychological Association.

■ Self-Explorations

1. How comfortable are you about revealing personal information to others? Is this related to your family or cultural values? Have you ever disclosed something to a person and later wished you had not? What did you disclose and why did you regret it? How has the experience affected your comfort with self-disclosure?

2. Describe some situations in which you have had to set limits on others. How comfortable are you in limit setting in your relationships with others?

3. Do you know anyone who has been involved in a sexual or romantic relationship with an authority figure, such as a coach, teacher, priest, or relative? How did it happen and what were the effects of that relationship?

■ Essay Questions

1. What factors should a clinician consider if a client requests more meeting time?

2. From your reading in this chapter about boundary maintenance, discuss the benefits and risks of getting to know clients in non-work-related ways.

3. How should a clinician respond if a client directly raises his or her romantic feelings toward the clinician?

■ Key Terms

Gifts as symbolic messages

Limit setting

Professional boundaries

Proscribed conversation

Self-disclosure

Unplanned contacts

CHAPTER 13

Working with People in Crisis

Crisis intervention has much in common with other forms of clinical work. It requires attending and listening, support and empathy, exploration and elaboration, and careful assessment and working agreements. We use many of the same skills to help clients gain insights, make meaning of events, and change behaviors. As in all clinical work, we pay careful attention to the relationship. However, crisis intervention requires modifications in some of the customary timing, focus, and forms of clinical interviewing.

In this chapter, we begin by describing what is meant by *crisis*. We explore crisis intervention and the skills clinicians use in working with individuals and communities in crises. Finally, we discuss how crisis intervention work can create unique stresses for clinicians, who must cope with vicarious or secondary trauma.

■ Crisis

Crisis is ubiquitous in the twenty-first century. War, famine, political upheaval, sudden population dislocations, slavery, disasters, accidents, abuse, torture, and widespread violence make crisis an inescapable reality in the lives of millions of people around the globe. Violence, poverty, racism, religious prejudice, large-scale unemployment, and other forms of hardship and oppression also create hazardous conditions that prime people for crisis reactions to precipitating events that easily overwhelm already stressed coping resources. The constant stream of distressing media images of traumatizing domestic and international crises and their focus on dire consequences perpetuate a climate of crisis that is hard to avoid.

The ravages of trauma and crisis cut across all class, color, ethnocultural, political, and international boundaries. No one is immune, whether in large urban areas, small towns and villages, rural settings, desert habitats, or remote islands. From epidemiological research, Martin Deahl (2000) estimates that over two-thirds of the world's population are exposed at some point to traumatizing events severe enough to meet the DSM "stressor" criterion for **Posttraumatic Stress Disorder (PTSD)**. Symptoms of PTSD include (1) reexperiencing the traumatic events through intrusive thoughts or dreams; (2) experiencing hyperarousal through difficulty sleeping, hypervigilance, inability to concentrate, or irritability; and (3) avoiding reminders of the event through detachment, efforts to avoid thoughts or feeling, numbing, or withdrawal from social contact. The reported rate of PTSD among combat veterans and first-line emergency responders is over 30 percent (Deahl, 2000). It is clear that over the course of our clinical careers, we will be called upon time and again to help people in crisis. All clinicians must be prepared to provide speedy, well-crafted, and well-coordinated interventions in collaboration with others.

The word **crisis** comes from a Greek root meaning "to decide." Murray Levine and David Perkins (1997) state that "the term means a critical turning point in the progress of some state of affairs in which a decisive change, for better or worse, is imminent" (p. 208). The father of crisis intervention, psychiatrist Erich Lindemann, first described crisis reactions after observing the acute grief expressed by persons who survived or were affected by the 1942 Cocoanut Grove nightclub fire in Boston—a sudden conflagration that took the lives of nearly 500 revelers in less than 10 minutes. He also studied and worked with similar reactions in relatives of deceased armed forces personnel and medical patients, and he counseled patients who had lost a relative in the course of psychiatric treatment.

Trauma is the term often used to describe a catastrophic crisis that involves events so sudden, massive, extraordinary, uncontrollable, or dehumanizing that they overwhelm cognition and meaning making, feeling regulation, biological processes, habitual adaptive mechanisms, and relational capacity. Traumatic events significantly affect overall functioning and can shatter people's assumptions about how the universe operates and how people behave toward one another (Janoff-Bulman, 1992). Judith Herman (1997) notes that:

Traumatic events call into question basic human relationships. They breach the attachments of family, friendship, love and community. They shatter the construction of the self that is formed and sustained in relation to others. They undermine the belief systems that give meaning to human experience. They violate the victim's faith in a natural or divine order and cast the victim into a state of existential crisis. (p. 51)

From an ecological perspective, Patricia Harney, Leslie Lebowitz, and Mary Harvey (1997) believe that there are multiple possible outcomes to trauma, not just psychological harm, depending on the interaction of the traumatic event, individual variables, and the environment in which these factors play out. Among the environmental factors that influence posttrauma adaptation, we emphasize family, cultural, friendship, and spiritual support, plus provision of sufficient emergency income to help people restabilize, rebuild, and mitigate stress with renewing activities.

Jessica Henderson Daniel (2000) has called for a widening of the definition of trauma to include persistently distressing memories or continual experiences of race- or color-based "microaggressions" (p. 130). Daniel notes that, in addition to the prejudicial policies and practices of organizations and institutions, racism also occurs in subtle and "equally troubling, individual everyday acts" (p. 128), whose cumulative effects are widely traumatizing for people of color and many others identifying with them. As noted previously, these frequent aggressions include acts of exclusion, victimization, harassment, verbal abuse, stereotyping comments, intimidation, and injustice as well as what Sue and colleagues have labeled as "microinvalidations"—those behaviors that negate or discount the psychological thoughts, feelings, and racial reality of Black Americans (Sue et al., 2008).

In a similar vein, Joan Hertzberg (1996) speaks of the cumulative traumatizing effects of class-based oppression through both subtle and overt acts of dominance. "The effects of malignant, internalized oppression can be devastating and the cumulative impact can constitute what Root (1992) refers to as **insidious trauma,** one that evolves from the ongoing experience of denigration based on social status or identity" (p. 133). For example, Weaver (2005) discusses the historic traumatic effects on Native Americans of the theft of Indian lands and resources, the forced breakup of families and tribal groups, the massive removal of children from their families to Indian schools, the outlawing of ancient spiritual practices, and the destructive effects of the introduction of alcohol into tribal life.

EXERCISE 13.1 Oppression-Based Traumas

In your journal, discuss oppression-based traumas you have either directly experienced or have observed as they happened. Share your experiences in class. Notice how you react to telling or hearing about these incidents. Imagine the feelings and coping strategies of others who may experience these aggressions on a regular basis. How does this exercise improve your clinical understanding of responsiveness with victimized people?

The term **secondary trauma** is used to describe a traumatic response to hearing about or witnessing others' traumatic experiences. Charles Figley (1983) first used the term to describe the stressful reactions of families and friends in response to knowing about a traumatic event experienced by a significant other. In addition, individuals can experience secondary trauma in response to events that happen to people they hardly know because these events awaken their own vulnerabilities or repressed traumatic experiences of a similar nature (Figley, 2002).

Shortly after the shooting in Columbine High School, my son Miguel started having nightmares and would awake screaming that "they" were coming after him. He was scared to go to school, and his mother and I didn't know how to reassure him. This lasted for a couple of weeks. Every now and then, he still has the same dreams.

Hate crimes can create secondary trauma for those who are not the direct victims of the attack. Peter Finn and Taylor McNeil (1987) define hate crimes as "words or actions intended to harm or intimidate an individual because of her or his membership in a minority group; they include violent assaults, murder, rape, and property crimes motivated by prejudice, as well as threats of violence and other acts of intimidation" (p. 2). Hate violence is a form of terrorism that traumatizes not only the direct victim but all members of the targeted group. Hate crimes affect the rest of us by reminding us of the sudden malice with which our lives can be ended or turned upside down by forces beyond our control.

The United States has passed hate crimes legislation which originally defined hate crimes as those motivated by the victim's race, color, religion, or national origin. In the fall of 2009, the U.S. Congress expanded the definition of hate crimes to include those committed because of gender, sexual orientation, gender identity, or disability.

The counseling center at the college reported seeing a number of lesbian, gay, bisexual, and transgender students who came in because they were having anxiety symptoms and wanted to talk about what happened to Matthew Shepard, a gay college student who was beaten and left to die hanging on a barbed wire fence in Laramie, Wyoming.

* * *

In the weeks following the racially motivated dragging death of James Byrd, Jr., an African American in rural Texas, the parents of African American kids at our day care center decided to meet to talk about how to handle the anger, fear, and despair they felt for their children.

■ Common Features of a Crisis

Some suggest that, whenever clients come to us, they are in crisis (James, 2008). Although that may be true on one level, we are referring to a more limited and specific use of the term *crisis*. We believe that crises have some very specific features.

1. *There is a precipitating or triggering event.*   People face numerous events that could precipitate a crisis. Crisis theorists describe many different types of crises arising from different **precipitating events**. We find it helpful to delineate four: situational, developmental, environmental, and compound.

Situational crises may be precipitated by extraordinary incidents, such as fires, acts of violence, diagnoses or episodes of mental or physical illness, or abrupt changes in established systems in which people feel secure. **Predisposing factors** such as poverty, social isolation, racism, and gender bias put people at risk for specific situational events. For example, living in an impoverished inner-city neighborhood may put people at higher risk of being exposed to violence and health hazards.

Erik Erikson (1963) notes that normal growth and life-cycle developmental events can generate **developmental crises** of adaptation to new people and challenges. Developmental transitions include the birth of a child, marriage, divorce, going to school, finding and developing job opportunities, aging, and death. Of course, different cultures have different developmental transitions and may attribute different meanings to them.

Environmental crises affect groups of people who may share a common living environment. Richard James (2008) refers to these as **"ecosystemic crises"** (p. 14). They may be precipitated by **natural disasters** (e.g., storms, tornadoes, floods, hurricanes, tidal waves, earthquakes, volcanoes) or **human-made disasters** (e.g., oil spills, toxic waste dumps, biohazards, nuclear accidents, or arson fires that devastate vast tracts of land and destroy homes and wildlife). James suggests that ecosystemic crises can also include biologically based disasters (disease, epidemics), politically based disasters (war, refugee crisis, ethnic cleansing), or economically based disasters (severe economic depression, mass unemployment due to plant closings or job outsourcing).

Many have noted that a crisis often rekindles unfinished business from previous crises (Lindemann, 1965; Parad, 1965). Cynthia Poindexter (1997) refers to this phenomenon as a **compound crisis,** while James (2008) refers to it as a transcrisis state. A person whose mother died when she was 5 may find she reexperiences the crisis at age 60 when her sister dies. Lindemann (1965) writes of **delayed grief reactions,** in which survivors of a recent loss may suddenly experience grief from an earlier loss. Sometimes delayed grief reactions occur when people reach the age of the deceased at the time of his or her death.

Precipitating events do not have to be big. "The straw that broke the camel's back"—a small thing that is the last in a series of upsetting events or hazardous circumstances—can overwhelm the individual or system. After nine pregnancies, a tenth may be a crisis. The precipitating event may not be as severe as the events or conditions preceding it, but it can be overwhelming physically, emotionally, or psychologically. A person may be able to cope with numerous hazardous conditions and events. For example, a woman may be able to cope even though she loses her job, becomes ill, and her partner dies, but, like the straw that broke the camel's back, the breakdown of the water heater overcomes her.

2. *The person perceives the event as a danger, loss, or threat.*   Howard Parad (1965) notes that the event that precipitates a crisis must be perceived as a threat. The key thing is not the event but the meaning that individuals attribute to it and its anticipated effect on the future. Perception of danger and reactions to it are idiosyncratic. Two people exposed to the same event may perceive the threat quite differently.

> *I worked in a school in which a student brought a gun to class. One of the students, Hunter, was quite frightened at the time, shaking and crying. The next day, his mother said that he didn't want to go to school. He feigned sickness. For weeks after the event, he was jumpy and emotional. Jamil was in the same class. He didn't seem at all anxious at the time, nor did he have any visible follow-up reactions.*

Culture often influences the way people understand and make meaning of events, signaling them about the kind and level of distress they should experience and express in reaction to events. Spiritual beliefs, too, can influence responses. Lindemann (1965) discovered that surviving family members who thought events were connected with God's divine plan recovered more quickly than those who could find no way to understand why their loved ones had been taken. Hinduism and Islam teach that life is determined by fate or by the will of God or Allah. It is possible that subscribing to these beliefs may help protect people from the more severe and lasting effects of trauma and crisis.

3. *Customary coping methods do not work or are inadequate to the degree of threat.*   **Coping mechanisms** are methods people use to overcome, reduce, or accommodate the demands of stress. In a crisis, people often attempt to use their customary coping methods, but, in the face of a novel or extreme situation, they may try new methods. In fact, the failure of familiar or customary coping mechanisms may precipitate a crisis in and of itself or may exacerbate an existing crisis.

Coping mechanisms can be healthy or maladaptive, and they can also be effective or ineffective. During a crisis, a person may try a healthy but ineffectual method of coping. For example, talking to friends can be a helpful coping strategy. But if these friends have not had a similar experience and/or do not grasp its meanings and effects, talking to them may not help.

> *Eileen was a very resilient and social young woman. In times of crisis, she would often talk things through with her family and her boyfriend, get their input, and decide how to proceed. But after she was raped, that coping strategy no longer worked. Her family thought that she shouldn't "dwell on it," and, although her boyfriend was willing to listen, he would soon be shaking with rage at the man who did this to her.*

At the same time, it is possible to have an effective but paradoxically maladaptive response to a crisis.

> *After the fire, Lucas found that he couldn't sleep. He was nervous and jittery. He found that having a couple of drinks helped him feel less anxious and sleep through the night. While he was able to drown out the images of the fire, his drinking began to interfere with his work and family relationships and eventually led to his being fired from his job and to major marital difficulties.*

4. *The person feels overwhelmed, anxious, disoriented, or uncertain.*   When faced with a crisis, the person is thrown into a state of disequilibrium, feeling overwhelmed, disoriented, anxious, or uncertain. Unsettling reactions are manifest in statements such as:

"I can't breathe."
"I'm on the verge of a nervous breakdown."
"I feel numb, empty, nothingness."
"I'm losing it."
"My world is turned upside down."
"I can't eat, I can't think, I can't feel."
"Why me?"
"Nothing matters anymore."

These reactions to a crisis may take the form of a number of common physiological, emotional, cognitive, and relational responses.

- *Physiological:*   Tightness in chest and heart palpitations; tiredness; headaches; digestive or appetite changes; sleep problems; high blood pressure; frequent sighing, blank staring, and hand-wringing.
- *Emotional:*   Numbing; feelings of sadness, anxiety, anger, crankiness, and impatience; periods of tearfulness; loss of pleasure in people, things, and activities; feelings of estrangement or of not being like other people.
- *Cognitive:*   Distorted thinking; self-blame; inability to concentrate; narrowed perception; foggy thinking and disorganized thoughts; perseveration; expecting the worst.
- *Relational:*   Withdrawal from usual social contact to avoid too much stimulation or the expectations of others; or the opposite—having the need to be with, or in touch with, others constantly for reassurance, calming, advice, or resources; loss of confidence in authority figures, community leaders, and spiritual groups.

5. *The destabilization inherent in a crisis provides the opportunity to restabilize at a higher or lower level of functioning.*   In every crisis, there exists both danger and opportunity. In a crisis, a person can **decompensate**, engaging in self-harm and other maladaptive behaviors. However, a crisis also affords the opportunity to learn, grow, and establish new connections, behaviors, and skills that can be useful in the future. The destabilization of a crisis can result in a decline in functioning or provide an opportunity to restabilize at new levels of knowledge, resilience, and coping.

The vulnerability experienced in a crisis may also leave people open to new ideas. In addition, although a new crisis may carry with it the risk of evoking unresolved crises from the past, it can also provide an opportunity for people to rework those past issues and feelings as they emerge in the present situation (Lindemann, 1965; Parad & Caplan, 1965).

Yoshi came to see me when a lover of seven years left her with very little warning. It turned out that this was the second time someone who seemed so caring and ready to settle down had begun to cool and then left her high and dry, and suddenly seeming so cold in the process. "Where did I miss the warning signs?" she wondered miserably. Over several meetings, it became clear that she had been raised by a distant and work-involved single mom whose premature death in an automobile accident removed any chance for this client, a child at the time, to express her sadness and anger about being so left out in the cold, second fiddle to a job. She came to see that perhaps she had chosen these lovers in an unconscious replay of her feelings of abandonment by her mother. Maybe her antennae were out, searching for another person who couldn't really stay by her over time, in order to have a different ending this time. Yet here she was, "high and dry" again. A lot of our work, then, was to have her revisit her powerful longings for her mom not to leave her, but to hold her close and say that nothing would make mom happier than to spend her days with this lonely child. The client cried a lot and was eventually able to put words to her unexpressed childhood grief about her mom's distance and death.

While working with clients in crisis, it is easy to focus on the pain and suffering that people experience. Yet some clients report a new appreciation for life, new adaptive skills, and new friends or activities borne of the crisis and its aftermath. For example, someone who made a serious suicide attempt and was hospitalized for recovery and treatment may, on reflection, speak of how much value he or she now puts on life, having very nearly lost it. Perhaps visiting friends, well-wishing cards, and the support of the clinician and staff renew the client's hope that a better life can be had with support than in isolation. Maybe someone who went through a hurricane or deadly landslide and was moved to a new locale, hating that he had to go, now realizes that he has much better opportunities for work and friendships in the new locale than in the old one, and finds better housing and employment that gives him a great new start there.

Richard Tedeschi and colleagues (Tedeschi, Park, & Calhoun, 1988) coined the term **posttraumatic growth** to describe the positive changes arising from a struggle with trauma. Since their original presentation of that term, many positive psychologists and trauma theorists have written about the factors that contribute to these growth outcomes (See Calhoun & Tedeschi, 2006).

Our awareness that people can indeed rise from the ashes and use their new adaptive strengths to create greater good for themselves and others means that clinicians need to listen to the range of responses to traumatic life situations and not just anticipate that everyone will be depressed and broken for life when horrible things happen.

How one copes with a crisis is influenced by situational factors, such as material and social supports and culture, and psychological factors, such as coping capacities and resilience. **Resilience** is the capacity to adapt competently despite or because of adverse or hazardous conditions. Bonnie Benard (1997) identifies caring, communication skills, humor, and the ability to make and sustain strong peer relationships as important assets of resilient individuals and families. "Resilience is not a trait that people either have or do not have. It involves behaviors, thoughts, and actions that can be learned and developed in anyone" (APA, 2007, p. 2). Supportive and caring relationships with family, friends, and others who offer trust, encouragement, and reassurance can also strengthen resilience (APA, 2007). After 9/11, there was a surprising underuse of psychological assistance by New Yorkers directly impacted by the Twin Towers disasters. Trauma response planners underestimated the resilience of New Yorkers and their preference for using friends, family, work associates, school-based services, and survivor networks to work through the horrors they experienced and witnessed (McNally, Bryant, & Ehlers, 2003).

6. *There is a window of opportunity during a crisis when the person is particularly amenable to assistance.*   There is a period of several weeks following a crisis during which feelings of vulnerability may make people more open to growth and development. They may reach out to others for assistance or be unusually amenable to help offered by neighbors, community agencies, or emergency service providers. Crisis theorists suggest that after about eight weeks, people often will find some way to lower or eliminate their stress and tension and that help after that time is less effective. As Lydia Rapoport (1965) states, "(a) little help, rationally directed and purposively focused at a strategic time, is more effective than more extensive help given at a period of less emotional accessibility" (p. 30).

■ Crisis Intervention

Characteristics of Crisis Intervention

Crisis intervention has much in common with other forms of clinical work, yet due to the rapid and intense nature of crisis work, there are some differences.

1. *Crisis intervention is immediate.*   We know that, unless help is provided rapidly, people under significant stress can worsen their situations through impulsive action based on incorrect information, by taking their feelings out on those around them, through the use of substances to numb or express intense emotions, or by retreating into angry, hopeless isolation. For these reasons, the National Center for Posttraumatic Stress Disorder (NCPTSD) calls for post-crisis **psychological first aid**, recognizing that immediate intervention after a traumatic event can increase significantly one's coping ability.

2. *Crisis intervention is brief.*   Crisis intervention involves a rapid evaluation and time-limited provision of services to support coping and the resumption of precrisis relationships and activities. Brief interventions mobilize, reinforce, and focus clients' strengths to reduce the likelihood of becoming anxious, depressed, and helpless under stress. Key needs and activities designed to meet them are identified and carried out in short-term interventions, with more long-standing needs and problems identified but often sidelined for now. If they wish, clients may do further work of greater complexity later when the immediate crisis has passed.

3. *Crisis intervention is specifically focused.*   The clinician working with a client in crisis often provides more structure than in other types of clinical work. Once there is an agreement to meet, work immediately focuses on

eliciting a clear, organized description of precipitating events; on discussing related client interpretations and reactions; on planning action to meet any urgent needs for concrete resources, such as shelter, clothing, and food; and on thinking about clear next steps to be taken in the days and weeks ahead. We are less likely to explore for links between current events and those earlier in life unless clients introduce such links and press to discuss them to find some measure of relief.

4. *Crisis intervention may require more frequent meetings and meetings of varying durations.*   Meetings are often scheduled at shorter intervals to help calm and organize thinking, to relieve pressure from urgent feelings that might promote impulsive behaviors, and to bring about a speedier resolution of crisis-related problems. Initial sessions may be longer than usual to allow the client to tell the whole story and get some initial relief, while later sessions may take the form of brief check-ins. As the crisis abates, the intervals between sessions usually become increasingly longer, allowing clients continued support while resuming their lives.

5. *Crisis intervention may require more clinician activity and direction than usual.*   Clinicians often inform, guide, structure, and advise clients in crisis more than they normally might. We may also accompany clients to meetings or hearings to provide support or take action on behalf of clients too destabilized at present to speak or act for themselves. Because people are sometimes in crisis because they have lost their homes, loved ones, pets, or means of making a living, we are very active in helping them find shelter, food, transportation, links with loved ones near and far, assistance in finding pets, and temporary funds to sustain them until more secure arrangements can be developed.

What Clinicians Do in Crisis Intervention

The clinician's tasks are many in the immediate work of engagement and assessment. All interventions should be carried out with empathy, patience, and carefulness, so as not to further destabilize things, and with a commitment to doing all that we can to alleviate stress and feelings of dislocation from the familiar. A major activity of crisis responders in recent natural disasters such as Hurricane Katrina was to provide donated cell phones to separated survivors and arrange for the national media to show photos of separated children and elderly so that survivors could try to locate each other and reestablish supportive communication. Another important activity was to provide legal aid assistance to displaced residents who had encountered racism in some sectors of the real estate industry when seeking temporary apartments until they could rebuild back home.

1. *Help the client tell a coherent story.*   One of the first tasks of the clinician in any crisis work is to help the client organize a coherent and meaningful narrative of critical events at hand. Initial conversations can be disorganized, laden with emotion, and overwhelming for both the client and the clinician.

Initial assessment conversation can quickly clarify for the clinician and team whether a particularly confused or distressed client should be encouraged to get into vivid detail and upset feelings, or hold off on that processing for now, instead helping the client restabilize psychologically by focusing on concrete needs and actions to take to stay safe and comfortable.

In other situations in which clients' moods and states of mind signal readiness to describe and feel more intensely, we first help clients talk about triggering events by providing structure for the conversation. Gentle questions focusing on the specifics of what has happened, to whom, and with what consequences can help organize the pressured stream of feelings and information. This patiently guided conversation can be important in helping the client re-establish a sense of capacity and control, even if only by creating a coherent story for self and others.

EXAMPLE

In the following exchange, the clinician is working with a teenager who was the lone survivor of a car crash in which friends died.

Client [weeping]: I don't know what happened.

Clinician: You were in an accident.

Client: I tried to get Bobby out but I couldn't. Oh, God . . . he was . . . there was . . . I can't do this . . . they were all over the place but him . . .

Clinician: Let's stop for a second. I think it may help to just go back and start by describing the accident itself.

Client: I am so confused. There was all this blood and the horn.

Clinician: Who was in the car with you?

Client: Bobby, Grace, and Jerry.

Clinician: Where were you going?

Client: I don't know . . . wait . . . it was to the movies.

Clinician: What road were you on?

Client: Route 128 . . . near Bordenville.

Clinician: Then what happened?

Client: The accident.

Clinician: What do you remember right before it occurred?

Some postcrisis clients may be mute, shocked, and silent. Others may show "the thousand yard stare"—a numb, wide-eyed look often seen on the faces of trauma survivors. Bessel van der Kolk, Jennifer Burbridge, and Joji Suzuki (1997) note that certain biological changes affect how clients remember and talk about what occurred: "Because traumatic experiences appear to be stored primarily as somatic sensations and intense affect states, they may be least accessible to semantic processing" (p. 110).

Critical Incident Stress Debriefing (CISD) (Mitchell, 1983) consists of immediate postcrisis ventilation, meaning making, support, and suggestions for coping, and has been a popular form of working with trauma survivors and first responders to crises. Marwan Dwairy (2005) studied the use of CISD to help Palestinians with their stress reactions following terrorist events. He concluded that individual debriefing is not appropriate in collectivist cultures that are group or family focused. Individuals and groups should not be forced to attend CISD sessions.

A number of studies have identified client complaints about being overwhelmed and "retriggered" by the intensity of the CISD experience. These studies have also revealed a lack of rigor in the research intended to empirically validate CISD (Devilly, Gist, & Cotton, 2006). The Department of Veterans Affairs stated that "recent research indicates that psychological debriefing is not always an appropriate mental-health intervention" (United States Department of Veterans Affairs. 2009, p. 1). While helping clients organize their crisis stories, we need to be careful not to retraumatize them by having them dwell on the more horrific specifics of events. If they don't feel like talking about upsetting details, we don't push, but rather reassure them that as time goes on they will know best what they do and don't want to talk about.

CLIP 13.1
Helping Clients
Tell Their Stories

EXERCISE 13.2 Helping to Structure the Story

In class, role-play the initial conversations between a client and crisis worker in which the client is disorganized and overwhelmed by feelings and the clinician attempts to help the client structure a coherent story about the event. Use as many clinical skills as you think useful (gentle guiding questions, reflection, clarification, limit setting, calming, empathic statements, changing the subject).

---

2. *Focus on safety and concrete needs.* One of the urgent first tasks of crisis responders is to help people reestablish their resource base through advocacy and action on their behalf. For example, the first task in work with people who have lost everything in a fire is to help them find surviving loved ones following the rush to escape, and then work together to find shelter, food, clothing, and other needed resources.

Concrete needs also include safety from outside harm. Judith Herman (1997) notes that for those who experience violence, rape, and other forms of abuse, the first task is the establishment of safety: "This task takes precedence over all others, for no other therapeutic work can possibly succeed if safety has not been adequately secured" (p. 159). Safety work may involve making sure that the survivor of partner abuse finds a place to stay in a domestic violence shelter with an undisclosed address, that an abused child is never left alone with a known abuser, or that the victim of a sexual assault at home installs secure locks on windows and doors.

> *Jacki said it was very hard to leave Aidan and go to the shelter with her daughter Kelly because Aidan would be unable to manage alone, and, in spite of beating her, he could be so thoughtful and loving when sober. We talked many, many times about such a move before she was able to move out. What finally got to her was my underscoring that, if he seriously harmed her or Kelly, he would have to live with the consequences for the rest of his life. She was so centered on his interests that thinking of him in prison or separated from them by a court order moved her to go into the shelter. It also helped to review that he would leave them during benders for days at a time—evidence that he could "manage alone." I knew that her problems of low esteem and inability to protect herself would require longer-term work, but the pressing need was to prevent injury or death at the hands of a violent man.*

CLIP 13.2
Establishing a
Sense of Safety

3. ***Validate events and distress reactions.*** People in a state of crisis often feel uniquely upset, troubled, and different from others because of what has happened to them. They commonly wonder whether they are making up or exaggerating events or overdramatizing effects and reactions. It is thus essential to validate and normalize universal human feelings and behaviors in a crisis to help decrease feelings of differentness and worries about being mentally ill. For example, a message helpful to many men and boys from cultures that celebrate male power and invincibility is that of permission and encouragement to express their feelings directly rather than suppressing them, acting them out aggressively, or using substances to numb them. If feelings are taboo for any individual, family, or group, we can explore for current thoughts, reactions, and possible bodily complaints that may be somatic expressions of pain.

We also validate how normal it is not to want to trigger more upset feelings once people believe they are finally calmer. If the individual's culture or local gender norms discourage the expression of strong emotions, we do not push—the last thing that people need when feeling vulnerable. Rather, we can work with the client on other things while helping them understand that any upsets they feel in the future could be the normal remnants of the current crisis and that they may talk with someone in the future if they

4. ***Help clients contain feelings and reduce stress.*** When working with clients who have experienced trauma, clinicians need to help clients protect themselves from overwhelming intrusive feelings and thoughts. There is widespread misperception in popular culture that emotional catharsis brings about immediate healing. However, encouragement to ventilate tumultuous feelings may not be indicated until clients have developed better coping strategies for containment and stress reduction.

Workers should be prepared to explain to clients the wisdom of strengthening self-protecting and containing capacities before putting further pressure on already overburdened adaptive capacity. An important message to communicate is that all people need to exercise the capacities to both have and not have emotional reactions because both capacities—expression and self-restraint—are required throughout life. Expression makes sense when people are able to self-soothe and contain extremes of feeling or behavior that would otherwise destabilize them or others around them.

Stress-reducing strategies help cushion the recall of especially disturbing events such as rape, family violence, and massively distressing disasters where life and property are lost in the blink of an eye. Some people forget to breathe when stressed, but they can be coached to find safe and calming images or "places to go" in their minds to contain distress and quickly exit from distressing preoccupations. From prior spiritual or meditative practice, many people already know how to focus on and regulate their breathing to calm and reach meditative states. During any crisis, these practices can be revived and strengthened, first using them with the clinician and then resuming meditative calming on their own. We also discuss and encourage physical self-strengthening through gym activity and other exercise like skating, walking, jogging, and good diet and health practices. We then encourage the use of spiritual resources and increasing the time spent with positive people and on positive activities.

We can practice containment and relaxation strategies with the client in our meetings, so that these can also be tried with increasing success and frequency at home or on their own. These strategies include our intervening during a session to limit the subject matter, the feeling reaction, or the amount of time spent on feeling or thinking about upsetting material. Stress reduction strategies can also be taught, practiced together, and applied outside of the meetings, with reports back about the strategies' personal or cultural appropriateness and ease or difficulty of use.

I generally tell my clients to start with those relaxing/soothing skills that have worked for them in the past. If they typically use jogging, hot baths, and TV shows to relax or take care of themselves, I encourage them to do that rather than take up a new skill or activity. When faced with the stress of a crisis, clients don't need the added stress of learning a new activity. On the other hand, for some clients, focusing on a new skill may help to distract them from perseverating on the crisis. It depends on the individual client.

EXAMPLES

Client A: I just keep having these images in my mind of the tornado ripping everything apart, and our sheep flying through the air and then turning up dead, miles away.

Clinician A: Whenever you get those images, you might try focusing on your breath and your breathing. Imagine a calm and comfortable place of complete safety. Keep enlarging this in your mind, screening out all concerns. It's a way of distracting and refocusing your thoughts. The slowing and lengthening of your breathing also calms anxiety all by itself. Let's try it together.

* * *

Client B: I can't sleep at night. I feel anxious and scared of being alone in the house.

Clinician B: That's hard. Let's think together about things you could do to feel safer. First tell me what you are doing prior to sleep.

Client B: I watch TV.

Clinician B: That might be a good idea if it isn't violent. Does it help?

Client B: Not really. I find I can't go to sleep.

Clinician B: Doing arduous exercises about an hour before bed can help your body relax. Exercise induces endorphins that calm and soothe.

EXERCISE 13.3 Eliciting and Containing Feelings

In groups of three or four, rotate the roles of interviewer and client. Do two different role-plays. In the first, the client recounts a traumatic event, displaying very little affect. The clinician attempts to elicit feelings and validate the feelings as normal. In the second role-play, the client is dramatically spilling thoughts and feelings in a relatively incoherent way. The clinician practices helping the client to contain and self-soothe.

Whenever feasible, we encourage clients in crisis to try to avoid or reduce contact with situations and people who introduce more stress into their lives. Since some work and home stresses are natural and unavoidable, we can suggest ways of minimizing hassles by focusing on one task at a time, getting through one hour or day at a time, and giving maximum attention to activities with others that are likely to minimize conflict. Ironically, volunteering to help others in crisis actually helps people feel better because the recipients are usually grateful for the help and the activity gets them out of their isolation and usual routines. The skill is in finding the right activities that affirm and soothe the self without unduly taxing it.

Following the hurricane that tore through their area and left many homeless, Maxine practically had to be dragged by her sister to help serve turkey dinners to senior citizens on Thanksgiving Day. She felt she had nothing left to give to anybody after many weeks in a shelter and a bout of the flu. She agreed to go and later said it was the best thing she ever did, because she had forgotten that some people were worse off than she was and were thankful for any little thing people did for them. She later went back and offered to do Bible study one day a week to take her mind off things, and reading the Testament with others helped her remember how calming that was.

CLIP 13.3
Stress Reduction

5. *Quickly establish a baseline of previous functional capacity.* To develop a sound assessment of current client assets and set realistic goals, we also take a brief history of client relational patterns, educational and work levels, coping strategies, and crisis management experiences prior to the present crisis. Clients' past aspirations and plans, ideas about self, and expectations for the future are also important to elicit, as they often inform the client's current reactions and capacities for readjustment following a destabilization. Since helplessness, confusion, and inadequacy are common reactions to destabilizing events, it is important to ask clients whether these attitudes, feelings, or self-assessments are new or were a pattern prior to the triggering event. If new, they may benefit from focus and countering by the clinician, whereas if they indicate ongoing personality patterns, they may require more work at another time.

This rapidly gathered information constitutes a functional baseline with which to compare important aspects of client functioning during and following the current crisis. For example, if a man is newly using substances to calm himself for sleep since the onset of a crisis, planning and goals will be different than if he had a history of episodic problem drinking unrelated to particular stress levels.

6. *Focus on the effects of the crisis on relationships and feelings of relatedness.* Because people in crisis often isolate themselves to avoid further emotional stimulation or conflict, clinicians should periodically check in with them about the nature and extent of their relationships with family, friends, and others. It is not unusual for clients to become irritable or sad when encouraged to have more contact with people. At times, relating makes them remember people or things they have lost, so they may feel it is wiser to hunker down alone to avoid remembering.

A good relational experience with a clinician or other compassionate friend or helper is one of the best antidotes for isolation because it can rekindle longings for more contact with others. If ever there were a need for a "holding environment," it is with people recovering from crisis and trauma who have for all intents and purposes given up on themselves and others. If we provide unfailing support, positive regard, carefulness of approach, and sensitivity to mood and timing, it can help restore the client's understanding that, while many bad things happen to people, all people are not bad.

Additionally, the very focus on relating itself brings the importance of human ties back to mind and offers clients a chance to grieve for their losses as well as to entertain fleeting thoughts of restoring positive ties with others over time. In this work, we listen for subtle signs of disengagement or reengagement (e.g., spending too much time alone or beginning to come out of one's shell one step at a time). Tiny signs of progress can be missed unless there is routine checking-in about relationships and activities involving more time outside the home. People who feel damaged often need a longer time to take the risk of reconnecting more openly with others, especially if they have to explain the crisis event to others before reaching some level of understanding, self-acceptance, and peace about it.

7. *Involve family and friends in the intervention.*   Friends and family (biological and chosen) can be rich sources of information about the crisis and about the presence or absence of natural helping resources currently available to the client. Resilient people often return rather rapidly to familiar routines and responsibilities if these make sense and are still available in a daily life altered by crisis. Family, friends, and fellow members of faith communities can all reach out, support, and assist crisis-stressed loved ones in reintegrating themselves into the familiar, thus decreasing feelings of estrangement and "being ill." However, crises may both stress and isolate clients from their usual bases of support by virtue of some stigma, fear, or overwhelming sense of separateness caused by triggering events.

> *After some grief work with me right after the loss of her husband, Ida went back to work pretty quickly because she loved lunches with her fellow workers at the counseling center. Yet, even though music had always comforted her, she couldn't bring herself to sing in her church choir again at this time because she wanted to "be mad at God a little longer" for taking her husband from her at too young an age.*

If the crisis is related to or caused by family or friends (e.g., domestic violence, sexual abuse, rejection by family for being gay), it may not be appropriate to involve them in the work. It is important to assess with the client whether including family or friends in the work would be more distressing than productive.

Charles Figley (1995) observes that significant others in the person's life may experience **emotional contagion,** that is, they may "catch" or absorb the loved one's distress and be in crisis as well. Thus, we try to involve significant others early in any crisis work when family members and friends of the person in crisis may also need support, information, and an opportunity to discuss events and reactions.

8. *Focus on strengths.*   A common problem of people in crisis is that they easily forget their strengths and reliable resources, especially if these have not initially led to the immediate resolution of crisis conditions. We thus ask about client strengths—small or large—demonstrated prior to the crisis. We communicate the normalizing beliefs that crisis discombobulates everyone and that the resulting confusion and disequilibrium are not a confirmation of personal deficits or problems too huge to resolve.

Workers responding quickly and knowledgably to crises have to be careful to maintain a strengths perspective even while using benign authority to create a sense of calm, orderly process, and hope for change. Overwhelmed and exhausted people often feel better and more competent if they can assist in their own recovery or need-meeting efforts and not just stand by while turmoil unfolds around them. Furthermore, if we become too directive or controlling, clients' feelings of being overwhelmed and out of control may be reinforced rather than dissipated.

9. *Help the client make meaning of the events.*   Clinicians help clients use their cognitive skills to make meaning of their crisis experiences. We noted earlier that one of the first tasks is to help the client tell a coherent story. Later, the clinician helps the client create a fuller understanding of the events and situations around the crisis. This often involves challenging perceptual distortions as well as helping clients feel in charge of their lives.

Locus of control refers to one's perceptions of personal power and place in the world. It also concerns the extent to which people see themselves as capable of effectively influencing outcomes and accomplishing their desired goals. When people experience a crisis, when their perceptions and expectations of themselves and their world are shattered, they frequently experience life as essentially out of their control or as controlled by cruel fate, a god, or a karmic destiny playing itself out. People often ask themselves "Why me?" and come up with answers that are a fulfillment of their worst suspicions about themselves. Survivors of sexual assault, for example, often describe themselves as damaged goods and can feel somehow responsible for the assault ("I should have left when the others did," "I shouldn't have gone there that late at night"). Lone survivors of accidents almost universally struggle with the question of why they survived and others ("nicer than me") did not.

As we do routinely in our work to help people alter distorted beliefs and perceptions, we can gently challenge harsh posttraumatic self-judgments by exploring the evidence on which they are based, by asking for alternative explanations of why events happened, by actively suggesting other interpretations or implications of events, and by sharing stories of anonymous survivors of similar events to illustrate different conclusions for the client to consider.

> *I find it tricky to talk about others who have been in a similar experience because it may make my clients worry about confidentiality. Clients may worry that "if she is telling me about someone else's story, what does she tell other clients about my story?" Stressing anonymity helps somewhat, but I have chosen to say, "I read about people in a similar situation once. . . ."*

Clients also have to find a way to integrate the crisis experience into their lives and identities so that it becomes one part of their story instead of the whole story. Some people may not be able to get beyond the destabilizing event, but many others can be helped by individual, family, or group work after the initial crisis is resolved. For example, the U.S. Defense Department has sponsored effective trials of online cognitive behavioral self-management treatment to help traumatized veterans work through the traumas of war (Litz et al., 2007).

C L I P   13.4
Making Meaning
of Events

10. *Maintain a here-and-now focus on the present crisis.*   Because of the compound nature of many crises, the discussion of events, reactions, and interpretations often leads naturally to past crises being rekindled by the present one. For example, a stressful job change may remind a man of an earlier crisis he went through when switching from a public to a private high

school. Being resettled in public housing near a noisy airport may rekindle a Bosnian family's frightening memories of planes pulverizing their village. Our goal is to find the right balance between here-and-now focus and there-and-then exploration so that clients do not become overwhelmed by the powerful combination of past and present review.

We may speak of past losses if such expression will not destabilize current efforts to cope. Judgments are formed by evaluating the client's emotional stability when talking about the past. If clients can tolerate linkages between the past and present, they need to feel free to grow at times through making useful connections between feelings now and feelings then or through comparing adaptive strategies available in the past with more (or less) sophisticated and helpful resources available now. A clinician's main consideration is to try to confine work to a focus on present concerns, needs, and reactions so that situations are resolved as quickly and constructively as possible.

11. *Check regularly for suicidal or other self-harming behaviors.* We regularly check in with clients in crisis about their distress levels, moods, and preoccupying thoughts. We listen for signs of despair, hopelessness, wishes to escape or to rejoin lost ones, or for mentions of means of self-harm such as pills, weapons, risky behaviors, or fantasies of driving into bridge abutments or jumping off nearby cliffs. We are also alert for behaviors such as suddenly giving away possessions or money or suddenly presenting as strangely relieved and happy—sometimes the result of a decision to end life. Discussions with supervisors may need to be augmented by consultations with appropriate psychiatric staff, with an eye to possible hospitalization if the client remains suicidal. We discuss suicide more thoroughly later in this chapter.

> *When her husband died suddenly, Micah ingested so much aspirin that it made her sick and she threw up. Interestingly, she did this at the time her best friend was to pick her up for lunch, which suggested to me that she was at least ambivalent about killing herself— a good sign. However, when she was subsequently hospitalized, I did note with the inpatient physician that I thought her gesture had been a serious one and asked if he could only give her very limited prescriptions for antidepressants to make it harder for her to use the medication to kill herself.*

12. *Use rituals and other marker events.* An important reintegrative tool that clinicians have learned from people undergoing recovery from traumatic shock is the importance of rituals in restoring feelings of agency, dignity, and connections. Some survivors and relatives of those lost in the 9/11 attacks have helped design memorial sites and tributes honoring those lost. Survivors of terrorist bombings and deadly earthquakes and tsunamis have created remembrance ceremonies by weaving thousands of flowers, sympathy notes, and images of the deceased into fences around affected areas as an ongoing expression of grief and respect. Some 9/11 survivors have participated in memorial plans that honor their dead. Websites about murdered hate crime victims offer opportunities to participate in virtual rituals as well

as providing education about hate crimes. The honoring ceremonies given to deceased veterans as their caskets return from abroad and are buried with dignity and grief are further examples of rituals that help people remember, honor, and cope.

The AIDS Memorial Quilt has achieved a similar result in bringing loved ones and survivors together to honor those lost and to connect thousands of people in support of programs and research to improve victims' lives and chances of survival. Annual services that celebrate the lives of national heroes like the Reverend Martin Luther King, Jr., Cesar Chavez, and Rosa Parks also serve as uniting experiences and beacons of hope for those still struggling for respect, rights, and improved economic opportunities.

> *When a longtime school administrator died last year, two colleagues devised a touching ritual in which her picture, flowers, and candles were placed on a table around which a large group collected in a remembrance circle, each recalling aloud something precious about the deceased.*

E X E R C I S E 13.4 Rituals for Healing

In class, discuss rituals you have participated in or learned about that help survivors of trauma honor losses and begin to heal. What thinking and planning needs to take place before enacting a ritual? How will you decide who should participate and in what manner? Can you think of any rituals you witnessed that did not appear to serve their stated purpose? How would you have carried out the ritual differently? Has your family passed on to you any rituals of healing that you would like to share with the group?

---

13. ***Refer to mutual aid groups.***   It often helps people in crisis to speak with and learn from others like themselves who have been through similar ordeals. Joyce West Stevens (1997) underscores the importance of helping African American adolescent females develop and sustain strong kinship and reference group connections as they deal with societal devaluations (microaggressions) based on racism and gender bias. Women with new breast cancer diagnoses can benefit from talking with others in Reach to Recovery Programs, and men who have experienced heart attacks may utilize Heart to Heart groups in rehabilitation settings. The very process of mutual aid—the exchange of caring, coping tips, and reinforcing support for persistence—is revitalizing for all members as they feel themselves able to help others in spite of their own stress and self-doubt (Shulman, 2009).

It has become common for relatives of people lost in jetliner crashes to form support groups following the crash. These groups not only place flowers at the crash site and devise religious services and memorials, but they also have advocated successfully to get airlines to improve their notification and support processes following airline accidents.

In areas without such group programs, clinicians can start mutual aid groups simply by asking clients who need support and education if they would be interested in meeting with other affected people about ways they cope with a shared crisis. Very often, if child or elder care and transportation are provided as needed, men and women are ready to give support groups a try.

These groups are now more frequently referenced in the media, creating more awareness of their benefits in reducing isolation and increasing awareness of resources and coping strategies to help with stress. Katherine Briar-Lawson (1998) estimates that some 25 million people in the United States are served by the "giving and benefiting ethos" of self-help groups promoting "non-elite and non-hierarchical peer power" (p. 546).

14. *Prepare the client for ending.*   Usually, crisis intervention is understood by participants to be purposely short term. As the work progresses, the clinician should mention preparation for ending more frequently. He or she moves to a less active stance, encouraging the client to assume more responsibility for the meetings and to devise problem-solving strategies for use in the future. Crisis intervention usually ends when clients have returned to precrisis levels and modes of functioning and have reestablished a reliable base of adequate resources, social support, and work or other meaningful activities.

Bonds can be unusually strong in crisis intervention, so both clinicians and clients should carefully attend to the ending work. Discussions at ending can include honoring the relationship and the work they have done together, as well as their meaning to each participant. They should discuss the client's plans for the future, as well as the support and resources that the client has established. (See Chapter 14 for a fuller discussion of endings and transitions.)

The multiple disasters caused by the 2005 back-to-back hurricanes Katrina and Rita have demonstrated that this benign concept of a well-planned ending to crisis intervention is not always accurate. While thousands of people eventually received housing and other resources from shelters and relief centers around the United States, many of those who survived remain in what might rightly be called a "second state" of posttraumatic marginalization, outrage, and despair.

15. *Provide follow-up and ongoing support.*   Clinicians and crisis response teams should plan periodic check-ins with "recovered" clients to assess well-being and coping capacities over time. Clients may also reach out to clinicians at anniversaries of important crises, such as deaths or disasters.

Cindy called me every fall, not mentioning what I knew—that this time of year was the anniversary of the deaths of both her mother and father. Often we simply caught up by phone, with her disclosing a new achievement or work stress getting her down. This year, I invited her to come in and see me, and she talked about the fact that I seemed like "good family" to her, and she hated to think of me dying or moving away "out of reach" when I retire, a prospect she's aware of. She herself could tie these feelings into missing her dad, her closest supporter of many years, and she was able to experience a little more sadness with me over his death. We reviewed with delight her good work in maintaining a happy marriage over many years and the presence of a few really good friends in her life. I made sure she understood how much I've enjoyed working with her and that I am always glad to hear from her about how she is. To ease an eventual transition, I referred her to a younger colleague for some specialized work I don't do, and she agreed.

When Ongoing Clients Experience Crises

Crises can and do arise in the lives of ongoing clients. When they do, they often (not always) displace other work at hand. Clinicians need to shift gears to attend to the crisis, support coping, and mobilize any resources that might assist the client's adaptation to the new circumstances and challenges. Often clients use what has been learned in ongoing work to manage crises more quickly and resourcefully. We can also help them find similarities between a current crisis and upsetting situations they have resolved previously so that the current challenge feels less daunting or unmanageable.

■ Suicide Prevention as a Special Form of Crisis Intervention

Suicide as a Global Issue

The World Health Organization (WHO) estimates that a million or more people commit suicide each year, with a death by suicide every 40 seconds. More people die from suicide than from armed conflict. (WHO, 2008, p. 1). In the past, suicide rates were highest among elderly males, but today, suicide rates among young people make them the highest-risk group in one-third of both developing and developed countries (WHO, 2008).

The gravity of the aggregate suicide data is heightened when we consider the severe worldwide economic downturn of 2008 and its global impact. Millions have lost their jobs, income sources, homes, savings, retirement safety nets, and bright prospects for the future. These economic events have unfolded simultaneously with numerous destabilizing wars, natural disasters, and desperate population migrations in Asia, Africa, and the Middle East. Loved ones have been lost to famine, disease, disasters, interethnic violence, and economic stress-related suicides and homicides. Confidence in larger systems, political leadership, and once-reliable institutions has declined.

Feelings of traumatic loss, hopelessness, and helplessness and loss of reasons for living have been correlated with high risk for suicidal thinking and behaviors. This is especially true when combined with easy access to toxic substances or firearms, and/or major thought or mood disorders (Gunnell & Lewis, 2005; Jobes, Rudd, Overholser, & Joiner, 2008; Knox, Conwell, & Caine, 2004; McKenzie, Serfaty, & Crawford, 2003).

Suicide in the United States

The Centers for Disease Control (CDC) report that there are some 32,000 suicides annually in the United States (CDC, 2005). The clinical significance of this rate is heightened when we consider that there are 25 suicide attempts for every suicide completion. A completed suicide impacts an estimated six family members or friends, referred to as *suicide survivors,* who may need clinical follow-up themselves for the traumatic effects of sudden suicidal loss (American Association of Suicidology, 2008).

Suicide rates vary by gender, age, race, and ethnicity. Males complete suicide at a rate four times that of females, but females attempt suicide three times more often than males. Firearms are the most commonly used method of suicide among males and poisoning is the most common method of suicide for females (CDC, 2005). The highest suicide rates occur among White elderly males aged 75 and older who are seriously ill and/or isolated, and adolescents aged 15–24, at risk due to sexual orientation identity struggles, bullying, lack of family and social support, and substance use. Thousands of veterans returning from international war zones with psychological and physical trauma and disabilities are also at risk for suicide. The suicide rate among U.S. veterans has continued to rise over the last four years. By 2008, it was at its highest level in three decades (Alvarez, 2009).

While it is important to know about group risk factors, Paula Clayton and Tracey Auster (2008) note that "individuals of all races, creeds, incomes, and educational levels die by suicide. There is no typical victim" (p. 16). This understanding underscores the need for clinicians and prevention specialists to work to prevent suicides through macro-level prevention activities around the globe and by learning how to carry out effective suicide risk assessments and timely interventions.

It is highly likely that at some point most clinicians will encounter a situation in which a distraught client or a member of a highly stressed group contemplates suicide (that is, has **suicidal ideation**) or attempts suicide (sometimes called **parasuicide**) as an exit from what he or she believes to be unbearable situations that they cannot alter or influence. Assessing risk and attempting to prevent suicide are among the most daunting tasks a clinician faces.

Key Issues in Working with the Suicidal Client

1. *Prepare for the unexpected.*   An ethical standard across the human service professions is that professionals should not take on client situations that are beyond their competence. You would not join a crisis team or work on a suicide hotline without training. So prepare yourself with knowledge about suicide risk assessment and intervention steps, because we can never know when suicide might arise in our caseloads. For example, you might be working with clients on daily life issues when a crisis develops unexpectedly,

hidden suicidal ideation is newly revealed, and you must respond appropriately, in concert with others, to this new challenge.

> *Clarice came to see me about her work situation. She was having difficulties with her*
> *boss. She did not seem depressed, hopeless, or suicidal when we started working together.*
> *However, during our brief work together, her husband left her and she became suicidal.*

You should not delay learning more about crisis and suicide interventions until you are suddenly faced with a serious crisis situation. Ask your
supervisor and instructors what steps you should take if one of your clients suddenly expresses suicidal thoughts or intentions. Read about interventions such as we are presenting here, and attend professional workshops
and presentations on these subjects in order to begin to prepare for the unexpected. Do not be reassured by an agency colleague's certainty that "we
never get suicidal people here, so don't worry about that." No setting or
population is immune.

2. *Use empirically supported assessment tools and protocols to assess for risk factors, warning signs, and protective factors.*   Rudd (Jobes, Rudd, Overholser, &
Joiner, 2008) distinguishes between suicide warning signs and suicide risk factors. "As with other conditions, like heart attack and stroke, **warning signs**
connote imminent risk, risk that is evident over the next few minutes, hours,
or days. In contrast, **risk factors** are related to what can best be described as
lifetime risk, with the time periods covered in the extant literature ranging anywhere from a year to several decades (cf. Rudd, Joiner & Rajab, 2004)" (p. 409).

Several risk factors for suicide include membership in a high risk group,
such as adolescents struggling with issues of sexual orientation, victims of
parental rejection or gay bashing, disabled and traumatized veterans returning from war, victims of traumatic loss, multiple attempters of suicide, and clients with multiple DSM diagnoses. (Sommers-Flanagan & Sommers-Flanagan,
2009; Jobes et al., 2008).

Alcohol and substance abuse increase risk of suicidal behavior by reducing one's ability to inhibit impulsive behavior, reducing adaptive problem
solving, exacerbating ongoing stressors, and leading potentially supportive
persons to withdraw from the individual (Freeman, Martin, & Ronen, 2007).
Other risk factors include "living in areas where there is low concentration
of one's own group; socioeconomic stress; thwarted aspirations; racism; hostile environments and acculturation stresses; difficulty with identity formation; loss of religious or social affiliations; and loss of family and community
support" (McKenzie, Serfaty, & Crawford, 2003, p. 101).

David Jobes and colleagues (2008) have identified "suicide warning
signs [that] include hopelessness, rage, reckless behavior, a feeling of being
trapped, increased alcohol/drug use, social withdrawal, anxiety/agitation,
dramatic mood change, and the lack of a sense of purpose in life" (p. 406).
They also believe that specific hopelessness and lack of reasons for living are
greater signs of suicidal risk than severe depression.

There are a number of validated assessment tools with which to measure
suicide potential, degree of risk, and counterbalancing reasons for living.

Common measurements include the Scale for Suicide Ideation (SSI) (Beck, Kovacs, & Weissman, 1979) and the Linehan Reasons for Living Scale (RFL) (Linehan, Goodstein, Neilsen, & Chiles, 1983).

In 2003, the American Association of Suicidology (AAS) gathered together a team of internationally renowned clinical researchers for the purpose of agreeing on and describing common warning signs of suicide. They developed the mnemonic **IS PATH WARM** for use in evaluating suicide warning signs. This framework can assist clinicians in eliciting clients' more private, inner-circle revelations about risky behaviors, worrisome states of mind, and/or clear preparations for suicide (see Box 13.1).

Sommers-Flanagan and Sommers-Flanagan wisely state that "the goal of a comprehensive suicide assessment interview is not to predict suicide, but to predict risk and then manage the risk effectively" (2009, p. 254).

As noted earlier, if a client reveals suicidal thinking, intent, or self-harming behaviors, the interviewer must calmly explore whether clients are having or have had suicidal thoughts, intentions, plans, and means, or have made suicide

---

BOX 13.1 American Association of Suicidology's Suicide Warning Signs

I	Ideation	Expressed or communicated ideation
		Threatening to hurt or kill him/herself, or talking of wanting to hurt or kill him/herself; and/or
		Looking for ways to kill him/herself by seeking access to firearms, available pills, or other means;
		Talking or writing about death, dying or suicide, when these actions are out of the ordinary
S	Substance Abuse	Increased substance (alcohol or drug) use
P	Purposelessness	No reason for living; no sense of purpose in life
A	Anxiety	Anxiety, agitation, unable to sleep or sleeping all the time
T	Trapped	Feeling trapped (like there's no way out)
H	Hopelessness	Hopelessness
W	Withdrawal	Withdrawal from friends, family, and society
A	Anger	Rage, uncontrolled anger, seeking revenge
R	Recklessness	Acting reckless or engaging in risky activities, seemingly without thinking
M	Mood Change	Dramatic mood changes

Reprinted with permission of American Association of Suicidology (2008).

attempts in the past. To find out more about possible suicide plans, Sommers-Flanagan and Sommers-Flanagan suggest the use of the acronym **SLAP** (2009, p. 265) to guide questions about the suicide plans:

Specificity
Lethality
Actual availability of imagined method
Proximity of social helping resources (p. 265)

Protective factors lower the risk of suicide. These factors include "a satisfying family and social life . . . constructive employment or use of leisure time . . . purpose and meaning for living . . . religious and ethnic beliefs that provide hope" (Collins & Collins, 2005, p. 124). Focusing only on suicide-related content can get both the client and the clinician down, and can obscure hopeful and energizing aspects of the client's life. Ask clients about any special relationships, beliefs, affiliations, activities, spiritual practices—even heroes, models for living, or TV characters or series—that may buffer him or her against acting out suicidal thoughts or fantasies. Ask whether there were other times in life when the client may have enjoyed living. Were there even little things the client accomplished, or people who were proud and encouraging of him or her? Pets that diminished loneliness and were grateful for caregiving? A favorite song, poem, book, or inspirational setting that were invigorating?

Sometimes people are surprised by the way their thinking has constricted due to depression or anxieties, and that they've just walled off or out their best protective people or strategies. You may have to persist for some time in order to elicit these positives. If you continue with these clients over time, be sure to bring up these pluses whenever it is fitting to do so, to keep them in the client's mind and help sustain them during difficult times. Sometimes clients benefit from bringing in photos of people, pets, or happy travel destinations and describing the good these represent.

> *I visited Luleen in a hospital psych unit where she'd gone voluntarily that because she felt like killing herself to end many years of depressive feelings that really brought her "down into the pits." I asked her what had stopped her from killing herself with the gun she'd held in her hand for an hour or so, thinking about it. She finally said she thought what kept her alive was thinking of her little boy and how horrible it would be for him to see her dead: "Now, he is the one thing I live for and get as much back from as I put out." I said that he's more than that—he's also not depressed, not anxious . . . is really smart, funny, and full of himself, and that these traits are the result of her care as she raised him and showed him a different way to live than people had shown her. And she should be very happy about these qualities she imbued in him and nurtured. She said she is so busy chastising herself that she forgets the good she's capable of. I then brought up all the homeless people who thanked her for her help to them as a volunteer on a health bus—the men were always giving her little things to thank her.*

3. *Directly address suicidal ideation.*   Some clinicians have worried that bringing up the topic of suicide and asking detailed questions about risk factors may trigger suicide. Such fears have no empirical support (Jobes et al., 2008). It may be that many clinicians are fearful of asking about suicide

because they may hear more about it from the client than they feel prepared to deal with, or that they'll be in over their heads. In fact, many clients are relieved to talk about their suicidal thoughts and impulses. A clinician who calmly explores for suicide ideation may help the client feel confident that the clinician is accepting of clients contemplating suicide, isn't afraid to talk about suicide, and knows that talking about it is not the same as carrying it out.

EXAMPLE: ELABORATING CONTENT ABOUT THINKING AND PREPARATION

Clinician: You've said several times that you don't feel like going on.

Client: Why should I? Mariasia and I were joined spiritually. I just want to be with her again . . . really, be with her forever.

Clinician: And how do you picture that happening?

Client: Well . . . if I took an overdose. I feel her presence around me at night. I would just join her, is all.

Clinician: How often are you thinking about this joining her in death?

Client: I guess a lot. At night, really. And I have enough medication to do an overdose, if you really want to know.

Clinician: How much medication do you have?

Client: About 70 tablets I've saved up over the months.

Clinician: How ready are you to do this?

Client: I think about it a lot, but I'm not ready yet. It would kill our daughter.

In this example, the clinician takes her time eliciting detail about the nature, strength, specificity, and likelihood of suicidal wishes and intention to enact them. As the story develops, she will ask about many other things, including any past attempts at self-harm, any previous evaluations for depression or suicidality, any other ways the client has thought of killing himself, and any mitigating positive factors other than the daughter. The client's ambivalence is already starting to show in his caring about the consequences for his 20-year-old should he kill himself. Sometimes people are so severely depressed that they aren't able to care about those left behind after suicide. This client shows caring in the moment—but that doesn't mean that he may not act anyway, on a lonely or longing impulse if, for example, the daughter goes away on holiday. We simply emphasize here the importance of gently following clues in a client's story, into the middle circle of risk information gathering—a painstaking process of patiently and kindly staying close to the details in the client's story.

Some clients come voluntarily and speak freely and with worry about what has brought them to the point of thinking about killing themselves. Others may be depressed and irritated about questions asked, or may be in a "what's the use of talking?" mood. Others may be so tired from sleep-blocking rumination and ambivalence that they wait for the clinician to lead them and have little to say in response. If coming from cultures in which self-harm is taboo, individuals and families may be intensely uncomfortable, embarrassed, and even in denial and temporarily dismissive about the possibility of self-harm by a family member.

> *A family from India was to visit their daughter at an American Ivy League college when the parents got a call from the college health service. The social worker there reported that the daughter had attempted to overdose in the dorm the previous evening, but was found by her roommate soon after. The daughter, who was old enough to make her own decisions, was now on a psychiatric unit at a nearby hospital. The worker asked the parents if they had seen serious depression or suicidal behavior in their daughter before, and they were adamant that no one in the family or its history had ever had "mental problems like this." They insisted it must be school stress that was prompting such behavior, and they decided that they shouldn't come for a visit until the daughter was "healthy" again. When the student was discharged and came to see the social worker for follow-up therapy, she recounted that she had been depressed throughout her secondary education because she felt unattractive. Her father had paid for her to see a psychologist in Mumbai but told her to "tell no one about it" so as not to shame the family. She now felt that the parents' refusal to come over at this time was a "little punishment for being depressed out loud."*

4. *Offer both empathy and hope.* People who are suicidal commonly wonder whether they are making up or exaggerating events or overdramatizing effects and reactions. For example, suicidal clients may suddenly ask questions such as: "Am I sounding self-pitying?" "Do you think I'm just trying to get attention by threatening to kill myself?" "If I'm crazy enough to want to die at my young age, wouldn't it be better to just have me gone from the Earth?" or "I don't have a single reason to keep living—isn't that pathetic?"

Many people are accustomed to friends or loved ones telling them things like, "Everybody has problems, we're lucky to be alive," "What's done is done, crying over spilled milk is useless, let's move on," or "How about the rest of us, how do you think we feel when we see you wanting to kill yourself?" The clinician can make empathically aligned comments such as, "So much has been taken away from you in the blink of an eye." or "I'm so glad you told me about how hopeless you're feeling today. With so much going wrong, I can see why a person might feel like giving up, even though there could be some options he hasn't had time to think about like I have."

In addition to empathy and openness to the client's unhappy story, be direct and honest with the client about being moved or touched by the content you are hearing as the story proceeds. Sometimes sympathy can be as important as empathy in helping clients feel heard and appreciated when under siege by powerful feelings of despair: "My heart goes out to you in your struggling about life and death—I can feel the power of the struggle right here in the room, so it must be terrible for you to feel it most of the time."

As in all crisis intervention, validation of the clients' struggles, dilemmas, and hardships conveys respect and appreciation of the fact that they came in to consult with someone instead of killing themselves and ending their pain.

> *I was working with a client who was quite hopeless about her life "ever getting better."*
> *I reflected her pain and hopelessness, but I told her that while there was no guarantee*
> *her life would get better, there was a guarantee that if she killed herself her life definitely*
> *would not get better. I was quite hopeful that if we worked together she had a possibil-*
> *ity of happiness. I realize that I had to use this approach selectively because some people*
> *believe that committing suicide will transport them to a better life.*

5. *Focus on immediate safety.*   Get the specifics of where and with whom the client is living, and the contact information of people who may be willing to help buffer against suicidal acts and thinking in isolation. If the assessment shows a high risk of suicide, try to get the client's immediate permission to phone at least one "emergency contact" with whom both clinician and client can talk, describing the client's state of mind and its implications for the return home. If it helps allay security concerns, try to ensure that the client can live with supportive others for a time, unless and until the situation is clarified or resolved satisfactorily.

Clinicians who think a client may be actively suicidal should get a consultation with a supervisor or psychiatrist. David and Diane Sue (2008) urge that a suicidal client not be left alone in an interview room while the clinician leaves to get consultation—at least until it has been determined by consultants that there is no immediate risk of self-harm.

> *I assessed a 35-year-old anxious male who came as a walk-in at our psych clinic. I*
> *thought he was at risk for suicide and asked the psychiatrist to evaluate him for po-*
> *tential hospitalization. The psychiatrist evaluated him as having bipolar disorder and*
> *agreed to the hospitalization that the client was seeking in order to calm himself down.*
> *The client asked me if he could use my office phone to make one short call to his mother*
> *before going to the hospital. I said, "Of course, I'll just step outside so you can talk*
> *privately," thinking to show him some respect. The moment I stepped outside, I could*
> *hear him lock my office door. I could hear him loudly open my window—I was terrified.*
> *I called out to him: "What are you doing? Please give us a chance to help you before you*
> *hurt yourself." The secretary seated by my office heard the commotion and called secu-*
> *rity. Luckily they arrived in time to open the door and prevent the client from jumping.*
> *I never left a suicidal client alone again!*

Bring the client with you to the consultation and encourage his or her active participation in the ensuing conversation. Clients' participation in decision making often reduces fears or suspicions about what professionals are saying behind their backs and what will happen next. An invitation for him or her to join in also implies that the client must and can be active in planning and problem resolution, an idea that can help undercut hopeless or helpless feelings. Moreover, if the consultant appears to the client to look and sound older and wiser than the younger or less seasoned clinician, that appraisal can be a source of relief as the client feels "in good hands," or "having two shrinks, not just one." Sometimes a client may ask to have the consultant as his therapist rather than an intern or less experienced clinician, and such may be the arrangement if all parties believe this change is in the best interest of the client.

> *My middle-aged male psychiatrist-supervisor agreed to take on an 80-year-old Irish American suicidal male newly released from an inpatient unit because the client felt more comfortable with and better served by a male psychiatrist than a female social worker, whom he saw as a potential welfare worker in his country of origin. Ego should not be a factor where working with suicide is concerned.*

Though agencies and hospitals may still try to enlist the client in signing a "No Suicide Contract," Jobes and colleagues (2008) critique such a contract as "an utterly inadequate intervention for suicide risk" (p. 406). David and Diane Sue (2008) state that "'no-harm' agreements, even when willingly signed by the client, are by no means a guarantee against suicidal behavior" (p. 295).

If a client is at serious risk of harming himself or herself, we should discuss the possibility of hospitalization with the client. We have both a legal and ethical responsibility to attempt to protect clients from self-harm, even if it is against the client's will. If on assessment the clinician and consultant concur that the client is not safe, but the client refuses hospitalization, the client may be required to undergo **legal commitment** to an appropriate psychiatric facility for further assessment and treatment for a legally specified period of time before mandatory court reevaluation.

In terms of **risk management,** you should document in detail the important information gleaned from your assessment with the client, and to these chart notes attach a copy of the summary that the consultant will provide after the conjoint consultation. If you are a student, make certain your supervisor reads and cosigns any ongoing interview notes, diagnostic conclusions, and intervention recommendations and cosigns anything you add to the chart going forward. This serves as validation that you are being supervised by qualified staff and are not working alone on a matter as serious as suicide.

6. *In suicide prevention work, follow the intervention recommendations given you by your consultants and supervisors;* don't decide that you know best. In suicide emergencies, seek immediate consultation about what to do. Especially when you have worked with someone for a while and have a good relationship, it is easy to think that you know the client better than anyone else and can tell whether the client would actually commit suicide or not. This is not possible for anyone to do.

> *A nurse at our inpatient unit had watched over a man in confinement for many weeks. He was psychotic and had tried to blind himself and cut himself with plastic dinner knives. Now he'd been stripped of all clothes and was in a padded room so that he couldn't injure his head. On a freezing cold night in winter, he convinced the nurse to give him a warm blanket. She knew this was forbidden, but she proceeded to do it because she could feel the cold of the room. He thanked her profusely and warmed up, relieving her. Later, when she was walking the building doing room safety checks, she discovered that he had suffocated himself with the blanket.*

We all like to think that no one in a trusting and supportive relationship is going to kill her- or himself. One of the hazards in suicide work is that, for the very reason that clients often like and respect their clinicians so much, they may kill themselves without giving any warning ahead of time precisely because they don't want to upset the clinician or put him or her through a lot of prevention work when they really are prepared and ready to die.

7. *Self-care.*   Crisis work is very stressful, and working with suicidal clients is extremely stressful. We are mandated by law and professional standards to try to prevent by all legal means client harm to self or others. We can feel an awesome sense of responsibility, as though holding someone's life in our hands.

Clinicians who have worked diligently with a client who has committed suicide are often greatly affected. They often come together to express grief and discuss lingering concern and anguish around the questions "What steps did we take to prevent this?" and "Could we have done anything more or differently to prevent this death?" Colleagues, supervisors, and consultations can help clinicians review the situation, what steps were taken to support the client, and what actions one could take in the future. Although the clinician may have wished to do some things differently, it is important for him or her to know that the client made the decision to end life; it is not the clinician's fault, and to date, there are no means of predicting when someone will actually commit suicide.

■ Community Crises

Environmental or ecosystemic crises usually affect very large groups or communities, as when a flood destroys most of the housing in a village, a toxic waste accident causes terminal illnesses in many people living nearby, or a terrorist attack shuts down public transportation. Responses to these widely affecting crises vary, depending on the strengths, needs, and resources available in local areas, on the community's beliefs about and access to outside services and helpers, and on the willingness and ability of insiders and outsiders alike to help in ways that feel empowering rather than overwhelming and demeaning.

Characteristics of Community Crises and Interventions

Environmental or ecosystemic crises can affect a community in many destabilizing ways. Initially, they shake the fundamental beliefs of all affected regarding the predictability of daily life and the immutability of familiar support networks and resources. Other effects, such as the sudden break-up of families, the loss of pets and livestock, and the loss of most means of making a living, are equally distressing and combine with the following factors to devastate a community and trigger outside intervention.

The Entire Infrastructure of a Community Can Be Lost or Destabilized

Loss of customary support systems. Often people turn to their friends, families, and social and spiritual networks for help in times of crisis. However, during overwhelming community crises such as tornadoes that destroy everything in a town, the most basic networks may all be experiencing trauma at the same time and be unable to help each other as soon or as well as in the past. Television demonstrates this phenomenon graphically through postcrisis images of groups of neighbors and families in shock, staring fixedly at ruins, crying with each other or digging fruitlessly for personal belongings long gone. Yet within hours or days, communities often pull together collectively to establish communication and order, to help each other with shelter, food, and the rescue of animals, and to seek governmental help for specific collective needs.

Crises have a way of revealing the nature and extent of any community's organization and disorganization, its power centers, and its marginalized groups in need of further inclusion and empowerment. In another apparent race- and class-based microaggression, the poor and many people of color in New Orleans affected by Hurricane Katrina have been largely sidelined again in planning for the safety and reconstruction of their traditional residential areas. It is in just such situations that clinicians can ally with community groups, political activists, and supportive politicians to work to create an inclusive process for the reconstruction of meaningful opportunities and networks when such devastating disasters strike.

Loss of leadership and community resources. When calamity strikes a whole community, skilled leadership in the community may be disabled or destroyed. Community leaders may be killed, injured, or in a crisis state over their own losses and unable to respond to the needs of the community.

There may be no phone service, electricity, or sanitation, and there may not even be enough food and water for the number of people in need. Roads, bridges, and transportation systems to other people and resources may be out of commission for a long time, meaning that basic supplies and means of sheltering people and communicating have to be flown in on a continuous basis until the foundations of community life are restored. Such effects have been observed in the Southeast Asian and African tsunamis of 2004 and the earthquakes in China in 2008 and in Haiti in 2010. It has been estimated that it will require two decades to restore community structures, institutions, and resources to those affected by these events.

Political and legal authorities themselves can be paralyzed by the degree of loss and devastation and may have difficulty providing immediate protective and reorganizing responses, causing people to panic about their survival. For example, as floodwaters rose rapidly during Hurricane Katrina, numerous policemen abandoned their posts to save their families from widespread flooding, and others were among the citizens photographed looting local stores for food and water.

Clinicians, too, may be traumatized by losses and unable to respond for a time as helpers of others. In addition, their agencies may no longer be standing or operative, and colleagues may have been injured or killed. Mary Pulido (2007) speaks of clinicians in New York City at the time of the 9/11 attacks who were traumatized by what they saw and heard that day. Then they were retraumatized by the gruesome stories of client-survivors trying to describe what traumatized them. Some workers threw up or cried after sessions; many couldn't sleep or stay focused on work. Many withdrew socially because of compassion fatigue. These are all normal responses when a community crisis strikes everyone, and the wise clinical practice setting prepares in advance to offer its staff crisis support.

Loss of a sense of agency, purpose, and meaning in life. Devastating community crises leave members feeling that life is out of their control. They may feel that much of what anchored their lives and gave them meaning and purpose has been lost forever and that little can be trusted or counted on anymore, including people offering support and assistance. This despairing worldview often leads to anguished and aimless pacing or searching for lost people and possessions; to numb passivity, excessive sleep, and bouts of crying; or to angry protests and unreasonable demands for the immediate restoration of life as it used to be. Some members may abandon the community temporarily or permanently, moving away to recover with relatives in another locale, yet finding it hard either to forget or to reclaim their roots.

People from Outside the Community May Come to Help

When damage to people, institutions, and property is severe and widespread, outsiders, including the Red Cross, the Federal Emergency Management Agency (FEMA), Homeland Security, the National Guard, the military, and a host of state and regional agencies trained to provide emergency assistance may be called in to help. The focus of these helpers is on the most basic survival needs of the whole community and on meeting the needs of all people, not just powerful ones or insiders. Clinical professions also participate in community interventions. For example, the American Psychological Association's Disaster Response Network consists of trained volunteer professionals flown into various locales beset by crisis. The Red Cross and many social work and counseling organizations have crisis response training for workers in disasters and school emergencies.

Culturally effective helping. James (2008) observes that when crises strike, we usually do not have the culturally suitable resources needed to help the many people who are suddenly affected. "However, we do know that deeply held cultural beliefs and previously learned ways of dealing with the world rapidly surface when individuals are placed under a crisis" (James, 2008, p. 25). It is important that clinicians be culturally responsive. Each locality should be preparing both human and concrete resources for their specific populations. If disaster response planners are aware that a large number of elderly live in their community, they should include plans for the evacuation of the elderly and disabled. If a community is composed of mostly Spanish-speaking individuals, planners should be sure that information is available in Spanish. Even if no culturally appropriate resources are available, James suggests that establishing a relationship built on hope, trust, and credibility can be a starting point and a key ingredient in helping survivors begin to access resources and to cope. The support of friends, family, and other allies has proved to be remarkably effective in helping people stabilize and develop beneficially after crisis (Tedeschi & Calhoun, 1995).

Suspicion of strangers.   Small, isolated, or poor communities may lack the expertise and financial resources to respond adequately to widely affecting crises, yet may be suspicious of outsiders. This is especially true if the outside helpers are from a different cultural, religious, or language group than the affected community or if they treat the community as too inept to engage in meaningful joint assessment and planning.

Under crisis conditions, those affected may knit together more tightly in their behaviors and beliefs to survive with traditions intact and may not be comfortable depending on outsiders to meet most of their basic needs. People can quickly feel sidelined by outsiders and "experts," who may be suspected of not really understanding who the survivors are and what they are up against. A we–they perspective is easy for people to develop under unremitting stress, and families or groups may "circle their wagons" to ward off further distress. It can take a while for people to accept and believe in newcomers, especially when crises have destroyed their faith in other human beings.

Although nonlocal clinicians may be the most experienced and skilled at counseling around certain crises in the life of a community or region, they may be seen as unwelcome intruders. Thus, we must respond with sensitivity to our outsider status, and community leaders should be observed bridging outsiders to insiders through demonstrations of positive regard and gratitude. Indigenous leaders must be seen requesting outsiders' help, welcoming them publicly at a gathering of the community, and familiarizing outsiders with local beliefs about the nature of disasters and the locally sanctioned ways of seeking or receiving help. News of the positive ways outsiders do actually help must be widely disseminated informally to encourage residents to use the help offered.

Utilizing the community's own power.   From the onset of crisis, community members must be empowered to act on their own behalf at every opportunity to prevent the malignant effects of passivity and despair in the aftermath of community crises. Restoration of a sense of agency and worth in people who have lost their sense of a secure base, as well as their sense of control over life events, is a first priority in the prevention of further personal, familial, or systemic disorganization. Sometimes large-group process is the best and only way to help people ventilate feelings and concerns because it is an efficient means of enabling people to experience their commonalities and provide mutual aid. The more people come to know about each other's feelings, ideas, caring, and coping, the stronger their community can be once it is reconstituted, and the readier it can be to face adversity in the future.

Interventions by both insiders and outsiders must value and ensure the active collaboration of ordinary community members in decision making, planning, and reconstructive action all along the way. Unfortunately, citizens with power often find it easier to exclude their already marginalized fellow citizens in order to speed the process of reconstruction by allocating planning power and emergency funding to better known, well-connected insiders. James notes that much research indicates that, when disaster strikes, a community's natural altruism does not extend as readily to the elderly, poor, less educated, or ethnic minority residents. He further observes that "disaster plans as they are currently formulated put the poor, the elderly, the sick and other disenfranchised individuals who are not physically able to rebuild, relocate or rebuild at extreme risk" (p. 590).

Listening and responding quickly and sympathetically to all requests for special forms of help signals respect for all those affected and an appreciation that they often know better than outsiders what is most helpful in restoring their faith in people and in collective action.

> One thing our community asked for right away and got was an expanded rescue force rowing around the area rescuing beloved pets stranded on barn roofs, housetops, and slabs of high ground. After we insisted, rules designed to maintain healthy environments were changed in the shelters so that families could have their pets with them as familiar sources of support. Some livestock were also rescued and secured in separate areas, representing the promise of restored livelihood over time.

Many helpers, many complications.   Community interventions necessarily involve many helpers and agencies, each providing different but necessary services. Efficiency and the prevention of wasteful duplication require a great degree of close relating, coordination, and trust in each other to follow through as planned. That many strangers can come together in unfamiliar locales and rapidly provide excellent reconstructive and lifesaving services is a testimony to the professional dedication and preparation of so many skilled helpers, including clinicians.

James (2008) describes instances of "too much helping" that can impede or complicate a community's collective efforts to reconsolidate through mutual aid and reorganization. He deplores what he describes as well-intentioned but sometimes misguided "trauma tourism," (p. 31), in which throngs of well-meaning helpers and the trauma industry flood in, uninvited and uncoordinated, to help people they automatically assume will be panicky, inept at coping, and in need of guidance and protection. McNally et al. (2003) report that more than 9,000 counselors streamed unbidden into New York City following the World Trade Center collapse, setting up counseling sites that very few people used except to get claim forms.

Coordination.   The coordination of services and providers is vital to marshal quickly a variety of interventions while conserving precious resources. A group of community and agency leaders identifies community needs and designates interventions and roles. A crucial aspect of this coordination is deciding on the goals and steps of various interventions and then collectively assigning and carrying out roles so that efforts are not duplicated or wasted. In this way, people get the timely and appropriate forms of the help they need without being deluged with helpers. It is not a good idea to jump into a disaster scene doing whatever feels natural.

Uncoordinated emergency interventions can add to the chaos and confusion, can send conflicting messages, can wastefully duplicate services for some while others get nothing, and can undermine careful centralized planning and the equitable distribution of resources. Chaotic service provision and lack of accountability also allow unscrupulous people—both survivors and "helpers"—to siphon off resources for their own profit. For example, an entrepreneur in New Orleans actually devised tour bus trips to take curious visitors through the city's ruins as numbed fellow citizens move out trash and try to rebuild.

Communication. Rumor and misinformation are two great destabilizing forces in the period following a community crisis. People can be unsettled by misinformation and begin to react in ways that further destabilize already pressured systems. For example, following a flood, if citizens are mistakenly informed by panicky neighbors that their homes are being looted, they may unwisely try to reach their homes alone and be drowned in a subsequent tidal surge.

Emergency communications need to be clear, specific, and limited to the important information people need to feel safe, informed, and heard by authorities. After a disaster, media hype may saturate victims with traumatic images, information, and rumors. On the other hand, after the terrorist bombing of the U.S. Embassy in Kenya, TV, radio, and newspapers informed residents about possible psychological symptoms and how to get help for them (Vasterman, Yzermans, & Dirkzwager, 2005). Unless invited to do so and well informed by the response leadership as to what should be communicated, clinicians and other emergency workers should not get involved in speculative discussions with clients about things to come or hoped-for services that have not yet materialized.

Intervention staff members usually establish a centrally located communications center that collaboratively produces informational reports for leaflet and media distribution. If media infrastructure has not been devastated by the disaster, clarifying reports are broadcast regularly on radio, TV, and the Internet at set intervals and in the multiple languages used in the area. Trusted native language speakers may also be called on to move from area to area, answering questions and providing the latest news. Crisis response leadership may request that clinicians wishing to participate in the crisis intervention be speakers of the area's primary languages. They may also ask willing community members to act as translators once they have been briefed on the counseling process and goals, as well as the need for confidentiality.

■ The Clinician in Crisis

Clinicians' reactions to working with people in crisis are commonly observed and have been variously referred to as "emotional contagion" (Miller, Stiff, & Ellis, 1988), "secondary traumatic stress" (Figley, 2002), "traumatic countertransference" (Herman, 1997), "compassion fatigue" (Figley, 2002), and "vicarious traumatization" (McCann & Pearlman, 1990). Figley (1995) argues that we get these secondary stress, or **vicarious trauma,** reactions because "the process of empathizing with a traumatized person helps us to understand the person's experience of being traumatized, but, in the process, we may be traumatized as well" (p. 15). He observes that clinicians who have the greatest capacity for empathy may also be at the greatest risk of developing what he calls "compassion stress." We can at times experience symptoms similar to those of our clients in crisis, including difficulty sleeping, nightmares, anxiety, and intrusive thoughts.

For those of us who work with violence and abuse, repeated stories of the brutality people inflict on one another can shake our faith in human relationships. This can affect both professional and personal relationships outside work as we take upset responses home with us. For example, according to Figley (1995), women who work with rape survivors "often develop a general disgust for rapists that extends to all males" (p. 1). As Herman (1997) notes:

> Repeated stories of human rapacity and cruelty inevitably challenge the therapist's basic faith. It also heightens her sense of personal vulnerability. She may become more fearful of other people in general and more distrustful even in close relationships. She may find herself becoming increasingly cynical about the motives of others and pessimistic about the human condition (p. 141).

Workers can experience vicarious trauma from empathizing with clients in crisis but can also experience crises in their professional lives—for example, when their place of employment closes down on short notice, when a client commits suicide, or when there is violence against a colleague in the workplace. In addition, we can experience direct stress and trauma from the hazards of working long hours in stressful or high-risk situations without adequate support and supervision.

Community crises can also affect clinicians, who may be struggling with the loss of their own loved ones, pets, or material goods at the same time as they are trying to help others cope with similar losses. While encouraging others to express themselves freely, we may not think that we, as self-styled models of resilience, should express distress in public. Yet everyone may be staying in close proximity in a public place such as a gym or an armory.

Clinicians who have experienced previous crises in their own lives can have unfinished business stirred up by working with clients in a similar crisis (Figley, 1995). Finally, we may be facing our own current personal life crises, such as the illness or death of loved ones, becoming depressed or distractible and wondering how we can continue to provide good service to others. As clinicians, we need to attend to how our own crises, past or present, affect our abilities to work effectively with clients in crisis.

I took a man on in treatment who had been through a number of things that I also had in my own childhood. During one memorable period of time, he began to have nightmares of a man attacking him in the dark. Shortly after that, without realizing that his story had evoked my own childhood trauma, I began to have scary illusions when entering my apartment that an attacker was waiting for me in the shower or the closet. I actually had to go check each time to make sure no one was there and was very embarrassed yet gripped by these ideas, and I distinctly remember wishing that the client generating these fears would drop out of treatment. That would fix everything, I thought.

Herman (1997) notes that the therapist "empathically shares the patient's experience of helplessness. This may lead the therapist to underestimate the value of her own knowledge and skill, lose sight of the patient's strengths and resources, lose confidence in the power of the therapeutic relationship . . . feel de-skilled" (p. 141). She also believes that therapists can experience "profound grief" (p. 141) in working with victims of childhood sexual abuse and trauma.

Mary Ann Dutton and Francine Rubenstein (1995) note that clinicians may detach from clients, distancing by judging, labeling, or pathologizing the traumatic reaction, "which creates the illusion that the client's reaction to the traumatic event is in some way different from that of a 'normal' individual. Other forms of detachment include adopting a personal and emotional distance from the client . . . being chronically late or frequently canceling appointments, or allowing frequent interruptions during appointments" (p. 87).

Herman (1997) believes that another way of detaching is "to feel contempt for the patient's helplessness, or paranoid fear of the patient's vindictive rage" (p. 145). A less obvious form of detachment is that of actually taking on so many assignments involving traumatic stress that no one person or story can truly engage us deeply because we are always moving rapidly in and out of contact to serve so many people. Detachment is also observed in those of us who try to identify a domain of practice in which there will—hopefully—be no work with trauma. No such domain exists.

Self-Care to Counter Worker Stress

Clinicians and other crisis responders now recognize that we, too, need help to digest, make meaning of, and move on from the often overwhelming sensory and emotional experiences involved in trauma work. An important aspect of such self-care is setting some limits on the number of clients in severe crisis to be seen at any one time. Some jobs do not permit such a limit because the clinician's role is precisely that of emergency room or neighborhood crisis responder, and crisis is the specific purpose and focus of the work. Even then, if we are taxed beyond the ability to perform our duties in a professional manner, it is our ethical responsibility to negotiate with superiors for periodic relief from taking on new clients, if only temporarily.

When an agency does, however, permit more balance in assignments, it is important that we take advantage of the opportunity to diversify assignments. Supervision and consultation are musts in crisis and trauma work. Just as clients need help and support in dealing with crises, so do clinicians. Informed, safe, and reliable supervision provides a unique opportunity to ventilate and receive knowledge and support following upsetting experiences with clients and communities. Rescue urges, overidentification, detachment, and judgmentalism can be spotted, identified, and worked on so that workers are less likely to burn out in the work.

Supervisors can normalize periodic feelings of hopelessness, helplessness, anger, or guilt about not having suffered as much as others, not having saved people, and not always providing the "just right" intervention with people deeply in crisis. Whenever working alone with highly stressed and disorganized families presents more challenges than an individual clinician can respond to adequately, supervision can redirect clinicians to work in teams. Supportive supervision, teamwork, continuing support from friends and family, and periodic respite from work can all play a role in sustaining crisis responders.

CLIP 13.5
Community Crises

■ Conclusion

Crisis affects everyone: No one is immune. When beliefs, familiar people, structures, and resources are suddenly gone, crisis reactions call for brief, immediate, well-focused, and sensitive interventions to re-establish a sense of connection and capacity to cope. Only with awareness, information, and care can clients and clinicians alike minimize stress and destabilization from repeated crises and maximize the opportunity for healing and growth. Rituals, social support, and restorative activity with others can refocus survivors' strengths and altruism in empowering ways that rekindle feelings of efficacy and safe belonging.

"Worldwide, the prevention of suicide has not been adequately addressed due basically to a lack of awareness of suicide as a major problem and the taboo in many societies to discuss openly about it. In fact, only a few countries have included prevention of suicide among their priorities. Reliability of suicide certification and reporting is an issue in great need of improvement. It is clear that suicide prevention requires intervention also from outside the health sector and calls for an innovative, comprehensive, multi-sectoral approach, including both health and non-health sectors, e.g. education, labor, police, justice, religion, law, politics, the media" (WHO, 2009, p. 1).

■ Suggested Readings

Daniel, Jessica H. (2000). The courage to hear: African American women's memories of racial trauma. In Leslie C. Jackson & Beverly Greene (Eds.), *Psychotherapy with African American women* (pp. 126–144). New York: Guilford.

Herman, Judith. (1997). *Trauma and recovery.* New York: Basic Books.

James, Richard. (2008). *Crisis intervention strategies* (6th Ed.). Belmont, CA: Thomson Brooks/Cole.

Knight, Carolyn. (2009). *Introduction to working with adult survivors of childhood trauma: Techniques and strategies.* Belmont, CA: Brooks/Cole Cengage.

McNally, Richard J., Bryant, Richard A., & Ehlers, Anke. (2003). Does early psychological intervention promote recovery from posttraumatic stress? *Psychological Science in the Public Interest, 4*(2), 45–79.

Ting, L., Sanders, S., Jacobson, J. M., & Power, J. R. (2006). Dealing with the aftermath: A qualitative analysis of mental health social workers' reactions after a client suicide. *Social Work, 51,* 329–341.

van der Kolk, Bessel A., Hopper, James W., and Osterman, Janet E. (2001). Exploring the nature of traumatic memory: Combining clinical knowledge with laboratory methods. *Journal of Aggression, Maltreatment, & Trauma, 42,* 9–31.

Webb, Nancy Boyd (Ed.). (2007). *Play therapy and children in crisis: Individual, group and family treatment* (3rd Ed.). New York: Guilford.

■ Self-Explorations

1. Have you personally experienced a traumatic event? In your journal, record the event and your reactions to it. Ronnie Janoff-Bulman (1992) believes that trauma shatters people's assumptions about the world. Do you think the trauma you experienced affected your worldview? In what ways?

2. Discuss a traumatic event that happened to someone else but had a significant impact on you. It could be something that happened to a member of your family or someone close to you, or it could be an event that happened to someone you did not know. Discuss how it affected you.

3. Make a list of the common ways you cope with crisis. You might use different coping mechanisms in different situations, but list the ones you use most often. What determines the strategies you use and when you use them?

4. Have you ever experienced a crisis that, at the time, you thought of as a negative event, but from which there later emerged productive outcomes and personal growth? Discuss the events and what came of them for you personally.

■ Essay Questions

1. Define *vicarious trauma.* How does it affect the clinician's cognitive schemas? List and discuss some ways that clinicians can resolve or balance the vicarious trauma in their lives.

2. Define *environmental traumas* and *human-made traumas*. Discuss the differences between them. What local or national factors can cause the two kinds of traumas to occur together? Can you give an example?

3. Describe a specific natural disaster you witnessed, were a part of, or know a lot about. If it were to occur again and you could give advice to intervention teams who are about to go in and try to help, what suggestions and cautions would you give them?

4. In what circumstances would you encourage clients to tell their crisis stories immediately, welcoming whatever feelings were present? In what circumstances would you advise clients to go slowly so as not to be retraumatized by the unsettling content or intense flooding of emotion?

5. This chapter explained that crisis presents both danger and opportunity. Discuss what that means, giving examples of crisis components that illustrate your discussion.

■ Key Terms

Compound crisis

Coping mechanisms

Crisis

Critical Incident Stress Debriefing (CISD)

Decompensate

Delayed grief reactions

Developmental crises

Ecosystemic crises

Emotional contagion

Environmental crises

Hate crimes

Human-made disasters

Insidious trauma

IS PATH WARM

Legal commitment

Locus of control

Natural disasters

Parasuicide

Posttraumatic growth

Posttraumatic Stress Disorder (PTSD)

Precipitating events

Predisposing factors

Protective factors

Psychological first aid

Resilience

Risk factors

Risk management

Secondary trauma

Situational crises

SLAP

Suicidal ideation

Trauma

Vicarious trauma

Warning signs

CHAPTER 14

Endings and Transitions

Inevitably, clinical work comes to an end. As often as possible, endings are planned and are a natural part of a stated contract. For example, the clinician and client in an employee assistance program may agree to meet for a fixed number of sessions, a social worker in a halfway house may agree to meet with a client only as long as the client is attending other specified programs, or a college student may graduate and no longer be eligible for services at the college counseling center. But endings can also happen in an unplanned way. They may be the result of unanticipated circumstances, as when the client has to move away, the clinician becomes too ill to work, the client discontinues the relationship, or the agency closes.

Either the client or the clinician may initiate endings. Endings may seem to be a natural and timely closure to the work together, or they may seem precipitous. Regardless of the reason, we try to undertake a formal process of ending to assist the client in summarizing and integrating the work with the clinician and to assist in planning for the future. This formal termination process may be brief or carried out over a number of sessions.

Termination is the term traditionally used in clinical work to describe the process of ending. The term was conceived in a much earlier era of practice that was heavily influenced by the psychoanalytic theory of therapy. Traditional psychoanalytic theory anticipated so thorough and productive a therapeutic restructuring of client dynamics, defenses, and character that work could be terminated with the expectation of little future need for further work.

We believe that termination represents a transitioning process through which clients gradually move to other systems of support and problem solving, such as family; ethnocultural and spiritual networks and practices; and mutual aid, political action, and recreational groups. Clients often take the work and the relationship away with them as sustaining inner resources available for use in the future. But we also recognize that termination may not be the last time the clinician sees the client.

We realize how often environmental stressors and socioeconomic inequities contribute to the problems clients face. Clients with few resources, complex problems, or new objectives for work together sometimes come back to see the same clinician with whom they ostensibly terminated or finished up. Therefore, although clinicians often use words such as *termination*, *ending*, and *transition*, we believe that the process is often one of finishing work "for now." If we think of life and circumstances as forever fluid and dynamic, then the idea of cycles of work at different points in time makes perfect sense in the lives of many people.

■ Even Before We End: Foreshadowing

It is important that clinicians and clients have as much lead time as possible to discuss ending and to allow for the processing and digestion of the transition from this special form of caring and collaboration. Thus, whether or not there is a specified plan for ending, we occasionally **foreshadow the ending** during the working relationship. This is particularly true in work with clients whose many prior relational losses make separations or endings difficult.

Whenever possible, an agreed-upon, planned ending is the best way to wrap up work together because it provides many opportunities to review, compare expectations with realities, look ahead, and both regret and celebrate concluding this cycle of work. When there is a projected date for an ending, we foreshadow it by occasionally noting the date so that all can be alert to it and can plan the focus and pace of the discussion accordingly.

EXAMPLES

Clinician A: Before we begin work today, I wanted to review with you that it's the end of March, just seven weeks before my placement ends and I leave here to continue my education.

* * *

Clinician B: We said we would finish up after Christmas, and since Christmas is just three weeks away, I thought it might be good today to look at where we are and whether that still seems to be a good idea. If so, let's figure out how we can plan ahead for it so it doesn't just suddenly happen without us getting ready for it, especially here at the holidays.

* * *

Clinician C: This is our fifth of eight sessions; what would you like to accomplish by the time our meeting ends today?

CLIP 14.1
Foreshadowing
the Ending

When the contract is somewhat more open and continues over time, clinicians may periodically review goals, accomplishments, and remaining issues and more frequently mention "when our work together is finished" to help clients keep the relationship and work in perspective.

Here time is well used as both a boundary and an incentive for efficient use of work.

■ Initiating Endings and Transitions

Whatever the reason for or the nature of the ending, clinicians can use several skills to ease the process of change for the client, maximize gains to date, and help make the transition to other supportive connections and activities. Because the skills used to end the work are much the same as those used in transitions and breaks, we begin by elaborating ending skills and then demonstrate how these skills can be adapted for planned and unplanned transitions and interruptions in the work.

EXERCISE 14.1 When Clinicians Should Initiate Endings

Before reading more about endings, pause to identify some of your ideas about them. In your journal, describe the circumstances in which you think the clinician should initiate the ending of the clinical relationship.

Clinician-Initiated Endings

Sometimes clinicians initiate the process of ending. This may be appropriate in a number of situations. For example, a clinician may initiate ending because the goals have been accomplished and it is simply time to end work together. Beginning clinicians should always consult with supervisors as to the appropriateness of ending before raising the subject with the client.

Whenever possible, initiate the conversation about ending early in a given session so that the client does not feel that you want to end the relationship because of something the client has just revealed or done. Whenever suggesting the possibility of ending for now, it is important to leave room for the client's responses and, in the absence of any immediate ones, keep an eye out for nonverbal and indirect themes. The following are several useful ways of introducing the topic of ending when the goals of the relationship have been met.

EXAMPLES

Clinician A: Anna, things have gone so well for a while now. Is it time for us to think about the possibility of our bringing our work together to a close?

* * *

Clinician B: Miguel, you've been wondering when our work will be through. Should we decide on a date, far enough away to give you a few more weeks to reestablish yourself back in the community?

* * *

Clinician C: By spring, Brian, I expect you'll be ready to try things without seeing me every week. I'd like us to keep things as they are for now, to support you through the holidays, but we might plan on ending our work together in March. What do you think?

We may also initiate ending the relationship if we believe that, although the client could still use some assistance, we are unable to help because we do not have the expertise necessary to work with the client on a specific issue.

> *I was working with a woman at the family planning clinic. We were meeting about birth control methods and STD prevention. She disclosed that she had been sexually abused. I knew that this would be an important topic for her to explore, but I certainly wasn't trained to work with it. I referred her to a more knowledgeable mental health counselor at the clinic.*

When we feel that we can no longer work with a client because the client's issues are beyond our expertise, we must carefully make a **referral.** This can be difficult because the client may feel rejected or reluctant to see another clinician. Using the prior example, the clinician might proceed in the following way.

E X A M P L E

Clinician: Serafina, I was thinking about what you told me at our last meeting about what happened to you in your family.

Client: Yeah.

Clinician: I think that having been sexually abused must have been an awful experience that you haven't gotten much help for.

Client: You're the first one I told about it.

Clinician: I appreciate your confidence in me.

Client: Yeah, I couldn't believe that I told you.

Clinician: What does it feel like to have told me?

Client: It felt okay . . . but I've been thinking about it a lot.

Clinician: You know, I think it would be really good if you could talk about what happened to you with a colleague of mine who has a lot of experience helping women who have been abused.

Client: I couldn't imagine talking to anyone but you. Can't you help me with it?

Clinician: Serafina, I really want to help you, but I haven't had any experience working with women who have been sexually abused. I think the best thing I could do for you would be to help you talk to Brenda at the Women's Health Collaborative. She is a wonderful counselor whom I like a lot.

Client: Do you mean I can't see you anymore?

Clinician: Well, we were finishing up our work about birth control and safe sex practices, so we would be stopping anyway. I know it can be hard to think about saying good-bye to someone with whom you've shared so much.

Client: Yeah. I always hate good-byes.

Clinician: What I would like to do is to set up a meeting for you with Brenda. I would meet with you for one last time after you've seen her to find out how it goes and to say good-bye.

E X E R C I S E 14.2 Thinking About Ending

In your journal, record your reactions to the preceding scenario. How do you think the client feels? How do you think the clinician feels? What would you have done differently?

EXERCISE 14.3 Referral Role-Plays

Role-play a scenario in which you discuss referring a client to another person or agency because you are unable to help the client with the issues he or she has uncovered. Video record the role-play. Watch the video with your team and then debrief: Discuss what it felt like to be the clinician and what it felt like to be the client.

Clinicians may need to initiate the end of the relationship if they feel that a client is not making use of the relationship. This is a very complex and difficult issue, and such an ending should be undertaken only after careful review with a supervisor.

EXAMPLE

Clinician: Leo, we've been meeting for a while about your problems finding a job, and we don't seem to have accomplished much. I am not sure that our continued meeting would be helpful to you.

Client: Well, I like meeting.

Clinician: I don't think it is a good use of your time and money. I have the feeling that you aren't sure that you really do want to work on getting a job.

Client: Yeah, I do.

Clinician: Well, I've noticed that you haven't followed through on any of the assignments we've agreed might help. We've explored this a lot, and I'm still not sure why that is. However, why don't we stop meeting for a while. Then, if you feel ready to practice job-hunting skills, I'll be happy to work with you again.

Client-Initiated Endings

Clients, too, can initiate endings for a variety of reasons. They may feel that the goals of the relationship have been met and that they are ready to try things on their own or to transition to another kind of work. Clients may also suggest ending if they feel that the clinician is getting ready to end the relationship and they themselves want to be the first to leave. In addition, clients can end work because they are at odds with the clinician or agency, because the issue being addressed in the work makes them feel uncomfortable, or because they feel they are not being helped. The clinician may or may not agree with the client's decision and must carefully explore the situation with the client to make sure that he or she is not initiating ending because of discontent with the clinician or clinical process. We attempt to explore the issue while respecting a client's right to decide.

> *I remember a client who came in quite angry one week and said that he was leaving our counseling sessions. He said I hadn't helped him and he decided that he was through. My first instinct was to say, "Okay." I felt like I didn't want to seem defensive by pushing him as to why he wanted to go, and I worried that maybe I hadn't helped him. But then I remembered my supervisor saying, "You have to explore it." So I did and kept saying to myself, "Don't be defensive . . . keep the focus on him . . . try to be empathic . . . this is a learning opportunity." It worked. He really felt I listened, and then he said he was mad at me for something I had said that had pushed his buttons. We explored those buttons and continued our work. I was glad I hadn't given in to my first instinct to say, "Fine, bye."*

Sometimes it becomes clear that the client wants to end, even against the clinician's best judgment. In such situations, we believe that, after carefully exploring the issues, the clinician should help the client end as well as is feasible, highlighting any positives to date and not being punitive about the decision to leave. This avoids contributing to the client's potential feelings of failure or guilt. In addition, we try to keep the door open for future work or referrals.

EXAMPLE

> *Clinician:* Well, it sounds as if you're really feeling that this is the time to stop. You've used the relationship well [summarizing the way client has used it]. While you may want to do some more work later, this feels to you like it is enough for now. I'd be happy to help you or make a referral if you decide that you want to do more work on this in the future.

At times we become concerned that the client is self-sabotaging or playing out an old pattern of breaking off relationships just when they are working. A clinician might want to raise the possibility that such dynamics may be at work. The client may disagree but at least the clinician has left him or her with something to think about. We may not feel good about this sort of ending, but it is important to recognize that decisions still rest with the client. Maximizing client self-determination is always important. Sometimes clients learn things through the process of ending that they have not been able learn in the relationship.

E X A M P L E

> *Clinician:* Wayne, I'm worried that you may be doing with me what you've described doing so many times before: that whenever you get close to somebody, you take off.
>
> *Client:* What's it to you?
>
> *Clinician:* If at some point you don't let someone in and keep them in, I worry you're going to be lonely for the rest of your life. You've already told me how much that hurts.
>
> *Client:* I have to see on my own how it goes.

Outside Forces May Precipitate Ending

Clients or counselors may also have to initiate ending because of external circumstances. Insurance limits may necessitate an ending. Clients may no longer be able to afford the care being offered. A significant other may insist that the client end the relationship. Unexpected events can result in a client or clinician having to move away or change jobs. Participants can become too ill to attend meetings, or an agency might close with very little notice.

When an agency is closing, restructuring, or discontinuing some services, both clinician and client may feel displaced and upset. At times, our own anger or fears may seep into the clinical work with clients, escalating their worries and feelings of loss. We need to find other places to work out our own distress so that our work remains centered on the client's experience rather than on our own. Supervisors can indicate any instances in which it might be useful to share clinicians' own reactions to changes in the agency.

> *I was working in a methadone clinic in a hospital where there was some talk of a merger with a larger teaching hospital. The clients picked up on it somehow. There were lots of rumors that the clinic would be closed. I remember Philip saying, "I'm just gonna go back to using when they close this place." We had to spend lots of time reassuring them that we weren't closing.*

* * *

> *I know that closing an agency is tough on the staff as well as on the clients, but I was shocked to hear that some of the staff just started not showing up and began using their sick time right before the agency closed. I felt so bad for the clients. It wasn't their fault, but they were the ones who were losing out. They didn't even get to say good-bye to some of the staff.*

When external circumstances necessitate a transition or ending, the client and clinician may both feel that things are beyond their control, especially if their work is not completed or if it is at a crucial point. Some people are barely fazed by ending this kind of relationship, but others—clinicians included—may need to grieve the loss of the relationship, at the same time appreciating all that they have been able to accomplish in whatever time they have had.

> *Nonie and I had worked together for a couple of years on maintaining her at home in spite of a history of episodes of bipolar disorder. She was in her early thirties, had a child by someone she had had a fling with at the mental hospital, and was being supported by Rehabilitation funds to go back and finish college. Right at the point when she was trying to enter school and worrying about being accepted by her peers, I was offered a job that I could not resist at another agency. It meant moving from a mental health to a medical setting, where I would not be allowed to see my current clients. I loved Nonie, and we had been through so much together with her getting in jams and then out again. It gets to you to have to step away from someone you care about and who is counting on you to be there with them. We did some work on ending well in advance of my leaving, but Nonie went off her meds, as I feared, and landed back in the hospital just when I left the agency. I felt terrible and poured this out fairly regularly in supervision. My supervisor helped me to see that Nonie had probably gotten herself readmitted to have familiar people around to help her with her sadness. The staff at the hospital confirmed that this was what she was absorbed with in their meetings with her. As life would have it, a month after I left, I was shopping in the area market when I wheeled my cart around an aisle and literally ran smack into Nonie. I was so happy to see her again, but she burst into tears and could not stop crying. We sort of went off into an empty corner and did more talking about moving on to her new worker at the clinic, someone I knew would be great with her. Over the next six months, she called me twice at home to ask me to please see her, and I just continued gently to underscore her strengths and encourage her back to her new worker. She did follow through as hoped.*

Initiating Ending Too Soon or Too Late

Sometimes either a client or a clinician may suggest ending the relationship too soon.

Clinician or Organizational Factors End the Work Prematurely

Work between a clinician and client may be ended prematurely by the clinician's geographic move, change in jobs, retirement, illness, or death. During times of organizational change, agencies may merge or close, necessitating an end of work. **Managed Care Organizations** (MCOs) are part of an industrialization of health care that creates incentives to limit treatment. MCOs may arbitrarily terminate work with clients whose coverage has expired (Acuff, et al., 1999). Clients may need to terminate treatment when their insurance benefits stop paying.

Although infrequent, client abandonment is another example of the clinician ending the work prematurely. The term **client abandonment** describes a clinician's "failure to take the clinically indicated and ethically appropriate steps to terminate a professional relationship" (Younggren & Gottlieb, 2008, p. 500). It can also be a thinly disguised process of passing along to other professionals clients who have an obvious need of service but with whom the clinician finds it difficult or unprofitable to work. For example, a client may be constantly demanding, critical, threatening, or consistently unwilling to carry out agreed-upon roles or tasks that would forward the work. Abandonment can also occur if a clinician fails to assess for imminent risk before ending with clients who have been impulsively self-harming, suicidal, or violent in the recent past, or if the clinician terminates with someone who is at the peak of a crisis (Freeman, Felgoise, & Davis, 2008). Clinicians can be subject to licensing board investigation and civil suits for client abandonment.

Risk management when ending interventions against the client's will involves the steps of documenting fully in the client's record the thoughtful preparatory conversations you have with the client about why the work together should end; documenting the content of any consultations you have around a reasonable rationale for ending sooner than expected; suggesting and/or arranging appropriate follow-up care for clients who wish it; and not continuing to work with someone whose needs are beyond your competence just to try to avoid that client's complaints to management if a referral to a more expert provider is suggested appropriately (Younggren & Gottlieb, 2008).

As a routine part of contracting for work, the clinician should provide an explanation of what he or she can and cannot do with and for the client, as well as the rights of and expectations for the client in order to coevolve the intervention. Part of the discussion might be that if either clinician or client believes that progress is not being made, after a thoroughgoing discussion of the situation, a referral to an appropriate colleague or agency may be required.

The Client Unilaterally Ends the Work

Research reveals that 30 to 57 percent of clients drop out of agreed-upon interventions earlier than initially planned (Reis & Brown, 2006; Vasquez, Bingham, & Barnett, 2008). Some expressed reasons given by clients for premature termination include a feeling of being mismatched with a clinician; longer-than-expected waits to be seen when in crisis; moving to another area; and lack of income, insurance, and transportation that would support the work. Others may feel pessimistic about the treatment offered to them, may not like its demands or effects, or may feel stigmatized for receiving mental health services (Edlund, Wang, Berglund, Katz, Lin, & Kessler, 2002). Clients who do not have a clinician who shares their ethnicity, culture, or native language may be less satisfied with the relationship and may end the relationship or just stop coming without explanation.

It is important that clinicians also ask themselves what they have done that may have led to premature termination. When clinicians work with clients whose culture is different from theirs, they may feel threatened, not know how to proceed, and become defensive (Pedersen, Crethar, & Carlson, 2008). Sometimes dropouts are prompted by the clinician's unhelpful attitudes and behaviors: missing the client's nonverbal cues, impatience eliciting the client's stories, or interrupting the client when he or she is detailing a concern the clinician doesn't deem important.

Brendali Reis and Lillian Brown (1999) believe that the number of drop-outs can be reduced by preintervention preparatory conversation about what is being offered, what will be expected from the client and the clinician, and any differences in perspectives about expectations and roles. Reis and Brown (2006) demonstrated good client continuance after presenting to new clients a brief preintervention video that illustrated what clinician–client encounters look like, and some expectations and benefits of open and frank clinical interactions.

Some clients who are feeling anxious about the work may suggest ending just when things are "getting hot" or when they are on the verge of making a significant change. They may use compelling language to justify their leaving.

> *Lorinda was a woman who came to the women's center for counseling about her relationship with an abusive husband. She was beginning to talk about the possibility of leaving him and had even asked me to look into some shelters for women who were victims of domestic violence. Lorinda and I had been meeting for about three weeks when she announced that she thought she needed to stop coming because she couldn't get a baby-sitter for her 1-year-old child and there was "just no way I can keep coming." We talked about the difficulty she was facing (it was true that she had no sitter), but as we explored it in more detail, Lorinda said that perhaps she didn't want to come because she was scared she was on the verge of making a major change in her relationship with her husband.*

On the other hand, both clinician and client may enjoy the work and the relationship and may want to hold on to the relationship for longer than necessary. Sometimes the clinician may continue to see a client for financial reasons because of the income the client provides or because the client is an "easy" client—someone the clinician likes and enjoys working with. Some clinicians find the work of ending so painful that they repeatedly delay talking about an approaching ending, thus shortening the time for the important reflection and conversation that could greatly benefit the client.

Moreover, clinicians and clients may not want to give up the caring warmth and wonderful experience of having someone who is there to listen in such a relationship-centered way. It is no favor to clients, however, to delay the modeling and development of a necessary life skill: concluding a relationship knowing that there will be other important relationships and that important aspects of this one can be stored forever in the hearts and minds of the participants.

> *I had seen Simcha off and on for several years for various problems related to leaving home, getting established in a career, and partnering in a big city full of risks for young adults. We had become as comfortable in our work together as two old shoes and clearly enjoyed each other. When it finally felt right not to come anymore, Simcha said laughingly that there must be some ethical rule that a social worker can't say no if a client wants to pay to come and be with the worker because it just feels so good, period.*

Sometimes clients can feel dependent on professionals, as though unable to make it alone. Others may have suffered serial losses and may understandably resist experiencing another. For some clients, contact with the clinician is perhaps the most interesting experience they have all week. Isolated individuals refusing referrals to other groups and activities outside their homes may even tell the clinician that, when he or she stops home visiting, they will have little other human contact, which makes ending very painful. Periodic conversations with clinical supervisors can help ensure that clinicians and clients end relationships in a compassionate but timely manner.

EXERCISE 14.4 Your Own Experiences with Endings

In your journal, discuss a time in the past when you ended a relationship. It might have been the ending of your own work with a clinician or the day you graduated from school or had a school friend who moved very far away. Record the circumstances of the ending and the things you experienced or said during the ending process. Looking back, what thoughts and feelings come to mind now about the ending process?

■ The Tasks of Endings and Transitions

The tasks and skills involved in ending are many, and you may have noted some of them as you recorded your part in the endings you wrote about in Exercise 14.4. Although we discuss the skills of ending in a particular order, they often overlap and ebb and flow. The work around endings can occur purposefully over a number of sessions, weeks, or months—or even in one meeting, if that meeting is all we have.

Announcing the Process: "Now We Are Ending"

Whether at the end of an interview or at the end of the work, the responsibility for verbally marking the ending time rests with the clinician. Because clinicians are responsible for marking the end of a session, they may say: "We have to be finishing shortly, so let's take a moment to review what we've said today, where we are, and what's ahead." Similarly, and using many of the same skills, the clinician has to say at a designated point in the work that, because the work and relationship are ending soon, it is time to acknowledge the ending and to do some work together specifically about ending. The subject of ending is gently yet confidently broached as a natural and inevitable part of life and work.

Clients with serious cognitive limitations may not be able to grasp the concept of ending or understand the nuances of a discussion focused on ending. Sometimes the best that the clinician can do is to mark off the sessions on a calendar or chart, as a visual indicator of time moving ahead and finally running out. Often a loved one close to the client and skilled in communication with him or her can accompany the client and help the client understand the clinician's intent and tasks to be done.

As time and ability permit, the clinician notes with clients that they can still take beneficial steps during the ending time: dealing with reactions, reviewing accomplishments and remaining issues, planning ahead, and making any necessary arrangements to ease the way for the client. Sometimes the introduction of focused ending work is an occasion for relief and excitement; at other times, the client may react with shock or dismay.

EXAMPLE

Clinician: Well, Roland, we are coming to the end of our work together.

Client: I can't believe how quickly the time has gone.

Clinician: Me either.

Client: So we're "terminating." What do we do when we're finishing?

Clinician: Well, I think it's a good time to remember where you were when we first met, to think about what we have done and where you are now in relation to the issues you came in with. It's also a time to think about how you may handle things in the future. We get to see if there are any loose ends that we want to talk about before you leave, and finally we say good-bye.

Acknowledging and Exploring Reactions to Ending: "How Does It Feel?"

Clients who see a dentist or an internist a number of times do not usually "work through" the ending of their work together. Even after a lengthy hospital stay, the staff do not usually ask, "How do you feel about our discharging you?" or "Did you have feelings about the people who assisted you while you were here?" A formal termination process is a phenomenon particular to clinical relationships, and many clients may not be used to focusing so intensely on ending a professional relationship. In addition, both clients and clinicians may be surprised at the intensity of their emotional reactions to ending—the more so if the contacts were initially mandated by others or laden with other complexities. For many clients, the ending phase of work is a great opportunity to celebrate their achievements, to honor a valued relationship, and then to move on. Joseph Walsh (2003) notes that in solution-focused and narrative therapies, in which the whole emphasis of the work is on helping clients author more positive and hopeful narratives that look toward more empowering futures, the focus at ending is on celebrating the success of these activities and how they are already playing out constructively in everyday life.

We can help by normalizing feelings and reactions related to endings and by helping clients express these feelings as the process of ending unfolds.

Some clients take endings in stride and have few reactions beyond mild regret at ending contact with someone they respect. Other clients, especially those who are loss sensitive or isolated, may feel sad and apprehensive as they imagine ending work with the clinician. Feelings may be overwhelming or intolerable, especially when the ending stirs up many unresolved losses from the past.

Some clients may threaten to harm themselves or others in response to the clinician's leaving, sending up an unmistakable **cry for help.** Clinicians are alert to these possibilities, particularly in clients who may have had a history of harming themselves or others before undertaking clinical work. Many people use the term **regression under stress** to describe the familiar phenomenon of outgrown behaviors returning under pressure because they are familiar, almost knee-jerk outlets for distress that cannot at the moment be expressed verbally. Clinicians wisely discuss with supervisors a range of potential responses in case client emergencies arise during ending work.

Sometimes client actions around endings take the simpler form of losing things: schedule books, keys to the house or car, important papers, and so on. Clients who previously expressed sadness or loss through bodily symptoms may react to the ending by once again experiencing somatic symptoms. We can use the skills of examining the moment, processing the process, or directly addressing indirect references to the ending process. If we can help clients see connections between their behaviors during ending and certain unexamined feelings underlying them, in the future they may be able to recognize their customary distress signals sooner and perhaps speak out, rather than acting out, their feelings.

EXAMPLE

> *Clinician:* Roland, have you noticed that you have started to lose things a lot lately? Last week, you said you lost your car keys and today you lost your gloves.
>
> *Client:* Yeah, I'm scattered.
>
> *Clinician:* Do you think it could have anything to do with losing our relationship soon? Sometimes it's easier to have feelings about lost things than about lost people.

Some clients may miss a session or two at this time, perhaps to abbreviate or draw out the process of ending, to avoid the pain of reflecting on loss, or perhaps even to register protest. In such instances, it is often helpful to reach out by phone or letter, suggesting a possible link between the missed sessions and the process of ending. Here the clinician can gently ask the client to try to come back in so that things can be discussed together rather than thought about alone (the way that many clients have learned to deal with unhappy events).

Gary had suffered from a serious form of schizophrenia, but over a 3-year period, he let me in so that we developed very good talks about his hopes for the future. It came time for me to make a change, and I moved to another town. I could not get Gary to come in to talk with me about this. Instead, he took off for Florida on his motorcycle and sent me a note on a restaurant napkin to say, "Hi there." In response, I sent a letter to his parents' home, telling him what my last day would be and hoping to see him. He just appeared in the waiting room that day, in motorcycle leather and helmet, and when we sat together to say good-bye, he pulled his helmet visor down over his face and talked with me through it. I could see the tears running down his cheeks behind the visor but did not comment, as I knew how hard this was for him. He was able to say that, when you lose friends, it is sad. At the end, we hugged each other good-bye and wished each other well. For a time, I could see him sitting on his bike outside the agency, loudly racing his motor. I was sorry to end with him, and he saw it in me as I saw it in him.

Reactions to ending provide an important opportunity for clinician and client to attend to the client's way of dealing with change and, time permitting, to explore unresolved feelings from past losses, educating the client as to how these feelings may be emerging in current reactions to ending. Clients who can appreciate human reactions to loss and change, as well as the possibility of taking good experiences with them in memory, are helped to cope better with loss and change. They can learn to anticipate common reactions to future changes and develop in advance good alternatives for managing their reactions with a minimum of harm to self or others.

Remembering: "Where Were You When We Began?"

Client and clinician review goals and accomplishments in relation to the client's issues and circumstances when the work began: "Let's go back and look at where you were when we first met." Some clients remember very accurately, and others not so well. In some situations, it can be useful to bring in process notes from early encounters and review them together to refresh the clients' memory of what they described as their situation and what feelings they had when they first came in. If they filled out an intake problem list or were asked to provide a written narrative regarding problems and goals, these materials can also be reviewed. A discussion of the goals and accomplishments can be the source of much pleasure, as clients remember how stuck they felt and how much further along they feel now.

E X A M P L E

Clinician: Roland, I was thinking about where you were when we first met. You were having anxiety attacks.

Client: Yeah. I was having about three a week. It was awful.

Clinician: And it was affecting your work and home life.

Client: I kept missing work and I thought Isabelle was going to leave me.

Reviewing Highlights of the Work Together: "What Have We Gotten Done?"

Client and clinician review salient developments during their work together for the purpose of identifying changes, honoring persistence and achievement, affirming client strengths, and discussing the transferability of developed skills. Embedded in this generally upbeat review is the notion that change in concert with others is now clearly possible. This review also gives the clinician a chance to note that the client's convictions about hopelessness and "stuckness" have lost some of their power. Perhaps the future can now be tackled more hopefully and assertively. During this review, clinician and client may also explore the main features and dynamics of their relationship, particularly where changes or improvements have occurred that augur well for the client's future efforts to relate with others.

EXAMPLE

> *Clinician:* You did a lot of work here.
>
> *Client:* I remember during our first meeting when you said that you thought you could help. I didn't really believe it.
>
> *Clinician:* Well, you really worked hard at it in spite of that.
>
> *Client:* I remember when we started those relaxation tapes . . . [They continue to discuss events in the course of their work together, including setbacks or failures.]

Evaluating Current Status: "Where Are You Now?"

In evaluating the current status of the client and his or her situation and prospects, the clinician and client discuss where the client is in relation to the originally described issues, assets, and problems. They may also evaluate the client's current functioning, outlook, and circumstances, highlighting the client's strengths and supports and checking for any risks to well-being. These discussions act as a reminder of the gains the client has made during their work together.

EXAMPLE

> *Clinician:* So, how would you say you're doing with the anxiety attacks at this point?
>
> *Client:* Well, you know . . . I haven't had one in almost two months.

Clinician: Nice work! And how would you describe things with Isabelle?

Client: Well, we still have our tensions. I thought she would be so relieved that my anxiety attacks were gone that everything would be great with her. But she still gets on my case sometimes. [They continue to talk about his home and work life.]

Foreshadowing the Future: "Where Are You Heading?"

As part of the ending process, the clinician and client explore what the client anticipates and what kinds of issues might arise in the future. They discuss how the client might respond to old familiar challenges if they should arise again. To double-check on shared understandings, the clinician often asks the client to recount what he or she will do in a particular crisis and to review more specifically whom he or she will rely on in the future for support, advice, and comfort to buttress and maintain growth.

EXAMPLE

Clinician: What will you do two months from now if you find that the anxiety attacks come back?

Client: Well, I certainly hope they don't. I thought I was better.

Clinician: I hope they don't, too, but in case they do, it's important to know what you would do to handle them.

Client: Well, I guess I would go back to that self-talk exercise you gave me and I would use the tapes. And I can talk to Isabelle, she's good at listening.

Clinician: And if that doesn't work?

Client: I would call you. Would that be okay?

Clinician: Of course it would.

Checking for Unfinished Business: "Is There Anything We Should Cover Before We End?"

The clinician and client always double-check to see whether they need to take care of anything before ending. We keep an eye out for things that might need saying or doing—things the client might not have mentioned or thought of.

I have a little visualization I use with clients when we are ending. I ask them to imagine that they are walking down the stairs after leaving my office for the last time and to think about whether or not there is anything else they would have liked to have said to me but didn't. I invite them to say it now.

Giving and Eliciting Feedback About the Meaning of the Relationship: "What Has This Meant?"

As we mentioned in our discussion of the skills of examining the moment and processing the process, the clinical relationship provides an opportunity to talk about the relationship itself. In the ending phase of the work, we often give clients direct feedback about how we have experienced and valued them and their work with us.

EXAMPLE

Clinician: One of the things I noticed about you, Roland, is how persistent you are. Things would look pretty gloomy, and you were still having lots of anxiety attacks, but you kept at it. You continued to use the relaxation exercises and self-talk when a lot of people would have given up.

Client: Some people would say I'm stubborn.

Clinician: I think hanging in there is a very important thing when it works for you. Are there times when it doesn't?

Client: Well, sometimes I have a hard time knowing when it's a matter of persistence that will get me somewhere and when it's a matter of me being too rigid to let go of something. [Clinician and client explore.]

The clinician purposely sets time aside to review with the client special aspects of their relationship and what it has meant to them both. This is often a time when both clinician and client share what they have appreciated about each other. We advise clinicians to hold off on these discussions for a time, lest any resulting "love fest" prevent clients from telling clinicians about any anger they may have about ending, especially when a circumstance in the clinician's life is making termination necessary. Exploration could be initiated using a number of different statements or questions.

EXAMPLES

"Before we finish, Eda, I'd like us to have a chance to talk about our relationship and what it's meant to both of us."

"We have gone over just about everything except how it's been for us to work together, Dan. Can we do that this morning?"

"Graciela, should we take some time now to review the relationship we've had here and what it says about your new ability to work closely with someone?"

"One of the things we haven't said much about, Denise, is the relationship we've developed. It's special, and I'm going to miss working with you."

"It was an honor to work with you, Kwame. Your courage in getting your family here from your homeland during wartime and carving out a new life for all of you has touched me deeply."

"Chou, you have really taught me a lot about the benefits of silence! I have even started to meditate, thanks to the little book you gave me. I am very grateful."

We make a point of expressing what we have gotten from the work with the client because we unfailingly learn or grow from parts of the experience. If the relationship has been difficult, we may not say that in parting but instead say, for example, "Even though we've had our moments, I'm glad we kept working together and were able to get some things done that you felt helped your son." We try never to fake goodwill or meaning that clearly has not characterized the meetings. Inauthenticity does not feel right, and clients can usually see through it. Instead, we try to remain cordial and polite, no matter what has happened.

EXERCISE 14.5 Giving Positive Feedback

Divide into small groups. Think about a person in your life with characteristics that you find unpleasant. Briefly describe the relationship, as well as the negative characteristics that make this relationship unpleasant for you. Think of one honest, positive piece of feedback that you could give to this person. Role-play giving this positive feedback to that person. Discuss whether the statements were well framed and believable.

Addressing Issues Around Future Contact

Both clients and clinicians may have a hard time parting. Clients may express this difficulty by asking whether, now that clinical work is ending, the clinician can become a friend: "You're just the kind of person I like" or "You and I have so much in common—can't we do anything together after this? It seems such a shame."

Clients often picture the client-centered relationship occurring in social settings—a far cry from the mutuality of real friendships. Moreover, once clients come to experience the "warts and all" of the real person who is the clinician out of role, they may be surprised or regretful.

> *When I told a beloved therapist that I often wished we knew each other in some other ways, she recounted a lunch she'd had with a therapist of hers after finishing up their clinical work. She was appalled to see how slovenly his dress was, and how his tie was covered with soup stains, and that he droned on a lot about himself. She reminded me that we see what we want to in people. That was the last contact she ever wanted with that therapist. I wondered what this hinted I might see in my own therapist if she became a friend, and I pretty much gave up the idea.*

One of the good things about leave-takings is that, when done well, they teach us how to develop ending skills. Joan Fleming and Therese Benedek (1966) suggest that the current relationship can be "metabolized into a memory" (p. 174) so that energy invested in it can be released to other relationships and activities. Moreover, this memory can act as a precious resource to be called upon when people face future adversity or challenge.

Clients sometimes ask if they can call or write the clinician in the future. Clinicians are of many minds about this request, and it is helpful to talk over options and their implications with a supervisor. Often the very idea that one can have contact makes the contact unnecessary: The idea itself is the comfort. Decisions have to be made individually. When working in smaller settings or locales, be careful not to choose some clients to favor with continued contact, denying others whose feelings may be quite hurt should they learn of the distinction.

Since we believe that much clinical work is ongoing, we often choose to let clients know that they can attempt to contact us in the future if they decide that they would like to do further work. Hung-Tat Lo and Kenneth Fung (2003) state that it is especially important to "leave the door ajar" for isolated ethnic minority families from cultures that believe that authentic relationships last over a long time and "are rarely terminated artificially" (p. 165). However, we must be careful that we do not make promises we cannot keep. Aware of how situations and schedules can change, we do not promise that we will always be available to work with clients in the future. We can suggest that the agency and others like ourselves will be available if we are not.

Giving and Receiving Mementos

Sometimes the clinician gives a gift to the client at the end of the relationship as a memento or symbol of the work together. For example, we may give a client who is beginning to feel her own strength a magic wand representing the client's power, or we may give a book of nature poetry to a client who uses nature as a comfort during times of loss. The gifts that clinicians give to clients need not be concrete. A gift could be the sharing of a blessing (e.g., the Irish blessing "May the wind be always at your back."). It could be a memory of something strong or soothing (watching the sunset at water's edge) or a mental picture of a significant scene from the client's life (imagining being held by a beloved parent).

Clients may ask for a picture or for mementos of the work together. Again, depending on the client's cultural traditions, the agency's and worker's theoretical orientation, the agency policy, and the worker's and client's individual styles, pictures or mementos may or may not be given. Clinicians—especially those who work with children, teens, or groups—may join clients for a photograph that acts as memory of a cherished experience together. If the clinician and client have been video recorded during their work, the client may request a copy of the video: "You know how we did that video recording? Well, could I get you and me on video so I can have something to remember from what we did?" or "Can I get a shot on my cell phone?" It would be wise to consult with a supervisor before acting on such requests and prepare in advance for things that may come up that might require an immediate response.

It may at times be validating to send a client a letter or card underscoring the client's accomplishments and wishing him or her well on the road ahead.

> *When Moses left the residence, I wanted him to have something to hang onto if things got tough when he went home. I wrote him the following letter:*
>
> *Dear Moses,*
> *It was good yesterday to watch you leave the house—and our work together—with such good confidence and skills for your life back in your "real" home. I could see how excited your dad was to get you back. You said you never got a letter, so I thought I would send this short note to say, "Way to go!" I want you to hang onto this and check it out if you get low. We all think you have what it takes to make it, and we're wishing you luck and courage every step of the way.*
> *High fives from all of us at The Grove,*
> *Your Counselor,*
> *Kareem Batts*

Clients may bring ending gifts to us. People from many cultures believe that gifts symbolize a natural and well-deserved "thank you" for services rendered by a hardworking professional. As with other gifts, carefully address their suitability and meaning.

> *I don't ask, "Why did you feel you needed to bring me a gift?" But as I open the gift, I do ask the client what they were thinking when they decided to bring me a gift. They always have interesting and useful things to say without it becoming a big deal. I always open the gift and am thankful for it with the client present. If it's food and the client asks me to taste it on the spot, I say that I will only eat some if the client will join me, and they usually do.*

Some community agencies may have bulletin boards on which pictures of clients and activities are displayed. Clinicians need to think carefully about confidentiality and get clients' permission before displaying any pictures in which clients are visible. We should also think about the effects on all clients if only some clients' pictures are displayed or if gifts from some clients are visible.

In many collectivist societies and cultures, showing and sharing come naturally. Thinking back on endings he regrets, Walsh (2003) describes a very traumatized and isolated Burmese war veteran he encouraged to use his good cooking skills to connect with a roommate. He did so and felt much better. When gains were made and the time came to end, this young man invited Walsh to share a meal at his apartment, which the clinician declined due to his sense of his code of ethics. The client was crushed, and Walsh now believes he conveyed a double message about food and relating. Now he wishes he had at least asked the man what cooking for Walsh would have meant to him and whether he would like to bring in some food that they could share in the office together.

Saying Good-Bye

In time-limited or task-focused clinical work, saying good-bye is a fairly straightforward and simple task that occurs much as it does in regular good-byes following any association. Participants acknowledge the end of the meeting or meetings, appreciate what each has contributed, and wish each other well. Handshakes and light hugs are often exchanged, the counselor walks the client to the door or waiting room, observing their customary practice of leave-taking. Deeply emotional reactions and protests about ending are rarely anticipated, since the focus of ending work has been on a review of the work, the tasks accomplished, and the client's reliance on self, family, and community resources more than it has been on the counselor's presence.

By contrast, when the clinical relationship itself has been a primary focus or an important therapeutic holding environment, the last meeting may follow searching and wide-ranging discussions of achievements, regrets, work yet to be done, past losses, gains, and readiness to proceed without the clinician. Whereas earlier ending discussions may have had a graver or more affective coloration, the final good-bye is usually more interactive and upbeat—a positive send-off after much good work together. Sometimes a quiet celebration or other ritual (e.g., an exchange of small gifts) is used to focus on the good-bye as a kind of celebratory launching.

While we recognize that the final good-bye may be sad, we always attempt to refocus clients on achievements and possibilities. We find it helpful to say that we will be picturing them doing something they have longed for and intended to do, such as graduate, stay clean and sober, or parent successfully. We attempt to have clients remember us as someone who is permanently in their corner, who believes in them, and who is rooting for them.

CLIP 14.2
Tasks and Skills
of Ending

EXERCISE 14.6 Saying Good-Bye

Divide into small groups. Practice in pairs the final moments of saying good-bye and exiting. Practice several kinds of good-byes, including those from public places, from office settings, from a client's apartment, or after a shared subway ride following a meeting at another agency. Discuss your experience and feelings as both clinician and client. What have you learned from this exercise?

■ Follow-Up and Evaluation

Many clinicians and agencies conduct **follow-up evaluations** after the end of clinical work. These evaluations may be formal, involving tests and other assessment measures as discussed in Chapter 8, or they may be informal check-ins. Follow-up evaluations can occur a month, six months, or even years after the initial work. At times, these follow-up meetings may serve as a reinforcement of the previous work together, reminding clients of the strengths and resources they have and the skills they developed during the course of the clinical relationship. As a side benefit, follow-up evaluations give the client a chance to discuss and honor how he or she is able to use the learning from the clinical relationship to resolve other problems.

EXAMPLE

Client: Well, it's been six months since I saw you.

Clinician: How's it been going, Roland? [The clinician explores Roland's anxiety attacks and how he is doing at work and with Isabelle.]

Client: You know, Isabelle has gone back to school. The other night she was a wreck about an exam she had to take. I taught her those relaxation exercises you taught me, and she calmed down. It was neat to be the helper for once.

Clinician: I'm glad they were helpful. What a great thing you did for her.

Client: Yeah, I'm pretty proud that I can use what I learned here.

■ Planned Breaks, Interruptions, Transfers, and Abrupt Endings

Planned Breaks

Sometimes a clinician and client decide together that a great deal has been accomplished and that it is now time for a **planned break,** during which the client goes for a time without face-to-face visits with the clinician.

In advance of the break, they schedule a future appointment in which to review the client's interim experience and to decide only then whether further professional assistance is indicated. Sometimes these planned breaks are a part of the termination process.

> *At the clubhouse, a day program for people who have been in an inpatient psychiatric hospital, we have a gradual termination process. We slowly decrease the number of days that the client comes to the clubhouse until they are coming only once a week. After a while, we will suggest that the member take a one-month "vacation" from the center, but we always set up a follow-up visit to see what the experience was like. Often a client will take repeated "vacations" before he or she finally feels ready to leave for good.*

Interruptions

Sometimes the work between clinician and client is interrupted, occasioning a need for immediate work on the process of ending contact, either temporarily or permanently. A clinician or client may become ill, pregnant, or take a long trip—all of which may require an interruption, although a return is anticipated.

> *I had been working as a rehabilitation counselor at a nursing home for three years when my husband got a sabbatical from his college teaching job. He was offered a six-month fellowship in Montana, and we decided that I would join him there. I took a leave from my job, and let me tell you, it was hard to say good-bye to all the clients. I wasn't sure which of them would still be there when I returned. I reassured the clients that I would be returning in September. I told them where I was going, and I said I would think of them.*

The use of a symbolic **transitional object** is helpful in sustaining a feeling of connection between the client and the clinician. This is especially true with children, who may need a concrete reminder of the clinician's existence, but it is often supportive for adults as well.

> *When the college interns leave the preschool for winter break, we actually use it as a learning experience. Kalina was going home to Hawaii, so we took out a world map and showed the children where Kalina was going. We brought in pictures of Hawaii and had Kalina send postcards each week. That way the children would remember her when she returned.*

Even when the interruption or break is anticipated or time limited, client and clinician may go through a process similar to other endings. We prepare the client for the interruption, leave room to talk about the feelings the interruption evokes, and attempt to get some closure for the work completed. Although we plan to return, the client may not be there when we do so. In fact, a clinician might not return.

> *A couple of years ago, two therapists were murdered while they were on vacation. I was one of a team of clinicians who stepped in to work with their clients after their deaths. It really brought home to me how important it is to realize that you can never promise you will be back. You can promise you will try, but never that you will always be there.*

In a similar vein, when a clinician is suddenly diagnosed with a life-threatening illness and is subject to periods of treatment absence, of low energy, and of low emotional availability, the clinician is faced with tough choices about whether and how to keep working with clients. Careful work with supervisors and regular support from a group of supportive colleagues can help guide decision making about the disclosure of the illness, as well as temporary or ongoing needs for scheduling changes (Morrison, 1997; Philip, 1994).

Clients are usually very understanding and accommodating, yet the question lingers with the clinician as to whether they would be better served by another clinician. If the illness is serious or life threatening, clients are often helped to say goodbye and transfer to another colleague or group if further work remains to be done. For the client's sake, the transfer work is usually done before the clinician's functioning deteriorates markedly. It is not unusual for clients to attend memorial or funeral services whose rituals afford an opportunity to get some closure on the loss of an important relationship. Public processes also help clients mourn without having to disclose the nature of their relationship with the deceased clinician.

Transitions to Another Clinician

On other occasions the client may be transferred to another clinician. This can happen during a planned interruption, as with illnesses, in which case it is anticipated that the original clinician and client will reconnect. It can also happen when the client sees another clinician after terminating with the original one. If the client is terminating, the clinician can offer to speak with the new clinician. This can facilitate the new work, help the clinician learn about the client, and perhaps avoid old pitfalls. Some clients like to have a sense of continuity in the work, and they may hope that this conversation will prevent them from having to repeat everything with the new clinician. Other clients may refuse permission for the clinicians to speak with each other, preferring to start with a clean slate.

When the client is seeing another clinician, the original clinician can help the client prepare for work with the new clinician.

EXAMPLE

Clinician: Last week you told me that you and Isabelle are going to see a couples therapist after we finish our work together.

Client: Yeah, Isabelle wants to work on "our communication," as she calls it.

Clinician: What do you think that will be like? [They explore Roland's anticipations and fears.]

Clinician: Do you think you will talk about our work together?

Client: I don't know.

Clinician: I want you to know that I feel fine about your talking about what worked and didn't work in our relationship. Sometimes people feel that they are betraying their old counselor if they talk to their new counselor about stuff they did or feelings they had with their old counselor. It can help future work to explore with your new counselor—both the things that helped and those that didn't.

If the client is seeing another clinician only temporarily and anticipates continuing with the original clinician, the two clinicians usually speak but, again, only after the client has given written permission, which is kept in the client's file. It can ease transitions if the original clinician introduces the client to the **covering clinician** before leaving.

The covering clinician can often feed useful information about the relationship back to the original clinician, although being careful never to compete to be the "better helper." Any concerns or questions that the covering clinician has about the work should be shared directly with the clinician rather than with the client. The covering clinician becomes a team member and assumes the same ethical and legal obligations as though he or she were the primary clinician.

When one of my partners was taking an extended vacation, she asked me to see a client of hers. She described the client as someone who was very shy and had a hard time talking. I was quite surprised when I met the client, who seemed anything but shy. After I had met with him a couple of times, I told him that I had expected him to be much more reticent because that was how his therapist had described him to me. He told me that he felt very uncomfortable talking to any women, specifically professional women. He was comfortable talking with me because I was a man. We explored the issue and discussed how he might raise the issue with his therapist when she returned. When she did return, she told me how great it was that her client had seen me. He had talked with her about what we had discussed, and it really changed the nature of their work together. She threatened to go away again so that I could "do consultations" with all her clients.

Transitions to Family and Community Support Systems

When clients end therapy, they often continue to receive support and caring from their natural helping networks, such as family, friends, neighborhood resource centers, religious or spiritual communities, or mutual aid groups. As noted previously, Taylor and colleagues (2000) have delineated the vital roles that black churches play in providing connections, activities, emotional support, and guidance. Delgado (1997) has noted that small businesses and Latino-owned beauty parlors act as social and informational support centers in Latino communities. Community centers and clubs, after-school programs, literacy and citizenship initiatives, cultural associations, and neighborhood action groups also offer opportunities to lessen isolation and strengthen individual and family esteem and pride.

A clinician's knowledge of and solid relationship with a wide variety of these resources are important in helping clients connect with them as they transition from the clinical relationship. Some of these programs and support centers may have staff who reach out to clients. Sometimes the clinician may explain what services are offered and even accompany clients to their first contacts with community resources. Doman Lum (2004) considers the ability to connect clients with meaningful resources to be a bedrock of clinical competence in working cross-culturally. Ideally, the clinician uses these resources throughout the work together, and not just as the clinical relationship is drawing to a close.

Abrupt Endings

The client may abruptly leave a session, simply not show up, or cancel future appointments. If a client stops coming, we usually attempt some sort of **outreach:** a phone call, a letter, or, in some cases, a home visit. Decisions about outreach should be discussed with a supervisor. If the client does not return, we can try to get some closure through a **letter of termination.**

EXAMPLE

Dear Juan,

I haven't heard from you since our last meeting on July 23. I have tried to contact you by phone and letter. I will assume that you have made the decision to stop our work at this time.

If you decide that you would like to return to get more closure on our work or if you feel that I can be of help to you in the future, please feel free to contact me at the agency.

It has been a pleasure getting to know you. I hope that you will have success in getting your GED as you planned.

Sincerely,
Davra Nawan

We all need to prepare ourselves for the fact that sometimes clients suddenly drop out of the work and never call or write to explain why. They may not respond to any of our outreach to them. These unexplained exits can leave us blaming ourselves, doubting our abilities, and feeling upset that a client we have worked hard to engage has just left us high and dry. Sometimes reviewing our work with a supervisor can help us understand problems that we did not see or subtle messages from the client that might have signaled ambivalence or intention to stop.

> *At a day treatment center, when a member dropped out, we would hold what we called a "group autopsy." We would discuss the member, his history in the program, and his relationship with staff and peers. Sometimes we could figure out why the member left—for example, because he was having difficulty with another member or one of the staff, or because of things changing at home. Sometimes there was no way of knowing. At least in these meetings, we could identify what we needed to change to respond more effectively to our members or we could console each other that we had done the best we could.*

We can fret for a long time about what we did or did not do to make things end this way, and doing so can make it hard to get closure. While it is good to explore which of our actions may have contributed to this sudden ending, we have to be able to let go and move on.

> *I remember one supervisor telling me that it was narcissistic to think that the reason a client left was because of something I had done. He reminded me how small we actually can be in a client's extremely complicated life.*

■ The Clinician Feels the Loss

Abrupt endings are particularly difficult for a clinician, but all endings evoke feelings in us. As the time to end approaches, we may find that, like the client's feelings, our own feelings may come out in behavior. We may lose our car keys or appointment books, double-book a client who is ending, or find ourselves feeling sad, anxious, or relieved. Clinicians working in health or hospice settings often encounter the very moving experience of working closely with clients with terminal health conditions. These clients know they have little time left and understandably do not want to lose a clinician with whom they are able to share whatever they wish about their dying.

Under special circumstances, a clinician who wishes to do so may arrange with the agency to continue to meet with a dying client even after leaving the agency and other clients. Consultation with a supervisor can help resolve dilemmas about whether and with whom to continue and how to arrange to keep seeing a client until death occurs. This is clinical work at its most human, characterized by flexibility, availability, and respectful adaptation to the needs of clients and their loved ones.

As clinicians, we form attachments to our clients and can have a great investment in their well-being, just as they are often strongly invested in the work with us and in our presence, caring, and encouragement. This is a human relationship of some intensity as well as a working partnership, and its attenuation or ending affects clinicians as well as clients.

> *I hated ending with Charysse. I had literally watched her grow up. She had been in the after-school program at the center when I was a rec counselor, and I had coached her on the basketball team. Then she'd been one of the kids in the alcohol and drug group, and she eventually became a peer counselor. Now, she was having a baby and moving to*

CLIP 14.3
Clinicians'
Reflections

Des Moines with Raffie. (I knew him, too.) When our last meeting was over, I walked into my supervisor's office and just cried. I was so happy for her and for the new life she was starting, but it was so sad to see her go.

■ Conclusion

Whether planned or unplanned and whether initiated by client, clinician, or outside forces, the ending of the clinical relationship provides an opportunity for new learning and growth. Good endings can help clinicians and clients increase their relational capacity, knowledge, and sensitivity. Both can take the work and the relationship away with them as internalized and sustaining inner resources, available for use as long as there is memory.

In Chapter 15, we discuss the ongoing education and self-care that clinicians need to remain fit and effective in work with clients. We highlight many professional issues, challenges, and benefits that await clinicians over the course of a long and active career. We also discuss the importance of professional affiliations and support.

■ Suggested Readings

A theoretically inclusive book that discusses ethnocultural considerations in ending is:

Walsh, Joseph. (2003). *Endings in clinical practice: Effective closure in diverse settings*. Chicago: Lyceum.

Further readings about endings include:

Edlund, Mark J., Wang, Philip S., Berglund, Patricia A., Katz, Stephen J., Lin, Elizabeth, & Kessler, Ronald C. (2002). Dropping out of mental health treatment: Patterns and predictors among epidemiologal survey respondents in the United States and Ontario. *American Journal of Psychiatry, 159,* 845–851.

Fair, Susan M., & Bressler, Joanna M. (1992). Therapist-initiated termination of psychotherapy. *The Clinical Supervisor, 10,* 171–189.

Gutheil, Irene A. (1993). Rituals and termination procedures. *Smith College Studies in Social Work, 63,* 163–176.

Reis, Brendali F., & Brown, Lillian G. (2006). Preventing therapy dropout in the real world: The clinical utility of videotape preparation and client estimate of treatment duration. *Professional Psychology: Research and Practice, 37,* 311–316.

Vasquez, Melba J. T., Bingham, Rosie P., & Barnett, Jeffrey E. (2008). Psychotherapy termination: Clinical and ethical responsibilities. *Journal of Clinical Psychology, 64,* 653–665.

Younggren, Jeffrey, & Gottlieb, Michael. (2008). Termination and abandonment: History, risk, and risk management. *Professional Psychology: Research and Practice, 39,* 498–504.

■ Self-Explorations

1. Recall a time when you were part of an ending that was not done well. What happened? Why? How do you think you or the other person could have handled it better?

2. Do you think you would be more likely to end a relationship too soon or too late? Why?

3. How do you deal with endings at this point in your life? What are your strengths in this area? What are the challenges for you?

4. Sometimes people do funny things during a period of transition in their lives—acting in ways that may be considered expressions of loss—misplacing keys, locking themselves out, leaving a personal item behind so that they have to go back to retrieve it. Has this ever happened to you? How do you understand it?

■ Essay Questions

1. List and briefly describe five major tasks of ending the clinical relationship and work.

2. Discuss the benefits and risks of giving and receiving mementos at the end of the work or the construction of an ending ritual (a celebration, a drawing, a picture taking, or a video recording) with the client.

3. Discuss mistakes clinicians can make when ending clinical relationships and work.

4. What are the steps clinicians take to ensure the best possible referral for a client with ongoing needs for service? What things can clinicians do to determine whether an agency they have never used before is one that would provide effective follow-through with the client?

■ Key Terms

Client abandonment	Outreach
Covering clinician	Planned break
Cry for help	Referral
Follow-up evaluation	Regression under stress
Foreshadow the ending	Termination
Letter of termination	Transitional object
Managed care organizations	

CHAPTER 15

Professional Issues: Ongoing Education and Self-Care

To be effective, clinicians have to develop and sustain high degrees of understanding, compassion, skill, and commitment, which requires lifelong education, personal growth, and careful attention to the care of the professional self. This chapter addresses the professional issues of ethical practice, self-care, and ongoing education.

■ Self-Care: Taking Care While Giving Care

If you believe in quality clinical work and the contributions it can make to a better world, then it is important that you not only survive but also thrive as a compassionate, effective, and ethical provider. Only then can you perpetuate clinical practice at high levels of commitment and competence. You must come to the work with your eyes wide open, prepared to nourish and renew yourself and to connect with others for support, validation, relaxation, and enjoyment.

Stresses of Clinical Work

All work is stressful to some degree. In complex societies, most working people have to contend with the stresses of time and resource pressures, of complex communication networks, of working within systems of unequal power and privilege, and of compromises to ideals that must be made to get work done.

Certain stresses are unique to clinical work in the human services. Assignment loads can be very large and call for work both within and outside the agency, often separating clinicians from their collegial support for many hours of the week. In economic downturns, clinicians may be laid off or let go just like other workers are. Those who remain then inherit the caseloads of those departing, on top of work for which they are already responsible. Agencies may also require that clinicians rotate evening and weekend emergency beeper coverage. It is often hard to put the work down at day's end, especially when emergencies suddenly arise that only worsen if left unattended to. For example, in continuous work with great numbers of victims at disaster sites, there may be no "day's end" for clinicians or disaster teams, and only weak supervisory support to mitigate stress (Pulido, 2007). Consequent reductions in "getaway" rest and relaxation with family and friends can be extremely wearing on relational people.

Research on the etiology of professional distress indicates that many clinicians may have learned early in life to overdo for others to earn love or to avoid conflict in their troubled families of origin (Sussman, 1992). To help the family stay organized if parents were absent or dysfunctional, these youngsters were inducted into self-sacrificing roles carried out for the good of others, roles that often play out again in the selection of demanding/rewarding human service work as a career path (O'Connor, 2001).

This preparation for sacrifice and for helping others may underlie much of the workaholism that seems to characterize the working style of many agencies and clinicians. The very other-centeredness that is the hallmark of so much good clinical work can also strain our resources and draw our attention away from our own survival needs. Periods of emotional exhaustion, fatigue, detachment, and depression may cycle with sustaining feelings of accomplishment, role satisfaction, and the pleasure of engaging with memorable clients and colleagues (Figley, 2002; Norcross, 2000; Rupert & Kent, 2007).

> *I used to tell people that I worked two or three jobs because I needed the money, but really, I think now that it was because I didn't know any other way of being. In visiting my siblings more, I began to notice that none of us could really just sit still for long and talk with each other. We had to get up while talking and be busy "doing something useful." We regularly drove each other crazy asking repeatedly, "Are you hungry?. . . can I get you anything while I'm up? . . . if you need anything, please just say."*

Historically, clinicians have been underpaid, undervalued, and undersupported. At the same time, we are very aware that many other professions and occupations enjoy greater pay, benefits, and respect than we do. This occurs in spite of our years of education and experience, the importance of our services to communities, our advanced degrees, and our willingness and commitment to work with populations that are often marginalized by other professions.

> *After a master's degree and 30 years of experience, I am making less money than my nephew, who's a year out of college and working in a big accounting firm. It does bug me sometimes, but I always try to remember why I chose to do this work in the first place. I still love it—but I do fret about pay inequities.*

Clinicians often work with stories of tragedy, violence, cruelty, and human indifference to suffering. These stories can continue disconcertingly to haunt our thoughts—sometimes even our dreams. As noted in Chapter 13, clinicians repeatedly exposed to traumatic stories may absorb clients' experiences so extensively that they develop symptoms of vicarious traumatization (Figley, 2002; McCann & Pearlman, 1990).

Burnout, or **compassion fatigue,** is an occupational hazard in the helping professions (Figley, 1995; Pulido, 2007). It often results from clinicians' interacting intensely with people with many severe problems over a long period and with poor support. The symptoms of compassion fatigue include physical, mental, and emotional exhaustion ("I'm worn out"); insensitivity to others ("I don't care anymore"); a sense of futility or hopelessness about one's actions ("Going out there to visit them will change nothing"); and a sense of isolation and invalidation ("Who cares what we do anyway?"). At times you may experience a kind of disempowerment, lack of control, and disenchantment similar to that experienced by many of our clients when they work hard under tough conditions.

Work stresses often compromise the immune system, contributing to emotional and physical disorders and symptoms such as head, stomach, and back pain; insomnia; and a pervasive feeling of uneasiness or tension (Borysenko & Dveirin, 2006; Domar & Dreher, 2000). Over the years, some clinicians turn to substance use to cope with the pressures of the job and develop addictions and serious relationship problems at home (Siebert, 2005). In extreme circumstances, some find release in unethical activities or relationships with clients involving financial or sexual exploitation. The stresses of clinical work can take their toll unless we are vigilant about our own well-being. All professions now have confidential help lines for impaired colleagues, and some urban AA groups are specifically for clinicians, so that they can participate in mutual aid without encountering clients.

EXERCISE 15.1 Stresses in Clinical Work

In your journal, record the major stresses that affect clinicians in your agency or area. What impact have you seen these stresses have on colleagues? What stresses have affected *you* so far? What can you do to diminish their impact on your own life and work?

Strategies of Self-Care

Whereas the physician uses the stethoscope and X-ray, or the plumber a wrench and pliers, clinicians use the professionally developed self to relate with clients, conduct assessments, and develop meaningful responses and interventions. Personal awareness, attunement, empathy, and readiness to listen and respond to others are a clinician's basic "tools of the trade." To preserve the precious instrument of self, we have to become as responsive to ourselves as we are to our clients.

1. *We need to identify clearly the people, activities, and forces that sustain us and those that do not.* Work to find work settings and colleagues that can consistently appreciate and support you while helping you learn how to set some limits on what you are able to do with and for others—and stay on this side of exhaustion. Clinicians in public agencies experience much greater stress than those working in nonprofit settings (DiFranks, 2008), so be mindful of environmental supports and hazards when making employment decisions. Unless you consider these important steps of self-advocacy with the same concern and energy with which you would advocate for any client, your gifts of attunement, caring, empathy, and responsiveness can actually become hazards to your long-term well-being.

Frederick Sweitzer and Mary King (2009) list eight kinds of support you may need from various allies over the years: someone who just listens without advising; sound advice when it's needed; praise from "fans"; friends to relax and play with; "chicken soup people" who comfort; people who challenge you to go further or deeper; the companionship of "buddies" with whom you can say or do anything without fear; and affirmation and validation from people who've had similar feelings or experiences (p. 27).

The overuse or misuse of an instrument leads to its deterioration. Furthermore, when we are tired, distracted, or resentful of work's burdens, clients can see this and then quietly suffer from diminished caring, attention, and responsiveness, just as we do when we see that our usual support is "not there" due to stressful preoccupations.

2. *We need to develop and sustain self-empathy.* Judith Jordan (1991b) describes **self-empathy** as the capacity to notice, care about, and respond to our own felt needs as generously as we attend to the needs of others. Just as with clients, the strategies of self-care involve valuing yourself, thinking about your needs differently, and connecting with others in order to experience rest and renewal, support and validation, self-actualization, and effectiveness at home and at work.

3. *We need to be good to ourselves and to take time and space for ourselves without feeling selfish, guilty, or that we are wasting time.* We often find out the hard way that overworking and overgiving always have a physical and emotional price, often paid in physical symptoms and relational disconnects. It is important to relax and nurture yourself, rather than feeling driven to always be doing something for others. Since doing for others is also a very rewarding part of our lives and work, what we are urging is more self-care

and balance in how you organize your life. We would like to see self-care become routine in the lives of caregivers rather than incidental to "more important things."

> *I get up an hour earlier than I used to, in order to do yoga stretches in the quiet of the morning before the others come down. Everyone knows this is "mama's time."*

* * *

> *Every day I pretend to get on a scale that shows how much my burdens weigh today instead of how much I do. If they weigh a lot, I laugh and plan what little treat I can work into the day to pick up my spirit. It is usually something chocolate!*

* * *

> *I thank my angels every morning for love and strength, and again every night. You can never have too many angels.*

4. *Fundamental to self-care are good health practices, which sustain both energy and the body's natural immune responses to protect against physical, mental, and emotional problems.* You can stay fit through regular exercise and healthy dietary practices, minimizing the use of substances like caffeine, nicotine, alcohol, or drugs, which trigger high-low cycles that in turn affect energy, concentration, and mood. When work is largely confined to interior or closed spaces with poor air quality and artificial lighting, take brief breaks outside in fresh air and sunlight, and bike or walk to and from work whenever feasible. You can also carve out a few moments to walk down hallways or between floors instead of always phoning or emailing colleagues. Just a little bit of exercise refreshes mind and body between tasks, but we have to make a habit of it.

> *A neighbor who walks every morning helped me get started walking, too. It didn't have to be far or long; it just had to be. Then the trick was to set up my own workday so that there would be time for walking in it. If the weather was bad, I learned to walk around the five floors of my agency.*

5. *Using the power of humor to sustain and refresh is another useful strategy in reclaiming efficacy.* Clinicians often develop shared bulletin boards on which they post favorite cartoons or sayings that make everyone laugh and reflect on the follies of the human condition or the pomposities some people are capable of. We are always careful not to use humor that hurts or offends.
6. *Connections with others, especially with people who don't talk about workplace stress all the time, are also crucial to good self-care.* These connections can be with friends and family, or they can occur through activities in which people with similar interests come together to share or create. Some clinicians take great satisfaction in working together in social action and public health campaigns aimed at changing social conditions. Singing and theater arts groups, dance, exercise, and meditation groups—all can provide channels for creative expression, feedback, and friendship. Cultural rituals or spiritual retreats may also provide comfort.

> *Some of our staff go out dancing on Friday nights—one loves to salsa dance. Four play bridge once a month. One man sings in a gospel choir, and another plays trombone in a little jazz café the next town over. All of them say how much this eases them up and helps them be more present for clients all week.*

7. *Many clinicians find that spiritual connections through meditation or formalized religious practice help them when stressed.*   Meditation programs, videos, workshops, and literature are widely available for use in relaxation and stress reduction, and you can practice physically relaxing activities at the beginning, middle, or end of a day or during a lunch break. Health care research is affirming the therapeutic potential of mindfulness meditation, and in a study of mental health workers in a demanding DBT program, participants heralded their program's mindfulness training and practice as their most effective stress relief strategy (Perseius, Kaver, Ekdahl, Asberg, & Samuelsson (2007). In any 24-hour period, there are 96 fifteen-minute blocks, leaving us few excuses for not relaxing. Just 10 to 15 minutes of focused meditation can induce a peacefulness and bodily rest that help alleviate sleep problems due to worry as well as daytime stress on the job.

8. *You must also purposely make time for doing creative things you are good at and find especially pleasing.*   Gardening, working out, sports, painting and drawing, quilting or knitting, listening to music or playing an instrument, cooking special foods, writing or composing poetry, and reading are some of the many ways that people find to enjoy themselves through self-expression.

> *I saved up and got a keyboard and told my friends about how much I liked writing little songs for people's birthdays—it was so different from my usual routines, in which I encourage others' creativity and growth. Occasionally I play simple duets with a friend who's just now taking cello lessons at 70.*

9. *When you feel depleted, use staff or professional meetings to talk more about your positive feelings about your work and the things that are going well.*   Although angry or negative ventilation in peer groups may be a good release, too much negative ventilation can also leave participants feeling cynical or hopeless. Always try to find a way to balance excessive negativism with recall of *what you like and value* in the work and the things you admire in special people with whom you work.

10. *In hard times, remember your competencies and contributions, and relate to an ongoing base of support that revives your spirit.*   Mind-body specialists Alice Domar and Henry Dreher (2000) emphasize that, to maintain health and spirit, self-care always has to have "two aspects: one in solitude, one in relationship" (p. 11). But too much isolation when distressed can dismantle your energy, spirit, and perspective on the world and your place in it.

> *Sometimes I like to eat my lunch by myself outside the school, looking out at the nearby lake. This is when I'm tired of listening and talking and I just want to have some private, silent time to get myself together before I go back to class. Other times I like to go eat Thai food up the street with my program friends. We get silly together and catch up on news and gossip.*

If you are "one of a kind" (the only lesbian, the only African American, the only Muslim) in your work setting, make sure that you find and nurture support within you own cultural institutions and activities. Feeling "at home" at the deepest levels is very uplifting.

EXERCISE 15.2 Preventing Compassion Fatigue

In small groups, discuss how you recognize compassion fatigue in yourselves, and describe some of the things you do successfully, alone and with others, to prevent it.

■ Ongoing Education

Clinical education does not end with a diploma; it is a lifelong learning process. It is your professional obligation to continue your education through supervision, consultation, personal therapy, reading about current clinical research and intervention techniques, and attending continuing education and professional development courses. All of these collaborative activities contribute to an important maturational process that you are likely already beginning to experience.

Supervision

Clinical internships usually provide weekly supervision. In some settings, you may have two or more supervisors, who select and assign cases that advance learning, arrange coverage, oversee the general work of clinicians, and attend to the development of students' values, knowledge, and skills in clinical practice with clients. Agencies sometimes have group supervision in which all interns gather to review their work with each other.

Supervision is an essential part of your continuing growth throughout your career. We believe that all clinicians should have some form of ongoing supervision, whether it is individual, group, or peer supervision.

Individual Supervision

Good individual clinical supervision parallels a good clinical relationship in several respects. It provides a sustaining environment for learning and growth; it helps potentiate the learner's strengths, skills, and development; and it models relational, assessment, and problem-solving skills. While primarily task focused, a worker and supervisor may also examine the moment or process the process of their relationship. Because of supervisors' considerable ongoing knowledge of a worker's clients, goals, and stories to date, they often cover with clients when their supervisees are away, occasionally seeing a client or two who may need support during the worker's absence.

Supervisors act as a backstop in times of crisis, and they frequently model critical thinking, composure, and purposeful behavior under fire.

> *I remember the first time I was working with a client who was suicidal. I felt quite out of my depth. I called my supervisor to tell him what my client had just said about thinking about killing herself. His response was, "Well, let's think how we should respond." I can't tell you how relieved I felt with his use of the word "we." It made me feel that I wasn't alone. I felt I could relax into the comfort of our team. He was in this with me.*

Your supervisors also help you learn professional values and work with you to resolve contradictions and dissonance between the values of your upbringing and those of the profession you have chosen (Cascio & Gasker, 2001). Supervisors are often selected because of their sound values and standards and their effective role modeling of well thought-out approaches to complex problems.

Supervisors can help you learn how to be effective as you work with culturally diverse clients in a multicultural world. They can inaugurate you into the professional culture you will be a part of for the rest of your career.

Regular supervision is one of a clinician's best ways to monitor clients' progress toward goals and personal actions and reactions in relation to clients and client material (Kadushin & Kadushin, 1997). Reviewing the content and sequencing of clinician–client exchanges in interviews also helps us develop reflective practice skills (Graybeal & Ruff, 1995). That is, you will come to see that moment-to-moment transactions between yourself and clients generate knowledge about both of you and can provide direction for the next steps in the interview, in the overall work, and for your clinical learning. The process of good supervision is similar to the clinical skills learning process suggested in this text, with a parallel focus on examining and trying out skills and receiving feedback from others that enhances understanding and skill execution.

Because age, race, culture, locale, and gender all affect communication styles, no single counseling style will be appropriate for the diverse populations you will be serving (Derald Sue & Sue, 2008). Supervision can give you feedback about the ways you may affect clients and help you change your behaviors so as to align yourself better with clients from many different cultures.

Supervisors will help you recognize and attend to subtleties of themes and expression in your conversations with clients, supervisors themselves, colleagues, and others. They often model the attitudes, reactions, and listening and responding skills that they hope you incorporate into your developing practice repertoire. Certainly, effective supervisors listen closely to the supervisory process, trying to join with both your perspective and that of the client (Dean, 1984; Sweitzer & King, 2009).

Your supervisors may also focus on steps in the overall problem-solving work with clients: what is or is not being resolved, and where agreed-on plans may have gotten derailed. Thinking things out together can generate new goals or strategies. Before the meeting closes, you and the supervisor summarize plans for future sessions. You will often be asked to hazard guesses about what may occur next, to develop your capacity to anticipate events accurately so as to be more prepared to work with them. In time you will become more comfortable and adept at spotting problems *as* they occur and more able to take corrective action.

Although **"therapizing" supervisees** (probing for painful details of personal history) is avoided, supervisors are usually open to hearing a brief outline of a clinician's problems or experiences if they are disrupting learning or work with clients. Because problems with interviewing inevitably arise as a result of the complex dynamics of human exchange, supervisors try to find the right blend of minimal exploration of the learner's story and respect for the learner's privacy and personal boundaries (Kaiser, 1997).

> *Cora was a 42-year-old woman who came to the clinic to get some help with child rearing. While I was seeing her, her father was diagnosed with bone cancer, adding even more stress to her caregiving responsibilities. I didn't specifically talk about the issue with Duane, my supervisor, but it came up in passing as I said something about how Cora was late because she stopped at the hospital to visit her father. Duane started asking me questions, and it became clear that I hadn't talked with Cora enough about how her father's illness was affecting her. My supervisor said he was curious about my lack of follow-through on this, and then I told him about my mother's recent cancer diagnosis.*
>
> *We talked a little about how my own feelings as a daughter of someone who was dying of cancer may have gotten in the way of my attending to an important issue for Cora. Throughout the conversation, I thought Duane was being careful to look at the interface but not to push me too hard to talk about my mother. While he was caring, he made it clear that he was interested in talking about my mother's illness only to the extent that it might be affecting my work. At the end of our meeting, he said that I might want to talk to a counselor myself about all the stresses I was coping with. I started to cry and said I thought he had a good point.*

To normalize the struggles of the learning process, clinical supervisors may occasionally share some of their own missteps and dilemmas as continuing learners. They may also periodically assign readings about the process of clinical work or learning. Supervisory discussions may incorporate learning from the intern's concurrent course readings or training programs, and supervisees may bring in materials that give the supervisor new information or perspective, heightening a feeling of reciprocal influence and respect.

> *I brought in an article from my clinical class for my supervisor to read, about new research detailing the effects of trauma on children's neurology. After we looked at the research in relation to two kids I'm working with, she brought in an article for me to read, about research on love and empathy that shows that they have the potential to alter neurological development favorably.*

Sometimes supervision is really hard; for example, when a supervisor may have to tell you that something you have said or done is inappropriate and that you must change your behavior. This might occur if your continuing statements or work practices demonstrate unethical bias or prejudice; if you consistently miss client appointments; or if several colleagues complain that your approach to them is rude or offensive. Limit setting is designed to help you realign your behaviors with the standards of the profession. You will come to appreciate how professional guidance and limits help you work with others more productively.

The diversity of students and clients today reflects the changing demographics of the twenty-first century in ways that practicum supervisors, training faculties, and agency staff may not because the human services have been as slow as other sectors of the economy in hiring and promoting ethnocultural minorities. Students thus may or may not be able to find the range of diversity in colleagues and mentors that they might wish to have as models (e.g., people of color; gay, lesbian, or transgender persons; people with disabilities). Whether supervision is intra- or intercultural, supervisors work to help learners develop a range of models and provide students the opportunity to speak frankly about problems the setting may pose for them.

> *I always wished I had a gay or lesbian supervisor with whom I could talk over my questions about whether and how I might come out to my clients, and whether it would be okay to talk in the lunchroom about activities with my partner when everybody else talked about their weekends. I had heard there were other gay people in the agency, but they weren't out, and I couldn't be sure of correctly identifying them by myself, so I didn't know what to do.*

EXERCISE 15.3 Reactions to Supervision

In your journal, record your positive and negative reactions to supervision you have received in the past. Based on your experience, make a list of guidelines or watchwords that you would give to a new supervisor. Note any special needs that arose for you in your work and whether your supervision was helpful or unhelpful. Be prepared to discuss your experiences in class.

Group Supervision

You can also benefit greatly from weekly **group supervision**—education and support meetings in which discussions of clinician–client dialogues, learning dilemmas, techniques, and case-planning concerns affirm the mutuality of the learning process. This kind of back-and-forth exchange of knowledge and practical tips can help to build both your comfort and "voice" in groups and get feedback from trusted colleagues.

Supervisors can often arrange for interns and counselors in several neighboring agencies to come together at intervals for education and support. The agency may also be able to arrange for you to be supervised by more than one person or discipline to vary the learning experience, tap many sources of expertise, and enrich the feedback and exchange process between individuals and disciplines.

Isaac was a great individual supervisor. He taught me tons of stuff about how to work with clients. I felt like I could share all my concerns with him and that he would help me figure out what to do. But I was also glad that I was in group supervision. I liked hearing about how other people were doing things. The group gave me an opportunity to get lots of different feedback, and then with Isaac I could sit down and see which felt right to me.

Peer Supervision

Following completion of formal education, clinicians continue to use supervision to enhance their effectiveness. You can establish **peer supervision** groups, in which two or more clinicians share their work and offer feedback and support as they would do in an agency supervision group. Many such groups last for 20 years or more.

When I worked at the community mental health agency, about four of us were considered senior clinicians. We were the supervisors to the new staff and student interns, but we realized that we also wanted support and help with our own work. We set up a peer supervision group where we took turns presenting our cases to each other.

EXERCISE 15.4 Peer Supervision

Many of the exercises in this book have suggested that you get feedback from peers. In small groups, give positive feedback to your colleagues about the peer supervision you have received. Be as specific as possible about what you have gained from them.

The amount and quality of supervision beginning clinicians can anticipate after completing formal degree studies are varied, depending on local resources and developments in managed care. There is a widespread impression that the quality and extent of supervision are diminishing in many settings because of agency cutbacks and administrative demands that supervisors provide more direct service or case management functions and devote less time to non–income-producing supervision, staff education, and interagency collaborations.

State licensure in the helping professions usually mandates specified hours per week of advanced clinical supervision, but finding employment in agencies that reliably provide it is another matter entirely. Some clinical job applicants make supervision a bargaining chip in employment negotiations when they can. Others ask that part of their hiring package be money for outside supervision at the requisite level to assist them in meeting licensing requirements. Many recently graduated clinicians must purchase private supervision or settle for inconsistent supervision on the job. Whether supervision is provided at work or not, it is still your responsibility to continue advancing your knowledge and skills through supervision, specialized training, and workshops. Local and state clinical societies and organizations can be very helpful in locating appropriate resources.

Consultation

Consultation is a process whereby clinicians at all levels of experience reach outside their normal learning and supervisory relationships to benefit from the perspective and advice of a seasoned mentor, who is valued for special knowledge and skills in certain areas of practice. Consultation is often sought when the clinician feels unusually stuck or confused in work with a client. The consultation may focus on the client, on the clinician, on the relationship, or on the surrounding systems influencing care.

The contact with the consultant is often short term, for purposes of ad hoc brainstorming and the formulation of strategies for problem resolution. The clinician or other involved parties present a thumbnail sketch of the client, the ongoing work, the relationship, and the reason for consultation. The consultant may interview the client separately, with the clinician, or in front of a staff group to elicit information or demonstrate strategy. Consultation has several different uses.

EXAMPLES

A clinician in a group home for latency-aged children seeks a consultation on how to handle a specific client's bed wetting. Others on the staff ask to attend to learn more about the problem in general.

* * *

A teen client assigned to a clinical intern is showing signs of psychotic thinking. The intern's supervisor has not worked with psychosis before and so refers the intern to a colleague in the clinic's outpatient psychiatric services for consultation about the client. The consultant may advise additional outpatient evaluation of the client to see whether medication or further family involvement is indicated.

* * *

A Cambodian psychologist makes monthly medical rounds at a neighborhood health clinic, commenting on any special ethnic issues or concerns arising in work with Cambodian patients of the clinic.

* * *

After an unexpected client death upsets many staff, a practitioner specializing in trauma work with teams is invited to consult with the staff as a group, with an agenda of dealing with the death and the staff's sense of loss and failure.

If you seek outside consultation about a client, remember that ethically you must protect the client's right to confidentiality. You are ethically required to conceal all identifying information about the client, and, if the consultant is to see a video or hear an audio recording of a session, you must obtain the client's written approval first.

Sometimes the consultant focuses entirely on your concerns and needs, sometimes on the teaching of a new skill, and at other times on dealing with an issue that has arisen in the course of work with a client. Finally, you and your supervisor might seek informal consultation with experienced colleagues if tensions between you disrupt the supervisory learning process. While you are in school, you and your supervisor can usually consult directly about problems with faculty liaisons to placement sites. In such instances, to assure just process, be sure to ascertain that the liaison is not a close friend of any of the participants in the problem resolution.

Agencies and supervisors may be legally and ethically responsible for your behaviors, and therefore they usually have the final say in the conduct of professional practice. An exception is an agency asking staff to carry out unethical practices. In such circumstances, contact your local, state, or national professional association or licensing board for information about available resources for assistance.

Personal Therapy as a Learning Experience

Your own therapy might make a significant contribution to your clinical education and practice. In fact, some graduate programs suggest that interns have personal therapy. Furthermore, interns often seek therapy because their clinical learning stimulates curiosity and interest in exploring their own stories further.

The experience of being a client can also heighten your appreciation of the dynamics and skills involved in the helping process. In addition, you can use your own therapy to explore the personal dynamics and blind spots that may interfere with your effective use of self in relationships with clients. Finally, you might decide to seek therapy if a client's issue stimulates unresolved issues of your own that affect your functioning both on the job and in your private life. A supervisor may help identify such issues; then you can decide whether you want to explore them more thoroughly in therapy. In rare instances, a student or clinician who becomes unable to discharge duties because of serious impairment can be asked to take a leave to get help in order to meet professional responsibilities. In fact, clinicians have an ethical responsibility to assist colleagues whose physical, mental, or emotional problems affect their work.

A supervisee of mine was having difficulties at work. I began to wonder if she was drunk. She sometimes slurred her speech, she came late to meetings and missed two sessions with clients. I asked her what was happening. At first she said she was fine but I persisted (using all my clinical skills of reflection and confrontation). She eventually told me that she was hooked on narcotics. I told her that she needed to get help for lots of reasons, but one was that it was clearly affecting her ability to be a responsible social worker and that, if she didn't, she could lose her job. She was admitted to a detox hospital. When she came back in about six weeks, she seemed different and motivated to live a clean and sober life. She carried out responsibilities well after that, and saw an addictions specialist to learn more about herself. It turns out that, while she was in detox, someone told her about a group for impaired social workers sponsored by our local association and she joined that group.

Clinicians usually seek therapy outside their work environments because professional codes of ethics and standards for practice prohibit dual relationships with supervisors. In addition, we are likely to relate our own problems more comfortably and fully with therapists than with workplace supervisors who participate in performance evaluations and periodic administrative discussions of how students and staff are handling their responsibilities.

Professional Resources

An important way to keep up with advances in the fields of counseling and psychotherapy is by continuing to read the professional literature. Clinicians often subscribe to the major professional journals in their discipline, some of which are provided as a benefit of membership in professional organizations. The *Journal of Counseling and Development* is a benefit of membership in the American Counseling Association, just as the journal *Social Work* comes with membership in the National Association of Social Workers. All members of the American Psychological Association receive the *American Psychologist*.

Clinicians working in specific fields often subscribe to journals whose subject matter ranges from child welfare, alcohol and drug abuse, family therapy, and multicultural practice to school guidance counseling, vocational and rehabilitation counseling, and health and hospital practice. These journals give us the opportunity to stay abreast of innovative developments and model projects in practice and research in our fields. Professional organizations often have newsletters and magazines (e.g., *Counseling Today, The NASW Newsletter,* and the *APA Monitor*) that provide current information about what is happening in the professions.

In addition to journals and newsletters, we read books about special areas of treatment and topics of interest. Reading is a vital part of the professional's ongoing responsibility to maintain expertise and to practice competently.

I have a growing library of books and articles. While I was a student, I started a file folder in which I put articles that I found particularly helpful. Over the years, that file folder has become a file cabinet! We often share articles at the clinic. There's a space on the bulletin board where we can post something we find useful.

The Internet increasingly eases our access to a great deal of information. The major clinical professional organizations have Websites, blogs, and chatrooms. There are listservs and online discussion groups on numerous topics of interest to clinicians. Because anyone can assert anything on the Web without verification, you need to carefully check the credentials of the people involved in these lists and the accuracy of postings and articles making impressive claims.

> *With the advent of the World Wide Web, when I want information about a particular topic, I can do a PsychInfo search. But I also belong to a number of psychology listservs. I was looking for a good article on termination the other day and put my request on the listserv. I got back some great leads from colleagues across the country.*

Continuing Education

Most states require clinicians to take specific amounts of approved continuing clinical education to maintain their licenses. **Continuing education** programs may focus on working with particular client populations (disabled veterans, the elderly, refugees), with specific problems or disorders (trauma, sexual abuse, compulsive behaviors, depression), or with specific methods or techniques (short-term interventions, EMDR techniques, play therapy, journal writing) and in different modalities (face-to-face, online). There are now continuing education "webinars" to advance knowledge about specific problems and best practices.

Continuing education affords an ongoing opportunity to grow in understanding, self-awareness, and the purposeful use of self; to learn new skills; and to develop our competencies. They also provide very useful practice-related bibliographic resources. After some presentations, learners divide into small discussion or role-play groups in much the same way that formal educational programs ask students to do.

Continuing education programs also provide important venues for networking with other clinicians.

> *Continuing education programs have given me wonderful opportunities for new knowledge and skills, and they have also given me unexpected chances to meet and learn from leading clinical figures I thought I would only ever encounter in books and articles. Over the last couple of years, I have taken continuing education institutes on DBT with Marsha Linehan, on ADD with Ted Hallowell, on cognitive behavioral therapy with Dave Barlow, and on multiracial identity with Maria Root. Now when I read their work, I feel like I know them.*

A special form of continuing education is offered by advanced certificate programs, postgraduate internships, fellowships, and specialty training. These programs sometimes allow enrollees to see clients with designated problems (domestic violence, alcoholism, trauma), at specialized sites, and under senior supervision for the advancement of knowledge and skills.

Contributing to the Education of Others

As clinicians we are not just consumers of education; we also contribute to the education of others through teaching, research, public speaking, consultation, writing for the media, supervision, and academic scholarship. These pursuits may begin while individuals are still in school, and are often carried out with colleagues or mentors. Educational exchange and feedback among clinicians (as when attending and presenting papers at annual professional meetings) provide rich satisfaction and can be a stimulating addition to work.

> *When three colleagues and I presented at a statewide conference on gay adoption, two respected therapists from the West Coast were there to hear more about issues and research in this area of interest. After our presentation, they asked to meet with us over coffee to talk more about our topic. It was great giving them information for a change—we have used so many of their articles about counseling adolescent parents.*

There will be many more international exchanges over the decades ahead, as technological advances narrow the distances between human service providers, clients, researchers, and educators around the world.

■ Conclusion: What Lies Ahead

A graduation is called a "commencement" with good reason, because it marks the beginning of learning for life. Completing a course or text on clinical interviewing is also a commencement; it marks the beginning of lifelong learning about clinical knowledge, methods, and roles. We believe that the most effective clinical learning is embedded in relationships. Working alone, you cannot see your blind spots and therefore cannot get help from others about them. You also miss the "Aha!" moments that occur with colleagues and mentors in the lively exchange of confirming and opposing ideas. In addition, you miss chances to develop comfort in giving and receiving feedback.

Contact with others also increases the probability of generating completely novel possibilities that none of us think of alone. Empathy, intuition, perception, judgment, and timing are also improved by feedback from colleagues. Because we often work behind closed doors and supervisors can know only what they observe and we and others tell them, our learning and work call for a high degree of integrity, respect for the rights of others, the exercise of self-restraint, and a readiness to act to protect others from harm.

Advancing your clinical knowledge and skills always involves review, review, review and practice, practice, practice. Nothing beats being seasoned through the mastery of a variety of learning challenges with the help of wise and caring mentors and colleagues. In addition to your own personal advocacy to obtain the best teaching available, you can seek out the help of professional organizations to obtain needed resources and advanced training and education. Ultimately you, too, may be one of their continuing education presenters in your own specialty.

We believe that informal learning is equally as important as formal education in the intentional refinement of clinical skills. A crucial part of informal learning is widening the influences to which you let yourself be exposed—to be "out there" with many different kinds of people and belief systems, interacting with human suffering, struggle, and triumph. When you confront the extent of poverty, discrimination, and injustice around you, you may be drawn to social activism. Becoming involved in political action campaigns, working for justice and equality, and extending your ethic of care to all living things and resources on our planet are also natural extensions of your clinical work and professional values.

Another major influence on the shaping of your professional self and skills is your interactions with clients as teachers. Clinical work is never just a simple process of thinking ahead that "She'll do this and then I'll do that." It is precisely the relationship between the participants, and the effects of cultural differences and relationship dynamics on the evolution of each conversation and activity, that plays such an important role in both clinical work and learning. Clients teach and shape us by their comments, by their looks and other nonverbal messages, by their complaints or requests that things be said or done differently, and by their refusals to go down useless pathways that look so good to us as outsiders to their stories. They also beam and credit us when we "get it right," commend our faithfulness in making important visits after hours, and acknowledge the importance of our concern and efforts as they work to improve their situations and relationships. They will teach you to laugh and cry with them, to persist when it is hard to go on, to take a look at yourself while you are looking at them. They will help you change, and these changes will sharpen your vision and soften your edges. Some clients will stay within you forever, as they have for us, just as some of who you are will stay within them.

So clinical skill and relational capacity are much, much more than what we *do* at work; they are importantly who we *become* through work, thanks to the way clients affect us through the interactive process that is the clinical relationship. Clinical learning will be a life-changing process for you. No one participating in a process of human exchange can emerge from that exchange unaltered in important ways. Once you get "clinical ears"—the ability to hear and read the metacommunication in human transactions and an ability to recognize and appreciate multicultural communication—you are likely to become a more sensitive and attuned listener and responder in your personal relationships. Furthermore, meeting new and varied people throughout your career usually stimulates heightened curiosity and interest in others and may impel you into domains of practice you might never have imagined yourself engaging in when you started out. While many challenges await you as clinicians, so do the many rewards and benefits of working with and for others.

CLIP 15.1
Conclusion

■ Suggested Readings

Good sources for information on professional development include:

Dean, Ruth G. (1984). The role of empathy in supervision. *Clinical Social Work Journal, 12,* 129–139.

Dillon, Carolyn. (2003). *Learning from mistakes in clinical practice*. Pacific Grove, CA: Brooks/Cole.

Domar, Alice & Dreher, Henry. (2000). *Self-nurture: Learning to care for yourself as effectively as you care for everyone else.* New York: Penguin Books.

Gottlieb, M. C., Robinson, K., & Younggren, J. N. (2007). Multiple relations in supervision: Guidelines for administrators, supervisors, and students. *Professional Psychology, 38,* 241–247.

Jansson, Bruce S. (2007). Becoming an effective policy advocate: From policy practice to social justice. Pacific Grove, CA: Brooks-Cole.

McCann, Lisa, & Pearlman, Laurie Ann. (1990). Vicarious traumatization: A framework for understanding the psychological effects of working with victims. *Journal of Traumatic Stress Studies, 3,* 131–149.

Sweitzer, H. Frederick & King, Mary A. (2009). *The successful internship.* Pacific Grove, CA: Brooks/Cole Cengage.

■ Self-Explorations

1. What originally attracted you to clinical work? Describe the differences between what you expected and some of the realities in professional life and work of which you are now more aware.

2. List the activities in your personal life that can help balance out the stresses in your professional or student life. Discuss the activities you actually make time for now, as well as the ones you need to carve out time for in the future so that you stay fit and smart over the long haul.

3. What do you find are your most common missteps at this point in your clinical learning? What are the sources of these mistakes, and how can you remedy them? Discuss situations or techniques that are proving especially challenging for you at this point.

4. List your own personal qualities that you will work assiduously to preserve. Discuss any personal qualities you want to alter, soften, or eliminate to be more effective as a clinician. Finally, what aspects of the clinical professions make personal qualities so important?

■ Essay Questions

1. Discuss clinician burnout. Define *burnout* and elaborate its major causes. Is burnout inevitable for all human service workers? Why or why not? What are the signs of burnout in a professional clinician? Finally, discuss the numerous things human service workers can do to prevent burnout in spite of ongoing stresses and challenges in the work.

2. What are the benefits of and differences between individual and group supervision?

3. Discuss the advantages and disadvantages of peer group supervision. Should friends join a group where they will be giving supervision to each other? Discuss the "dual roles" concept and its implications for this situation.

4. Debate the premise that all clinicians should show evidence that they have had personal therapy. Should educational programs mandate therapy for students? Why or why not?

■ Key Terms

Burnout	Group supervision
Compassion fatigue	Peer supervision
Consultation	Self-empathy
Continuing education	"Therapizing" supervisees

Multicultural Counseling Competencies

The following guidelines were developed by the Association for Multicultural Counseling and Development and have been endorsed by the American Counseling Association (ACA). Reprinted with permission from ACA.

I. Counselor Awareness of Own Cultural Values and Biases

A. Attitudes and Beliefs

1. Culturally skilled counselors believe that cultural self-awareness and sensitivity to one's own cultural heritage is essential.
2. Culturally skilled counselors are aware of how their own cultural background and experiences have influenced attitudes, values, and biases about psychological processes.
3. Culturally skilled counselors are able to recognize the limits of their multicultural competency and expertise.
4. Culturally skilled counselors recognize their sources of discomfort with differences that exist between themselves and clients in terms of race, ethnicity, and culture.

B. Knowledge

1. Culturally skilled counselors have specific knowledge about their own racial and cultural heritage and how it personally and professionally affects their definitions and biases of normality/abnormality and the process of counseling.
2. Culturally skilled counselors possess knowledge and understanding about how oppression, racism, discrimination, and stereotyping affects them personally and in their work. This allows individuals to acknowledge their own racist attitudes, beliefs, and feelings. Although this standard applies to all groups, for White counselors it may mean that they understand how they may have directly or indirectly benefited from individual, institutional, and cultural racism as outlined in White identity development models.
3. Culturally skilled counselors possess knowledge about their social impact on others. They are knowledgeable about communication style differences, how their style may clash with or foster the counseling process with persons of color or others different from themselves based on the A, B, and C Dimensions and how to anticipate the impact it may have on others.

C. Skills

1. Culturally skilled counselors seek out educational, consultative, and training experience to improve their understanding and effectiveness in working with culturally different populations. Being able to recognize the limits of their competencies, they

(a) seek consultation, (b) seek further training or education, (c) refer out to more qualified individuals or resources, or (d) engage in a combination of these.

2. Culturally skilled counselors are constantly seeking to understand themselves as racial and cultural beings and are actively seeking a nonracist identity.

II. Counselor Awareness of Client's Worldview

A. Attitudes and Beliefs

1. Culturally skilled counselors are aware of their negative emotional reactions toward other racial and ethnic groups that may prove detrimental to the counseling relationship. They are willing to contrast their own beliefs and attitudes with those of their culturally different clients in a nonjudgmental fashion.

2. Culturally skilled counselors are aware of their stereotypes and preconceived notions that they may hold toward other racial and ethnic minority groups.

B. Knowledge

1. Culturally skilled counselors possess specific knowledge and information about the particular group with which they are working. They are aware of the life experiences, cultural heritage, and historical background of their culturally different clients. This particular competency is strongly linked to the "minority identity development models" available in the literature.

2. Culturally skilled counselors understand how race, culture, ethnicity, and so forth may affect personality formation, vocational choices, manifestation of psychological disorders, help-seeking behavior, and the appropriateness or inappropriateness of counseling approaches.

3. Culturally skilled counselors understand and have knowledge about sociopolitical influences that impinge upon the life of racial and ethnic minorities. Immigration issues, poverty, racism, stereotyping, and powerlessness may impact self-esteem and self-concept in the counseling process.

C. Skills

1. Culturally skilled counselors should familiarize themselves with relevant research and the latest findings regarding mental health and mental disorders of various ethnic and racial groups. They should actively seek out educational experiences that enrich their knowledge, understanding, and cross-cultural skills for more effective counseling behavior.

2. Culturally skilled counselors become actively involved with minority individuals outside of the counseling setting (e.g. community events, social and political functions, celebrations, friendships, neighborhood groups, and so forth) so that their

perspective of minorities is more than an academic or helping exercise.

III. Culturally Appropriate Intervention Strategies

A. Attitudes and Beliefs

1. Culturally skilled counselors respect clients' religious and/or spiritual beliefs and values, including attributions and taboos, because they affect worldview, psychosocial functioning, and expressions of distress.

2. Culturally skilled counselors respect indigenous helping practices and respect minority community intrinsic help-giving networks among communities of color.

3. Culturally skilled counselors value bilingualism and do not view another language as an impediment to counseling (monolingualism may be the culprit).

B. Knowledge

1. Culturally skilled counselors have a clear and explicit knowledge and understanding of the generic characteristics of counseling and therapy (culture bound, class bound, and monolingual) and how they may clash with the cultural values of various cultural groups.

2. Culturally skilled counselors are aware of institutional barriers that prevent minorities from using mental health services.

3. Culturally skilled counselors have knowledge of the potential bias in assessment instruments and use procedures and interpret findings keeping in mind the cultural and linguistic characteristics of the clients.

4. Culturally skilled counselors have knowledge of family structures, hierarchies, values, and beliefs from various cultural perspectives. They are knowledgeable about the community where a particular cultural group may reside and the resources in the community.

5. Culturally skilled counselors should be aware of relevant discriminatory practices at the social and community level that may be affecting the psychological welfare of the population being served.

C. Skills

1. Culturally skilled counselors are able to engage in a variety of verbal and nonverbal helping responses. They are able to send and receive both verbal and nonverbal messages accurately and appropriately. They are not tied down to only one method or approach to helping but recognize that helping styles and approaches may be culture bound. When they sense that their helping style is limited and potentially inappropriate, they can anticipate and modify it.

2. Culturally skilled counselors are able to exercise institutional intervention skills on behalf of their clients. They can help clients determine whether a "problem" stems from racism or bias in others (the concept of health paranoia) so that clients do not inappropriately personalize problems.

3. Culturally skilled counselors are not averse to seeking consultation with traditional healers and religious and spiritual leaders and practitioners in the treatment of culturally different clients when appropriate.

4. Culturally skilled counselors take responsibility for interacting in the language requested by the client and, if not feasible, make appropriate referrals. A serious problem arises when the linguistic skills of a counselor do not match the language of the client. This being the case, counselors should (a) seek a translator with cultural knowledge and appropriate professional background or (b) refer to a knowledgeable and competent bilingual counselor.

5. Culturally skilled counselors have training and expertise in the use of traditional assessment and testing instruments. They not only understand the technical aspects of the instruments but are also aware of the cultural limitations. This allows them to use test instruments for the welfare of culturally different clients.

6. Culturally skilled counselors should attend to as well as work to eliminate biases, prejudices, and discriminatory contexts in conducting evaluation and providing interventions, and should develop sensitivity to issues of oppression, sexism, heterosexism, elitism, and racism.

7. Culturally skilled counselors take responsibility for educating their clients to the processes of psychological intervention, such as goals, expectations, legal rights, and the counselor's orientation.

Clinician-Client Privacy Agreement

This Agreement contains important information about professional services and business policies. It also contains summary information about the Health Insurance Portability and Accountability Act (HIPAA), a federal law that provides privacy protections and client rights with regard to the use and disclosure of your protected health information (PHI) used for the purpose of treatment, payment, and health care operation. HIPAA requires that we provide you with a Notice of Privacy Practices for use and disclosure of Protected Health information (PHI). The law requires that we obtain your signature acknowledging that we have provided you with this information. It is very important that you read all this document carefully. You can discuss any questions you have about the procedures with your clinician at any time.

When you sign this document, it will also represent an agreement between us. You may revoke this Agreement in writing at any time. That revocation will be binding on your clinician unless he/she has already taken action or if there are obligations imposed on us by your health insurer in order to process or substantiate claims made under your policy; or if you have not satisfied any financial obligations you have incurred.

LIMITS ON CONFIDENTIALITY The law protects the privacy of all communications between a client and a clinician. In most situations, a clinician can only release information about your treatment to others if you sign a written authorization form that meets certain legal requirements imposed by HIPAA. There are other situations that require only that you provide written, advance consent. Your signature on this Agreement provides consent for the use and disclosure of PHI for the purposes of treatment, payment, and health care operations and for those activities, as follows:

1. Your clinician may occasionally find it helpful to consult other health and mental health professionals about a case. During some of these consultations, every effort will be made to avoid revealing your identity. The other clinicians consulted are also legally bound to keep the information confidential. All consultations will be recorded in your Clinical Record.
2. You should be aware that there are other mental health providers and administrative staff at our agency. In most cases, we will need to share protected information with these individuals for both clinical and administrative purposes, such as scheduling, billing and quality assurance. All of the mental health professionals are bound by the same rules of confidentiality. All staff members have been given training about protecting your privacy and have agreed not to release any information outside of the practice except as is allowed by HIPAA for the treatment, payment, and healthcare operations.

There are some situations where a clinician is permitted or required to disclose information without either consent or Authorization:

1. If you are involved in a court proceeding and a request is made for information concerning your diagnosis and treatment, such information is protected by the clinician-client privilege law. A clinician cannot provide any information without your (or your legal representative's) written authorization, or a court order. If you are involved in or contemplating litigation, you should consult with your attorney to determine whether a court would be likely to order your clinician to disclose information.
2. If a government agency is requesting the information for health oversight activities, clinicians may be required to provide it for them.
3. If a client files a complaint or lawsuit against his/her clinician, the clinician may disclose relevant information in order to defend him/herself.
4. If a client files a worker's compensation claim, we must, upon appropriate request, provide appropriate information, including a copy of the client's record, to the client's employer, the insurer or the Department of Worker's Compensation.

There are some situations in which clinicians are legally obligated to take action and reveal some information about a client's treatment in order to protect the client and/or others from harm. In our experience, these situations do not occur often:

1. If a clinician has reasonable cause to believe that a child under age 18 is suffering physical, sexual or emotional abuse resulting in harm or substantial risk of harm to the child's health or welfare, the law requires that a report be filed with the Department of Social Services. Once such a report is filed, the clinician may be required to provide additional information.
2. If a clinician has reason to believe that an elderly or handicapped individual is suffering from abuse, the law requires that a report be filed with the Department of Elder Affairs. Once such a report is filed, the clinician may be required to provide additional information.
3. If a client communicates an immediate threat of serious physical harm to an identifiable victim or if a client has a history of violence and the apparent intent and ability to carry out the threat, clinicians are required to take protective actions. These actions may include that the client write a safety contract, notifying the potential victim, contacting the police, and/ or seeking hospitalization for the client.
4. If a client threatens to harm himself/herself, clinicians are obligated to request a client to sign a safety contract, to seek hospitalization for him/her, or to contact family members or others who can help provide protection.

If such situations arise, your clinician will make every effort to fully discuss it with you before taking any action and he/she will limit the disclosure to what is necessary.

PROFESSIONAL RECORDS   You should be aware that, pursuant to HIPAA, we keep Protected Health Information about you in two sets of professional records.

One set constitutes your Clinical Record. It includes information about your reasons for seeking therapy, a description of the ways in which your problem impacts on your life, your diagnosis, the goals that we set for treatment, your progress towards those goals, your medical and social history, your treatment history, any past treatment records that are received from other providers, reports of any professional consultations, your billing records, and any reports that have been sent to anyone, including reports to your insurance carrier. You may examine and/or receive a copy of your Clinical Record if you request it in writing unless your clinician believes that access to it would endanger you. In those situations, you have a right to a summary and to have your record sent to another mental health provider or your attorney. Because these are professional records, they can be misinterpreted and/or upsetting to untrained readers. For this reason, we recommend that if you request to examine them, you initially review them with your clinician, or have them forwarded to another mental health professional so you can discuss the contents.

In addition to the Clinical Record, your clinician might keep a set of Psychotherapy Notes. These Notes are for the clinician's own use and are designed to assist him/her in providing you with the best treatment. While the contents of Psychotherapy Notes vary from client to client, they can include the contents of therapy conversations, analysis of those conversations, and how they impact on your therapy. They also contain particularly sensitive information that you may reveal to your clinician but is not required to be included in your Clinical Record. These Psychotherapy Notes are kept separate from your Clinical Record.

While insurance companies can request and receive a copy of your Clinical Record, they cannot receive a copy of the Psychotherapy Notes without your signed, written Authorization. Insurance companies cannot require your Authorization as a condition of coverage nor penalize you in any way for your refusal. You may examine and/or receive a copy of the Psychotherapy Notes unless your clinician determines that it would adversely affect your well-being. In that case you have a right to a summary or to have your record sent to another mental health provider or your attorney.

CLIENT RIGHTS   HIPAA provides you with several new or expanded rights with regard to your protected health information. These rights include requesting that your clinician amend your record; requesting restrictions on what information from your Clinical Record is disclosed to others; requesting an accounting of most disclosures of protected health information that you have neither consented to nor authorized; determining the location to which protected information disclosures are sent; having any complaints you make about policies and procedures recorded in your records; and the right to a paper copy of this Agreement. You are welcome to discuss any of these rights with your clinician.

MINORS AND PARENTS   Parents and clients should be aware that the law allows parents to examine the treatment records of children who under 18 and who are not legally emancipated, unless the clinician believes this review would be harmful to the client and his/her treatment.

Because privacy in psychotherapy is often crucial to successful progress, particularly with teenagers, it is sometimes our policy to request an agreement from parents that they consent to give up their access to their child's records. If they agree, during treatment, the clinician will provide them only with general information about the progress of the child's treatment, and his/her attendance at scheduled sessions. Any other communication will require the child's Authorization, unless the clinician feels that the child is in danger or is a danger to someone else, in which case, he/she will notify the parents of the concern. Before giving parents any information, the clinician will discuss the matter with the child, if possible, and do his/her best to handle any objections the client might have.

INSURANCE REIMBURSEMENT

You should also be aware that your contract with your health insurance company requires us to provide it with information relevant to the therapy you receive. Your clinician will be required to provide a clinical diagnosis. Sometimes he/she will be required to provide additional clinical information such as treatment plans or summaries, or copies of your entire clinical record. In such situations, your clinician will release only the minimum information about you that is necessary for the purpose requested. This information will become part of the insurance company files and will probably be stored in a computer. Though all insurance companies claim to keep such information confidential, we have no control over what they do with it once it is in their hands. In some cases, they may share the information with a national medical information databank. If you request it, you can be provided with a copy of any report your clinician submits. By signing this Agreement, you agree that your clinician can provide requested information to your insurance company. Your signature below indicates that you have read this agreement and agree to its terms. Your clinician will also sign this agreement, indicating a contract between you and him/her.

Name of Client (Print)

Signature of Client   Date

Name of Clinician (Print)

Signature of Clinician   Date

Glossary of Key Terms

Advanced empathy The process of hypothesizing (after some experience with the client) about themes, patterns, or feelings of the client that he or she may not yet have verbalized or even been aware of.

Advocacy Clinicians' work with social action groups, service agencies, and institutions to increase benefits, access, opportunities, justice, and rights for people.

Alternative perspectives Novel explanations or ways of thinking about people and situations that may broaden clients' definitions of self, others, and prospects for the future.

Ambivalence Having two or more opposing ideas, feelings, or impulses simultaneously, which often leads to feeling stuck and immobilized.

Anticipatory empathy Before meeting with clients, the clinician thinks about the information available about the clients, anticipates their feelings and reactions, and adjusts his or her ways of interacting accordingly.

Anxiety hierarchy The cognitive-behavioral technique of having the client rate frightening stimuli on a scale of 1 to 100 in terms of their intensity and psychological power in the client's life.

ASL interpreters American Sign Language interpreters for deaf or hard-of-hearing people who use a combination of signing, finger spelling, and body language to convey meaning and tone.

Assertiveness training Learning to develop greater self-affirmation and voice through education, support, and new skills rehearsal to prepare for challenging or formerly disempowering interactions.

Assessment interview An information gathering conversation that includes client self-reports and the clinician's experience in the interview. Assessment interviews may be unstructured, semi-structured, or structured.

Assessment summary A psychological report summarizing assessment findings and case conceptualization.

Aversive racism A term describing the thinking and actions of those who espouse egalitarian values and find racism offensive while being unaware of their own unconscious, unintentional racist behaviors.

Behavioral rehearsal The clinical technique of practicing new behaviors in the safety of the clinical interview, trying them out with the clinician's feedback and encouragement before trying them out elsewhere.

Bibliotherapy The clinical strategy of referring clients to specific readings, books, articles, or Websites relevant to issues they are working on.

Borrowed environment Any nonoffice setting or locale adopted for interviewing purposes.

Brainstorm Putting numerous alternative explanations or possibilities on the table for discussion without judging them as they emerge.

Bubble of calm A circumscribed and focused atmosphere of quiet and safety conducive to clinical conversation and reflection on the work.

Burnout An occupational hazard in the helping professions (often called compassion fatigue) resulting from repeated, intense interactions with people with many severe problems. Symptoms include exhaustion, insensitivity to others, hopelessness, irritability, and frequent absences from work.

Case conceptualization The integration and analysis of assessment data from which hypotheses about the person, situation, and possible interventions are based.

Central relational paradox The Stone Center principle asserting that individuals accustomed to invalidation or rejection often try to connect with others by holding back parts of their experience and feelings for fear that disclosure of these parts of themselves will lead to more rejection.

Certification A process by which a professional group confirms that a practitioner has met a set of advanced educational and practice standards established by the certification agency or board.

Checking-in A sustaining technique in which the clinician asks how things feel or seem to the client after a period of exploration.

Circular causality A principle of systems theory asserting that events in complex systems often exist as both causes and effects of each other.

Client abandonment The unethical practice of "dumping" or deserting clients with whom the clinician has found it hard to work.

Client gestalt A client's values, beliefs, and personal background in the larger social, cultural, and familial contexts.

Client information variables Important information about client demographics including age, gender, ethnicity, and presenting problem.

Client rights Principles of client care to ensure a mutually respectful partnership, including the right to information necessary to make decisions about treatment options, confidentiality, and professional courtesy.

Clinical interviewing The process of structured, purposeful, client-centered, ethically guided conversations with clients aimed at identifying problems as well as assets and resources that may help in problem resolution.

Clinical intuition A clinician's informed hypotheses, combined with preconceived ideas and feelings about clients and their narratives.

Clinical judgment Informed decision making about how to proceed clinically, based on client data, relevant theory and research, hunches, intuition, and cumulative experience with situations such as the one at hand for the client and the team.

Clinical listening A form of attending closely to verbal and nonverbal communication, to themes and patterns, and to the context in which clients' stories take place. This process includes attending to the relationship and to the clinician's own inner process.

Clinical record A formal, legally protected client file, which includes assessment data (including the reason the person has come for help, test results, and social and medical history); the formulation (including diagnosis and goals for the work); and treatment plans (including progress towards goals). The clinical record also includes any forms completed by the client (including HIPAA documents and permission releases), reports received from other providers, and any reports about the client that are sent to anyone else, including reports to insurance carriers.

Clinical repose The relaxed, attentive, reassuring steadiness of the clinician, which helps the client to relax and feel confident of the clinician's reliability.

Clinician gestalt A clinician's values, beliefs, and past experiences, mediated by familial and cultural background.

Closed-ended questions Focused questions that can usually be answered with a word or two.

Compassion fatigue Often referred to as burnout, this biopsychological fatigue is an occupational hazard in the helping professions, often resulting from clinicians' intense interactions with people with many severe problems over a long period and with poor support.

Complementary medicine Holistic health specializations whose techniques are designed to bring about the harmonious integration of mind and body resources. Complementary practices include acupuncture, meditation, herbal remedies, homeopathy, naturopathy, reflexology, and chiropractic.

Compound crisis A situation in which a current crisis rekindles unfinished business from previous crises.

Confidentiality A professional ethical standard ensuring the privacy of client–clinician communications, with special exceptions designed to protect both the public and professionals from specified perils.

Congruence Clinicians are genuine and authentic with clients, free of pretense and hypocrisy, and not hiding behind a mask of professionalism.

Consecutive interpretation Language interpretation in which one party speaks, the interpreter conveys what was said, and then the other party speaks, followed by the interpreter's translation. Both the clinician and client need to leave space after speaking so that the interpreter can work with clarity and accuracy.

Consequences Responses that reinforce or encourage a behavior, or that serve as disincentives to it.

Consultation A clinical learning process in which clinicians reach outside their normal supervisory relationships to benefit from the perspective and advice of a seasoned practitioner or expert valued for special knowledge and skills in certain areas of practice.

Content of the assessment Identifying the specific problems, participants, incentives, and goals for the change process, while also elaborating clients' strengths and resources for use in problem solving.

Contingency contract A clearly articulated behavioral plan that outlines roles, responsibilities, action steps, and rewards and consequences to promote and maintain specified behaviors.

Continuing education Advanced clinical learning programs continuously required for licensure and often focused on enhancing knowledge and skills for work with particular populations, on problems or disorders, or on specialized or newly developing methods and techniques.

Contracts Working agreements that enumerate goals, roles, and responsibilities; proposed intervention methods; duration and costs of meetings; and plans for measuring progress and evaluating outcomes.

Coping mechanisms The methods people use to overcome, reduce, or accommodate the demands of stress.

Coping questions Clinical questions that focus clients on how they have been successful in the face of adverse circumstances.

Corrupt contracts Contracts in which multiple service providers, working separately and without communicating with each other, make different or conflicting working agreements with clients (or clients with them) that are thus inauthentic for all practical purposes.

Countertransference A term from psychodynamic theory to describe an unconscious process in which the clinician views the client as representative of an important figure from the clinician's past, then behaves toward the client as thought he or she *were* that person.

Covering clinician A clinician who carries out supportive work with a client whose primary clinician is away for a time and who later provides the primary clinician with useful feedback about the client's reactions and work during the absence.

Crediting client strengths The technique of stopping conversation to give clients deserved appreciation for their courage, determination, and accomplishments to sustain them at hard points of the work.

Crisis An important turning point in events when action must be taken to avoid disaster or significant distress. The destabilization in a crisis provides an opportunity to restabilize at a higher or lower level of functioning.

Critical incident review process A formalized and retrospective team process in which members review incidents of threats or harm to staff and plan strategies for managing such incidents in the future.

Critical Incident Stress Debriefing (CISD) The immediate and brief posttrauma process of education, ventilation, and validation of personal experiences, along with the preparation of survivors for ongoing coping around the complex aftereffects of the trauma.

Critical thinking A form of theoretical critique that divides theories into their conceptual constructs, assumptions, and hypotheses; attempts to understand the history and context that inform these constructs; and evaluates their strengths, limitations, and practice implications.

Cry for help A client's self-harming or threatening behaviors that signal a need to elicit a response from the clinician or others. This may occur during the ending process and reflect strong reactions to the clinician's anticipated departure.

Culturagram A clinical assessment matrix elaborating the complexities and interwoven influences of family, cultural, and contextual relationships, as well as the family's efforts to engage with cultural institutions for support.

Cultural competencies Specific values, attitudes, techniques, and strategies to guide working with people in culturally responsive ways.

Cultural formulation A listing and brief discussion of cultural issues to consider before a clinician from one culture diagnoses and plans treatment for apparent "disorders" manifested by someone from another culture. Recommended in the DSM-IV.

Cultural racism The ways in which the cultures of people of color are denigrated and the culture of the dominant group is imposed on ethnic or racial minorities.

Cultural relativism A philosophical perspective asserting that diagnostic categories are social constructions used to explain Western psychiatric phenomena, with limited applicability in diverse settings around the world. Universal standards of normality or abnormality cannot be applied to all societies.

Cultural strengths Individual, interpersonal, and environmental sources of support that are derived from identification, membership, and activities in one's cultural group.

Cultural universalism A philosophical perspective that asserts the Western biomedical diagnostic framework as universal and attempts to identify similarities in illness patterns across cultures.

Culture A group's shared history, language, behaviors, traditions, customs, symbolic expressions, rituals, and expectations of one another, transmitted from generation to generation.

Culture bound The sociological principle asserting that human behaviors are shaped by the culture in which they are lodged and that their meanings can be understood only in the context of that culture.

Culture-bound syndromes Recurrent and locality-specific patterns of behavior and experience that are considered to be illnesses or afflictions but that do not seem to have an attributable and identifiable organic base. It is assumed that these behaviors are influenced by local cultural factors.

Decisional balance sheet A Motivational Interviewing tool for clarifying a client's beliefs and readiness for change through a cost-benefit analysis that weighs the client's investment in current troubling behaviors against proposed new behaviors.

Decompensate The gradual process of becoming less organized and able to cope with adversity.

Delayed grief reaction Lindemann's term to describe the phenomenon in which survivors of a recent loss suddenly experience grief from an earlier loss.

Desired outcomes Goals agreed upon by clinician and clients that express the positive aims of the working relationship. Goals should include clearly defined outcomes that are observable and measurable and can be used in assessing the effectiveness of interventions.

Developing new metaphors Helping clients create alternative perspectives by helping them exchange the negative or powerless metaphors that structure their versions of reality for more positive visions that can help them move rapidly toward positive change.

Developmental crises Crises triggered by normal but stressful growth and life cycle transitions.

Diagnosis A shorthand summary of a complex set of human behaviors and characteristics, often using medical or psychological terms to describe disorders and important related social factors for purposes of intervention planning and ongoing research.

Diagnostic reliability The level of agreement between two or more clinicians about whether an individual meets the criteria for a psychiatric diagnosis, and if more than one diagnosis is applicable, about which diagnosis is the primary one.

Dialectical Behavior Therapy A specially tailored cognitive-behavioral program developed by Marsha Linehan, that teaches hopefulness, self-acceptance, emotional stability strategies, and other coping skills to people whose powerful, poorly regulated feeling states and self-destructive impulses haves made life hard for them and for people around them.

Direct influence Employing the symbolic power of clinical roles to pressure clients, subtly or overtly, to behave in given ways deemed important to their well-being or safety.

Discrepancies Inconsistencies between two statements, between thoughts and feelings, between intentions and behaviors, and between verbal and nonverbal communication.

Discrimination The unfair treatment of people because of prejudice, usually based on color, class, age, gender, sexual orientation, size, or ability, or on racial, ethnic, or religious group membership.

Diversity The rich variations, permutations, and complex overlaps within the multiple identities of people.

Dot-dot-dot reflection An interview response in which the clinician repeats back the last thing said and hangs it, unfinished, in midair for the client to complete.

Double questions Clinician questions that confuse clients by asking them to reply to a stream of two or more questions at once.

DSM The Diagnositic and Statistical Manual is the American Psychiatric Association's multiaxial classification of mental disorders in which clinical syndromes are listed with a set of symptom criteria. Axis I covers Clinical Syndromes; Axis II, Developmental and Personality Disorders; Axis III, Physical Conditions; Axis IV, Psychosocial and Environmental Stressors; and Axis V, Global Assessment of Functioning.

Duty to warn A therapist's legal and ethical responsibility to warn intended victims of any serious threat to their life or safety that is expressed by a client of the therapist. In addition, the clinician may be required to notify police and other authorities of such a threat.

Eclectic   A clinical practice approach incorporating aspects of more than one theoretical perspective and requiring knowledge and experience to implement effectively.

Ecological   A systems perspective describing the interactive and interdependent relationships between people, all other living and nonliving things, and the systems of which they are all a part.

Ecomap   A clinical assessment tool that reflects the nature and extent of reciprocity in client relationships with others.

Ecosystemic crises   An environmental crisis caused by natural or human-made disasters, diseases, epidemics, or severe economic depressions.

Elaboration   A technique by which the clinician encourages the client to expand on, deepen, and enrich the details the story.

Electronic medical records   Confidential health information-sharing technology systems that allow consumers, providers, insurers, and hospitals to access individuals' health and mental health records.

Emotional contagion   The experience of catching or absorbing a loved one's distress and subsequently becoming distressed oneself.

Empathic echo   A verbal reflection of both the content and the affect within a client's story, to signal that the clinician is attending closely to what the client says and does in the moment.

Empathic failures   Clinical interactions in which clinicians reflect the wrong content, feeling, or meaning; miss important themes; pile on too much sympathy; confuse one client's story with another; or seem disingenuous.

Empathy   The process of experiencing the world from another's subjective perspective while maintaining one's own perspective as an outside observer. Clinical empathy involves a constant oscillation between observing the client, feeling and thinking as if one *were* the client, and then feeling and thinking *about* the client's experience in order to develop hypotheses about it.

Empirically supported treatment (EST)   A specific method or technique that has been demonstrated through empirical research to be effective with a particular problem or disorder when used with clients from a clearly defined population.

Empowerment perspective   A practice philosophy that emphasizes the centrality of client participation and self-determination. Thus, the helping process is viewed as an "exchange among equals."

Environmental assessment   Gathering information about the neighborhood and community of the client. For home visits, it includes determining which routes to the home are safest at various hours, how area residents regard outreach workers, being aware of who is in the home and whether weapons may be present, as well as the location of exits in case danger arises within or outside a residence.

Environmental crises   Incidents in which natural disasters or biologically based, politically based, or economically based disasters seriously destabilize those who share a common living environment.

Ethical dilemmas   Conflicts arising between institutional and professional policies and ethics; between parts of an ethics code; between law and ethics; or between a professional's personal and professional values and an ethics code.

Ethical principles   Ethics code statements that describe overarching professional values, aspirational in nature, that are to serve as enduring benchmarks for professional conduct with clients and colleagues.

Ethical standards   Ethics code statements that clearly elaborate professional behaviors that are prescribed as well as specific professional conduct that is proscribed.

Ethics   A branch of philosophy that deals with moral judgments and perceptions of right and wrong.

Ethnicity   The common ancestral, cultural, linguistic, religious, geographic, or national characteristics by which large groups of people distinguish and organize themselves.

Ethnocultural transference   A relational process in which previous inter- or intracultural experiences are unconsciously displaced onto the clinical relationship by both the client and the clinician, distorting their interactions.

Evaluation   The measurement of the appropriateness, progress, and effectiveness of clinical work both during and following interventions.

Evidence-based practice (EBP)   The clinician uses evidence based on the scientific method to make decisions about clinical work, including decisions about therapeutic models and techniques, clinician characteristics, and client needs.

Examining the moment   The technique of addressing what is happening in the clinician–client relationship at a given point in time.

Exception questions   A solution-focused technique of eliciting information about situations or times in which the client's usual behaviors or problems have not occurred.

Exploration   The gathering of information through the use of questions, prompts, or probes.

Exploring indirect references   The technique of addressing a client's remarks about other situations or experiences that the clinician thinks may obliquely refer to the clinical relationship or represent issues or feelings arising in it.

Exposure therapy   The client is exposed to specifically identified anxiety-provoking stimuli with the goal of eliminating anxiety through habituation. Exposure can be done in imagination, in real life (*in vivo*), or using virtual reality and Second Life technologies.

Extrospection   The process in which clinicians stand away and observe themselves in action with clients in order to see where the power in the interview is at the moment. They then adjust themselves as needed so that power stays with the clients.

Faith-based organizations   Religious organizations that provide community services, support, and activities.

Feeling-thinking   A term developed by relational-cultural theorists to describe the intertwined bundles of thoughts and feelings that play off of and feed into each other powerfully and inseparably.

Fiduciary relationship   A safe, reliable, confidential relationship that enables the client to have confidence that the clinician is trustworthy.

Focal opening lines   A clinician's opening remarks that lend structure to initial clinician–client interactions and often provide a conversational framework, agenda, and tone.

Follow-up evaluations   Interviews, tests, and other assessment measures used to determine how well client strengths, resources, and prospects are holding up over time after the termination of the clinical relationship.

Foreshadow the ending   The technique of forecasting an ending so that both clinician and client can prepare and pace their discussion accordingly.

Formal contracts   Written, highly specific, and concrete agreements that specify each goal's component objectives and the tasks, steps, participants, and timelines for accomplishing each.

Formal diagnosis   The process of determining if the client's problems or symptoms meet the specific DSM criteria for a disorder.

Formal observations   Target behaviors are clearly defined and their antecedents and consequences are viewed and noted.

Formulation   Summary statements that condense and attribute meaning to all the rich data emerging from the assessment process, providing a practical and meaningful guide for work.

Genogram   A clinical assessment tool (like a family tree) that reflects multigenerational family relationships, patterns, and intergenerational transmission of assets and issues.

Gifts as symbolic messages   Client gifts to the clinician may often express subtle or unconscious client needs, dynamics, or hopes in regard to the clinician.

Goals   The desired results or outcomes of the clinical work and relationship.

Group supervision   A group of clinicians hire a supervisor for regular meetings focusing on education and support, where discussions of clinician–client dialogues, learning dilemmas, techniques, and case-planning concerns affirm the mutuality of the learning process.

Hate crimes   Hateful words or actions intended to harm or intimidate an individual because of her or his membership in a minority group. Actions include violent assaults, murder, rape, and property crimes motivated by prejudice, as well as threats of violence and other acts of intimidation meant to terrorize all members of the targeted group as accounts of the violence spread.

Heterosexism   A value system that prizes heterosexuality, assumes that it is the only appropriate manifestation of love and sexuality, and that devalues homosexuality and all that is not heterosexual.

Hidden agendas   Secret aims of the clinician or client that are unexpressed and that can negatively affect the work together.

Hierarchical transference   A relational process in which people with histories of subordination may manifest feelings of powerlessness and helplessness in response to perceived clinician power and authority whether the power is real or not.

HIPAA   (Health Insurance Portability and Accountability Act) Federal law protecting the privacy of those receiving health and mental health services. HIPAA requires that clinicians provide clients with a Notice of Privacy Practices and information about the use and disclosure of Protected Health Information, which must be signed by the client before the work begins.

Holding environment   The anchored, client-centered, and caring clinician presence that allows the client to stay self- and problem-focused without distraction or fear of judgment or abandonment.

Homework   Client work assigned between sessions, such as journaling, meditation, behavior logs, and meeting attendance, to support client strengthening beyond the presence of the clinician.

Homophobia   The hostility, contempt, or hateful speech and acts directed toward gay men and lesbian women because of their real or perceived sexual orientation.

Human-made disasters   Events such as oil spills, toxic waste dump or biohazard lab leaks, nuclear accidents, global transmission of viruses, and wartime use of chemical weapons that leave widespread illness, disability, and fear of death.

Hunches   Informed guesses or working hypotheses about the client and his or her situation.

ICD   The World Health Organization's International Classification of Diseases, which is often used by clinicians outside the United States.

Identity   An individual's self-conceptualization as well as the ways in which one defines oneself as part of larger groups or communities.

Idiographic   Information that focuses on one specific individual.

Imaginal rehearsal   Mentally practicing new behaviors and developing plans of action and new skills for responding to future challenges.

Immediacy   Gerard Egan's term for examining the moment.

Inclusive cultural empathy   Clinical empathy that incorporates exploration of and respect for the client's various cultural influences as well as a recognition of the clinician's. The ability to appreciate all of the cultural teachers who influence the client and those who influence the clinician.

Indigenous helpers   Individuals in a culture who are prized for their gifts of wisdom, spirituality, and healing and to whom community members turn for advice, healing, and consolation.

Individual racism   Discriminatory behavior on the part of an individual.

Informal observation   Observation of the client in the interview or in a natural setting, in order to obtain general impressions of client behaviors. Informal observations do not require the specific identification of target behaviors, antecedents, and consequences.

Information sharing   The introduction of new concepts or information the client may be unaware of, as a means of widening possibilities or extending opportunities.

Informed consent   A professional ethical standard requiring that clients be fully informed about the benefits and risks of specific recommended interventions before these may be implemented.

Insidious trauma   A kind of trauma that steadily evolves from the ongoing experience of denigration based on color, social status, or some devalued aspect of one's identity.

Insight development   Gaining a new or clearer perspective on complex issues, dynamics, feelings, or relationships.

Institutional racism   Social or governmental policies, structures, and activities that subordinate and harm people of color.

Intentional use of self   The clinical process of acting in a self-aware, considered, deliberate, and goal-focused manner with clients.

Interpersonal Therapy   A brief, 16–20 week client–clinician process with a therapeutic focus on resolving or reworking clients' current, here-and-now interpersonal problems, losses, and transitions. It encourages expression of depressed and angry feelings and teaches coping skills through role-play interactions, discussion, and homework.

Interpreters   Trained professionals knowledgeable about the client's culture, the counseling process, and confidentiality, who are prepared to interpret both words and their meanings in a culturally sensitive way.

Interrater reliability   The level of agreement between two appropriately qualified observers rating the same behaviors.

Interval of respite   A break in intense exploration or elaboration that protects the client from being overwhelmed.

Intervention plan   A statement of the agreed-upon goals of the clinical work and the proposed methods and resources for achieving these goals.

Introspection   The reflective process of looking within oneself to appraise the nature, intensity, and meanings of feelings, thoughts, and dynamics that can affect interpersonal behaviors and relationships.

IS PATH WARM   A mnemonic for use in evaluating suicide warning signs.

Islands of possibility   Small client successes that can be amplified through review and discussion that kindle hope and further work toward goals.

Labeling   Reducing the rich complexity of a person to a few behaviors, then categorizing the person based on those behaviors.

Legal commitment   A judicial process by which a person may be mandated to an appropriate psychiatric facility for further assessment or treatment for a specified period of time.

Letter of termination   A letter the clinician writes to a client after the client's abrupt and unexplained disconnection from clinical work, reassuring the client that the clinician or agency will be available for future contact if needed.

Levels of inference   Proximity of clinical inferences and conclusions to the data on which they are presumed to be based. Low levels of inference stick close to the facts while high levels of inference are more hypothetical.

Life chart   A clinical assessment tool that provides a birth-to-present-day timeline of dates and ages at which major life experiences impacted the client, both positively and negatively.

Life records   Previous treatment records or notes, school records and reports, health reports, and other written documents describing client development and performance of everyday tasks.

Lifespace interviews   Observations of and conversations with clients in their everyday environments.

Limit setting   The technique of restricting, with respect and caring, a client's inappropriate or destructive comments, behaviors, or requests in order to maintain clear and comfortable boundaries.

Locus of control   A psychological principle referring to one's perception of personal power and place in the world, and the extent to which people see themselves as capable of effectively influencing outcomes and accomplishing desired goals.

Long-term goals   Desired results that require extended time, work, and resources to accomplish.

Managed care   A cost-driven structure of health and mental health service provision which attempts to decrease costs by limiting the number, length, and type of visits for defined health or mental health problems and improve the quality of care by careful review of services.

Managed care organizations.   Health care programs that attempt to reduce the cost of providing health benefits and improve the quality of care by reviewing the medical necessity of specific services and limiting the number, length, and type of visits for defined health or mental health problems.

Mental disorder   A behavior or psychological syndrome associated with (a) emotional distress, (b) impaired functioning or disability, or (c) behavior that puts the person at risk of pain, suffering, disability, death, or loss of freedom.

Metacommunication   Implicit messages about the communication, as well as about the relationship between the communicators.

Metaphor   A word or phrase (not meant literally) that clients or clinicians can use as a symbolic representation of experience.

Microaggressions   Acts of exclusion, victimization, harassment, verbal abuse, stereotyping comments, intimidation, and injustice, including everyday acts of racism whose cumulative effects are widely traumatizing.

Mind/body programs   Wellness-oriented programs that emphasize and work to harmonize the connections between people's physical, spiritual, and emotional states.

Minority status   A term denoting the social position of a numerically smaller or politically powerless group in relation to a larger, controlling, and politically dominant majority.

Miracle question   Steve DeShazer's solution-focused technique of asking clients: "If a presenting problem were magically resolved while you were sleeping, what would be different on waking that would indicate that the problem is resolved?"

Mirroring   A physical form of reflection in which the clinician subtly matches the client's posture, facial expression, and gestures, while careful not to mimic or parrot.

Modeling   The principle that people will learn new behaviors, attitudes, values, and feelings by observing others who seem similar to themselves or who are respected authorities.

Motivational Interviewing   Miller and Rollnick's structured process for increasing motivation for change by helping clients understand and resolve their ambivalences and patiently structure and time their change activities.

Multiaxial diagnostic system   The use of the five axes or domains of human experience of the DSM diagnostic system to represent relevant health and mental health diagnoses, past and present levels of personal and social functioning, and social or other stresses affecting functioning.

Multicultural practice   Clinical practice within and between a wide variety of cultures and backgrounds.

Multidisciplinary team   A collaborative group representing a variety of clinical disciplines whose case conceptualizations and formulations benefit from the specialized knowledge, skills, and biopsychosocial perspectives that each member contributes to the evaluation and planning process.

Multiethnic   A term denoting that an individual's or group's identity incorporates more than one ethnic heritage.

Multiple dimensions of identity   An individual's core sense of personal identity develops in the context of various identity dimensions, including family background, sociocultural conditions, and other social influences.

Multiple realities   A principle of systems theory positing that individual participants in a transaction will have unique and sometimes conflicting views of what is occurring, how and why it developed, and the way it ought to evolve.

Multiple relationships   A clinical boundary crossing in which a clinician has more than one kind of relationship with a client or a client's family members or friends.

Multiracial   A term indicating that an individual's or group's identity incorporates more than one race.

Mutual aid   The provision of caring, encouragement, and support for one another by members of a self-help group.

Mutual empathy   The relational process of reciprocal caring and attending that leaves both clinician and client feeling seen, understood, and moved by the other.

Mutual empowerment   The relational process wherein clinician and client both develop better relational skills through mutual empathy and the exchange of authentic feedback about what happens between them.

Mutuality   The interview process phenomenon in which client and clinician come to affect each other's ideas and behaviors, growing and changing through caring and authentic give–and–take.

Natural disasters   Widely unsettling events in nature such as severe storms, tornadoes, floods, hurricanes, tidal waves, earthquakes, and volcanic eruptions.

Natural helpers   Instinctively attuned, empathic, and responsive people to whom others easily turn for help and support.

Negative cognitive triad   An unhappy self-appraisal in three domains of experience: view of self ("I'm a loser"); view of the world ("My people never get a real break"); and view of prospects for the future ("My jail time will always keep me from succeeding").

Negative transference   An unconscious relational process in which a client expresses or reenacts in the moment old, unhappy, stuck scenarios with the clinician, as though the latter were actually the punisher, exploiter, molester, or indifferent parent of the past. The client, feeling angry or betrayed, may proceed to misinterpret the clinician's motives and behaviors.

Nomothetic   Information about a group of individuals that can be generalized to others.

Nondirective opening lines   A clinician's opening remarks that are deliberately open ended to give clients greater opportunity to set the agenda, pace, focus, and tone.

Nonverbal communication   A form of communication that includes physical appearance, body posture, gestures, movements, and facial expressions.

Not-knowing perspective   A viewpoint expressing two important aspects of clinical knowledge building: (1) It is okay not to know, and (2) clients often know more than we do about the realities of their experience and of everyday life.

Objectives   The specific and concrete component parts of goals that are observable and measurable and that can be used in assessing the effectiveness of interventions.

Observation   A method of clinical assessment in which the clinician evaluates the client's behaviors and interactions in the interview setting, a lab, or a natural lifespace.

Online counseling   Delivering "e-therapy" services to clients at a distance utilizing evolving communication technologies such as email, Skype, videoconferencing, chat rooms, and videophones.

Open-ended questions   Nondirective questions that keep clients in the driver's seat of the conversation by giving them more opportunity or flexibility in responding and elaborating.

Oral interpretation   A specialized form of verbal interpretation for people who are deaf or hard of hearing and who lip-read instead of signing.

Outreach   The technique of reaching out to clients by phone, letter, or Internet. Outreach can be used to try to bring closure and reassurance to the client when he or she has abruptly stopped coming before or during the ending process.

Overidentification   A psychological process in which clinicians emphasize the similarities between themselves and their clients, while minimizing or denying things that would reveal differences between them.

Paralinguistic cues   How things are said—the culturally influenced tone and pitch of voice; rate of speech; emphasis; and stuttering, sighing, and other vocalizations that give nuance and meaning to interpersonal communication.

Parasuicide   Repeated nonlethal suicide attempts.

Partialize   The technique of breaking broad goals down into their concrete and measurable component parts.

Patterns   Repeated behavioral or affective sequences.

Peer supervision   A gathering in which two or more clinicians meet regularly to share their work and offer feedback and support about their clinical dilemmas and concerns.

Personal space   An invisible area around people that serves as a protective emotional barrier against the unwanted approaches of others.

Perspective   The viewpoint or position one takes when envisioning self in relation to others and to the wider world.

Perspective taking   The ability to understand the intentions, desires, and beliefs of another person, resulting from reasoning about the other's state.

Physical attending   The physical manifestation—literally, the embodiment—of the clinician's interest in and openness to the client, to the story, to the relationship, and to the work to be done together. It readies the interviewer to listen.

Planned break   A period of time in which the client purposely goes without face-to-face contact with a clinician, often used as a "dry run" before ending.

Positive mirror   The technique of seeking out and reflecting an alternative positive view of the client, crediting small achievements the client may have overlooked or undervalued, and emphasizing positive connections that clients may already have in their lives.

Positive Psychology   A clinical theory that focuses on identifying and enhancing a client's positive traits, emotions, and activities.

Positive Psychology Interventions   Clinical work that enhances feelings of well-being and happiness by building and expanding client's positive emotions, engagement with others, and capacity to lead a meaningful life.

Positive transference   A relational process in which the client idealizes the clinician and may experience him or her as incomparably wise, caring, and helpful.

Positivity portfolios   Collections of inspirational pictures, cards, objects, and sayings related to each of the emotions of joy, gratitude, serenity, interest, hope, pride, amusement, inspiration, awe, and love. Clients turn to these collections to ward off emotional downturns.

Posttraumatic growth   The positive changes arising from a struggle with trauma.

Posttraumatic Stress Disorder (PTSD)   A reaction to a serious or life-threatening event in which the person (1) reexperiences the traumatic event through dreams, intrusive thoughts, or flashbacks, (2) avoids stimuli associated with the event, and (3) has persistent symptoms of arousal such as sleep disturbances and hypervigilance.

Posture of attention   The physical manifestation or embodiment of the clinician's interest in and openness to the client, the story, the relationship, and the work together.

Precipitating events   The incidents or circumstances that set off a crisis. They may be catastrophic incidents or small things that are the last in a series of upsetting circumstances that leave the person feeling overwhelmed and unable to cope.

Predisposing factors   Poverty, health hazards, social isolation, marginalization, racism, widespread prejudice, and other conditions that leave people vulnerable to traumatic events and crisis states.

Prejudice   Positive or negative bias, poorly informed opinions, or unjustified assumptions about individuals who belong to a certain group or who fit into a particular socially constructed category.

Prioritize   The technique of ranking goals and objectives in the order of their urgency, importance, and likelihood of achievement.

Privileged communication   Federal or state legal protections of confidentiality for certain types of client–clinician relationships or in specified situations.

Process of the assessment   The use of exploration techniques to gather, organize, and analyze client-situation information relevant to the problems presented and to the strengths and resources available for use in problem resolution.

Process recording   Written or recorded verbatim transcripts of clinician–client interviews, useful in clinician–supervisor reflection on both the unfolding work and relationship, and on the skill development of the clinician.

Process the process   The technique of discussing the overall course of the relationship to point out themes, patterns, or notable developments in the work.

Professional boundaries   Lines of demarcation between clinician and client as they come together in a work-focused relationship.

Professional clinicians   Practitioners who have completed formal clinical education at or beyond the bachelor's or master's degree, who are appropriately licensed, and whose work is guided by clinical theory, research findings, ethics, and laws.

Professional code of ethics　A formal set of principles and standards of conduct that elucidate the values of a discipline or profession, prescribing certain behaviors and specifically forbidding others.

Professional license　A certification by a state demonstrating the practitioner's completion of required advanced course work and a set number of hours of advanced practice under supervision, in addition to successful testing in advanced clinical knowledge and competencies in specialized areas of practice.

Projection　A psychodynamic term to describe the clinical process in which clinicians disavow and repress their own unpleasant or taboo feelings, then attribute these feelings to clients or others ("I'm not angry, she is!").

Prompts　Minimal interview responses by the clinician that encourage the client to continue with the story or to add to what has already been said.

Proscribed conversation　An interview in which there are external restrictions on topics or content areas that clinicians can discuss with clients.

Protective factors　Strengths and supports that mitigate risk.

Pseudoquestions　Clinician directives or commands disguised as questions.

Psychological attending　The discipline of putting aside personal distractions, worries, and self-concerns and setting up "radar" to receive the signals the client is sending.

Psychological first aid　Immediate intervention after a traumatic event to enhance one's coping ability.

Psychological report　A term often used to describe an assessment summary.

Race　A social construct often used to classify people based on geographic origin and presumed shared physical characteristics like skin color, hair texture, and facial features. While the concept of race is socially meaningful, there is no biological basis for racial categorization.

Racial microaggressions　Unintentional, often unconscious, racist behaviors toward people of color, including microassaults, microinsults, and microinvalidations. Each of these behaviors devalues, offends, and injures its targets.

Racism　A powerful force of race-based prejudice and discrimination with institutional power behind it that can be found in individuals, families, cultures, and sociopolitical structures and institutions.

Random acts of kindness　A technique in Positive Psychology Interventions in which clinicians ask clients to derive pleasure and good feelings from virtue-based acts such as charitable contributions and supportive gestures towards people in need of help. Clients are asked to undertake 15 such acts per week and record the effects on themselves and others.

Randomized clinical trials　Studies to evaluate the effectiveness and safety of interventions by monitoring their effects on participants who are randomly assigned to different treatment groups.

Ratatat questioning　Clinician questions that barrage the client with one rapid-fire question after another. No topic is pursued long enough to develop any real depth or meaning.

Reciprocal influences　A principle of systems theory describing the ways in which every member of an interaction affects and is affected by the other participants.

Reciprocal inhibition　Wolpe's behavioral theory that one response (anxiety) can be inhibited by the occurrence of another response (relaxation) that is mutually incompatible with it. Reciprocal inhibition is a basic principle of systematic desensitization.

Referral　Giving the client names of particular providers or agencies that can meet a client's specific needs, either during the clinician's and client's work together or after the work ends.

Reflecting discrepancies　The technique of pointing out to clients perceived inconsistencies between two statements, between thoughts and feelings, between intentions and behaviors, and between verbal and nonverbal communication.

Reflection of affect　Clinician statements that accurately represent the client's stated or implied feelings.

Reflection of content　Clinician statements that accurately represent the client's statements about behaviors, thoughts, and interactions, as well as about the contexts in which they are embedded.

Refocusing　The technique of returning the client to a desired topic by gently intruding on client remarks and inserting the topic into the conversation once again.

Reframing　The general term applied to a group of skills that clinicians use to help clients gain new perspective and shift their ways of thinking about a situation, opening up new possibilities and potential solutions.

Regression under stress　A psychological process in which clients return to outgrown behaviors under pressure because they are familiar, knee-jerk outlets for distress.

Reinforcers　Consequences or events that occur after a behavior, increasing the probability of its recurrence.

Relational tending　A relational technique of accurately noticing, addressing, and working through issues in the clinical relationship.

Reliability　The degree to which an assessment measure is consistent over time or in different settings or if used by different assessors.

Resilience　The capacity to adapt competently to adverse or hazardous conditions.

Resistance　The client's reluctance or refusal to follow the clinician's leads or suggestions.

Response-ability　Janet Surrey's term for understanding what relationships require, developing relational skills, and remaining faithful to relationships even if it is not always easy to do so.

Review of life records A clinician's review of the records of clients' previous treatments, their school records, and other written documents including previous test reports. These records may not necessarily provide an accurate reflection of the client in the past nor provide a valid picture of the client as he or she is now.

RE-VIEW PRACTICE Method The authors' suggested method of mastering clinical practice knowledge and skill application by reading about clinical concepts and techniques, seeing them applied by clinicians, then trying them out and receiving useful feedback from instructors and colleagues.

Risk factors Those characteristics or activities that increase a person's chances of a disease, injury, or harm in the future.

Risk management Activities designed to reduce clinician liability.

Role-play Relational behavior simulations in which clinicians help clients prepare for difficult interactions with others by alternating roles and feedback in a brief scenario of exchanges similar to those the client faces elsewhere.

Sabotage An act in which one member of a treatment team, who does not believe in the goals and plans that the team has established, encourages a client to undermine or act against the treatment plan.

Salience of identity The importance and meaning of an individual's or group's identity varies depending on the situation.

Scaling questions Clinical questions that ask clients to estimate the intensity of their emotional arousal, desire for change, or other variables on a scale of 1 to 10 or 1 to 100.

Scientist/practitioner model The model that recognizes that clinicians conduct research, develop and carry out interventions, and evaluate treatment procedures and programs to determine best practices. They also stay abreast of current developments in psychology and human services, medical and psychiatric services, and political and economic spheres.

Secondary trauma A traumatic response to hearing about or witnessing others' traumatic experiences that awaken one's sense of vulnerability, sometimes causing the witness to develop posttraumatic symptoms too.

Self-disclosure Clinicians' purposeful sharing of their own personal demographic information, experiences, and reactions with clients.

Self-empathy The capacity to notice, care about, and respond to our own felt needs as generously as we attend to the needs of others.

Semistructured interviews Assessment interviews that may be guided by a list of content areas that the clinician should cover.

Shaping Breaking a task into its component parts, then rewarding successive approximations (small steps) in the direction of the desired behavior.

Short-term goals Desired results that can be accomplished relatively quickly in the near term.

Silence A form of communication, not just a blank space between communications. It may serve as a natural breather between topics or as a period of thoughtful reflection, and it can indicate comfort, discomfort, anger, calm, or many other things.

Simultaneous interpretation In this mode, the interpreter speaks at the same time as one of the parties in an interaction or presentation is speaking, closely following the speaker's words. This kind of interpretation rarely occurs in clinical interviews, and is used largely when dignitaries or heads of state meet, as in the United Nations Assembly.

Situational crises Crises triggered by ordinary events such as fires, acts of violence, diagnoses or episodes of mental or physical illness, or abrupt changes in established systems in which people feel secure.

SLAP A mnemonic for framing questions regarding a person's suicide plan, questions about *specificity, lethality, actual availability of imagined method, and proximity* of social helping resources.

Slowdowns A sustaining technique in which the clinician "taps the brakes" on the interviewing process, modeling patience and carefulness with self by signaling clients that there is no need to rush the unfolding story or feelings.

Social construct Meaning created and recreated though human interactions and use of language. A shift in power often leads to a redefinition of meaning.

Social justice perspective A point of view asserting that clinicians have a primary social responsibility to work for equal rights, resources, and opportunities for all people. Clinicians should also nourish structures and processes that encourage growth and development while opposing all forms of oppression and environmental degradation.

Societal norms Widely held standards and expectations codified into laws, to which all members of society are expected to adhere.

SOLER Psychologist Gerard Egan's acronym for sitting squarely in an open posture, leaning forward, making eye contact, and relaxing into the moment.

Spontaneous remission The natural process by which client symptoms end or improve greatly without any assistance from professionals or programs.

Stakeholders Friends, family, and others important to the client and to the problem-solving process and who have vested interests in the outcomes of the intervention.

Stereotype A fixed, oversimplified, often biased collective image of members of a particular group based on its characteristics, beliefs, practices, or aspirations.

Stigma The negative assumptions and prejudices attached to people because of their membership in particular devalued groups.

Strength-based genogram A clinical assessment tool that clarifies important intergenerational models and sources of individual, family, and group assets and accomplishments.

Strengths perspective A view of human development and functioning that highly values client assets and potentials. Clinicians identify and underscore the often undervalued or unnoticed strengths that clients have used successfully to resolve problems, as well as highlighting and utilizing new strengths and supports.

Structured interview An assessment interview consisting of a set of standardized questions that are to be asked in a specific order.

Suicidal ideation Contemplation of or preoccupation with suicide.

Summarizing An interview technique in which the clinician pulls together in condensed form the major ideas, themes, or patterns that have just been discussed and reflects them back to the client.

Supportive sounds Brief utterances and encouragements that mark the clinician's active listening and close following of the client's narrative.

Sustaining techniques Interviewing strategies that offer clients support as they explore and elaborate more deeply.

Symbolic power The power, expertise, and influence clients may attribute to clinicians by virtue of their roles and authority.

Synchrony A response to rapport in which people involved in ongoing conversation begin without awareness to manifest similar tones, postures, gestures, and other nonverbal behaviors.

Systematic A systems perspective asserting that people are best understood in the context of the relationships, resources, opportunity systems, and barriers to well-being in their lives.

Systematic desensitization Gradual step-by-step exposure to the feared stimulus on an anxiety hierarchy is paired with a relaxation strategy, which gradually extinguishes the fear through reciprocal inhibition.

Tactile signing Interpreting for people who are blind as well as deaf by making manual signs into a person's hands, using cued speech, and signing exact English.

Tangential questions Clinician questions that veer from the main topic of the interview, taking side roads without good reason and creating an aura of aimless or poorly focused conversation.

Termination The term traditionally used in clinical work to describe the process of ending.

Testing A method of clinical assessment in which the clinician uses intelligence and personality tests, symptom checklists, and other evaluative tools to measure client capacities and problems in functioning.

Test-retest reliability The scores a person receives on a test should be consistent even if the test is given by different examiners or administered at different times.

Themes Repeated or recurring sets of ideas and beliefs reflecting an underlying organizing principle.

Theory A systematic set of principles used to understand and explain observable phenomena and to guide clinical work with clients.

"Therapizing" supervisees A supervisor's inappropriate probing for painful details of a supervisee's personal history that could be related to current interviewing missteps.

Three good things The Positive Psychology technique of helping clients counter depressive episodes by writing down for a week three good things that went well each day. Then they are asked to reflect on their own role in the daily three good things: what they may have done or said that contributed to the good things happening, and what that behavior leaves them feeling now.

Timing A clinician's developed instinct and cultural sensitivity for what and how much to ask, when to ask it, and whom to ask.

Token economy A specific form of contingency contracts in which clients earn tokens or points for desired behavior and pay tokens for designated misbehavior. Self-defined reinforcements can be purchased with tokens or points.

Transferability of skills The clinical concept asserting that one's strengths, talents, or methods of coping in one situation might work well in others.

Transference A psychodynamic term referring to an unconscious relational process in which a client's earlier unresolved relational dynamics or conflicts are unwittingly displaced or "transferred" onto the current relationship with the clinician and then reenacted or expressed as though appropriate or real in the moment.

Transitional object A symbolic representation of the clinical relationship or work, often given to the client at ending to sustain a feeling of connection and support.

Trauma An extraordinary and overwhelming event in which a person's usual coping mechanisms are insufficient to meet the challenge or threat. Such events can shatter people's assumptions about how the universe operates.

Treatment by objectives An intervention structured by partialized, prioritized, and measurable objectives and by the particular tasks, steps, timelines, and responsibilities for accomplishing each objective.

Treatment manual An empirically validated treatment guide that spells out step-by-step instructions, timing, and techniques to resolve a particular set of problems.

Treatment plans Treatment or intervention plans that spell out agreed-upon goals for the work to come and the people, methods, and resources proposed to achieve the goals. These plans serve as a road map to help guide clients and clinicians throughout the intervention process.

Triggers People, circumstances, ideas, feelings, and events that stimulate behavioral reactions.

Unconditional positive regard The appreciation and affirmation of clients as people of worth. The clinician communicates nonjudgmental acceptance and genuine care for the client.

Underlining An interview response in which the clinician underscores important content or experience by the strategic use of verbal or nonverbal emphasis, often rendered through tone, facial expressions, or emphatic gestures.

Universalizing A technique in which the clinician verbally situates the client in a community of people sharing similar feelings, experiences, or opinions.

Unplanned contacts Unintended encounters between clinicians and clients when they see each other outside their usual meeting place.

Unstructured interviews Assessment interviews that are flexible in focus so as to allow the clinician to follow the lead of the client.

Using direct influence Employing the symbolic power of clinical roles to pressure clients, subtly and overtly, to behave in given ways deemed important to their well-being or safety.

Validation The clinician's endorsement and appreciation of the realities of the client's story.

Validation of the difficulty of disclosure The sustaining technique of recognizing and appreciating personal and cultural reluctance to share private matters with an outsider such as a professional interviewer.

Validity How well an assessment measures what it intends to measure and how accurate a picture it gives of the person(s) assessed.

Value differences Often unseen and unspoken differences in the way people attribute meaning and worth to other people, events, institutions, cultural practices, beliefs, group aspirations, and the like.

Vicarious trauma Clinicians' secondary trauma reactions due to empathizing with and absorbing the stories and symptoms of numerous traumatized people. It is also known as emotional contagion and can result in compassion fatigue.

Virtual Reality Exposure Therapy A Wii-like technology-based exposure treatment that immerses severely anxious or traumatized clients in a computer-generated virtual environment relevant to each client's particular anxiety, with the sights, sounds, smells, and challenges the client would face in a real-world exposure. The therapist has a parallel set of controls and can rapidly diminish the anxiety stimulus when necessary to calm the client.

Warning signs Events or behaviors that connote imminent risk of suicide over the next few minutes, hours, or days.

Watchwords A clinician's helpful self-reminders of some simple do's and don'ts about potential personal behaviors, relational dynamics, or reactions in an upcoming interview.

Working alliance The form of a clinician–client bond that is focused on problem-solving work.

References

Abu-Ras, Wahiba, Gheith, Ali, & Cournos, Francine. (2008). The Imam's role in mental health promotion: A study at 22 mosques in New York City's Muslim community. *Journal of Muslim Mental Health, 3,* 155–176.

Acuff, Catherine, Bennett, Bruce E., Bricklin, Patricia M., Canter, Mathilda B., Knapp, Samuel J., Moldawsky, Stanley, et al. (1999). Considerations for ethical practice in managed care. *Professional Psychology: Research and Practice, 6,* 563–575.

Addams, Jane. (1910). *Twenty years at Hull House.* New York: Macmillan.

Alvarez, Lizette. (2009, February 5). Army data shows rise in number of suicides. *New York Times,* p. A12.

American Association of Suicidology. (2008). *Is Path Warm?* Accessed December 12, 2009 from www.suicidology.org/web/guest/stats-and-tools/warning-signs

American Counseling Association. (2002). *Multicultural counseling competencies.* Alexandria, VA: Author.

American Counseling Association. (2005). *The American Counseling Association code of ethics.* Alexandria, VA: Author.

American Psychiatric Association. (2000). *Diagnostic and statistical manual of mental disorders IV-TR.* Washington, DC: Author.

American Psychological Association. (1990). *Guidelines for providers of psychological services to ethnic, linguistic, and culturally diverse populations.* Washington, DC: Author.

American Psychological Association. (2002a). *Guidelines on multicultural education, training, research, practice, and organizational change for psychologists.* Washington, DC: Author.

American Psychological Association. (2002b). *Ethical principles of psychologists and code of conduct.* Washington, DC: Author.

American Psychological Association. (2007). Record keeping guidelines. *American Psychologist, 62,* 993–1004.

Amodeo, Maryann, Grigg-Saito, Dorcas, & Robb, Nancy. (1997). Working with foreign language interpreters: Guidelines for substance abuse clinicians and human service practitioners. *Social Work, 15,* 75–87.

Amodeo, Maryann, & Jones, L. Kay. (1997). Using the AOD cultural framework to view alcohol and drug issues through various cultural lenses. *Journal of Social Work Education, 34,* 387–399.

Anderson, Harlene, & Goolishian, Harry. (1992). The client is the expert: A not-knowing approach to therapy. In Sheila McNamee & Kenneth Gergen (Eds.), *Therapy as a social construction* (pp. 25–39). Newbury Park, CA: Sage.

Anderson, Timothy, Ogles, Benjamin M., Patterson, Candace L., Lambert, Michael J., & Vermeersch, David. (2009). Therapist effects: Facilitative interpersonal skills as a predictor of therapist success. *Journal of Clinical Psychology, 65,* 755–768.

APA Presidential Task Force on Evidence-Based Practice. (2006). Evidence-based practice in psychology. *American Psychologist, 61,* 271–185.

Aponte, Harry. (1994). *Bread and spirit: Therapy with the new poor—diversity of race, culture, and values.* New York: Norton.

Arredondo, Patricia, & Glauner, T. (1992). *Personal dimensions of identity model.* Boston: Empowerment Workshops, Inc.

Arredondo, Patricia, Toporek, Rebecca, Brown, Sherlon P., Jones, Janet, Locke, Don C., Sanchez, Joe, et al. (1996). Operationalization of the multicultural counseling competencies. *Journal of Multicultural Counseling and Development, 24,* 42–78.

Atkinson, Donald R. (2004). *Counseling American minorities* (6th ed.). New York: McGraw-Hill.

Atkinson, Donald R., Bui, Uyen, & Mori, Sakurako. (2001). Multiculturally sensitive empirically supported treatments—an oxymoron? In Joseph G. Ponterotto, J. Manuel Casas, Lisa A. Suzuki, & Charlene M. Alexander (Eds.), *Handbook of multicultural counseling* (pp. 542–574). Thousand Oaks, CA: Sage.

Ault, Amber, & Brzuzy, Stephanie. (2009). Removing gender identity disorder from the Diagnostic and Statistical Manual of Mental Disorders: A call to action. *Social Work, 54,* 187–189.

Baird, Brian N. (2007). *The internship, practicum, and field placement handbook: A guide for helping professionals* (5th ed.). Upper Saddle River, NJ: Pearson.

Baker, F. M. Diagnosing depression in African-Americans. *Community Mental Health Journal, 37,* 31–38.

Bandura, Albert. (1969). *Principles of behavior modification.* New York: Holt Rinehart & Winston.

Bandura, Albert. (1976). Effecting change through participant modeling. In John Krumboltz & Carl Thorenson (Eds.), *Counseling methods* (pp. 248–265). New York: Holt, Rinehart & Winston.

Barak, Azy, Hen, Liat, Boniel-Nissim, Meyran, & Shapira Na'ama. (2008). A comprehensive review and a meta- analysis of the effectiveness of Internet-based psychotherapeutic interventions. *Journal of Technology in Human Services, 26,* 109–160.

Bargh, J. A., McKenna, K. Y. A., & Fitzsimons, G. M. (2002). Can you see the real me? Activation and expression of the "true self" on the Internet. *Journal of Social Issues, 58,* 33–48.

Barlow, David, & Durand, Mark. (2009). *Abnormal psychology* (5th ed.). Belmont, CA: Wadsworth.

Barnett, Jeffrey E., Lazarus, Arnold A., Vasquez, Melba J. T., Moorhead-Slaughter, Olivia, & Johnson, W. Brad. (2007). Boundary issues and multiple relationships: Fantasy and reality. *Professional Psychology: Research and Practice, 38,* 401–410.

Barnett, Jeffrey E., Wise, Erica H., Johnson-Greene, Doug, & Bucky, Steven F. (2007). Informed consent: Too much of a good thing or not enough? *Professional Psychology: Research and Practice, 38,* 179–186.

Barrett, Janie Porter. (1926). The Virginia Industrial School. *Southern Workman, 55,* 353–361.

Bateson, Gregory. (1972). *Steps to an ecology of mind.* New York: Chandler.

Bateson, Gregory. (1979). *Mind and nature.* New York: Dutton.

Bateson, Gregory, Jackson, Don, & Weakland, John. (1963). A note on the double bind. *Family Processes, 2,* 154–161.

Beck, Aaron. (2005). The current state of cognitive therapy: A 40-year retrospective. *Archives of General Psychiatry, 62,* 953–959.

Beck, Aaron T., Kovacs, M., & Weissman, A. (1979). Assessment of suicidal intention: The Scale for Suicide Ideation. *Journal of Consulting and Clinical Psychology, 47,* 343–352.

Beck, Judith. (1995). *Cognitive therapy: Basics and beyond.* New York: Guilford.

Benard, Bonnie. (1997). Fostering resiliency in children and youth: Promoting protective factors in school. In Dennis Saleebey (Ed.), *The strengths perspective in social work practice* (pp. 167–182). White Plains, NY: Longman.

Benefield, Hope, Ashkanazi, Glenn, & Rozensky, Ronald H. (2006). Communication and records: HIPAA issues when working in health care settings. *Professional Psychology, Research and Practice, 37,* 273–277.

Benson, Herbert, & Klipper, Miriam. (1976). *The relaxation response.* New York: Morrow.

Behnke, Stephen H., & Warner, Elizabeth. (2002). Confidentiality in the treatment of adolescents. *Monitor on Psychology, 33*(3). Accessed September 24, 2009 from www.apa.org/monitor/mar02/confidentiality.html

Bersoff, Donald N. (2008). Record keeping guidelines. In Donald N. Bersoff (Ed.), *Ethical conflicts in psychology* (4th ed.) (pp. 536–542). Washington, DC: American Psychological Association.

Birdwhistell, Ray L. (1970). *Kinesics and context.* Philadelphia: University of Pennsylvania.

Blanco, Carlos, Clougherty, Kathleen, Lipsitz, Joshua, Mufson, Laura, & Weissman, Myrna. (2006). Homework in interpersonal psychotherapy (IPT): Rationale and practice. *Journal of Psychotherapy Integration, 16,* 201–218.

Blom, Bjorn. (2009) Knowing or un-knowing? That is the question: In the era of evidence-based social work practice. *Journal of Social Work, 9,* 158–177.

Boehm, Amnon, & Staples, Lee H. (2004). Empowerment: The point of view of consumers. *Families in Society, 85,* 270–280.

Borysenko, Joan. (1987). *Minding the body, mending the mind.* New York: Addison-Wesley.

Borysenko, Joan, & Dveirin, Gordon. (2006). *Saying yes to change: Essential wisdom for your journey.* Carlsbad, CA: Hay House.

Briar-Lawson, Katherine. (1998). Capacity building for integrated family-centered practice. *Social Work, 43,* 539–550.

Bridges, Nancy. (2005). *Moving beyond the comfort zone in psychotherapy.* Lanham, MD: Jason Aronson.

Bronfenbrenner, Urie. (1979). *The ecology of human development: Experiments by nature and design.* Cambridge, MA: Harvard University Press.

Brown, Chris, & Trangsrud, Heather B. (2008). Factors associated with acceptance and decline of client gift giving. *Professional Psychology, 39,* 505–511.

Brown, Laura. (1994). *Subversive dialogues: Theory in feminist therapy.* New York: Basic Books.

Bureau of Labor Statistics. (2008). *Interpreters and Translators.* Accessed October 3, 2009 from www.bls.gov/oco/ocos175.html

Burke, Brian, Arkowitz, Hal, & Menchola, Marisa. (2003). The efficacy of motivational interviewing: A meta-analysis of controlled clinical trials. *Journal of Consulting and Clinical Psychology, 17,* 843–861.

Burns, Andrea B., Brown, Jessica S., Sachs-Ericsson, Natalie, Plant, E. Ashby, Curtis, J. Thomas, Fredrickson, Barbara L., et al. (2008). Upward spirals of positive emotion and coping: Replication, extension, and initial exploration of neurochemical substrates. *Personality and Individual Differences, 44,* 360–370.

Burns, David D. (1999). *The feeling good handbook.* New York: Plume-Penguin.

Burns, George. (2005). Naturally happy, naturally healthy: The role of the natural environment in well-being. In Felicia A. Huppert, Nick Baylis, & Barry Keverne (Eds.), *The science of well-being* (pp. 405–431). New York: Oxford.

Burns, George (Ed.). (2007). *Healing with stories: Your casebook collection for using therapeutic metaphors.* Hoboken, NJ: Wiley.

Calhoun, Lawrence, & Tedeschi, Richard (Eds.). (2006). *Handbook of posttraumatic growth: Research and practice.* Mahwah, NJ: Lawrence Erlbaum.

Canda, Edward, & Furman, Leola. (1999). *Spiritual diversity in social work practice: The heart of helping.* New York: Free Press.

Caplan, Paula J. (1995). *They say you're crazy: How the world's most powerful psychiatrists decide who's normal.* Reading, MA: Addison-Wesley.

Carlo, Gustavo, Koller, Silvia, Raffaelli, Marcela, & de Guzman, Maria R. T. Culture-related strengths among Latin American families: A case study of Brazil. *Marriage & Family Review, 41,* 335–360.

Cascio, Toni, & Gasker, Janice. (2001). Everyone has a shining side: Computer-mediated mentoring in social work education. *Journal of Social Work Education, 37*(2), 283–293.

Cashwell, Craig S., Scherbakova, Julia, & Cashwell, Tammy H. (2003). Effect of client and counselor ethnicity on preference for counselor disclosure. *Journal of Counseling and Development, 81*(2), 196–202.

Centers for Disease Control and Prevention (CDC). (2005). *Web-based Injury Statistics Query and Reporting System (WISQARS)* [Online]. National Center for Injury Prevention and Control, CDC (producer). Accessed December 12, 2009 from www.cdc.gov/ncipc/wisqars/default.htm

Chambless, Dianne L., Baker, Mary J., Baucom, Donald H., Beutler, Larry E., Calhoun, Karen S., Crits-Christoph, Paul, et al. (1998). Update on empirically validated therapies, II. *The Clinical Psychologist, 51*(1), 3–16.

Chambless, Dianne L., & Hollon, Steven D. (1998). Defining empirically supported therapies. *Journal of Counseling and Clinical Psychology, 66*(1), 7–18.

Chan, Sam, & Lee, Evelyn. (2004). Families with Asian roots. In Eleanor W. Lynch & Marci J. Hanson (Eds.), *Developing cross-cultural competence: A guide for working with children and their families* (3rd ed.) (pp. 219–298). Baltimore, MD: Brookes.

Chang, Valerie, Scott, Sheryn, & Decker, Carol. (2009). *Developing helping skills: A step-by-step approach.* Belmont, CA: Brooks/Cole Cengage.

Chao, Christine M. (1992). The inner heart: Therapy with Southeast Asian families. In Luis Vargas & Joan D. Koss-Chioino (Eds.), *Working with culture: Psychotherapeutic interventions with ethnic minority children and adolescents* (pp. 157–181). San Francisco: Jossey-Bass.

Chu, James. (1991). The repetition compulsion revisited: Reliving dissociated trauma. *Psychotherapy, 28*(2), 327–332.

Clark, David A., & Beck, Aaron T. (2009). *Cognitive therapy of anxiety disorders: Science and practice.* New York: Guilford.

Clayton, Paula, & Auster, Tracey. (2008). Strategies for the prevention and treatment of suicidal behavior. *FOCUS: The Journal of Lifelong Learning in Psychiatry, 6*(1), 15–21.

Coleman, Daniel. (2000). The therapeutic alliance in multicultural practice. *Psychoanalytic Social Work, 7*(2), 65–90.

Collins, Barbara G., & Collins, Thomas M. (2005). *Crisis and trauma: Developmental-ecological intervention.* Belmont, CA: Wadsworth.

Collins, Lynn H. (2008). Practicing safer listserv use: Ethical use of an invaluable resource. *Professional Psychology, 39,* 690–698.

Comas-Diaz, Lillian, & Greene, Beverly (Eds.). (1994). *Women of color: Integrating ethnic and gender identities in psychotherapy.* New York: Guilford.

Comas-Diaz, Lillian, & Jacobsen, Frederick M. (1991). Ethnocultural transference and countertransference in the therapeutic dyad. *American Journal of Orthopsychiatry, 61,* 392–402.

Compton, Beulah, Galaway, Burt, & Cournoyer, Barry. (2005). *Social work processes* (7th ed.). Belmont, CA: Brooks/Cole.

Comstock, Dana. (2004). Reflections on life, loss, and resilience. In Maureen Walker & Wendy B. Rosen (Eds.), *How connections heal: Stories from relational-cultural therapy* (pp. 83–101). New York: Guilford.

Congress, Elaine. (2004). Cultural and ethical issues in working with culturally diverse patients and their families: The use of the Culturagram to promote cultural competent practice in health care setting. *Social Work in Health Care, 39,* 249–262.

Constantine, Madonna, & Sue, Derald Wing (Eds.). (2005). *Strategies for building multicultural competence in mental health and educational settings.* Hoboken, NJ: John Wiley.

Corey, Gerald, & Corey, Marianne Schneider. (2007). *Becoming a helper* (5th ed.). Pacific Grove, CA: Brooks/Cole.

Corey, Gerald, Corey, Marianne Schneider, & Callanan, Patrick. (2007). *Issues and ethics in the helping professions* (7th ed). Belmont, CA: Brooks/Cole Cengage.

Corey, Gerald. (2009). *Theory and practice of counseling and psychotherapy* (8th ed.). Belmont, CA: Wadsworth.

Cournoyer, Barry R. (2004). *The evidence-based social work skills book.* Boston: Allyn & Bacon.

Cournoyer, Barry. (2005). *The social work skills workbook* (4th ed.). Pacific Grove, CA: Brooks/Cole.

Cross, William E., Jr. (1971). The Negro-to-Black conversion experience: Towards a psychology of Black liberation. *Black World, 20,* 13–27.

Cross, William E., Jr. (1991). *Shades of black: Diversity in African American identity.* Philadelphia: Temple University Press.

Cross, William E., Jr., & Fhagen-Smith, Peony. (2001). Patterns of African American identity development: A life-span developmental perspective. In Charlaine J. Wijeyesinghe & Bailey W. Jackson, III (Eds.), *Reflections on racial identity development: Essays on theory, practice, and discourse* (pp. 243–270). New York: New York University Press.

Cross, William E., Jr., Smith, Lakesha, & Payne, Yasser. (2002). Black identity: A repertoire of daily enactments. In Paul B. Pedersen, Juris G. Draguns, Walter J. Lonner, & Joseph E. Trimble (Eds.), *Counseling across cultures* (pp. 93–108). Thousand Oaks, CA: Sage.

Cross, William E., Jr., & Vandiver, Beverly J. (2001). Negrescence theory and measurement: Introducing the Cross Racial Identity Scale (CRIS). In Joseph

G. Ponterotto, J. Manuel Casas, Lisa A. Suzuki, & Charlene M. Alexander (Eds.), *Handbook of multicultural counseling* (pp. 371–393). Thousand Oaks, CA: Sage.

Cuijpers, Pim, van Straten, Annemicke, & Andersson, Gerhard. (2008). Internet-administered cognitive behavior therapy for health problems: A systemic review. *Journal of Behavioral Medicine, 31*, 69–177.

Daniel, Jessica H. (2000). The courage to hear: African American women's memories of racial trauma. In Leslie C. Jackson & Beverly Greene (Eds.), *Psychotherapy with African American women* (pp. 126–144). New York: Guilford.

DeAngelis, Tori. (2009). Virtual healing. *Monitor on Psychology, 40*(8), 36–40.

De Jong, Peter, & Berg, Insoo Kim. (2001). Co-constructing cooperation with mandated clients. *Social Work, 46*(4), 261–374.

De Jong, Peter, & Miller, Scott D. (1995). How to interview for client strengths. *Social Work, 40*, 729–736.

de la Cancela, Victor, Jenkins, Yvonne M., & Chin, Jean Lau. (1993). Diversity in psychotherapy: Examination of racial, ethnic, gender, and political issues. In Jean Lau Chin, Victor de la Cancela, & Yvonne M. Jenkins (Eds.), *Diversity in psychotherapy: The politics of race, ethnicity, and gender* (pp. 5–15). Westport, CT: Praeger.

de Mello, Marcelo F., de Jesus Mari, Jair, Bacaltchuk, Josue, Verdelli, Helen, & Neugebauer, Richard. (2005). A systematic review of research findings on the efficacy of interpersonal therapy for depressive disorders. *European Archives of Psychiatry and Clinical Neuroscience, 255*(2), 75–82.

de Shazer, Steve. (1988). *Clues: Investigating solutions in brief therapy.* New York: Norton.

de Shazer, Steve. (n.d.). *The Miracle Question.* Accessed February 1, 2006 from www.brief-therapy.org/steve_miracle.htm

Deahl, Martin. (2000). Psychological debriefing: Controversy and challenge. *Australian and New Zealand Journal of Psychiatry, 34*(6), 929–939.

Dean, Ruth G. (1984). The role of empathy in supervision. *Clinical Social Work Journal, 12*(2), 129–139.

Decety, Jean, Michalska, Kalina J., & Akitsuki, Yuko. (2008). Who caused the pain? An fMRI investigation of empathy and intentionality in children. *Neuropsychologia, 46*, 2607–2614.

Delgado, Melvin. (1997). Role of Latina-owned beauty parlors in a Latino community. *Social Work, 42*, 445–453.

Delgado, Melvin. (2007). *Social work practice with Latinos: A cultural assets paradigm.* New York: Oxford University Press.

DePoy, Elizabeth, & Gilson, Stephen French. (2004). *Rethinking disability: Principles for professional and social change.* Belmont, CA: Thomson-Brooks/Cole.

Devilly, Grant J., Gist, Richard, & Cotton, Peter. (2006). Ready! Fire! Aim! The status of psychological debriefing and therapeutic interventions: In the work place and after disasters. *Review of General Psychology, 10*(4), 318–345.

Devore, Wynetta, & Schlesinger, Elfriede G. (1996). *Ethnic-sensitive social work practice* (4th ed.). Boston: Allyn & Bacon.

DiFranks, Nikki N. (2008). Social workers and the NASW Code of Ethics: Belief, behavior, disjuncture. *Social Work, 53*, 167–176.

Dillon, Carolyn. (1999). A relational perspective on mutuality and boundaries in clinical practice with lesbians. In Joan Laird (Ed.), *Lesbians & lesbian families: Reflections on theory and practice* (pp. 283–303). New York: Columbia University Press.

Dillon, Carolyn. (2003). *Learning from mistakes in clinical practice.* Pacific Grove, CA: Brooks/Cole.

Dolgoff, Ralph, Loewenberg, Frank M., & Harrington, Donna. (2009). *Ethical decisions for social work practice* (8th ed.). Belmont, CA: Brooks/Cole Cengage.

Domar, Alice, & Dreher, Henry. (2000). *Self-nurture: Learning to care for yourself as effectively as you care for everyone else.* New York: Penguin.

Duckworth, Angela Lee, Steen, Tracy A., & Seligman, Martin E. P. (2005). Positive psychology in clinical practice. *Annual Review of Clinical Psychology, 1*, 629–651.

Dutton, Mary Ann, & Rubenstein, Francine L. (1995). Working with people with PTSD: Research implications. In Charles R. Figley (Ed.), *Compassion fatigue: Coping with secondary traumatic stress disorder in those who treat the traumatized* (pp. 82–100). New York: Brunner/Mazel.

Dwairy, Marwan. (2002). Psychotherapy in competition with culture: A case study of an Arab woman. *Clinical Case Studies, 1*, 254–267.

Dwairy, Marwan. (2005). Stress management among collective societies: The case of the Palestinian Arabs in Israel. *Australian Journal of Disaster and Trauma Studies, 1*, n.p.

Dwairy, Marwan. (2009). Culture analysis and metaphor with Arab-Muslim clients. *Journal of Clinical Psychology, 65*, 199–209.

Edlund, Mark J., Wang, Philip S., Berglund, Patricia A., Katz, Stephen J., Lin, Elizabeth, & Kessler, Ronald C. (2002). Dropping out of mental health treatment: Patterns and predictors among epidemiological survey respondents in the United States and Ontario. *American Journal of Psychiatry, 159*, 845–851.

Egan, Gerard. (2010). *Essentials of skilled helping: Managing problems, developing opportunities.* Belmont, CA: Brooks/Cole.

Ehrenreich, Jill, Fairholme, Christopher, Buzzella, Brian, Ellard, Kristen, & Barlow, David. (2007). The role of emotion in psychological therapy. *Clinical Psychology, 14*, 422–428.

Eisenberg, Nancy, Spinrad, Tracy L., & Sadovsky, Adrienne. (2006). Empathy-related responding in children. In Melanie Killen & Judith G. Smetana (Eds.), *Handbook of moral development* (pp. 517–549). Mahwah, NJ: Lawrence Erlbaum.

Eldridge, Natalie S., Mencher, Julie, & Slater, Suzanne. (1997). The conundrum of mutuality: A lesbian dialogue. In Judith V. Jordan (Ed.), *Women's growth in diversity: More writings from the Stone Center* (pp. 107–137). New York: Guilford.

Ellis, Albert, & MacLaren, Catharine. (1998). *Rational emotive behavior therapy: A therapist's guide.* Atascadero, CA: Impact.

Ellis, Priscilla, & Murphy, Bianca Cody. (1994). The impact of misogyny and homophobia in therapy with women. In Marsha Mirkin (Ed.), *Women in context: Toward a feminist reconstruction of psychotherapy with women* (pp. 48–93). New York: Guilford Press.

Epston, David, & White, Michael. (1990). *Narrative means to therapeutic ends.* New York: Norton.

Erikson, Erik. (1963). *Childhood and society.* New York: Norton.

Everett, Joyce C., Homstead, Kerry, & Drisko, James. (2007). Frontline worker perceptions of the empowerment process in community-based agencies. *Social Work, 52,* 161–170.

Fadiman, Anne. (1997). *The spirit catches you and you fall down.* New York: Farrar, Straus & Giroux.

Fair, Susan M., & Bressler, Joanna M. (1992). Therapist-initiated termination of psychotherapy. *The Clinical Supervisor, 10,* 171–189.

Faver, C. A. (2004). Relational spirituality and social caregiving. *Social Work, 49*(2), 241–249.

Ferdman, Bernado M., & Gallegos, Placida I. (2001). Racial identity development and Latinos in the United States. In Charmaine L. Wijeyesinghe & Bailey W. Jackson, III (Eds.), *New perspectives on racial identity development: A theoretical and practical anthology* (pp. 32–66). New York: New York University Press.

Fhagen-Smith, Peony E. (2003). Mixed Ancestry Racial/Ethnic Identity Development (MAREID) model. Wellesley College Centers for Women Working Paper #413. Wellesley, MA: Wellesley College Centers for Women.

Figley, Charles. (1983). Catastrophe: An overview of family reactions. In Charles R. Figley & Harris I. McCubbin (Eds.), *Stress and the family: Vol 2. Coping with catastrophe* (pp. 3–20). New York: Brunner/Mazel.

Figley, Charles (Ed.). (1995). *Compassion fatigue: Coping with secondary traumatic stress disorder in those who treat the traumatized.* New York: Brunner/Mazel.

Figley, Charles R. (2002). Compassion fatigue: Psychotherapists' chronic lack of self care. *Journal of Clinical, 58*(11), 1433–1441.

Finn, Peter, & McNeil, Taylor. (1987). *The response of the criminal justice system to bias crime: An explanatory review.* Cambridge, MA: Abt Associates.

Finn, Jerry, & Schoech, Dick. (2008). Introduction. *Journal of Technology in Human Services, 26,* 105–108.

First, M. B., Spitzer, R. L., Gibbon, M., & Williams, J. B. W. (1997). *Structured Clinical Interview for DSM-IV Axis I Disorders, clinician version (SCID-CV).* Washington, DC: American Psychiatry Press.

Fisher, Celia B., & Fried, Adam L. (2003). Internet-mediated psychological services and the American Psychological Association Ethics Code. *Psychotherapy: Theory, Research, Practice, Training, 40,* 103–111.

Fisher, Roger, Ury, William L., & Patton, Bruce. (1991). *Getting to yes: Negotiating agreement without giving in* (2nd ed.). New York: Penguin.

Fleming, Joan, & Benedek, Therese. (1966). *Psychoanalytic supervision.* New York: Grune & Stratton.

Frank, Ellen, Novick, Danielle, & Kupfer, David J. (2006). Antidepressants and psychotherapy: A clinical research review. *Dialogues in Clinical Neuroscience, 7,* 263–272.

Fredrickson, Barbara L. (2001). The role of positive emotions in positive psychology: The broaden-and-build theory of positive emotions. *American Psychologist, 56,* 218–226.

Fredrickson, Barbara L. (2009). *Positivity: Groundbreaking research reveals how to embrace the hidden strength of positive emotions, overcome negativity, and thrive.* New York: Random.

Freedberg, Sharon. (2007). Re-examining empathy: A relational-feminist point of view. *Social Work, 52,* 251–259.

Freeman, Arthur, Felgoise, Stephanie, & Davis, Denise. (2008). *Clinical psychology: Integrating science and practice.* New York: Wiley.

Freeman, Arthur, Martin, Donna, & Ronen, Tammie. (2007). Treatment of suicidal behavior. In Tammie Ronen & Arthur Freeman (Eds.), *Cognitive behavior therapy in clinical social work practice* (pp. 421–445). New York: Springer.

Gallo, Fred P. (2002). *Energy psychology in psychotherapy: A comprehensive source book.* New York: Norton.

Garcia Coll, Cynthia, Cook-Nobles, Robin, & Surrey, Janet. (1997). Building connection through diversity. In Judith V. Jordan (Ed.), *Women's growth in diversity: More writings from the Stone Center* (pp. 176–198). New York: Guilford.

Garvin, Charles, & Seabury, Brett. (1997). *Interpersonal practice in social work: Promoting competence and social justice.* Boston: Allyn & Bacon.

Gately, Laura A., & Stabb, Sally D. (2005). Psychology students' training in the management of potentially violent clients. *Professional Psychology: Research and Practice, 36,* 681–687.

Germain, Carel B., & Gitterman, Alex. (1996). *The life model of social work practice.* New York: Columbia University Press.

Gerson, Randy, McGoldrick, Monica, and Petry, Sueli (2008). *Genograms: Assessment and intervention* (3rd Ed.). New York: Norton.

Goffman, Erving. (1963). *Stigma: Notes on the management of spoiled identity.* Englewood Cliffs, NJ: Prentice Hall.

Goldfried, Marvin, & Eubanks-Carter, Catherine. (2004). On the need for a new psychotherapy research paradigm: Comment on Westen, Novotny, and Thompson-Brenner (2004). *Psychological Bulletin, 130,* 669–673.

Goldstein, Eda. (1997). To tell or not to tell: The disclosure of events in the therapist's life to the patient. *Clinical Social Work Journal, 25,* 41–57.

Gorden, Robert, & Kline, Paul. (1997). Should social workers enroll as preferred providers with for-profit managed care groups? In Eileen Gambrill & Robert Pruger (Eds.), *Controversial issues in social work ethics, values, and obligations* (pp. 52–62). Boston: Allyn & Bacon.

Gorini, Alessandra, & Riva, Giuseppe. (2008). Virtual reality in anxiety disorders: The past and the future. *Expert Review Neurotherapeutics, 8,* 215–233.

Gottlieb, M. C., Robinson, K., & Younggren, J. N. (2007). Multiple relations in supervision: Guidelines for administrators, supervisors, and students. *Professional Psychology, 38,* 241–247.

Graybeal, Clay, & Ruff, Elizabeth. (1995). Process recording: It's more than you think. *Journal of Social Work Education, 31*(3), 169–181.

Griffin, William. (1995). Social worker and agency safety. In Richard L. Edwards (Ed.), *Encyclopedia of social work, Vol. 3* (pp. 2293–2305). Washington, DC: National Association of Social Workers Press.

Grisso, Thomas, & Applebaum, Paul S. (1998). *Assessing competence to consent to treatment: A guide for physicians and other health professionals.* New York: Oxford University Press.

Guadelupe, Krishna L., & Lum, Doman. (2005). *Multidimensional contextual practice: Diversity and transcendance.* Belmont, CA: Thompson Brooks/Cole.

Gunnell, D., and Lewis, G. (2005). Studying suicide from the life course perspective: Implications for prevention. *British Journal of Psychiatry, 187,* 206–208.

Gutheil, Irene A. (1993). Rituals and termination procedures. *Smith College Studies in Social Work, 63*(2), 163–176.

Haight, Wendy L. (1998). "Gathering the spirit" at First Baptist Church: Spirituality as a protective factor in the lives of African American children. *Social Work, 43,* 213–221.

Hall, Edward. (1959). *The silent language.* New York: Fawcett.

Handelsman, Mitchell M., Knapp, Samuel, & Gottlieb, Michael C. (2002). Positive ethics. In C. R. Snyder & Shane J. Lopez (Eds.), *Handbook of positive psychology* (pp. 731–750). New York: Oxford.

Hanson, Meredith, & Gutheil, Irene. (2004). Motivational strategies with alcohol-involved older adults: Implications for social work practice. *Social Work, 49,* 364–372.

Harney, Patricia A., Lebowitz, Leslie, & Harvey, Mary R. (1997). A stage by dimension model of trauma recovery: Application to practice. *In Session: Psychotherapy in Practice, 3*(4), 91–104.

Harper, Robert G., Wiens, Arthur N., & Matarazzo, Joseph D. (1978). *Nonverbal communication: The state of the art.* Hoboken, NJ: Wiley.

Harris, Daniel. (1997). *The rise and fall of gay culture.* New York: Hyperion.

Hartl, Tamara L., Zeiss, Robert A., Marino, Catherine M., Zeiss, Antonette M., Regev, Lisa G., & Leontis, Arrie. (2008). Clients' sexually inappropriate behaviors directed toward clinicians: Conceptualization and management. *Professional Psychology, 39,* 674–681.

Hays, Pamela. (2008). *Addressing cultural complexities in practice: Assessment, diagnosis, and therapy* (2nd ed.). Washington, DC: American Psychological Association.

Heard, Heidi L., & Linehan, Marsha M. (1994). Dialectical behavior therapy: An integrative approach to the treatment of borderline personality disorder. *Journal of Psychotherapy Integration, 4,* 55–82.

Hecker, Jeffrey E., & Thorpe, Geoffrey L. (2005). *Introduction to clinical psychology: Science, practice, and ethics.* Boston: Allyn & Bacon.

Hein, Grit, & Singer, Tania. (2008). I feel how you feel but not always: The empathic brain and its modulation. *Current Opinion in Neurobiology, 18,* 153–158.

Helms, Janet E. (1985). Cultural identity in the treatment process. In Paul B. Pedersen (Ed.), *Handbook of cross-cultural counseling and therapy* (pp. 239–245). Westport, CT: Greenwood.

Helms, Janet E. (1990). *Black and White racial identity: Theory, research, and practice.* New York: Praeger.

Helms, Janet E. (1995). An update of Helms's white and people of color racial identity models. In Joseph Pontoretto, J. Manual Casas, Lisa Suzuki, & Charlene Alexander (Eds.), *Handbook of multicultural counseling* (pp. 181–191). Thousand Oaks, CA: Sage.

Henrichsen, Gregory. (2008). Interpersonal psychotherapy as a treatment for depression in later life. *Professional Psychology: Research and Practice, 39,* 306–312.

Hepworth, Dean H., Rooney, Ronald H., Dewberry Rooney, Glenda, Strom-Gottfried, Kimberley, & Larsen, Jo Ann. (2010). *Direct social work practice: Theory and skills* (8th Ed.). Pacific Grove, CA: Brooks/Cole.

Herdt, Gilbert (Ed.). (1992). *Gay culture in America: Essays from the field.* Boston: Beacon.

Herek, Greg. (1986). The social psychology of homophobia: Toward a practical theory. *Review of Law and Social Change, 14,* 923–934.

Herman, Judith. (1997). *Trauma and recovery.* New York: Basic Books.

Hernstein, Richard, & Murray, Charles. (1994). *The bell curve: Intelligence and class structure in American life.* New York: Free Press.

Hertzberg, Joan F. (1996). Internalizing power dynamics: The wounds and the healing. In Marcia Hill & Esther Rothblum (Eds.), *Classism and feminist therapy: Counting costs* (pp. 129–148). New York: Harrington Park.

Hill, Clara, Sim, Wonjin, Spangler, Patricia, Stahl, Jessica, Sullivan, Catherine, & Teybar, Edward. (2008). Therapist immediacy in brief psychotherapy: Case study II. *Psychotherapy Theory, Research, Practice, Training, 45,* 298–315.

Hill, G. William, IV. (1998). *Activities and Videos for Teaching Cross-cultural Issues.* Accessed November 23, 2009 from www. lemoyne.edu/OTRP/otrpresources/otrp_ccissues.html

Hill, Marcia. (2004). *Diary of a country therapist.* Binghamton, NY: Haworth.

Hodge, David R. (2003). *Spiritual assessment handbook for professionals.* Botsford, CT: North American Association of Christians in Social Work.

Hodge, David R. (2005a). Social work and the house of Islam: Orienting practitioners to the beliefs and values of Muslims in the United States. *Social Work, 50,* 162–173.

Hodge, David R. (2005b). Developing a spiritual assessment toolbox: A discussion of the strengths and limitations of five different assessment models. *Health & Social Work, 30,* 314–323.

Hodge, David R. (2006). A template for spiritual assessment: A review of the JCAHO requirements and guidelines for implementation. *Social Work, 51,* 317–326.

Horse, Perry G. (2001). Reflections on American Indian identity. In Charlaine M. Wijeyesinghe & Bailey W. Jackson, III (Eds.), *New perspectives on racial identity development: A theoretical and practical anthology* (pp. 91–107). New York: New York University Press.

Hunsley, J. (2007). Addressing key challenges in evidence-based practice in psychology. *Professional Psychology, 38,* 113–121.

Hunsley, J., & Lee, C. M. (2007). Research-informed benchmarks for psychological treatments: Efficacy studies, effectiveness studies, and beyond. *Professional Psychology, 38,* 21–33.

Iglehart, Alfreda P., & Becerra, Rosina M. (1995). Ethnicity, race, reform, and the evolution of social work. In Alfreda P. Iglehart & Rosina M. Becerra (Eds.), *Social services and the ethnic community* (pp. 107–148). Boston: Allyn & Bacon.

Ivey, Allen E., & Ivey, Mary Bradford. (2007). *Intentional interviewing and counseling: Facilitating client development in a multicultural society* (6th ed.). Pacific Grove, CA: Brooks/Cole Thomson.

Ivey, Allen E., Ivey, Mary Bradford, & Zalaquett, Carlos P. (2010). *Intentional interviewing and counseling: Facilitating client development in a multicultural society* (7th ed.). Pacific Grove, CA: Brooks/Cole Thomson.

Jacobson, Wendy B. (2001). Beyond therapy: Bringing social work back to human services reform. *Social Work, 46,* 51–61.

James, Richard K. (2008). *Crisis intervention strategies* (6th ed.). Belmont, CA: Thomson Brooks/Cole.

Janoff-Bulman, Ronnie. (1992). *Shattered assumptions: Towards a new psychology of trauma.* New York: Free Press.

Jansson, Bruce S. (2007). *Becoming an effective policy advocate: From policy practice to social justice.* Pacific Grove, CA: Brooks-Cole.

Jayaratne, Srinika, Croxton, Tom A., & Mattison, Debra. (2004). A national survey of violence in the practice of social work. *Families in Society: The Journal of Contemporary Social Services, 85,* 445–453.

Jensen, Arthur R. (1969). How much can we boost IQ and school achievement? *Harvard Educational Review, 39,* 1–123.

Jobes, David A., Rudd, M. David, Overholser, James C., & Joiner, Thomas E., Jr. (2008). Ethical and competent care of suicidal patients: Contemporary challenges, new developments, and considerations for clinical practice. *Professional Psychology: Research and Practice, 39,* 405–413.

Joe, Jennie R., & Malach, Randi S. (2004). Families with American Indian roots. In Eleanor W. Lynch & Marci J. Hanson (Eds.), *Developing cross-cultural competence: A guide for working with children and their families* (3rd ed.) (pp. 109–134). Baltimore, MD: Brookes.

Johnson-Greene, Doug. (2007). Evolving standards for informed consent: Is it time for an individualized and flexible approach? *Professional Psychology: Research and Practice, 38,* 183–184.

Jones, Susan R., & McEwen, Marylu K. (2000). A conceptual model of multiple dimensions of identity. *Journal of College Student Development, 41,* 405–414.

Jordan, Judith V. (1990). *Courage in connection: Conflict, compassion, creativity. Work in Progress #45.* Wellesley College, MA: Stone Center Working Paper Series.

Jordan, Judith V. (1991a). The meaning of mutuality. In Judith V. Jordan, Alexandra G. Kaplan, Jean Baker Miller, Irene Stiver, & Janet Surrey (Eds.), *Women's growth in connection: Writings from the Stone Center* (pp. 81–96). New York: Guilford.

Jordan, Judith V. (1991b). Empathy and self-boundaries. In Judith V. Jordan, Alexandra G. Kaplan, Jean Baker Miller, Irene Stiver, & Janet Surrey (Eds.), *Women's growth in connection: Writings from the Stone Center* (pp. 67–80). New York: Guilford.

Jordan, Judith V. (2004a). Relational resilience. In Judith V. Jordan, Maureen Walker, & Linda M. Hartling (Eds.), *The complexity of connection: Writings from the Stone Center's Jean Baker Miller Training Institute.* New York: Guilford.

Jordan, Judith V. (2004b). Relational awareness. In Judith V. Jordan, Maureen Walker, & Linda M. Hartling (Eds.), *The complexity of connection: Writings from the Stone Center's Jean Baker Miller Training* Institute (pp. 47–63). New York: Guilford.

Jordan, Judith V., Kaplan, Alexandra G., Miller, Jean Baker, Stiver, Irene P., & Surrey, Janet L. (Eds.). (1991). *Women's growth in connection: Writings from the Stone Center* (pp. 81–96). New York: Guilford.

Joseph, Stephen, Linley, P. Alex, & Maltby, John. (2006). Positive psychology, religion and spirituality. *Mental Health Religion and Culture, 9,* 209–212.

Kabat-Zinn, Jon. (1994). *Wherever you go, there you are: Mindfulness meditation in everyday life.* New York: Hyperion.

Kadushin, Alfred, & Kadushin, Goldie. (1997). *The social work interview.* New York: Columbia University Press.

Kaiser, Tamara. (1997). *Supervisory relationships: Exploring the human element.* Pacific Grove, CA: Brooks/Cole.

Kazdin, Alan E. (2001). *Behavior modification in applied settings* (6th ed.). Pacific Grove, CA: Wadsworth.

Kazdin, Alan E. (2008). Evidence-based treatment and practice: New opportunities to bridge clinical research and practice, enhance the knowledge base, and improve patient care. *American Psychologist, 63,* 146–159.

Kessler, Laura E., & Waehler, Charles. (2005). Addressing multiple relationships between clients and therapists in lesbian, gay, bisexual, and transgender communities. *Professional Psychology: Research and Practice, 36,* 66–72.

Kim, Bok-Lim C. (1996). Korean families. In Monica McGoldrick, Joseph Giordano, & John Pearce (Eds.), *Ethnicity and family therapy* (pp. 349–362). New York: Guilford.

Kim, Jean. (2001). Asian American identity development theory. In Charmaine Wijeyesinghe & Bailey W. Jackson, III (Eds.), *New perspectives on racial identity development: A theoretical and practical anthology* (pp. 67–90). New York: New York University Press.

Kiselica, Mark S., & Robinson, Michelle. (2001). Bringing advocacy counseling to life: The history, issues, and human drama of social justice work in counseling. *Journal of Counseling and Development, 79,* 387–397.

Knaevelsrud, C., & Maercker, A. (2006). Does the quality of the working alliance predict treatment outcome in online psychotherapy for traumatized patients? *Journal of Medical Internet Research, 8*(4), 31.

Knapp, M. L., & Hall, Judith A. (2009). *Nonverbal communication in human interaction* (7th ed.). Belmont, CA: Wadsworth.

Knapp, S., Gottlieb, M., Berman, J., & Handelsman, M. M. (2007). When laws and ethics collide: What should psychologists do? *Professional Psychology, 38,* 54–59.

Knapp, S., & VandeCreek, L. (2008). When values of different cultures conflict: Ethical decision making in a multicultural context. *Professional Psychology, 39,* 660–666.

Knight, Carolyn. (2009). *Introduction to working with adult survivors of childhood trauma: Techniques and strategies.* Belmont, CA: Thomson Brooks/Cole.

Knox, Kerry L., Conwell, Yeates, & Caine, Eric. (2004). If suicide is a public health problem, what are we doing to prevent it? *American Journal of Public Health, 94,* 37–45.

Koob, Jeffrey J. (2003). Solution-focused family interventions. In Allie C. Kilpatrick & Thomas P. Holland (Eds.), *Working with families: An integrative model by level of need* (3rd ed.). Boston: Pearson Education.

Kopp, Richard R. (1995). *Metaphor therapy: Using client-generated metaphors in psychotherapy.* New York: Brunner/Mazel.

Kutchins, Herb, & Kirk, Stuart. (1995). Should DSM be the basis for teaching social work practice in mental health? No! Response to Janet Williams and Robert Spitzer. *Journal of Social Work Education, 31*(2), 153–158.

Kutchins, Herb, & Kirk, Stuart. (1997). *Making us crazy: DSM: The psychiatric bible and the creation of mental disorder.* New York: Free Press.

Kwan, Karl, & Kwong-Liem. (2001). Models of racial and ethnic identity development: Delineations of practice implications. *Journal of Mental Health Counseling, 23*(3), 269–279.

La Fromboise, Teresa D., Berman, Joan Saks, & Sohi, Balvindar K. (1994). American Indian women. In Lillian Comas-Diaz & Beverly Greene (Eds.), *Women of color: Integrating ethnic and gender identities in psychotherapy* (pp. 30–71). New York: Guilford.

Lambert, Michael J., & Barley, Dean E. (2002). Research summary on the therapeutic relationship and psychotherapy outcome. In J. C. Norcross (Ed.), *Psychotherapy relationships that work: Therapist contributions and responsiveness to patients* (pp. 17–32). New York: Oxford University Press.

Larson, Paul S. (2008). Deep brain stimulation for psychiatric disorders. *Neurotherapeutics, 5*(1), 50–58.

Lazarus, Arnold. (1981). *The practice of multimodal therapy.* New York: McGraw-Hill.

Lazarus, Arnold, & Zur, Ofur. (2002). *Dual relationships and psychotherapy.* New York: Springer.

Leathers, Dale, & Eaves, Michael. (2008). *Successful nonverbal communication: Principals and applications* (4th ed.). Hoboken, NJ: Wiley.

Lebow, Jay. (2006). *Research for the psychotherapist: From science to practice but nothing else.* New York: Routledge.

Levine, Murray, & Perkins, David. (1997). *Principles of community psychology: Perspectives and applications.* New York: Oxford University Press.

Lewis, C. A. & Cruise, S. M. (2006). Religion and happiness: Consensus, contradictons, comments and concerns. *Mental Health, Religion and Culture, 9,* 213–225.

Lindemann, Erich. (1965). Symptomatology and management of acute grief. In Howard J. Parad (Ed.), *Crisis intervention: Selected readings* (pp. 7–21). New York: Family Service Association of America.

Linehan, Marsha M., Comtois, Katherine Anne, Murray, Angela, Brown, Milton Z., Gallop, Robert J., Heard, Heidi, et al. (2006). Two-year randomized controlled trial and follow-up of dialectical behavior therapy vs therapy by experts for suicidal behaviors and borderline personality disorder. *Archives of General Psychiatry, 63,* 757–766.

Linehan, M. M., Goodstein, J. L., Nielsen, S. L., & Chiles, J. A. (1983). Reasons for staying alive when you are thinking of killing yourself: The reasons for living inventory. *Journal of Consulting and Clinical Psychology, 5,* 276–286.

Litz, Brett T., Engel, Charles C., Bryant, Richard A., & Papa, Antony. (2007). A randomized, controlled proof-of-concept trail of an Internet-based, therapist-assisted self-management treatment for posttraumatic stress disorder. *American Journal of Psychiatry, 164,* 1676–1683.

Lo, Hung-Tat, & Fung, Kenneth P. (2003). Culturally competent psychotherapy. *Canadian Journal of Psychiatry, 48,* 161–170.

Lowen, Alexander. (1975). *Bioenergetics.* New York: Penguin.

Luepker, Ellen. (2003). *Record keeping in psychotherapy and counseling: Protecting confidentiality in the professional relationship.* New York: Brunner-Routledge.

Luey, Helen Sloss, Glass, Laurel, & Elliot, Holly. (1995). Hard of hearing or deaf: Issues of ears, language, culture, and identity. *Social Work, 40,* 177–182.

Lum, Doman. (2004). *Social work practice and people of color: A process-stage approach* (5th ed.). Belmont, CA: Thomson-Brooks/Cole.

Lum, Doman. (2007). *Culturally competent practice: A framework for understanding diverse groups and justice issues* (3rd ed.). Belmont, CA: Thomson-Brooks/Cole.

Lynch, Eleanor W. (2004). Developing cross-cultural competence. In E. W. Lynch & M. Hanson (Eds.), *Developing cross-cultural competence: A guide for working with children and their families* (3rd ed.) (pp. 41–77). Baltimore, MD: Brookes.

Lyubomirsky, Sonja. (2007). *The how of happiness: A scientific approach to getting the life you want.* New York: Penguin.

Mackelprang, Romel, & Salsgiver, Richard. (1999). *Disability: A diversity model approach in human service practice.* Pacific Grove, CA: Brooks/Cole.

Maheu, Marlene, Pullier, Myron L., Wilhelm, Frank H., McMenamin, Joseph P., & Brown-Connolly, Nancy E. (2005). *The mental health provider and the new technologies: A handbook for practice.* Mahwah, NJ: Erlbaum.

Malgady, Robert G., & Zayas, Luis H. (2001). Cultural and linguistic considerations in psychodiagnosis with Hispanics: The need for an empirically informed process model. *Social Work, 46,* 39–49.

Maslow, Abraham. (1968). *Toward a psychology of being.* Princeton, NJ: Van Nostrand.

Maturana, Humberto. (1978). Biology of language: The epistomology of reality. In G. A. Miller & E. Lennonberg (Eds.), *Psychology and biology of language and thought.* New York: Academic Press.

Mayberg, Helen S., Lozano, Andres M., Voon, Valerie, McNeely, Heather E., Seminowicz, David, Hamani, Clement, et al. (2005). Deep brain stimulation for treatment resistant depression. *Neuron, 45,* 651–660.

McCann, Lisa, & Pearlman, Laurie Ann. (1990). Vicarious traumatization: A framework for understanding the psychological effects of working with victims. *Journal of Traumatic Stress Studies, 3,* 131–149.

McCarty, Dawn, & Clancy, Catherine. (2002). Telehealth: Implications for social work practice. *Social Work, 47*(2), 153–162.

McIntosh, Peggy. (1989, July/August). White privilege: Unpacking the invisible knapsack. *Peace and Freedom,* 10–12.

McKenzie, Kwame, Serfaty, Marc, & Crawford, Michael. (2003). Suicide in minority groups. *British Journal of Psychiatry, 183,* 100–101.

McNally, Richard J., Bryant, Richard A., & Ehlers, Anke. (2003). Does early psychological intervention promote recovery from posttraumatic stress? *Psychological Science in the Public Interest, 4*(2), 45–79.

Meichenbaum, Donald. (1996). Stress inoculation training for coping with stressors. *The Clinical Psychologist, 49,* 4–10.

Mezzich, Juan, & Kleinman, Arthur (Eds.). (1996). *Culture and psychiatric diagnosis: A DSM-IV perspective.* Arlington, VA: American Psychiatric Press.

Middleton, Renee A., Stadler, Holly A., Simpson, Carol, Guo, Yuh-Jen, Brown, Michele J., Crow, Germayne, et al. (2005). Mental health practitioners: The relationship between White racial identity attitudes and self-reported multicultural competencies. *Journal of Counseling & Development, 83,* 444–456.

Midkiff, Donna M., & Wyatt, W. Joseph. (2008). Ethical issues in the provision of online mental health services (etherapy). *Journal of Technology and Human Services, 26,* 310–332.

Miller, Dusty. (1996). Challenging self-harm through transformation of the trauma story. *Journal of Sexual Addiction and Compulsivity, 3,* 213–227.

Miller, Jean B. Jordan, Judith V., Stiver, Irene P., Walker, Maureen, Surrey, Janet L., & Eldridge, Natalie. (2004). Therapists' authenticity. In Judith V. Jordan, Maureen Walker, & Linda M. Hartling (Eds.), *The complexity of connection: Writings from the Stone Center's Jean Baker Miller Training Institute* (pp. 64–89). New York: Guilford.

Miller, Jean B., & Stiver, Irene P. (1997). *The healing connection: How women form relationships in therapy and in life.* Boston: Beacon.

Miller, K. I., Stiff, J. B., & Ellis, B. H. (1988). Communication and empathy as precursors to burnout among human service workers. *Communication Monographs, 55,* 336–341.

Miller, William R., & Rollnick, Stephen. (2002). *Motivational interviewing: Preparing people for change* (2nd ed.). New York: Guilford.

Miltenberger, R. G. (2004). *Behavior modification: Principles and procedures* (3rd ed.). Pacific Grove, CA: Brooks/Cole.

Mio, Jeffery Scott, Barker Lori, & Tumambing, Jaydee. (2009). *Multicultural psychology: Understanding our diverse communities.* Boston: McGraw-Hill.

Mitchell, J. T. (1983). When disaster strikes . . . : The critical incident stress debriefing process. *Journal of Emergency Medical Services, 8*, 36–39.

Moreno, Jacob L. (1946). Psychodrama and group psychotherapy. *Sociometry, 9*, 249–253.

Morrison, Amy L. (1997). Ten years of doing psychotherapy while living with a life-threatening illness: Self-disclosure and other ramifications. *Psychoanalytic Dialogues, 7*(1), 225–241.

Mumm, Ann Marie, & Kersting, Robert C. (1997). Teaching critical thinking in social work practice courses. *Journal of Social Work Education, 33*, 75–84.

Munk, Melanie. (2005). Spiritual development. In Dana Comstock (Ed.), *Diversity and development: Critical contexts that shape our lives and relationships* (pp. 319–335). Belmont, CA: Brooks/Cole Cengage.

Murphy, Lawrence, Paranass, Paul, Mitchell, Daniel L., Hallett, Rebecca, Cayley, Paula, & Seagram, Samantha. (2009). Client satisfaction and outcome comparisons of online and face-to-face counselling methods. *The British Journal of Social Work, 1*, 1–14.

National Association of Social Workers. (1999). *Code of ethics of the National Association of Social Workers.* Washington, DC: Author.

National Association of Social Workers. (2001). *Standards for cultural competence in social work practice.* Washington, DC: Author.

National Organization for Human Services. (1996). *Ethical standards for human service professionals.* Austin, TX: Author.

Nemeroff, Charles B. (2008). Recent findings in the pathophysiology of depression. *Focus: The Journal of Lifelong Learning in Psychiatry, 1*, 3–14.

Netting, F. Ellen, Kettner, Peter M., & McMurtry, Steven L. (2008). *Social work macro practice* (4th ed.). Boston, MA: Allyn & Bacon.

Neukrug, Edward S., & Schwitzer, Alan M. (2006). *Skills and tools for today's counselors and psychotherapists: From natural helping to professional counseling.* Belmont, CA: Brooks/Cole.

Neumann, Melanie, Bensing, Jozien, Mercer, Stewart, Ernstmann, Nicole, Ommen, Oliver, & Pfaff, Holger. (2009). Analyzing the "nature" and "specific effectiveness" of clinical empathy: A theoretical overview and contribution towards a theory-based research agenda. *Patient Education and Counseling, 74*, 339–346.

Nietzel, Michael, Bernstein, Douglas, Kramer, Geoff, & Milich, Richard. (2003). *Introduction to clinical psychology* (6th ed.). Englewood Cliffs, NJ: Prentice-Hall.

Norcross, John C. (2000). Psychotherapist self-care: Practitioner-tested, research-informed strategies. *Professional Psychology: Research and Practice, 31*, 710–713.

Norcross , John C. (2002a). Empirically supported therapy relationships. In J. C. Norcross (Ed.), *Psychotherapy relationships that work: Therapist contributions and responsiveness to patients* (pp. 3–16). New York: Oxford University Press.

Norcross, John C. (Ed.). (2002b). *Psychotherapy relationships that work: Therapist contributions and responsiveness to patients.* New York: Oxford University Press.

Norcross, John C., Beutler, L. E., & Levant, R. F. (Eds.). (2006). *Evidence based practices in mental health: Debate and dialogue on the fundamental questions.* Washington, DC: American Psychological Association.

Nordal, Katherine C. (2009*)*. Protecting privacy in the electronic world. *Monitor on Psychology, 40*(3), 53.

O'Connor, Michael F. (2001). On the etiology and effective management of professional distress and impairment among psychologists. *Professional Psychology: Research and Practice, 32*, 345–350.

Okun, Barbara, Fried, Jane, & Okun, Marcia. (1999). *Understanding diversity: A learning-as-practice primer.* Pacific Grove, CA: Brooks/Cole.

Okun, Barbara F., & Kantrowitz, Ricki E. (2008). *Effective helping: Interviewing and counseling techniques.* Belmont, CA: Thomson Brooks/Cole.

Otto, Michael W., Smits, Jasper A. J., & Reese, Hannah J. (2005). Combined psychotherapy and pharmacotherapy for mood and anxiety disorders in adults: Review and analysis. *Clinical Psychology: Science and Practice, 12*, 72–86.

Padden, C. (1989). The deaf community and the culture of deaf people. In S. Wilcox (Ed.), *American deaf culture: An anthology* (pp. 1–16). Burtonsville, MD: Linstock.

Padesky, Christine, & Greenberger, Dennis. (1995). *Mind over mood: Change how you feel by changing the way you think.* New York: Guilford.

Parad, Howard J. (Ed.). (1965). *Crisis intervention: Selected readings.* New York: Family Service Association of America.

Parad, Howard, & Caplan, Gerald. (1965). A framework for studying families in crisis. In Howard J. Parad (Ed.), *Crisis intervention: Selected readings* (pp. 53–72). New York: Family Service Association of America.

Parker, Robin, & Chambers, Pamela Smith. (2005). *The anti-racist cookbook: A recipe guide for conversations about race that goes beyond covered dishes and "Kumbah-yah."* Roselle, NJ: Crandall, Dostie, & Douglass.

Parker-Oliver, Debra, & Demiris, George. (2006). Social work informatics: A new specialty. *Social Work, 51*, 127–134.

Parsons, Thomas, & Rizzo, Albert. (2008). Affective outcomes of virtual reality exposure therapy for anxiety and specific phobias: A meta-analysis. *Journal of Behavior Therapy and Experimental Psychiatry, 39*, 250–261.

Pedersen, Paul. (1991). Multiculturalism as a generic approach to counseling. *Journal of Counseling and Development, 70*(1), 6–12.

Pedersen, Paul B., Crethar, Hugh C., & Carlson, Jon. (2008). *Inclusive cultural empathy: Making relationships central in counseling and psychotherapy.* Washington, DC: American Psychological Association.

Pedrotti, J. T., Edwards, L. M., & Lopez, S. J. (2008). Working with multiracial clients in therapy: Bridging theory, research, and practice. *Professional Psychology, 39,* 192–201.

Peebles Wilkins, Wilma. (1995). Janie Porter Barrett and the Virginia Industrial School for Colored Girls: Community response to the needs of African American children. *Child Welfare, 74*(1), 143–161.

Perez, Ruperto, DeBord, Kurt, & Bieschke, Kathleen. (2007). *Handbook of counseling and psychotherapy with lesbian, gay, and bisexual clients.* Washington, DC: American Psychological Association.

Perseius, K.-L., Kaver, A., Ekdahl, S., Asberg, M., & Samuelsson, M. (2007). Stress and burnout in psychiatric professionals when starting to use dialectical behavioural therapy in work with young self-harming women showing borderline personality symptoms. *Journal of Psychiatric and Mental Health Nursing, 14,* 635–643.

Peterson, Christopher, Park, Nansook, & Seligman, Martin. (2006). Strengths of character and recovery. *Journal of Positive Psychology, 1,* 17–26.

Philip, Claire E. (1994). Letting go: Problems with termination when a therapist is seriously ill or dying. *Smith College Studies in Social Work, 64*(2), 169–179.

Plante, Thomas G. (1999). *Contemporary clinical psychology.* New York: John Wiley.

Poindexter, Cynthia C. (1997). In the aftermath: Serial crisis intervention for people with HIV. *Health & Social Work Journal, 22,* 125–132.

Polack, R. J. (2004). Social justice and the global economy: New challenges for social work in the 21st century. *Social Work, 49,* 281–290.

Ponterotto, Joseph G., Casas, J. Manuel, Suzuki, Lisa A., & Alexander, Charlene M. (Eds.). (2009). *Handbook of multicultural counseling* (3rd ed). Thousand Oaks, CA: Sage.

Pope, Kenneth S., & Keith-Spiegel, Patricia. (2008). A practical approach to boundaries in psychotherapy: Making decisions, bypassing blunders, and mending fences. *Journal of Clinical Psychology, 64,* 638–652.

Pope, Kenneth S., Sonne, Janet L., & Greene, Beverly. (2006). *What therapists don't talk about and why: Understanding taboos that hurt us and our clients.* Washington, DC: American Psychological Association.

Pope, Kenneth S., & Vasquez, Melba J. T. (2007). *Ethics in psychotherapy and counseling: A practical guide* (3rd ed.). San Francisco: Jossey-Bass.

Poulin, John. (2005). *A strengths-based generalist practice* (3rd ed.). Belmont, CA: Wadsworth Cengage.

Prochaska, James O., & Norcross, John C. (2007). *Theories of psychotherapy: A transtheoretical approach.* Belmont, CA: Brooks/Cole.

Prochaska, James O., Norcross, John C., & DiClemente, Carlo C. (1994). *Changing for good.* New York: Morrow.

Pryor, Karen. (1984). *Don't shoot the dog! How to improve yourself and others through behavioral training.* New York: Bantam.

Pulido, Mary L. (2007). In their words: Secondary traumatic stress in social workers responding to the 9/11 terrorist attacks in New York City. *Social Work, 52,* 279–281.

Qin, Dongxiao, & Comstock, Dana. (2005). Traditional models of development: Appreciating context and relationship. In Dana Comstock (Ed.), *Diversity and development* (pp. 1–23). Belmont, CA: Brooks/Cole Cengage.

Ragusea, Anthony S., & VandeCreek, Leon V. (2003). Suggestions for the ethical practice of online psychotherapy. *Psychotherapy: Theory, Research, Practice, Training, 40,* 94–102.

Ram Dass, & Gorman, Paul. (1985). *How can I help? Stories and reflections on service.* New York: Knopf.

Rapoport, Lydia. (1965). The state of crisis: Some theoretical considerations. In Howard J. Parad (Ed.), *Crisis intervention: Selected readings* (pp. 22–31). New York: Family Service Association of America.

Rappaport, Julian. (1987). Terms of empowerment/exemplars of prevention: Toward a theory for community psychology. *American Journal of Community Psychology, 15,* 121–148.

Reamer, Frederic. (1995). Malpractice claims against social workers: First facts. *Social Work, 40,* 595–601.

Rebuffat, Gaston. (1965). *Between heaven and earth.* New York: Oxford University Press.

Reik, Theodor. (1948). *Listening with the third ear.* New York: Farrar & Straus.

Reis, Brendali F., & Brown, Lillian G. (1999). Reducing psychotherapy dropouts: Maximizing perspective convergence in the psychotherapy dyad. *Psychotherapy, 36,* 123–136.

Reis, Brendali F., & Brown, Lillian G. (2006). Preventing therapy dropout in the real world: The clinical utility of videotape preparation and client estimate of treatment duration. *Professional Psychology: Research and Practice, 37,* 311–316.

Renn, K. A. (2007). LGBT student leaders and queer activists: Identities of lesbian, gay, bisexual, transgender, and queer identified college student leaders and activists. *Journal of College Student Development, 48,* 311–330.

Reynolds, Amy L., & Pope, Raechele L. (1991). The complexity of diversity: Exploring multiple oppressions. *Journal of Counseling and Development, 70*(1), 174–180.

Richards, P. Scott, & Bergin, Allen E. (Eds.). (2000). *Handbook of psychotherapy and religious diversity.* Washington, DC: American Psychological Association.

Rizzo, Albert et al. (2009). VR exposure therapy results with active duty OIF/OEF combatants. In J. D. Westwood et al. (Eds.), *Medicine meets virtual reality 17* (pp. 277–282). Amsterdam, The Netherlands: IOS Press.

Roazen, Paul. (1992). *Freud and his followers.* New York: Da Capo.

Robb, Christina. (2007). *This changes everything: The relational revolution in psychology.* New York: Picador-Ferrar, Straus & Giroux.

Robinson, Tracy L. (2005). *The convergence of race, ethnicity, and gender: Multiple identities in counseling* (2nd ed.). Upper Saddle River, NJ: Pearson.

Rochlen, Aaron B., Zack, Jason S., & Speyer, Cedric. (2004). Online therapy: A review relevant definitions, debates and current empirical support. *Journal of Clinical Psychology, 60,* 269–283.

Rogers, Carl. (1957). The necessary and sufficient conditions of therapeutic personality change. *Journal of Consulting Psychology, 21,* 95–103.

Rogers, Carl. (1958). The characteristics of a helping relationship. *Personnel and Guidance Journal, 37,* 6–16.

Rogers, Carl. (1980). *A way of being.* Boston: Houghton Mifflin.

Rogers, Carl, & Sanford, R. C. (1985). Client-centered psychotherapy. In Harold Kaplan, Benjamin Sadock, & Arthur M. Friedman (Eds.), *Comprehensive textbook of psychiatry* (pp. 1374–1388). Baltimore, MD: Williams & Wilkins.

Rollock, David, & Gordon, Edmund W. (2000). Racism and mental health into the 21st century: Perspectives and parameters. *American Journal of Orthopsychiatry, 70*(1), 5–13.

Root, Maria P. P. (1992). The impact of trauma on personality: The second reconstruction. In Laura Brown & Mary Ballou (Eds.), *Theories of personality and psychopathology: Feminist reappraisal.* New York: Guilford.

Root, Maria P. P. (1996). *The multiracial experience.* Thousand Oaks, CA: Sage.

Root, Maria P. P. (2001). Negotiating the margins. In Joseph G. Ponterotto, J. Manuel Casas, Lisa. A. Suzuki, & Charlene M. Alexander (Eds.), *Handbook of multicultural counseling* (pp. 113–121). Thousand Oaks, CA: Sage.

Rose, Stephen M. (2000). Reflections on empowerment-based practice. *Social Work, 45,* 403–412.

Rosenhan, David L. (1973). On being sane in insane places. *Science, 179,* 250–257.

Roszak, Theodore, Gomes, Mary E., & Kanner, Allen D. (Eds.). (1995). *Ecopsychology: Restoring the earth, healing the mind.* San Francisco: Sierra Club.

Royal, Germain, & Dunstan, Georgia. (2004). Changing the paradigm from "race" to human genome variation. *NatureGenetics, 36*(11), S5–S7. Accessed April 15, 2006 from www.nature.com/ng/journal/v36/n11s/pdf/ng1454.pdf

Rupert, Patricia A., & Kent, Jamie S. (2007). Gender and work setting differences in career-sustaining behaviors and burnout among professional psychologists. *Professional Psychology: Research and Practice, 38,* 88–96.

Saleebey, Dennis. (2001). The Diagnostic Strengths Manual. *Social Work, 46,* 183–192.

Saleebey, Dennis. (2005). *The strengths perspective in social work practice* (4th ed.). Upper Saddle River, NJ: Pearson.

Schamess, Gerald. (1999). Therapeutic love and its permutations. *Clinical Social Work Journal, 27,* 9–26.

Schiller, Linda. (2007). Not for women only: Applying the relational model of group development with vulnerable populations. *Social Work with Groups, 30,* 11–26.

Schutz, William. (1967). *Joy: Expanding human awareness.* New York: Grove.

Schwartz, Thomas L. & Parks, Tricia L. (1999). Assaults by patients on psychiatric residents: A survey and training recommendations. *Psychiatric Services, 50,* 381–383.

Seabury, Brett. (1976). The contract: Uses, abuses, and limitations. *Social Work, 21,* 16–21.

Seligman, Martin. (2002). *Authentic happiness: Using the new positive psychology to realize your potential for lasting fulfillment.* New York: Free Press.

Seligman, Martin, Steen, Tracy A., Park, Nansook, & Peterson, Christopher. (2005). Positive psychology progress: Empirical validation of interventions. *American Psychologist, 60,* 410–421.

Sharifzadeh, Virginia-Shirin. (2004). Families with Middle Eastern roots. In Eleanor W. Lynch & Marci J. Hanson (Eds.), *Developing cross-cultural competence: A guide for working with children and their families* (3rd ed.) (pp. 373–410). Baltimore, MD: Brookes.

Sheafor, Bradford, Horejsi, Charles, & Horejsi, Gloria. (1997). *Techniques and guidelines for social work practice.* Boston: Allyn & Bacon.

Sheldon, Kennon, & Lyubomirsky, Sonja. (2004). Achieving sustainable new happiness: Projects, practices, and prescriptions. In P. A. Linley & S. Joseph (Eds.), *Positive psychology in practice* (pp. 127–145). New Jersey: Wiley.

Shih, Margaret J., & Sanchez, Diana T. (2005). Perspectives and research on the positive and negative implications of having multiple racial identities. *Psychological Bulletin, 131,* 569–591.

Shulman, Lawrence. (2009). *The skills of helping individuals, families, groups, and communities* (6th ed.). Belmont, CA: Brooks/Cole.

Siebert, Darcy C. (2005). Help seeking for AOD misuse among social workers: Patterns, barriers, and implications. *Social Work, 50*(1), 65–75.

Slattery, Jeanne M. (2004). *Counseling diverse clients: Bringing context into therapy.* Belmont, CA: Brooks/Cole.

Smith, Janna Malamud. (2000). Psychotherapy with people stressed by poverty. In Alex N. Sabo & Leston Havens (Eds.), *The real world guide to psychotherapy practice* (pp. 71–92). Cambridge, MA: Harvard University Press.

Snowden, Lonnie R., & Cheung, F. K. (1990). Use of inpatient mental health services by members of ethnic minority groups. *American Psychologist, 45,* 347–355.

Sommers-Flanagan, John, & Sommers-Flanagan, Rita. (2009). *Clinical interviewing* (4th ed.). Hoboken, NJ: Wiley.

Spencer, Patricia C., & Munch, Shari. (2003). Client violence toward social workers: The role of management in community mental health programs. *Social Work, 48,* 532–544.

Sperry, Len. (2007). *Ethical and professional issues in counseling and psychotherapy practice.* Boston: Allyn & Bacon.

Stevens, Joyce West. (1997). African American female adolescent identity development: A three-dimensional perspective. *Child Welfare, 76*(1), 145–172.

Stiver, Irene P. (1991). The meaning of care: Reframing treatment models. In Judith V. Jordan, Alexandra Kaplan, Jean Baker Miller, Irene P. Stiver, & Janet Surrey (Eds.), *Women's growth in connection: Writings from the Stone Center* (pp. 250–267). New York: Guilford.

Stokoe, W. (1989). Dimensions of difference: ASL and English-based cultures. In S. Wilcox (Ed.), *American deaf culture: An anthology* (pp. 49–59). Burtonsville, MD: Linstock.

Stone, Michael. (1997). *Healing the mind: A history of psychiatry from antiquity to the present.* New York: Norton.

Sue, David, & Sue, Diane M. (2008). *Foundations of counseling and psychotherapy: Evidence-based practices for a diverse society.* Hoboken, NJ: Wiley.

Sue, Derald W. (2003). *Overcoming our racism: The journey to liberation.* San Francisco, CA: Jossey-Bass.

Sue, Derald W., Arredondo, Patricia, & McDavis, Roderick. (1992). Multicultural counseling competencies and standards: A call to the profession. *Journal of Counseling & Development, 70,* 477–484.

Sue, Derald W. Capodilupo, Christina M., Torino, Gina C., Bucceri, Jennifer M., Holder, Aisha M. B., Nadal, Kevin L., et al. (2007). Racial microaggressions in everyday life: Implications for clinical practice. *American Psychologist, 62,* 271–286.

Sue, Derald W., Capodilupo, Christina M., & Holder, Aisha M. B. (2008). Racial microaggressions in the life experience of Black Americans. *Professional Psychology, 39,* 329–336.

Sue, Derald W., Ivey, Allen E., & Pedersen, Paul B. (1996). *A theory of multicultural counseling and therapy.* Pacific Grove, CA: Brooks/Cole.

Sue, Derald W. & Sue, David. (2003). *Counseling the culturally diverse* (4th ed.). Hoboken, NJ: Wiley.

Sue, Derald W. & Sue, David. (2008). *Counseling the culturally diverse: Theory and practice* (5th ed.). Hoboken, NJ: Wiley.

Surrey, Janet. (1991a). Relationship and empowerment. In Judith V. Jordan, Alexandra G. Kaplan, Jean B. Miller, Irene P. Stiver, & Janet L. Surrey (Eds.), *Women's growth in connection: Writings from the Stone Center* (pp. 162–180). New York: Guilford.

Surrey, Janet. (1991b). The self-in-relation: A theory of women's development. In Judith V. Jordan, Alexandra G. Kaplan, Jean B. Miller, Irene P. Stiver, & Janet L. Surrey (Eds.), *Women's growth in connection: Writings from the Stone Center* (pp. 51–66). New York: Guilford.

Sussman, Michael B. (1992). *A curious calling: Unconscious motivations for practicing psychotherapy.* Northvale, NJ: Jason Aronson.

Swartz, Holly, Zuckoff, Allen, Grote, Nancy, Spielvogle, Heather, Bledsoe, Sarah, Shear, Katherine, et al. (2007). Engaging depressed patients in psychotherapy: Integrating techniques from motivational interviewing and ethnographic interviewing to improve treatment participation. *Professional Psychology, 38,* 430–439.

Swartz, Leslie. (1998). Language diversity and mental health care. In L. Swartz (Ed.), *Culture and mental health: A South African view* (pp. 25–51). New York: Oxford.

Sweitzer, H. Frederick, & King, Mary A. (2009). *The successful internship: Personal, professional, and civic development.* Belmont, CA: Brooks/Cole Cengage.

Swenson, Carol R. (1998). Clinical social work's contribution to a social justice perspective. *Social Work, 43,* 527–537.

Syme, Gabrielle. (2006). Fetters or freedom?: Dual relationships in counseling. *International Journal for the Advancement of Counselling, 28,* 57–69.

Szasz, Thomas. (1960). The myth of mental illness. *American Psychologist, 15,* 113–118.

Tafoya, Terry. (1989). Circles and cedar: Native Americans and family therapy. *Journal of Psychotherapy and the Family, 6,* 71–98.

Taylor, Robert, Ellison, Christopher, Chatters, Linda, Levin, Jeffrey, & Lincoln, Karen. (2000). Mental health services in faith communities: The role of clergy in Black America. *Social Work, 45,* 73–87.

Tedeschi, Richard, & Calhoun, Lawrence. (1995*). Trauma and transformation: Growing in the aftermath of suffering.* Thousand Oaks, CA: Sage.

Tedeschi, Richard, Park C., & Calhoun, Lawrence. (1988). *Posttraumtic growth: Positive change in the aftermath of crisis.* Mahwah, NJ: Lawrence Erlbaum.

Thakker, Joanne, & Ward, Tony. (1998). Culture and classification: The cross-cultural application of the DSM IV. *Clinical Psychology Review, 18,* 501–529.

Ting, Laura, Sanders, Sara, Jacobson, Jodi M., & Power, James R. (2006). Dealing with the aftermath: A qualitative analysis of mental health social workers' reactions after a client suicide. *Social Work, 51,* 329–341.

Tischler, Carl L., Gordon, Lisa B., & Landry-Meyer, Laura. (2000). Managing the violent patient: A guide for psychologists and other mental health professionals. *Professional Psychology: Research and Practice, 31,* 34–41.

Torrey, E. Fuller. (1972). What western psychotherapists can learn from witchdoctors. *American Journal of Orthopsychiatry, 42,* 69–76.

United States Department of Health and Human Services. (2001). *The Surgeon General's Report on Mental Health: Culture, Race and Ethnicity.* Washington, DC: Author

United States Department of Health and Human Services. (2009). *Understanding HIPAA Privacy.* Accessed October 5, 2009 from www.hhs.gov/ocr/privacy/hipaa/understanding/index.html

United States Department of Veterans Affairs. (2009). *Types of debriefing following disasters.* Accessed December 13, 2009 from www.ptsd.va.gov/professional/pages/debriefing-after-disasters.asp

Valle, Ramon. (1980). Social mapping techniques: A preliminary guide for locating and linking to natural networks. In Ramon Valle & William Vega (Eds.), *Hispanic natural support systems: Mental health promotion perspectives* (pp. 113–121). Sacramento: State of California Department of Mental Health.

van der Kolk, Bessel A., Burbridge, Jennifer A., & Suzuki, Joji. (1997). The psychobiology of traumatic memory: Implications of neuroimaging studies. *Annals of the New York Academy of Sciences, 821,* 99–113.

van der Kolk, Bessel A., Hopper, James W., & Osterman, Janet E. (2001). Exploring the nature of traumatic memory: Combining clinical knowledge with laboratory methods. *Journal of Aggression, Maltreatment, & Trauma, 42,* 9–31.

van der Kolk, Bessel A., & van der Hart, Onno. (1991). The intrusive past: The flexibility of memory and the engraving of trauma. *American Image, 48*(4), 425–454.

Van Dierendonck, D., & Mohan, K. (2006). Some thoughts on spirituality and eudaimonic well-being. *Mental Health, Religion and Culture, 9,* 227–238.

Vasquez, Melba J. T. (2005). Independent practice settings and the multicultural guidelines. In Madonna G. Constantine & Derald Wing Sue (Eds.), *Strategies for building multicultural competence in mental health and educational settings* (pp. 91–108). Hoboken, NJ: John Wiley.

Vasquez, Melba J. T., Bingham, Rosie P., & Barnett, Jeffrey E. (2008). Psychotherapy termination: Clinical and ethical responsibilities. *Journal of Clinical Psychology, 64,* 653–665.

Vasterman, Peter, Yzermans, C. Joris, & Dirkzwager, Anja J. (2005). The role of the media and media hypes in the aftermath of disasters. *Epidemiological Reviews, 27,* 107–114.

Vinson, T. S., & Neimeyer, G. T. (2000). The relationship between racial identity development and multicultural counselor training. *Journal of Multicultural Counseling and Development, 28,* 177–193.

von Bertalanffy, Ludwig. (1968). *General systems theory: Foundation, development, application.* New York: Braziller.

von Foerster, Heinz. (1981). *Observing systems.* Seaside, CA: Intersystems.

Walker, Maureen. (2004). How relationships heal. In Maureen Walker & Wendy Rosen (Eds.), *How connections heal: Stories from relational-cultural therapy* (pp. 3–21). New York: Guilford.

Walker, Maureen, & Rosen, Wendy B. (Eds.). (2004). *How connections heal: Stories from relational-cultural therapy.* New York: Guilford.

Walsh, Froma (Ed.). (1999). *Spiritual resources in family therapy.* New York: Guilford.

Walsh, Joseph. (2003). *Endings in clinical practice: Effective closure in diverse settings.* Chicago: Lyceum.

Walsh, Joseph. (2009). *Generalist social work practice: Intervention methods.* Belmont, CA: Brooks/Cole-Cengage.

Weaver, Hilary N. (2005). *Explorations in cultural competence: Journey to the four directions.* Belmont, CA: Brooks/Cole.

Webb, Nancy Boyd (Ed.). (2007). *Play therapy and children in crisis: Individual, group and family treatment* (3rd ed.). New York: Guilford.

Weick, Ann. (1983). Issues in overturning a medical model of social work practice. *Social Work, 28,* 467–471.

Weinger, Susan. (2001). *Security risk: Preventing client violence against social workers.* Washington, DC: National Association of Social Workers Press.

Weissman, Myrna, Markowitz, John, & Klerman, Gerald. (2007). *Clinician's quick guide to interpersonal psychotherapy.* New York: Oxford.

Westen, Drew, Novotny, Catherine, & Thompson-Brenner, Heather. (2004). The empirical status of empirically supported psychotherapies: Assumptions, findings, and reporting in controlled clinical trials. *Psychological Bulletin, 130*(4), 631–663.

White Kress, Victoria, Eriksen, Karen, Rayle, Andrea Dixon, & Ford, Stephanie J. W. (2005). The DSM-IV-TR and cultures: Considerations for counselors. *Journal of Counseling and Development, 83,* 97–105.

Whitson, Susan. (2009). *Principles and applications of assessment in counseling* (3rd ed.). Belmont, CA: Brooks/Cole-Cengage.

Wijeyesinghe, Charmaine L. (2001). Racial identity in multiracial people: An alternative paradigm. In Charmaine L. Wijeyesinghe & Bailey W. Jackson, III (Eds.), *New perspectives on racial identity development: A theoretical and practical anthology* (pp. 129–152). New York: New York University Press.

Williams, Janet B., & Spitzer, Robert. (1995). Should DSM be the basis for teaching social work practice in mental health? Yes. *Journal of Social Work Education, 11,* 148–153.

Winerman, Lea. (2006). Bringing recovery home. *Monitor on psychology, 37*(4), 32.

Wolpe, Joseph. (1958). *Psychotherapy by reciprocal inhibition.* Sanford CA: Stanford University.

Wong, Y. Joel. (2006). Strength-centered therapy: A social constructionist, virtues-based psychotherapy. *Psychotherapy: Theory Research, Practice, Training, 43,* 133–146.

World Health Organization. (2008). *World Suicide Prevention Day Statement, September 10, 2008.* Accessed December 13, 2009 from www.who.int/mediacentre/events/annual/world_suicide_prevention_day/en/index.html

World Health Organization. (2009). *Suicide Prevention; SUPRE.* Accessed December 13, 2009 from http://www.who.int/mental_health/prevention/suicide/suicideprevent/en/

Yan, Miu Chung. (2008). Exploring cultural tensions in cross-cultural social work practice. *Social Work, 53,* 317–328.

Young, Mark E. (2005). *Learning the art of helping: Building blocks and techniques.* Upper Saddle River, NJ: Pearson.

Young, Mark, & Chromy, Samantha. (2005). *Exercises in the Art of Helping.* Upper Saddle River, NJ: Pearson.

Younggren, Jeffrey N., & Gottlieb, Michael C. (2008). Termination and abandonment: History, risk, and risk management. *Professional Psychology, 39,* 498–504.

Index

Note: Page numbers followed by b indicate Boxes